Logion Press Books

Stanley M. Horton, Th.D.
General Editor

ELEMENTS OF A CHRISTIAN WORLDVIEW

Elements of a Christian Worldview

Compiled and Edited by Michael D. Palmer

General Editor: Stanley M. Horton

LOGION PRESS

Springfield, Missouri
02-0491

3rd Printing 2010

© 1998 by Gospel Publishing House, 1445 N. Boonville Ave, Springfield, Missouri 65802. All rights reserved. No part of this book may be reproduced, stored in a retrieval system, or transmitted in any form or by any means—electronic, mechanical, photocopy, recording, or otherwise—without prior written permission of the copyright owner, except brief quotations used in connection with reviews in magazines or newspapers.

Logion Press books are published by Gospel Publishing House.

Library of Congress Cataloging-in-Publication Data

Elements of a Christian worldview / compiled and edited by Michael D. Palmer ; general editor, Stanley M. Horton.
     p.   cm.
   Includes biographical references and index.
   ISBN 978-0-88243-874-0
    1. Christianity—20th century.   I. Palmer, Michael D., 1950–
II. Horton, Stanley M.
BR121.2.E44   1998
261—DC21

98-19264
Rev.

Printed in the United States of America

For my parents,
Don and Thelma Palmer,
who successfully passed the faith to me
and who encouraged me to seek the truth,
and
for my 18-year-old son,
Bradley Charles Palmer,
who, at the time of his tragic death
on November 22, 1997
was already well on his way
toward understanding many of the
central concepts in this book.

Table of Contents

Foreword

Much of the English vocabulary comes from the Greek and Latin languages. Words as common as *agenda* or *exit* come straight from classical times. Other words, however, march into English, unnoticed, from some other culture. *Khaki* stems from a Pakistani term. *Bureau* is pure French. *Corridor, patio,* and *plaza* are unadulterated Spanish, and *chocolate* right out of Aztec.

Worldview, the focus of this book of essays, reaches English as no less such a linguistic emigrant. The German language has a penchant for compound words. Just to take an extreme example, here is the German word for a military tank: *Schützengrabenzerstörungsautomobil.* A synonym, by the same language laws: *der Panzer.* "Worldview" puts two English equivalents side by side as literal translations of the German term *Weltanschauung*—a term with a long and noble philosophical heritage.

Invented by German philosophers, *Weltanschauung* describes a way of viewing the world. Someone might take it that the world is an illusion; things aren't really real. Another could say, as do idealists of all ages, that there's more to the world than what you can see. Still another might conclude the world is inhospitable and hopeless, leading to despair.

Instead of Anglicizing *Weltanschauung* as "worldview," the perpetrators would have done English-speaking peoples a favor by being a little less complicated. Translating *Weltanschauung* as "outlook" or even "attitude" wouldn't have been far from the mark, except that the German technical term specifically refers to one's attitude toward the world.

Which "world"? The vast reaches of starry universes? The full complement of human cultures on our globe? Or possibly the "world" that comes in for some bad press in Scripture? The German philosophical tradition certainly had in mind the material and the invisible universe, the visible world and the galaxies of intellect. People's notions of reality constitute their worldview.

As far as I can tell, there is no biblical word that could be called the equivalent of "worldview." But there surely lie on the pages of Scripture the contours of a normative attitude toward the world, visible and invisible. There exists, though theologians don't make much of it, a theology of the world.

Cosmology qualifies as one term describing how people think about the world. Astronomers and related scientists use the term to define a science of the distant universe. Theologians use the same term to assemble biblical doctrines related to the origin and destiny of the visible world—called in Greek (including New Testament Greek) the *cosmos.* ("Cosmetic" got its flavor of beauty from the Greeks' awe over the stunning symmetry of the heavens.)

The other chief word in the Greek New Testament for "world" goes a different direction. *Oikoumenê* describes the sum total of human cultures. Since this word first defined a family household, it's easy to understand how it came to mean organized society, leading to the word "economy" on the one hand and to "ecumenical" on the other. So the biblical words used to describe the world have been taken over by other common meanings. We'll just have to speak of a theology of the world.

I detect in the New Testament a double usage of the idea of the world and how Christians should view it. There is a Johannine view of the world—an organized system of human, even demonic, sinful opposition to God. From this viewpoint, according to a cluster of passages from the Gospel of John, the Letters of John, and the Revelation, true believers are counseled to "avoid the world"—which can be called "this evil world," a sector of society which lies opposite the church. This is the world to avoid, to shun, and its existence makes holiness or separation from the world necessary.

The other strand of the idea of the world in Scripture I think of as Pauline. Paul's view of the world is more sanguine than John's. That difference may reflect their respective life experiences. John traditionally has been thought of as a rural fisherman; Paul, a sophisticated, well-traveled citizen of Rome. There are conspicuous contrasts in the attitudes of John and of Paul toward the world. Both, nurtured in the Jewish Scriptures, see God as the creator of all that is. Both view God as in control of all human events. Both know that the present world system is transient, soon to pass away. Both, with Peter, expect a new heaven and a new earth.

The difference lies in what to make of the realm of human culture *at the present time.* John can hardly find anything good in the present world of people and things. Paul, on the other hand, rises to majestic rhetoric in praise of God's control of all human enterprise, which he views as tarnished but authentic reflections of the image of God resident in every human person and therefore in all human culture. Both John and Paul, of course, take sin to be the fundamentally correct analysis of the flawed human condition. Both look to divine transformation metaphors of biology—new birth, second birth, vines and pruning, eternal life, and the like. Paul, trained as a lawyer, prefers judicial language—guilt, judgment, adoption, justification, acquittal.

Thinking Christians can draw help from both Paul and John. The machinations of fallen humankind do indeed cluster in pockets of human culture—pornographic art, unjust laws, systematic cheating in business or education, to name but a few. Christians from Arminian traditions, which accent human freedom, seem to incline toward dark views of the world as something to avoid, a realm from which to separate. Such inklings have gotten theologized especially in the Methodist, Holiness, and Pentecostal sectors of the church.

But equally biblical notions about human culture emerge from the pen of the apostle Paul and appear in parts of the church affected by the Reformed tradition. Take, for example, this mind-stretching affirmation given by Paul in a context of advice to Corinthian Christians who limited themselves to favored ambassadors of Christian truth: "All things are yours, whether Paul or Apollos or Cephas or life or death or things present or things to come—all things are yours, and you are Christ's and Christ is God's" (1 Corinthians 3:21–23).

"All things are yours," the heritage of the Christian. All of human culture: all art, all music, all heroic acts of self-sacrifice, all nobility, all compassion. Nothing omitted. Everything belongs to the Christian. The baseball heroes. The master violinist. Makers of fine-silver filigree. The eloquent evangelist. Mother Teresa. Albert Einstein. Tiger Woods. Paul, Apollos, and Cephas: The Lord didn't intend for any to limit openness to any one of God's creatures. All are yours: all people, even all things.

The editor of the essays in this book, and the essayists themselves, here provide thoughtful resources by which to construct a full-orbed worldview that blends both Paul and John. These wise words will help reflective followers of Jesus know what to avoid in the world, what to shun. But they will aid also in the expansion of appreciation for all that is good in human culture, the collected reflections of God's highest creatures who, however tarnished and alone among all living beings, embody the image of God.

I commend these essays to thoughtful Christians everywhere, and especially to young adults who are beginning to learn the immensity and diversity of God's world.

—RUSSELL P. SPITTLER
Provost and Professor of New Testament
Fuller Theological Seminary

Preface

The preface is often the least read part of a book. I hope this one will be an exception, because the aims of the book and the philosophical concerns that inspired it are explained here.

As the title implies, this book considers certain components or factors—*elements,* as I call them—that constitute a *worldview.* It is a book by Christian scholars intended for Christians who seek thoughtful responses to those fundamental questions they find confronting them in many facets of life. More particularly, it is written for young adults who have been powerfully confronted by such questions, perhaps for the first time. Some of the chapters focus on academic disciplines—natural science, behavioral science, literature—that one typically encounters in colleges and universities. Other chapters deal with everyday issues of living, such as work and leisure. Still others center on cultural phenomena: music, films, and politics. As I've thought of the relative placement of the chapters and the connections among them, the most descriptive word that comes to my mind is *montage:* separate pictures combined to form a composite picture. Although the chapters are linked to each other in various ways (both obvious and not so obvious), each can be read independently.

Consequently the reader will look in vain for a single, sustained argument from beginning to end. It is not that sort of book. Still it does exhibit a certain recurring, if not conspicuous, theme: the integration of faith, learning, and life. To integrate is to form, coordinate, or blend into a functioning, unified whole. To integrate faith, learning, and life means to develop for oneself a thoroughly Christian way of thinking about and responding to issues and all kinds of life-situations. It means developing a distinctively Christian perspective on all matters of faith, all modes of inquiry, and all of the profound questions life evokes.

Integration in its richest expression—thinking and acting in a thoroughly Christian way—is neither easily achieved nor achieved once and for all. In fact, it is best not thought of as an achievement at all. It is really more a process that continues throughout life as we reflect on the meaning of our faith and try to let it shape our responses to new ideas and experiences.

Unfortunately, what we see more often than integration is some form of juxtaposition. To juxtapose two things is to set them alongside each other. The interaction between them may be real in certain specific ways, but the scope of interaction is limited and the two are never truly unified. The psychology student is merely juxtaposing her faith and her college major if she fails to think carefully about how her Christian beliefs relate to the theories of personality she is studying in the classroom. The young business manager is merely juxtaposing his faith and his career if he fails to let the moral implications of his Christian belief system inform his management policies. In general, we juxtapose our faith and our college major, or our faith and our career, or our faith and any other aspect of our life, when we hold our faith in such a way that it makes no evident difference in the way we think about or express ourselves in any of these other areas.

When we speak of faith making an evident difference in how we think and express ourselves, we mean more than simply being able to state our beliefs clearly and succinctly. Indoctrination can achieve these results. But integration and indoctrination are not at all the same. Indoctrination seeks unquestioning acceptance of answers developed by someone else, usually an authority figure. Integration requires discovering answers for oneself, even if mentors, friends, or colleagues assist along the way. Indoctrination, even when well intentioned, inhibits the assumption of responsibility, because it restricts the questioning process which forms the basis of all sound decision-making. Integration, even when difficult and painful, promotes mature faith, because it involves assessing competing ideas and seeks to understand how the Christian faith speaks to such ideas.

With these distinctions in mind, I hasten to note that this book is a deliberate attempt to address those for whom indoctrination is not an acceptable response to life's great (and difficult) issues. It is a book that explores ideas, concepts, and principles, some of which are controversial and all of which resist easy answers. It therefore presumes a measure of maturity on the part of the reader. Moreover, it both presupposes and encourages an integrational approach to the subjects it addresses.

The first chapter sets forth the basic elements of any worldview. They are, as I conceive them, (1) ideology, (2) narrative, (3) moral and aesthetic norms, (4) rituals, (5) experience, and (6) the social element. The remainder of the chapters deal in one way or another with these six elements as we see them developed in a Christian worldview. In every case, the authors of the chapters have attempted to do more than provide information about their respective disciplines and fields of expertise. They have attempted to model what it means to think Christianly— to truly integrate faith and learning and life. It is my hope that their words will serve as a stimulus to many young Christians to live out the meaning of their faith in every aspect of their lives.

—MICHAEL D. PALMER
Professor of Philosophy
Evangel University

Acknowledgments

Authors regularly absolve all the people who helped them from responsibility for any errors or deficiencies in the text. That certainly must be done here as well. But while the errors and deficiencies are mine, much credit belongs to many friends and colleagues. And I am not saying this *pro forma*. We are all very much the products of what other people have helped us to become. Regarding this book, many people have helped along the way—from forming the initial idea to producing the final product—and I wish to acknowledge my considerable debt to them.

The editorial board of Logion Press deserves credit for the confidence they placed in me in taking on this project and for their patience and support along the way. David Bundrick, chairman of the editorial board when this book was first proposed, worked hard to ensure that the project had a good beginning. Dayton Kingsriter, who succeeded Bundrick as chairman of the editorial board, devoted many hours to this project. I thank him for his work as a facilitator. Jean Lawson, managing editor, and Glen Ellard, book editor, were helpful, pleasant to work with, and professional in every way. Thanks to Leta Sapp for her design of the layout and text. Kim Kelley did an excellent job coordinating the layout and design of the book. I wish to express special thanks to Dr. Stanley Horton, general editor, for the careful attention he gave to the various drafts of each chapter. Additionally, I wish to thank him for the moral support and patience he extended to me during the development of the book. I have come to have deep affection for him as a person and considerable respect for his ability as an editor. He is a man in whom there is no guile—a gentleman in the truest sense of the word—and I count it a privilege to have worked with him.

What a delight it has been to work with the contributing authors! Their writing has stimulated my thinking beyond anything I had imagined at the outset.

Locally, Evangel University has been a wonderful place for me to mature as a scholar since I first arrived on campus in 1985. From the inception of this project, Dr. Glenn H. Bernet, Jr., Vice President for Academic Affairs, provided encouragement for the project—and money! He is the prime mover in my receiving a grant from the university's Faculty/Alumni Project Fund to underwrite various expenses associated with the development of the book.

Many students at Evangel University also contributed to the overall quality of this book. During two summer sessions (1996 and 1997), students in a general education course entitled Christian Philosophy read earlier versions of some of the chapters that appear here and offered helpful comments. I am gratified that they took seriously my invitation to comment on all aspects of the manuscript.

I am indebted to several colleagues who read and commented on certain chapters. Larry Dissmore, Music Department, commented on the chapter on music. Turner Collins, Science and Technology Department, offered numerous helpful comments on the chapter on science. I literally could not have written my own lead chapter on worldview without the generous help of Twila Edwards (Biblical Studies) and James Edwards (Humanities). When at one point in the development of the chapter I reached an impasse, they devoted almost an entire weekend to reading the manuscript and discussing with me numerous organizational and substantive issues. Michael Buesking, Humanities Department, produced virtually all of the artwork in the text. His pen sketches are a continuing source of satisfaction and pride for me. I am honored to have them appear in this book. Stan Maples, Humanities Department, designed the cover for the book. I thank Stan for his patience in listening to my ideas for the cover design and acknowledge his considerable skill in transforming my imprecise ideas into eye-catching images.

To my colleagues in the Department of Biblical Studies and Philosophy who encouraged me to undertake this project and who extended help along the way I express thanks. Gary Liddle, whose usual teaching duties are in biblical studies but who is really a Renaissance-style generalist, is the unsung hero behind this book. He believes in the concepts, understands them in some ways better than I do, and therefore his words carried special weight at crucial junctures along the way. He offered extensive analysis of several chapters. His questions were searching and his comments enormously helpful.

My wife, Connie Marie, is my encourager and my favorite companion—in the development of this book, as in so much else, *sine qua non.*

—M. D. P.

List of Contributors

Billie Davis, Ed.D. (Administration & Sociology, University of Miami, Florida), is Professor Emeritus and former chair of the Department of Behavioral Sciences at Evangel University in Springfield, Missouri.

Twila Edwards, M.A. (English Literature, Southwest Missouri State University), M.A. (Biblical Literature, Assemblies of God Theological Seminary), is Associate Professor of Biblical Studies at Evangel University in Springfield, Missouri.

Johnathan David Horton, Ph.D. (Music, George Peabody College for Teachers), is Professor of Music at Lee University in Cleveland, Tennessee.

Cheryl Bridges Johns, Ph.D. (Christian Education, Southern Baptist Theological Seminary), is Associate Professor of Discipleship and Christian Formation at the Church of God Theological Seminary in Cleveland, Tennessee.

Edgar R. Lee, S.T.D. (Theology, Emory University), is the Vice President for Academic Affairs at the Assemblies of God Theological Seminary in Springfield, Missouri.

Terrence Lindvall, M.Div. (Fuller Theological Seminary), Ph.D. (Communication, University of Southern California), is Professor of Film and Communication Studies at Regent University in Virginia Beach, Virginia.

Lawrence T. McHargue, Ph.D. (Biology, University of California, Irvine), is Professor of Biology at Southern California College in Costa Mesa, California.

Dennis McNutt, Ph.D. (Government, Claremont Graduate School), is Professor of History and Political Science at Southern California College in Costa Mesa, California.

J. Matthew Melton, Ph.D. (Regent University) is Chair of Communication and the Arts at Lee University, Cleveland, Tennessee.

Gregory J. Miller, Ph.D. (Religious Studies–History of Christianity, Boston University), is Associate Professor of Church History at Valley Forge Christian College in Phoenixville, Pennsylvania.

Charles W. Nienkirchen, Ph.D. (History, University of Waterloo), is Professor of Christian History and Spirituality at Rocky Mountain College in Calgary, Alberta, Canada. He also serves as Adjunct Professor on the graduate faculty of several Canadian seminaries.

Michael D. Palmer, Ph.D. (Philosophy, Marquette University), is Professor of Philosophy and Chair of the Department of Biblical Studies and Philosophy at Evangel University in Springfield, Missouri.

Miroslav Volf, Th.D. (Systematic Theology, Eberhard-Karls Universitat, Tübingen), is Henry B. Wright Professor in Theology at Yale University, New Haven, Connecticut.

Vardaman W. White, Ph.D. candidate (Theology and Ethics, University of Iowa), lives and works in Atlanta, Georgia.

1

Elements of a Christian Worldview

Michael D. Palmer

I t isn't often that I read a book that surprises me, less often one that makes a decisive impression. But I was both surprised and impressed by Chiam Potok's novel *The Chosen*. At the outset of the novel Reuven, the narrator, confesses: "For the first fifteen years of our lives, Danny and I lived within five blocks of each other and neither of us knew of the other's existence."[1] My own childhood and early adult years passed in a medium-sized town in the mountains of western Montana where I knew all the neighbors for several blocks in all directions. So when I encountered Potok's sentence, my imagination was piqued. I discovered, as I read, that Reuven and Danny were blocked from friendship because their closest friends, family, and especially their fathers, embraced competing worldviews. Experiencing the collision of these worldviews captured my imagination and marked a turning point in my reflection on the major forces of belief and feeling that animate my own Christian worldview.

Two Boys, Two Worlds

Reuven Malter and Danny Saunders were Jewish boys who grew up in the 1940s in a densely populated neighborhood in Brooklyn. Until their teen years, they knew nothing of each other because they belonged to different sects, or branches, of Judaism with marked differences in worldview. Danny's family and friends were deeply conservative Hasidic Jews with origins in Russia. In their daily life, they communicated in Yiddish and observed certain cultural practices that unmistakably identified them as Hasidim. The men, for instance, wore black hats and long black coats and grew full beards and earlocks; boys grew side curls and had fringes on the outside of their trousers. Reuven's family and friends, by contrast, practiced a less con-

Hasidism

Hasidism is a Jewish movement founded in Poland in the eighteenth century by a man known as Baal Shem Tov. The name "Hasidism" derives from a related word, *Hasidim*, meaning "the pious ones." The Hasidic movement arose in reaction to persecutions and to the academic formalism of rabbinical Judaism. From its inception, it encouraged joyous religious expression through music and dance, and taught that purity of heart was more pleasing to God than learning. In 1781, the Talmudists declared Hasidism heretical. However, the movement continued to grow and is today a strong and vital presence in Jewish life.

---

[1]Chaim Potok, *The Chosen* (Greenwich, Conn.: Fawcett Publications, 1967), 9.

Yiddish

Yiddish is a High German language written in Hebrew characters that developed during the Middle Ages. The word "Yiddish" is short for *Yiddish daytsh*, literally "Jewish German." Linguists categorize the language as a member of the West Germanic group of the Germanic subfamily of the Indo-European family of languages. Before the annihilation of 6 million Jews by the Nazis during the 1940s, Yiddish was the tongue of more than 11 million people. Although it is not a national language, Yiddish is today spoken by more than 4 million Jews all over the world, especially in the United States, Israel, Argentina, Canada, France, Mexico, Russia, Ukraine, and Romania.

servative Jewish orthodoxy. In their daily life, they communicated primarily in English, wore ordinary American clothing, and grew no beards or earlocks. While the Malters and the Saunderses both longed for the return of the Jews to their homeland, their ideologies dictated very different paths for that to happen. Danny's father, Rabbi Saunders, like others in the Hasidic community, held that the Jews could return to their homeland only after the arrival of their long-promised Messiah. Reuven's father, on the other hand, joined Zionism, an ideological movement that worked to establish the state of Israel. In addition to differing over major political issues, the Saunderses and the Malters differed over everyday activities such as entertainment. Danny and Reuven would never have met at a theater because Rabbi Saunders' worldview forbade attendance of movies.

Torah

Torah means "teachings" or "learning." Jews have used the word in two related but distinct ways. First, Torah is the Hebrew name for the Pentateuch, the first five books of the Bible. The Torah, or Written Law, which Orthodox Jews believe was revealed directly by God to Moses on Mount Sinai, laid down certain laws of moral and physical behavior. Second, Torah is used in a wider sense to refer to all teachings of Judaism, including the entire Hebrew Scripture, the Talmud, and any generally accepted rabbinical interpretation.

Danny's Hasidic branch of Judaism and Reuven's Orthodox branch both believed in God and stressed the importance of the Torah. Yet the Hasidim viewed Reuven's people with suspicion. They called them *apikorsim*, a term of derision used to refer to Jews who abandoned traditional cultural practices and denied certain basic tenets of the Jewish faith like the existence of God, revelation, and the resurrection of the dead. It also referred to Jews who read the Torah in Hebrew rather than Yiddish, an unpardonable sin in the eyes of the Hasidim because Hebrew was the Holy Tongue. To use it in ordinary classroom discourse was considered a desecration of God's name. Reuven's people, of course, did not deny the existence of God. Their education, however, did differ importantly from that of the Hasidic children. While the Hasidic worldview confined education mainly to approved religious subjects, the orthodox added to religion such studies as modern science and psychology, topics profoundly suspect to Rabbi Saunders.

In the early 1940s, with the country fully committed to the war effort, some of the teachers of English in the Jewish parochial schools *(yeshiva)* felt a need to make a statement to "the gentile world." They wanted to show that yeshiva students, known for their studious lifestyle, were as physically fit as anyone else. To do this, they organized the neighborhood schools into a softball league. Not unexpectedly, the rabbis who taught in the yeshivas viewed baseball with skepticism. To them, it was an evil waste of time. They feared its strong appeal, feared it would lure the young people to give up their Jewish identity, feared it would make the young people want to assimilate themselves to American ideas and culture. The young people themselves embraced the game and embraced the thought of being Americans. For them, an inter-league baseball victory "came to take on only a shade less significance than a top grade in Talmud." Success in baseball allowed them to consider themselves full participants in the nation's life: "It was an unques-

Talmud

The word *Talmud* means literally "learning" or "instruction." In Judaism it is the name for a work composed of two parts: Jewish Oral Law and the accompanying rabbinical commentaries. The text of the Oral Law (written in Hebrew) is called the Mishna; the text of the accompanying rabbinical commentaries (written in Aramaic) is called the Gemara. The Gemara developed out of the interpretations of the Mishna by the Jewish scholars (Pharisees of A.D. c.200–c.500), whose hairsplitting arguments made the work a valuable source of supplemental information and comment.

tioned mark of one's Americanism, and to be counted a loyal American had become increasingly important to us during these last days of the war."[2]

Danny and Reuven first met during baseball competition between their two schools. During the game, Reuven's eye was seriously injured when it was struck by a ball hit by Danny. The interaction of the boys, including their eventual friendship following the accident, provides a concrete basis for considering what it means to hold a worldview. It also provides a useful model for thinking carefully and accurately about the main lines of a Christian worldview. Indeed, the story of these Jewish boys merits consideration because the questions it raises—the important ones—are the same ones Christians face today: questions about God, about ourselves, about our community, about what we can hope for, about what we must do. In the pages that follow, we shall explore what it means to have a worldview in general and in particular what it means to have a *Christian worldview*. When we are finished, we will have (like Danny and Reuven) both a deepened appreciation of the questions and a better grasp of the way our worldview hangs together.

What Is a Worldview?

As an initial definition of our topic, we can say that a worldview is a set of beliefs one holds. However, not every set of beliefs forms a worldview. Some sets of beliefs are merely random collections or odd assortments of beliefs. As I look at the books on a shelf in my study, I see one called *Triviata*. Its subtitle describes it as *A Compendium of Useless Information*. A friend gave me the book as a joke. The disconnected statements of fact it contains surely do not constitute a worldview. The beliefs in a worldview hang together, cohere, in a certain way. Rather than standing as a list of disconnected ideas (a compendium of useless information, so to speak), these beliefs fit together in a unified way and form a whole. On this point, one could hardly find a more stark contrast than between *Triviata* and the Talmud. In the Jewish tradition the Talmud represents a centuries-long attempt by many rabbinical commentators to arrive at a unified interpretation of the Jewish oral law. Even when the rabbis differ in their interpretations of the oral law, they continue to strive for a unified interpretation that contains no contradictions.

At the very least, then, a worldview is a set of beliefs that are consistent with each other and form a unified point of view. But even this description is not adequate. For example, a set of beliefs about geometry, balancing the national budget, or navigating a major computer network like the Internet may exhibit both consistency and unity of perspective, but none of these sets of beliefs constitutes a worldview. This is so for at least two rea-

---

[2]Ibid., 12.

sons. First, although consistent and unified in their point of view, they are rather narrow in their focus and deal primarily with technical issues. By contrast, the core beliefs of a worldview address concerns central to the meaning of human life. Second, beliefs about geometry, the national debt, or the Internet have few direct connections to other things we believe or do. The geometer does not have to apply his knowledge to building houses; a theory about balancing the national budget might well never see the light of day beyond the door of the economist who developed it; knowing how to negotiate the Internet says nothing about what kind of information one should seek or share. By contrast, the core beliefs of a worldview have important implications for many other beliefs and practices in daily life. In Danny's Hasidic community, for example, belief in God profoundly affected every other belief and practice.

> **"A worldview is a set of beliefs and practices that shape a person's approach to the most important issues in life."**

Similarly, because they believed Torah to be God's law, the Hasidim also believed they should gather regularly at the synagogue for prayer and study. In addition, they expressed their faith and community loyalties by their rituals (rites of passage such as *bar mitzvah* for boys), dress (black hats and long black coats), outward appearance (full beards and earlocks), and traditional practices (marriages arranged by parents). In short, the core beliefs of a worldview are not narrow in focus but touch almost every other belief and practice of those who adhere to the worldview.

The questions faced by people like Danny and Reuven in the Jewish tradition and by thoughtful people in the Christian tradition are really questions about our most basic beliefs and practices. Whether we are aware of it or not, our core beliefs and practices form a point of view or perspective that is distinctively ours. This distinctive perspective constitutes our *worldview;* our various core beliefs and practices are the *elements* of that worldview. A worldview, then, is a set of beliefs and practices that shape a person's approach to the most important issues in life. Through our worldview, we determine priorities, explain our relationship to God and fellow human beings, assess the meaning of events, and justify our actions. Our worldview even speaks to the most ordinary practices in everyday life, including the types of things we read and view, the types of entertainment and leisure activities we seek, our approach to work, and much more.

Who Has a Worldview?

In one respect, the answer to the question "Who has a worldview?" is quite easy: Everyone capable of considering the question already has a worldview. The ways we speak and act give evidence that we have a worldview. They show that we hold certain core beliefs, that we have adopted a certain set of priorities, that certain stories strike us as particularly telling and seem to move us, and that certain practices and social arrangements have special importance for us.

Of course, it is *not* true that everyone who has a worldview possesses it in precisely the same way. Some people possess a worldview only in the sense that they have inherited a set of beliefs and practices from their family and immediate community. They do not understand their beliefs and they do not grasp the larger significance of their actions. They believe and act in an uncritical, naive manner rather than in a self-reflective way. Often as not they will explain why they believe or do something by referring to their family traditions, church standards, or political party affiliation. In short, they have a worldview only in the sense that someone else has imposed it on them, not because they have thoughtfully considered the important issues and chosen their worldview.

It is not uncommon for people who have merely inherited a worldview to assume that everyone else's beliefs and practices are similar to their own. Unchallenged by any other point of view, they may grow apathetic toward their own. In the mid-1960s, in a song entitled "Nowhere Man," the Beatles captured the sense of life for a person who has grown indifferent to his worldview.[3] According to the song's lyrics, *nowhere man* occupies a place in *nowhere land* making pointless plans for *nobody.* To all appearances, he has no idea where he is going. In perhaps the most poignant line of the song, we hear that nowhere man "doesn't have a point of view." The line raises a compelling question: Is it possible to have no point of view? Probably not. More likely, nowhere man's real problem is not that he literally has no point of view. His case is worse than that. He is indifferent to the only point of view familiar to him. He therefore might as well not have a point of view, because he has no idea where he is going in life.

> **"Who has a worldview? Everyone capable of considering the question."**

The discovery that not everyone follows patterns of belief and practice similar to one's own can come as an abrupt awakening. When it does, two types of response are common. Some people respond defensively. They retreat behind memorized dogmas and familiar clichés and generally adopt the position that they have nothing to learn from outsiders. (In *The Chosen,* the Hasidim—particularly the young teenagers—adopted this

---

[3]Beatles, "Nowhere Man," original track released in 1965 by Northern Songs, Ltd.

posture toward non-Hasidic Jews.) Other people respond with embarrassment. By comparison to the beliefs or practices of others, their own may seem unimportant, trivial, or unsophisticated. They may try to downplay them or even hide them when interacting with outsiders. (One of the issues Danny faced when he went away to the university was whether he should cut his earlocks and wear clothing that did not identify him as a Hasidic Jew.) Defensiveness and embarrassment often signal immaturity. They indicate that the persons in question are not completely comfortable with their own worldview.

> "We are the captains of our fate and the masters of our soul in our ability to be deliberative about the life we lead."
>
> —*Vincent E. Rush*

We have been talking about the way people acquire their worldview. Some people, we said, merely inherit their worldview. Those who acquire their worldview only in this limited way may well grow apathetic or indifferent to it. Or if they unexpectedly encounter someone who has a different worldview, they may respond defensively or with embarrassment. By contrast, a worldview can be acquired through *choice.* To choose, in the sense intended here, does not mean merely that one selects a worldview from among several available options—as if one were a child picking out a puppy at a pet store. Choosing also does not mean that one rejects one's inherited worldview. Choice refers to a deliberative process that is almost more a style than an action. Alertness, awareness, self-reflection, being present to the alternatives—all of these signify what is meant by choice. Choosing means that one is not tossed about like flotsam and jetsam on the sea of life. As one author has pointed out, "We may not be the captains of our fate and the masters of our soul with total ability to control the environment around us, but we are the captains of our fate and the masters of our soul in our ability to be deliberative about the life we lead . . ."[4] In short, the person who *chooses* is the opposite of the Beatles' *nowhere man.*

Everyone capable of reflecting on worldview issues already has a worldview. The critical question is how one finally acquires that worldview. To acquire it as an inheritance from one's immediate family and community may be a good way to begin. Indeed, that is the way everyone first acquires a worldview. But in an important sense an inherited worldview is not yet fully one's own. To have it fully as one's own—to live it with conviction and believe it with understanding—requires that one *choose* it. The person who chooses a worldview by making it a matter of deliberate, reflective selection will not be apathetic or indifferent toward it. Nor is that person likely to be either

---

[4]Vincent E. Rush, *The Responsible Christian* (Chicago: Loyola University Press, 1984), 94.

defensive or embarrassed about it. Finally, the person who chooses a worldview is better placed both to evaluate deficiencies in his own worldview and to learn from other worldviews.

Elements of a Worldview

A well-developed worldview typically provides a broad picture of life's essential concerns. A well-developed worldview, thus, usually exhibits certain major components, or *elements*. In a science like chemistry, an element is a fundamental substance that consists of atoms of only one kind. We use the word *element* in this way when we speak of chemical elements such as hydrogen or helium in the periodic table. In mathematics an element is a basic member of a mathematical or logical set. In the Christian faith, we use the word *elements* (plural) to refer to the bread and wine associated with remembering Christ's last supper. Within the context of talking about a worldview, however, an element is more like a definable aspect of how human beings

Holmes's Description of a Worldview

In recent decades Christians have found themselves facing formidable intellectual challenges on several fronts. Not the least of these has been the challenge to articulate a worldview that at once remains true to the central faith tenets of Christianity and at the same time responds adequately to contemporary developments in empirical science, moral theory, the arts, and philosophy. One of the leaders in meeting this challenge during the second half of the twentieth century is the philosopher Arthur Holmes. In the following passage, Holmes provides a summary of the main criteria of an intellectual framework that merits being called a worldview.

"An overall world view, then, will have the following characteristics:

1. It has a *wholistic* goal, trying to see every area of life and thought in an integrated fashion.

2. It is a *perspectival* approach, coming at things from a previously adopted point of view which now provides an integrative framework.

3. It is an *exploratory* process, probing the relationship of one area after another to the unifying perspective.

4. It is *pluralistic* in that the same basic perspective can be articulated in somewhat different ways.

5. It has *action outcomes*, for what we think and what we value guide what we will do."

This passage is excerpted from *The Making of a Christian Mind, A Christian World View & the Academic Enterprise* (Downers Grove, Ill.: InterVarsity Press, 1985), 17. Other notable works by Holmes are *All Truth is God's Truth* and *Contours of a Christian Worldview*.

explain and practice what they believe. A well-developed worldview typically exhibits at least six distinct elements.[5] They may be briefly described as follows.

1. Ideology. The ideological element of a worldview consists of core beliefs. These beliefs are usually expressed in a formal and precise way such as in philosophical propositions, statements of a creed, authoritative formulas, or doctrines. The ideology of a worldview is also usually expressed in a systematic way, meaning that some attempt is made to ensure that the key statements are consistent with each other. In *The Chosen*, Rabbi Saunders taught Danny the ideologies of Hasidism through intensive study of the Talmud.

2. Narrative. The narrative element of a worldview recounts certain significant events in the history of those who hold the worldview. In some cases, narratives also deal with future events. Narratives may be about many things, for example, a famous person, the founding of a people or a nation, the beginning of the world, or someone's interaction with God or gods. Narrators often express these events in sacred writings, myths, historical accounts, stories, legends, or even lyrics of a hymn. Artists sometimes also represent narrative themes in paintings or other forms of art. If ideology expresses core beliefs in precise and formal language, narrative expresses core beliefs by example, image, symbol, or metaphor. The biblical stories of Abraham, Isaac, and Jacob are central to the Hasidic worldview.

3. Norms. A norm is a standard of some kind. When we talk about a worldview, two of the most important kinds of norms are *moral, or ethical,* norms and *aesthetic* norms. Aesthetic norms provide a basis for making decisions about what is beautiful, pleasing, or sublime.[6] Moral norms establish requirements for

---

[5]My thinking about the general categories of belief and practice that make up a worldview was stimulated by Ninian Smart, *Worldviews, Crosscultural Explorations of Human Beliefs,* 2d ed. (Englewood Cliffs, N.J.: Prentice Hall, 1995).

[6]Chaim Potok has nothing significant to say about aesthetics or aesthetic norms in *The Chosen*. However, aesthetics is a major theme in two of his novels about a painter named Asher Lev: *My Name Is Asher Lev* (New York: Alfred A. Knopf, 1989) and *The Gift Of Asher Lev* (New York: Alfred A. Knopf, 1990). Since biblical times, orthodox Judaism has expressed mixed feelings about art and artistic beauty. On the one hand, the Scriptures report that God himself dictated much of the design of the ancient tabernacle and the artifacts that it housed. We are told that He even identified the skilled artisans who were to make the various ceremonial utensils and priestly garbs. So Judaism clearly has a historical interest in items of beauty and the judgments that relate to what is beautiful. On the other hand, the Scriptures forbid the making of "graven images." In orthodox Judaism, this commandment has been interpreted to forbid the making of pictures, especially portraits of persons. Jewish artists have, therefore, tended to slant their art toward highly symbolic forms.

right conduct, stipulate our responsibilities, and generally explain to us what kind of person we should be. In *The Chosen*, the place of moral norms in Judaism emerges powerfully at one point when Reuven meets Danny in the hospital for the first time after the eye injury. Angry at Danny, Reuven at first refuses to speak but then blurts out: "You can go to hell, and take your snooty bunch of Hasidim along with you." When Mr. Malter learns of Reuven's unkind remark, he says. "You did a foolish thing, Reuven. You remember what the Talmud says. If a person comes to apologize for having hurt you, you must listen and forgive him."[7]

These three elements of a worldview—ideology, narrative, and norms—form an intricate pattern of beliefs. However, this pattern does not exist merely in the abstract. It becomes vital and dynamic within the context of experience and practice. In Orthodox Judaism, for example, the beliefs about God (ideology) are not merely concepts about some neutral and remote deity regarded as the Master of the Universe.[8] He is a being who is actively worshiped. The Hasidim portrayed in *The Chosen* pray to Him in the neighborhood synagogues and talk about Him in their homes, on the streets, and in the shops. His influence is felt in all facets of their lives, for they believe themselves to be His chosen people. The story (narrative) they recount of His deeds in the history of their people is celebrated and reenacted in certain rituals such as those associated with the Passover and Hanukkah. The central narratives together with traditional rituals evoke powerful experiences for the believer.

> **"These three elements of a worldview—ideology, narrative, and norms—form an intricate pattern of beliefs."**

4. Ritual. A ritual is a ceremonial act performed periodically on special occasions. It is designed to reenact or recall a special event. A ritual can be somber or festive, formal or informal. In any case, rituals provide an occasion to reflect on the meaning of one's core beliefs and to evoke an affective response to those beliefs. Both functions are intended to integrate the patterns of belief into the fabric of one's inner life and character. Observing the Passover, for example, involves celebrating, and in a sense reliving, the liberation of the Hebrews from Egyptian bondage described in the Book of Exodus.

5. Experience. When we speak of the experiential element of a worldview, we mean the way that someone becomes acutely aware of the truths expressed in the core beliefs. The beliefs no longer seem abstract and distant. Instead, they become immediately present. The Hasidim are famous for nurturing highly mystical and personal experiences.

---

[7]Potok, *The Chosen*, 63–64.

[8]The expression "Master of the Universe" is commonly used by Jewish people to describe God.

6. Social Element. The core beliefs of any worldview will evaporate like fog in the morning sun if they are not embedded in a social setting. This is so because the social setting provides the organizational structures and other means that allow the beliefs to be perpetuated from one generation to another. One of the most striking features of *The Chosen* is the way Potok provides insight into Hasidic community life. Each Hasidic sect had its own rabbi, its own synagogue and yeshiva, its own customs, its own fierce loyalties. In a poignant comment on community life, Reuven says, "On a Shabbat [Sabbath] or festival morning, the members of each sect could be seen walking to their respective synagogues, dressed in their particular garb, eager to pray with their particular rabbi, and forget the tumult of the week . . ."[9]

We noted earlier that a worldview is a set of beliefs and practices that shape a person's approach to the most important (and many other) issues in life. Everyone, we said, has a worldview. We also briefly described six of the most important elements of a worldview. In what follows we shall examine these six elements in greater detail in preparation for describing a Christian worldview.

The Ideological Element

Worldviews ordinarily arise out of experience and the narratives that exemplify and elaborate on that experience. But experiences vary from one person to another, and narratives by their very nature lend themselves to multiple interpretations. For these reasons, worldviews commonly develop a set of authoritative statements that constitute their ideological element. These statements form a central framework, or system, for explaining reality. Already, we have referred to them as *core beliefs*. Orthodox Judaism, for example, expresses several core beliefs, among them: There is only one God, God created the world, God is actively involved in history. These essential beliefs are part of the ideological element of Orthodox Judaism. These tenets (and other important ones) explain the nature of God and His relationship to the rest of creation, including human beings.

GENERAL FUNCTIONS OF IDEOLOGY

The ideological element of a worldview serves several functions. One function is to bring order and coherence to the wide array of data given in experience. On their surface, the things we experience often seem to have no relationship to each other. Moreover, one person's experiences often seem unrelated to those of other people, especially if the other people live in another country or lived in the past. But ideology can provide a

---

[9]Potok, *The Chosen*, 9.

sense of the connections among seemingly disparate events and among persons separated geographically and temporally. This point is vividly evident in the ideology of Judaism. During the time Moses was trying to secure the freedom of the Hebrews, the plagues that came upon the Egyptians were not simply random, isolated catastrophes. They were part of a larger destiny: God's work in historical events. Judaism has also always nurtured a strong sense of the identity of its people. Jews are not simply isolated individuals, but members of a historical people. The books of the Law remind them of this historical connection to their ancestors. In the Book of Deuteronomy, as Moses is about to articulate the commandments of God,

> **"Worldviews commonly develop a set of authoritative statements that constitute their ideological element."**

he says, "The Lord our God made a covenant with us at Horeb [Mt. Sinai]. It was not with our fathers that the Lord made this covenant, but with us, with all of us who are alive here today" (Deut. 5:2–3). The people these words were spoken to were not present when the covenant was made at Horeb. Nevertheless, the covenant is for them every bit as much as it was for their ancestors, because they are part of a people chosen by God from time immemorial. In short, one function of ideology is to bring order and coherence to experience.

A second function is to provide a basis for assessing the values, insights, and knowledge claims of others. There have been few times in human history when adherents of any given worldview lived an entire generation, much less several generations, without encountering people whose worldview differed radically from their own. Even the most isolated peoples have, on occasion, interacted with outsiders. In point of historical fact, most peoples have interacted with outsiders frequently and in diverse ways, from trade, to war, to cultural exchange. Whenever interaction occurs between one people and another, the question naturally arises: How shall we evaluate and make sense of what these people (outsiders) say and do? The ideology of one's worldview provides a frame of reference for responding to the question. When Daniel and other young members of the Jewish nobility were taken captive in Babylon in the seventh century B.C., they maintained their identity and coped with the worldview espoused by their captors in part because they were well founded in their own worldview. They judged what was good and bad, right and wrong, forbidden, permissible, or required of them in terms of the core beliefs of their own worldview. Without a clear understanding of those core beliefs they might easily have been assimilated into Babylonian life and culture.

A third function of the ideological element is to define the community. In other words, ideology helps separate insiders from outsiders, those who belong from those who do not belong. In each worldview, the beliefs typically accepted by those who hold to the worldview form a framework, a skeleton, that gives shape to the world as perceived by the members of the community. While there is usually some latitude in precisely how to interpret and apply the core beliefs, anyone who stretches the limits too far risks being separated from the community. Major differences in core beliefs usually cannot be tolerated indefinitely. Consider, for example, that the earliest Christians were practicing Jews. A profound ideological split occurred almost at once, however, because the followers of Jesus declared Him to be divine and equal to God—an ideological notion unacceptable to orthodox Jews.

GENERAL IDEOLOGICAL CONTENT

Worldviews that otherwise differ from each other in their specific content—even ones that are radically opposed to each other—exhibit an interesting similarity in the way they develop their general ideological content. In other words, worldviews tend to talk about similar topics. For instance, naturalistic worldviews (like Marxism or atheistic existentialism) and theistic worldviews (like Judaism or Christianity) differ on many important points. They are so different on some points that they conflict with, even contradict, each other. Nevertheless, they talk about similar topics. For instance, they both express ideological views about what exists and they both advance claims about human nature. Let us examine these topics more closely.

Karl Marx

Karl Marx (1818–1883) was a German social philosopher and revolutionary who lived and wrote at the height of the Industrial Revolution in the nineteenth century. He and Friedrich Engels are generally regarded as the founders of modern socialism and communism. With Engels he wrote the *Communist Manifesto* (1848) and other works that broke with the tradition of theorists like John Locke who appealed to natural rights to justify social reform. Marx invoked instead what he believed to be laws of history that lead inevitably to the triumph of the working class. Marx was exiled from Europe after the revolutions of 1848. In his monumental work *Capital* (3 vol., 1867–94), which he wrote while living in London, he presented a trenchant criticism of capitalist economic theory and developed his own economic theory.

For more information about Marx, see Appendix 3, "Karl Marx," on page 470.

Background Theory About What Exists

General ideological statements about what exists constitute what we may call a *background theory* about the nature of the universe. A background theory addresses at least three topics: the *cosmos, God,* and *history.*[10]

The Cosmos. The expression *cosmos* was used first by the ancient Greeks to refer to something beautifully and systematically arrayed—like the threads in a tapestry. The opposite of cosmos was chaos, or disorder. Early on, the Greeks used the term to describe the orderly and harmonious arrangement of the stars and planets as they appeared in the night sky. Today the meaning of the term has been extended to include not only the arrangement of the celestial bodies but the universe at large—quite literally, everything that exists. It includes things we readily see as well as things difficult to see, for example, electrons. It also includes things we cannot see at all but can only think about, such as numbers, concepts, laws of nature. Despite these changes in its usage in modern times, the term *cosmos* still raises questions that the ancient Greeks pondered. If the celestial bodies in the night sky are arrayed in an orderly and harmonious way, what explains their order and harmony? Has someone or something arrayed them according to some plan, or is their appearance only a chance arrangement? A *naturalistic worldview* is one that denies that any event or object has any supernatural significance. Modern naturalistic worldviews hold that scientific laws or principles are adequate to account for all phenomena such as the arrangement of celestial bodies and the movement of electrons. A *theistic worldview,* by contrast, is one that embraces the idea that supernatural powers play a role in the unfolding of events. Theistic worldviews today, therefore, reject the claim that scientific laws alone can explain the world and our experience of it. Marxism and atheistic existentialism are examples of naturalistic worldviews. Judaism, Islam, Hinduism, and Christianity are examples of theistic worldviews.

God. Quite clearly not all worldviews recognize the existence of God. However, all major worldviews assert, or at least imply, a position regarding the existence of God. Judaism, Islam, and Christianity as theistic worldviews have a good deal to say in their ideological, that is, doctrinal, statements about the existence of God, his attributes, his activities. Not unexpectedly Marxism as a naturalistic worldview has less to say about God. Nevertheless, it is not silent on the subject, nor is it neutral.

---

[10]The expression "background theory" comes from Leslie Stevenson, "Rival Theories," chap. 1 in *Seven Theories of Human Nature,* 2d ed. (New York and Oxford: Oxford University Press, 1987). I have also adapted parts of Stevenson's general framework for discussing rival theories of human nature.

Marx himself denied the existence of God. Indeed, he is famous for the claim that religion is "the opium of the people," by which he seems to have meant that the life of faith is deceptive and delusional: It offers no hope of solving life's problems but only succeeds in covering them up temporarily.

History. Every major background theory of the universe also asserts or implies something about history in its ideology. Theistic worldviews emphasize the work of God in the flow of history. They highlight the way God uses people and events at specific times and in specific locations to fulfill His ultimate purposes, which are timeless. For instance, Hasidism, both in point of fact and as described in Potok's novel, identifies a man called the Baal Shem Tov as one specially called by God about the year 1750 to live a pious life and to teach others to live piously. (*Hasidim* means "the pious ones.") Judaism in general also has a strong sense of God's intervention in history: God created the universe and human beings (Gen. 1,2), gave a historical promise to Abraham ("I have made you a father of many nations" [Gen. 17:5]), and even used the enemies of the Hebrews (for example, Pharaoh and Cyrus) to accomplish His purposes. A Christian worldview departs from any Jewish worldview in one crucial respect: Jesus, at once divine and human, is the central figure in the account of God's dealing with humankind.

Naturalistic worldviews assert a blindly mechanical view of history. History is the product of human beings interacting with each other and with impersonal natural forces. However, naturalists are divided as to whether history exhibits patterns—either progress or regress. The French philosopher Jean-Paul Sartre rejected any notion of the natural order "participating in" or being responsible for anything like historical progress. For him, nature has no ultimate purposes, no intentions, no direc-

Jean-Paul Sartre

Jean-Paul Sartre (1905–1980) was a French philosopher, playwright, and novelist. Beginning in 1936 he published philosophical studies and novels, the most notable being *Nausea* (1938) and *The Wall* (1939). During World War II he completed his most important philosophical work, *Being and Nothingness* (1943). Partly because of his involvement with the French resistance forces and partly because of his philosophical brilliance, Sartre emerged after the war as the dominant figure in the French existentialist movement. Sartre himself was an atheist. During the early postwar years he wrote a number of novels and plays, which brought him worldwide fame.

For additional information, see Appendix 2, "Jean-Paul Sartre," on page 468.

tion—it simply exists. Karl Marx, on the other hand, who certainly rejected any notion of divine purpose or plan to history, claimed that nature itself exhibits patterns of progress. Human beings are part of nature; they therefore also exhibit patterns of progress in their history.

Account of Human Nature

Besides providing a background theory of the universe, worldviews offer a general account of what it means to be human. This account will echo certain main themes in the background theory. For example, if the background theory rejects (or is silent on) the notion that the universe has purpose and an ultimate destiny, then the associated account of human nature will also reject (or be silent on) whether the individual person has a purpose or an ultimate destiny. Similarly, if the background theory says that the universe has a purpose and an ultimate destiny, then the associated account of human nature will express the same view about the individual person. Sartre, an atheistic existentialist, portrays the universe as totally lacking purpose and ultimate destiny. Nature does not exist *for* human beings. Indeed, nature does not exist *for* anything. It simply exists—without plan, purpose, intention, hope, or destiny.[11] (A character in one of Sartre's novels, realizing this point as he ponders the roots of a giant chestnut tree, is revulsed by the thought and vomits.[12]) Consistent with this view of the universe, Sartre asserts that human beings, at the outset of life, also lack any essential purpose or destiny. Neither God nor nature gives life meaning. If life ever comes to have a purpose or meaning, it will happen only because one chooses to make it meaningful.

By way of contrast, Judaism and Christianity hold that God created the universe, that He is at work in the universe to bring about His purposes, and that the universe has an ultimate destiny according to His plan. And does humankind fit into God's ultimate scheme for the universe? Yes, indeed! The Book of Genesis, sacred to both Judaism and Christianity, declares that we are made in the image of God. Potok, referring to the man who founded Hasidism, says, "He taught them that the purpose of man is to make his life holy—every aspect of his life: eating, drinking, praying, sleeping."[13]

---

[11]Jean-Paul Sartre's most notable philosophical views are set forth in *Being And Nothingness, A Phenomenological Essay on Ontology,* trans. Hazel E. Barnes (New York: Washington Square Press, 1992; published by arrangement with Philosophical Library, c. 1956). This text is the principal philosophical text of modern atheistic existentialism.

[12]Jean-Paul Sartre, *Nausea,* trans. by Lloyd Alexander (New York: New Directions, 1949 and 1964).

[13]Potok, *The Chosen,* 103.

Clearly, a worldview that describes the individual as having a purpose and an ultimate destiny will also express a set of ideals for each person. These ideals can be inner character traits. For example, the apostle Paul, speaking in the first century A.D., describes the task of each person as one of conforming to the image of Christ. He establishes certain character ideals by reference to Jesus. Each person must endeavor to embody the character ideals modeled by Jesus, including personal integrity, humility, gentleness, patience, love, and compassion. Ideals can also be expressed as social conditions. The ancient Jewish prophets, for example, extolled justice as a social ideal. For them, the just society would be one in which the poor and the weak were adequately cared for.

If purposive worldviews seem naturally to express ideals for their adherents, do naturalistic worldviews also offer ideals? The answer seems to be a qualified yes. As we noted earlier, Marx denied the existence of God. He therefore allowed no place in his worldview for a concept of divine purpose for human beings. In that sense, humankind has no destiny and no ideals to achieve. But Marx claimed to discover patterns of progress in human history: He thought that human beings have progressed from ancient barbarism through stages of slavery and feudalism to capitalistic forms of society and economy. The final stage he believed to be one in which workers would come to control industry and other means of production. Control of these economic forces would allow them to change social and political institutions for the better and thereby bring about the best possible (that is, the ideal) relationships among all human beings. In short, although Marx's worldview is certainly nonpurposive, it does seem to identify certain ideals and to advocate striving for them.

Albert Camus, like Jean-Paul Sartre, rejected not only the notion of purpose as it appears in theistic worldviews, but also anything like the patterns of progress described by Marx. For him, reality is absurd—totally lacking meaning, purpose, or plan. This means that, for Camus, human choices are ultimately arbitrary. Things and events are what we make them to be, and there is really no reason for making them one way rather than another. Does this mean that Camus recognized no ideals? The answer is—Indeed, he did recognize ideals. In his most famous ideological publication, *The Myth of Sisyphus And Other Essays*, Camus adapts to his own philosophical purposes the ancient Greek myth about Sisyphus.[14] According to the myth, Sisyphus, King of Corinth, one day incurred the relentless wrath of Zeus. In Hades, the underworld, Zeus punished Sisyphus by compelling him to roll a rock uphill and to repeat this cycle forever.

---

[14]Albert Camus, *The Myth of Sisyphus And Other Essays,* trans. Justin O'Brien (New York: Random House, Vintage Books, 1955), 88–91.

For Camus, Sisyphus is "the futile laborer of the underworld." His activity is utterly senseless, completely devoid of purpose. Should Sisyphus—should those whose lives mirror Sisyphus's life—despair? Camus thinks not? Joy is an option: "One must imagine Sisyphus happy."[15] But how? And where is the ideal in this depiction of the human condition? Joy is possible because the *meaning* of fate is finally a matter to be settled by human beings. Zeus can dictate our fate, but only we can determine what that fate shall mean for us and whether it will undo us. "Sisyphus," says Camus, "teaches the *higher fidelity* that negates the gods and raises rocks."[16] Camus' ideal—his heroic figure—is someone who at once recognizes that the universe is implacably cold and indifferent to human concerns but who nonetheless resolves to achieve a kind of "absurd victory" by determining for himself what his experiences have meant.

Ideals establish what kind of people we should be and exemplify what is worth achieving. Ideals represent reality and the human condition as they ought to be, not as they are. The implication is that things can be better than they are. Thus, when a worldview includes a set of ideals, it also customarily offers an explanation as to why people fail to achieve those ideals. In Jewish and Christian worldviews human beings ideally exist in fraternal communities with each other and in harmony with

Albert Camus

Albert Camus (1913–1960) was a French novelist and man of letters. Born in Algiers, Algeria, much of his intellectual life was devoted to exploring his belief that the human condition is absurd. This fact, together with his association with the French philosopher Jean-Paul Sartre, led many to identify him as a member of the existentialist movement, though his particular brand of humanism distinguished him from that movement. The figures in his plays and novels are certainly presented as recognizing the absurdity and meaninglessness of their situation (a prominent existentialist theme); at the same time, they assert their humanity by rebelling against their situation (Camus's distinctively humanistic turn). Camus's most notable works are the novels *The Stranger* (1942), *The Plague* (1947), and *The Fall* (1956) and the essays *The Myth of Sisyphus* (1942) and *The Rebel* (1951). In 1957 Camus was awarded the Nobel Prize in literature. He died in an automobile accident in 1960. At the time of his death, he was working on an autobiographical novel, published posthumously in 1995 under the title *The First Man*.

---

[15]Ibid, 91.

[16]Ibid.

their Creator. These ideal relationships existed in the beginning, in a garden-like setting. They have been shattered because of human choices to reject God's purposes. In an existentialist worldview like that of Sartre or Camus, human beings ideally live authentic lives carrying out projects that they have chosen freely. They fall short of the ideal because they refuse to accept the burden of their own freedom and because they fail to take full responsibility for the vast range of choices implied by that freedom. In the Marxist worldview, human beings ideally exist in harmony (rather than in competition) with each other, work at satisfying (rather than demeaning) tasks, and enjoy the fruit of their labor (rather than have it taken by others and used against them). The ideal escapes their grasp because of certain underlying capitalist economic arrangements and because of the social and political structures that reinforce capitalist economy. In general, each worldview not only articulates certain ideals, it also explains why human beings fail to achieve them.

> **"In general, each worldview not only articulates certain ideals, it explains why human beings fail to achieve them."**

Ordinarily, when a worldview articulates a set of ideals and then explains how human beings and their social institutions fall short of the ideals, it also offers some solution. If the ideals (or something like them) once existed, then the worldview will explain how to regain what was lost. For example, Judaism identifies a time under kings David and Solomon when Israel was a unified nation. If this time was not quite ideal, it certainly represented a political and social high-water mark for the Jews. The ideal was lost when foreign armies repeatedly invaded their homeland. The ideal can be regained only when the Jews prepare themselves spiritually and God intervenes in history to provide the Messiah.

For some worldviews, of course, the principal ideals never actually existed. They exist only in the future, on the horizon of time. In this case, the worldview will explain how to achieve them. Marxism is just such a worldview. Marxists believe there never was a time in human history when most human beings did not in some way experience a lack of community, did not suffer the indignities of coerced labor, did not lose control over their tools and the products of their labor. But with unrestrained capitalism at the height of the industrial revolution in Europe and the United States in the nineteenth century, these conditions worsened. Women worked in miserable sweatshops and died prematurely. Men competed with each other for low paying jobs. Even children labored excruciatingly long hours in filthy conditions. For Marx, both the cause and the solution were economic. Unrestrained capitalism, rather than social or political arrangements, was responsible for the prevailing misery and alienation. A better life—indeed, the *ideal* life—can be achieved only in the future as economic conditions are changed.

Summary

In this section, we have discussed the ideological element of a worldview. First, we cited three general functions of ideology: (1) to bring order and consistency to the data given in experience, (2) to provide a basis for assessing the values, insights, and knowledge claims of others, and (3) to define the community. These functions of ideology are not unique to one worldview. Rather, they are common functions of any worldview. Next we provided a sketch of the general ideological content of a worldview. Here again, we noted that however different worldviews may be in their specific content, they talk about similar topics. They provide, for instance, a background theory about what exists. Three central topics of the background theory are the cosmos, God, and history. Worldviews also provide a general account of human nature. This account will explain whether or not human life has purpose, what ideals are worth achieving, in what respect human beings fall short of the ideals, and how the ideals can be achieved. The ideological content of a worldview is ordinarily expressed in philosophical propositions, statements of a creed, authoritative formulas, or doctrines. It is also usually expressed in a systematic way, meaning that some attempt is made to ensure that the key statements are consistent with each other. The formal propositional nature of ideology distinguishes it from another important element of a worldview, *narrative,* which commonly has a story-like quality.

The Narrative Element

We pointed out earlier that the narrative element of a worldview recounts certain past or future events having to do with those who hold the worldview. Worldview narratives, however, are not simply records of coincidental happenings or summaries of interesting but chance events. They are stories that tell something special about the worldview or about the people who hold it. They may be about a famous person, the founding of a people or a nation, the beginning or end of the world, someone's interaction with God or gods, or some other event integrally tied to the worldview.

Narratives are a well-recognized feature of religious worldviews. All major world religions abound with them. The narrative element of Christianity, for example, focuses on the creation of the world; the alienation of the first man and woman from God; the subsequent covenants between God and humankind; the birth, death, and resurrection of Christ; the formation of the Church; and the promise that Christ will return to earth to orchestrate the final events of history. But narratives are not limited to religious worldviews. Secular worldviews also contain an important narrative element. Marxism, for instance, tells a rather elaborate narrative focusing on the unfolding of human history, the impersonal forces that shape human nature, the various ways human beings experience alienation, the ways economic and political arrangements come into being and change, and the prospects for a better life under new economic and political arrangements.

GENERAL FUNCTIONS OF NARRATIVE

There are two overriding functions of worldview narratives. First, they reinforce and embellish central ideological themes. We might compare a worldview's ideology and its central narratives to the skeleton and flesh of a body. This comparison will mislead, however, if it is taken to imply that one element is somehow more basic or fundamental than the other. Skeleton and flesh together are necessary for a living body; ideology and narrative together are necessary for a flourishing worldview.

Second, worldview narratives provide patterns, or models, for the adherents of the worldview. The language of ideology by its very nature tends to be abstract, technical, and somewhat sparse. In well-developed worldviews, ideology's role is crucial, but the average person finds little delight or encouragement in navigating its intricacies and nuanced distinctions. Narratives, by contrast, engage and capture the imagination. They inspire not only the mind but also arouse the emotions. They invite the hearers to envision and vicariously feel what it would be like to live out the ideological content of the worldview. If the Torah and Talmud set forth the relevant ideological framework for traditional Judaism, the stories of Abraham, Moses, Joshua, David, and Solomon provide its narrative content.[17] If the didactic teachings of Jesus and Paul, James and Peter, and the Apostles' Creed constitute part of the ideological dimension of Christianity, the parables and deeds of Jesus and the accounts in Acts form a crucial part of its narrative content. If the value theory of labor is part of Marx's ideology, the stories of child labor, women suffering and dying in sweatshops, and men laboring long hours in unsanitary and dangerous conditions (all recounted in his book, *Capital*) provide part of the narrative content of his worldview.[18] Narratives may make us laugh or cry; they may amuse or shock our sensibilities. In any case, they provide models—for character development, for how and how not to behave, for what are and are not acceptable social arrangements.

---

[17]In Potok's novel, Mr. Malter is a Zionist partly because the land of Israel is the site of the stories about persons and places important to Judaism: Abraham and Isaac, Jericho and Solomon's temple.

[18]Karl Marx, *Capital*, vol. 1, ed. Frederick Engels, trans. Samuel Moore and Edward Aveling (New York: International Publishers, 1967). See especially Chapter X, "The Working Day."

Types of Narrative

The burden of narrative is to recount the central events, past and future, of a people and their worldview. The function of narrative is to reinforce central ideologies and to provide models for the adherents of the worldview. Having said this, however, we should note that the narrative content of a worldview may take several forms. We briefly discuss five of them here.

Sacred Writings

In any tradition, sacred writings (believed to be divine words) are distinctive from other cultural stories or legends in (1) the authority they command, (2) the religious purposes they serve, and (3) the extent to which all orthodox thinkers in the tradition must square their thought with them. In some theistic worldviews, the most important narratives appear in texts regarded as sacred writings. Thus, for example, in Judaism the narratives central to the faith—the accounts of Abraham, Moses, Joshua, the judges, kings, and prophets—are recounted in texts whose scriptural status is unquestioned among orthodox Jews. Christians believe the same about narratives found throughout the Bible but especially those of Jesus and the apostles in the New Testament. In the Hindu tradition, the most important and well-known worldview narrative appears in the *Bhagavad Gita (Song of the Lord)*, a small fragment of scared dramatic poetry which forms part of a larger epic poem.[19] In it, a man named Arjuna, the hero of the narrative, seeks the advice of Krishna, the principal Hindu deity, as Arjuna is about to enter an important battle involving all the people of India.

Myth

A perfectly good word, *myth* has come to have a bad reputation in some circles. It derives from the Greek word for stories, *mythoi.* The Greek *mythoi* were most often about the gods and their interaction with human beings. Over time, Greek culture (including its religion) fell into disrepute. Its myths came to be viewed as stories not based in fact, "false stories." Among scholars today, however, the word *myth* refers strictly to a narrative in which divine beings play some role. Using it in this way does not address the issue of whether or how the narrative can be considered true. In other words, evaluation of the truth of a myth is a separate issue from the question of the role it plays in the worldview. Moreover, even if it is not historically

---

[19]The Bhagavad Gita is unquestionably a sacred writing, but strictly speaking it is not considered Scripture (i. e., divinely revealed sacred writing) in the Hindu tradition. Among sacred writings of Hinduism, only the four Vedas (ancient books of psalms) and certain of the Upanishads (ancient books of philosophy) are regarded as Scripture.

factual, it may still function as a narrative that contributes importantly to a worldview.[20]

Myth is a distinct category from sacred writings. In the ancient world, sacred writings were primarily used in religious rites and ceremonies. At special sacred convocations, ordinary people would hear the sacred text read by a priest for purposes of encouragement and instruction.[21] Of course, myths are not without their religious element. They are, after all, stories about the interaction of divine beings with human beings. But historically they have not served the same priestly functions served by sacred writings, especially Scripture. Rather, they found their place in the public assembly, the market place, and the outdoor theaters of the ancient world.[22]

One can hardly understand ancient worldviews without coming squarely to grips with their myths. This point certainly holds in the case of the ancient Greeks. For instance, Homer's myths, in the form of two epic poems, the *Iliad* and the *Odyssey*, are undoubtedly the most famous and influential from the ancient Greek world. The *Odyssey* is the story of Odysseus, the last Greek warrior to return home following the defeat of Troy. At every turn in the tale, Odysseus encounters strange mythical creatures: a giant one-eyed Cyclops, sea nymphs, lotus-eaters, sirens. And at each turn of the tale, his way is either hindered or facilitated by some god. When he finally arrives at his own island-home, he must defeat a corps of men, suitors, who seek to possess his property and take his wife for their own. On the years-long journey home, Odysseus—full of cunning and guile, the daring and impetuous warrior—must learn to approach life's challenges with a new frame of reference. Gradually, he learns patience, temperance, and humility. Only when he learns these lessons does he finally arrive on Ithaka, his beloved island-

---

[20]For a more complete discussion of myth see Joseph Campbell, *The Hero With a Thousand Faces*, 2d ed. (Princeton, N.J.: Princeton University Press, Bollingen Series XVII, 1968), and Joseph Campbell and Bill Moyers, *The Power of Myth* (New York: Doubleday, 1988).

[21]Sacred writings in any tradition, including Judaism and Christianity, were not readily available to ordinary people until long after the invention of movable type in the fifteenth century. Today's availability of the Bible in bookstores, libraries, computer CDs, and hotel rooms gives a completely misleading view of what it was like in the ancient world to have a sacred text.

[22]The Bhagavad Gita, in the Hindu tradition, is an example of epic poetry that came to be absorbed into a religious framework and made to function in subordination to a religious doctrine. Homer's epic poems, the *Iliad* and *Odyssey*, in the Greek tradition are more nearly myths in the sense described here. Homer's epic poems, though recited on religious occasions and incorporated into festivals and public convocations having religious significance, are poems first of all, not vehicles for conveying religious themes.

home, and become reunited with his devoted wife, Penelope.

Why did this story have such power for the Greeks and resound so eloquently for succeeding generations in Western civilization? Ninian Smart suggests a partial answer, that the ultimate meaning of myths has to do with deep impulses in our psyche: "[Myths] have to do with how we can come to terms with our feelings, and how we can achieve personal integration and wholeness."[23] Odysseus's journey home is really a journey toward a sort of wholeness of the self not possible under the old Greek warrior model. But, as Smart also points out, myth traditionally has an overriding communal meaning: "A myth is not just about me: it is about us."[24] The story of Odysseus, then, is about one man who found his way home and in doing so discovered a new way of living; but it is also the story of an entire people. Indeed, it is a story of how to approach life. Late in the poem, for instance, Homer has Odysseus say:

> Of mortal creatures, all that breathe and move,
> earth bears none frailer than mankind . . .
> No man should flout the law,
> but keep in peace what gifts the gods may give.[25]

Quite simply, Homer's *Odyssey* spoke to the Greeks, and it has spoken to successive generations in the West, because its themes transcend the story of one warrior.

Homer

Homer (eighth century B.C.) is the most famous poet (bard, or singer) of the archaic period of Greek history. According to ancient tradition, Homer was blind. Also according to ancient tradition, he composed two epic poems from material carried down from the thirteenth century B.C. by a long oral tradition: the *Iliad* and the *Odyssey*. Today these poems are considered the prototypes for all epic poems and are counted among the greatest works of Western literature. The *Iliad* tells of an episode lasting a few days in the ten-year-long war between the Greeks and the Trojans: the wrath of Achilles and its tragic consequences, including the deaths of Patroclus and Hector. The *Odyssey* begins ten years after the fall of Troy. It recounts how one of the Greek heroes, Odysseus, finally makes his way home to Ithaca where he is reunited with his wife, Penelope, and his son, Telemachus.

---

[23]Ninian Smart, *Worldviews*, 94.

[24]Ibid.

[25]Homer, *The Odyssey*, trans. Robert Fitzgerald (Garden City, N.Y.: Anchor Books, Doubleday & Co., 1963), 340.

Historical Narrative

Myth remains a viable form of narrative in today's world. But since the beginning of the scientific era, and especially since the advent of modern techniques for writing history, the power of myth-telling has diminished. Poised as we are to step into the twenty-first century, we seem to have a strong need to discover and retell what the past was actually like. We desire to place persons and events together in a coherent order. Ken Burns's ten-hour PBS television history "The Civil War" and his more recent eighteen-hour television story "Baseball"—both immensely popular—make the point. Part of their appeal, and part of the appeal of historical works generally, is that they answer our desire to know something about ourselves. For to know something of the story of our group is to know something of ourselves.

But even as we speak of knowing ourselves, we confront two competing interests in the production of historical works. First, we tend to seek the same answer to our historical questions that was sought by the evil queen in the fairy tale *Snow White*. "Mirror, mirror on the wall, who is the fairest of them all?" she asked, expecting that the mirror would name her the fairest woman in the land. We tend to romanticize the past, finding heroes at crucial junctures. In so doing, we make *ourselves* look better than perhaps we deserve. If George Washington refused to lie about cutting down the cherry tree, then his virtue accrues in some small way to all Americans. If one of my ancestors in the nineteenth century ran for the office of Vice President of the United States, then his fame somehow becomes an occasion for me to boast.

The second interest in producing a work of history is to establish an accurate record of events and persons based on empirical evidence and appropriate documentation. When history is pursued with this interest in mind, great heroes sometimes seem less brilliant, less virtuous.[26] Perhaps one of our heroes from the founding of our democracy turns out to have owned slaves.

So historical narratives elicit competing interests. On the one hand, history is about more than the past; it is about *us*. It is in our interest to know our history, because it is in our interest to know about ourselves. But this interest encourages us to inflate the past, make it something more and better than it was. On the

---

[26]However, one should be aware of an issue in writing history: revisionism, "a tendency in American historiography in the 1960s and early 1970s to rewrite the history of the cold war and shift the blame for it onto the U.S.A." (*Harper Dictionary of Modern Thought*, Alan Bullock and Oliver Stallybrass, eds., New York: Harper & Row, 1977, 541ff). In effect, one should realize that even histories are written (and rewritten) by people who may have their own spin on the material. (See, for example, Francis Fitzgerald, *America Revised* [New York: Random House, 1980].)

other hand, history approached critically and scientifically represents an attempt to view the past accurately. It is in our interest to achieve accuracy because history can then serve as a partial guide to the future by helping us avoid past mistakes. But this interest in accuracy can have the effect of deflating the past, making it seem mundane or ordinary and therefore not worthy of our attention.

The two competing interests discussed here—the interest in knowing about ourselves and the interest in accuracy—raise a compelling question: If the critical, scientific approach to history succeeds so often in deflating our cherished images of persons and events in our past, why pay attention to those who produce such histories? The answer is that history which results from critical inquiry has authority for us. The modern historian is part of what Smart calls "the fabric of modern scholarship and science which for us have an entirely convincing air."[27] It is precisely this authoritative and "convincing air" of modern history that makes it like ancient myths. Today, we look to historical narratives and biographies for illumination in the way people once looked to myths that told the story of the human race.

Literature and Drama

Histories and biographies play a more important role in the modern era than at any other time in the past. This is not to say that modern people look to them exclusively or even primarily for illumination on the human situation. Literature and drama (whether on the stage or the screen) have proven to be particularly compelling media for providing us significant stories about the human condition. As such they also serve as powerful instruments for reinforcing ideology and for providing models.

Stage drama and certain oral and written stories, of course, have been used from the beginning to fulfill these two functions. Ancient Greek tragedy is famous for its portrayal of persons who reached beyond the bounds of appropriate human behavior. In the Greek tradition, honor, pride, and a quick wit were considered desirable qualities. But hubris, or boastfulness, excessive pride, and mental skill without self-reflection were considered character flaws. Sophocles' tragic drama *Oedipus the King* dramatically presents the consequences of a life lived presumptuously. Oedipus, according to Greek legend, was a man who fulfilled an ancient prophecy that he would kill his father and have children with his own mother. As Sophocles presents the story, Oedipus came to fulfill the prophecy because he relied too much on his own talents and acted without true wisdom. In the last lines of the play, the leader of the chorus summarizes the chief conclusions to be drawn from Oedipus's experience:

---

[27]Smart, *Worldviews*, 81.

> Let every man in mankind's frailty
> Consider his last day; and let none
> Presume on his good fortune until he find
> Life, at his death, a memory without pain.[28]

Oedipus the King reminded the Greeks of important expectations laid down by the dominant worldview, and Oedipus himself served as a model for how not to live life. The Old Testament account of Samson serves a similar purpose. Despite his religious upbringing and despite repeated reminders of his spiritual status as a moral force, Samson cavalierly forgot the source of his strength—God. In the end, he was to be more pitied than admired. Thus, his story also constitutes a powerful, negative model.

In the twentieth century, novels have become prominent vehicles for presenting, reinforcing, or examining ideology and for providing models. In 1906, Upton Sinclair published *The Jungle*, a novel that presented a vivid and realistic picture of dangerously unhealthy working conditions in the Chicago stockyards and meat packing industry. The novel also clearly

Sophocles

Sophocles (496–406 B.C.) was a playwright, a respected public figure, a general, and a priest in the classical Greek period. During a career that saw him compose approximately 123 dramas, he won numerous prizes. Compared to other playwrights of his time, Sophocles was known as an innovator. For instance, he added a third actor, increased the size of the Chorus, and introduced scene painting. Although we have more than 1,000 fragments from his works, only seven complete plays survive. His best-known works are *Antigone* (c.441), *Oedipus the King* or *Oedipus Tyrannus* (c.429), and *Oedipus at Colonus* (401). Sophocles's characters are dramatically interesting in that their destinies are determined more by their own character traits than by the Greek gods. Partly for this reason, Sophocles's work has profoundly influenced Western tragedy. The fourth century B.C. philosopher Aristotle, in his work *Poetics*, treated *Oedipus Tyrannus* as an ideal example of Greek dramatic irony.

---

[28]Sophocles, *Oedipus Rex*, in *The Oedipus Cycle*, trans., Dudley Fitts, and Robert Fitzgerald (New York: Harcourt, Brace & World, Harvest Book, 1939 and 1949), 78.

expresses Sinclair's socialist convictions.[29] He wished to denounce unregulated capitalism as an acceptable economic arrangement in any worldview. Earlier, we discussed Camus's philosophical work *The Myth of Sisyphus,* in which he expresses the view that reality offers no overarching purposes to support or explain human existence but that human beings can determine for themselves what meaning life will hold. He develops these same themes in much more powerful imagery in his literary works *The Stranger, The Plague,* and *The Rebel.* The characters in these works, although keenly aware of the meaninglessness of the human condition, assert their humanity by rebelling against their circumstances. C. S. Lewis, famous for his reasoned defense of the Christian faith in works like *Mere Christianity* and *The Problem of Pain,* also wrote substantial novels (*That Hideous Strength* and *Perelandra*) that embodied distinctly Christian themes. Chaim Potok's *The Chosen,* the novel referred to many times already, and a good many other novels of his, offer profound insights into modern Jewish life and its worldview in America.

If the modern novel stands at the forefront of literature as a vehicle for articulating worldview themes, film has almost eclipsed stage drama. This is not to say stage drama is languishing; it is not. But the film industry has become a multibillion-dollar industry, and its powerful influence on the minds of young and old alike shows no signs of abating. Norman McLean's poignant novella *A River Runs Through It* achieved critical acclaim but only a modest readership when it was published in 1976 by the University of Chicago Press. It became a worldwide box office hit when Robert Redford released his film version in 1994. *The Bridges of Madison County* initially received only limited attention as a novel. As a 1995 film starring Clint Eastwood and Meryl Streep, it gained an immediate and widespread viewership.[30] Without question, film has captured the imagination of modern audiences in a way that literature and drama never approached. It has therefore become the most powerful medium of the twentieth century for presenting, reinforcing, or examining ideology, and for providing models.

Narrative in Visual Art

Narrators (writers, storytellers) express their narratives verbally—in sacred writings, myths, historical accounts, novels,

---

[29]*The Jungle* demonstrates that authors do not control how readers will interpret their work. Instead of convincing Americans of the need for socialism, *The Jungle* provided added impetus for passage of pure food and drug laws.

[30]Notably the film stands on a worldview that allows a bored housewife to have an adulterous encounter. Partly as a result of the widespread success of the film version, the novel went on to sell more than ten million copies.

and other literature. Sometimes they combine the spoken word with choreographed action, as in drama and film, or combine lyrics with music, as in a ballad. However, words are not essential to the expression of narrative. Using nonverbal symbols, artists can express the central narrative themes of a worldview in media as diverse as painting, sculpture, icon, or architecture. The Hebrew Scriptures describe in vivid detail the construction of the ancient Hebrew tabernacle, the tentlike facility used for worship prior to the construction of the temple under king Solomon. The tabernacle itself together with the priestly vestments and sacred utensils used inside it all expressed—without words—the narrative of the sacred covenant between the Hebrew people and Yahweh.

A twentieth century Russian Jewish painter, Marc Chagall, eloquently expresses the modern Jewish experience and worldview in his paintings. One painting, "White Crucifixion," depicts a crucifixion scene. The man on the cross wears a crown of thorns and a Jewish prayer shawl for a loincloth. All around the crucifixion scene are small images of modern Jewish persecution, including depictions of unspeakable atrocities associated with the Jewish Holocaust of World War II.

Secular worldviews also express themselves through art. Marxism expresses itself in a particular genre known as social realism that suffuses matter with a certain brilliance, or shining quality. Paintings in this genre present human figures in heroic poses and emphasize the importance of production or revolutionary war. With social realism we have art in the service of politics: painting furthers the socialist worldview and points toward the consummation of human history.

SUMMARY

In this section, we have discussed the narrative element of a worldview. First, we cited two functions of worldview narratives: (1) they reinforce and embellish central ideological

Marc Chagall

Marc Chagall (1887–1995) was a painter, printmaker, designer, sculptor, ceramicist, and writer. He was born in Belorussia and preferred to be known as a Belorussian artist. (His artistic works are noted for their consistent use of folklore imagery.) However, after being exiled from Belorussia in 1923 (when it was part of the former Soviet Union), he became recognized as a major artist in France.

themes, and (2) they provide patterns or models for those who hold the worldview. Just as the functions of the ideological element are not unique to one worldview, so too the functions of narrative are not unique to a single worldview. We also briefly discussed five different forms worldview narratives can take: sacred writings, myth, historical narrative, literature (including drama), and art. These forms are not necessarily the only forms worldview narratives can take, but they are among the most important and common ones.

The Normative Element

A norm is a standard of some kind. We encounter standards in virtually every area of life. For example, when we write, or read what someone else has written, we encounter grammatical standards. When we drive down the highway, we encounter legal standards (in the form of traffic signs and patrol cars). When we cook, or eat someone else's cooking, we encounter culinary standards. Our judgments and evaluations of all kinds of human behavior are made in terms of norms. "Your sentence is unintelligible," "You were driving too fast," "That chili you made is fantastic"—all these evaluations imply reference to a norm, a standard. When we talk about a worldview, two of the most important kinds of norms are *moral* and *aesthetic*.

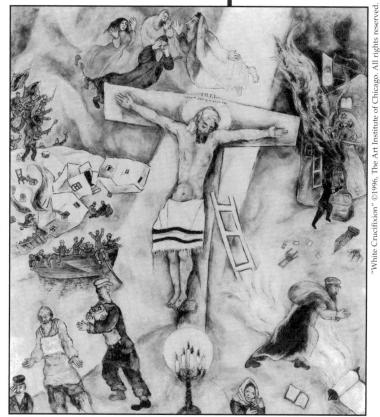

White Crucifixion, the painting shown here, was produced in 1938, three years after Chagall visited Poland and came face to face with the virulent anti-Semitism of that time and place.

Moral norms govern our behavior and character development. They are standards that require, prohibit, or allow certain kinds of behavior or the development of certain kinds of character traits. They can be either *specific* or *general*. Prohibitions against lying, stealing, and injuring are all examples of specific moral norms. The Torah (the Mosaic law) expresses many of the specific moral norms that have been recognized in Judaism throughout history. Ten of these—the "Ten Commandments" or

Decalogue—have had a profound and lasting influence not only on Judaism and Christianity but also on Western civilization at large. Christians believe that Jesus summarized the entire Mosaic law in two commandments: to love God and to love one's neighbor (including one's enemy) as oneself. General moral norms are called moral principles. They include principles of rights, justice, and utility. General moral principles, such as concern for the welfare and fair treatment of the poor, are evident throughout the Hebrew prophetic writings.

> **"When we talk about a worldview, two of the most important kinds of norms are *moral* and *aesthetic*."**

Aesthetic norms are standards by which we judge what is beautiful, pleasant, or sublime. Western culture today seems gripped by the belief that aesthetic judgments are merely expressions of personal taste and that taste is not open to dispute. Either you like something (find it beautiful, for example) or you do not. No standards can be brought to bear in making a judgment or in asking others to evaluate the phenomenon in question. This view, however, seems more an extension of a certain prevalent ideology than a sound aesthetic insight. Moreover, the worldviews that have dominated civilization historically, as well as many that exist today, have not shared the view that taste is indisputable.[31] At the very least, critical thinkers have recognized the important relationship between a worldview's ideology and its aesthetic dimension. If ideology is primarily intellectual, then aesthetics is at least affective: Music, painting, sculpture, and other forms of art have a powerful potential to move us. They can be employed to reinforce the core beliefs of a worldview. Of course, the corollary is that they also have the potential to undermine those core beliefs.

What, then, is the relationship between the normative elements of a worldview and the other elements? Quite simply, the normative elements both shape and are shaped by the other elements. The ancient Hebrews, for example, experienced God as a powerful, creative, dynamic, and often mysterious deity. At times they even feared Him. But their dominant impression was not of a vengeful and capricious deity but of a good, loving, holy, and righteous one. Moreover, the traits they believed Him to possess they eventually came to view as moral mandates for themselves. He expected obedience and sacrifice to himself, but He also expected due attendance to the needs of the poor; He expected proper observance of the Sabbath, but He also expected upright conduct. Nor was correct conduct alone sufficient.

---

[31]Among the ancient Greeks, for example, the philosopher Plato stands out as someone who devoted considerable critical attention to challenging this view. See Plato's dialogues *Symposium* and *Republic*.

He wanted the Hebrews' behavior to reflect an upright character. As for the aesthetic dimension, the God who led the Hebrews out of bondage in Egypt and into the desert also commanded them to erect a tabernacle, a special place where He would meet them. This structure (not so much a building as an elaborate tent) was to be developed according to His own detailed instructions, under the guidance of the most skilled and artistic craftsmen among them. We know about these things, of course, because they have been transmitted to us by important narratives in the Hebrew Scriptures. What we see in this example is that the normative elements of a worldview along with experience, ideology, and narrative are woven together into a single fabric of life for the ancient Hebrews. Similar relationships in these elements would hold for the worldviews of other peoples as well.

The Ritualistic Element

With our discussions of the ideological, narrative, and normative elements of a worldview, we have taken account of the core beliefs and values that enter into our lives. But a worldview consists of more than these beliefs. A vital and dynamic worldview also inevitably includes certain rituals. If the worldview is secular, its rituals might include parades or public re-enactments of politically or nationally significant events (e.g., Independence Day, Memorial Day, New Year's Day). If it is theistic, its rituals will probably include specific acts of worship or special ways of celebrating important religious dates or events (e.g., Hanukkah, Passover, Christmas, Easter).

What separates rituals from any other kind of human behavior, and what makes them have special significance for us? One way to begin to answer these questions is to consider briefly some of the common but often ignored features of our language and behavior.

In the early 1960s, Oxford philosopher J. L. Austin wrote a book that called attention to the special role words play in our language and daily life. Some words, of course, are simply names or labels for objects. Others, *performatives,* Austin noted, actually do things.[32] When a friend asks me to meet her at a certain time and place, and I say "I will, I promise," I have done more than express my feelings or predict my conduct. I have *made* a promise. The same is true when I say "I congratulate you . . ."; "I apologize for . . ."; "I christen this ship . . ."; "I accept your offer . . ." Saying the words constitutes the act itself. Put another way, saying the words actually amounts to performing an act.

---

[32]J. L. Austin, *How to Do Things with Words* (London: Oxford University Press, 1962).

Elaborating on Austin's line of reasoning, we can extend the notion of performatives to include gestures. A soldier recognizes the authority of an officer by saluting, a hostess greets by smiling, a teacher agrees by nodding, a parent denies permission by shaking the head, a man and woman seal their marriage by exchanging rings and kissing.

Now in the last analysis, rituals commonly use both words and gestures performatively. They are a special class of words and deeds that actually do things. A ritual is a ceremonial act performed periodically on special occasions. It is designed to reenact or recall a special event. A ritual can be somber or festive, formal or informal.

> **"A ritual is a ceremonial act performed on special occasions, designed to reenact or recall a special event."**

Not all rituals function in precisely the same way. Indeed, based on the way they function, we can identify at least three different kinds of rituals. One form of ritual is intended to renew bonds. In doing so, it enhances the group. In the United States, we see both the renewing of bonds and the enhancement of the group during Independence Day celebrations each year. Speeches by prominent public figures, family and community picnics, setting off fireworks at the end of the day—all of these are rituals that remind Americans of their common political heritage. In so reminding them, the ritual celebrations renew and strengthen the national bonds that bind Americans together as a people.

Another form of ritual celebrates rites in a way that recreates an event, making it real in the present. One prominent feature of the American Independence Day celebration—setting off fireworks at night—actually serves this function in addition to the function described earlier. Setting off fireworks is a stylized reenactment of battle (muskets firing, cannons blasting) during the Revolutionary War that secured the political independence from England so boldly declared in the famous document of July 4, 1776.

A third type of ritual facilitates transition from one status to another. Bar mitzvah, for example, is the Jewish ceremony in which a young male (traditionally at age 13) is initiated into the religious community and performs his first act as an adult, reading in the synagogue from the weekly portion of the Torah. Graduation ceremonies at educational institutions are a secular means of marking the transition from student to graduate.

All rituals seem to have at least two essential features in common: (1) they provide an occasion for reflection on the meaning of one's core beliefs, and (2) they are intended to evoke an affective response to one's core beliefs. Both functions integrate the intricate patterns of beliefs, narratives, and norms into the fabric of one's inner life and character.

The Experiential Element

When we consider the way a team of programmers develops a new computer operating system or the way a logician derives the conclusion of a logic proof or the way a mathematician solves an equation, we notice at once that these tasks are primarily intellectual tasks. The problems in each case are strictly rational in nature and do not require the involvement of the emotions to solve them. Of course, it is not uncommon to hear experts in technical fields speak with passion about their work. But when we hear them talk this way, we do not confuse their enthusiasm with their intellectual ability to carry out their tasks. Whether or not computer programmers, mathematicians, or logicians are affected by the technical tasks that face them is not strictly pertinent to the completion of those tasks. The same is not true when we broaden the discussion beyond technical fields and begin to consider the relationship people have with their worldview. Generally speaking, when people embrace a worldview, they do so with their whole person. This means that when they embrace a worldview they commit themselves not just intellectually but also emotionally and spiritually. Where this is so, the importance of certain affective and spiritual experiences will rival the importance of ideology, the rational element of a worldview.

Affective and spiritual experiences also often play a major role in the birth and development of a worldview. In this connection, it is notable that Judaism and Christianity, both of which have highly developed ideologies, look back to Abraham of the Old Testament as a source of inspiration. Abraham spent his early years in Ur, a place whose inhabitants (Chaldeans) probably recognized many gods. It seems plausible to speculate that, in those days, Abraham's ideology, like that of the people around him, was polytheistic (recognizing many gods). What, then, explains the fact that at the age of 75 he decided to leave his country, his people, and his father's house and set out for a land he had never seen before? The Scriptures do not attribute the move to a change of ideology. Rather they describe an experience: God spoke to him (Gen. 12: 1–3). Abraham's beliefs about God (part of his ideology) seem to have changed and matured only after he responded faithfully to the voice of God. In short, Abraham's experience gave birth to a new way of thinking.

> **"When people embrace a worldview, they commit themselves not just intellectually but also emotionally and spiritually."**

Most religious worldviews give a prominent place to experience. It is commonly regarded as a driving force in their birth and development. Does the same hold true for philosophical worldviews? In many cases, the answer is yes. A common misconception about philosophical worldviews is that they are exclusively a product of the intellect. The ancient Greek philosopher Plato advanced a more accurate view when he asserted that philosophy begins in wonder. In other words, philosophical reasoning is commonly motivated by experiences that profoundly affect us. The birth of a child, the death of a dear friend, political upheaval, encounters with majestic or fearful natural phenomena—these experiences and countless others as well can lead us to ponder questions of ultimate concern. When reflection on such issues deepens sufficiently, a philosophical worldview may emerge.

The development of Plato's own philosophical worldview illustrates the point. Plato was born in 428 B.C., not long after the beginning of the war between Sparta and Athens, which lasted for nearly three decades (431–404 B.C.). During his youth he experienced the demise and eventual collapse of political institutions in Athens and experienced firsthand the social chaos the city fell into. These experiences of his youth seem to have had a powerful impact on his philosophical development. Later, in his mature years, he wrote the *Republic,* one of the chief political and philosophical documents in Western literature. In it, he not only articulates his vision of an ideal society where justice prevails but also provides the central themes of his worldview.

More recent philosophical worldviews, such as Marxism and atheistic existentialism, exhibit a similar pattern. Marxism is generally regarded as an ideology, and this is certainly not an inaccurate way to think of it. But, like Platonism, it did not develop in a social vacuum. Marx himself seems to have been profoundly affected by what he saw and read of the working conditions endured by laborers in nineteenth-century Europe, particularly England. In his major work, *Capital,* he sets out the economic theory he has become famous for. However, he also details the wretched conditions of women who lived (and often died) as virtual slaves in sweatshops, children who toiled in foundries, and men who labored long hours for minimal wages in mills and factories. In short, Marxism emerged as a prominent social ideology in part because Marx himself was deeply moved by what he experienced. Jean-Paul Sartre, widely regarded as the founder of modern atheistic existentialism, lived in France during and between the First and Second World Wars. Many of his most prominent ideological claims—reality has no purposes beyond those we impose on it, human relationships are dominated by power struggles—are rooted in his experiences of that period. Clearly, for people like Plato, Marx, and Sartre, their ideologies were continuous with their experiences, not separate from them.

Two main points emerge from our discussion of the experiential element of a worldview. First, experience is not an incidental feature of a worldview. For the typical adherent of a worldview, it is as important as ideology. Second, experience is integrally bound up with ideology. In some cases, it even serves as the wellspring of ideology.

The Social Element

As we have discussed worldview elements to this point, we have viewed them *synchronically*. In other words, we have ignored their placement in history and discussed them as though they existed in a narrow time period. But of course, this approach is misleading in several ways. For one thing, worldviews do not remain unchanged throughout their history. Therefore, to view them only synchronically means that we are

Plato

Plato (428–348 B.C.) was a Greek philosopher of the classical period. As a young aristocrat headed for a career in politics, the single most important acquaintance he made was that of Socrates, whose life, personality, and teachings profoundly influenced him. Within a few years after the execution of Socrates in 399 B.C. by the Athenians, Plato began to write philosophical works in the form of dialogues (conversations). Many of them feature Socrates. About 386 B.C. near Athens, Plato founded the most influential school of the ancient world, the Academy, where he taught until his death. His most famous pupil there was Aristotle.

Plato's philosophical dialogues fall into three main groups. The early, or Socratic, dialogues, (e.g., *Apology, Crito,* and *Euthyphro*) present Socrates in lively conversations with prominent Athenians over important issues such as piety and courage. Often the views placed in the mouth of Socrates seem to be consistent with what the historical Socrates is believed to have held. The middle period, or mature, dialogues (e.g. *Republic, Phaedo,*

Symposium) still feature Socrates as a powerful thinker and conversationalist, but the views he advances are believed to be those of Plato the mature philosopher. The late period, or critical, dialogues (e.g. *Timaeus, Parmenides,* and *Laws*) seem to retain the dialogue form in name only and bear more resemblance to treatises than dialogues. Often Socrates is not the protagonist; sometimes he makes only a cameo appearance; in the *Laws* he does not appear at all. The later dialogues are called critical dialogues because in them Plato evaluates and challenges his own earlier philosophical views.

Plato's dialogues touch upon virtually every important problem that has occupied subsequent philosophers. His teachings are regarded as among the most influential in the history of Western civilization, and his writings are counted among the world's most important literature.

likely to ignore or overlook the importance of changes in a worldview that occur over time. But also, to view them only synchronically increases the likelihood that we will fail to appreciate one of the most difficult but important tasks facing the adherents of any worldview: successfully perpetuating the core beliefs and practices from one generation to the next. For these and other reasons, scholars have found value in considering cultural phenomena as they occur or change over a period of time. This is called taking a *diachronic* approach. One way of examining a worldview diachronically is to examine the social arrangements and institutions of its adherents.

Max Weber (see sidebar in chapter 5, p. 198) was the first person to undertake a systematic examination of the social arrangements and institutions of religious worldviews. He noticed that religions move in historically cyclical patterns. In the first part of a cycle, a charismatic leader (a prophet, mystic, or clergyman, for example) plays a prominent role. This person conveys a new and powerful vision to people who are prepared to receive it. After they accept the message of the charismatic leader and become his or her disciples, these people enter a phase of consolidating and formalizing the leader's insights. This phase is commonly marked by traditionalism: the followers struggle to maintain the power and vitality of the message as received from the founder. Novelty gives way to routine. Spontaneity gives way to institutionalization. Social gatherings and events that once required little promotion or prior notification now occur according to a fixed schedule. Over time the followers separate into identifiable factions in the group: those who cautiously adhere to the routines of the institution and those who try to recapture the vitality of the founder's original message. The tension between these two factions may last a long time, but eventually a split occurs and the cycle begins again when a new charismatic figure exploits the tension.

Weber's account helps explain many interesting phenomena in religious worldviews. For instance, it helps explain the existence of religious sects. In Judaism, Hasidism originated in Poland in the eighteenth century as a movement responding to persecution and reacting against the academic formalism of rabbinical Judaism. Its charismatic founder was the man called Baal Shem Tov, who encouraged joyous religious expression through music and dance and taught that purity of heart was more pleasing to God than the mechanical repetition of rituals and intensive study of the Scriptures and Talmud. But subsequent generations of Hasidim experienced precisely the kinds of cyclical dynamics identified by Weber. As leaders and sect members alike attempted to consolidate the insights of their founder, they paid increasing attention to external factors that identified them as "pious ones." Almost immediately, clothing and hairstyles (described so eloquently by Potok) began to stand out as identifying traits of the Hasidim. In addition, worship that was once cherished for its spontaneity, joy, and lack of formalism began to take on specific patterns and routines. Even intense study of the Scriptures and Talmud, played down by early leaders, finally became an important feature of Hasidic life. Indeed, study became such an obsession that within a few generations of its inception, Hasidism had produced several great Talmudists. At various historical junctures, the tension between those who faithfully but mechanically held to the traditions and those who attempted to recover the spirit and vitality that animated the Baal Shem Tov broke into the open. Splits occurred over points of doctrine and practice and new branches of Hasidism were formed, usually under the direction of a powerful new leader.

In *The Chosen*, Potok, who is himself a Jew and who is intimately acquainted with the tensions and stress-points within Judaism, speaks with authority when he explains how the Hasidim viewed the many great leaders in their tradition: "The Hasidim had great leaders—*tzaddikim,* they were called, righteous ones . . . They followed these leaders blindly. The Hasidim believed that the *tzaddik* was a superhuman link between themselves and God."[33] Deep affection for their leaders, fierce loyalty to each other, and a strong sense of tradition made it possible for the Hasidim to survive centuries of persecution in eastern Europe. On the other hand, these same traits also engendered within them attitudes of spiritual superiority regarding other Jews and led them to define group membership exclusively. Those whose views they rejected they stigmatized with labels: *Goyim* for gentiles, *apikorsim* for Jews.

Sects like Hasidism are hardly unique to Judaism. If Weber is correct, all major religions have them because all major religions undergo the social cycles he describes. What is more, these cycles do not seem to be limited to religious communities. Secular social groups commonly exhibit the same dynamics. The historical development of communism both in Russia and China makes the point well. Vladimir Lenin (1870–1924) was a Russian revolutionary, founder of Bolshevism, and a major force in the founding of the Soviet Union. Mao Tse-Tung (1893–1976) was a Chinese revolutionary and founder of the People's Republic of China. Both men were known as visionaries and charismatic leaders. Yet within their own lifetime, both men saw their personal vision of socialism undergo transformation. The political organizations and governments charged with carrying out the vision of these men in their respective countries quickly became heavily bureaucratic, even totalitarian. Mao lived long enough to understand how far the political institutions and government bureaucracy had departed from

---

[33]Potok, *The Chosen,* 104.

his vision. Partly as a response he instigated the so-called cultural revolution (1966–1969), a period of widespread agitation which he seemed to regard as an occasion for recapturing the revolutionary spirit of earlier decades.

No worldview can survive apart from a social setting that bridges multiple generations. In other words, a worldview that lasts only one generation is hardly worth the name. Thus, the social element is indispensable to the long-term success of any worldview. Those who are concerned about passing on a vital worldview to the next generation have utilized the elements discussed earlier: ideology, narrative, moral and aesthetic norms, rituals, and experience. Teachers attempt to transmit an understanding of ideology and norms, parents tell stories, community leaders attempt to nurture an appreciation for rituals, and everyone works together to provide social events and institutions that will elicit the experiences that are vital to the worldview.

> **"No worldview can survive apart from a social setting that bridges multiple generations."**

Of course, there is no guarantee that each successive generation will understand and remain faithful to its heritage. If Weber is right about the developmental phases of a worldview, then every generation faces two daunting tasks: (1) the task of faithfully transmitting to the next generation insights from its past (as articulated in the founder's vision), and (2) the task of helping the next generation cope with cultural (social, political, religious) trends in the present. The Hasidim portrayed in *The Chosen* attempted to meet the first task, in part, by establishing yeshivas, requiring daily rigorous study of the Talmud, and gathering regularly for prayer in the synagogues. They attempted to accomplish the second task, in part, by adopting a distinctive style of dress, restricting their association with outsiders, limiting the range of subjects taught in school, and forbidding their children to attend movies.

There are innumerable ways to fail to transmit a worldview in all its richness. The allure of contemporary popular culture can be a major distraction. This was precisely why Potok had the rabbis in *The Chosen* object to letting the Hasidic children attend movies and play baseball. The fact that Danny and Reuven met for the first time on a baseball diamond testifies to the power of contemporary popular culture. In addition to the siren-call of popular culture, the strategies for transmitting a worldview may be flawed or ineffectively executed. Teaching methods appropriate for one person or one generation, for example, may be inappropriate to another. Rabbi Saunders taught Danny by imposing a rule of silence: from the time Danny was four years old, Rabbi Saunders spoke to him only in formal settings such as when they studied the Talmud. He was using a method employed by his own father. The purpose was to ensure that his brilliant son would learn suffering (through imposed silence) and thereby learn to empathize with others who suffer. In Danny's case, the technique almost misfired, nearly alienating him.

Clearly, there are many difficulties associated with the task of transmitting a worldview from one generation to the next. In a relay race there are many ways to drop the baton. Given the innumerable difficulties associated with the task, we should not be amazed that some worldviews fall into disrepute and cease to play a vital role in the lives of a people. Rather, we should be amazed that some worldviews have been transmitted successfully from one generation to the next for thousands of years.

Elements of a Christian Worldview

Throughout this chapter we have cited examples from several worldviews to illustrate the various components of a worldview. Some of the examples have been drawn from our Christian heritage. We have proceeded on the assumption that Christianity is a worldview and that it exhibits elements common to other worldviews. We are now in a position to explicitly affirm (and not simply assume) that Christianity is indeed a worldview. Like other worldviews it provides a comprehensive approach to life's essential concerns. Moreover, like other worldviews it exhibits all six of the elements discussed in the preceding sections. In what follows, we recapitulate the six elements of a worldview in order to highlight the core beliefs and practices of a Christian worldview.

The Ideological Element

Ideology is a general term used to describe the core beliefs of any worldview. The more customary name given to ideology in the Christian tradition is "doctrine." Another way to make the point is to say that, in the Christian tradition, doctrinal statements have been the primary instruments for stating the ideology of a Christian worldview.

Like other major worldviews, Christianity articulates what we earlier called a background theory about the nature of the universe. This background theory includes accounts of the cosmos, God, and history. Christianity also offers a general account of human nature.

THE COSMOS

In the Christian worldview, the cosmos is created by God. This position separates Christianity from naturalistic worldviews inasmuch as they do not recognize divine activity in the cosmos. But it also separates Christianity from certain other worldviews that do recognize the existence of divine beings. The ancient

Greeks, for example, believed that gods existed, that they were immortal, and that they were active in the cosmos. At the same time, the Greeks did not believe that the gods created the cosmos. In ancient Greek cosmology, the most primitive existing thing was a *primordial unity,* an undifferentiated mass. The first stage of development was the emergence of a *gap* (literally, "chaos"), a separation into two parts of the original unity. The two parts became Heaven and Earth. The gods of popular mythology appeared only much later.[34] Here then we have a notable difference with Christian doctrine, according to which God existed first and later created the cosmos: "In the beginning God created the heavens and the earth." (Gen. 1:1) In addition, orthodox Christianity holds that the cosmos is continually sustained by God and that what He created is good. The Greeks believed that their gods were active in the cosmos, but they attributed to them no responsibility for the continued existence of the cosmos. Nor did they believe that the gods were capable of determining the moral qualities of anything that exists.

GOD

The Christian doctrines about God are numerous, complex, and often subtle and highly refined. We cannot summarize all of them here. However, we can reiterate a few of the most important ones. To begin with, in Christian doctrine, God is the central figure. Not only was everything created *by* Him, everything was created *for* Him. He is the source of everything in the cosmos, and in the end everything in the cosmos will fulfill His purposes according to a plan orchestrated by Him from time immemorial. God is also good. Moreover, He is without beginning and without end. In this respect, the Christian account of God differs importantly from the ancient Greeks' account of their gods. The Greek gods were not uniformly good. Indeed, with few exceptions, they were not morally superior to human beings. It is true that the Greek gods were held to be immortal. But immortality was a limited concept. It meant only that the gods would not die, not that they had no beginning.

HISTORY

According to Christian doctrine, God did not create the cosmos and then abandon it. Quite to the contrary, He is intimately involved in the unfolding of historical events. In Greek cosmology, fate and chance were assigned prominent roles. But these were fundamentally blind and impersonal forces over which neither gods nor mortals exercised much control. In Christian doctrine, God, who controls the destiny of everything,

---

[34]Hesiod, *Theogony,* II. 114–138, trans. Richard Latimore, in *Hesiod* (Ann Arbor, Mich.: University of Michigan Press, 1959).

is neither blind nor impersonal. He is insightfully and personally at work in history in a way that will eventually, in His timing, bring about His purposes. On this point, of course, Christian doctrine differs markedly not only from limited theistic views like those of the ancient Greeks but also from naturalistic worldviews (such as Marxism or existentialism), which assert that historical events are exclusively the result either of blindly mechanical forces or human endeavor.

Human Nature

We noted earlier that major worldviews give not only a background theory of the universe but also a general account of human nature. Christianity also provides such an account. This account coincides with what Christianity asserts about the cosmos at large: God created humankind, He is not detached and distant but rather intimately and personally acquainted with each individual human being, and He is working out His ultimate purposes in the lives of individual human beings. But here the similarity between humankind and the rest of the cosmos ends. Stars and planets, rivers and mountains, salmon and grizzly bears, protons and neutrons, all operate according to a certain order. In every creature there are certain natural forces and inclinations that move it toward ends and enable it to act in certain ways. This order is one that God imposed on the creatures when He instilled in them the tendencies they have, and it is an expression of His eternal law that governs the cosmos. Human beings, of course, are part of nature, and as such they also exhibit natural inclinations that move them toward ends and enable them to carry out bodily and mental activities.

But human beings are ordered toward their ends and activities in a way that differs profoundly from other creatures. Human beings have reason and therefore have the capacity (albeit a limited capacity) to discover for themselves what they must do to achieve their ends. Unlike other creatures, they also have the capacity to ignore or reject ends that are appropriate to them. In other words, they can elect not to direct themselves toward ideals that God has set before them. Tragically, they have elected to do precisely that and have thus become estranged from God, the Creator of all good things. In Christian doctrine, this choice not to aim at the ideals established by God is called *sin* (translating Greek and Hebrew words that mean to miss the mark or the goal).

What are the ideals and how can human activity be reoriented so as to aspire toward them once again? Some of the most basic and important ones are inner traits that define one's character, fraternal relationships with fellow human beings, and a harmonious relationship with God himself. If human beings are capable of steering a course away from the divinely ordained ideals, they are not similarly capable of redirecting their own course toward those ideals and reestablishing a harmonious relationship with God. Only God can accomplish that, and He chose to effect the reconciliation through the life, death, and resurrection of Jesus.

Where do the doctrines of the Christian worldview come from? Preeminently, they come from the Bible. Since all parts of the Bible are considered sacred and divinely inspired, all parts of it are also potential sources of doctrine.[35]

The Narrative Element

In the Christian worldview, narratives may be divided into two general categories—*primary* and *secondary*—reflecting the relative importance and authority of the sources. Primary narratives are found in the Bible. They include stories about God's creation of the cosmos; the alienation of the first man and woman from God; the subsequent covenants between God and humankind; the birth, death, and resurrection of Jesus; the formation and expansion of the Church; and the final events of history. They also include stories of some of the most notable persons of faith, such as Abraham, Jacob, Moses, Joshua, David, Daniel, Peter, and Paul.

Secondary narratives reflect the continuing experience of Christians throughout the centuries since the formation of the Church. They include accounts of the death of martyrs, stories of saints, reports of miracles, and testimonies of God's faithfulness in small and large affairs.

Secondary narratives sometimes take the form of historical accounts. Two popular modern examples are Corrie ten Boom's *Hiding Place* (about a Christian family who hid Jews and thus saved them from death at the hands of the Nazis) and David Wilkerson's *Cross and the Switchblade* (about a young minister who went to the streets and slums of New York to preach the gospel to teenage gang members and drug addicts). Sometimes secondary narratives take a literary form. Dante Alighieri's epic poem *The Divine Comedy*, John Bunyan's allegory *Pilgrim's Progress*, John Milton's epic poem *Paradise Lost*, Flannery O'Connor's short story "Revelation," and C. S. Lewis's novels *The Chronicles of Narnia* are all notable examples of literary pieces that articulate a distinctly Christian worldview.

Secondary narratives sometimes even appear in visual arts. The medieval Gothic cathedral in Chartres, France, eloquently

---

[35]As a matter of historical fact, however, not all parts of the Bible have received equal attention in the development of doctrine. Passages that have typically received the most attention are those that deal with the nature of God, His acts of creation (including the creation of humankind), the rejection of God by humankind (called the Fall), God's plan to restore humankind through the death and resurrection of Jesus, and God's plan for the final events in history.

embodies a Christian worldview. The building is laid out in the shape of a cross; the stained glass windows depict events from the Old and New Testaments; sculpted figures set in the portals remind us of famous biblical persons; its spires reach toward heaven. Every visible feature of the cathedral's architecture reminds us of the central narratives of Christianity and thereby reinforces the doctrines and teachings of the medieval Church.

In a Christian worldview, primary narratives are both more important and more authoritative than secondary narratives. This is due to the fact that they appear in sacred Scripture, which is held to be divinely inspired. However, secondary narratives are certainly not unimportant. Moreover, primary and secondary narratives serve similar functions. Like narratives in other worldviews, they reinforce and embellish core ideological, i.e., doctrinal, themes and provide patterns, or models, for believers to emulate.

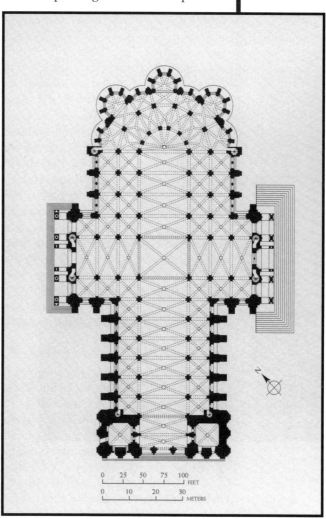

Plan of Chartres Cathedral. (After Frankl.)

The Normative Element

We noted earlier that a norm is a standard of some kind, that we encounter norms in virtually every facet of life (from grammar to the culinary arts to law), and that our judgments and evaluations of all human behavior and character rest on norms. We also noted that two of the most important kinds of norms are *moral (ethical)* norms and *aesthetic* norms. A Christian worldview includes both kinds of norms.

THE MORAL DIMENSION

For Christians, moral norms derive from the Scriptures. This happens in at least two ways. Sometimes the Scriptures explicitly forbid or require a certain kind of behavior. The Ten Commandments, set forth in Exodus 20, and Jesus' two commandments to love God and to love one's neighbor are good examples of specific proscriptions and prescriptions. But important norms are not always set forth in the form of specific commands. Sometimes they are articulated more vividly and powerfully in the narratives of men and women who appear in Scripture. The seventh commandment forbids adultery (Exod. 20:14); the story of Joseph fleeing Potiphar's wife (Gen. 39) dramatically exemplifies what it means to live by it. The tenth commandment forbids coveting things that belong to one's neighbor (Exod. 20:17); the story of David's desire for Bathsheba, the wife of Uriah the Hittite, vividly reminds us of the tragic results of acting on one's covetous desires (2 Sam. 11). The Levitical law requires God's chosen people to love their neighbors as themselves (Lev. 19:18); the story of Jonathan and David eloquently describes the meaning of deep and abiding love: "Jonathan became one in spirit with David, and he loved him as himself" (1 Sam. 18:1). Centuries later, when a rich young man asked Jesus the requirements for achieving eternal life, Jesus reminded him that the commandments required him to love his neighbor as himself and then told him to sell all his possessions and give them to the poor. The young man left sad. If the story of Jonathan's love for David exemplifies loving one's neighbor, the story of the rich young man makes evident how other things can lay claim to our affections and pull us away from the ideal. Throughout the Bible, narratives bring to life the meaning of moral norms that would otherwise appear as stark and formal commandments.

THE AESTHETIC DIMENSION

If narrative plays a prominent role in showing moral norms for the Christian, it plays an even larger role in demonstrating *aesthetic norms*—the norms by which we judge what is beautiful, pleasing, or sublime. Whereas the Scriptures provide a wealth of commandments to guide our behavior and character development in the moral sphere, they provide few explicit commandments about what is expected in the aesthetic sphere. But this relative lack of specific instruction does not mean that the Scriptures are silent on the matter of judging what is beautiful, pleasing, or sublime. They express important principles in the form of narrative. The detail for building the tabernacle in the Book of Exodus[36] leaves no doubt that God places a high value

---

[36]See especially chapters 35 through 39.

on beauty. Moreover, we can infer from statements about Bezalel, the chief artist of the project, that skilled craftsmanship and artistry are gifts from God. Moses, speaking to the people, says of him: "See, the Lord has chosen Bezalel . . . and he has filled him with the Spirit of God, with skill, ability and knowledge in all kinds of crafts—to make artistic designs for work in gold, silver and bronze, to cut and set stones, to work in wood and to engage in all kinds of artistic craftsmanship" (Exod. 35:30–33).

If craftsmanship and artistic talent are gifts from God, the narrative in Exodus makes clear that the products that come from applying those gifts were not intended to be set aside in museums. Museums—buildings erected to protect and display artifacts and works art—are largely a modern invention. Even as they protect and display art objects they give silent testimony to the fact that those objects no longer belong to everyday life. The Old Testament Tabernacle (and later, Solomon's Temple) were not museums. They were places of worship, prayer, and (sometimes) celebration. This means that the artifacts and works of art diligently brought forth by people like Bezalel should not be considered objects produced merely for the sake of having a pure aesthetic experience—not, so to speak, "art for the sake of art." Rather they were artifacts and works of art whose significant context was a place of worship. In other words, contemplation of beautiful artifacts and works of art—including priests' garments, goblets and bowls, altars, the ark of the covenant—was continuous with the act of worship. The same God who called Bezalel and other craftsmen to make beautiful artifacts and works of art also called the people to enter worship in the confines of (or at least near) a beautiful structure and close to beautiful objects. But of course the worship was not worship of beauty *per se*, but of God, the Creator of all things good and beautiful.

We have not attempted to provide a complete outline of a Christian aesthetic. Our point has been much simpler: Although the Bible gives few clear directives or instructions for evaluating art, its narratives provide a rich source of examples that can help us develop a Christian aesthetic. Another way to make the same point is this: In the absence of explicit biblical instructions about judging things beautiful, pleasing, and sublime, we should not conclude that God cares nothing about aesthetics. Nor should we conclude that art is simply a matter of personal taste and that no standards (norms) can be brought to bear in judging what is presented as art. The biblical narratives assist the patient reader in thinking about appropriate standards. They do this, for example, by providing models of significant contexts (such as worship or celebration) within which artifacts and works of art were exhibited. Understanding these contexts can provide clues about the limits of artistic endeavor and artistic appreciation for a Christian.

The Element of Ritual

The ideological, narrative, and normative elements of Christianity articulate its core beliefs. But Christianity is much more than a set of beliefs. As a living faith and worldview it also includes distinctive rituals that help integrate the core beliefs into the fabric of the behavior and character of the believers.

Earlier we identified three functions of rituals: (1) to reenact events so as to make them real in the present, (2) to facilitate transitions from one status to another, (3) to renew bonds among members of a group. The major rituals in Christianity serve all three functions.

The most prominent example of a ritual that reenacts a past event is the celebration of Communion, the Lord's Supper. Evidently this ritual was important from the earliest days of the Church. By the time Paul wrote his first letter to the Corinthian believers, the celebration was already being abused (1 Cor. 11). It seems that some believers were using it for a time of feasting and drinking; others went hungry. For these reasons, Paul reminded the Corinthian believers of the purpose and meaning of the celebration. It is not, he pointed out, an occasion for gregarious eating and drinking. Rather, it is an occasion to remember Christ's sacrifice on the cross and to reflect on one's own

The Christian Ritual of Celebrating the Lord's Supper

All four Gospels recount a supper that Jesus had with his disciples near the time of the Jewish Passover Feast and immediately before His crucifixion: Matt. 26, Mark 14, Luke 22, John 13. This supper was evidently considered important, because from the earliest days of the Church it was remembered and commemorated on a regular basis. To minimize abuse and distortion of this commemorative event in the early Corinthian church, Paul set forth simple instructions, which have become a standard for all subsequent celebrations of the Lord's Supper:

"For I received from the Lord what I also passed on to you: The Lord Jesus, on the night he was betrayed, took bread, and when he had given thanks, he broke it and said, 'This is my body, which is for you; do this in remembrance of me.' In the same way, after supper he took the cup, saying, 'This cup is the new covenant in my blood; do this, whenever you drink it, in remembrance of me.' For whenever you eat this bread and drink this cup, you proclaim the Lord's death until he comes" (1 Cor. 11:23–26).

spiritual condition. Over the centuries, participating in the Lord's Supper has been defined in terms of Paul's description of it to the Corinthians: "Whenever you eat this bread and drink this cup, you proclaim the Lord's death until he comes" (1 Cor. 11:26).

Rituals also facilitate the transition from one status to another. The most notable expression of this ritual function in Christianity is the practice of baptism. Baptism marks the transition from one set of loyalties to another, from identification with the old Adam, the first man, to identification with the new Adam, Christ.

Baptism also serves the third function of rituals: strengthening bonds with a group. Notably, baptism is a *public act*. It is carried out not in secret but in the presence of witnesses. Thus, when the convert plunges beneath the water and emerges once again, two things occur. First, the convert, having symbolically died with Christ, rises to life with Christ through His resurrection. Second, the convert also becomes part of a community of believers. Baptism thus establishes a bond with all Christians (the Church universal). At the same time, those who witness the baptism are reminded of the common faith that ties them to all believers, living and dead.

The Christian Ritual of Baptism

Baptism is an ancient ritual, dating back to the earliest days of the Church. Marking a break from identification with the old Adam (the first man) to identification with the new Adam, Christ, baptism is the most important ritual of transition in Christendom. As a publicly enacted ritual it also serves to establish and strengthen bonds with members of the immediate community of faith as well as with Christians everywhere at all times (the Church universal). Evidence for the importance of baptism is seen in the fact that Jesus' own baptism is recorded in the Gospels.

John the Baptist told his followers,

"I baptize you with [in] water for repentance. But after me will come one who is more powerful than I, whose sandals I am not fit to carry. He will baptize you with [in] the Holy Spirit and with fire. His winnowing fork is in his hand, and he will clear his threshing floor, gathering his wheat into the barn and burning up the chaff with unquenchable fire."

Then Jesus came from Galilee to the Jordan to be baptized by John. But John tried to deter him saying, "I need to be baptized by you, and do you come to me?"

Jesus replied, "Let it be now; it is proper for us to do this to fulfill all righteousness." Then John consented.

As soon as Jesus was baptized, he went up out of the water. At that moment heaven was opened, and he saw the Spirit of God descending like a dove and lighting on him. And a voice from heaven said, "This is my Son, whom I love; with him I am well pleased" (Matt. 3:11–17).

Before leaving the ritual element, we should pause for a moment and reflect on the meaning of rituals for the Christian. Rituals, at their best, are publicly observable expressions of attitudes, intentions, and dispositions that are essentially unseen. When heeded attentively and thoughtfully they become the vestments (ceremonial robes) of spiritual acts. Of course, rituals can also be enacted thoughtlessly and mechanically. In that case, they become mere routines and lose their spiritual power. What makes the difference? What determines their vitality? Rituals that realize their promise are informed by sound doctrine and grounded in experience.

The Experiential Element

When we speak of the experiential element of Christianity, we have in mind primarily the ways in which someone encounters God. The Bible is sprinkled liberally with narratives that describe such encounters. In addition, the encounters do not all follow any simple model or formula. Evidently, God makes His presence known in numerous and varied ways. Nevertheless, several of the biblical descriptions of encounters with God exhibit patterns of experience that seem to recur in common types of experience in the history of Christianity. We will touch here briefly on four examples: Paul on the road to Damascus (Acts 9), Isaiah in the temple (Isaiah 6), the apostles gathered on the Day of Pentecost (Acts 2), and Elijah in the cave at Horeb (1 Kings 19).

Paul's experience on the road to Damascus was one of radical conversion. It occurred in the early days of the formation of the Church, when the Church was spilling out of its birthplace in Jerusalem and spreading to many parts of the ancient Near East. At that time, the Church was also beginning to experience organized opposition. Paul (known then as Saul) was a devout and zealous Jew with a good deal of religious training in the tradition of the Pharisees. For reasons we do not fully understand, he sought to arrest and imprison any Christians he might find in Damascus. The Scriptures say that as he neared Damascus a light from heaven flashed around him. Falling to the ground blinded, he heard the voice of Jesus: "Saul, Saul, why do you persecute me?" The voice instructed him to continue to Damascus. There, after three days, he was met by a Christian named Ananias who prayed for him to receive his sight. Upon regaining his sight, Paul was baptized and almost immediately began to preach in the synagogues that Jesus is the Son of God. Paul's experience was one of the early, dramatic conversions to the Christian faith. Apart from being baptized, none of the specific features of Paul's conversion experience (the flash of light, falling to the ground, hearing the voice) became a standard for other conversions. At the same time, the fact that he encountered God (in the person of Jesus Christ) in a transforming way is widely regarded among Christians as a fundamental experience defining what it means to be a Christian.

Isaiah's experience in the temple bears a certain resemblance to Paul's experience on the road to Damascus: Both men had a visual experience and heard a voice. Paul saw a blinding light and heard the voice of Jesus; Isaiah saw the Lord "seated on a throne, high and exalted" and heard the voice of seraphs saying: "Holy, holy, holy is the LORD Almighty; the whole earth is full of his glory" (Isa. 6:1–3). But Isaiah's experience was notably different from Paul's. Paul's was a conversion experience that radically transformed him from being an enemy of Christ and His church to being a follower of Christ and a leader in the community of believers. On the other hand, Isaiah was not an enemy of God; indeed, he was a devout Israelite at the time of his temple experience. His experience is therefore best described not as a conversion but as a commissioning. Isaiah heard and answered God's call to speak a prophetic message in God's behalf to the people of Israel. Just as conversion is commonly recognized among Christians as a defining spiritual experience, so too being called and commissioned to a life in service to God is recognized as a common Christian experience. To be sure, not everyone's experience is as arresting and overpowering as Isaiah's. But Christians in every era of the Church have borne witness to encounters with God in which they believed they were commissioned to a life of service.[37]

> **"The prophet Joel told of a time to come when God would pour out His Spirit on all of His servants, both men and women."**

Isaiah's temple experience was by no means unique among Old Testament figures. Other prophets also experienced unusual—even overpowering—encounters with God that led to their commissioning. Amos, Jonah, and Jeremiah (to name only three) had such experiences. Still, the prophets of old are more remembered for the singular nature of their experiences than for any pattern they established for Christians. The prophet Joel, however, told of a time to come when God would pour out His Spirit on all of His servants, both men and women (2: 29). Centuries later, on the Day of Pentecost following Jesus' resurrection, Peter found occasion to recall Joel's prophecy. In the second chapter of Acts, Luke describes a phenomenon that transformed a small band of timid followers of Jesus into a courageous and vital community of believers who understood themselves to be commissioned by God to bear witness to the resurrected Christ. "When the day of Pentecost came, they were all together in one place. Suddenly a sound like the blowing of a violent wind came from heaven and filled the whole house

---

[37]Notable examples include Augustine (354–420), Francis of Assisi (1181–1226), Ignatius of Loyola (1491–1556), and John Wesley (1703–1791).

where they were sitting. They saw what seemed to be tongues of fire that separated and came to rest on each of them. All of them were filled with the Holy Spirit and began to speak in other tongues as the Spirit enabled them" (Acts 2:1–4). Isaiah's temple experience shows vividly that God commissions individuals from time to time and gives them a prophetic voice. The experience of the believers on the Day of Pentecost demonstrates that Isaiah's experience is not limited to a few: The tongues of fire separated and came to rest on *each of them* and *all of them* were filled with the Holy Spirit.

Paul's conversion, Isaiah's commissioning, the believers' empowerment on the Day of Pentecost—all these encounters with God's presence model an important strand of religious experience. In each instance, God's appearance was majestic: marvelous in power and glory. For Paul, God presented himself as a blinding light from heaven and the authoritative voice of Jesus—to which Paul responded, "What shall I do, Lord?" For Isaiah, God presented himself as a royal, enthroned figure—to which Isaiah could only say, "Woe to me! . . . I am ruined! . . . my eyes have seen the King, the Lord Almighty" (Isa. 6:5). On the Day of Pentecost, it was the sound of a rushing wind and tongues of fire. And the response was a declaration of "the wonders of God."

Rudolph Otto coined a special word for the kind of encounter with God experienced by Paul, Isaiah, and the apostles on the Day of Pentecost. He called it "numinous," from the Latin word *numen,* a spirit.[38] For Otto, the numinous experience is the experience of something that is mysterious and awe-inspiring, at once fearful and fascinating. For Otto, the *something* in question—that which we experience as mysterious and awe-inspiring, marvelous in power and glory—is properly called holy. God is not just good. He is *holy.* This seems to be the point of what the seraphs affirm when they say: "Holy, holy, holy is the LORD Almighty" (Isa. 6:3).

We have highlighted three instances of human beings experiencing the presence of God. Paul's conversion experience helps us understand the meaning of radical transformation. Isaiah's temple experience leads us to consider what it means to be commissioned to speak prophetically. The events on the Day of Pentecost remind us that the empowering of the Holy Spirit is for everyone. While these three experiences accentuate different facets of religious experience, they also exhibit certain similarities that may give us a misleading impression of how God's presence can be experienced. Paul, Isaiah, and the apostles felt God's presence in what can fairly be described with such words as *fearful, fantastic, overwhelming, majestic, glorious.* Their re-

---

[38]Rudolf Otto, *The Idea Of The Holy,* trans. John W. Harvey (London, Oxford, New York: Oxford University Press), chapter III, 'Numen' And The 'Numinous,' 5–7.

sponses were appropriate to their respective experiences: Paul fell down, blinded; Isaiah cried out "Woe to me . . . I am ruined;" those gathered together on the Day of Pentecost broke forth in Spirit-inspired utterances. But does God make his presence known only in fantastic and overwhelming ways? And what, too, of the range of our responses to God?

The experience of Elijah at the mouth of a cave at Horeb suggests an important addition to what we have noticed so far. The writer of 1 Kings describes a time in Israel's history when the people began to worship Baal, one of the fertility gods recognized by peoples of the ancient Near East. Following several years of drought, Elijah, the prophet of God, summoned four hundred and fifty prophets of Baal to a mountain, where he arranged a contest. The god who consumed a sacrificial bull by fire would be recognized as the true God. Would it be Baal or Yahweh? After Baal failed to answer the prayers of his prophets, Elijah uttered a prayer eloquent in its simplicity and brevity. The Scriptures describe a scene no less awe-inspiring than anything experienced by Isaiah, Paul, or the apostles on the Day of Pentecost: fire from heaven burned up the sacrificial bull, the wood and stone under it, and the surrounding soil. Almost immediately, Elijah commanded that the prophets of Baal be put to death. Soon the rains resumed and the drought ended. While most people in Israel rejoiced, the king's wife, Jezebel, was deeply angered by the slaughter of Baal's prophets. When she threatened to kill Elijah, he fled many days south to Horeb, "the mountain of God," where he sought refuge in a cave. The next day, God commanded him to stand at the mouth of the cave, where He showed Elijah three fantastic phenomena: a powerful wind, an earthquake, and a fire. In each case, the Scriptures say that the Lord was not in the phenomenon. But after the fire, we are told, God spoke to Elijah in "a gentle whisper" (1 Kings 19:12).

On this occasion at least, God was not present in the fantastic displays of nature. Rather, He made himself known in a voice so soft as to be almost inaudible. In response, Elijah did not shout for joy or break forth in a victorious anthem. He simply covered his head with his cloak. We can only wonder what meditation or prayer may have entered his mind at that moment. For many Christians throughout the history of the Church, God has made his presence known in the way he did to Elijah at Horeb. For if God reveals himself in a blinding light or as an exalted monarch or in tongues of fire, He also reveals himself in the gentle whisper.

The Social Element

Any treatment of the social element of a Christian worldview must take into account the Church, for the simple reason that the Church is the primary social institution of Christianity. Its birth is described in the Book of Acts. From humble beginnings in

Palestine, it gradually spread to all parts of the Mediterranean basin. Having endured persecution from the Romans at various times during its first three hundred years, its being endorsed by Constantine I (A.D. 313) in the fourth century represented a new challenge. In the East, the Church became centered in Constantinople where it became largely subordinated to the emperor; in the West at Rome it remained an independent force under Papal rule. From both centers, it grew to embrace all of Europe. During the so-called Dark Ages, when the light of rational inquiry seemed nearly extinguished due to disease, poverty, and changing political alignments, the Church kept learning alive in monasteries and schools. Gradually, a break developed between East and West, and became permanent after 1054. In the West, the growing power and corruption of the Church contributed to a struggle within it to reclaim its spiritual heritage. Numerous movements inspired by reformers like Martin Luther (1483–1546) and John Calvin (1509–1564) eventually broke away from the Roman Church and formed separate branches of Christianity. Today, the Church is worldwide—crossing cultural, racial, and ethnic boundaries and encompassing many denominations.

> **"Knowing the words of Jesus or the doctrines of the Church is not the same as comprehending their meaning."**

What we said earlier about worldviews in general has been true for the Church historically and remains true today: Each generation faces two formidable tasks. The first is the task of faithfully transmitting its heritage to the next generation. As we have seen already, Christianity's heritage is a complex pattern of core beliefs, narratives, norms, rituals, and experiences. Successfully transmitting this complex pattern involves teaching doctrines, telling (and retelling) stories, modeling the appropriate moral and aesthetic values, reenacting rituals, and bearing witness to spiritual experiences. In short, it involves integrating the various elements into the recipient generation's daily rhythm of thought and practice. To approach the whole of life from this integrated perspective is the sum and substance of what it means to have a Christian worldview.

The second task is to help the next generation cope with contemporary cultural trends. Helping to cope means several things. To begin with, it means teaching persons to understand the *meaning* of their core beliefs within a contemporary setting. Knowing the words of Jesus or the doctrines of the Church is not the same as comprehending their meaning.[39] It is entirely

---

[39]The following analogy, though not perfect, helps make the point. Many people are familiar with Albert Einstein's famous formula $E = mc^2$. Only a fraction of these people know what the letters in the equation stand for, and very few people actually grasp its meaning well enough to apply it.

possible to be familiar with an important teaching and yet not really grasp its meaning or be able to apply it with understanding. This distinction lies at the heart of the troubling fact that Christians sometimes blur the line between a familiar teaching and a popular ideological trend in the prevailing culture. A simple example from the moral realm illustrates the point. One of the most famous passages in the Bible is Jesus' commandment: "Do not judge, or you too will be judged" (Matt. 7:1) The context suggests that Jesus is addressing himself to the tendency of some to exaggerate the faults in others and then pronounce condemnation on them. The context does not imply that Jesus categorically forbids us to assess (accurately evaluate) what other people say and do. But today Jesus' familiar saying stands in danger of being assimilated to the moral relativism pervasive in Western culture. For more than a few in the Church today it has come to mean: "Because everyone's tastes and values are different, therefore no one has a right to evaluate (judge) the moral merit of what anyone else says or does."

> **"'Thou has made us for thyself, O God, and our hearts are restless until they rest in thee.'"**
> —*Augustine*

So the Church's task of helping the next generation cope with contemporary culture requires that it provide ample opportunity both for extended, thoughtful reflection on the meaning of its core beliefs and for critical analysis of prevailing ideological trends. But it also means creating a social environment agreeable to our nature. In Jean-Paul Sartre's existentialist worldview, human beings are starkly alone. They live as isolated individuals, always in competition with each other. In a Christian worldview, precisely the opposite is true: We are relational beings. Preeminently, we have been created for a relationship with God. We bear His image, and we have been created to need Him. In the words of Augustine: "Thou has made us for thyself, O God, and our hearts are restless until they rest in thee."[40] But we have also been created for relationships with each other. We are not like so many marbles held together for a brief time in a pouch only to scatter in all directions when the pouch is opened. The more appropriate metaphor is found in the New Testament: together, *inter*dependent rather than *inde*pendent, we are the *body of Christ*. If we are relational beings, then helping the next generation cope with contemporary cultural trends means, in part, creating environments conducive to nurturing relationships. Specifically, if we are relational beings, then a primary function of the Church is to provide opportunities for persons both to encounter God and to interact with one another.

---

[40]Augustine, *The Confessions of Saint Augustine,* trans. Edward B. Pusey (New York: Random House, The Modern Library, 1949), 3.

Why is it not enough simply to understand what we believe and to have the ability to critically evaluate the trends in popular culture? Why must the Church also nurture relationships? Because, although developing critical, analytical, and reflective skills is crucial to our overall development as persons, in the final analysis we are governed not so much by what we know as by what we most love. Developing relationships with God and fellow believers is finally an endeavor of nurturing a love for both.

Conclusion: The Case for Limited Pluralism

We began this chapter by considering two Jewish boys, Reuven Malter and Danny Saunders, and their respective worldviews as presented by novelist Chaim Potok. Actually, it would have been more accurate to speak of two boys living out alternate versions of the same worldview, Judaism. True, until they got to know one another, Reuven and Danny viewed each other with suspicion and a measure of disdain. Danny's Hasidic community even spoke disparagingly of Reuven's people. Despite their differences, however, Reuven and Danny both lived well within the mainstream of orthodox Judaism. They both believed in God and accepted the Hebrew Scriptures as God's revelation to humankind. Their differences centered mainly on the relative weight they gave to certain points of interpretation in the Torah and the Talmud as well as the choices they made concerning cultural matters, like clothing and hairstyle. Their story is really very much like our own. Christianity is populated with its own Reuvens and Dannys, each representing a distinctive interpretive tradition and a distinctive set of cultural practices. What explains this kind of diversity, and should we be willing to live with it?

Christianity exhibits diversity for at least three reasons. First, a Christian worldview is a product of how we integrate the various elements described earlier: ideology (doctrine), narratives, moral and aesthetic norms, rituals, experience, and community life. Given differences of personal temperament and experience, some degree of diversity in the way we bring about this integration is virtually assured. The experiences of Christians at various times and places in history, for example, have led them to articulate their faith in ways that led to different theological traditions. Lutheran theology, for example, differs from Thomistic theology, and both differ from Reformed theology and Pentecostal theology. Moreover, differences of experience and theology have made for differences in ritual and community life. The formal liturgy of Episcopalians differs markedly both from the simplicity of worship found in Quaker meetinghouses and from the animated worship in Pentecostal churches.

Diversity is also explained by the different ways Christians interact with other contemporary non-Christian worldviews and culture. In the early centuries of the Church, Christians found themselves in constant dialogue with Greek and Roman mystery religions and philosophies. The specific views of these religions and philosophies led them to adjust certain aspects of their worldview to meet the challenges of the day while retaining their overall framework of belief and norms. During the Renaissance (fourteenth–sixteenth century), Christians encountered new issues, including the rise of new political institutions, the transition from a barter to a money economy, and advances in scientific method. As they did in earlier centuries, Christians had to make adjustments in their worldview to meet the new challenges, and they had to do it within a biblical framework. The responses that once allowed them to cope with ancient mystery religions no longer spoke adequately to important issues in the fourteenth, fifteenth, and sixteenth centuries. Today, Christians must also articulate a worldview that explains how to think Christianly about current trends in philosophy and psychology, literature and art, ethics and politics, science and technology. Since the Christian framework is sufficiently broad to accommodate more than one approach to these disciplines, a certain amount of diversity is to be expected.

> "A vital and functioning worldview can never be considered a finished product."

Finally, diversity in the Christian worldview is inevitable because a vital and functioning worldview can never be considered a finished product. A worldview is like a natural language: Wherever it is currently in use it will undergo modification to meet the needs of the situation. Modifications will occur at different times by different people with varying levels of skill in response to constantly changing events. Because no one version of a Christian worldview can be considered final, diversity can hardly be avoided.

So diversity within a Christian worldview is virtually inevitable. But is diversity a good thing? In many respects, yes. To begin with, diversity is due in part to our human limitations—our limited abilities to perceive, to think, and to critically evaluate, and the narrowness of our interests. Diversity, therefore, reminds us of our place in the cosmos: higher than the creatures but lower than God. Diversity, says Arthur Holmes, "reminds us of our finiteness, our creatureliness, our humanity; without that awareness a worldview could not be Christian at all."[41]

Second, diversity is a good thing because when attentively attended it actually enhances one's understanding and wisdom by deepening one's appreciation of the important questions. One of the great perennial debates in Christianity centers on the

---

[41]Arthur Holmes, "Toward a Christian View of Things," in *The Making of a Christian Mind*, ed. Arthur Holmes (Downers Grove, Ill.: InterVarsity Press, 1985), 16.

tension between the free will of humankind and the sovereignty of God. Historically, Jacob Arminius took one side of this debate and John Calvin the other side. Now it is possible that one side or the other in this debate actually has hit upon the correct theological position in its entirety. More likely, each side has grasped a part of a great mystery. Those persons, therefore, who attentively attend the various sides of the debate place themselves in a good position to appreciate the profundity of the questions that lie at the center of the debate. This kind of deepened appreciation for the questions represents a primary step toward growing in wisdom and understanding.

Finally, diversity reminds us that Christianity is not a closed system of thought and practice but a vital, exploratory approach to life. In this chapter, we have set forth some of the chief elements of a Christian worldview. These elements have been articulated as a general framework of core beliefs and practices. Over the past two millennia, Christian thinkers have brought this general framework to many different situations in different cultural and historical settings. What we notice in case after case is that Christians have distinguished themselves in their ability to adapt a basic framework of biblically based beliefs and practices to an ever changing environment.[42] While there have been lapses, false turns, and mistakes, the overwhelming record is one of constancy to the biblical tradition and remarkable openness and flexibility to an ever changing social and intellectual environment.

Review and Discussion Questions

1. In a single sentence, define *worldview*. Who has a worldview? Explain why the answer to this question is more complicated than it seems at first.

2. In your own words, provide brief definitions or descriptions of the following elements of a worldview: ideology, narrative, norm, ritual. Along with each definition or description provide your own example.

3. In the section on ideology, the author uses the expressions "background theory" and "account of human nature." What do these expressions refer to and how are they related?

---

[42]Some in the Christian tradition have rejected new ideas and tried to isolate themselves from non-Christian influences, the Amish, for example. The isolation of their farm-based settlements, their rejection of modern technological devices, the eighteenth-century style of their clothing, and their continued use of a European language, remind us of the Hasidic communities in Judaism. Although their reasons for trying to isolate themselves may have some justification, the Amish represent a declining minority among Christians. See Ruth Hoover Seitz, *Amish Ways* (Harrisburg, Pa.: RB Books, 1991).

4. Explain the differences between sacred writings and myths.

5. Compare and contrast myths and historical narratives. Provide your own example of each.

6. Identify a novel, short story, drama, or film that expresses an ideology. The piece you choose should be one that you are familiar with but is not mentioned in the chapter. Identify the ideology and explain how the piece expresses it.

7. What is a norm? What kinds of norms are important to a worldview?

8. Explain the notion of a *performative* statement or act. How does this notion fit with the ritualistic element of a worldview? Give an example not mentioned in the chapter.

9. Why is experience important to a worldview? What is the relationship of experience to ideology?

10. Summarize Max Weber's account of the way religions move in cyclical patterns. Do you think his theory applies to Christianity? Support your answer with examples and reasons.

11. The author argues for "limited pluralism" in a Christian worldview. What does this expression mean? Do you agree that a Christian worldview can accommodate limited pluralism? Explain your answer. If you believe that limited pluralism is possible, what are the limits?

Extended Projects for Reflection

1. Read Chaim Potok's novel *The Chosen*. Note the similarities and differences in the respective worldviews of Danny Saunders and Reuven Malter. Identify two people in your own faith tradition who exhibit a comparable set of similarities and differences of worldview.

2. Discuss other literary or artistic works that exemplify one or more of the elements of a worldview discussed in the chapter.

Selected Bibliography

Blamires, Harry. *The Christian Mind.* London: S.P.C.K., 1966.

Holmes, Arthur. *Contours of a Worldview.* Grand Rapids: William B. Eerdmans Publishing Company, 1983.

Holmes, Arthur, ed. *The Making of a Christian Mind, A Christian Worldview & the Academic Enterprise.* Downers Grove, Ill.: InterVarsity Press, 1985.

Nash, Ronald. *Worldviews in Conflict, Choosing Christianity in a World of Ideas.* Grand Rapids: Zondervan Publishing House, 1992.

Sire, James. *The Universe Next Door, A Basic Worldview Catalog.* Downers Grove, Ill.: InterVarsity Press, 1976.

Smart, Ninian. *Worldviews, Cross-cultural Explorations of Human Beliefs.* 2d ed. Englewood Cliffs, N.J.: Prentice Hall, 1995.

Stevenson, Leslie. *Seven Theories of Human Nature.* 2d. ed. New York and Oxford: Oxford University Press, 1987.

Wuthnow, Robert. *Christianity in the 21st Century, Reflections on the Challenges Ahead.* New York and Oxford: Oxford University Press, 1993.

2

The Role of the Bible in Shaping a Christian Worldview

Edgar R. Lee

The proverbial "sawdust trail" was my road to freedom and reality when, as a 16-year old, I heeded the appeal of a dynamic tent evangelist and knelt at a simple altar to confess my sins and invite Jesus Christ to be the Lord of my life. As I prayed, the deepest peace and security I had ever known flooded my consciousness. Somehow I knew without any doubt my sins were forgiven. I was indeed a new person, and Christ in some mysterious yet powerful way was now Lord of my life. My feet hardly seemed to touch the ground on Sunday evening as I walked the few short blocks back to my home. Through the years, that single event has continued to be the defining moment of my life.

Immediately the Bible came alive to me. I began the first of many journeys from Genesis through Revelation finding ever widening circles of insight and meaning as biblical truths rippled continuously through my life. Long before that fateful evening, however, the Bible began to shape what I now understand to be my *worldview*, "a set of beliefs about the most important issues of life."[1] I had learned smatterings of biblical teachings as a small boy in a Baptist Sunday school and from the monthly sermons of the pastor as he made the rounds of the small churches on his charge. And then there was the lazy summer when, on my annual visit to my uncle's farm, I discovered the Bible in comic book form. I sat for hours in the front porch swing devouring stories and pictures that vividly described the unfolding of God's revelation. Without my being consciously aware of technical worldview issues, the Bible began to fill in my understanding of the origin of humankind, the meaning and purpose of our life on earth, and the nature of our eternal destiny. So early on I learned that God is Creator of everything, human beings have fallen into sin and are in desperate need of redemption, Jesus Christ died and rose again for our sins, and He is coming again to finally reconcile the universe to himself. When the evangelist called for my "decision," I already knew the basic elements of a Christian worldview.

Building a worldview may be a little like putting together a complex jigsaw puzzle. Much like a child who finds all the straight edges and quickly puts in place the outer frame of the puzzle only to labor longer and more intensely to fill in the center scene, a new believer quickly from Scripture locates the basic framework of faith only to begin the process of learning the details. Scripture is at once simple and complex. Its narratives[2] wonderfully transform the mysteries of the ages into simple

> **"Building a worldview may be a little like putting together a complex jigsaw puzzle."**

---

[1] Ronald H. Nash, *Worldviews in Conflict: Choosing Christianity in a World of Ideas* (Grand Rapids: Zondervan Publishing House, 1992), 16.

[2] See chapter 1 for a discussion of this term.

stories readily grasped by the uneducated. At the same time, a fuller comprehension of the text through careful exegesis and theological interpretation is the demanding work of a scholar's lifetime. In this section, en route to that fuller comprehension, we want to think somewhat more intentionally about the role Scripture plays in the formation of our worldview.

Exegesis, **the process of explaining a Bible text by analysis, context, and the customs and culture of the time.**

The Nature of the Bible

Christians have always found the Bible to be compellingly relevant as the story of God's dealings with humankind through the ages. In terse narrative style laden with rich symbolism, the opening Book of Genesis rapidly sketches God's creation of the "heavens and the earth," a theological explanation of their origins. The divine, creative activity is spelled out simply in the words, "And God said, 'Let there be . . .'" (Gen. 1:3ff.) with the creative work following, "And it was so" (Gen. 1:6ff.). In six days, God's spoken word brought planet earth from a darkened formless waste to a garden teeming with verdant plant and animal life.

Almost immediately the narrative moves to an explanation of human origins with the introduction of the first pair, Adam and Eve (Gen. 1:26–29; 2:1–25). Created directly by God from the elements of the earth in an apparent state of innocence, they were placed in the Garden of Eden and commissioned to multiply and subdue the earth. But Adam and Eve quickly discovered, with a little help from the serpent, the exercise of their own free will, disobeyed the direct command of the Creator, and lost their paradise. Not only they but also their world was now fallen and resistant to their efforts to make both a living and a life. The curse of their self-will and disobedience was now let loose on the race to follow. Their first son committed the first murder; human depravity finds its explanation in the first book of the Bible.

These narratives, however, are only the preface to the Bible and the human condition. Genesis moves quickly to trace from the moral rubble the rise of a righteous line through Noah. Sensitive to the voice of God, he with his immediate family, survives a catastrophic flood of divine judgment to receive again the commission of the Creator to fill and rule over the earth (9:1–17). Following the story of the Tower of Babel with its explanation for the multiplicity of languages and ethnic groupings (11:1–9), attention turns to Abram. It is he whom God calls to father a great nation to be a source of blessing to all peoples on earth (12:1–3). From this point, the books of the Old Testament become a continuing saga of the way God gradually through the centuries forms an elect covenant people through whom Adam's fallen race will be restored.

And what a story it is! The patriarchs Abraham, Isaac, and Jacob grow ever so slowly into men of faith even as they exhibit human foibles along the way. Joseph, a man of outstanding character, providentially leads the famine threatened family to the safety of Egypt. Under a later Pharaoh, however, Egypt becomes not a refuge but a crucible in which this adolescent Semitic family can forge its identity in the midst of suffering and slavery. Enter Moses, a fugitive from the royal court, whom God now calls from tending sheep to lead His people out of bondage and into national identity through a fiery covenant at Sinai.

Courageous Joshua has the formidable task of guiding the people of God back into the land God had promised centuries earlier to the wandering patriarchs. Subsequently, during the anarchy in the period of the Judges, the prophet Samuel becomes God's instrument for selecting the first king, Saul, who proves to be more astute at warfare than at establishing a nation. But David follows Saul and combines in a unique way the military genius of an empire builder with the passion and vision of a prophet. Through him, God promises to bring an eternal kingdom (2 Sam. 7:5–16) though He reserves the building of Israel's temple for David's son, Solomon, renowned as the wisest man who ever lived.

In the succession of kings following David and Solomon, the Old Testament traces the often repeated stories of apostasy and revival, the splintering of the kingdom, palace revolts, wars that crisscross strategic Palestine, the fall and deportation of the Northern Kingdom, and finally the destruction of Jerusalem and its temple. A surviving remnant is marched off to a 70-year exile in Babylon. The hardships and sufferings, according to the great prophets of Israel, who spoke out boldly against the sins of their contemporaries, are the result of rebellion against God and failure to keep his covenant. But always forgiving, God acts to restore a chastened people, reestablish them in their land, rebuild their temple, and reiterate His promises of a coming Messiah through the seed of David.

After centuries of prophetic silence, the promise of Messiah is finally fulfilled in Jesus of Nazareth whose exciting story we find in the four Gospels. Spirit-conceived and virgin-born in ways mysterious even to faith, Jesus turns the popular notions of a messianic leader upside down. He is more prophet and teacher than the political deliverer His people expect. His mission is to proclaim the good news of God's salvation to the poor. To the dismay of the Jewish leaders, the people find His words corroborated in His miracles of compassion. Finally, to the utter consternation of His followers, He is arrested and condemned by the ruling aristocracy and handed over to the Roman governor to be crucified as a blaspheming messianic pretender and revolutionary.

But tragic crucifixion is followed by triumphant resurrection, the central miracle of the Bible. The apostles declare the risen Jesus to be truly the Messiah promised through David (Acts 2:29ff.). Both Lord (God) and Christ, He is the one who brings forgiveness of sins and the gift of the Holy Spirit to all humankind (2:38). Spirit-baptism, first given at Pentecost, both empowers believers and makes them the Church, the spiritual descendants of Israel, to whom all the blessings of divine salvation are now available. The remainder of the New Testament sets forth the story of the geographic and spiritual growth of the Church as the apostles and their believing colleagues evangelize the first century world. Along the way, guided by the Holy Spirit, they produce the letters of the New Testament for the guidance of their fellow believers and, providentially, ourselves. The Bible closes with the Book of Revelation which, whatever its apocalyptic mysteries, foretells the final eschatological consummation of the kingdom of God and the final reconciliation of both Adam's heirs and Adam's world.

Eschatological (Gk. *eschatos,* "last," and *legein,* "study"), referring to the end times and the future fulfillment of God's eternal plan and purpose.

In so confidently telling the story of God's patient work with humanity, the Bible presents itself as an inspired and authoritative book, initiated and written under the oversight of God himself. "All Scripture is God-breathed" (2 Tim. 3:16) wrote the great apostle, Paul, in what has become the cornerstone of the Christian doctrine of inspiration. Sometimes translated "inspired" (KJV), the word "God-breathed" is a literal translation of the Greek *theopneustos,* a compound from two words, *theos* meaning "God" and *pneô* meaning "to breathe." The sense of the passage is that God has so personally and intimately involved himself in the writing of Scripture that it can be thought of as His exhalation. Paul, writing long before the formal definition of the New Testament canon at the Council of Carthage in A.D. 397,[3] was probably thinking first of the scriptures of the Old Testament, which he usually had in his possession. However, his statement is strategically positioned in the canon and has come to be applied in the Christian tradition to the entirety of Scripture.[4] In fact, even during Paul's lifetime, his fellow apostles referred to his writings as Scripture. Thus 2 Peter observes that "Paul also wrote you with the wisdom that God gave him" but his letters are distorted by "ignorant and unstable people . . . as they do *the other Scriptures*" (2 Pet. 3:15–16).[5]

The letters of Peter reveal much the same understanding of and emphasis about the origin and inspiration of Scripture.

---

[3]For a good overview of the process of canonization, see Alan F. Johnson and Robert E. Webber, *What Christians Believe: A Biblical and Historical Summary* (Grand Rapids: Academic Books/Zondervan Publishing House, 1989), 36–40.

[4]Donald G. Bloesch cites the argument of Fred D. Gealy in *Interpreter's Bible* (New York: Abingdon, 1955) 11:504–506, to the effect that this passage implies Paul's writings, and perhaps all the New Testament writings, are to be understood as Scripture. Cf. *Holy Scripture: Revelation, Inspiration, & Interpretation* (Downers Grove, Ill.: InterVarsity Press, 1994), 317.

[5]Gealy notes this passage played an important role in "establishing the place of the Pauline corpus in the emerging N.T." Ibid., 506.

Synoptic, "seeing together," referring to Matthew, Mark, and Luke because these Gospels have so much in common.

"Above all, you must understand that no prophecy of Scripture came about by the prophet's own interpretation. For prophecy never had its origin in the will of man, but men spoke from God as they were *carried along* [Gk., *pheromenoi*] by the Holy Spirit" (2 Pet. 1:20–21). If Paul used the metaphor of the "breath" of God, Peter used the maritime image of a boat "carried along" on its course by the wind. Just as the wind fills the sails of a ship and propels it across the sea, God's Spirit moved sensitive persons to understand and write precisely what he wished. The apostolic tradition was emphatic in insisting that the initiative for the production of Scripture lies in the will of God. Never is its genius to be attributed to human beings.

These apostles and their colleagues who wrote the New Testament followed the example and teaching of Jesus himself in their regard for and use of Scripture. Several passages from the Gospels may be cited to demonstrate. In a crucial saying on divorce, Jesus quoted from Genesis 2:24, "For this reason a man will leave his father and mother and be united to his wife, and the two will become one flesh" (Matt. 19:4–5). The Genesis text does not directly attribute the saying to God. However, Jesus simply observes, as though in passing, that God, the Creator, *said* it. In a similar vein, when Jesus quoted from Psalm 110:1 which has been traditionally attributed to David, he said "David, himself, *speaking by the Holy Spirit,* declared . . ." (Mark 12:36). John W. Wenham has said, "So truly is God regarded as the author of scriptural statements that in certain contexts 'God' and 'Scripture' have become interchangeable."[6] A careful examination of the Gospels shows that Jesus did indeed hold an extraordinarily high view of His Scriptures, the Old Testament. For instance, He did not merely accommodate himself to what has sometimes been construed as a primitive understanding on the part of His contemporaries. Instead, He actually showed his own true feelings for Scripture by turning to it for direction and authority in the most crucial moments of His own personal life.[7] In His temptation, He put the devil to flight with quotations from Scripture (Matt. 4:6,10). Likewise, He interpreted the final movements of His betrayal with the words "it is written" (Mark 14:21,27). So interwoven into Jesus' life and consciousness was the Old Testament that there are no less than sixty-four quotations or allusions in the Synoptic Gospels alone.[8]

---

[6]Cited in Alan F. Johnson and Robert E. Webber, *What Christians Believe: A Biblical and Historical Summary* (Grand Rapids: Academic Books/Zondervan Publishing House, 1989), 23.

[7]Ibid., 24.

[8]Leon Morris, *I Believe in Revelation* (Grand Rapids: William B. Eerdmans Publishing Company, 1976), 59, citing the study of R. T. France, *Jesus and the Old Testament* (London: The Tyndale Press, 1971), 27.

In any theological debate, Scripture was always the final authority. So confident was Jesus of its permanent validity that He said, "[U]ntil heaven and earth disappear, not the smallest letter, not the least stroke of a pen, will by any means disappear from the Law until everything is accomplished" (Matt. 5:18). In one of His debates with the Jewish leaders He pointed out, "[T]he Scripture cannot be broken" (John 10:35).

Though faithful to the Old Testament and never contradicting its teachings, Jesus nonetheless saw himself as the fulfillment of the Old Testament. (Matt. 5:17; Luke 24:27,44–46; John 5:39–47). He is superior to its greatest prophets, Moses and Elijah (Matt. 17:1–11). His own teaching is authoritative as compared to the interpretations of His day (cf. Matt. 5:22,28,32,34,39,44). He did not hesitate to assume a position of superior authority in interpreting the Old Testament. For example, He conceded that Moses permitted divorce. Nonetheless on His own authority, He clarified the Old Testament teaching on divorce to assert that from the beginning it was not the will of the Creator (Matthew 19:8–9). Jesus' personal authority is also demonstrated in His understanding that His words will judge men on the last day (John 12:48).

> "In lifting up the Bible's claims for divine authority, however, we must never lose sight of the fact that it is also a human book."

The Old Testament, which Jesus treated with such reverence, is written as the Word of God who frequently reveals himself in it in direct speech. "The Spirit of the Lord spoke through me; his word was on my tongue," said David (2 Sam. 23:2). "The Lord Almighty has spoken . . ." was Micah's testimony (4:4). Amos begins his book, "This is what the Lord says" (1:3). The prophets regularly reported that "the word of the Lord" came to them (Hos. 1:1; Joel 1:1; Jon. 1:1; Zeph. 1:1). And so it goes through many of the thirty-nine books.

In lifting up the Bible's claims for divine authority, however, we must never lose sight of the fact that it is also a human book with the distinctive personalities of its human writers apparent on almost every page. To be sure, God is sometimes shown as writing certain things like the Ten Commandments (Exod. 31:18; cf. 34:1). On occasion He even speaks in a way that sounds very much like our modern dictation. For example, He apparently gave direct instructions to Moses for building the tabernacle (Exod. 25 through 27). He dictated a few words to Isaiah, "Take a large scroll and write on it with an ordinary pen: Maher-Shalal-Hash-Baz" (Isa. 8:1). But He more commonly spoke through the prophets in such a way as to utilize their own distinct personalities. Thus we must also emphasize the humanity of the Bible. It is indeed *theopneustos!* Nevertheless, the God-breathed word also came through the experiences and the words of mortal human beings. On the one hand, they "spoke from God" and "were carried along by the Holy Spirit" (2 Pet. 1:21). On the other, they were still fully conscious, cooperative, diverse, and talented human beings. Everywhere in the Bible one is aware that the personalities with whom God is dealing and through whom he is speaking or writing are unique. It shows the patriarchs, Abraham, Isaac, and Jacob, taking halting and sometimes wrongheaded steps in attempting to follow the Living God who was revealing himself progressively to them. It presents Moses both as the Egyptian-educated shepherd and as the prophet of Israel. Job's suffering is chronicled in elegant Hebrew poetry. David wails his complaints to God through powerful psalms as Saul incessantly pursues him. Proverbs de-picts the penchant of humans to distill their experience and advice in wise aphorisms. The lover's language is found in the Song of Solomon, and the cynic's search is detailed in Ecclesiastes. Isaiah provides unique human language for an exalted encounter with the transcendent God

> **"The God-breathed word also came through the experiences and the words of mortal human beings."**

(Isa. 6), while Jeremiah's eyes and words fill with tears as he traces the downward plunge of apostate Israel. The strange prophet Ezekiel acts out his prophecies in ways that sometimes make him appear to be almost mentally ill, while the simple but brilliant shepherd, Amos, captures the message of God in crisp agrarian metaphors.

Similarly, the New Testament, like the Old, bears the marks of its human authors. The Gospels illustrate this point. Together they make up a literary form quite different from other writings in the New Testament. They tell of Jesus Christ, the God-man, who wrought human redemption through His incarnation, ministry, death, and resurrection. But each of the four Gospels, though telling a common story from somewhat different perspectives, displays distinct characteristics of its author. For example, the Gospel of Luke bears evidence of careful research (1:3) by a writer who was apparently not personally an eyewitness and who may have been a physician (Col. 4:14). He emphasizes aspects of the life and ministry of Jesus largely ignored by the others. Examples include his interest in the work of the Holy Spirit, the poor and downtrodden, the dignity of women and their importance in the divine economy. Each of the writers of the New Testament letters has a unique approach. Paul writes one way with a profound and yet sometimes herky-jerky style. The letter to the Hebrews betrays the hand of a polished master of the Greek language who is steeped in the Septuagint, and who carefully organizes his argument. The letter of James with its many agrarian metaphors and practical bent may well reflect the basic needs of the churches in the Palestinian countryside within a few decades after the death and resurrection of Jesus. The letters of Peter appear to address more theological issues for the churches in Asia Minor. John in Revelation predicts the end

Septuagint, the Greek translation of the Old Testament made in Alexandria, Egypt, before the time of Christ. A later tradition said it was done by seventy men; hence, "Septuagint," from L. *septuaginta*, 70.

of the age in a series of highly symbolic visions, the precise meaning of which still intrigues eager students.

The presence of both divine and human elements in the Bible requires what biblical scholars often call an organic view of inspiration. "The Spirit enters into the history and culture of the writers and does not simply superimpose truth on them."[9] This account means that God prepared each biblical writer in such a way that the person's individuality would not be violated. Nonetheless, the inspired writer communicated precisely the message God desired in appropriate language for the intended audiences. The case of Moses illustrates the point. By every human standard, even had he escaped Pharaoh's infanticide, Moses should have grown up poor and uneducated, knowing nothing of the ways of the Egyptian court. Instead, the waters of the Nile carried him into the arms of Pharaoh's daughter who hired his own Israelite mother to nurse him. The princess raised him in the palace as her own son (Exod. 2:1–10), insuring that he was "educated in all the wisdom of the Egyptians" (Acts 7:22). Only after the privileges of the royal court were tempered by the spartan shepherd's life in the Sinai peninsula would God give Moses the inaugural revelation of the burning bush (Exod. 3) and the fiery covenant of Mount Sinai (Exod. 19). All of those experiences uniquely prepared Moses to write the messages of God to his people in a language and frame of reference they could understand.

While the Bible was written and compiled by many different authors and editors over hundreds of years, it displays remarkable unity in progressively revealing God and His will for human beings. Its various books all have a unique origin and historical setting. But each one cumulatively adds to our knowledge of the nature of God and His redemptive efforts on our behalf. James Orr summarized the complex historical unity of the Bible nicely: "The Bible is the record of God's revelations of Himself to men in successive ages and dispensations (Eph. 1:8–10; 3:5–9; Col. 1:25f), till the revelation culminates in the advent and work of the son, and the mission of the Spirit. It is this aspect of the Bible that constitutes its grand distinction from all collections of sacred writings . . . in the world."[10]

The truthfulness and authority of Scripture, though vigorously challenged by critics both ancient and modern, have largely been considered self-evident to men and women of faith. To be sure, Christian scholars have ably demonstrated that the Bible is amazingly accurate for such an ancient book compiled over such a long period of time and touching on so many facts of history.[11]

---

[9]Donald G. Bloesch, *Holy Scripture: Revelation, Inspiration, & Interpretation* (Downers Grove, Ill.: InterVarsity Press, 1994), 122.

[10]*The International Standard Bible Encyclopedia*, rev. ed., Geoffrey W. Bromiley, ed. (Grand Rapids: William B. Eerdmans, 1979), s.v. "Bible."

[11]See Donald G. Bloesch's comments and bibliography, *Holy Scripture: Revelation, Inspiration, & Interpretation* (Downers Grove, Ill.: InterVarsity Press, 1994), 323–24.

Those who seek the truth need not fear that in embracing the Bible they are adopting baseless myths or legends. However, the Bible remains largely irrelevant if the God of whom it speaks does not reveal himself to human beings in their own time and space. Just because something is true, or factual, does not make it relevant and meaningful. The authority of Scripture is finally demonstrated only in a personal encounter with the God of Scripture. In the words of the great reformer, John Calvin, "[T]he highest proof of Scripture derives in general from the fact that God in person speaks in it."[12] Calvin went on to add, "[T]he testimony of the Spirit is more excellent than all reason. For as God alone is a fit witness of himself in his Word, so also the Word will not find acceptance in men's hearts before it is sealed by the inward testimony of the Spirit."[13]

Distinguishing Its Worldview

Even a casual reading of the Bible will enable one to distinguish its worldview from several competing worldviews common in modern society. We here briefly consider the contrast with three modern worldviews: naturalism, pantheism, and deism.[14]

NATURALISM

In Western society, the dominant worldview has come to be what we might call naturalism. In this view, ultimate reality is

Calvin on Scripture

"God, the Artificer of the universe, is made manifest to us in Scripture . . ."

"Thus, the highest proof of Scripture derives in general from the fact that God in person speaks in it."

"For as God alone is a fit witness of himself in his Word, so also the Word will not find acceptance in men's hearts before it is sealed by the inward testimony of the Spirit."

"Let this point therefore stand: that those whom the Holy Spirit has inwardly taught truly rest upon Scripture, and that Scripture indeed is self-authenticated; hence, it is not right to subject it to proof and reasoning. And the certainty it deserves with us, it attains by the testimony of the Spirit."

(Material taken from Calvin's *Institutes of the Christian Religion,* vol. xx.)

---

[12]John T. McNeill, ed., *Calvin: Institutes of the Christian Religion.* Trans. Ford Lewis Battles. The Library of Christian Classics (Philadelphia: Westminster Press, 1960), 20:78.

[13]Ibid., 79.

[14]Existentialism is another view prominent today. See the discussion in chapter 1.

material, the "stuff" the universe is made of. Everything in the universe occurs naturally from the intrinsic potential of the elements themselves. Naturalism[15] is an outgrowth of the scientific mind-set coming from the Enlightenment.

The naturalistic perspective affirms belief only in those things that can be empirically tested and explained. Everything in the universe around us, including ourselves, is considered to be an accidental product of time and the processes of change implicit in the universe. Naturalism recognizes neither a place nor a need for an omnipotent, omniscient creator. The universe and we who inhabit it evolved through chance combinations of chemical forces. Any idea we have of a creator God is simply a projection of our imagination on the gigantic screen of a confusing universe. This view may also be referred to as *materialistic* because of the way it regards the physical matter of the universe as ultimate. It may also be regarded as *atheistic* because of its rejection of the idea of God. It may be thought of as *humanistic* because of its exclusive association of any ultimate value or morality with human beings. If there is no ultimate spiritual reality beyond human beings themselves, then the death of human beings is presumably the end of their personal existence. There is therefore no basis for belief in eternal life.[16]

By and large, naturalism dominates the curricula of secular universities and colleges today. There, God is largely unknown and usually considered to be either nonexistent or unknowable. The universe is a closed system, undisturbed and undisturbable; supernatural events, like miracles, cannot intrude. The Bible is merely a book like all other ancient books, filled with

Enlightenment, an eighteenth-century philosophical movement that emphasized the free use of reason, the empirical method of science, and questioned traditional doctrines and values.

Atheistic, Gk., *a* = without; *theos* = god

Luther on Scripture

"The Scriptures, although they also were written by men, are not of men nor from men, but from God."

". . . the Word of God is greater than heaven and earth, yea, greater than death and hell, for it forms part of the power of God, and endures everlastingly; we should, therefore, diligently study God's Word, and know and assuredly believe that God himself speaks unto us."

"How can we know what is God's Word, and what is right or wrong? . . . You must determine this matter yourself, for your very life depends upon it. Therefore God must speak to your heart: This is God's Word; otherwise you are undecided . . .

(Material taken from *A Compend of Luther's Theology,* Hugh T. Kerr, ed.)

---

[15] See chapter 1 for a discussion of this term.

[16] For a helpful critique of naturalism, see Ronald H. Nash, *Faith and Reason: Searching for a Rational Faith* (Grand Rapids: Academic Books/Zondervan Publishing House, 1988), especially pp. 256–59.

myths and mistakes, to be interpreted by whatever "scientific method" is currently in vogue. Its reported experiences of God are largely explorations of the writers' own inner feelings or desires. Modern students quickly grasp that, if there is no divine lawgiver, ethics and morality can never to be viewed in absolute terms. One's behavior is purely a matter of personal choice or social constraints. Naturalism inevitably leaves human beings adrift on a sea of ethical relativism and subjectivity.

By contrast, the Bible teaches with powerful certainty that God exists and calls everything into being by His powerful word. Thus its first book, Genesis, begins simply and elegantly, "In the beginning God created the heavens and the earth" (1:1). "The heavens declare the glory of God; the skies proclaim the work of his hands" (19:1), adds the Psalmist. So obvious does God's creative power and rule appear to be that another of the Psalmists adds, "The fool says in his heart, 'There is no God'" (53:1).[17] The God of the Bible not only creates, He continues to intervene in the world, calling Abraham, leading His people out of Egypt, establishing a covenant with them at Sinai, even giving a code of conduct they are to live by. He effects His purposes throughout biblical history until the fulfillment of His promises in Christ and the Church. Through Christ, the Church is assured of God's continuing presence and power until the end of the age and the consummation of all things. The vast biblical data supporting an understanding of God's intervention in His world on behalf of His own purposes has historically been expressed in the Christian doctrine of providence. Millard Erickson defines this doctrine as "the continuing action of God by which he preserves in existence the creation which he has brought into being, and guides it to his intended purpose for it."[18]

PANTHEISM

Another common worldview, native to many Eastern religions and growing in influence in the West, is *pantheism*. In this view, humankind is indeed god. But, then, so is a goat, or a tree,

---

[17]The Bible never attempts to prove the existence of God through rational proofs. However, Christian thinkers have done so with varying degrees of acceptance at different times in the church's history. The best known arguments are the *ontological*, based on our ability to conceive of a perfect being who must of necessity exist if perfect; the *cosmological*, based on the apparent need for a creator of our complex universe; the *teleological*, based on the apparent design of our universe; and the *moral*, based upon the presence of moral capacity in human beings. For a clear exposition, see Stanley J. Grenz, *Theology for the Community of God* (Nashville: Broadman & Holman Publishers, 1994), 40–45.

[18]Millard J. Erickson, *Christian Theology* (Grand Rapids: Baker Book House, 1983–85), 387.

or an asteroid. In the pantheistic system, God is totally immanent, or present, in the creation and indistinguishable from it. Pantheism discounts any sense of transcendence in which God is in some way separate from and greater than His creation. It also discounts the possibility of miracles or supernatural intervention. As to the future of humankind, this view is often associated with reincarnation, the belief that after death the individual is reborn in another life, the circumstances of which are determined by the net results of good and evil deeds in the earlier life.[19]

Pantheism, Gk., pan = all; theos = god; thus "all is God" or "God is in everything."

The Bible does teach that God is immanent in His universe in the sense that He is everywhere present and active. He actually went so far as to assume human flesh in the person of Jesus of Nazareth. Unlike pantheism, however, the Bible presents God as also transcendent: While creating and stooping to involve himself in His world, He nonetheless exists apart from it in the sense that His divine essence is not to be confused with anything He has made. God is not the same as His world.

Christianity is congruent with and indeed teaches what may be called a *theistic* worldview. In a theistic system, the ultimate reality is a god, or gods, who brings the universe into being and, in some sense, transcends it. The God of the Bible is not only personal but also an eternal reality. He existed before any material entity in the universe and brought into being from nothing everything that exists outside himself. "By faith we understand that the universe was formed at God's command, so that what is seen was not made out of what was visible" (Hebrews 11:3).

Theistic, from Gk., theos, "god."

In contrast to polytheistic (hence "many gods") systems which feature a number of gods, the writers of the Bible describe a monotheistic[20] belief powerfully expressed in the ancient Hebrew affirmation of faith, called the Shema, "Hear [Heb, *shema'*], O Israel: The Lord our God, the Lord is one" (Deut. 6:4). The idea of one God who is both invisible and intolerant of physical images, or idols, in an ancient world replete with numerous capricious deities made in the image of human beings of both sexes was revolutionary indeed!

Polytheistic, monotheistic; poly meaning "many"; mono, "one" or "only."

But Christianity is a special kind of monotheism. While believing firmly in one God, Christians at the same time affirm without any sense of contradiction that their one God is also triune in His essential nature and redemptive work.[21] Thus Paul, as a devout Jew, could write at one moment "there is no God but one" (1 Corinthians 8:6) and almost immediately add, "yet for us there is but one God, the Father . . . and . . . one Lord,

Triune, "three Persons in the one divine Being."

---

[19]See *The Encyclopedia of Religion*, Mircea Eliade, ed. (New York: Macmillan Publishing Company, 1987), s.v. "reincarnation."

[20]See *Evangelical Dictionary of Theology*, Walter A. Elwell, ed. (Grand Rapids: Baker Book House, 1984), s.v. "monotheism."

[21]See G. W. Bromiley, s.v. "trinity."

Jesus Christ" (v. 6). He frequently alternated the triune names as in his references to Spirit, Lord, and God in the conferral and operation of spiritual gifts (1 Corinthians 12:4–6).

DEISM

Deism, from the Latin *deus*, "god" and -ism.

Christian theism in its historic orthodox expressions has been understood to be supernaturalistic in that God not only creates the universe but also sustains it by His power and intervenes directly in it to accomplish His purposes. However, a variation of Christian theism arose in early seventeenth-century England, which we have come to know as *deism*[22] and which still surfaces from time to time in many subtle, and sometimes not so subtle, ways. Highly rationalistic, the early deists abandoned the revelatory knowledge of the Bible to posit a universe in which God was reduced to the role of "first cause." Using the imagery of the watchmaker, they claimed that God originally created the world, "wound up" its natural processes, and spun it out into the universe, where He abandoned it. In such a belief system, there is little need for such classical Christian doctrines as the Trinity, the incarnation of Christ, atonement, miracles, or inspired Scripture. Basically, in this view, God equipped spaceship earth for its voyage and left it to whatever adventures may occur. Since divine intervention is hard to predict or verify, this view has a certain appeal for people who sense the need for a Creator but think that He is absent from daily life. In popular usage, the word *deistic* is sometimes applied to orthodox expressions of Christian faith that limit God's will or capacity to intervene miraculously in His world.[23]

By contrast, the Bible demonstrates throughout that God not only created the world but is constantly involved in its preservation. In the revival of Nehemiah's time, the Levites prayed, "You alone are the Lord. You *made* [past tense] the heavens . . ." But they added, "You *give* [present tense] life to everything . . ." (Neh. 9:6). The theme of the Old Testament might well be, "The Lord has established his throne in heaven, and his kingdom rules over all "(Ps. 103:19). Daniel noted, "He changes times and seasons; he sets up kings and deposes them" (Dan. 2:21). Similarly, the New Testament teaches that Christ is "before all things, and *in him all things hold together*" (Col. 1:17) and that he as Son of God "is . . . *sustaining all things by his powerful word*" (Heb. 1:3).

Both Testaments show God's care for the world. In Psalm 104,

---

[22]Ibid., s.v. "deism."

[23]See Kirk Bottomly, "Coming Out of the Hangar: Confessions of an Evangelical Deist," in *The Kingdom and the Power: Are Healing and the Spiritual Gifts Used by Jesus and the Early Church Meant for the Church Today?* Gary S. Greig and Kevin N. Springer, eds. (Ventura, Calif.: Regal Books, 1993), 257–274.

God "makes springs pour water into the ravines" (v. 10) and "grass grow for the cattle" (v. 14). The rain is stopped and similarly resumed at his pleasure (1 Kings 17:1; 18:1,45). In the words of Jesus, it is God who sends sun and rain on both the good and the evil (Matt. 5:45) and who cares for birds, lilies, and grass (Matt. 6:26–30).

God also keeps individual persons: David when pursued by Saul (1 Sam. 23:9–12; 26:24); Shadrach, Meshach, and Abednego in the fiery furnace (Dan. 3:28); Paul through storm and shipwreck (Acts 27:23–24). While deism may seem an attractive view to those who have difficulty tracking scientifically the path of supernatural intervention in the universe, it cannot be sustained by a careful reading of the Bible.

Filling Out the Worldview

To say that the Bible presents a comprehensive and unified worldview is to overstate the case and to misunderstand the nature of biblical literature. While all cultures have a worldview, be it simple or complex, mythically or abstractly stated, randomly scattered and orally preserved or carefully written in a document, no one way of stating a Christian worldview would meet the needs of all cultures at all times. Rather the Bible is essentially the written witness to God's creation and governance of the universe insofar as it relates to human beings. It is also the record of the ways God has revealed himself and His will for humankind. As an authoritative document which witnesses to the nature of God, the world, and human beings, the Bible is a source from which a reasonably comprehensive worldview may be constructed. Many narratives or teachings of Scripture speak directly to the various elements of a worldview. Where matters are not specifically addressed by Scripture, reasonable inferences may be drawn from relevant and abundant narrative sources. For example, the Genesis narratives of creation (chapters 1 through 3) presuppose that God created everything that exists. But they do not directly address the question as to whether God created the world in six literal 24-hour days about 6,000 years ago, as many have believed, or over long age-days as many others believe. One's particular theory on the manner and chronology of the earth's creation will be established on inferences drawn from careful study of the biblical text as compared with the evidence of the physical and biological sciences.

IDEOLOGY

Christians have historically found it necessary to identify the core beliefs of their faith through careful study of the Bible and then to express those beliefs in terse and easily memorized statements of faith, which are commonly called creeds.

Kenosis, **Christ's conde-scension to earthly humiliation, so named from the Greek** *kenoô*, **"to empty," in verse 7.**

Incarnation, **the taking of human form, both fully human as well as fully divine.**

Exaltation, **the restoration of Jesus to His glory at the Father's throne.**

Not infrequently, tersely worded statements of Scripture dealing with key doctrinal issues served as the first creeds, and continue to serve in that way today. Thus, in the Shema mentioned earlier, we have a core belief of Judaism and, subsequently, Christianity, "Hear, O Israel: The Lord our God, the Lord is one" (Deut. 6:4). When a prominent Jewish rabbi questioned Jesus as to which of the many commandments of the Old Testament was the greatest, he had devised a clever ruse to determine the essence of Jesus' belief system. Apparently without hesitation, Jesus quoted from Deuteronomy 6:5, "Love the Lord your God with all your heart and with all your soul and with all your mind," and followed up with a second quotation from Leviticus 19:18, "Love your neighbor as yourself" (see Matt. 22:34–40). Jesus understood those passages to contain essential elements of Israel's faith.

The first Christian preachers naturally looked to key passages of the Old Testament to express important aspects of their belief in the risen Christ as in Peter's quotation from Psalm 16:8–11 (see Acts 2:25–28) or Paul's quotation of Psalm 16:10 (see Acts 13:35). Paul is often thought to have quoted an early Christian creed in Philippians 2:5–11 when using the *kenosis* as an example to encourage believers to emulate the humility of their Lord. Another example appears in 1 Timothy 3:16, which emphasizes both the incarnation and exaltation of Jesus.[24]

From those early beginnings has flowed a steady stream of creedal development intended to restate the core beliefs of Christian faith in easily repeatable form. The purpose was to respond to the particular challenges of each historical era. The best known of the early creeds is the so-called *Apostles' Creed*, still in widespread use today. Though not composed by the apostles, as legend suggests, its earliest forms probably reach back to an early period in church history, the end of the second century.[25] It is an eloquent but simple affirmation of biblical faith framed around statements of belief in "God the Father almighty," "Jesus Christ, his only Son, our Lord" and "the Holy Spirit."

From simple beginnings, creeds slowly grew in complexity and sophistication to offset the particular heresies of their times. With the Reformation era, they became quite lengthy as the emerging Protestant traditions attempted to clarify their beliefs on the basis of Scripture as opposed to those of Roman Catholicism. The *Augsburg Confession* of 1530 takes up more than forty pages. Approximately one-third is a creedal statement of belief; the remainder has to do with doctrinal matters

---

[24]For further information see John H. Leith, ed., *Creeds of the Churches: A Reader in Christian Doctrine from the Bible to the Present*, 3d ed. (Louisville, Ky.: John Knox Press, 1982), 12–16.

[25]Ibid., 22–25.

then in dispute.[26] Each of the major traditions prepared creeds refined to state what were believed to be crucial scriptural beliefs important to them but omitted or contradicted by others. The *Westminster Confession of Faith* (1646), influential in the Reformed tradition, strongly emphasizes God's predestination of those whom he has elected to salvation.[27] By contrast the Anglican *Thirty-Nine Articles of Religion* (1563)[28] placed little emphasis on predestination. Its Methodist revision into *The [twenty-five] Articles of Religion* (1784) also largely ignores the issue.[29] The historic creeds all represent an attempt to draw out the direct or implied teachings of the Scriptures on key affirmations their authors were contending for. Scripture is usually understood as the authoritative basis from which they are developed and argued.

BIBLICAL NARRATIVE

Creeds tend to be abstract and philosophical. They therefore appeal mainly to educated adults interested in distilling and transmitting the key theological pillars of faith. Much of the vitality of faith is transmitted, however, in the narratives of the Bible, which tend to be colorful, dramatic, and easily remembered. Biblical narratives are never just an end in themselves. They always contain important theological or ethical lessons. For example, the simple but dramatic stories of Adam and Eve (Gen. 1 through 3) address some of the most vital questions of human existence. A personal, transcendent, and all-powerful God created the first human pair in His own image (1:27) from elements of the earth (2:7). He made them a family unit (2:24) and defined their existence by certain instructions for worship (3:8–9), service (1:26; 2:15), and ethical behavior (2:17). But if humans are noble, they are also ignoble. Thus the story tells of Adam's and Eve's temptation by the serpent (3:1–7) and how they were later expelled from the Garden, the place of their origin. The narrative gives an explanation for suffering (3:16) and hard work (3:17–19) and even foreshadows the redemption of humankind.[30]

As even a novice reader soon learns, the Bible gives us much

---

[26]Ibid., 63–107.

[27]Ibid., 193ff.

[28]Ibid., 266ff.

[29]Ibid., 353ff.

[30]The narrative seems to presume that animals were slaughtered in order to make clothing from the skins, foreshadowing later practices of animal sacrifice for the atonement for sin. It also promises that the woman's offspring will bruise the head of the serpent (3:15). This promise has been historically understood as the *protevangelium* ("first gospel") pointing forward to the death and victory of Christ.

more than doctrines, commands, and precepts. From Genesis (the book of beginnings) to Revelation (John's Apocalypse), the Bible communicates its messages in evocative narratives as captivating as a Shakespearean drama or as luminous as an Impressionist painting. The stories of Abraham begin a saga of a covenant people vital to God's plan of redemption (Gen. 12 through 25:11). The stories of Moses chronicle miraculous deliverance, the establishment of the covenant, the institution of prophecy, and the formation of the nation. The future Savior is foreshadowed in the stories of King David, under whom the people of promise defeated their enemies on every side and established an empire. Along the way, the narratives of heroes like Joseph and Samson incorporate both positive and negative ethical lessons along with important theological insights.

> "The Bible is not only the source for doctrine or theology in the Christian worldview, it is also the source for a consistent and benevolent ethical system."

In the New Testament, the narratives of the birth of Jesus contain the crucial elements of the Christian doctrine of the incarnation in which God takes human form in order to redeem Adam's fallen posterity. The stories of His baptism, endowment with the Spirit, temptation, and ministry all recount how God lived among human beings teaching the way of salvation. The story of the crucifixion is more than a sad account of a tragic miscarriage of justice. It is the story of how God forgives the sin of the race. The narrative of the resurrection is the capstone of the Gospel story, showing how God overcomes the death of Jesus to finish the work of redemption. The narrative of the Book of Acts recounts the beginnings of the Church. In fascinating detail it describes both that the Living God dwells within His people (rather than in a tabernacle or temple) and that He sends them out as responsible partners in the reconciliation of the world. The apocalyptic scenarios of the Revelation tell of the consummation of all things with final judgment for the unrepentant and eternal blessedness for the redeemed.

NORMATIVE ELEMENTS OF SCRIPTURE

The Bible is not only the source for doctrine or theology in the Christian worldview, it is also the source for a consistent and benevolent ethical system. Ethical instruction is to be found throughout the Bible, from the first Book of Genesis where Adam is commanded by God not to eat the fruit of the tree of the knowledge of good and evil (2:17), to the final Book of Revelation where the hearer is commanded neither to add to nor to take away from its prophecies (22:18–19). Beginning in the Pentateuch and continuing through the Bible, ethical teach-

Pentateuch, from Gk. *penta*, "five," and *teuchos*, "book."

ings range from carefully codified laws as specific and practical as a prohibition against usury (Deut. 23:19) to sweeping general principles like "Love your neighbor as yourself" (Lev. 19:18).[31] Biblical ethics is both personal, having to do with the way individuals relate to God and each other as in the preceding examples, and social, spelling out actions which contribute toward the well-being of society as a whole. Thus Amos bitterly censures his fellows who "trample on the poor" (5:11) and calls for "justice in the courts" (5:15). Much of the content of the Bible is ethical in nature, directly concerned with the way people live in relation to God and each other.

Usury, "charging exorbitant interest."

The heart of biblical ethics is found in the Ten Commandments, or the "Ten Words" as the Hebrew text literally puts it (as does the Greek: "Decalogue"), which God himself wrote on tablets of stone and gave to Moses (Exod. 20:1–17; Deut. 5:1–22). Far more than a simple set of legal proscriptions, the Decalogue is a covenant (Deut. 5:3), structured in the covenant language of the ancient Near East: The Lord as the Great King who has delivered Israel from Egypt sets the terms his people are to live by. Properly speaking, the commands call for a response of disciplined love and gratitude to the Lord, not a tedious legalistic system.

The Decalogue divides naturally into two sections.[32] The first section, comprising commandments one through four, has to do with what might be called vertical relationships, those between man and God. Thus Israel is to (1) have no other Gods, (2) make (worship) no idols, (3) permit no misuse God's name, and (4) observe the Sabbath day. The second section, comprising commandments five through ten, have to do with horizontal relationships, those between persons. Thus Israel is to (5) honor parents, (6) not murder, (7) not commit adultery, (8) not steal, (9) not give false testimony, (10) not covet anything that belongs to a neighbor.[33] In a time of rampant idolatry and ethical confusion, the Decalogue was a far more revolutionary document than can be imagined by our culture, which has been powerfully influenced by the Judeo-Christian tradition.

The importance of the Decalogue is emphasized by the way it is used in the New Testament. Jesus regarded its commandments as the basic ethic of the kingdom of God. In debate with

---

[31]However, note the way in which the Old Testament ethical command is set within the life of the community to prevent revenge and grudges against fellow Israelites. Jesus and Paul, by contrast, seem to universalize this command.

[32]Some scholars, noting the attitudinal nature of the tenth commandment, identify it as a third section.

[33]See *Evangelical Dictionary of Theology*, s.v. "Ten Commandments." Note that Craigie, the author, includes the fifth commandment to honor parents with those relating primarily to God since the parents are responsible to teach the law of God to their children.

His opponents, He reiterated the Decalogue. But in so doing, He lifted it far above a mere set of rules when He summarized the first table as a command to love God and the second table as a command to love one's neighbor (Matt. 22:34–40). Jesus' concern for the Decalogue is repeatedly demonstrated. For example, He rehearsed the second table to a rich but apparently covetous and legalistic young man (Matt. 19:18–19). The clear implication was that the man had lost sight of what it meant to love both God and neighbor. On other occasions, He said, "[D]o to others what you would have them do to you, for this sums up the Law and the Prophets" (Matt. 7:12). Here again He dynamically restates the second table as love of neighbor and shows its centrality in the will of God. For Jesus, the essence of the Decalogue as love for God and neighbor is eternally valid and universally commanded.

> "Jesus regarded the Decalogue's commandments as the basic ethic of the kingdom of God."

Paul, and for that matter the New Testament community at large, followed the example of Jesus in perpetuating the ethic of the Decalogue. Paul repeated four commandments from the second table and like Jesus before him reduced them dynamically to the law of love. "[W]hatever other commandment[s] there may be," he says, "are summed up in this one rule: 'Love your neighbor as yourself.' . . . Therefore love is the fulfillment of the law" (Rom. 13:9–10). Far from being legalistic, however, Paul understood that love is the gift of God by His Spirit (Rom. 5:5) and that the Spirit both breaks the power of sin (Rom. 6:12; 8:2; 8:13; Gal. 5:16) and provides the motivation to live out the ethics of the Kingdom of God (Rom. 8:4; Gal. 5:22). Moreover, one's relationship to God is not based on perfect adherence to commandments (Rom. 3:20), important as they are as obedient responses to God, but on a righteousness freely provided through faith in the redeeming work of Jesus Christ (Rom. 3:21–26).

The Bible does not leave us with a legalistic code of ethical behavior that gives specific prescriptions for every difficult situation. Rather, it bears witness to a personal God, awesome in holiness, who commands humankind to love both Him and each other out of a grace He provides. The Decalogue, and other specific commandments of the Bible, becomes a set of authoritative guiding principles that are amazingly resilient and applicable to every situation through prayer and the wisdom of the Holy Spirit.

RITUALS DERIVED FROM SCRIPTURE

The biblical narratives are replete with powerful rituals by which the people of God invoked His blessings and observed

His commands for worship and service. From the simple sacrifices of Abram at the outset of God's covenant with him (Gen. 15), to the elaborate tabernacle in the wilderness with its carefully prescribed sacrificial and ritual systems (Exod. 35 through 40; Lev. 1 through 27), to the gilded and even more complex temple of Solomon (1 Kings 5 through 8), Israel developed what she understood to be the manner of worship ordered by her great King as an appropriate demonstration of His will in the lives of His people. Thus the temple liturgy came to symbolize Israel's election and special privilege as the unique people of God. The destruction of the temple by the Babylonians in 586 B.C. effectively spelled out God's rejection and punishment for their sins. Subsequently, pious Israelites longed for the restoration to divine favor implied in their regathering and rebuilding of the temple.

The importance of the rebuilt temple in the lives of Jews following the exile is seen in the way Jesus himself frequented the temple and participated in its services (Matt. chs. 21 through 24; Mark chs. 11 through 13; Luke 2:27,41–49; 19:45–46; chs. 20 through 23; John 2:13–16; 7:14ff. etc.). This was true despite His contempt for the wickedness of its leaders (cf. Matt. 23) and the rampant commercialization of its sacrifices (Matt. 21:12–13; John 2:13–16). Jesus also foresaw a time when the splendid temple of His day, magnificently renovated by Herod the Great, would again be destroyed (Matt. 24:1–2; Mark 13:1–2; Luke 21:5–6). Early Christians regularly used the temple for their gatherings (Acts 3:1ff.; 5:12; 5:42) and took part in its rituals (Acts 21:26) but, even so, understood that forgiveness of sins was now accomplished through the death of Jesus (Acts 2:38; 5:30–31) rather than temple rituals as such (cf. Heb. 9).

> **"The biblical narratives are replete with powerful rituals by which the people of God invoked His blessings."**

The fact that early Christians increasingly attached less significance to temple ritual (together with Jesus' prediction of the destruction of the temple) may have led to tensions between them and Jewish leaders. For instance, Stephen was charged with speaking against the temple (Acts 6:13,14). In response, he eloquently pointed out that, although God had given the Jews possession of the tabernacle and later the temple, they eventually turned a deaf ear to His commandments and laws. Stephen then insisted, "the Most High does not live in houses made by men" (7:48). In any event, by the time the temple was destroyed in A.D. 70, worship in it was no longer vital to Christian faith.

The rituals of temple and synagogue undoubtedly had an important influence on the ritual practices[34] of Christianity in such features as music and singing, giving, prayer, the reading

---

[34] See chapter 1 for a discussion of this term.

Eucharist, **from the Greek verb** *eucharisteô,* **"give thanks."**

Sacrament, **from Lat.** *sacrere,* **"to consecrate."**

Ordinance, **a prescribed ceremony; in theology, those commanded by Christ.**

of Scripture, and preaching. Jewish antecedents abound for each of those practices, and the Bible either directly teaches their importance or provides precedent for their use in worship.

The two most obvious ritual practices taught in Scripture are baptism and the Eucharist, or Holy Communion, as it is often called. Liturgical churches tend to regard these events as sacraments, believing that grace is actually mediated through them. Those in the free church tradition usually call them ordinances, desiring to get away from any magical connotations of grace that may detract from the necessity of faith and obedience in the observance.

Baptism in water as a sign of repentance and commitment to God appears to have been first introduced into the Jewish tradition in the ministry of John the Baptist (Matt. 3:6). Jesus himself submitted to the baptism, not as a sign of repentance but "to fulfill all righteousness" (Matt. 3:15). It also became the occasion for His anointing by the Spirit (Matt. 3:16–17). Jesus' disciples appear to have baptized others on occasion (John 3:22–26; 4:2). Baptism is commanded in conjunction with the Great Commission that Jesus gave His disciples (Matt. 28:19) and was a part of Christian ritual practice from the beginning (Acts 2:38; 8:12,38; 9:18; 10:48). The language of baptism appears occasionally in the Epistles to speak of death to the old life of sin and disobedience prior to coming to faith in Christ (Rom. 6:1–4; 1 Pet. 3:21). (See the sidebar on baptism in chapter 1, p. 67).

The ritual practice of Holy Communion derives from the Christian understanding that Jesus himself commanded it in the accounts of His last supper with the disciples, found in the Synoptic Gospels (Matt. 26:17–30; Mark 14:12–26; Luke 22:7–23) and in Paul's first letter to the Corinthians (11:17–34), probably our earliest written record of the event. In the climactic moments of that meal, Jesus took bread and, after giving thanks, directed the disciples to eat it, saying, "This is my body." Similarly, He distributed the cup of wine, saying, "This is my blood of the [new] covenant, which is poured out for many." Jesus clearly identified this ceremonial occasion with His impending death and understood it to symbolize uniquely the way in which His death would become an atonement for the sins of humankind. Both Luke's and Paul's witness have Jesus connecting the bread to His body given for us (Luke 22:19; cf. 1 Cor. 11:24). His blood is "my blood of the covenant, which is poured out for many" (Mark 14:24). Matthew adds, "for the forgiveness of sins" (26:28). Both Luke (22:19) and Paul (1 Cor. 11:24) specifically recall that the supper is to be repeated "in remembrance of me." (See the sidebar on Communion in chapter 1, p. 66).

Other practices are often inferred from the Bible as appropriate ways to celebrate and observe one's faith. Such practices include regular meetings, singing, use of musical instruments, praying, preaching, use of spiritual gifts in worship, and so forth. Different churches place differing values on particular rituals, depending on their reading of the Bible.

SPIRITUAL EXPERIENCE

Four powerful examples of biblical religious experiences have been investigated in the previous chapter (see pages 68–71). The biblical narratives indeed abound with stories of the ways in which God has encountered human beings in life transforming ways. What needs to be added here is that the Bible presents a living, personal, and loving God who desires to enter into relationship with all who are willing to come to Him in repentance and faith. This point is perhaps supremely made in the Fourth Gospel's description of the incarnation: "The Word became flesh and made his dwelling among us" (1:14). Dwelling among human beings, Jesus entered into warm and personal relationships with them. Even as He prepared for death, the Gospel writers note Jesus' concern for continuing relationships. "And I will ask the Father and he will give you another Counselor to be with you forever . . . I will not leave you as orphans; I will come to you" (John 14:16–19). In other words, in the comforting presence of the Holy Spirit whom He would send, Jesus would once again enter into vital personal contact with His people.

The experience of the early believers as recorded in the Book of Acts builds upon the Gospel promise. Luke reports,

The Elements of the Lord's Supper

There has been a great deal of debate throughout the history of the church over precisely how to understand the elements of bread and wine in relation to the actual body and blood of Jesus. Roman Catholics have historically described their view as *transubstantiation*, claiming that in the celebration of the mass the elements of bread and wine are actually transformed into the body and blood of Jesus. Lutherans have followed the German reformer Martin Luther (1483–1546) in arguing for *consubstantiation*, believing that the body and blood of Jesus are actually present in, with, and under the elements of bread and wine. Most Protestants have followed to some extent the *memorial view* of the Swiss reformation leader Ulrich Zwingli (1484–1531), believing that the elements are simply symbols of the body and blood of Jesus. They often temper Zwingli's memorial understanding with the insight of John Calvin that Christ is really present in the communion in a mystical sense through the activity of the Holy Spirit.

"The disciples were filled with joy and *with the Holy Spirit*" (Acts 13:52), decisively connecting their joy with the Spirit. The hallmark of early faith was a joyous experience of Christ through His Spirit (Acts 2:46–47; 8:8,39). Throughout the New Testament, there is a striking connection between the person and presence of the Holy Spirit and Christian experience. In Paul's thought, God pours love into one's heart by the Spirit (Rom. 5:5) who also nurtures the additional "fruit" of joy and peace as well as other character attributes (Gal. 5:22; cf. Rom. 15:13). Hope is another contribution of the Spirit (Rom. 15:13). This indwelling presence of the Spirit gives assurance by which believers know God loves and accepts them. Thus Paul writes, "The *Spirit himself* testifies with our Spirit that we are God's children" (Rom. 8:15–16; cf. Gal. 4:6). In a similar vein, the first letter of John adds, "And this is how we know that he lives in us. We know it *by the Spirit* he gave us" (1 John 3:24). Early Christians also spoke just as easily of Christ's being in the believer (Rom. 8:10; Gal. 2:20; Eph. 3:17).

> "'Church' often denotes a building, a usage not found in the Bible and which tends to deflect attention from the Church as an entity headed by Christ."

To sum up, Christian experience is one of sensing God's power in the inner person in a way that strengthens faith (Eph. 3:16, 20; Col. 1:11) and contributes to one's peace of mind (Phil. 4:7).

THE CHURCH AS A SOCIAL INSTITUTION

The primary social entity associated with Christian faith is the Church, the rationale for which is deeply embedded in Scripture. Biblically, the word *church* is used both to denote a local group of Christian believers and the universal Church, the aggregate of all true believers throughout the ages. In modern life, *church* often denotes a building in which a particular group of Christians meet, a usage not found in the Bible and which tends to deflect attention from the essential nature of the Church as a spiritual entity headed by Christ, composed of his people, and indwelt by his Spirit. We also use the word today to speak of particular denominations, for example, the Presbyterian Church. Each denomination will be defined by its distinctive emphasis in the Bible and the unique way it understands its history. Our purpose here is to inquire about the impact of the Bible on our unique experience of Church.

The Bible shows that God has always dealt with humankind on an individual and personal level. At the same time, He placed them in social groups. After the creation of Adam, God quickly pronounced "It is not good for the man to be alone. I will make a helper suitable for him" (Gen. 2:18). The creation of Eve and the establishment of the family unit followed (2:21–24). God's call to Abram came with the promise to make him a great nation

(Gen. 12:1–3). The story of the Old Testament is the story of the creation of Israel as a unique people of God through whom He could further His purposes for humankind. The Christian Church came into being with the understanding that it was the culmination of many of God's promises to and through Israel.[35]

According to the New Testament, Jesus himself anticipated the creation of the Church (Matt. 16:18; 18:17) and prefaced His ascension with a commission that would result in its growth (Matt. 28:18–20). The Church is not simply a voluntary association, as many people in a democratic society commonly believe. Scripturally, it is an organism created by the Holy Spirit as men and women respond in faith to the preaching of the word of God. One does not so much elect to become a part of the Church as to be placed there by the action of Christ in the salvation event. "By one Spirit we were all baptized into one body . . . and we were all made to drink of one Spirit" (1 Cor. 12:13). The head of the Church is Christ himself (Eph. 1:22–23; Col. 1:18) and the most descriptive biblical metaphor for the Church is "body of Christ" (Rom. 12:5; 1 Cor. 12:12, etc.). Thus the Church, biblically speaking, is the universal body of believers indwelt by God's Spirit and obedient to Jesus Christ as head.

The Church exists to accomplish several ends in the divine purpose. First, it exists to worship and serve God. Peter, with a vivid mix of metaphors, sees the people of God as living stones built into a spiritual house, or temple, and at the same time they are a holy priesthood offering spiritual sacrifices to God (1 Pet. 2:5). Paul also describes the Church in similar terms (1 Tim. 3:15). Second, the Church exists to evangelize the world. Jesus uniquely constituted His people as a mission people and directed them to "go and make disciples of all nations" (Matt. 28:19). Third, the Church is charged with the nurture and growth of its members. It is to be the place where "the body of Christ may be built up until we all reach unity in the faith and in the knowledge of the Son of God and become mature . . ." (Eph. 4:12–13). A biblical worldview can be properly articulated and experienced only from the corporate reality of the Church.

Conclusion

There have been few days in the years since my tent meeting conversion that I have not actually opened the Bible to read from its wisdom for either devotional or academic needs. There have been none where the memory of its message did not guide and illuminate my thoughts and actions. The puzzle of a consistent and satisfying worldview has been filled out as I have discovered over and over again the dynamic congruence of my

---

[35]Many specific promises to Israel will be fulfilled in the Millennium. See Stanley M. Horton, *Our Destiny: Biblical Teachings on the Last Things* (Springfield, Mo.: Logion Press, 1996), 190–197.

personal relationship with God, the word He has spoken in the Bible, and the world He has created. To be sure, both my way of thinking and behavior have often been painfully challenged. I have often faced the need to repent and to renew on both fronts. Moreover, I do not yet have completely satisfactory answers to every conceivable question that may be posed for my belief system. Certainly no worldview is without difficulties. But I find fewer in a Christian approach based on Scripture. Rather than requiring a sacrifice of my intellect, I find that the Bible continues to move me on in the quest for a more complete understanding of its teachings. And I find that living out its message brings joy and satisfaction on a personal level, which more than rewards the cost of a believing obedience. For me, the Bible has truly proven itself to be *theopneustos*, "God-breathed." Like Calvin, I have found "God in person speaks in it."

Review and Discussion Questions

1. How would you tell the story of the Bible in a few brief sentences?

2. Discuss the meaning and importance of the Greek word *theopneustos* found in 2 Timothy 3:16.

3. How do the biblical writers usually think of the origin and authority of their writings?

4. What is the significance of the fact that the Bible appears simply to assume the existence of God without any necessity of rational proofs of his existence? Why do you suppose later Christian thinkers—Anselm, Thomas Aquinas, Paley—feel a need to offer such proofs?

5. Compare and contrast the worldview of the Bible with that of naturalism, pantheism, and deism.

6. How do the historic creeds of the Christian church relate to the Bible and our worldview?

7. How do the narratives of the Bible inform our worldview? What precautions must be exercised in forming a worldview from narratives?

8. How are we to understand the significance of the Decalogue for our ethical lives today?

9. What are the two major ritual practices that almost all Christians observe and what is their significance? Also, in what ways can these rituals become "mere" rituals? What ways can you think of to help today's church avoid treating them as mere rituals?

10. Discuss the Holy Spirit's role in the experience of Christian faith.

Selected Bibliography

Bloesch, Donald G. *Holy Scripture: Revelation, Inspiration, & Interpretation.* Downers Grove, Ill.: InterVarsity Press, 1994.

Elwell, Walter A., ed. *Evangelical Dictionary of Theology.* Grand Rapids: Baker Book House, 1984.

Eliade, Mircea, ed. *The Encyclopedia of Religion.* New York: Macmillan Publishing Company, 1987.

Hoffecker, W. Andrew, and Gary Scott Smith, eds. *Building a Christian World View.* 2 vols. Phillipsburg, N.J.: Presbyterian and Reformed Publishing Company, 1986, 1988.

Horton, Stanley M., ed. *Systematic Theology.* Rev. ed. Springfield, Mo.: Logion Press, 1995.

Johnson, Alan F,. and Robert E. Webber. *What Christians Believe: A Biblical and Historical Summary.* Grand Rapids: Academie Books/Zondervan Publishing House, 1989.

Leith, John H., ed. *Creeds of the Churches: A Reader in Christian Doctrine from the Bible to the Present.* 3d ed. Louisville: John Knox Press, 1982.

McNeill, John T., ed. *Calvin: Institutes of the Christian Religion.* Translated by Ford Lewis Battles. The Library of Christian Classics, vol. 20. Philadelphia: Westminster Press, 1960.

Nash, Ronald H. *Faith and Reason: Searching for a Rational Faith.* Grand Rapids: Zondervan/Academie Books, 1988.

3

Voices From the Past: Historical Attempts to Shape a Christian Worldview

Gregory J. Miller

When most students arrive at college, they are not very excited about history. I think this is understandable. American college students not only live in a future-oriented culture, they are at a particularly future-oriented time in their lives. There is an exhilaration in being free from the constraints of past expectations, reputations, and even relationships. "The past is old news. What is really important is where we go from here, right?"

Well, not exactly. The past has shaped everything we are in the present. To know where we are and where we are going, we must know where we have been. This is as true for individuals as it is for institutions, nations, and civilizations. Although those who are ignorant of history may not be "doomed to repeat its mistakes," they are doomed to be dominated by historical forces they are only vaguely aware of.

In this sense, we are captives of the past. And the key to our freedom is knowledge of our captor. Knowing the past opens to us new worlds of possibilities for human thought and action; like a rest while on a mountain hike, when we turn to look back we are amazed by what we see. We learn that things have not always been as they are now, nor do they necessarily have to be. With increased perspective and maturity, we are able to straighten our path and clarify where we're headed.

This is especially true for believers. God provides a rich heritage to inspire and instruct us. The children of Israel were often commanded to "remember the deeds of the LORD" (Ps. 77:11). In the New Testament, for example, the "Faith Chapter" (Heb. 11) is essentially a history lesson in faithfulness to God and the faithfulness of God. When we remind ourselves that "we are surrounded by such a great cloud of witnesses" (Heb. 12:1), our faith is strengthened to "run with perseverance the race marked out for us." Similarly, any chapter in the history of the Church (beginning with the Book of Acts) displays God's provision and care. Since God intervenes in human affairs, history reveals something of the very nature and character of God. Despite heresy and division, difficulties and assaults, God's kingdom is not vanquished. Individuals and nations may rise and fall, but God remains in control. For the Christian, the study of history builds faith and increases hope.

> **"Understanding the past is essential for constructing a Christian worldview in the present."**

Understanding the past is essential for constructing a Christian worldview in the present. Christianity in the twentieth century is vastly different from the first century. We cannot naively attempt to recreate the Apostolic Age. Instead, we learn from twenty centuries of church history what factors have led us to believe and act as we do. The failures of the past warn us of possible dangers. The triumphs of the past encourage us to follow their examples.

Overview of Church History

History is more easily understood if a solid framework is first established. You do not need to memorize long lists of dates. Rather, concentrate on key dates to provide a frame of reference (the beginning and end of periods, for example) and seek to grasp the story line of the past. Historians generally divide church history into three main periods: (1) The Early Church: Pentecost–A.D. 500, (2) The Medieval Church: 500–1500, and (3) The Modern Church: 1500–present. These periods are not sharply divided but rather blend into one another with important transition times from A.D. 400–600 (the fall of Roman power in Western Europe) and 1450–1650 (the Renaissance and Reformation). (See illustration 1.)

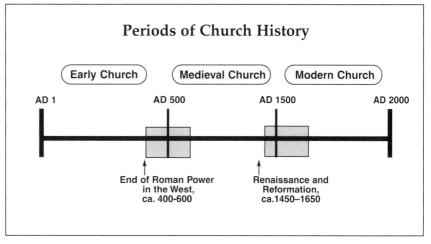

Illustration 1

In any brief summary of history, generalizations are unavoidable. It is therefore important to keep in mind that although history does display the work of God, its primary characters are human beings and institutions. Church history is neither a simple decline from a "golden Apostolic Age" to modern ruin, nor a continual triumphant march toward ever greater glory. Instead, in every period of the church and in every great leader, there have been weaknesses as well as strengths. One of history's more exciting lessons is that God works wonders through real people.

The Early Church

OVERVIEW

Whether they realize it or not, many Christians are familiar with events to about A.D. 60, because that is about the time the Book of Acts ends. However, the entire period of the Early Church (ca. 30–500) tells a fascinating story of the numerical and geographical expansion of Christianity. The first half of this period (see illustration 2), also known as the Age of Persecution, was a time of growing conflict with the Roman government. Because of Christians' refusal to participate in government-sponsored pagan worship, many Romans considered them traitors and feared their growing influence in society. At times Roman hatred erupted into brief periods of intense anti-Christian sentiment and outright massacre. The most severe of these persecutions, the Great Persecution begun by the Emperor Diocletian (303–311), aimed at nothing less than the annihilation of Christianity.

The second half of this period, also known as the Age of the Imperial Church, witnessed the dramatic victory of the Church. In a surprising turn of events, the next man after Diocletian to control the entire Roman Empire, Constantine the Great (ca. 274–337), made a public declaration in favor of Christianity. His unexpected conversion seems to have been connected to a dream (or vision) of a cross in the sky the night before a major battle. After Constantine ordered his troops to put the Christian symbol on their shields, they won a critical victory even though they were outnumbered (Battle of Milvian Bridge, 312).

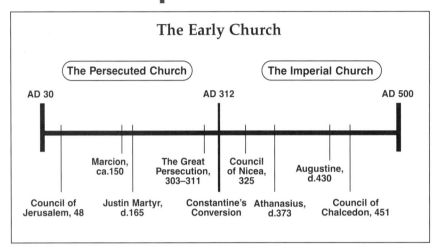

Illustration 2

When Constantine gained control of the Roman Empire, many declared it to be the dawning of a glorious new era in the history of the Church. The Church historian Eusebius, a great admirer of Constantine, likened his reign to the millennial rule of Christ. In many ways it was a tremendous triumph. For three hundred years Christians had been a suspect minority. Still only some 15 percent of the total Roman population by A.D. 300, the Church quickly assumed a dominant role in society after Constantine's conversion. By A.D. 400, the Church was no longer a *persecuted* minority, but a *persecuting* majority. The Church Fathers had wrestled with many critical issues, a strong institutional structure had been built, and a good part of the Christian worldview was already in place.

This great victory radically changed the character of the Church. In the opinion of many contemporaries, the structured, state-sponsored Church of the Imperial Age represented a significant cheapening of the faith.

Official Christianity was not the only thing changing from 312–500. Even as the Church was gaining influence in the Roman world, the Roman Empire itself was collapsing. The traditional date for the "Fall of the Roman Empire" in Western Europe is A.D. 476. The process was actually a long one, beginning in the early

400s and lasting until the 600s. By A.D. 500, invading Germanic tribes had brought with them a new political and social order and ushered in a new period in the history of the Church.

SHAPING A CHRISTIAN WORLDVIEW

The Early Church era is also known as the patristic period. "Patristic" (Latin *pater* = father) is a title of respect and refers to the importance of a few outstanding theologians and ecclesiastical leaders who are collectively known as the Fathers of the Church. As Christianity expanded into the Roman world, the Early Church faced many new issues and challenges. The Fathers wrote and taught, individually and in assembled councils, in an attempt to answer these questions. Many of their solutions still form an essential foundation for theological reflection, church organization, and Christian living.

Among the contributions of the Early Church to the shaping of a Christian worldview, four areas have been particularly important: (1) self-definition, that is, the understanding of what it means to be a Christian in reference to Judaism, (2) the relationship of Christianity to non-Christian culture as explored by the Apologists, or defenders of the faith, (3) the Christian view of God and of Jesus the Christ in the early ecumenical councils, and (4) the relationship of Christianity to government.

Christianity and Judaism

From the beginning, the newborn Church found itself in a multicultural world. Its immediate context and its first members, however, were almost exclusively Jewish. One initial concern that the community of believers faced was their relationship to first century Judaism. Did one have to become a Jew to be a true follower of Jesus? Did identification with the believing community free one from all traditional Jewish expectations? What about the Jewish Scriptures? Were the Scriptures superseded in whole or in part by Jesus the Christ?

These concerns were foremost in the minds of the New Testament authors, especially Paul. As "Apostle to the Gentiles" Paul was particularly concerned that Greeks and Barbarians (non-Greeks), Jews and Gentiles, would be allowed equal standing in the community of faith (Gal. 3:28; Col. 3:11). The Council of Jerusalem in about A.D. 48–49 (Acts 15) recognized the value of his diligent work in writing letters, traveling, and preaching. The importance of this Council can scarcely be exaggerated: Gentiles were to be accepted into the community on the basis of faith in Christ (Acts 15:7,9,11). The apostles urged moral living and Christian unity, but did not require believers to participate in the ritual life of Judaism or physically identify themselves with the Jews through circumcision.

Despite the relaxation of ritual requirements, early Chris-

The Septuagint (abbreviated LXX) was translated between 250 and 150 B.C. by Jewish scholars in Alexandria, Egypt, a leading intellectual center of the day. It was used initially for study and evangelism by Jews whose primary language was Greek. After it was adopted by Christians as their Scripture, it was largely abandoned by the Jewish community.

tianity continued to be influenced significantly by its Jewish origin. This is clearly seen in the importance of the Hebrew Scriptures (the Old Testament) in the life of the Church. It took a long period of time (about 350 years after the birth of the Church) for the diverse collection of writings that we call the New Testament to be standardized and universally accepted. During this time, the Old Testament recounted the history of God's relationship with humankind and prophesied concerning the coming of Jesus the Messiah. In its Greek translation, called the Septuagint, early Christians could demonstrate to people throughout the Roman Empire that Christianity was no new teaching, but the culmination of God's ancient promises. Christianity was not a mere "sect of the Jews," but the very fulfillment of God's covenant with Abraham, Isaac, and Jacob.

The view that Christianity was the New Covenant of the God of Israel did not go unchallenged. Marcion, a second-century businessman in the Church of Rome, attempted to sever Christianity completely from Judaism. For Marcion, only Paul and Luke had correctly understood Jesus' teachings, and even a portion of *their* writings had been corrupted by Jewish ideas. Marcion rejected the entire Hebrew Scriptures. He also claimed that the Yahweh of the Old Testament—a God that commanded animal sacrifices and even the slaughter of children, albeit of the enemy—was an evil, lesser spiritual being and not the absolute God of love revealed in Jesus. Marcion's teaching gained many adherents and appealed to those Christians in the Roman Empire who were not comfortable with a close connection with the frequently despised Jewish minority.

The Fathers of the Church were quick to defend the apostles' use of the Old Testament and their identification of Yahweh with God as revealed in Jesus Christ.[1] Following the example of the writings of the apostles, they responded to Marcion's criticism of the Old Testament with two interpretive techniques that had enormous influence in the history of Christian thought. First, writers prioritized certain Old Testament texts, emphasizing prophecies about Christ and demoting ceremonial instructions to historical significance only. Second, they interpreted hard-to-understand and technical passages allegorically. The descriptions of the wilderness Tabernacle, priestly garments, and events in the history of the Israelites prefigured the ministry of Christ and the Church. Later biblical interpreters such as Origen and Gregory of Nyssa would find

---

[1]As a result of the controversy with Marcion, the first known list of authoritative Christian writings, the so-called Muratorian Canon, was written. The Muratorian list includes most of our New Testament, although it demonstrates that the authority of certain books (for example, Hebrews, 1 and 2 Peter, 3 John) was still in question, probably because they either were short or had not been circulated among the majority of the churches yet.

"types" or "figures" of the New Covenant in nearly every verse of the Old Testament. Using these two interpretive strategies they preserved essential continuities both between the Old and New Testaments and between Judaism and Christianity. Following a middle position, the Apostles and Fathers understood Christianity to be both separate from and yet the fulfillment of Judaism.

Despite important connections, by the end of the second Jewish rebellion (known as the Bar Kochba Revolt, A.D. 132–135) Christianity had become thoroughly distinct from Judaism. This was the case in the minds of not only Christians and Jews, but also the Roman imperial government. Within one hundred years of the birth of the Church, Christianity had become a Gentile religion. This shift is dramatically illustrated by the fact that all of the New Testament writers (except one) are Jewish, and all of the post-New Testament authors of Christian literature are Gentile.[2] Before about A.D. 150 Christian writers frequently debated against Jews and energetically distinguished their teachings and worship from Judaism. After this time the Fathers of the Church turned their attention to questions of the relationship of Christianity to the Greco-Roman culture that surrounded them.

The Apologists and the Relationship Between Christianity and Culture

The response of the Early Church to the Greco-Roman culture was much more ambiguous. Celsus, a late second-century critic of Christianity, claimed that Christians seduced only the unlearned "women, children, and slaves." However, the personal and moral fulfillment of the faith increasingly attracted a significant number of educated and learned adherents. They recognized the truth and beauty of the gospel but were aware that pagan culture had produced works that also contained (at least) some truth and some beauty. Even today there is considerable debate about the proper attitude of Christians toward non-Christian art and learning. The Early Church helped to shape the Christian worldview in this area by establishing the boundaries within which the issue has been discussed throughout Church history.

Justin Martyr (died ca. 165) best reflects one end of the spectrum of Christian responses. Even after his conversion Justin continued to wear the traditional garb of a Greco-Roman philosopher. He also found much value in pagan philosophy, especially in Socrates and Plato. Not only did he use their concepts as a bridge to understanding for his educated Roman audience, Justin also claimed that the Greek thinkers had un-

---

[2]There are one or two possible exceptions. See Jaroslav Pelikan, *The Christian Traditions, vol. 1, The Emergence of the Catholic Tradition* (Chicago: University of Chicago Press, 1971).

derstood, albeit only partially, the real truth of God. He viewed classical learning as a kind of preparation for the gospel. Justin therefore sifted through ancient culture, appropriating those concepts that he considered compatible with Christianity and using them in his learned defenses. Following in this path, the Alexandrian scholars Clement and Origen, as well as many others, greatly aided the spread of the gospel by translating Christian concepts into terms understandable to the Roman world. Their work also gained intellectual respectability for the faith. On the negative side, in the translation process Christian thinking was influenced and shaped by Greco-Roman thought. At worst, some Christian teachers came to express worldviews more in common with earlier Greek philosophers (like Plato) than with the teachings of Jesus.

The Syrian theologian Tatian (died ca. 180) represents another possible response to non-Christian culture. Despite being a student of Justin Martyr, Tatian later completely rejected non-Christian culture. Tatian denied the possibility of anyone outside of the faith discovering any independent truth or possessing any independent good. Tatian claimed that anything valuable that Socrates might have said was borrowed (or stolen) from Moses and the prophets. Those Christian thinkers who followed Tatian's strategy were more easily able to retain aspects of the Jewish heritage in Christianity and to avoid the sometimes damaging contentions that arose through speculative theology. However, they paid dearly for their cultural purity and isolation with a tendency to lapse into elitism, severe legalism, and a marginalization that ended their contribution to later Christian thought.[3]

Justin Martyr

A professional teacher thoroughly acquainted with Platonism and Stoicism, Justin Martyr (c.100–c.165) became a Christian as a result of encountering an old man while walking on a Samarian beach. Although Justin never became a church official, he wrote and debated extensively in the service of the gospel. The work he did in Ephesus and Rome, which led to his martyrdom, established him as the most important defender, or apologist, of Christianity in the second century. Important writings: *Dialogue with Trypho*, *First Apology* (dedicated to the Roman Emperor Antoninus Pius).

[3]It should be noted that the Christian community Tatian was a member of, the Encratites, made celibacy, and perhaps even vegetarianism, a requirement for all true believers.

Most of the Church Fathers fall somewhere between these two positions. As represented by their allegorization of the Exodus account, the Early Church "spoiled the Egyptians of their treasures" and used pagan learning to construct their Christian intellectual Tabernacle. At times this appreciation for Greco-Roman culture produced uneasy consciences. For example, Jerome, the translator of the most influential Latin version of the Bible (known as the Vulgate), once dreamed that God reprimanded him for being "more a Ciceronian [a famous Roman orator] than a Christian." Yet, when the North African theologian Tertullian asked, "What has Athens to do with Jerusalem?" like many others he did so with a methodology and in a style that betrayed just how influential Athens had become.

Councils and Creeds: The Christian View of God

At the very center of the Christian worldview is a unique conception of God as one (monotheism), yet in three persons: Father, Son and Holy Spirit. In this significant area the Early Church used every tool at its disposal (including Greek philosophy) to expound upon biblical concepts and to articulate authoritative statements concerning the nature of God and of Christ. The two most important statements, the Nicene Creed (325) and the Chalcedonian Creed (451), remain the basis for orthodox Christianity worldwide, even to the present.

When Constantine the Great finally brought the entire Roman Empire under his control, to his dismay he discovered that the Christian Church he supported was deeply divided by controversy: An Alexandrian churchman, Arius (died A.D. 336), was teaching that Jesus was God's first and best creation, but not coequal and coeternal with the Father. Because of its skillful use of some scriptural passages, the Arian position became popular. Its rationality was appealing and it removed the philosophic difficulties of the Trinity. To many, however, the Arian position was a deviation from the teachings of the Apostles and a denigration of Christ.[4] The conflict between the two parties was frequently heated and sometimes even violent. In 325 Emperor Constantine summoned all the Church leaders (bishops) throughout the Roman Empire to gather at Nicea in Asia Minor (modern Turkey) in order to settle the dispute and restore unity to the Church. This First Ecumenical (i.e., universal) Council of the Church rejected the Arian position and affirmed the mystery of the three-in-one. They declared that the Son is of the same essence (Gk., *homoousia*) as the Father, equal in His divinity, coeternal, begotten, not made, but at the same time a distinct person within the Godhead.

---

[4]See Kerry D. McRoberts, "The Holy Trinity," in *Systematic Theology*, rev. ed., ed. Stanley M. Horton (Springfield, Mo.: Logion Press, 1995), 162–168.

"We believe . . . in one Lord Jesus Christ, the only begotten Son of God, Begotten of the Father before all ages, Light of Light, true God of true God, begotten not made, of one substance with the Father."

—*Nicene Creed*

Although the issue remained very much in doubt over the next sixty years, the Nicene position eventually triumphed, thanks largely to the tireless battling of leaders like Athanasius of Alexandria (ca. 295–373). Since then the doctrine of the Trinity, Christianity's unique understanding of God, has been the central standard by which orthodoxy has been measured.

About one hundred years later, competing understandings of the relation of humanity and divinity in Christ caused another significant conflict. On one side stood a group largely from Egypt that tended to overemphasize the divinity of Christ. For these *monophysites* (Gk., "one nature"), Jesus' human qualities were relatively unimportant. Monophysites claimed that the humanity of Christ was swallowed in His divinity like a drop of water in a flask of wine.

Directly opposed to this were the followers of Nestorius (died ca. 451), a bishop of Constantinople. Nestorian teaching radically separated the two natures of Christ. Rather than seeing a union of natures (the traditional analogy was "like water and wine"), *Nestorians* saw the incarnation as a "conjunction" of divine and human persons. Therefore, characteristics of Christ's divinity could not necessarily be ascribed to the human Jesus. Mary could be described as the "Mother of Jesus," but not the "Mother of God" (*theotokos*).[5] Rather than the relation between the human and divine in Christ being like water and wine, Nestorians argued that it was more like water and oil.

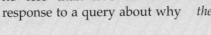

Athanasius of Alexandria

Athanasius of Alexandria (c.295–373), called the "Black Dwarf" by acquaintances due to his short stature and skin color, was one of the most important bishops and theologians in the Early Church. Most of his 45-year career as the bishop of Alexandria was devoted to the battle against Arianism. He was frequently in mortal danger and was exiled no less than five times. In response to a query about why he did not just give up because the whole world seemed against him, he is reputed to have responded, "Then it shall be Athanasius against the world!" He was convinced that Jesus Christ had to be *completely* God in order to achieve humankind's *complete* redemption. He was also influential in the popularization of monasticism in the East and West through his support of St. Anthony the hermit. Important Writings: *On the Incarnation of the Word, Life of Anthony*.

---

[5]Note that those who first called Mary "Mother of God" were saying something about Jesus rather than about Mary: Jesus is God, is divine.

The 4th Ecumenical Council at Chalcedon (451) rejected both of these extreme positions. The Creed of Chalcedon strongly affirms that Christ is both fully God and fully human (leaving as a mystery how this is possible). According to Chalcedon, Christ shares the same nature as God in all respects and shares the same nature as humankind in all respects except for sin.

Although these two controversies might seem to twentieth century Christians as nothing more than insignificant theological word-games, they certainly were not insignificant to Early Christians. Rather, these views were hammered out on the anvil of serious, passionate, intellectual discussion. Thanks to their intellectual labor and personal sacrifices, the unique Christian understanding of God had been preserved. Since the Early Church period, these guidelines have determined when one has gone beyond the boundaries of orthodox Christianity.

Saint Augustine and the Fall of Rome

The new power of the Church after Constantine was not without cost or danger. The Emperor's religion became popular. Unlike the earlier days of the Church, the "narrow gate" (Matt. 7:13) grew wide and many rushed in, some for questionable reasons. Large basilicas were constructed for formal, elaborate worship services. Congregations increasingly became more observers than participants, and a very distinct line was drawn between clergy and laity. Church leaders were often selected on the basis of political clout and economic status rather than on ministerial ability.

Perhaps the greatest danger lay in the assumed coextensiveness of Christianity and Roman power. The government of the Church nearly paralleled that of the State. Roman Emperors gave the chief ecclesiastical officials in each town, the bishops, considerable civic responsibilities. They often served as local judges and as representatives of Imperial power. In return, the State helped to enforce correct doctrine and provided financial support. Since everyone assumed that Rome was *Roma aeterna* (eternal Rome), they perceived this close connection to be a strength, not a weakness.

In A.D. 410 the Roman world was stunned to hear that the Visigoths, Germanic tribes from the north, had captured and pillaged the Eternal City. Rather than an isolated incident, for the next two hundred years various Germanic peoples overran Western Europe and Western North Africa. The Eastern part of the Empire was preserved (Greece, Asia Minor, Egypt, Syria-Palestine), but Imperial power collapsed in the West. The glorious civilization of Rome was destroyed and the lights of learning and culture began to be extinguished all over Western Europe.

Some blamed Rome's adoption of Christianity for its fall. Christians themselves were confused about the relation of the Church to government. In response to the crisis of Rome's

Jesus Christ is both "truly God and truly man . . . acknowledged in two natures without confusion, without change, without division, without separation."
—*Chalcedonian Creed*

decline, the greatest Christian teacher since Paul turned his attention to the subject. In his book *The City of God*, North African church father Augustine (354–430) differentiated between the human government and society (City of Man) and the invisible Church of all true believers (the City of God). The City of Man was God's temporal and temporary tool and could assume many forms throughout time. The City of God was invincible and would continue to triumph and accomplish God's will. In essence, men and nations would rise and fall, but God's kingdom would conquer all.

Augustine's teaching helped give the Church courage in a difficult time of transition. It has been a source of strength for many believers when faced with the collapse of a "Christian" government. The important concept that Christianity could continue despite the collapse of any particular societal or governmental form was one of the last contributions of the Early Church to the Christian worldview.

The Medieval Church

Overview

The designation Middle Ages was first used around A.D. 1500 as a derogatory name for a thousand year period of "ignorance and superstition" between the "golden age" of classical culture

Saint Augustine of Hippo

After a number of years seeking spiritual fulfillment and control over his sinful nature, Saint Augustine of Hippo (354–430) experienced a powerful conversion to Christianity in 387. His conversion prompted him to leave a prestigious position as a teacher of rhetoric in the important Italian city of Milan and return to his native North Africa. Although he desired a quiet life of prayer and study, he was soon ordained bishop of the city of Hippo (in modern Tunisia). From his desk and pulpit in Hippo, Augustine turned his well-trained mind and skillful pen to the critical issues of the day. Augustine's theological contributions are extensive and he is widely regarded as the most important individual in church history after the Apostolic period. He wrote numerous books, treatises, commentaries, and sermons but is perhaps best known for his moving spiritual autobiography, *Confessions*, which established the autobiographical genre and has been a source of inspiration to believers for centuries. Augustine's role as a transitional figure between the Roman and Medieval periods is highlighted by the fact that he died in 430 as the Germanic Vandal tribe was conquering the city of Hippo. Important Writings: *Confessions*, *City of God*.

and its "rebirth" (Renaissance). (The adjective "medieval," a name for the same era, first appeared in the early 1800s.) We now know that the Medieval Period was not necessarily the Dark Ages, but instead made many essential contributions to Western Civilization.

The period of the Medieval Church is divided into three sub-periods (see illustration 3). The Early Medieval period (500–1100) winessed the gradual development of the Germanic chiefdoms into kingdoms. The most important of these, the Frankish kingdom of Charlemagne, prompted a brief flourishing of culture and learning, known as the Carolingian Renaissance.

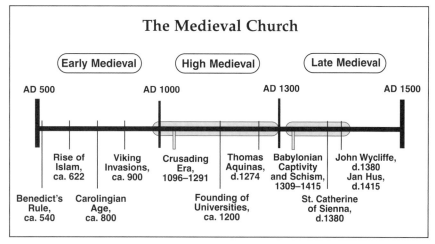

Illustration 3

In the Early Medieval period the authority of the Roman Church and its bishop (the Pope) over all West European churches was established (at least in theory). The number of monasteries increased rapidly, and they became the spiritual and educational centers for Christianity.

After the reign of Charlemagne (ca. 771–814), Western Europe plunged into its darkest period. The descendants of Charlemagne were not only unable to maintain his realm, but were hard pressed by attacks on three sides. A nomadic people from the steppes of central Asia, the Magyars, swept into Eastern and Central Europe. Striking out from the Arabian peninsula, Islamic warriors conquered the Roman East (Syria, Palestine, and Egypt), North Africa, and Spain (ca. 630–730). Muslim sailors made continual raids on Italy and the southern coast of France. Except for the Greek Peninsula and Asia Minor, the Mediterranean Sea became dominated by the Muslims. The most fearsome attacks came from the Northmen (Vikings). Descending from Scandinavia in their longboats, the Vikings were able to penetrate deep upriver. They looted and plundered villages, destroyed monasteries, and scattered the inhabitants before them. To the lonely monk sitting in his cell in the latter 800s and 900s, it looked as if the world was coming to an end. Marginal comments on manuscripts contained grave predictions concerning the turn of the millennium.

Climatic changes, population growth, and the redevelopment of trade allowed the High Middle Ages (1100–1300) to be a time of renewed vigor in the West. Christianity went on the offensive against Islam and attempted to regain lands lost to the initial Muslim conquest. These Crusades (primarily 1096–1291) encouraged the development of trade and commerce, which in turn stimulated the growth of towns and cities. Skilled artisans built magnificent castles and cathedrals. The first universities were founded. Members of new monastic orders, the Dominicans and Franciscans, wrote impressive theological and philosophical works.

The Late Middle Ages (1300–1500) is a complex, transitional time in Western history. Church government grew increasingly greedy and corrupt. Internal divisions and schisms nearly destroyed the institution of the papacy. In just three years (1346–1349), the Black Death (bubonic plague) killed nearly one-third of all Europeans. Wars ravaged the countryside and city. Yet, starting first in Italy around A.D. 1300, a Renaissance (rebirth) of classical learning and literature began to spread northward. In addition, calls from within the Church for reform gained strength and urgency. In the midst of the decay of the medieval way of life, a significant new culture was being born.

SHAPING A CHRISTIAN WORLDVIEW

To the modern person the Medieval Period is even more foreign than the world of classical Greece and Rome. The Middle Ages was more rural than urban, more communal than individual. As a whole it seems more superstitious than rational. Still, the Medieval Church made many significant contributions to the shaping of a Christian worldview. Among the most important of these are (1) monasticism and its view of Christian life and work, (2) the marriage of faith and reason by Scholasticism, and (3) the search for a direct encounter with the Living God through Christian Mysticism.

Saint Benedict of Nursia

Inspired by the examples of Eastern solitary monks, St. Benedict of Nursia (ca. 480–ca. 547) began a life of monasticism as a young man. Within a short time Benedict's reputation for sanctity grew and many other young men gathered around him for instruction. After some hesitation, Benedict formed his monks into a community south of Rome at Monte Cassino. For his community Benedict put together a *regula*, or rule, which was a guide or constitution for the community. *The Rule of St. Benedict* was to become one of the most influential documents of the Medieval period and became the model for monastic life.

Monasticism

Perhaps the single most important aspect of Christianity in the medieval West was monasticism. The forms of monasticism varied widely: Some monastics were contemplative, some were primarily active, some were solitary, some lived in communities. All monastics shared the defining characteristic of a rigorous separation from the world in order to live a life of devotion to God. Separation from the world required asceticism (denial of oneself), including (at a minimum) lifelong celibacy and the abandonment of private property. Often monastics underwent severe hardships to discipline their bodies and minds. To live a life totally separated to God was considered the highest form of the *imitatio Christi* (the imitation of Christ).

Although in the East monasticism had many adherents even under the Roman Empire, monasticism in Western Europe did not begin to flourish until the collapse of Roman power. Benedict of Nursia (died ca. 547) was instrumental in shaping and popularizing monastic life, especially through the example of his community and its *Rule*.

Benedict's *Rule* was similar to many monastic rules, both East and West. However, it did possess two unique characteristics that greatly impacted the development of Christianity in the West and Western civilization. First, especially in comparison with Eastern rules, the tone of St. Benedict's *Rule* is strikingly moderate. Unlike some of the bizarre and outrageous deprivations that occurred in the Syrian and Egyptian deserts, moderate community life became the norm in Western Europe. Monks were given enough to eat, adequate clothing, and moderate discipline. The elderly and infirm were treated with special gentleness. This moderate tone helped account for both the enormous growth of monasticism in Western Europe and for the long-term stability of the institution.

More important was Benedict's exceptional wisdom in making labor an essential part of the monastic devotion to God. The Benedictine slogan *ora et labora* ("pray and work") accurately summarizes the daily life of the monastic. For the monk, work became a type of prayer. One expressed devotion to God by every action of the consecrated life. The mundane became sacred. In itself this would have been a significant contribution to Christian thought. But Benedictine monasticism almost single-handedly rescued Western culture and learning when it advocated *intellectual labor* as a kind of work particularly suitable to the glorification of God.

With the collapse of the Roman city, scattered monasteries in the rural areas became the primary centers of learning. The Germanic kings relied on the monasteries to teach Latin reading and writing skills that were necessary for the maintenance of

"Idleness is the enemy of the soul. Therefore at fixed times, the brothers should be busy with manual work; and at other times in holy reading. . . . We intend to found a school to train men in the service of the Lord, but where we shall not make the rules too strict and heavy. . . . If we seem to be severe, do not get frightened and run away. The entrance to the path of salvation must be narrow, but as you progress along the life of the Faith, the heart expands and speeds with love's sweetness along the pathway of God's commandments."

—*The Rule of St. Benedict*[6]

---

[6]Adapted from Henry Bettenson, ed., *Documents of the Christian Church,* 2d ed. (London: Oxford University Press, 1963), 161–79.

government. Most importantly, the early medieval monasteries preserved the written records of culture: books and manuscripts. Particularly important in this development was a brief flowering of culture centered on the court of the greatest monarch of the early Middle Ages, the Frankish Emperor Charlemagne.

Through annual military campaigns, Charlemagne extended the domain of the Franks on all sides. He subdued most of France, Western Germany, and portions of northern Italy and Spain. One of Charlemagne's most significant accomplishments was to closely link his dynasty with the Roman Church. The Christmas coronation in A.D. 800 of Charlemagne as Holy Roman Emperor by Pope Leo III symbolizes this union. To better control his realm, Charlemagne supported monasteries as centers of learning and education. He used bishops as advisors and representatives of imperial power and coerced pagans in the newly conquered territories to convert to Christianity.

> "We owe a great deal of our knowledge about the ancient world to the painstaking labor of Medieval monks."

Of the many reforms that resulted from this union of forces, the one that had the greatest effect was a simple reform of handwriting. Because vellum (writing parchment prepared from animal skin, e.g., calf, goat) disintegrated over time, manuscripts had to be recopied to preserve their content. Since the handwritten page was the only means for preserving the written word, unreadable handwriting meant significant increases in the number of textual errors and even the complete loss of knowledge. Unfortunately, the general decline of learning after the fall of Roman power and the isolation of the monasteries caused a degeneration of handwriting. Under the threat of severe punishment for sloppiness or deviation, as a result of Charlemagne's reforms monks throughout Western Europe were taught how to write good, readable Latin. The number of manuscripts copied also increased significantly. The long-term effects are impressive: Of the oldest manuscripts of the ancient texts that are now extant, including biblical manuscripts, the majority of these are from the period of the Carolingian Renaissance. We owe a great deal of our knowledge about the ancient world to the painstaking labor of these monks.

Scholasticism and the Revival of Learning

The year 1000 came and went, and the few dire predictions concerning the end of the world did not come to pass.[7] Western Europe seemed to turn a corner. Culture and trade revived. Political power stabilized. Especially in Italy, cities began to

---

[7]Stanley M. Horton, *Our Destiny: Biblical Teachings on the Last Things* (Springfield, Mo.: Logion Press, 1996), 136–37.

grow again. Scholarship thrived in the High Middle Ages, stimulated by the rediscovery of classical Greek writings that were unknown to the West but had been preserved by the Muslims. This flourishing of learning, in combination with the needs of growing royal bureaucracies, produced the Western university. In the thirteenth century major universities were founded in Paris (France), Bologna (Italy), and Oxford and Cambridge (England).

In response to the new learning and the needs of urban life, a different kind of monasticism emerged. Monastic orders founded by St. Francis and St. Dominic (the Franciscans and Dominicans) did not seek refuge in rural areas but lived in and ministered to the urban population. Because they had no land on which to grow their food, these monks and nuns became known as *mendicants*, or begging monastics.

From the beginning, mendicants were intimately connected with the medieval universities. A wealth of learning, especially in theology and philosophy, began to pour forth from Dominicans

Saint Thomas Aquinas

Although he was known as the "dumb ox" by his fellow Dominicans because of his large physical size and slow seriousness, St. Thomas Aquinas (1225–1274) was one of the most powerful thinkers in church history. During his tenure as a teacher of theology in Paris and Rome, Thomas worked to reconcile faith (traditional Christian doctrine) and reason (including the newly discovered philosophical writings of Aristotle). According to Thomas, humankind's ability to reason was the "image of God" in which humankind was created (Gen. 1:26). His strong reliance upon human reason was based on his belief that the Fall corrupted only humankind's will and not its reasoning powers. Despite his philosophical focus, Thomas recognized the importance of Christian experience and of the Bible. Thomas

taught that reason can demonstrate the existence of God and the immortality of the human soul, but it cannot establish essential doctrines such as the deity of Christ. Although it can never contradict reason, faith in God's revelation is necessary for salvation and doctrine. *Thomism*, the theological system based on the writings of Thomas, was used extensively in the Roman Catholic response to the Protestant Reformation and has remained highly influential through the twentieth century. Many of Thomas's arguments, especially his "Five Ways" (proofs for the existence of God), have been used by both Catholic and Protestant defenders of the faith. Important Writings: *Summa theologiae, Summa contra gentiles*.

and Franciscans in the new academic centers. As a reference to the rigorous application of reason to theology, their methodology is called *scholasticism*. (See the sidebar on Scholasticism in ch. 4, p. 153). Many of these thinkers (for example, St. Anselm, Abelard, Peter Lombard) made significant contributions to the history of Christian theology. The individual who best represents the summit of Christian learning in the High Middle Ages, however, is St. Thomas Aquinas (1225–1274).

Starting from biblical data and the evidences of reason, Thomas constructed an edifice of Christian thought that in its realm rivaled the great medieval cathedrals. According to Thomas, some aspects of the faith might be beyond reason (that is, *nonrational*). However, because God is a God of reason and has built rationality into the universe, no part of orthodox Christian teaching can contradict reason (that is, be *irrational*). Using the rediscovered logical and analytical structure of Aristotle, Thomas attempted to provide a comprehensive, encyclopedic view of the world and knowledge from a Christian perspective. Politics, ethics, art, science, all had a place in Thomas's house of learning. Some later Christian leaders criticized scholasticism for exaggerating the ability of the human mind, not leaving enough room for mystery, and often spinning off into intricate debates about matters of little importance. Yet, the union of Christianity and Reason in scholasticism remains a significant accomplishment. Thomas's *Summa Theologica* continues to provide the foundation for much Roman Catholic belief and provides an essential foundation for modern Christian apologetics (the defense of the faith) by both Protestants and Catholics.

Christian Mysticism

The power of the Papacy and the institutional church also reached its summit in the thirteenth century. From his office in Rome, Pope Innocent III dictated policy to kings throughout Europe and demanded greater conformity among common believers. However, this drive for power left the Church without adequate political allies and vulnerable to greed and corruption. Weaknesses were particularly evident when a series of calamities in the fourteenth century deeply divided medieval Christendom.

Under pressure from King Philip the Fair of France, Pope Clement V left Rome and took up residence near the French border at Avignon. Although the Avignon papacy (1309–1377) developed into a highly organized and efficient bureaucracy, to many contemporaries it seemed that the spiritual head of Christendom had lost his independence. An attempt to end this "Babylonian Captivity of the Church" created multiple, competing popes instead. This competition resulted in a split in the church known as the Great Papal Schism (1378–1417).

A *Christian mystic* seeks a direct, unmediated experience or encounter with God. As opposed to Eastern mysticism, Christian mysticism upholds the ultimate transcendence of God. For example, when Christian mystics speak of an awareness of "oneness with God" or "possession by God," they are not meaning an absorption that destroys the self or the distinction between human beings and God. Various forms of Christian mysticism have been present throughout church history.

In the confusion of this period, some Christians turned inward. These *mystics* helped shape the Christian worldview by encouraging the direct experience of a loving yet almighty God. For them the worship of God and the life of the believer transcended human institutions and actions. If God was allowed to purge one's sin, this made possible His illuminating the heart and providing a means, if only for an instant, of gaining a sense of union with Him. The writings of the mystics, often filled with lover-beloved metaphors, are some of the most beautiful in all of Christian literature.[8]

For many women especially, mysticism provided an opportunity for religious leadership and activity that had been blocked by the male-dominated institutional church. For example, St. Catherine of Sienna (ca. 1347–1380), one of the most profound and influential mystics, gained an international reputation for her sanctity, wisdom, and intimacy with God. Speaking on the basis of her charismatic authority, St. Catherine was instrumental in ending the "Babylonian Captivity" and returning the papacy to Rome.

Saint Catherine of Sienna

St. Catherine of Sienna (ca. 1347–1380) demonstrated strong spiritual sensitivity beginning in her early childhood in Florence (Italy). After a series of visions, at age 15 Catherine vowed to remain a virgin and withdrew to a life of prayer and contemplation in association with an order of Dominican lay sisters. She continued to have mystical experiences throughout her life. Her mystical teaching emphasized the redeeming blood of Christ and union with God through suffering by identification with Christ on the cross. Her unusual combination of contemplation and activity led to a mystical rapture that inspired her confident and aggressive action on behalf of the Church. Catherine spent most of her career fighting ecclesiastical abuses by teaching, preaching, and instruction. Although nearly illiterate, Catherine dictated hundreds of instructional letters, many prayers, and an important work on mystical experience. Her direct rebuke of Pope Gregory XI in Avignon helped build momentum for the return of the papacy to Rome. She died as a result of her labors in attempting to end the papal schism. Catherine was declared patron saint of Italy in 1939. Important Writing: *The Book of Divine Providence.*

---

[8]For example, the popular devotional author Richard J. Foster has been significantly influenced by Christian mystics. See Richard J. Foster, *Celebration of Discipline: The Path to Spiritual Growth.* rev. and expanded ed. (San Francisco: HarperCollins, 1988).

As the year 1500 approached, it became increasingly clear to many that mystic experience alone could not solve the serious problems within the Church. Despite the healing of the Great Papal Schism and the end of the "Babylonian Captivity," ministerial responsibilities were not being fulfilled. Immorality among the clergy was frequent. Often simply for financial gain, church officials encouraged common people to believe that relics (preserved portions of saints' bodies or possessions) could work miracles. A moral and governmental reform "in head and in members," that is, both in the hierarchy and in the life of the parish, was needed.

A few voices went further and demanded changes in doctrine. Early Reformers, including John Wycliffe (d. 1384) and Jan Hus (d. 1415), advocated new understandings of the sacrament of the Lord's Supper. Most importantly, they demanded that the Scriptures be available in the vernacular (the language of the people) and not only in Latin (the language of the elite). Although their activities were limited in number and geographical extent (England and Bohemia respectively), the reforms of Wycliffe and Hus were a sign of things to come.

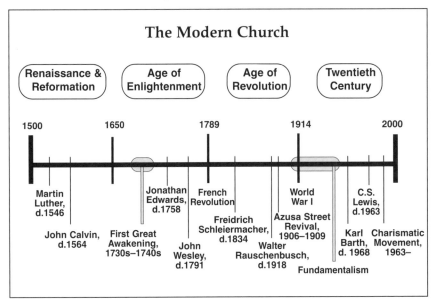

Illustration 4

The Modern Church

OVERVIEW

Rapid change and increasing complexity have characterized history over the last 500 years. The Renaissance spirit of individualism combined with the scientific advances of the Enlightenment produced a series of technological innovations that have revolutionized human life. Rather than solving the problems of the world, however, modern technology has created new challenges. In particular, the crises of the twentieth century have demanded a critical reevaluation of the future course of civilization. Western culture faces some difficult questions at the turn of the second millennium.

Historians divide the Modern Period into four subperiods

(see illustration 4). In the Early Modern Period (ca. 1500–1650), also known as the Renaissance and Reformation, a gradual transition from Medieval to Modern took place. European sailors like Columbus explored the world. The astronomical discoveries of Galileo Galilei and Johannes Kepler began the Scientific Revolution. The proliferation of the moveable-type printing press revolutionized mass communication. Beginning in 1517, long-standing demands for reform within the Church erupted into outright schism. Led by Martin Luther and others, Protestantism was established as a separate branch of Christianity independent of Roman Catholic control. By 1650, after a long military and political struggle, Protestantism was established in Northern Europe and North America.

During the Age of Reason (1650–1789), discoveries about the natural world encouraged the view that progress through science and technology was inevitable. Enlightenment leaders believed human reason could push back the veil of ignorance and superstition and reveal a beautifully ordered universe. The arts also reflected this new worldview by emphasizing structure, order, and symmetry. In politics, the founding of the United States seemed to demonstrate that rational human beings could work together to build a just and fair society. The worldview of *modernism*, based on the principles of individualism, human reason, and progress through science and technology, came to dominate Western civilization.

The Age of Revolution (1789–1914) witnessed a number of political and cultural changes. Beginning with the French Revolution (1789), common citizens used both politics and violence to destroy ancient aristocratic privileges. Led by the example of the United States, democracy gradually triumphed in Western Europe. In culture, Romanticism rebelled against the "dry" rationalism of the Enlightenment. Artists, musicians, and writers glorified the *Sturm und Drang* (storm and stress) of nature and human emotion. The Romantic spirit also impacted theology. Classic Protestant liberalism with its emphasis on the subjective, immanent elements of religion came to dominate the mainstream churches and seminaries.

In addition to political changes, a series of technological advances, collectively known as the Industrial Revolution, transformed Western society in the nineteenth century. New methods of energy conversion (specifically the steam engine) enabled large-scale manufacturing and transportation. Entire populations shifted as laborers migrated from rural to urban areas and across national boundaries. As a result of the new economic conditions, the middle-class began to grow. Extensive urbanization produced the consumer-oriented modern city. While technology and manufacturing brought a higher standard of living to many, to others the new economic conditions in the cities brought only crime, poverty, and depersonalization.

> *Modernism* is the worldview that has dominated Western thinking since the Enlightenment. The primary characteristics of modernism include (1) reliance on the power of human reason, (2) faith in progress and development, primarily through science and technology, and (3) belief in the absolute sovereignty of the individual.

Postmodernism is a worldview that increasingly has gained influence over *modernism* during the last century. Postmodernism continues to emphasize the absolute sovereignty of the individual, but is pessimistic concerning human progress and doubts the ability of human reason to produce objective truth. Where there is no objective truth, there are only (political) power relationships. Therefore, the intellectual debates of postmodernism have centered around issues concerning the control and interpretation of culture.

The technological advances that enabled rapid industrial development also gave the West (Western Europe and the Americas) a military advantage over the Middle and Far East for the first time. Both in search of raw materials and markets for their manufactured goods and feeling a duty to civilize non-European "savages," the Western powers extended control over much of the world through colonization or intimidation in the late 1800s. Christian missions closely followed the European colonial conquests, and sometimes even preceded them. From a global perspective the nineteenth century was the "Great Century" for Protestantism; Christian churches were established throughout the world. By 1914, the West was politically powerful, increasingly democratic, and economically prosperous. With technological advances in every field, it looked to many as though the promises of triumphant modernism, a just and rational society, were within reach of humankind.

The loss of a generation of young men in World War I (1914–1918) was the first major blow to modernist hopes. The Great Depression, the totalitarianism of Hitler and Stalin, World War II (1941–1945), and the Holocaust demonstrated that advances in science and technology did not automatically bring a better world. After the end of the Second World War the United States and parts of Western Europe enjoyed a time of unparalleled prosperity. By the mid-1970s, however, American economic prosperity and cultural stability had already begun to unravel. Despite the technological advances of the information and computer age, the world is still plagued by crime, poverty, oppressive governments, and environmental disasters.

In theoretical science as well as in culture, the modernist confidence in human reason and progress has melted into postmodern anxiety and confusion. Although *postmodernism* retains Western culture's elevation of the individual, it holds that truth is subjective, dependent on personal or cultural perspective, and is therefore completely relative.

The lack of objective truth leads to the lack of objective meaning. Postmoderns are subsequently left to find their own way in a world that is not necessarily going anywhere.

SHAPING A CHRISTIAN WORLDVIEW

The rapidly changing modern world has presented a number of significant challenges to the Church. Many more individuals and events have made important contributions to the shaping of a Christian worldview in the Modern Period than can be mentioned in a few pages. In addition, because of the direct nature of their influence, Protestant attempts to shape a Christian worldview will be emphasized. Among the most important of these are (1) the Reformation and the birth of Protestantism, (2) the Puritan synthesis, (3) the 19th Century Responses to Modernism, (4) the renewal of orthodox Christian thinking in the twentieth century, and (5) Pentecostal and Charismatic movements and the reality of supernatural Christianity.

The Reformation and the Birth of Protestantism

In 1517, a young monk and university professor in Wittenberg, Germany, became greatly distressed over outrageous claims made by a Dominican indulgence salesman, John Tetzel. Tetzel claimed that for their "good deeds" of contributing money to the Church (that is, purchasing indulgences), God would reward the givers by forgiving their sins. If needed, one could obtain forgiveness in advance of the intended sin or for an already deceased loved one (to speed them through purgatory). There was even a sliding scale depending on the severity of the sin and the ability to contribute.

Martin Luther (1483–1546) considered this to be no less than marketing the grace of God for a price. Luther's written response to the indulgence trade, the *95 Theses on the Efficacy of Indulgences*, helped to trigger a reform of doctrine throughout Europe. Within one generation, a majority of northern Europeans had radically separated from the Roman Church to form their own confessions and institutions. Much of modern Christianity is a direct result of this "protest" against the abuses of medieval Roman Catholicism.

Over the next few years after the *95 Theses*, Martin Luther gradually realized that he was advocating a complete change of authority for the Church. If the Pope and even Church councils (official gatherings of Church leaders) could err, as was the case concerning indulgences, how were believers to know what to do to please God? Luther's answer became the foundation for all subsequent Protestant thought. The final authority for the Christian life was Scripture alone (*sola scriptura*). Using the *sola scriptura* principle, Luther saw no basis for indulgences, purgatory, relics, pilgrimage. In short, the entire medieval Roman Catholic system of forgiveness and merit before God was built on a false foundation.

> **"The final authority for the Christian life was Scripture alone (*sola scriptura*)."**

Luther did find the complete forgiveness of God given freely, not on the basis of what an individual had done but based on faith alone (*sola fides*) in who Christ is. For an individual like Luther who had struggled intensely with his personal sense of guilt before God, this "Reformation discovery" was like the dawning of a new day. No longer was endless religious exercise necessary to earn the favor and forgiveness of God. This had already been given because of Christ's work on the cross. The believer could not contribute one thing to his or her eternal salvation except to humbly receive God's forgiveness in Christ by faith. For Luther, this gave the believer tremendous freedom to live a life of service to God motivated by love, and not by guilt or responsibility.

In one of the first successful uses of mass media, the newly developing printing industry took Luther's message and broadcast it throughout Europe. Many political and religious leaders joined his call for reform. In large portions of Northern Europe, much of the previous one thousand years of Christian practice and doctrine was swept away. Monasteries, in places containing a significant proportion of the population and possessing tremendous amounts of land and wealth, were closed. (Being a monastic earned no special favor with God and was seen as a kind of works-righteousness.) Clergymen also lost their special status as mediators of the grace of God. Ultimately, everyone was his or her own priest before God. The person at the plow received the same grace and pleased God just as much as the most dignified saint.

What then was the role of good works? Himself no stranger to sin, Luther knew that love of God alone would not sufficiently motivate most people to do what is right. Even after grace there was a need for the law, as long as people did not again drift back into believing that their good deeds saved them. The law was a

*M*artin *Luther*

Martin Luther (1483–1546), the father of Protestantism, is generally recognized as one of the most important individuals in Church history. He  was born in central Germany to well-to-do peasant parents, who intended that he study law. However, as a result of a vow made during a narrow escape from a lightning storm, at age 23 Luther joined an Augustinian monastery in nearby Erfurt (Germany). Luther excelled in monastic discipline and academic studies; at the same time, he experienced a sustained spiritual crisis because he felt that he could never satisfy God. Both as a recognition of Luther's abilities and as an attempt to meet his spiritual needs, in 1508 his monastic order transferred him to the new university at Wittenberg to continue his academic studies. Four years later he received the Doctor of Theology degree and was appointed to the chair of biblical studies. Over the next five years, largely through the preparation of lectures on Psalms, Romans, and Galatians, Luther came to understand that the righteousness of God was not something that one had to earn on the basis of his or her own merits, but was credited to the believer by faith through Christ's work on the cross. As Luther explored the consequences of this Reformation "cornerstone," monitoring the controversy over indulgences and engaging in the debates that followed (especially the Leipzig Disputation, 1519), he realized

guide to behavior and a restraint to sin. Reflected in human governments, laws preserved peace and order. The kingdom of heaven and the kingdoms of the earth, though separate, could and should coexist in harmony. Each believer possessed dual citizenship with responsibilities in each realm.

Of the many other important reformers who helped to shape the Christian worldview, John Calvin also deserves specific mention. Like Luther, Calvin held to justification by faith alone but centered this justification in the absolute sovereignty of God. Since God was in control of all things, the basis of salvation was in God's choices, not humankind's.[9] On this basis, to his great comfort, Calvin could now energetically and confidently pursue the crusade against sin and darkness without fear of the loss of grace due to failure. Calvin would allow no challenge to his authority and had no tolerance for open sin. Sin and false belief must be cut out of the Christian community like cancer from the body.

Luther had been suspicious of human reason and wary of the grand systems of Thomas Aquinas and the scholastics. John

---

[9]See Daniel B. Pecota, "The Saving Work of Christ," in *Systematic Theology*, ed. Stanley M. Horton, 356.

that much of medieval Roman Catholicism was based upon a works-righteousness that was contrary to biblical Christianity. Since the Pope and many Church authorities had supported these practices, Luther was obliged to argue that they could err and that Scripture alone must be the authority for faith and practice. Luther was declared a heretic by the Pope (1520) and an outlaw by the Holy Roman Emperor (1521), but received political support from German princes, which enabled him to reform many churches along biblical lines independent from Roman control. By Luther's death in 1546, territories from Switzerland to Scandinavia had followed Luther in his "protest" against the Roman Catholic Church. Not all "Protestants" agreed with Luther on all points, and the movement soon splintered into many factions. However, Martin Luther's importance as the originator and champion of the Reformation is undeniable. Luther's works include over fifty volumes of sermons, biblical commentaries, and theological writings. His most important written contribution, however, may be his translation of Scripture into German. Because it was the first translation into German, Luther's German Bible was a milestone in the history of biblical translation and was a significant influence on the development of the German language itself. Important writings: *Freedom of a Christian*, *Babylonian Captivity of the Church*, German translation of the Bible.

Calvin had a much greater confidence in the illumined Christian mind. The high moral tone and brilliant use of the mind made Geneva the education center of Protestantism. In the words of the Scottish reformer John Knox, Calvin's Geneva was "the best school of Christ since the Apostles." The sense of God's control over destiny gave those who studied in Geneva a great confidence in the correctness of their cause. This confidence enabled those who followed Calvin to have a profound impact on Western culture, not only in continental Europe but also to a great extent in Britain and America.

The Puritan Synthesis

During the Enlightenment of the 1600s and 1700s, advances in science and technology drove a wedge between faith and reason for many people. Enlightenment leaders such as Voltaire understood religion to be synonymous with superstition. Religion produced bondage; reason created freedom. Some of these Enlightenment thinkers, called *Deists*, retained Christian ethics but rejected any supernaturalism in religion. Although God was seen as a transcendent creator, His role was likened to

John Calvin

Many of Luther's ideas were taken up and developed by the greatest systematizer of the Reformation, John Calvin. Calvin (1509–1564), a Frenchman, had trained for a legal career but he was forced into exile because of his growing attraction to Reformation ideas. While traveling in exile he passed through Geneva, Switzerland, a town that had recently opted for Protestantism. Although he preferred the quiet life of a scholar, Calvin was persuaded to lead the Genevan reform. With a brilliant, piercing intellect, sharpened by legal training, Calvin made significant contributions to biblical studies, ministerial theory, and theology. *Institutes of the Christian Religion*, his magnum opus, remains one of the most important systematic theologies ever written. Calvin's Geneva became an important training center for Protestants, especially those fleeing persecution in France and England. Calvin's emphasis on the sovereignty of God encouraged his students to see themselves as specially chosen by God. This triumphant confidence enabled Calvin's style of reform to have a significant impact in Holland, Great Britain, and the New World. The denominations which are the successors to John Calvin today make up the single largest group of Protestants, and include Presbyterians, Dutch Reformed, and most Baptists. Important writings: Calvin's Biblical Commentaries and the *Institutes of the Christian Religion*.

that of a clock maker who constructed the intricate mechanism of the universe and stood aside from it. In the American version of deism, under the guise of "Providence," God also shaped the destinies of nations. However, the deists' God did not intervene in the lives of ordinary individuals nor did he reveal himself in an incarnate Son. Jesus was the greatest moral teacher and the Bible the best place for moral instruction, but Jesus was not divine and the Bible was merely the words of wise men.

In the midst of this difficult environment, one of the greatest contributions was made to the shaping of an orthodox Christian worldview. In the seventeenth century a group of English Protestants called *Puritans* settled the British colonies of New England. Dedicated to Reformation principles, they called for the purification of the Church of England from human invention (understood to be vestiges of Roman Catholicism) and the purification of themselves from sin. They placed a strong emphasis on the work of God in the community and in the lives of individuals. The Puritans emphasized a personal conversion and were immensely concerned about spiritual growth and development in the Christian life.

Jonathan Edwards

Jonathan Edwards (1703–1758) was a child prodigy, mastering Latin, Greek, and Hebrew and writing scientific and philosophical papers while just a teenager. After completing studies at Yale College, Edwards assumed the pastorate of the Congregational church at Northampton, Massachusetts, at age 24. It was from the pulpit at Northampton that Edwards supported and guided the American revival known as the Great Awakening. In addition to discharging pastoral responsibilities, Edwards was an indefatigable scholar, often working twelve- to fourteen-hour days in his study. He was also a man of deep religious experience, perhaps best illustrated by his emotional response to the Great Awakening, especially the revival preaching of George Whitefield. Although Jonathan Edwards is unfortunately best known for an atypical sermon, "Sinners in the Hands of an Angry God," his works on philosophy, psychology, and theology are among the most important in American church history. His support for scientific experimentation is tragically illustrated by his agreement to be injected with an early form of the smallpox vaccine. He died as a result, only three months after assuming the presidency of the College of New Jersey (Princeton). Important Writings: *A Faithful Narrative of the Surprising Works of God, A Treatise Concerning Religious Affections, Freedom of the Will.*

In addition to this moral and emotional focus, the Puritans also emphasized the importance of the intellect. They encouraged each other to love God with their hearts and also with their minds. They believed that education was the responsibility of the Christian community. People of faith should be taught to read so that they could read the Word of God for themselves. As leaders of the community, ministers needed both a personal experience of God and rigorous intellectual training. The fruit of this attempt to join "head and heart" as a Christian includes the founding of many important institutions of higher education.[10] Yet the impact of the Puritan synthesis goes far beyond higher education. To the extent that the United States of America has its roots in evangelical Christianity, it does so largely because of the contributions of the New England Puritans.

The summit of the Puritan attempt to shape a Christian worldview is represented by Jonathan Edwards (1703–1758), a Congregational pastor in Northampton, Massachusetts. From an early age he was interested in the exploration of the natural world and the development of the intellect. Edwards was convinced that if God was indeed creator of the natural universe and the giver of the intellect, then the rational exploration of the

---

[10]Beginning with Harvard (founded 1636) and including Yale (1701), Princeton (1746), Dartmouth (1769), and many others. See Mark Noll, *A History of Christianity in the United States and Canada* (Grand Rapids: Wm. B. Eerdmans Pub. Co., 1992), 97–105.

John Wesley

John Wesley (1703–1791) was the fifteenth child in a ministerial family of Epworth, England. John Wesley's father, Samuel Wesley, had been significantly influenced by English Puritanism and raised his children in strict discipline and Christian piety. While a student at Oxford University, John, his brother Charles, friend George Whitefield, and others began meeting for Bible study and mutual encouragement (1727). This "Holy Club," as they were called, later became the foundation from which the Methodist movement developed. Wesley's first independent experience as a parish minister ended in disaster; he was forced to leave his missionary position in the British colony of Georgia (1737). His unsuccessful venture, however, did result in an important contact with Anabaptist Moravians. The Moravians' assurance of salvation encouraged Wesley to seek a deeper experience of God. In 1738 Wesley received assurance of the forgiveness of his sins when his "heart was strangely warmed" while listening to a reading of Luther's preface to his commentary on Romans. This dramatic experience revolutionized Wesley's

world was an activity that in itself glorified God. He remained keenly interested in scientific discoveries and technological advances throughout his life.

Yet, Jonathan Edwards was not without a fervent personal faith. His support of the colonial revival known as the First Great Awakening (1730s–1740s) was essential for its success. His published defense of the emotional aspects of the revival, *A Treatise Concerning Religious Affections* (1746), remains an essential work for understanding the proper balance between emotion and reason in the Christian life.

Across the Atlantic in England, a contemporary of Jonathan Edwards was thinking along similar lines. John Wesley made significant contributions to the history of Christianity through his theological writings, use of outdoor preaching, and organizational genius. Although primarily known as the leader of a great English revival and the founder of Methodism, Wesley also was enthusiastic about science, technology, and the arts.

Nineteenth Century Responses to Modernism

In the years following the War for Independence (1775–1781) Christian activity in America was at a very low ebb. A series of revivals, known as the Second Great Awakening (ca. 1798–1820s), partially reversed this trend. However, the growing prestige of science and the difficulties of ministry on the frontier

life and ministry: The next year he began the scandalous practice of preaching outdoors to large crowds. The Methodist revival that followed impacted tens of thousands on both sides of the Atlantic. By the time of his death, Wesley had traveled over 250,000 miles, preached 42,000 sermons, and published over 200 books. The small Methodist societies that Wesley formed for the promotion of the Christian life have become today one of the largest denominations within Protestantism. John Wesley was the first significant churchman to adopt the theological position of the Dutch theologian Jacob Arminius (d.1609), which emphasizes humankind's responsibility in accepting Christ in salvation. (See Pecota, "The Saving Work of Christ," in *Systematic Theology*, ed. Horton, 368–72.) This, in combination with his doctrine of Christian Perfection (the cooperation of human will and the Holy Spirit leading to increasing sanctification and holiness) significantly laid the foundation for the Holiness and Pentecostal movements of the late nineteenth and early twentieth centuries. Important Writings: Wesley's Sermons and *Journal*, and *Notes on the New Testament*.

(early 1800s) and in urban centers (late 1800s) shifted America distinctly in the direction of secularism.

In Europe, the French Revolution and the various democratic and socialistic movements that followed it were even more devastating to Christianity. To make way for the autonomy of the common person, traditional structures of authority were swept away, in many cases including that of the Church.

In both Europe and America, new intellectual perspectives increased the drift toward secularism. Karl Marx (1818–1883) argued that religion was only a mask for power relationships between social classes. In *The Origin of Species* (1859), Charles Darwin (1809–1882) popularized an explanation for the order and structure of the biological world that did not require the activity of a divine architect. Together with the geological writings of Charles Lyell, Darwinism seemed to undermine the credibility of the scriptural account of creation.

There were two distinct responses within Christianity to these nineteenth century challenges. Partially under the influence of Romanticism, many Christians abandoned the intellectual defense of the faith and turned to its inner, subjective aspects. In *On Religion: Speeches to its Cultured Despisers* (1799) the German theologian Friedrich Schleiermacher (1768–1834) defined the essence of religion as a "feeling of dependence" on the "infinite." By appealing directly to human experience, Schleiermacher believed that he was preserving a role for religion in a world increasingly dependent on reason and science.

Religion certainly does involve emotions and personal experience. However, the theologians who followed Schleiermacher (generally known as "classical Protestant liberals") paid a very high price for their gains. The emphasis on religion as subjective experience blurred the distinctions between religions, made much of Christian doctrine irrelevant, and at times descended into outright pantheism, that is, seeing no distinction between God and the world. God was knowable as immanent, that is, active in the world, but not as transcendent, that is, above and separate from the world. For classical Protestant Liberalism, modern rationalism posed no threat. Christianity simply was not about the defense of particular doctrines, but about religious feeling and moral values.[11]

In the United States, churches were seriously divided in their response to modernism. Classical Protestant liberalism was attractive to many important church leaders and theologians who were seeking to accommodate Christianity to the modern world. Congregational minister Horace Bushnell (1802–1876) criticized revivalism and encouraged gradual Christian educa-

---

[11]In England a similar view of God compelled an influential group of clergymen under the leadership of John Henry Newman (1801–1890) to leave the Church of England for the more elaborate ritual of Roman Catholicism.

tion rather than dramatic conversion. In *Christian Nurture* (1847), Bushnell argued that humankind could overcome evil through Christian training, the moral influence of Christ, and the inner presence of the divine.

Similar ideas were developed by Walter Rauschenbusch (1861–1918). His experience as a pastor in New York City's notorious Hell's Kitchen left him with an acute understanding of the social aspects of sin. In *Christianity and the Social Crisis* (1907), Rauschenbusch popularized the understanding that the intent of Jesus' teachings was not the salvation of individuals, but the promotion of political and economic justice. For Rauschenbusch, true salvation meant social salvation, that is, the creation of a just social system. According to this social interpretation of the gospel, God and humankind working together would progressively destroy the tyranny of social evil. The Social Gospel was a bold effort to deal with the challenges of the industrial age and provided an important corrective to self-centeredness in the Church. However, like classic Protestant liberalism, it drifted from orthodox Christianity by neglecting doctrine, the authority of Scripture, and the supernatural.

More disturbing to many Christians was the damage done to biblical authority by higher criticism. Using the methodology of higher criticism, German scholars such as D. F. Strauss and F. C. Baur concluded that much of the New Testament was not an authentic product of the first century, but was an attempt by later Church leaders to mythologize their past. Belief in the verbal inspiration of the Bible and in the reality of biblical miracles was seen as an obstruction to genuine scholarship. Both in Europe and the United States many theologians embraced biblical higher criticism as the scholarly application of modern reason to Biblical studies.

In opposition to mainline liberalism with its acceptance of the new science and higher criticism, Christian Fundamentalism emerged in America in the late 1800s. The term *fundamentalism* is derived from a series of pamphlets called *The Fundamentals* (1909–1915), which were written to stake out common theological ground for all conservative Christians by providing an easily understood, brief guide to essential Christian doctrine. Those leaders that rallied to the cause of *The Fundamentals*, including the founder of Westminster Seminary, J. Gresham Machen, and former United States Presidential candidate William Jennings Bryan, invested much energy on the defense of traditional Christian tenets, especially the authority of Scripture, Christ's sacrificial atonement for sin, and the authenticity of biblical miracles.

While the fundamentalist defense of the necessity of doctrine and the authority of Scripture has been absolutely essential to the preservation of Christianity in the twentieth century, it too has not been without a price. Increasingly harsh rhetoric and at

Higher criticism starts from the assumption that the Bible can be analyzed like any other work of literature. In practice, biblical higher criticism has tended to question traditional views of authorship, dating, location, and historical context of specific books of the Bible.

Fundamentalism reacted against attacks on the Bible by defending the inspiration, infallibility, and authority of Scripture. Over the last several decades, however, the term *fundamentalism* has narrowed to mean an exclusive reliance on the literal interpretation of the Bible, or any dogmatic, rigid conservative position.

times rabid anti-intellectualism led to cultural isolation and a lack of national influence. By the 1920s, as illustrated in the famous John Scopes "monkey" (evolution) trial, many Americans believed that a person could not be an evangelical Christian and "modern" at the same time. One was either a superstitious, backward person of faith or a progressive, "up-to-date" person of reason.

The Renewal of Orthodox Protestant Christian Thinking in the 20th Century

Even though postmodernism has been gaining strength, for most of this century Christian thinkers have been fighting the old adversary of modernism. This is no easy fight. To many observers, from the 1920s to the 1960s it appeared that orthodox Christianity was nearly defeated. In almost every cultural institution of influence, classic Protestant liberalism with its emphasis on human subjectivity in religion was the dominant voice. In major universities theology departments often disappeared or were replaced by *religion* departments. By the 1960s, popular theologians were discussing the effects of the "death of God" on the modern "secular city."

Yet traditional, orthodox Christianity was far from finished. Due to the contributions of thinkers and church leaders in

Karl Barth

Although Swiss-German, Karl Barth (1886–1968) refused to be intimidated by the Nazi attempt to dominate religious life in Central Europe. Barth was a leading influence behind the formation of the German Confessing Church, which remained faithful to orthodox Christianity and opposed Hitler. After the war Barth continued to teach theology, often in the bombed-out remains of the German universities. His preaching, writing, and teaching had an enormous impact in both Europe and the Americas. His lectures and character inspired hope in a shattered and despondent society. For Barth, the horrors of the war could be understood only in terms of sin in need of redemption, not ignorance in need of knowledge, as classical liberalism taught. Humankind could have hope, but only on the basis of Christ's work on the cross. Karl Barth's most important contribution to Christian thought was a restoration of a God-centered theology based on the divine revelation of the Word of God in Christ, Scripture, and preaching. In the opinion of many Church historians, Karl Barth is the most important Protestant theologian in the twentieth century. Important Writings: *Commentary on Romans*, *Church Dogmatics*, *Credo*.

Europe, the United States, and the developing nations, the Christian worldview (specifically the evangelical Christian worldview) has made a remarkable comeback. There have been many significant contributors in this renewal of Christian thinking, but three deserve particular recognition.

Both in terms of the quantity and the quality of his scholarly work, Karl Barth (1886–1968) may be the single most important Christian theologian of the twentieth century. Although Barth had been attracted to classical Protestant liberalism early in his career, his experiences as a young pastor from 1911 to 1921 caused him to reverse his theological position. Barth's rejection of liberalism and its cheerful optimism about human nature was only deepened by the immense suffering of World War I (1914–1918). Significantly influenced by the writings of Martin Luther, Barth turned to the divine revelation of Scripture for truth. Unlike Protestant liberalism, which viewed Scripture as nothing more than human wisdom and beautiful literature, Barth emphasized that Scripture contained the revelation of an almighty, transcendent God. Barth was suspicious of the abilities of human reason and emphasized the necessity of the Holy Spirit to make the words of Scripture to be of spiritual value. In conjunction with other theologians, specifically Emil Brunner and the Americans Reinhold and Richard Niebuhr, Karl Barth skillfully articulated traditional Christian doctrines.[12] Through their work essential Christian doctrines such as the reality of sin and separation from God, the importance of redemption in Christ, and the belief in a transcendent God regained academic credibility.

In the United States one theologian more than any other has helped to reestablish the intellectual respectability of evangelicalism: Carl F. H. Henry. Despite coming from a conservative evangelical background, he was determined not to allow it to keep him from getting the most advanced education available.

Carl Henry's writings demonstrate sustained, serious Christian thinking on a wide variety of theological, philosophical, and cultural topics. Perhaps his greatest contribution has been his work in the formation of an evangelical scholarly community. Carl Henry served as public-relations coordinator and board member of the National Association of Evangelicals, president of the Evangelical Theology Society, and president of the board of the Institute for Advanced Christian Studies. Henry edited and supervised numerous projects of Christian scholarship. Under his leadership the magazine *Christianity Today* became a

---

[12]They, however, did not view Scripture as the objective written Word of God, but as human writings that could become the Word of God when the Spirit spoke existentially. Evangelicals consider this a deficient view of Scripture. See John R. Higgins, "God's Inspired Word," in *Systematic Theology,* ed. Horton, 112–13.

respected forum for evangelical news, discussion, and commentary. Along with the support of the popular radio evangelist Charles Fuller, Henry and like-minded scholars established Fuller Theological Seminary (Pasadena, California), a key center for evangelical thinking. As the elder statesman of the "new evangelicalism," Henry's careful thought, quality work, and Christian character have demonstrated to believer and nonbeliever alike that it is still possible in the modern world to worship God with the mind as well as with the heart.

Although Clive Staples (C. S.) Lewis (1898–1963) was not a theologian or clergyman, he has probably done more to restore the popular respectability of orthodox Christianity in the English-speaking world than any other writer in this century. He was raised in the Anglican Church, but by the time he began attending Oxford University (1917) he had become an atheist. C. S. Lewis earned degrees in literature from Oxford and served as tutor and lecturer there and at Cambridge for his entire professional career. Outside of his religious writings, he is best known for his scholarly work in Medieval and Renaissance English literature. As he describes in his autobiography, *Surprised*

Carl F. H. Henry

Carl Ferdinand Howard Henry (1913–   ), a son of German immigrants, was raised on a small farm on New York's Long Island. During the Depression years he served as an editor and writer for major New York newspapers, including the *New York Herald Tribune* and the *New York Daily News*. In 1933 he had a conversion experience, and two years later enrolled in the undergraduate program in philosophy at Wheaton College (Illinois). By 1949 Henry was an ordained Baptist minister and had received an M.A. (Master of Arts) in Philosophy from Wheaton, a Th.D. (Doctorate in Theology) from Northern Baptist Theological Seminary, and a Ph.D. in Philosophy from Boston University. In addition to his work at Fuller Theological Seminary, over the course of his career Henry also taught at several major evangelical institutions of higher education and served on the boards of numerous organizations. His writings have been recognized as distinguished contributions to Christian epistemology, ontology, and political philosophy. Henry was a frequent speaker and preacher, notably as lecturer-at-large for World Vision International from 1974–1986. Especially as the editor of *Christianity Today* magazine (1955–1968, thereafter editor-at-large), Henry served as the most important statesman and spokesman in American evangelicalism. Important Writings: *God, Revelation and Authority, The Uneasy Conscience of Modern Fundamentalism*, and his autobiography, *Confessions of a Theologian*.

by Joy, in 1931, after a long intellectual struggle, Lewis converted to Christianity. Gifted as a writer and thinker of substantial
clarity and style, Lewis became famous for his reasonable explanations of the Christian faith. He wrote more than 25 Christian books, including *The Screwtape Letters, Mere Christianity*,
and the children's fantasy series *The Chronicles of Narnia*. The
success of the 1993 motion picture based on the life of C. S.
Lewis, *Shadowlands*, demonstrates his continued popularity and
influence. (See the sidebar on Lewis in ch. 10, p. 370).

The Pentecostal and Charismatic Movements

As a worldview, secular modernism collides with Christianity in its most basic tenet: the reality of the supernatural.
No amount of Christian thinking would have carried the
churches through the difficult years of this century had it
not been for those believers that recognized the necessity of
Christian experience and the reality of God's direct, supernatural intervention in the lives of humankind. In a culture
that tends to be dominated by rationality, even within the
churches, an absolutely essential role in the shaping of the
Christian worldview has been played by Pentecostals and
Charismatics in the twentieth century.

Stressing the experience of God in conversion and also a
special empowerment by the Holy Spirit for Christian service and ministry (Acts 2:4, 1 Cor. 12), Pentecostals brought
energy to evangelism and world missions. Gathering momentum and national attention as the result of an extended revival
on Azusa Street in Los Angeles (1906–1909), the Pentecostal
denominations, led by the Assemblies of God, the Church of
God in Christ, and the Church of God, have gained large
numbers of adherents. From a worldwide perspective, Pente-
costalism has been the fastest growing movement in Christianity in the twentieth century.

Impacted by the vitality of Pentecostal life and worship,
members of other denominations also began to seek legitimate experiences of the supernatural power of God. The national attention surrounding the public support of charismatic
gifts by Episcopalian priest Dennis Bennett in 1963 encouraged many members of mainline churches to seek the gifts
of the Holy Spirit. While some of these Charismatics have
remained in their home churches and others have separated
to form independent fellowships, their growth has been phe-
nomenal. The Catholic Charismatic Renewal, born out of similar experiences in prayer meetings at Duquesne University
in 1967, has added millions of believers to the number of
those having a direct encounter with the living God.

It is important to note that due to a strong missions emphasis
the Pentecostal and Charismatic movements are now numeri-
cally larger outside the United States than inside it. Not only has

this helped to shape the Christian worldview by "dewesterniz-ing" Christianity, it has also bequeathed a vibrant, supernatural faith to global Christianity at this important juncture in world history.

Conclusion

History teaches many lessons. One of the most important lessons is that the world we live in as Christians has changed considerably. Christian truth does not change, but the audience that needs to hear that truth certainly does. The history of Christianity can give us confidence, however, when we note the Church responding to its surroundings by shaping and reshaping its worldview. This is no insignificant calling and requires great seriousness, intellectual labor, and Christian maturity. The essence of orthodox Christianity cannot be sacrificed, but unless its formulation is appropriate to its historical context, we lose our effectiveness in the world.

In recent decades significant gains have been made by Christianity against modernism. But modernism is a worldview that is already in decline. How will evangelicals respond to the new challenges of our age?

There are many reasons to be hopeful. As can be seen by the essays in this book, evangelical Christians are making important contributions in several academic disciplines. Many educational institutions are strong and evangelicalism has a growing publishing industry. We are learning how to integrate our faith and our learning once again. Many believers are taking up the call to love God with their mind and to "think like a Christian." It will be exciting to read the account of this generation's attempt to shape a Christian worldview. But that is a history yet to be lived and written.

Review and Discussion Questions

1. What would you select as the central identifying characteristic(s) of the Early Church? the Medieval Church? the Modern Church? How has the Church changed and how has it remained the same over the last two thousand years?

2. The Christian worldview has been hammered out on the anvil of conflict. What do you consider to be the most important challenges faced by the Church in each of its three main periods?

3. Constantine's conversion was a pivotal event in church history. In what ways would you consider this to have had positive consequences? Negative consequences?

4. How was the Medieval Church most like the Early Church? Most different? What accounts for both this continuity and these changes?

5. Medieval monks generally considered themselves to be living the highest form of the Christian life possible (the *imitatio Christi*). What was the *imitatio Christi* perceived to be in the

Early Church? In the Modern Church? What is the *imitatio Christi* today?

6. How is the Modern Church most like the Medieval Church? Most different? What accounts for both this continuity and these changes?

7. Martin Luther is recognized as the father of the Reformation, but would the Reformation have happened without him? Was it inevitable sooner or later?

8. After the Puritan and Wesleyan revivals, why did evangelicals generally turn away from scientific inquiry and the life of the mind? What evidence do you see that a renewal of "thinking as a Christian" may be taking place?

9. The Pentecostal and Charismatic movements are two of the most important events in twentieth century church history. Why have these movements grown so rapidly in the United States? Abroad? What might this tell us about human society in this century?

10. Based upon your understanding of contemporary culture, what do you consider to be the most important challenges that the Church will face in the next few decades? What aspects of the Christian worldview must be reshaped or reaffirmed to respond to these challenges?

11. Summarize at least three ways Christians have historically understood the relationship between faith and reason.

Selected Bibliography

GENERAL

Brauer, Jerald C., ed. *The Westminster Dictionary of Church History.* Louisville: Westminster, John Knox, 1971. Easy to follow and more American in emphasis, but contains no bibliographies.

Cairns, Earle E. *Christianity Through the Centuries.* Rev. and enlarged ed. Grand Rapids: Zondervan Publishing House, 1981. One of the most readable.

Chadwick, Henry, and G. R. Evans, eds. *Atlas of the Christian Church.* New York: Facts on File, 1987. The best geographic reference available.

Cross, F. L., ed. *The Oxford Dictionary of the Christian Church.* Oxford University Press, 1990. A standard reference work.

Douglas, J. D., ed. *Who's Who in Christian History.* Wheaton, Ill.: Tyndale House Publishers, 1992. A fine biographical dictionary.

Gonzalez, Justo L. *The Story of Christianity.* 2 vols. San Francisco: HarperCollins, 1984. Another very readable text.

McManners, John, ed. *Oxford Illustrated History of Christianity.* Oxford: Oxford University Press, 1990. Though overbalanced with British perspectives and the modern period, it provides some breathtaking visual images.

Pelican *History of the Church* series. 6 vols. New York: Penguin Books, 1954ff. Each book was written by a recognized expert in a major period of church history. The series is not technical, but makes use of excellent scholarship. The sixth volume, a separate history of missions by Stephen Neill, is a bonus.

Pelikan, Jaroslav. *The Christian Tradition*. 5 vols. Chicago: University of Chicago Press, 1971ff. The combination of Pelikan's melodic prose and his mastery of the primary source material make this series indispensable for the development of Christian thought.

MAGAZINE

Christian History. Each issue gives a colorful overview of a major individual or idea in church history. Although written for a wide audience, the scholarship is excellent and the bibliography provided makes this resource an excellent place for an undergraduate to begin research.

EARLY CHURCH

Ante-Nicene, Nicene, and Post-Nicene Fathers of the Early Church series. 38 vols. Peabody, Mass.: Hendrickson Publishers, Inc., reprint, 1994. The translation is dated but adequate, and there are many helpful indexes.

Ferguson, Everett, ed. *Encyclopedia of Early Christianity*. New York: Garland Publishing, Inc., 1990. A most important reference work.

Brown, Peter. *Augustine of Hippo*. New York: Dorset Press, 1967. The best biography on this important Church Father; provides a wonderful window on life in the late Roman Empire.

MEDIEVAL CHURCH

Catholic U. of America Staff. *New Catholic Encyclopedia*. 17 vols. New York: McGraw Hill Inc., 1967ff. Often the best source for the Middle Ages although written from a distinctly Roman Catholic perspective.

Ozment, Steven. *The Age of Reform, 1250–1550*. New Haven: Yale U. Press, 1980. An excellent survey of the Late Middle Ages, specifically in connection with the Reformation that followed.

Strayer, Joseph R. ed. *Dictionary of the Middle Ages*. New York: Charles Scribner's Sons, 1982ff. A helpful reference tool.

MODERN CHURCH

Bainton, Roland H. *Here I Stand: A Life of Martin Luther*. Nashville: Abingdon Press, 1950. A classic.

Burgess, Stanley M., and Gary B. McGee. *Dictionary of Pentecostal and Charismatic Movements*. Grand Rapids: Zondervan Publishing House, 1988. This is the standard reference on this subject.

Grenz, Stanley J., and Roger E. Olson. *20th Century Theology: God and the World in a Transitional Age*. Downers Grove, Ill.: InterVarsity Press, 1992. Actually begins with the rise of classical Protestant liberalism early in the nineteenth century; highly valuable due to its clear, concise summaries of the thought of modern theologians, who are sometimes difficult.

McGrath, Alister E. *Reformation Thought: An Introduction*. Cambridge: Blackwell Publishers, 1993. Surveys the major intellectual issues of the period.

Noll, Mark. *The History of Christianity in the United States and Canada*. Grand Rapids: William B. Eerdmans Publishing Co., 1992. This is the best survey of its kind.

Oberman, Heiko A. *Luther: Man between God and the Devil*. New York: Doubleday & Co., 1992. An eminently fascinating book.

4

The Christian and Natural Science

Lawrence T. McHargue

Biology is my life work and profession. I have been either a student or a professional in the field for the better part of four decades. During my years of study and work, I have encountered a wide range of responses among Christians to the practice of modern science. Some people, of course, are indifferent. They live in an era of unparalleled scientific research, but they ignore the practice of science and take its benefits for granted. Others are unabashed science enthusiasts. Or at least they enthusiastically embrace the products modern science makes possible. Still others seem dubious, suspicious, even hostile, about the practice of science.

Reflecting on these responses, I am reminded of how certain Christians once reacted to a friend of mine who felt called to pursue a career in natural science. Some took little note. Others were supportive and expressed genuine encouragement, though in general they had little idea what such a call might entail. A few expressed grave concern. His faith, they urged, would wither under the searing influence of atheistic scientists. Didn't he realize the risks involved in embarking on such a career? Their doubts did not deter him, but they did cause him considerable pain.

My friend's experience is not unique among Christians who have an interest in the natural sciences. Regardless of which way they turn, they encounter difficult questions and the centuries-old, allegedly irreconcilable conflict between modern science and the life of faith. Not uncommonly, they experience themselves as torn between two camps that seem determined to perpetuate a false dichotomy. One camp is inhabited by certain agnostic or atheistic scientists. In their eagerness to apply the scientific method rigorously to a broad range of important questions, they step beyond the bounds of the method that governs their daily research. To them, questions that cannot be answered by the scientific method are unimportant or irrelevant. They dismiss the notion that the universe at large (and human life in particular) is governed by an ultimate purpose, since such a purpose is not discoverable by the scientific method. Theirs is a thoroughly naturalistic conception of the universe. (See chapters 1 and 2 for discussions of naturalism.)

The other camp is inhabited by certain Christians who, though often sincere in their purposes, have a limited grasp of the methods of modern empirical science. They lump together science and naturalism. Then, in their haste to reject naturalism, they make erroneous claims against all science. They sometimes reason, for instance, that, since some important questions (e.g., questions about moral issues or God's existence) cannot be answered scientifically, science should not be regarded as holding the key to *any* important questions. (In other words, since naturalism is false, we should be skeptical about the scientific method embraced by naturalists.) Or again, since the scientific method is silent about whether the universe is governed by an ultimate purpose, these Christians sometimes infer that scientific questions are either trivial or dangerous to our faith commitments. In short, because their Christian worldview leads them to reject the basic tenets of naturalism, they believe they must also steer clear of the practice of modern science.

For the person who (like my friend) takes seriously both the life of faith and the practice of modern science, the task is to integrate the two within the framework of a Christian worldview. This task is difficult partly because it calls for a sound understanding of Scripture and theology and partly because it requires a solid grasp of basic issues related to the practice of modern empirical science. The most important of these issues may be framed as questions: How and why did modern science develop? What philosophical assumptions underlie the practice of natural science? What are the scope and limits of scientific method?

> "The task is to integrate the life of faith and the practice of modern science within a Christian worldview."

In the remainder of this chapter, we shall explore those questions. Our purpose is to mark out a path that leads to neither of the two warring camps. Modern empirical science is neither the sole source of answers to life's important questions nor a barrier to achieving such answers; neither a panacea for all our ills nor the devil's tool. In the last analysis, it is an extraordinarily powerful but limited method for advancing human knowledge. Understanding it and successfully integrating it into a Christian worldview call for hard work and patience—hard work because the issues are complicated and resist naive attempts to simplify them, and patience because the task cannot be completed in a short time. We cannot pretend to complete the task within the confines of this chapter. Nevertheless, we begin in the confidence that considering some of the key issues will at least point the way toward the sort of integration we seek.

The Greek Precursors of Modern Science

Theoretical natural science has a history that exceeds twenty-five hundred years. It began as a concern of Greek philosophers who preceded Plato and Aristotle. These philosophers were the first to explain the physical world in a reasoned and analytical way. They pondered the nature of matter, recognized physical laws, studied astronomy, began to formulate mathematical theory, introduced model-making to study natural phenomena, and proposed the first atomic theory. These early Greek philosophers also began the process of considering what we earlier called a background theory about the cosmos. (See chapter 1, pp. 33–35.) Their considerations opened the way for subsequent thinkers to study the world systematically rather than attribute all phenomena to irrational and unpredictable forces such as gods and goddesses.

ARISTOTLE

Aristotle is generally regarded as the philosopher whose thinking most affected the development of natural science in the Classical period (fifth through fourth century B.C.). Moreover, his arguments greatly influenced subsequent Western views about the nature of reality and what can be known of it. Indeed, his philosophical perspective profoundly affected scientific thought until the second half of the sixteenth century.

Aristotle's intellectual legacy is monumental. He made important contributions in many fields of learning including philosophy, logic, physics, biology, astronomy, literary theory, ethics, and political theory.

Aristotle recognized four categories of causes, or explanatory factors: the material, the formal, the efficient, and the final cause.[1] Roughly speaking, the *material cause* is the stuff something is made of. The *formal cause* is a thing's essence, nature, or structure. Aristotle believed that we can express an object's formal cause in a definition. The *efficient cause* is the agent, or pro-

Aristotle (384–322 B.C.), one of the most important philosophers of the ancient Greek world, is also generally regarded as one of the most important theorists in human history. He was born in Stagira, a town in the region of Thrace in northern Greece. At the age of seventeen he was sent to Athens to study at Plato's Academy, where he remained until Plato's death twenty years later. In 343 or 342, King Philip II of Macedon invited Aristotle to tutor his thirteen-year-old son, Alexander (later known as Alexander the Great), a position Aristotle held for several years. In 335 Aristotle returned to Athens, where he founded a school called the Lyceum. He ran the Lyceum until 323, when strong anti-Macedonian sentiment arose in Athens. Because he had long-standing connections with Macedon and because he feared retribution from angry Athenians, Aristotle decided to leave Athens for Chalcis on the island of Euboea, where he died in 322.

---

[1]Aristotle's primary discussion of causes or explanatory factors (Gk. *aitiai*) may be found in his *Metaphysics* BK VII and *Physics* BK II. For additional discussion, see George Sarton, *A History of Science,* vol. 1, *Ancient Science through the Golden Age of Greece* (New York: John Wiley & Sons, Inc., 1964).

cess, by which something is made. The *final cause* is the purpose for which it exists or the end (Gk. *telos*) toward which its action is directed. By way of example, consider the making of a statue. If it is to be made of marble, then marble becomes its material cause. But, of course, the statue will be more than merely a block of marble; it will have a certain structure, a prescribed shape. This will be its formal cause. It will have this prescribed shape because the sculptor will work on the marble with a chisel and a mallet: The impact of the chisel on the marble becomes the efficient cause of the statue. But we must not forget the reason the sculptor will make the statue. Perhaps it has been commissioned to commemorate the life of a famous person; this purpose, or end, explaining why it was made, will be the statue's final cause.

Aristotle made important and lasting contributions to philosophy, psychology, logic, and several other branches of inquiry. In biology, his classification scheme was essential for the development of taxonomy. His kingdoms are marvelously ordered, intricate, and interrelated.[2] His recognition of order is a basic assumption of modern science. He attempted to consider physical phenomena rationally and logically based on a perception of order. However, his enduring legacy in the sciences derives from his treatment of final causes (as described above). The view that the activities of things in nature are directed toward an end, a goal, a purpose, dominated his own accounts of both animate and inanimate objects. The same type of reasoning— called teleological explanation—eventually came to dominate the Medieval conception of physics in the twelfth and thirteenth centuries. Only in the latter half of the sixteenth century were teleological explanations in the practice of natural science finally and decisively replaced by mechanistic explanations of causation and the physical universe.[3]

The Medieval European Precursors to Modern Science

For the thousand years now known as the Medieval period (400–1400), the Church enjoyed unparalleled influence on the European continent. Its treasuries were full. Its buildings were the most impressive structures on the continent. Its leaders wielded remarkable political influence and in some cases exercised outright control over civil authorities. Most of the population at large labored long hours in the fields to stave off hunger; only a small minority had access to learning. Not surprisingly,

Teleology. Aristotle explained natural phenomena in *teleological* terms. Teleology is the study of the ends, or purposes, of things. To say that a worldview is teleological means that the worldview understands reality to be directed by ultimate purposes. Christianity can be described as a teleological worldview.

Aristotle's Unmoved Mover. Aristotle reasoned that there must be a first cause, or unmoved mover, who is eternal and unchangeable and is therefore not made of physical material. He taught that the unmoved mover is remote, does not occupy physical space, and is not infinite. Aristotle's unmoved mover is not the Creator of the Bible. However, the unmoved mover and ordained purposes (final causes) were later attractive to Christians. Medieval scholars, in particular Thomas Aquinas, reconciled Aristotelian teaching in philosophy and science with Christianity until the time of Galileo.

---

[2]Loren Wilkinson, ed., *Earthkeeping, Christian Stewardship of Natural Resources* (Grand Rapids: William B. Eerdmans Publishing Co., 1980), 109.

[3]This claim applies most accurately to the field of physics. In biology, teleological explanations were not supplanted until the nineteenth century.

the seats of learning were primarily in church institutions, such as monasteries and the few existing universities.

Early Medieval scholarship was influenced profoundly not only by the teachings of the Church but also by the powerful heritage of the Roman Empire. Scholars were familiar with the Roman poets and prose writers. Latin was the medium of discourse for all scholarly writing and discussion. The fact that early thinkers were affected both by Christian and Roman influences meant that they often found themselves attempting to reconcile the two traditions. Because the Greek philosopher Plato had influenced Roman philosophy, early attempts to reconcile Christian and non-Christian thought commonly sought to reconcile Christian teachings with certain features of Plato's philosophy, as understood by Roman philosophers. The most notable of these early attempts was done by Augustine (A.D. 354–430). (See the sidebar in chapter 3, p. 118.) His influence was unmatched until the thirteenth century.

> "Early Medieval scholarship was influenced profoundly by the powerful heritage of the Roman Empire."

Early Medieval European scholars were heavily influenced by Roman tradition and culture. At the same time, they had almost no direct knowledge of the extraordinary intellectual and cultural heritage of Classical Greece. But this heritage was so rich and varied that it gradually began to reshape Medieval thought and life when Europeans awakened to it. Its influence came in two stages. The first occurred in the twelfth and thirteenth centuries and is known as the Medieval Renaissance. It was spurred by the introduction into Europe of a few important Greek manuscripts. The second, known today as the Great Renaissance, began in Italy in the fifteenth century, and by the end of the sixteenth century had spread to all parts of Europe. This great "awakening" represented, in part, a response to an outpouring of translations of the works of ancient Greek poets, playwrights, scientists, and philosophers. Let us briefly review these two awakenings to better understand the cultural, theological, and philosophical context in which modern scientific method eventually emerged.

THE MEDIEVAL RENAISSANCE

The Medieval Renaissance of the twelfth and thirteenth centuries was mainly triggered by the rediscovery of important Greek texts. These included Euclid's work on geometry and Ptolemy's on astronomy, but especially Aristotle's on logic and scientific method. Until the twelfth century, European scholars knew of these writings only by reputation. Their rediscovery added new energy and direction to Medieval scholarship. In particular, Aristotle's writings emphasized the importance of observation, experiment, and logical argument. In this they represented quite a departure from the type of abstract speculation typical of the earlier Roman-Platonic tradition.

The influence of Aristotle's thought on Europe cannot be overestimated. It acted as a catalyst for a way of thinking that some four centuries later would take shape as the general model for modern scientific inquiry. At first, however, its primary influence was felt in theology. So persuasive was Aristotle's approach to a broad range of issues that theologians (or Schoolmen; see sidebar on Scholasticism) of the thirteenth century felt compelled to reconcile Christian theology with key tenets of his philosophy. More so than during any earlier period, they felt compelled to show that the claims of faith are consistent with the demands of reason. The most notable theologian to attempt this task was Thomas Aquinas. (See sidebar, p. 123.) Within a few decades of his death in 1274, his *Summa Theologica* became a primary source of instruction in theology.

By the fourteenth century, scholars increasingly asserted the legitimacy of pursuing rational explanations not specifically derived from nor directly tied to doctrinal considerations. Thomas Aquinas' attempt to demonstrate harmony between faith and reason was called into question in some quarters. In particular, William of Ockham argued that religious claims must be accepted purely on faith. Ockham also rejected traditional Medieval metaphysics and Scholastic theology. He held that non-

Scholasticism

Theologians of the late Medieval period are known as Schoolmen, or Scholastics. Scholasticism is distinctive in the Christian tradition for its commitment to the use of reason to deepen the understanding of what is believed on faith. Several of the most prominent scholastic thinkers sought to give a rational content to faith. Scholasticism began with Anselm (late eleventh century), who developed one of the most famous and enduring rational proofs for the existence of God (the so-called ontological argument). Abelard emphasized the rational approach in considering the most important philosophical question of the twelfth century, the question of whether universals such as "mankind" and "horse" are real (exist apart from human thought and language) or are simply names for grouping individuals. But the carefully reasoned theological system of Thomas Aquinas is regarded as the greatest achievement of the Scholastic age. It is distinctive and notable for its synthesis of faith and reason. Other Scholastic thinkers—particularly Bonaventure (1221–1274), John Duns Scotus (1266–1308), and William of Ockham (1285–1349)—rejected Aquinas' synthesis of faith and reason. As the Great Renaissance began to unfold across Europe, Scholastic methods were eventually rejected in the natural sciences, though they continued to be followed in politics and law.

revealed knowledge (knowledge found outside of Scripture) must be based on experience. In the fourteenth century, his approach became quite influential, especially at the Universities of Paris and Oxford. With Ockham, the disciplines of science and philosophy slowly but surely began to take on identities independent of theology. This trend continued into modern times.

THE GREAT RENAISSANCE

The idea that learning and knowledge could be independent of Church doctrines took firmer root during the Great Renaissance of the fifteenth and sixteenth centuries. The invention of the printing press (1450) and the exploration of new continents (beginning in the 1480s) were key developments that enlarged European conceptions of the world. These developments did so by encouraging a new cadre of professionals—men whose inquiring spirit took them far beyond the walls of ecclesiastical institutions. As their numbers grew, they began to ex-

William of Ockham

William of Ockham (c.1285–1349) was a member of the Franciscan order and an English philosopher. Ockham's teachings represent an important departure from earlier Medieval philosophy. He is most noted for holding a position called *nominalism*, the view that only particular perceptible objects (e.g., individual human beings or horses) exist. Universals (e.g., humanity or horseness) are not *real* (do not actually exist) except in people's minds and language. Ockham's nominalism stood in stark contrast to the Aristotelian *realism* of Thomas Aquinas, according to which universals do actually exist independently of people's minds and language. Ockham is also noted for rejecting the self-evidence of the Aristotelian notion of final cause. Also, although he believed in God, he did not believe God's existence is self-evident or a matter to be proved. Consistent with this view, he held that reason is not competent to judge matters of faith. In effect, he favored making a sharp distinction between matters of reason (such as the study of logic) and matters of faith. This position proved important in the development of scientific inquiry.

Ockham is famous for proposing a principle of parsimony commonly called Ockham's razor: "What can be done with fewer is done in vain with more." The meaning of his statement is that in any explanation of natural phenomena the simplest possible explanation or hypothesis that is consistent with the facts should be preferred. Any explanation that is inconsistent with the facts or observations should be rejected. Ockham's razor remains a basic feature of the scientific method to the present time.

change ideas through letters and travel. These new men of learning, known as humanists, led the way in the translation of a host of Classical Greek works beyond those of Aristotle. They also inspired new confidence in the human intellect and awakened a new sense of the worth and dignity of individual human beings.

Partly as a result of the growing confidence and liberating influence of the learned men of the Renaissance, two revolutions quietly unfolded. The first began within the Church and became public in 1517, when Martin Luther nailed his *95 Theses* to the door of the church in Wittenburg. (See sidebar, pp. 130–131.) The second was prompted by the work of Nicholas Copernicus, a Polish astronomer who developed arguments showing that the earth revolved around the sun. His so-called heliocentric theory of planetary motion challenged the traditional belief that the planets and stars revolved around the earth, taught by the Alexandrian astronomer Ptolemy (second century A.D.). The traditional conception assumed the earth to be at the center of the universe. Until the time of Copernicus, it had been sanctioned by the combined authority of Aristotle, Thomas Aquinas, and the commonly accepted interpretation of Scripture. Empirical evidence available at the time initially did not deci-

Exploration Beyond Europe

About the time Columbus reached the West Indies, exploration greatly expanded the European view of the world. Overwhelming numbers of strange and previously unknown animals and plants were brought back to Europe from the western hemisphere, Africa, India, and East Asia. Crop plants such as corn, beans, peanuts, peppers, squash, tomatoes, potatoes, sweet potatoes, papayas, mangos, and pineapples reached Europe for the first time. European naturalists gradually realized both that the world contained vastly more kinds of living things than they had ever imagined and that their classification schemes were woefully inadequate. The need to classify large numbers of living things was a major factor causing taxonomy, the science of naming and classification, to be the first branch of biology to be systematically organized. The same need led ultimately to the collapse of the concept of "fixed species."

Voyages to the southern hemisphere with its reversed seasons and different groups of animals and plants dispelled the Medieval notion that it was impossible to reach the southern parts of the world. Europeans observed southern hemispheric skies with brighter and more numerous stars than they could see at home. The discovery of distant lands, hosts of previously unknown animals and plants, culturally diverse peoples, and views of brilliant southern skies dispelled the notion of a self-contained earth having a fixed and relatively well understood order. The old ways of viewing the world, nature, and science began to change forever.

Developments in Astronomy

Major advances in astronomy and physics profoundly influenced all of science as the Modern era dawned.

Nicholas Copernicus (1473–1543), a Polish astronomer, laid the foundation for modern astronomy with his heliocentric theory of planetary motion. He first presented this theory about 1512 (perhaps earlier) in a short form in an unpublished manuscript entitled "Commentariolus." The fuller, refined version was published in 1543 in his landmark work *De revolutionibus orbium coelestium*.

Johannes Kepler (1571–1630), an ardent Lutheran, championed Copernican theory about sixty years later. Kepler differed

sively favor either the traditional account or Copernicus's theory. Yet the mathematical simplicity of the Copernican theory proved persuasive. Copernicus believed that God had imposed order and harmony on his creation, and he believed that its order was revealed in the language of mathematics.[4] Support for the Copernican revolution grew during the sixteenth century. Concurrently, the Medieval conception of physics, based largely on the writings of Aristotle, lost its persuasive hold on European thinkers. By the seventeenth century, it was overthrown.

The Emergence of Modern Science

The procedures and models of thought that eventually framed modern empirical science began to take shape in the fifteenth century with Copernicus and continued into the sixteenth century with other astronomers and mathematicians. The second half of the sixteenth century saw the beginnings of the Modern era and the steady supplanting of Aristotelian Scholasticism by modern science. This replacement of Aristotle's investigative method by scientific inquiry, culminating in the work of Sir Isaac Newton (1642–1727), is marked by several important and profound changes:

1. Observation and quantitative reasoning replaced authority. Until the late sixteenth century, a common form of scholarly argument for a thesis was to amass relevant supportive quotations and references from authoritative sources such as Classical and Medieval texts, especially those of Aristotle or the Church Fathers. However, astronomy and mathematics

---

[4]Nancy R. Pearcey and Charles B. Thaxton, *The Soul of Science, Christian Faith and Natural Philosophy* (Wheaton, Ill.: Crossway Books, 1994), 126–128.

from earlier astronomers in his unwavering loyalty to observed data. He accepted the validity of empirical data over the prevailing theory from the ancient world. He asserted that any hypothesis that does not seek to portray truth is inadequate in understanding God's universe. Kepler worked on principles of planetary motion using data collected by Tycho Brahe (1546–  1601), a Danish astronomer. Precise measurement and data were established as the basis for truth in the physical realm. Kepler held that observations of the universe are reliable because God had revealed himself in His creation.

required a different type of proof, and their development was therefore important to the process of replacing argument from authority with direct observation and quantitative reasoning. Francis Bacon urged researchers to reject arguments based on authority and to base their conclusions strictly on experiment and the direct study of nature. This approach fostered the use of empirical observation and provided a strong stimulus for the development of the experimental method.[5] Bacon recognized that the acquisition of scientific knowledge would proceed incrementally and be accomplished by many people. He understood that scientific experimentation would be needed to develop and provide support for new ideas in science. Bacon thus advocated the establishment of a scientific research program. He also outlined a methodology needed to produce practical results, though it would be fair to say that he was much too optimistic about the capacity of the method to yield continuous and reliable results.[6] His emphasis on observation marked a substantial shift in Western thought. Though his proposed method of conducting research lacks direction when viewed by today's standards, his proposals for research opened the way for subsequent workers to approach the physical world in a more systematic empirical fashion and without the constraints of arguments from authority.

[5]The effect of this new reasoning was to demystify nature and give permission to examine the creation, looking for causes. For additional discussion of this point, see Paulos Mar Gregorios, *Science for a Sane Society* (New York: Paragon House, 1987), 173. Sir William Cecil Dampier, *A History of Science and Its Relations with Philosophy and Religion* (Cambridge: Cambridge University Press, 1968), 319, 459.

[6]For Bacon, the object of scientific endeavor was the attainment of knowledge that could be put to practical use. The impetus for acquiring scientific knowledge was to exercise power over nature. See Wilkinson, *Earthkeeping*, 131–134.

2. Thinking in terms of qualitative analogies was replaced by purely quantitative reasoning. Medieval scholars commonly conceived the universe as a hierarchical, organic whole, with different levels of existing things—different levels of being, so to speak. Between these levels of being, between the macrocosmic universe and the microcosmic humankind, there existed affinities or correspondences. Accordingly, natural and social events were often interpreted as analogous to certain processes in the human body or in a living organism. Thus, for example, storms were viewed as expressions of divine anger, and the relation between the king and the nation was viewed as being patterned on the relation between God and His creation. During the sixteenth century, the hierarchical model and the analogical reasoning that went with it were replaced by a quantitative model. Galileo Galilei was prominent and influential in the attempt to quantify nature. According to him, science should concern itself exclusively with the measurable properties of the world, such as size, shape, and motion. Knowledge of nature, he thought, should be based on data that is transformed from the senses to numerical form. Indeed, he refused to work with data that could not be reduced to numerical form.[7] The quantitative approach to natural phenomena by Galileo and other like-minded researchers not only undermined the hierarchical view of the universe, but also hastened the acceptance of its replacement: a model whose language is mathematics. According to this model,

Francis Bacon

Francis Bacon (1561–1626) is credited with influencing the development of modern science by emphasizing observation and experiment rather than arguments based on authority. But he is also known for his desire to achieve practical results. He took careful note of several important facts of daily life in Europe: primitive living conditions, high mortality rates, high incidences of infectious diseases, and slow and uncertain communication and transportation. He was troubled that scientific knowledge had produced so little power, or control, over nature. He believed that God had given human beings dominion over nature, yet he saw little dominion being exercised. Bacon was critical of Aristotelian science, and he wanted to acquire knowledge that could be used to restore the dominion that had been lost in humanity's fall in Genesis 3. He is credited with recognizing that a dearth of knowledge about the natural world was an important factor in Europe's problems.

---

[7]Wilkinson, *Earthkeeping*, 124–128; Mar Gregorios, *Science for a Sane Society*, 173.

all natural things exist on the same level, subject to the same physical laws and differing only in quantitative ways. Of course, the acceptance of these changes in models of thought occurred over long periods of time and in fits and starts.

3. A radical shift occurred in the way Europeans explained natural phenomena. Since the first awakening in Europe in the twelfth century, Aristotle's account of four types of explanatory factors, or causes (material, formal, efficient, and final), dominated scholarly thinking. Of these, the final cause (explaining things in terms of their ends, or purposes) was commonly regarded as the most fundamental form of explanation. Many Medieval thinkers employed it to explain physical events, from the falling of stones to the orbits

Galileo Galilei

Galileo Galilei (1564–1642), an Italian astronomer, mathematician, and physicist, significantly altered the approach of science to the physical world. He is generally credited with bringing to prominence the view that knowledge of natural phenomena should be based on data that are reduced to a numerical form. When he was only nineteen, he discovered the principle of isochronism—the principle that each oscillation of a pendulum takes the same time despite changes in amplitude. Soon afterward he became known for inventing an instrument known as a hydrostatic balance and writing a treatise on the center of gravity of falling bodies. Until Galileo's time it had been assumed that if one thing weighed twice as much as another, then it would fall twice as fast. He found experimentally that this was not so. Traditionalists reacted hostilely to this conclusion because it contradicted the accepted teaching of Aristotle. Galileo also discovered that the path of a projectile is a parabola instead of a straight line. In addition he is credited with anticipating Isaac Newton's laws of motion. In 1609, he constructed the first astronomical telescope. His research with it led to the discovery of Jupiter's four largest satellites as well as

the stellar composition of the Milky Way. In 1632 he published a work that upheld the Copernican theory rather than the traditional Ptolemaic theory of planetary motion. His investigation of these matters marked a turning point in scientific and philosophical thought. But religious authorities did not view his discoveries favorably. In 1633 he was brought before the inquisition in Rome where he  was forced to renounce all his beliefs and writings supporting the Copernican theory.

Significant works: *Dialogue Concerning the Two Chief World Systems* (1632) and *Dialogues Concerning Two New Sciences* (1638). For additional discussion of Galileo's relationship to the Church as well as treatment of other related cases, see David C. Lindberg and Ronald J. Numbers, "Beyond War and Peace: A Reappraisal of the Encounter Between Christianity and Science" in *Perspectives on Science and Christian Faith* 39 (1987): 141–49.

of planets, in terms of their divine purpose. Gradually, however, this teleological view of explanation gave way to a mechanistic account of causation and a general interpretive model that viewed all of the physical universe as a vast machine.

The person who gave the most articulate and powerful expression to the mechanical model was Sir Isaac Newton. For example, to explain the movement of heavenly bodies as well as earthly objects, Newton proposed a hypothesis of universal gravitation and three laws of motion within the framework of a unified model of physics. In a radical departure from the Aristotelian tradition, he hypothesized that physical laws and processes are uniformly applicable to the entire universe.

Newton himself believed that the universe was created *ex nihilo* by a transcendent God, and that the universe and the laws that regulate it give evidence of God's design.[8] In other words, although Newton conducted his experiments strictly in accord with the methods of science and without reference to ultimate purposes (teleology), he himself subscribed to a larger world-view that allowed for such purposes. But many of his later followers advanced a completely naturalistic worldview according to which the universe is regulated solely by impersonal, mechanical laws.[9] They recognized no ultimate purposes,

Ex nihilo, **a Latin term meaning "from, or out of, nothing."**

Notable Scientific Discoveries in the Renaissance and Early Modern Period

Various scientific discoveries made during or shortly after Galileo's lifetime helped to shatter the Medieval view of nature (see p. 159, point 3), especially in physical science. William Gilbert (1540–1603) demonstrated that the earth is magnetic. Jean-Baptiste Van Helmont, a Christian physician, discovered gas and pneumatic chemistry while searching for a means to alleviate suffering. William Harvey (1578–1657) demonstrated the circulation of blood in the human body. Robert Hooke (1635–1703) was the first to observe cells. He also devised and improved several scientific instruments. Gassendi, a French priest, revived the atomic theory of Democritus and thus influenced later scientists. Each of these relied on careful observations and experimentation to reach his conclusions.

For additional information, see J. D. Bernal, *Science in History*, vol. 2, *The Scientific and Industrial Revolutions* (Harmondsworth: Penguin Books, 1969), 434–439, 459–464.

---

[8]Thomas F. Torrance, *The Christian Frame of Mind* (Colorado Springs, Colo: Helmers & Howard, 1989), 46.

[9]Margaret C. Jacob, "Christianity and the Newtonian Worldview," in *God and Nature, Historical Essays on the Encounter between Christianity and Science*, eds. David C. Lindberg and Ronald L. Numbers (Berkeley: University of California Press, 1986), 246–249.

divine or otherwise. On the contrary, they asserted that the universe is a vast and complicated machine whose movements conform to empirically discoverable laws. For them, reality was confined to measurable phenomena such as weight, mass, velocity, height, width, and physical force. The increasing prevalence of this naturalistic interpretation of the universe represents a major shift in Western thought. But while its increasing appeal in intellectual circles occurred concurrently with the rise of modern science, strictly speaking it does not follow directly from scientific thinking. It actually represents a worldview whose source lies beyond the scope of modern scientific method.[10]

Sir Isaac Newton

Sir Isaac Newton (1642–1727) was an English mathematician and physicist. He was unquestionably the premier scientist of his era and is generally regarded as one of the most astute scientific minds of all time. From 1669 until 1701 he taught mathematics at Cambridge University. In the mid-1660s he discovered calculus concurrently with W. G. Leibniz but independently of him. During the same period, he also articulated the law of universal gravitation and discovered that white light is composed of every color in the spectrum. In *Mathematical Principles of Natural Philosophy*, he showed how his principle of universal gravitation explained both the motions of heavenly bodies and the falling of bodies on earth. The same work explains dynamics (including Newton's three laws of motion), fluid mechanics, the motions of the planets and their satellites, the motions of the comets, and ocean tides. In a 1704 publication, *Optiks*, Newton argued that light is composed of particles. His theory dominated the field of optics for more than a century, until it was replaced by the wave theory of light. (In the twentieth century both theories were combined in the quantum theory.) In addition to his major accomplishments in physics, he built the first reflecting telescope, anticipated the calculus of variations, and devoted considerable attention to alchemy, theology, and history. He served as president of the Royal Society from 1703 until his death.

Major works: *Philosophiae naturalis principia mathematica* (Mathematical Principles of Natural Philosophy) (1687), and *Optiks* (1704).

---

[10]Pearcey and Thaxton, *The Soul of Science*, 93.

The Scientific Method

So far we have discussed certain historical developments that led to the emergence of modern science. We have also discussed some of the important and deep changes that marked the transition from investigative methods employed by Medieval thinkers (influenced by Aristotle) to the type of inquiry set in motion during the Renaissance and refined in the following centuries known as modern scientific inquiry. But, although we have identified some of its central features, we have not yet described its guiding principles and methodology. We turn to that task now.

Scientific advancement requires consistent methodology and reproducible results. Since the Renaissance, scientists have gradually perfected procedures by which they could gain knowledge and consistently study the physical universe. This methodology, called scientific method, involves the integration of two distinct elements, one empirical and one deductive. The empirical element requires that researchers actually examine natural phenomena, rather than merely speculate about them. The deductive element (consisting of the rules of mathematics and logic) places formal constraints on research and explanation, provides tools for analysis and prediction, and constitutes the formal language for communicating results.[11]

Scientific research can neither guarantee specific results nor ensure progress in acquiring knowledge on specific issues. But, as one philosopher of science has pointed out, "No competent scientist does pointless or unplanned experiments."[12] In other words, scientific research is not random. It is guided by an accumulated body of knowledge, the informed curiosity of researchers, prevailing scientific theories, and the constraints of the scientific method. Scientists interested in a particular question or problem must first determine the current state of knowledge about it before conducting any experiments. Accordingly they spend considerable time reading journals, monographs, books, and electronically stored material to ascertain the state of current knowledge in their areas of interest. Then, to approach their task systematically and to communicate effectively to others, they carefully attempt to define the problem they will focus their attention on. This task requires precise nomenclature for facilitating clear and unambiguous communication. Many of the key terms and concepts of this nomenclature typically derive from prevailing theories in the various sciences.

The term *nomenclature* refers to a system of standardized names (usually in Latin) used in biology for kinds and groups of kinds of animals and plants.

---

[11]During the time of the emergence of modern science, when science began to yield reliable results, philosophers and scientists alike recognized that both elements were necessary. They did not agree, however, on exactly how the two elements contribute to the formation of scientific knowledge. Indeed, theorists today still have reached no firm consensus on this issue.

[12]Stephen Toulmin, *The Philosophy of Science, An Introduction* (New York: Harper & Row Publishers, 1960), 66.

After considering what is known about the problem under investigation and after clarifying the precise question to be investigated, scientists construct a tentative explanation called a *hypothesis*. An acceptable hypothesis satisfies at least five criteria.

Relevance. No hypothesis is ever proposed for its own sake. It is proposed as an explanation for some fact or other. Therefore, to be acceptable, it must be relevant to the fact it is intended to explain. Relevance is determined by logical factors. "[T]he fact in question must be *deducible* from the proposed hypothesis—either from the hypothesis alone or from it together with causal laws that may be presumed to have already been established as highly probable, or from these together with certain assumptions about particular initial conditions."[13]

Testability. The hallmark of a scientific hypothesis (as against an unscientific one) is that it can be tested. The testability criterion means that the possibility exists of making an observation that would tend to confirm or refute the hypothesis. Of course, when we say observation, we do not necessarily mean direct observation. Often the testability criterion can be met only indirectly—as for instance when a hypothesis is articulated in terms of such unobservable entities as electromagnetic waves. In any case, for a hypothesis to qualify as a scientific hypothesis, it must ultimately be connected in some way with the facts of experience.

Compatibility with Previously Well-Established Hypotheses. This criterion is not only difficult to describe but also difficult to satisfy. At a minimum, compatibility means logical compatibility. As they attempt to explain more and more facts of experience, scientists aim at achieving a system of explanatory hypotheses. Of course, such a system is impossible if the hypotheses are logically inconsistent with each other. So at a minimum, any new hypothesis should be compatible with previously well-established hypotheses in the sense of being logically consistent with them. A note of caution is in order here. The task of science is not simply to make new hypotheses conform to old theories. The age of a hypothesis does not determine its truth. Unless this is so, science offers no prospect of making progress in advancing knowledge. The presumption in favor of older hypotheses holds only where they have received extensive confirmation. Where an older hypothesis and a more recent one both have extensive confirmation, and where the two hypotheses are inconsistent with each other, the only hope of a final resolution of the conflict lies with continued empirical testing.

> **"The hallmark of a scientific hypothesis (as against an unscientific one) is that it can be tested."**

---

[13]Irving M. Copi and Carl Cohen, *Introduction to Logic*, 10th ed. (Upper Saddle River, N.J.: Prentice-Hall, 1998), 547.

Explanatory or Predictive Power. The explanatory or predictive power of a hypothesis refers to its ability to support deductions about observable facts. The more observable facts that can be deduced from a hypothesis, the greater is its explanatory or predictive power. This point can be grasped by recalling our earlier references to Kepler, Galileo, and Newton. Newton's hypothesis of universal gravitation together with his three laws of motion had greater predictive and explanatory power than did either Kepler's or Galileo's hypotheses. We draw this conclusion because Newton's hypothesis allowed scientists to explain and predict everything explained and predicted by Kepler and Galileo and much more besides.

Simplicity. This criterion of modern science is directly attributable to the Medieval scholar William of Ockham (see the sidebar on p. 154). In its modern version, Ockham's principle of parsimony—Ockham's razor, as it is often called—says that if two hypotheses are equally relevant to the facts, testable, and compatible with previously well-established hypotheses, then the simpler of the hypotheses should be preferred over the more complex one.[14]

> "Since testing lies at the heart of the scientific method, experimental design is critically important."

When formulated, the hypothesis, or a part of it, is tested experimentally. Since testing lies at the heart of the scientific method, experimental design is critically important. In the simplest and most straightforward experimental design, an adequately controlled experiment must have two subjects: a control subject and an experimental subject. All variables remain the same in both except for one variable that is manipulated in the experimental subject. Scientists then take note of the effect of changing that variable. The best experiments are designed so that changing the one variable will test the hypothesis. If the results of manipulating the chosen variable are inconsistent with the hypothesis, the hypothesis is rejected. It is supported (though not necessarily fully accepted) if the experimental results obtained follow a pattern predicted by it. As a follow-up, scientists typically perform additional experiments to test the validity of a hypothesis.

Before concluding our brief description of scientific method, we must address two additional topics: law of nature and scientific theory.

Law of nature. The expression *law of nature* (or *scientific law* or *experimental law*) is widely used but has no single precise technical definition. Even scientists and philosophers of science have reached no consensus as to its exact usage. However, a few

---

[14]For a discussion of the difficulties associated with the simplicity criterion, see Copi and Cohen, 548–552.

general points can still be made. First, the expression is generally agreed to apply to a broad class of universal statements having to do with events in nature.[15] Thus, as the name suggests, laws of nature are about natural phenomena, not about logical or mathematical phenomena. Second, a law of nature articulates some systematic order underlying natural events. In other words, a law of nature articulates a pattern in what might otherwise seem like unrelated events. Third, a law of nature expresses a pattern that extends beyond the immediate data of a series of experiments; it formulates something universal. Finally, a law of nature is resilient. What this means can best be explained by noting that laws of nature often get incorporated into the fabric of a comprehensive theory. But also when this happens, they do not necessarily lose the uniqueness or distinctiveness of their explanatory and predictive power. They thus often survive the demise of the larger theory and find a place within the fabric of the successor theory. In this sense, then, they may be said to be resilient. By way of illustration, the twentieth century has seen the demise of the general Newtonian theory of the universe. At the same time, Newton's three laws of motion are still commonly accepted as valid for most areas of physics.

> **"The term *theory* is often misunderstood by people who have little direct acquaintance with science."**

Theory. The term *theory* is often misunderstood by people who have little direct acquaintance with science. For instance, it is a common misconception among nonspecialists outside the scientific community that a theory is simply a fanciful piece of speculation, a novel idea, or someone's unsupported guess. Actually, in scientific circles, to say that an explanation has reached the status of a theory is to say something quite significant about it. In science, a theory possesses much broader explanatory and predictive power than either a hypothesis or a law of nature. A scientific theory provides a broad perspective on the natural world that does far more than describe how it works. Hypotheses and laws can usually be articulated in a single proposition or mathematical formula. Theories, by contrast, are usually expressed in several related statements that are more general and inclusive. The most comprehensive scientific theories bring together

---

[15]Nineteenth century scientists commonly thought that nature was governed by "law." Their conception of law led them to believe that their principle task as scientists was to "discover" and record all the "laws of nature." Hundreds of these laws can be found in print from the period. Today, most valid "laws" are expressed as "principles" or "rules," and scientists no longer believe that they can arrive at a complete and satisfying account of natural phenomena simply by accumulating more and more "laws."

a wide variety of experimental laws and disparate data into a coherent whole. They can do this because they are essentially explanatory models (often mathematical) for connecting laws of nature to each other and to vast amounts of data including previously unexplained data. Scientific theories are certainly subject to confirming or disconfirming empirical evidence. But because they are essentially explanatory models that are expected to relate to a wide variety of phenomena, they are also judged on the basis of their comprehensiveness, overall coherence, and predictive power.

Basic Assumptions Underlying Science

An assumption is something taken for granted in a discussion, argument, or field of inquiry. Since assumptions form the beginning points of reasoning in any discipline, they are not usually the objects of proof. However, their presence is important, for they affect both the manner in which activities in a discipline are carried out and the conclusions that are reached. Sometimes they actually determine outcomes of thought processes in a discipline. The important assumptions that underlie natural science are those related to the method of science itself. These assumptions are common to all scientists, whether Christian or non-Christian. Here we briefly mention three of the most important assumptions underlying scientific method.

> "The important assumptions that underlie natural science are those related to the method of science itself."

Order in nature. Application of the scientific method assumes that things in the universe behave in an orderly way. Order shows itself in patterns and regularities that can be discovered. If the assumption of order in nature is correct, nature will be intelligible and subject to investigation. If it is incorrect, the scientific enterprise collapses.

Uniformity in nature. The assumption of uniformity means that laws of nature are valid over the entire universe in space and time. For instance, we assume that instruments sent deep into outer space, far beyond our familiar surroundings on earth, will operate and send reliable data back to us because our principles of physics and chemistry will be the same wherever we send them. As with the assumption of order in nature, the assumption of uniformity cannot be established conclusively. Nevertheless it would be impossible to conduct meaningful studies, if the fundamental nature of the universe varied from place to place.

Singularity of causes. It is a fundamental assumption in the study of nature that events do not just occur spontaneously, but happen only under certain conditions. One type of condition is called a *necessary condition:* a circumstance in whose absence the event cannot occur. Oxygen is a necessary condition for combustion, since in the absence of oxygen there can be no combustion. Another type of condition is called a *sufficient condition:* a circumstance in whose presence a certain event must occur. Oxygen alone is not a sufficient condition for combustion to occur. However, when virtually any substance is raised to a certain threshold temperature in the presence of oxygen, combustion (or another form of oxidation) will occur.[16] Thus, the substance reaching the threshold temperature in the presence of oxygen constitutes the sufficient condition for combustion of that substance. Clearly, it is possible for there to be several, even many, necessary conditions for the occurrence of an event. Moreover, all these necessary conditions must be included in the sufficient condition for the event. But what does all this tell us about the causes and effects in nature? Simply this: If we identify cause with sufficient condition, and if we regard the sufficient condition for an event as the conjunction of all the necessary conditions for that event, then we are led to the conclusion that there is a unique cause for every effect. Uniqueness, of course, does not imply simplicity. The cause may be quite complex and involve numerous factors. Even so, the prevailing assumption among scientists is that only a single set of such factors exists that can produce the effect in question.

> **"It is a popular misconception that a given event could have resulted from any number of alternative causes."**

The assumption of the singularity of causes seems counterintuitive to many. Indeed, it is a popular misconception that a given event could have resulted from any number of alternative causes. The man's death, we speculate, might have resulted from poisoning, a heart attack, an auto accident, a gunshot wound. So why assume a single cause? Because, scientists will say, if we subject an effect (the man's death, say) to careful scrutiny, and if we specify that effect precisely, the seeming plurality of causes will evaporate and we will find the single cause.

The Scope and Limits of Natural Science

Making the case that modern science has affected us in many profound, far reaching, and beneficial ways is easy to do. To begin with, since its birth in the Renaissance, it has introduced a degree of precision and focus in human knowledge unknown in the Classical and Medieval periods. Specifically, it has afforded us the capacity to answer certain kinds of questions with a high degree of probability. By way of simple illustration, we can point to the way scientists have steadily built a case since the

---

[16]There are exceptions to this general rule. Some substances are inert toward reaction with oxygen.

late 1950s that tobacco use is harmful to the user. Used as directed, it can be lethal. When the first report of the Surgeon General was released in the early 1960s, tobacco industry representatives insisted that the evidence against tobacco was scant and equivocal.[17] But continued scientific research over several decades has taken the debate far beyond the realm of surmise and speculation. Today even the tobacco industry's most ardent spokespersons do not dispute the scientific conclusions about the harmful effects of tobacco on its users.

Modern science has also permitted and facilitated applications that once could hardly have been dreamed of. The science fiction of the 1940s and 1950s seems today to be quaint and humorously primitive compared to today's actual applications. Advances in computer technology, ease and safety of travel, enhanced worldwide communication networks, control and eradication of many communicable diseases, improvements in medical and pharmacological products that extend life and improve its quality—these and myriad other examples amply demonstrate the power of modern science to affect our lives through the specific knowledge and technology it makes possible.

The power of modern science is directly related to the strict application of its method, its quantitative approach to nature, and its narrow focus on the processes of efficient (mechanical) causes of events in nature. But these sources of its power also imply certain notable limitations. We shall briefly mention three of them here. They all relate to science's inability to provide ultimate direction for its own activities.

The first limitation may be gotten at by considering the history of science. It is tempting to view the history of modern science as producing a coherent, interconnected, and steadily expanding body of knowledge. Our earlier description of developments in science since the Renaissance may even implicitly encourage this picture. Unfortunately, the picture is flawed and misleading. What passes under the name of progress in science actually discloses a major limitation of science. This limitation is captured succinctly in the old saying that insight is earned but not steered. Although there is a logic and a set of procedures for testing scientific hypotheses, none exists for conceiving them.[18] Francis Bacon's confidently expressed view in the early seventeenth century that progress in science could be almost a mechanical process is seriously misleading. When we review

---

[17]Investigations in the mid-1990s by news organizations and congressional committees indicate that tobacco industry managers actually already had strong evidence of the health hazards of their products several decades earlier. Their public statements during the 50s, 60s, 70s, and 80s in many cases lacked candor or were simply false.

[18]Charles E. Hummel, *The Galileo Connection, Resolving Conflicts Between Science & The Bible* (Downers Grove, Ill: InterVarsity Press, 1986), 155.

the historical record, we discover rather quickly that scientific discoveries—great and small alike—are not the product of any single formulaic approach. Rather, they typically emerged through a process in which persons of perceptive judgment fit together a possible explanation and the data, made revisions and modifications where necessary, and developed tests to confirm (or disconfirm) their hypotheses. Kepler intently scrutinized Tycho Brahe's observations for nearly five years before he finally detected the form of an ellipse in his diagram.[19] Only after thirty-four years of tireless research did Galileo feel confident in his hypothesis about constant acceleration.

A second limitation is related to the first but shows itself most prominently in the way major changes in scientific disciplines occur. The limitation in question may be described as a kind of scientific myopia or tunnel vision that befalls a community of scientists who conduct their research within the framework of

Albert Einstein

Albert Einstein (1879–1955), a German born and naturalized American citizen (1940), is recognized as one of the greatest theoretical physicists of all time. In 1905 he wrote a paper in which he developed his special theory of relativity, which dealt with systems or observers in uniform (unaccelerated) motion with respect to one another. In 1911 he asserted the equality of gravitation and inertia, and in 1916 he formulated a general theory of relativity that included gravitation as a determiner of the curvature of a space-time continuum. He also made important contributions to modern quantum theory. For his work in theoretical physics, notably on the photoelectric effect, Einstein was awarded the 1921 Nobel Prize in physics.

By 1914 Einstein came to hold the position of professor of physics and director of theoretical physics at the Kaiser Wilhelm Institute in Berlin. Because he was Jewish, the antisemitic Nazi government of Germany confiscated his property and revoked his German citizenship in 1934. From 1933 until his death in 1955, he held a post at the Institute for Advanced Study in Princeton. His time at Princeton was devoted largely to developing a unified field theory, according to which he hoped to explain gravitation and electromagnetism with one set of laws. He was unsuccessful in this attempt, and many prominent physicists today believe such a task cannot be accomplished in principle.

---

[19]Norwood Hanson, *Patterns of Discovery* (Cambridge: Cambridge University Press, 1961), 72–84.

commonly held models for solving problems in their discipline. Of course, at one level (the level of everyday operations) shared assumptions and shared problem solving techniques are beneficial, even necessary, if scientists are to make progress in their work. But at another (global) level, they may also pose limitations and restriction on the community of scientists who live and work by them. For instance, they may impose a narrow view of the problem or disguise possible solutions to the problem. In such a case, progress in the discipline may depend on someone from outside the discipline challenging the commonly held assumptions and offering a radically different model for continuing research in the field.

> **"The salient point here is that scientific method does not—indeed, cannot—determine the ends of human action."**

In a now classic work entitled *The Structure of Scientific Revolution*, Thomas Kuhn has described radical departures from traditional scientific models as scientific revolutions.[20] The models themselves (including assumptions, laws, theory, application, and instrumentation) he calls *paradigms*. The migration or transition from a time-honored model to a new model he calls a *paradigm shift*. The transition from Aristotelian physics to Newtonian physics at the outset of the Modern period would count as a paradigm shift, as would the twentieth century change from Newtonian physics to Albert Einstein's relativity theory.

The radical transition from an accepted model in favor of a new model—what Kuhn calls a scientific revolution—can neither be predicted nor planned. This inability to predict or plan shows that scientific discovery, and scientific progress in general, is not as orderly, refined, or linear a process as the uninitiated might suppose. And the fact that discovery and progress are not gradual and predictable but fitful, and sometimes arbitrary and accidental, exposes one of the major limitations on the scientific method.

The first and second limitations point to a third limitation: Scientific method can neither guarantee progress toward a complete and comprehensive body of scientific knowledge, nor properly address certain types of questions.[21] Specifically, modern scientific method lacks the capacity to evaluate or explain what issues ought to be addressed. In this sense, modern science does not count as a worldview—at least in the densely textured sense described in chapter one. For instance, it expresses

---

[20]Thomas Kuhn, *The Structure of Scientific Revolutions*, 2d ed. enl. (Chicago: University of Chicago Press, 1970).

[21]Del Ratzsch, *Philosophy of Science, The Natural Sciences in a Christian Perspective* (Downers Grove, Ill: InterVarsity Press, 1986), 97–105.

no clear and overarching ideology. It therefore cannot tell us what is worthy of attention, cannot tell us what we should aspire to or what we should hope for, and cannot tell us what finally matters in life.

Scientific method, for example, cannot tell us what kinds of technology to develop, nor can it tell us how to apply the technology that has already been developed. I walk on two artificial legs. The shanks and sockets of my artificial legs are made of a light and technically sophisticated carbon-graphite material developed by chemists. I would be unable to walk as I do now if I had lived in an earlier century with decidedly lower levels of technology. Naturally, I am grateful that advances in applied science have improved the quality of my personal life. But the scientific method itself did not dictate the application of knowledge toward this beneficial end. People with a larger vision of what is both possible and important developed the products that have improved my life. Directed by different motives and aims, they might just as well have produced technological devices antithetical to my interests or anyone else's. The salient point here is that scientific method does not—indeed, cannot—determine the ends of human action. Such ends are largely determined by the worldviews human beings, including scientists, subscribe to.

More generally, scientific method cannot tell us what kinds of social policies ought to be enacted. In the 1960s, sociologist George Lundberg asked this fundamental question: *Can science save us?*[22] His own answer to the question was that scientific

*S*cientism

The belief that we can reach ultimate truth by means of the scientific method is known as *scientism* or *scientific imperialism.* Scientism asserts that science is the primary model of rationality. Many advocates of scientism are openly hostile toward religion in general and Christianity in particular.

For additional treatment of scientism, see the following works:

J. P. Moreland, *Christianity and the Nature of Science* (Grand Rapids: Baker Book House, 1989), 103–104.

David N. Livingstone, "Farewell to Arms: Reflections on the Encounter Between Science and Faith," in *Christian Faith & Practice in the Modern World*, ed. Mark A. Noll and David F. Wells (Grand Rapids: William B. Eerdmans Publishing Co., 1988), 239–262.

Mary Midgley, "Can Science Save Its Soul?" *New Scientist*, 135 (1992), 24–27.

---

[22]George A. Lundberg, *Can Science Save Us?* 2d ed. (New York: David McKay Company, 1961).

> "The function of setting up goals and passing statements of value transcends the domain of science."
>
> *—Albert Einstein*

method, applied to all social problems, represents our best hope of achieving the better society we all desire. At the time of publication, one commentator allowed that Lundberg had made the strongest case he had ever seen yet for believing that science can guide the thinking and policy-framing of legislators, officials, and others in high office. Despite the optimism of the period in which the book was published, there is little evidence today that anything approaching Lundberg's vision is possible.[23]

The larger insight to be inferred from the three limitations on scientific method discussed here is that science is not self-directed. It requires the superintendence of an overarching perspective, or frame of reference. This kind of larger perspective, as we learned from chapter one, is a *worldview*. The scientific method itself is not a worldview. However, employing it (or the knowledge acquired through it or the applications gained from such knowledge) toward particular ends, or goals, inevitably presupposes a worldview.

Conclusion

We have come full circle to the reflections and questions set forth at the outset of this chapter. We have reviewed some of the notable touch points in the history of science from its beginnings in ancient Greece to the emergence of modern scientific method during the Renaissance and early Modern period. We also described modern scientific method and set forth some of the key assumptions underlying the current practice of the empirical sciences. Finally, we examined the scope and limits of science. What have we learned that bears on the centuries-old appearance of a conflict between the practice of modern empirical science and the life of faith? And what have we learned that bears on my friend's desire to answer God's call on his life by embarking on a career as a scientist?

The history of science shows us that Classical and Medieval science were teleological in orientation. They were dominated by an interest in the purposes of natural objects and events. But purposes are not necessarily readily apparent in natural phenomena, and thinkers whose investigations are oriented toward finding such purposes run the risk of imposing their own assumptions and expectations on the things they investigate. During the Classical and Medieval periods the concern to discover purposes had the practical effect of impeding scientific discovery by imposing certain philosophical and theological

---

[23]In a similar vein, Peter Atkins argued that we can obtain all truth and knowledge by means of the scientific method. He raises the fundamental question in the title of one of his publications: "Will Science Ever Fail?" *New Scientist* 135 (1833): 321–35, 1992. Atkins asserts that there are no limits to gaining knowledge by the use of reason and the scientific method. Atkins's thesis, like Lundberg's before him, seems overly optimistic.

assumptions on the processes of discovery. Investigations tended to be based on reasoning from first principles (whose sources were philosophical and theological) rather than on mathematical analysis of empirical data.

The European thinkers and practitioners who in the Renaissance and early Modern period began to articulate the modern method of science were mostly persons of faith. But they recognized that progress in the empirical sciences required them to remove all talk of teleology from their investigations. Accordingly, they sought to limit themselves to measurements of quantities like velocity, mass, and time; calculations based on observations and experiments; and descriptions in generalized mathematical formulas. Instead of looking for final causes, they restricted their inquiries to efficient (mechanical) causes.

For people like Newton, the new emphasis on formulating in mathematical terms the laws that describe the mechanisms of nature did not imply a complete rejection of teleology, only a rejection of its application in the empirical investigation of nature. Nor for them did the new emphasis on science imply that science could answer every question. Science, in their estimation, represented one perspective on natural phenomena. They claimed that it offered neither the only nor the entire explanation of nature, but simply one mode of explanation (albeit an important one). In this sense, their claims for science remained relatively modest.

Some of Newton's successors in the eighteenth century and later were less guarded. They not only followed Newton in expunging teleological explanations from empirical investigations but went beyond him in expunging them from all worldview considerations. They inferred that if the scientific method cannot discover purposes, then purposes must not exist (except perhaps in the minds of human beings). In short, they merged their views regarding the practice of empirical science with a completely naturalistic and mechanistic worldview. As should be evident from our discussion so far, this merger is neither necessary for science nor inevitable from a larger philosophical point of view.

Here we must turn once again to my friend's Christian acquaintances who urged him to abandon his plans to seek a career in science. In a way, they were making the same logical move as the eighteenth century naturalists: Because the method of empirical science does not allow us to investigate purposes, these Christians inferred that it necessarily and inevitably leads to a naturalistic worldview. And if the practice of science leads one toward naturalism, the reasoning goes, then surely Christians should steer clear of it. But this move to merge empirical science and the larger philosophical position of naturalism is no more warranted for Christians today than it was for naturalists in the eighteenth century.

When we detach empirical science from a naturalistic world-view, we have no reason to regard scientific research any differently than we do work in any other career-calling. One must always be on guard for the subtle ways one's worldview and personal integrity might be compromised. And though science cannot develop or verify moral principles, moral considerations can never be sidestepped by the practicing scientist, because moral issues pervade every career and every human endeavor. Having said this, we have no reason to regard the practice of science as less noble than any other calling. "The earth is the Lord's and the fullness thereof," and we are His children. If He can call some of us to preach the gospel; to build homes, schools, houses of worship; to answer to the needs of the poor; to write great literature, poetry, and music, then surely he can call others of us to study His creation.

> **"Though science cannot develop or verify moral principles, moral considerations can never be sidestepped by the practicing scientist."**

But, also, from a moral point of view based on Scripture, the study of nature seems a legitimate pursuit for the Christian. Perhaps in the larger sense we can even regard the study of nature as something of an ethical requirement for any Christian in today's world. Genesis 1:26–30 is often referred to as the *cultural mandate* to exercise dominion over the earth and thereby to be faithful to the Creator in whose image we are created.[24] From a moral point of view, the exercise of dominion in all its ramifications requires stewardship. (See Volf's treatment of this issue in chapter 6.) Given the ecological issues that face us in a fragile environment and given the pressing medical and nutritional needs of so many people around the world today, stewardship surely requires that we understand the natural world over which we are to exercise dominion. If this is so, we should hardly be surprised that some Christians would be called to careers as research scientists or that every Christian bears some responsibility to acquire at least a basic scientific understanding of the natural world we humans inhabit.[25]

---

[24]Richard T. Wright, *Biology Through the Eyes of Faith* (San Francisco: Harper and Row, 1989), 169.

[25]Michael Palmer assisted in the organization and development of this chapter. Gary Liddle, Associate Professor of Biblical Studies at Evangel University, and Turner Collins, Professor of Biology at Evangel University, read and commented on the text.

Review and Discussion Questions

1. Why is the thinking of ancient Greek philosophers in the area of natural science significant? Why do students still study it today?

2. In what ways did the thinking of Aristotle dominate natural science in Europe during the Middle Ages?

3. What factors or events caused major changes in European thinking about natural science?

4. In what order have the various disciplines that are concerned with physical reality developed up to the present time? Why did they follow that sequence of development? Was it due to the nature of the disciplines themselves or to other factors?

5. What did early modern scientists believe about the earth and the universe? How did their belief in God and the Scriptures affect their work?

6. Why were the use of observation and experimentation by researchers so important in forming the basis of modern science?

7. Why were Galileo, Bacon, and Newton so important in the development of the empirical sciences?

8. How did the intellectual climate of the Enlightenment of the eighteenth century affect natural science? In what ways does the thinking that was so dominant during that century still affect natural science today? Explain?

9. What is the scientific method? What implications do Thomas Kuhn's insights about scientific revolutions and paradigms have for our understanding of the scientific method?

10. Develop an argument for or against the following statement: Given time and sufficient research, the empirical sciences can attain a complete explanation of all aspects of reality.

11. What is an assumption? What are some of the assumptions of natural science?

12. Develop an argument for or against the following statement: The basic assumptions of natural science are in conflict with some of the basic assumptions of Christianity.

Extended Projects for Reflection

1. Galileo was censured by Church authorities and forced to renounce some of his scientific conclusions. What lessons for today's Christians can be gleaned from the confrontation between Galileo and those who censured him? Before you respond to this topic it may be wise to do some library research and review the historical record of the events in Galileo's day.

2. In the last part of this chapter, the author refers to something called the *cultural mandate.* Explain this mandate in more detail and develop more of its implications for a Christian view of the natural sciences.

3. Pick one of the following topics and explain how a Christian might deal with it in light of considerations developed

in this chapter: miracles, the theory of evolution, the human soul, the clear-cutting of tropical forests.

Selected Bibliography

Barbour, Ian G. *Religion in an Age of Science.* The Gifford Lectures 1989–1991, vol. 1. San Francisco: Harper and Row Publishers, 1990. This is a highly scholarly treatment of theology and science. Evangelicals may disagree with some of his ideas, but it is a thoughtful treatment of the subject.

Behe, Michael J. *Darwin's Black Box*: *The Biochemical Challenge to Evolution.* New York: Free Press, 1996. This work, written by a biochemist, argues that certain biochemical systems are irreducibly complex and therefore could not have arisen gradually in a Neo-Darwinian manner. Behe argues that these irreducibly complex systems indicate intelligent design and, by implication, a Designer.

Clark, Gordon H. "The Limits and Uses of Science." In *Horizons of Science: Christian Scholars Speak Out*, ed. Carl F. H. Henry. New York: Harper and Row Publishers, 1988. This is noteworthy as a work of a Christian philosopher.

Clouser, Roy A. *The Myth of Religious Neutrality.* Notre Dame: University of Notre Dame Press, 1991. This is an interesting work that considers several academic activities, including mathematics and physics. Clouser concludes that all human thinking is influenced by religious assumptions and understanding, whether or not they are acknowledged.

Dawkins, Richard. *The Blind Watchmaker.* New York: Norton Publishers, 1986. Dawkins argues against any possibility of design in nature. He is strongly opposed to any idea of creation or design.

Kuhn, Thomas. *The Structure of Scientific Revolutions*, 2d ed., enl. Chicago: University of Chicago Press, 1970. This book is now considered a classic in philosophy of science.

Lindberg, David C., and Ronald L. Numbers, eds. *God and Nature, Historical Essays on the Encounter between Christianity and Science.* Berkeley, Calif.: University of California Press, 1986.

Moreland, J. P. *Christianity and the Nature of Science.* Grand Rapids: Baker Book House, 1989. An excellent and worthwhile work on the philosophy of science written by an evangelical.

Pearcey, Nancy R., and Charles B. Thaxton. *The Soul of Science: Christian Faith and Natural Philosophy.* Wheaton, Ill.: Crossway Books, 1994. This is an excellent work, and is in some ways perhaps the best of this list. It is well written and can be readily understood with some concentration. It considers mathematics, physical science, and biology.

Ratzsch, Del. *Philosophy of Science: The Natural Sciences in Christian Perspective*. Downers Grove, Ill.: InterVarsity Press, 1986. A useful work that considers science from a Christian viewpoint.

Rothschild, Richard C. *The Emerging Religion of Science*. New York: Praeger Publishers, 1989. This is a work every Christian must profoundly disagree with, but it is worth reading because it represents the thinking of someone well trained in physical science who believes that there is no ultimate reality beyond physical phenomena.

Wright, Richard T. *Biology through the Eyes of Faith*. New York: HarperSan Francisco, 1989. Published for the Christian College Coalition (now known as the Coalition for Christian Colleges and Universities). The work represents a notable effort to address the Christian biology student's need to align science and faith.

5

A Perspective on Human Nature

Billie Davis

W hat makes real people?"

"What's the matter with you?" my dad asked in response to my question. "What kind of notion is that—real people?"

"People that live in houses," I tried to explain. "People that stay together in towns."

I had expressed in a child's artless way the basic human puzzle.

My family was among the original American homeless, now called migrant workers. I was born in the hopyards of Oregon, and with the seasons and years we followed the fruit and vegetable crops over routes later known as "migrant streams." We lived in tents at the edges of fields, or in rows of one-room shacks provided by the growers, or sometimes in strictly supervised government camps. The eldest child, living in these cramped confines, I knew the most intimate details of family life and economy. I watched the children being born, usually without outside attendants. There were eight besides me, and two of them died before my eyes.

I knew all about the Great Depression; that the government was full of graft; that rich people work the poor to death and then kick them in the teeth; and that a poor man's got no chance. Sometimes Dad said he was just fed up with doing the rich man's dirty work, so we made willow baskets and paper flowers to sell. The earliest thing I can remember is selling baskets

The Concept of Marginality

While the need to belong in association with others is basic to human nature, some persons experience social conditions that make them feel separated from any group. To describe this type of alienation, Robert Park (1864–1944) contributed the term *marginal man*. Park was a key figure in the Chicago school of sociology and coauthor, with Ernest W. Burgess, of the first significant sociology textbook, *An Introduction to the Science of Sociology*, 1921. In accordance with his lifelong interest in race relations, he took a position at Fisk, a Black university. His observations of intercultural situations led him to characterize as *marginal* those persons whose experiences kept them from adjusting completely to any social group. Such persons find themselves always on the "margins" rather than comfortably integrated. They can feel like strangers everywhere. The positive aspect of being marginal is that they can observe their own and other groups with considerable objectivity. Because of personal detachment, they can learn to accept differences, develop wide appreciations, and make mature adjustments. Some Christian scholars have compared this to "being in the world and yet not of it." Although Christians have a strong sense of belonging in the body of Christ (the Church universal), they must maintain a critical detachment from social values that are constantly changing.

The concept of marginality is most fully developed by one of Park's students, Everett Stonequist, in *The Marginal Man* (New York: Russell & Russell, Inc., 1961).

and flowers. Dad told me to go up one side of a street and back down the other throughout a town, knocking at every door and entering every place of business, saying, "Would you like to buy a basket? They are 25 cents apiece."

Basket peddling made me conscious of the life pattern in a settled community and the contrast between this and my own lifestyle, dress, language, and total condition. I heard people call us "gypsies," "migratory workers," "fruit tramps," "farm labor," "transients," and "Okies." The separation was so obvious that I began to conceive of the townsfolk as *real people*. Peddling through the streets I became aware of special buildings and facilities in the town pattern. Gradually I learned of a life where there were schools, churches, libraries, and parks, and began to understand that some were provided through community cooperation.

> **"My way of life caused me to have what students of society describe as a marginal experience."**

I asked "What makes real people?" because I had sensed, probably more deeply and quickly than most children, the vital concepts of being and belonging. My way of life caused me to have what students of society describe as a marginal experience. I moved in various worlds and could see contrasts that were hidden to those whose lives were more ordered and predictable. I wondered why I was different from the town kids and how people joined together in towns. I was driven to voice as a guileless minor what philosophers and theologians have always pondered: Why am I like I am? Who am I? Why am I here? Do I *belong* anywhere? How do I relate to others? What is a *person*? Out of attempts to answer questions like these grew the studies, discoveries, and theories of psychology and sociology.

What Does It Mean to Be Human?

As we have seen, an account of or perspective on human nature is an element in every *worldview*. It may be the most significant element to us personally, because what we believe about human nature substantially controls how we treat people and what we expect of them. Our success and happiness in friendship, school, career, marriage, parenthood, and even religion depend to a great extent on what we believe about ourselves and others.

Although we learn much from personal experience and the media, most of our formal knowledge about human nature and behavior comes from the fields of psychology and sociology. The purpose of this chapter is to help you understand and evaluate scholarly and popular ideas in the light of Christian truth. Practical outcomes should be, first, self knowledge that gives you confidence and control in your personal life and, second, appreciations and insights that enhance all your social relationships.

In the academic world and in everyday living, the nature of the human race is a key question. Psychology and sociology base their claim to be sciences on the assumption that elements of human nature can be isolated, like elements in chemistry, through observation and experimentation. But no method can be applied to human nature without first assuming something about it. That is why the histories of these disciplines seem to go in a circle. Initially, scholars tried to break away from philosophical and theological approaches so they could study humans as objects of scientific investigation. Eventually, many of them found they could not avoid the fact that the person is a whole being, having inner qualities that precise scientific theories could not fully explain. We see then why it is especially important to approach psychology and sociology with a Christian worldview: These disciplines treat the subjects of personhood, human behavior, and relationships, for which Scripture is the first and highest authority.

Psychological Perspectives

Psychology may be one of earth's most important ideas, yet the precise meaning of the term as it applies to the discipline is elusive. I first heard the word from my high school social studies teacher in 1938. He was big on definitions. "*Psyche,*" he explained, "comes from a Greek word that started out meaning 'breath,' and developed to 'soul' and 'spirit.' In English we use it to mean 'mind.' *Logy* also comes from the Greek, 'word' or 'speech.' It carries the idea of 'discourse,' 'expression,' and has come to include 'study' and 'science.' The term *psychology*, meaning 'science of the mind,' was first recorded in 1693 and began to be widely accepted in the 1830s."

My first college professor used the term *adjustment* to define psychology. He said it is most concerned with how individuals respond to various stimuli. Modern dictionaries define *psychology* as "The science that deals with mental processes and behavior."[1] Most recent textbooks refer to the lack of a single, generally accepted definition of psychology, and go on to list numerous branches and specialties. However, the two main concepts, mental processes and behavior, indicate the two main concerns of psychologists. The first is related to philosophy and deals with reasoning, thinking, feeling, and perceiving. The second is related to physiology and studies behavior as a function of the nervous system.

The Important Question of Methodology

Psychology began with questions about people and then quickly developed into questions about how to study people.

---

[1]*American Heritage Dictionary of the English Language*, 3d ed., s.v. "psychology."

Throughout recorded history people have wondered about relationships between mind and body, thinking and feeling. Theology and philosophy were the sources of knowledge and theories. Psychology as a separate study or science eventually developed from the same kind of human self-consciousness that had led to philosophical speculation. Thinkers proposed theories and suggested explanations about consciousness, reason, perception, memory, and the motives that determine behavior. Inevitably someone would ask, How can we really know? What is the best way to find the answers to our questions?

In the late eighteenth and nineteenth centuries, when the world was becoming excited about advances in natural science, the way seemed clear. Human phenomena could be observed and analyzed just as other aspects of nature. Social thinkers decided that philosophers' and theologians' questions must be restated in order to get away from religion.[2] Scholars should find a different basis for thinking about the human mind and behavior. Psychology should be an independent science. Historians generally give credit to a German philosopher, Johann Friedrich Herbart (1776–1841), for directing subsequent psychologists toward an empirical, rather than philosophical, approach to the study of psychological concerns. That is, he proposed that direct experience and objective observation were better methods for psychology than trying to analyze thoughts and feelings. Wilhelm Wundt (1832–1920), who established the first laboratory for experiments, was trained as a physician. His book *Principles of Physiological Psychology*, published in 1873, contributed much to establishing psychology as a distinct science.

But with its roots in philosophy and physiology, psychology had a problem. Certain philosophers had already convinced many scholars of dualistic theories of human nature.

Johann Friedrich Herbart

Johann Friedrich Herbart (1776–1841) was a German philosopher. Some scholars call him "father of psychology" because he gave the studies a name and declared they should be developed as a true science. Others say he should be called the "grandfather of psychology" because he did nothing but propose the idea on which others based research that created an independent science of psychology. His writings were not based on empirical investigation, but were what modern scientists call armchair speculation. In two books he argued for the separation of psychology from other disciplines: *A Textbook of Psychology* and *Psychology as a Science*.

---

[2] Gary R. Collins, *The Rebuilding of Psychology* (Wheaton, Ill.: Tyndale House Publishers, 1976), 137.

Most influential was René Descartes's thesis that a human being represents a union between a psychological mind and a mechanical body.[3] His dualistic thinking opened the way for three major conceptions: (1) Psychologists who considered psychology a mental science believed knowledge could be gained by introspection. (2) Others declared that to make psychology a true science only objective data, that is, observable sensory phenomena, should be used. They favored observing the behavior not only of adult humans but of lower animals and infants, incapable of self observation. Observing behavior, they contended, is the best way to understand the nature and processes of the mind. (3) Still others maintained that psychology should be a study of both mind and behavior. This school has never fully agreed on one scientific system, but today the most frequently cited definition of psychology includes both mental processes and behavior.

Psychology's history, therefore, is a story of attempts to reconcile rigid prescriptions of scientific investigation with the dynamics of humanity. One historian specifically com-

Wilhelm Wundt

Wilhelm Wundt (1832–1920) was a German scholar, son of a Lutheran pastor. Wundt studied medicine, and taught physiology at the University of Heidelberg. While there his interest turned to psychology, and he established a private laboratory for experiments. In 1879, as a professor of philosophy and psychology at the University of Leipzig, he developed the first university laboratory. His interest went beyond experimental investigations to include major studies regarding the influence of culture on the human mind. Wundt is more truly the father of psychology because his work became the model for the discipline. Students from all over the world went to Leipzig to learn about the new science. Many of them took his ideas and methods to their countries where they became the foundation on which psychology would develop.

Wundt published *Principles of Physiological Psychology* in 1873. His most ambitious work is a ten-volume treatment of cultural, or *folk*, psychology, *Volkerpsychologie*. The last volume was published in 1920. Translations of Wundt's works include *An Introduction to Psychology* (Rudolf Pintner, trans.), New York: Arno Press, and *Elements of Folk Psychology*, New York: Macmillan.

---

[3]Howard H. Kendler, *Historical Foundations of Modern Psychology* (Chicago: The Dorsey Press, 1987), 6–13. See also René Descartes, *Meditations on First Philosophy*, Meditation Two.

plains that the history of theoretical development is difficult because the early founders of psychology insisted on dealing with such topics as the meaning and purpose of human existence![4] His remark gives us a clue to how questions of methodology can lead to some unchristian views of human nature, leading to antagonism between psychology and religion. A brief examination of the major branches of psychology will help us to understand better how theories and methods always involve assumptions about human nature.

René Descartes

René Descartes (1596–1650), philosopher and man of letters, is generally regarded as the father of the Modern period (17th–19th centuries) in the Western intellectual tradition. He was born in La Haye (now called Descartes) in the region of Touraine in France. His early education, which he was quite proud of, took place at the Jesuit college at La Fléche in the region of Anjou. Later, in 1616, he completed a law degree at the University of Piotiers. Not satisfied with a law career, Descartes decided to travel. This decision led him to join the Dutch army in 1618. One day in November 1619, while on a military tour of Germany, he sat alone in a small stove-heated room reflecting on a new philosophical system that would unify all branches of learning and give them the certainty of mathematics. That night he had three dreams, which he said inspired him to construct this new system of knowledge and which seem to have remained an abiding motivation for all his later philosophical, scientific, and mathematical work. As Descartes's reputation grew over the years he was invited by Queen Christina of Sweden to come to Stockholm to tutor her in philosophy. After much hesitation, he reluctantly accepted the invitation in the fall of 1649. The harsh winter of 1649–1650, combined with the rigorous schedule imposed on him by the queen (e.g., philosophy lessons at five o'clock in the morning), adversely affected his health. In February 1650 he contracted pneumonia and died.

Given the relative brevity of his life, Descartes's body of writing is quite impressive. He wrote on subjects ranging from mathematics to optics to physics and philosophy. Even more impressive than the amount of writing he generated is the influence he had on later philosophers and the general public. His most famous writings are two philosophical works: *Discourse on the Method of Rightly Conducting One's Reason and Seeking the Truth in the Sciences* (1637) and *Meditations on First Philosophy in Which Are Demonstrated the Existence of God and the Immortality of the Soul* (1640).

---

[4]Ibid., 20.

EXPERIMENTAL PSYCHOLOGY

Early psychologists who considered psychology a science of the mind developed a technique for studying conscious awareness. Subjects were asked to describe what they experienced in various laboratory situations. They called the method *introspection*. Some scholars thought the results of such experiments were unreliable. Sigmund Freud was one who claimed it was not possible for a person to accurately observe his or her own mental life. He introduced to psychology the concept of the unconscious. The main proposition of his theory is that persons may be completely unaware of forces that control their thoughts, feelings, and actions.

Other early leaders in the field tried to turn psychology away from studies of inner consciousness. The school known as *behaviorism* developed from attempts to make psychology a study of observable behavior. Terms like *mind* and *will* were eliminated because they could not be observed. They were considered mental states that must be inferred from how people act. Behaviorism assumes that people can be studied as objects in a strictly empirical manner. People are organisms that

Sigmund Freud

Sigmund Freud (1856–1939) was born in Freiburg, Moravia (in the Austria-Hungary empire), the son of a Jewish merchant. He lived most of his life in Vienna. Freud studied at the medical school of the University of Vienna and decided to specialize in clinical neurology. His observation of patients led to his belief that the mind consists of three compartments: conscious, preconscious, and unconscious. He had to find a method for observing unconscious processes in order to support his theories. Psychoanalysis thus developed as a strategy for retrieving evidence from the patient's unconscious.

Freud's life was filled with pain and tragedy. His family was persecuted because of its Jewish heritage, four sisters executed in concentration camps, his books publicly burned, and he suffered horribly with cancer in his mouth. Undoubtedly a genius, his influence overflows the fields of medicine and psychology to significantly impact our culture. Freudian ideas and distinctive terminology impregnate every area relating to human nature and behavior: religion, philosophy, literature, visual and performing arts.

The book *Studies in Hysteria*, coauthored by Josef Breuer in 1895, marks the beginning of psychoanalysis. *The Interpretation of Dreams*, 1900, is called his most brilliant work. *The Standard Edition of the Complete Works of Sigmund Freud* was translated from the German under the general editorship of J. Strachey, in collaboration with Anna Freud, published by Hogarth Press, London, 1953–1956.

respond in mechanical ways to stimuli. Their actions are controlled by predictable laws.

B. F. Skinner, a leading behaviorist, said it is useless to make theories about mental processes that cannot be observed. He believed that psychologists should devote themselves to observing behavior and describing how stimuli bring about observable results. Out of his work came the concept of *reinforcement*, a technique for applying stimuli to get desired results in areas such as education and parenting. In its purest form, behaviorism views the person as a machine and behavior itself as being ultimately determined by forces beyond personal control.

CLINICAL PSYCHOLOGY

As a subspecialty in the field, clinical psychology is defined as the practice of therapy and counseling techniques, especially for handling mental and emotional problems. Clinical psychology has its beginnings with Sigmund Freud's treatment of patients by a method he called *psychoanalysis.* The term derives from the idea that people's experiences result in inner unknown

Burrhus Frederic "B.F." Skinner

Burrhus Frederic Skinner (1904–1990) was born in Susquehanna, Pennsylvania, into a conventional middle-class family. As an undergraduate Skinner majored in English, with the intent of becoming a writer. His biographers consistently declare him to be a brilliant and rebellious young man. He developed a technique to control his own behavior, but refused to respect sacred cows on the college campus or conform to imposed regulations. Unable to gain recognition for his writing and intrigued with the subject of behavior, he enrolled in Harvard's graduate program in psychology. Here he became a dedicated scholar, concluding his graduate work with a doctoral thesis proposal for research on *The Behavior of Organisms.* Publication in 1938 of a book with that title launched his career in behaviorism and won him acceptance as a leader in the field of psychology. He was a popular professor first at the University of Minnesota, then at the University of Indiana, and finally at Harvard. Skinner was imaginative and extremely active all his life. In addition to writing both scholarly and popular books he invented teaching machines and developed systems of behavior control for child rearing and self-management.

Among his many works are *Science and Human Behavior*, New York: Macmillan, 1953; *Contingencies of Reinforcement: A Theoretical Analysis*, New York: Appleton-Century-Crofts, 1969; *Beyond Freedom and Dignity*, New York: Alfred A. Knopf, 1971; and *About Behaviorism*, New York: Alfred A. Knopf, 1974.

feelings that can be brought into consciousness by analysis. Freud's view is that people are controlled by impulses below the level of consciousness. Many of these are sexual and aggressive urges, often related to early childhood experiences. Psychoanalysis aims to uncover the hidden causes of behavior and deal with life on a conscious level.

Today clinical psychology has what Gary Collins calls an "unclear" professional image. Parting from the determinism of Freud, modern professionals do not have a unified sense of direction. They are split into a diversity of theories, techniques, and opinions. "A clinical psychologist accepts the empirical method," Collins says, "but he may also admit that difficult-to-observe things like hope, meaning, values, motives, or goals do exist and do influence behavior."[5]

HUMANISTIC PSYCHOLOGY

The humanistic conception of persons emphasizes freedom of the individual to choose what to do and become. It incorporates the idea that people should be encouraged to realize their own potential. Some have called the development of potential *self-actualization*. People are responsible for their own lives, and the responsibility cannot be shifted to outside forces. The focus is mostly on the normal human being rather than on pathologies or problems. Applying animal research methods to humans is discouraged.

In this context the term *humanistic* implies a concept of man or woman that recognizes each as a person, irreducible to more elementary levels, and their unique worth as beings potentially capable of autonomous judgment and action. While secular

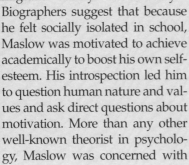

Abraham H. Maslow

Abraham H. Maslow (1908–1970) was one of seven children of an immigrant family in Brooklyn. Biographers suggest that because he felt socially isolated in school, Maslow was motivated to achieve academically to boost his own self-esteem. His introspection led him to question human nature and values and ask direct questions about motivation. More than any other well-known theorist in psychology, Maslow was concerned with values and ethical principles. His major method in developing the *Hierarchy of Needs*, for which he is best known, was to study specific persons he considered to be "self actualized." In this way he hoped to discover "moral imperatives" that accounted for moving persons beyond mere survival to meaningful fulfillment in life. His most often quoted books are *The Psychology of Science*, 1966, and *Motivation and Personality* (2nd ed.), 1970, New York: Harper & Row.

---

[5]Collins, *The Rebuilding of Psychology*, 48.

humanists omit the fact of God's creation, they defend the idea of human ability to transcend material and social conditions in ways that are unique to human beings. "The focus of humanistic psychology is upon the specificity of man, upon that which sets him apart from all other species. It differs from other psychologies because it views man not solely as a biological organism modified by experience and culture but as a person, a symbolic entity capable of pondering his existence, of lending it meaning and direction"[6]

Humanistic Psychology came to be called *Third Force Psychology* because it began in resistance to the first two *forces*: experimental and clinical psychology. Two leaders most often cited in this context are Abraham H. Maslow and Carl Rogers.

Psychology defined as the scientific study of behavior and cognitive processes minimizes the role of choice and free will, emphasizing environmental, physiological, and naturalistic determinants of behavior; Third Force Psychology, on the other hand, stresses human nature and is more philosophical and speculative than either experimental or clinical psychology. Some of its basic theoretical assumptions may be summarized as follows:

1. Human beings are free agents who have control over their own destiny. Environment plays a part, but we make significant choices that can change us into better persons.
2. In general, a *better person* is one who is self-actualizing, one who realizes one's own potential.
3. We can understand someone else's behavior to the extent we can identify with that person or share that person's worldview, a viewpoint very different from trying to understand behavior on the basis of stimulus-response analysis.
4. The usefulness of much empirical research is questioned. We should try to understand individuals rather than laws that govern the behavior of the species.
5. The here and now is stressed rather than the past or future. We should emphasize the choices of this moment rather than dwell on causes from the past.

Maslow's hierarchy of needs that motivate behavior represents a major contribution to what Third Force Psychology is. Maslow says humans are unique among animals because they exercise a measure of control over their own life and by choice may achieve or fail to achieve their highest potential. In Maslow's view, experiences of self-actualization (i.e., achievements of potential) give life meaning.[7]

---

[6]G. Marian Kinget, *On Being Human—A Systematic View* (New York: Harcourt Brace Jovanovich, 1975), preface, v.

[7]M. Ray Denny and Robert H. Davis, *Understanding Behavior— Foundations and Applications* (Geneva, Ill.: Paladin House Publishers, 1981), 228, 407.

CHRISTIAN THINKING ABOUT PSYCHOLOGY

In their determination to make psychology fit the natural science model, psychologists have generally rejected religious explanations. Students often get the impression from secular textbooks that religion and science are grossly incompatible. But theologians remind us that the creation account includes God's command for people to care for the earth and its creatures (Gen. 1:26–28). Menzies and Horton, for example, interpret this as biblical encouragement for the development of physical science "that would help people learn about the earth and how to use it properly." "It was the go-ahead," they declare, "for a biological science that would help people learn about all living organisms and how to treat them."[8] In part, theologians' affirmation that God's creation is orderly and consistent (in contrast to irrational imagining and mysticism) laid a foundation for the development of modern science.

> "Students often get the impression from secular textbooks that religion and science are grossly incompatible."

Similar thinking is revealed by Myers and Jeeves, who explain that Christians who study brain mechanisms are likely to see their science and their faith as complementary. "Science explores the natural processes underlying such phenomena, while faith helps one grasp the significance of the whole human system."[9] On the other hand, Christians who study general psychology or train to work as psychologists with troubled people see how the perspectives (or worldviews) of secular psychology can distort understandings about human nature. So while they warn students to be aware of hidden values and assumptions in secular writings, they also describe some "striking parallels between what researchers are concluding and what Christians believe."[10]

In answer to the question of the need for a Christian psychology, most Christian scholars offer in various terms the concept expressed in the title of the book by Myers and Jeeves: *Psychology Through the Eyes of Faith*. That is, we must examine psychological truth in the light of Christian truth, not apart from it. We can find every necessary truth in the Bible, but it is not a psychology textbook. God gives us fundamental principles, which guide our thinking, but He leaves it to us to think and apply knowledge. Christian psychologists note that every basic finding in scientific studies of human behavior reflects some biblical or theological truth. I have said, more crudely, that psychologists run panting along behind the Bible. An illumi-

---

[8]William W. Menzies and Stanley M. Horton, *Bible Doctrines* (Springfield, Mo.: Logion Press, 1994), 79.

[9]David G. Myers and Malcolm A Jeeves, *Psychology through the Eyes of Faith* (San Francisco: Harper and Row Publishers, 1987), 11.

[10]Ibid., 17.

nating example appears in a statement in a counseling theories textbook. The author calls "exciting" his discovery that people respond better when they believe life has meaning—even to the point of believing that suffering has a purpose.[11] I did not think that was a new idea. I heard it first as a child in Sunday school.

Christian psychologists consistently agree that the major theories of personality are closely related to religious issues. Most of the early theorists were personally involved in religion, especially Christianity, throughout their lives. Although many of their words and actions seem hostile to Christianity, their theories were influenced by it. One example is psychoanalytic theory, which provides guidelines for treating persons who suffer from feelings such as guilt, failure, inadequacy, or evil inclinations. The same conditions are dealt with in religion through the concepts of sin, forgiveness, and grace.

> **"We can find every necessary truth in the Bible, but it is not a psychology textbook."**

Paul C. Vitz, a professor of psychology and author of many journal articles, reminds us that the major theories of personality are closely related to religion. He mentions Freud, Jung, Adler, and Rogers as theorists who were personally involved in religion. He says that much of Carl Rogers's humanistic psychology can be clearly understood as translations of Christian concepts from the transcendent world of theology into the natural world of psychology. "I claim there is a field of Christian psychology," Vitz explains, "the purpose of which is to unpack the latent psychology found in Scripture and to coordinate that with valid psychological knowledge of both the scientific and nonscientific kind."[12]

Another strong proponent of a Christian psychology, Gary R. Collins, boldly declares a hope that psychology can be *rebuilt* on the foundation of Christian truth. He projects a psychology at once consistent with revealed biblical truth and truth discovered by scientific methods. He proceeds on the basis of four premises. First, psychology is worthwhile and useful as a tool for understanding the human mind and human behavior and for developing applications for treatment of human problems. Second, major weaknesses result in secular psychology because its theories do not adequately explain human realities. They cannot, because they are built on wrong assumptions about the origin and nature of people. Third, methods of science cannot answer essential questions such as those regarding human

---

[11]Lester N. Downing, *Counseling Theories and Techniques: Summarized and Critiqued* (Chicago: Nelson-Hall, 1975).

[12]Paul C. Vitz, "A Christian Theory of Personality: Covenant Theory," in Thomas J. Burke, ed., *Man and Mind: A Christian Theory of Personality* (Hillsdale, Mich.: The Hillsdale College Press, 1987), 199–202.

The word *sociology* was coined in 1830 by a French philosopher, Auguste Comte (1798–1857), who toyed first with the notion of *social physics*, to designate a scientific approach to the study of human associations.

meaning, purpose, and spiritual conditions. Fourth, if God does exist and has revealed crucial facts about human beings, then either we must incorporate such revelation into our inquiries or we will never form a complete view of human nature. Collins concludes that we need to rebuild psychology because "No other world view is as logical, internally consistent, or able to give meaning" as that of the Christian religion.[13]

Sociological Perspectives

We define sociology naively as a study of society. *Social* comes to us from a Latin term meaning "to follow." It includes the idea of people being connected, related to one another in patterns. Therefore it is more meaningful to say sociology is a study of institutions—the structures and processes formed by people in association. Institutions are constructed and perpetuated, reproduced, and changed as people act together, in cooperation or conflict, to meet real needs. Institutions usually treated by sociologists include family, government, economy, education, and religion. Recently health has been added, and sometimes sports and recreation.

For most of human history people lived in social organizations that were taken for granted. That is, most people did not question their social order. For example, in the ancient and

Auguste Comte

Auguste Comte (1798–1857) was born in Montpellier, France. He was secretary to and the adopted son of Claude Henri Saint-Simon, who inspired him to become a career philosopher. Because he had little formal education, Comte was not able to get the teaching positions he wanted. However, he persevered in study and writing and, with a minor lecturing position, was able to attract scholars to his ideas. Today he is generally recognized as founder of the philosophical school of positivism that assumes valid knowledge can be attained only by scientific methods. He coined the term *sociology*, by which he meant a kind of "social physics" that would uncover scientific laws of society. His theory was that if social institutions, such as government, were built on scientific principles, people would live in harmony instead of arguing over disputed claims of philosophy, metaphysics, and religion. The writings he is known for are *The Positive Philosophy*, in six volumes, published in 1842, and *System of Positive Philosophy*, in four volumes, 1851. An excellent source in English is *Auguste Comte and Positivism: The Essential Writings*, Gertrud Lenzer, ed., New York: Harper Torchbooks, 1975.

[13]Collins, *The Rebuilding of Psychology,* 138.

medieval eras of the Near East and Europe, few people questioned the social arrangement of kings, rulers, stewards, slaves, servants, rich, poor, and the hierarchy of priests. World population was small and scattered. There was little reason for most people to suppose their way of life was anything but natural. Then in the nineteenth century the world entered a period of ever accelerating change. Political revolutions upset traditional arrangements. The Industrial Revolution, with its technological advances, prodigious population growth, and multiplication of cities, was a major factor that radically changed human relationships. The resulting changes made people more aware, more ready to ask questions, than ever before.

Sociology developed during this period of change, much as psychology had. Philosophers and theologians asked the questions first: What makes society like it is? Why and how do people associate in patterns and form institutions? What forces keep social patterns stable? How and why do they change?[14] Influenced by the success of natural sciences in explaining the material world, some scholars decided to apply the same methods to a study of society. They believed that if natural science could disclose universal laws underlying the phenomena they studied, then a science of society should be able to discover and explain patterns in human association.

Founders of sociology as a science expressed more than a desire to analyze society. Perceiving turmoil and breakdown of traditional morals and values, they thought society could be improved if its structures and processes could be understood. Knowledge of social patterns should help scholars to define social "laws" similar to laws in nature, such as the law of gravity. They reasoned that solving social problems could be based on scientific knowledge alone. Such thinking has led to several theories that justify social policies and programs. Of interest here is the fact that defining a social problem involves assumptions about human nature. When we define a problem as *social* we imply that it is caused mainly by forces outside the individual. Is a person unemployed because of laziness or because of economic conditions? To what extent are divorce, homelessness, and unmarried motherhood, for example, to be defined as social problems?

Improving society motivated Emile Durkheim to study social phenomena. Much of his research aimed to demonstrate that social structures and processes could be treated as objects of scientific investigation. In this connection, he used the term *social facts*. For example, the family exists as a relationship. It is a

---

[14]In the fourth century B.C., the Greek philosopher Aristotle explored some of these questions (and others besides) in his *Politics*. In the thirteenth century A.D., the Christian theologian Thomas Aquinas examined questions about the nature of human beings and the laws (natural and civil) that govern them in Questions 90–92 of his *Summa Theologica*.

social fact. Durkheim saw the relationship factor, or society, as a distinct form of reality. Thus, for example, the concept *family* is different from the concept of several persons. He illustrated his point by reference to water. When the physical elements hydrogen and oxygen combine in proper proportions under certain conditions, a distinct product (water) emerges. Water has characteristics that cannot be attributed to either of its constituent elements. Neither oxygen nor hydrogen, for example, can put out fires, but water can. Similarly, when people interact to form a society (e.g., family, organization, state) collectively shared norms, beliefs, and values develop or emerge.[15]

Durkheim's concern for social order led him to study the origin and role of religion. He proposed that religion's function is to hold society together and to assure that individuals act in consensus for the common good. Therefore, religion is created by society for this purpose. Although he did not recognize a supernatural Being, he claimed religion was universal because persons must have shared moral values to survive as a society.

Durkheim's work did much to establish sociology as a unique study of human beings that cannot be reduced to the study of

Emile Durkheim

Emile Durkheim (1858–1917), a French philosopher who followed Comte, descended from a long line of Jewish rabbis. Reared to be a rabbi, he rejected personal religion to study it as a social phenomenon. Although Durkheim is known for his agnosticism, it was his interest in moral values in society that drove him into the field of sociology. He was concerned about moral degeneration in French society. His teaching area at the University of Bordeaux included moral education for school teachers. His interest in the scientific method was that he believed, like Comte, in the need to end moral disorder by discovering moral principles. He thought such principles could be applied to social conditions, racism, for example, just as knowledge of natural science is applied to improve physical living conditions. Comte had named sociology. Durkheim legitimized it in the academic world and became the first to bear the title professor of sociology. His work has had a profound influence on sociology as a science, an academic discipline, and a tool in social reform. He developed precise methodology and demonstrated it in studies that are still models for sociological theorizing and investigation. Notable works: *The Division of Labor in Society* (1895), *The Rules of Sociological Method* (1893), *Suicide* (1897), and *Elementary Forms of the Religious Life* (1915).

---

[15]David Ashley and David Michael Orenstein, *Sociological Theory: Classical Statements* (Boston: Allyn and Bacon, Inc., 1985), 95.

psychology. His major contribution to explanations of human nature is the idea of a "state of consciousness" that is not strictly individual. This state of consciousness, he says, comes from society, transfers society into us, and connects us with something that surpasses us, and turns us toward "ends that we hold in common with other men."[16]

Modern sociology is divided into many schools of thought; the majority incorporate in some way Durkheim's view of society as a determining force in the lives of individuals. Sociologists are most divided on the question of how people create society and then are created by it. Their theories differ from each other most on the degree and characteristics of social influence. The following three models generally form the working basis for modern sociological inquiry. Notice that each involves some presumptions about human nature.

STRUCTURAL-FUNCTIONAL MODEL

The structural-functional model is based on the view of society as a system of parts that work together to form a relatively stable whole. Society is composed of two parts: *structure* and *function*. *Structure* refers to persistent patterns, such as family, religion, government, or economic systems. Each structure has *functions* necessary for the stability and continuation of the society in its present form. A function is determined by finding the needs it meets within the whole system. Institutions grow out of society's need for control. The human body has been used as an illustration. Each part has structure and specific functions that contribute to the existence of the whole. In society, the separate institutions are interdependent, like the organs of the body, and they work together to maintain social organization and order. Structural-functional theorists focus on how society is unified and stabilized. (They fail to ask questions about conflict and social change.) This model originated from the work of Comte and Durkheim and has been further developed in the United States, especially by Talcott Parsons and Robert K. Merton.[17]

CONFLICT MODEL

Conflict theories emphasize conflict as a continuous factor in social life. Conflict, not unity, is the process that most influences the character of society and causes change. Society is viewed as fragmented, not integrated as a body. Major topics for concern include class inequalities and unequal distribution of resources and opportunities. People divide themselves into interest groups. Practically all social patterns favor some people over others, so society is in a constant struggle.

---

[16]Ibid., 117.

[17]George Ritzer, *Sociological Theory,* 3d ed. (New York: McGraw-Hill, 1992), 239–262.

I can illustrate from my childhood experience how functional and conflict theories differ in viewpoint. Migrant work is functional for the farming community as crops in various locations become ready for harvest in season. But it promotes a class system that leaves some people out of the community or town benefits and privileges. Karl Marx is the most important figure in the origin and development of conflict theory. Marx did not consider himself an academic sociologist, with a goal of studying society, but rather an activist, looking for ways to change and improve society. (See sidebar on p. 32 and Appendix 3, p. 470.) Later theories based on Marx's work emphasize how the parts of society contribute to change rather than stability, to conflict rather than agreement on values and laws.

SYMBOLIC-INTERACTION MODEL

"Symbolic interactionism" developed at the University of Chicago in the 1920s. The name was coined by Herbert Blumer, in a 1937 essay.[18] While a great variety of perspectives exist and

George Herbert Mead

George Herbert Mead (1863–1931), born in South Hadley, Massachusetts, was trained in philosophy and social psychology, and became a leader in the development of symbolic interactionism. After completing the bachelor's degree at Oberlin College, where his father was a professor, he taught in secondary education, then studied at Harvard and the Universities of Leipzig and Berlin. Although he never completed a graduate degree, he taught briefly at the University of Michigan and then for the rest of his life at the University of Chicago. Mead was best known for his teaching ability. Students rarely missed his classes and under his influence several became important sociologists.

In treating the concept of *self,* Mead, more directly and precisely than other theorists, addressed the question of what makes people. The self is the unique human ability to be both subject and object. Therefore it presupposes a social process: communication among humans. Self cannot develop without social contact, but when it has developed, it can continue to exist as a self-conscious mind. A person communicates, hears, and responds to himself.

Mead did not produce written works to the same degree as other major theorists. The work that outlines his thinking and has powerfully influenced sociology and social psychology was put together from his notes and papers, completed in 1934. It is *Mind, Self, and Society: From the Standpoint of a Social Behaviorist* (Chicago: University of Chicago Press, 1962).

[18]Herbert Blumer, "Social Disorganization and Personal Disorganization," *American Journal of Sociology* 42 (May): 1937, 871–877.

several roots are cited by scholars in the field, many sources name George Herbert Mead as the most influential contributor to the basic model.

Symbolic-interaction theories differ from the structural-functional and conflict models in one distinctive way: a concern with how people experience society more than with descriptions of society as a whole. This model provides a basis for the development of theories in social psychology: the study of how people relate, affect each other, and are affected by persons and groups. The scholars who framed it were seeking ways to avoid the idea that individual actions are directly determined either by internal psychological states or by structural forces of society. Instead, the person experiences society through contacts with others. Gestures and language—meaningful symbols—make communication possible. The mind and the self

> **"The underlying question of sociological inquiry: To what extent do we create society, and to what extent does society create us?"**

emerge out of these contacts. The ability to view oneself from the standpoint of others is essential for forming the self and organizing group activities. As people interpret the meanings of symbols and act according to their interpretations, patterns of interaction form the society. Again we see the underlying question that makes sociological inquiry important to us all: To what extent do we create society, and to what extent does society create us?

TWO TRADITIONS FORM MODERN SOCIOLOGY

Early American sociologists were divided in their answers to questions of human nature and the essential qualities of society. Following Comte and Durkheim, some clung to the concept of society as a thing in itself (separate from the individual person), to be studied objectively. Out of this thinking grows *naturalistic* (sometimes called *positivistic*) sociology. Sociologists study human behavior in the same way natural scientists study physical properties and interactions. They believe individual human beings are subject to laws that determine action, and they hope to articulate laws of society, much as natural scientists articulate laws of physics and chemistry. Persons are to a significant degree socially determined, acting out the demands and expectations of society. The naturalistic category includes both structural theory in sociology and behaviorism in psychology.

Other scholars believed more like Karl Marx and Max Weber, that society is composed of interacting persons in a complex dynamic of relationships. This approach leads to *humanistic* sociology. It rejects the idea that sociology must follow exactly the pattern of natural science. Investigating social problems is more important than structures or methodology. Persons are not passive objects of social forces but have will and choice. (This view shows up in Marx's analysis that economy is not so much a *structure* as it is the effect of class struggle.) People are potentially good and able to influence their environment if they are aware of conditions and possibilities. Social reform is a major concern for conflict theorists. In addition, a major purpose of sociological knowledge is to give people tools for designing a better world.

Recent commentators cite the continuing development of the two concepts, naturalistic and humanistic, as a problem for the future of the discipline. Modern sociology is neither a pure life science, like biology, nor simply a research-driven social reform movement. Some see an identity crisis for the discipline. They are disappointed in sociology's failure to fulfill the expectations of its founders. In its present state it is not an exact science, and it has failed to change the world to the degree that some of its early proponents had hoped.[19]

Max Weber

Max Weber (1864–1920), a German sociologist, is considered by most historians of sociology to have had more influence than any other one person on the development of Western sociology. Weber's father is described as a successful bureaucrat, attached to the political establishment and the earthly pleasures of middle-class society. His mother was a devout Calvinist who preferred an ascetic way of life. The tension between the two undoubtedly influenced Weber as he tried to reconcile the positivism of Durkheim, the conflict theories of Marx, and the influence on society of ideas such as the Protestant religion. Unlike Durkheim, he rejected the idea of a set of laws that would explain social behavior. Unlike Marx, he rejected the idea that the economic system is the primary determinant of human thought and relationships. He sought to develop a sociology that would account for the complex nature of social life. He stands between Durkheim and Marx as humanistic, but more scholarly than revolutionary.

Weber produced voluminous writings, of which the following are representative: *Essays in Sociology*, ed. H. H. Gerth and trans. C. Wright Mills, New York: Oxford University Press, 1946; *The Protestant Ethic and the Rise of Capitalism* (1904–1905) (New York: Charles Scribner's Sons, 1958); *Economy and Society*, ed. G. Roth and C. Wittich (Berkeley, Calif.: University of California Press, 1978).

---

[19]Joshua Glen, "Sociology on the Skids," *Utne Reader* (November/December, 1995): 28.

CHRISTIAN THINKING ABOUT SOCIOLOGY

Christians who study sociology see that the divisions and disputes among theorists result mainly from their misinterpreting human nature and origin. Both the naturalistic and the humanistic traditions out of which modern sociology has developed are limited in their attempts to describe reality because they omit the truth of creation and lack understanding of humankind's purpose. We might say ironically that what has been proved in the history of sociology is that science cannot replace religion and that human beings are willful actors. Several Christian scholars have taken advantage of the rift between naturalistic and humanistic sociology to suggest models based on biblical assumptions about human nature and purpose.

Margaret M. Paloma says, "It is the issue of the determined nature of person that holds the key for analyzing differing theoretical perspectives." She then outlines assumptions about the person from both naturalistic and humanistic sociology and proposes a synthesis that allows for biblical truths. A naturalistic theory, such as Durkheim's, contains two implicit assumptions: (1) that persons are fallen creatures whose redemption can be made possible by an ordered world, and (2) that persons are determined by social structures and norms. Humanistic sociology's chief assumptions are (1) that persons are more good than bad by nature and (2) that present evils can be eliminated by setting people free from oppressive constraints. Persons are not absolutely determined by society, but they must be stimulated into a consciousness of their situation so they can make changes.

> **"The divisions and disputes among theorists result mainly from their misinterpreting human nature and origin."**

Paloma believes that each of these perspectives agrees partially with the biblical image of person. Naturalistic assumptions are compatible with the concept of original sin but not with the doctrines of creation and free will. Humanistic assumptions are compatible with the view of creative humanity but not with the truth of fallen nature and the inability of humans to provide their own redemption. She suggests a Christian sociological model that accounts for (1) the reality of fallen humanity, shaped by social structure, and (2) the redeemed person who experiences salvation through Christ and then acts as an agent, through the power of the Holy Spirit, to influence society in accordance with the plan of God.[20]

"I always get a personal sense of excitement in the realization

---

[20]Margaret Paloma, "Theoretical Models of Person in Contemporary Sociology: Toward Christian Sociological Theory," in *A Reader in Sociology: Christian Perspectives*, ed. Charles P. De Santo, Calvin Redekop, and William L. Smith-Hinds (Scottdale, Pa.: Herald Press, 1980), 202–210.

that these scriptural principles were given by God long before some modern sociologist came across them in research." In this way Russell Heddendorf introduces his book *Hidden Threads*. As his words and the title imply, he believes essential truths about persons and society are to be found in the Bible. Sociologists discover some of this truth. Usually unconscious of its original source, they try to explain it in human terms. So, Heddendorf says, we can find "hidden threads" of Scripture as we study sociology. This approach will help us appreciate the thoughtful work of scholars even as we remind ourselves that flaws and contradictions can result from their unscriptural assumptions.[21]

Another advocate of learning to see human truth from a Christian perspective is Richard Perkins, author of *Looking Both Ways—Exploring the Interface Between Christianity and Sociology*. Studying sociology, he explains, promotes development of the human potential for reflexivity—the ability to observe oneself and look at life from more than one perspective. Often Christians feel threatened by sociology because its method is analytical. Instead of looking at human behavior from the one perspective of individual differences, sociology insists on considering many social factors. For example, we tend to think of people who fail academically as simply less intelligent or less ambitious; poverty is a personal failure; crime is a sin. Sociologists suggest that school failure and poverty could result from social injustice; that crime might grow out of poverty as well as personal immorality.

> "Often Christians feel threatened by sociology because its method is analytical."

Perkins believes sociology can help Christians become more insightful. He uses the term *marginal* as I have in thinking of my migrant experience. If we learn to think as Christian sociologists we can look both ways. Our tendency to think of religion only as personal salvation and faith can be corrected as we grasp the social implications of Jesus' life and teachings. "We need the reflexivity both biblical Christianity and sociology can provide—not simply each perspective learned, but both perspectives combined, so that one can act as a challenge for the other."[22]

David A. Fraser and Tony Campolo conclude their book *Sociology Through the Eyes of Faith* with suggestions for blending truths from sociology with Christian thinking. They express regret that some poorly informed Christians reject sociology completely, calling it "nothing but secular humanism," and

---

[21]Russell Heddendorf, *Hidden Threads: Social Thought for Christians* (Dallas: Probe Books, 1990), 14.

[22]Richard Perkins, *Looking Both Ways: Exploring the Interface Between Christianity and Sociology* (Grand Rapids: Baker Book House, 1987), 170.

they urge students not to overlook what the discipline has to offer. Conversely some are led by secular explanations to believe that religious phenomena are "nothing but the operation of social and psychological principles." Fraser and Campolo use the expression "partnership for truth" to describe their model for avoiding extremes. Christians can take advantage of useful sociological knowledge and at the same time help others to comprehend biblical verities. Their approach represents a strategy that creates dialogue partners in a conversation whose goal is to discover and express truth. "The major premise is that God's truth in the Bible and the truth of social realities are compatible, even when that compatibility is not always immediately obvious."[23]

Some Principles of Personhood

One of my college professors required students to leave all their belongings in the hall during tests. I remember looking at the piles of books and clothing and thinking, *He doesn't like us. He thinks we're all cheaters.*

What we believe to be true of people in general affects the way we approach individuals and groups. From the earliest records of human thought we learn that people have tried to analyze human nature in order to plan relationships and establish social order. Implicit in ancient writings from all civilizations is the concept that human goodness is somehow compromised. Great thinkers have sensed the potential for good and puzzled at people's inability to live up to their potential.[24] A common idea comes through from all the social philosophers: Human behavior is driven by a sense of need that must be satisfied, restrained, or directed.[25]

> **"Christians can take advantage of useful sociological knowledge and at the same time help others comprehend biblical verities."**

Attempts to apply knowledge from psychology and sociology have led to a similar strategy and conclusion. To know how to approach people and bring about desired changes, psychologists, social workers, and educators have had to ask, What are people really like? Many of them answer by describing human beings in terms of needs.

During my years in the field, scholars have used various terms, such as *wishes* and *drives,* to describe what most of them now call *needs.* They have devised various lists and theories explaining how need-meeting relates to behavior. On one prin-

---

[23]David A. Fraser and Tony Campolo, *Sociology Through the Eyes of Faith* (San Francisco: Harper/SanFrancisco, 1992), 300.

[24]The classical treatment of this issue appears in Aristotle's *Nicomachean Ethics,* Book VII, where Aristotle discusses the subject of moral weakness (Gk. *akrasia*).

[25]Howard Becker and Harry Elmer Barnes, *Social Thought from Lore to Science* (New York: Dover Publications, Inc., 1961), vol. 1: 78–79.

ciple they agree: All humans try in some way to meet their needs. Negative behavior results from not knowing what the real needs are, or from trying to meet real needs in wrong ways. Individual personalities develop from the way people perceive their needs and try to meet them.

NEED-MEETING THEORIES

Maslow's Hierarchy

Abraham Maslow's hierarchy of needs is the best-known model of a need-meeting theory. He lists five needs, beginning with what he considers most basic. His theory suggests that we are not motivated to meet higher needs until lower ones are met. For example, a hungry man would put getting food before being safe. A woman worried about her safety would care less about what people think of her. The hierarchy is, in brief,

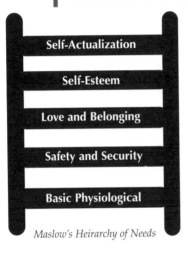

Maslow's Heirarchy of Needs

1. physiological needs—survival, physical functioning of the body
2. safety needs—security, stability, freedom from fear
3. belonging and love—affection, acceptance by others
4. esteem needs—self respect, sense of mastery and achievement
5. self-actualization—the need to develop full potential[26]

Brill's Model

Naomi I. Brill proposes a model in which two major categories of needs—the need for security and the need for opportunities to grow—are related to five aspects of the human personality: physical, emotional, intellectual, social, and spiritual.[27]

Unlike Maslow's model, hers does not place the needs in a hierarchy. Each category of need interacts with each aspect of personality.

The first primary need is for security. The physical aspect of personality expresses a need for material goods. The emotional aspect, a need for love and acceptance. The intellectual aspect, a need to know, to understand, and to master knowledge and skills. The social aspect, a need for meaningful relationships. Finally, the spiritual aspect expresses a need to have inner satisfactions.

---

[26]Abraham H. Maslow, chap. 4 in *Motivation and Personality* (New York: Harper and Row, 1970).

[27]Naomi I. Brill, *Working With People: The Helping Process* (New York: Longman, 1985), 27.

The second primary need is for opportunity to grow. People need something beyond security. They need opportunity to grow, develop maturity, and achieve potential in each of the five aspects of personality.

HUMANISTIC PERSPECTIVES

What makes real people? Although many scholars try to avoid it, all their theories hinge to some extent on this question. My research indicates that someone in every generation has tried to characterize human nature—describe the specific qualities and behaviors that set people apart from all other nature. Research in the social and behavioral sciences often concentrates on similarities between humans and lower animals. Anthropologists, for example, emphasize that both human beings and lower animals have the ability to learn, to make tools, to communicate, and to form social relations. Beyond agreeing on these abilities, anthropologists have reached little consensus. They disagree, for instance, over which characteristics are different only in degree and which are different in kind.

One ambitious exposition of humanistic psychology lists human characteristics in two categories: behavioral characteristics that are accessible to direct observation, and experiential characteristics that require subjective reports, inferences, and interpretation. Among the *behavioral characteristics* are these: language that is organized and governed by rules; tool making in the most encompassing sense, including the use of fire and unlimited inventions and technology; and culture making, meaning the endless variety of human adaptations, customs, laws, religion, and all activities developed to satisfy nonbiological needs. *Experiential characteristics* include reflective awareness, ethical concern, aesthetic urges, historical awareness, and metaphysical

EMOTIONAL   PHYSICAL

SPIRITUAL   **TOTAL INDIVIDUAL**   INTELLECTUAL

SOCIAL

SECURITY—to love and be loved, to relate to others, to have material needs met

OPPORTUNITY FOR GROWTH—to develop to maturity and achievement of maximum potential

Brill's Heirarchy of Needs

concern. Reflective awareness refers to the ability to know and to know that one knows, to engage in imagination, self-scrutiny, hypothesizing, philosophical speculation, and the development of self-concept. Ethical concern means a sense of right and wrong, good and bad, and many transcendent values that cannot be accounted for by social conditioning. Aesthetic urges are those expressed in activities that serve solely the purpose of sensory or symbolic enjoyment, devoid of utilitarian concern. Historical awareness, or a sense of time, refers to the ability to look back and plan ahead, and be aware of death. Finally, metaphysical concern leads to asking ultimate questions, the capacity to deal with infinity, eternity, ultimate origins and purposes, and the expression of religion.[28]

Biblical Perspectives

Two ideas emerge from all the studies and controversies about human nature. One is that religion is both behaviorally and experientially universal. The other is that scientists and scholars all recognize one human quality that stands significantly apart and to which all other human characteristics are related. It is our extraordinary capacity for dealing with symbols.[29] When secular researchers declare that language is a unique human instinct my respect for scholarship soars. I believe they have uncovered by diligent study and thinking what I cherish as the basic truth of divine-human relationship. God created us with the ability to understand and create language, or we never could have known the Word or the Word made flesh (John 1:14).

Are children born religious? Interpreting *religious* as a force toward relationship with God, I believe they are. I base my reasoning on two other questions: Are children born hungry? Why?

Psychology and sociology give us much valuable information, but fail to adequately explain how and why our actions result from our needs. Their attempts to explain fall short because they omit the fact of human purpose. Before we can answer the question of what makes people, we must face the larger question: What are people for? Only in Scripture can we find an adequate explanation. God formed human beings who would be capable of fulfilling their purpose. Unless we understand that purpose, nothing makes complete sense. That purpose is to glorify God, to love and be loved by Him, and to enjoy forever interacting with Him and His creation.

Think of the Genesis account. God created Adam and Eve in His own image. He invited Adam to join in creation by naming the animals. His first reflection about Adam was that he needed a companion. You might say God's first interaction with human beings was a teaching session: He told them to reproduce themselves and to fill the earth. He told them to care for His creation. He told them to work the ground and use its bounties for food. Not least, in telling them not to eat of a certain tree, He was

---

[28]Kinget, *On Being Human*, 3–4.

[29]See Steven Pinker, *The Language Instinct* (New York: William Morrow and Company, 1994). Pinker's reasoning supports the existence of a language instinct. Although to him "instincts" are biological qualities developed through evolution, I accept the facts of his research as support for God's purposeful creation.

telling them to restrain their impulses and be obedient to His authority.

We cannot go far in asking questions about human nature without making the basic statement that we are created by God for His own purposes. We share His image but, as a part of creation, we are subject to natural laws. Sometimes I shock my students by saying, "Suppose you were God. Given the stated purposes, what kind of people would you create? What essential qualities would you give them to make possible the fulfillment of their purpose?" The answer is that you would build into their nature, along with potential for development, *needs*—strong urges or appetites. So God created people with needs. He gave them hunger so they would eat and survive. He gave them sexual urges that would encourage human intimacy and ensure mating and procreation. Would He then leave them without a spiritual appetite to prompt them toward their ultimate reason for being? No. He created them with a God-need, to which His Spirit would speak, drawing them to Himself. Powerful needs for love and belonging move people to form caring relationships with Him and other humans.

> "'Suppose you were God. Given the stated purposes, what kind of people would you create?'"

Because humankind's basic purpose is to be with God, our primary need is to be in harmony with him. This need leads to searching and learning, and so we develop the *image of God* qualities. Our need to think and choose, to create, and to become all we were meant to be makes us potentially compatible with our Creator. The Bible begins with God creating humans and giving them instructions concerning His purpose for people and nature. From the Genesis creation account to the Great Commission recorded in Matthew's Gospel, the Bible is a story of how God works through people to generate and maintain His purpose. Our purpose is God's purpose. Sin entered our nature when this potential to be like God was misused. The fall of Adam and Eve is the original demonstration of how all evils and troubles come from not understanding real human needs or from trying to meet them in wrong ways.

THE CONCEPT **PERSON** INCLUDES RELATIONSHIPS

Consider the following statements about yourself and others. You share with others some needs and goals. You interact with these persons, working with them in various ways to meet your needs and reach your goals. You recognize a pattern in your relationships, including leadership and individual roles and responsibilities. You feel loyalty and a comfortable sense of attachment to these persons. In essence, these statements define group membership. You belong.

If you think seriously about the concept of *belonging* you may be startled to realize that almost all meaningful activity of your life requires some type of membership. Think of your name, address, nationality, class, profession. You are who you are and do what you do in a context of belonging. Consider your deepest needs and your highest objectives. What is important to you? What is pleasant and satisfying? In most cases you will find yourself thinking in terms of relationships: family, friends, church group, work group.

Most needs are met and goals are accomplished in the context of interpersonal interactions. This is so natural to human beings that it often goes unobserved. The highest gratifications come with sharing. And on the negative side, the most painful disappointments and most distressing problems rise out of interpersonal relationships, faulty communication, and real or perceived rejection—not belonging.

> **"Scripture clearly indicates that belonging and togetherness is the natural state of human beings."**

Scripture clearly indicates that belonging and togetherness is the natural state of human beings. God said, "Let us make man in our image" (Gen. 1:26). Here the idea of the plural and the idea of human nature are introduced simultaneously. God's creative statements up to this point are translated as impersonal commands: "Let there be light." "Let the land produce . . ." Then the style of expression changes completely with the creation of humans. It is no longer passive and impersonal, but intimate and plural. Note also that the record does not show God concerned with companionship for the lower animals. But He said it was not good for a person to be alone. And in spite of the fact that God is all-powerful and could offer Adam any sort of assistance, He introduces the remarkable concept that Adam needs a helper!

Rejecting naturalistic theories that present persons as products of society may sometimes lead us to depreciate dependency and cooperation. Placing strong emphasis on personal salvation, evangelicals tend to promote individualism, and may even neglect social responsibility. But Scripture teaches that belonging allows one to make meaningful contributions. A Christian person is a member of the Body of Christ.

Jesus said, "This, then, is how you should pray: Our Father . . . Give us today our daily bread. Forgive us our debts, as we also have forgiven our debtors. And lead us not into temptation, but deliver us from the evil one" (Matt. 6:9–13). The prayer Jesus taught us to pray is a group prayer. Perhaps our tendency to think of religion as an entirely individual experience blinds us to the fact that Jesus thought of His disciples as a group of interdependent persons. If this is so, then we can rightly conclude that His will is for us to care for each other. Who could say sincerely "Give us our daily bread" and not care that another person is starving? Who could say sincerely "Lead us not into temptation" and not care for those who are being deceived by godless value systems and social pressures?

In both Old and New Testaments some terms referring to one person or to God's people are interchangeable. Scripture describes behavior, such as sin, as both individual (e.g., 1 Sam. 25:17) and corporate (e.g., 1 Sam. 15:18). Also, biblical evidence unmistakably implies that people are intended to relate to one another: to care for one another, to interact, to cooperate, and to share experiences and responsibilities (e.g., 2 Cor. 1:3–7). Actually, it is impossible to be either fully human or Christian all alone.[30]

Social Changes Affect Relationships

While psychology and sociology cannot give complete answers unless they address the purpose of humanity, Christians cannot find complete answers unless we address the question of cultural influence. Studies in the behavioral sciences help us understand that relationships among people are determined more by customs and socially constructed attitudes than by human nature or individual personality traits.

In the first sociology class I ever attended, I learned a new word: *cohort*. It means a set of persons born in a certain time period, growing up under the influence of the same social and economic conditions, affected by the same historical events. "Generations are not so different from each other because people are young or old," the professor explained. "There's not that much change in the way people think as they grow from adolescence to adulthood. They are different because they belong to different cohorts."

Recently the idea of the cohort has been popularized. We name the generations, calling them, for example, Baby Boomers, Baby Busters, and Generation X. So it is not simply because they are old that your parents and grandparents seem to think so differently from you. They think differently because they belong to a different cohort, influenced by different government policies, styles, fads, ideas, media, technology.

The way people perceive their own situations today, and how they interpret the actions of others, usually reflects changes in how society views gender roles, divorce, sexual behaviors, unmarried motherhood. People feel offended, oppressed, or victimized in different ways because of changing values and customs. Words and actions that once were considered normal now form the basis for lawsuits. Words and actions that once were

> **"Christians cannot find complete answers unless we address the question of cultural influence."**

---

[30]Some material in this section has been adapted from Billie Davis, *The Dynamic Classroom*, 1987, and *Renewing Hope* (Springfield, Mo.: Gospel Publishing House, 1995).

considered evil and offensive now are accepted as normal.

Look back at the changes that have shaped your life: The technical advances that put you out of step with older people in a world that has come from radio to television to VCR to interactive computers. Moving. Divorce. Styles in music, dress, and dating. Economic changes and government programs. Consider how these phenomena change the way we relate to people. Much of our interpersonal turmoil is not entirely personal. How we relate to those around us—family members, friends, spouses, work supervisors, neighbors, fellow travelers on airplanes and highways, persons of various racial backgrounds, and poor people—is influenced by changing values and customs in our society.

> "How we relate to those around us is influenced by changing values and customs in our society."

History shows that social and economic changes influence how people relate to each other. In primitive societies, persons understood their interdependence. They knew they would all survive or starve together, so whatever they had was shared. Individuals related closely to the whole group. In the Old Testament period, God's laws made caring for others a religious obligation. The Lord commanded Hebrew societies to provide systematically for the poor. Failing to do so was a grievous sin, the subject of prophets' scolding and warning.[31] Families of several generations were responsible for each other, as well as for employees and strangers who needed hospitality. Jesus modeled and taught absolute equality in social status.

Today's world stands in marked contrast to the world of the Old Testament. In modern industrial societies we demand individual rights, emphasize individual possessions, and compete for status positions. People often feel no obligation to share what they have. If they do share, they commonly think of it as charity and put needy persons on a social level lower than themselves. Homelessness and single mothers' poverty have their roots in relatively recent attitudes about family cohesion and responsibilities.

How persons perceive each other, with either positive or negative outcomes, is affected or even dictated by social inventions. An example of changes that can have a significant effect on the way people think and act toward others is the law requiring equal access for disabled persons in schools and public facilities. Before the legislation, we carried people in wheelchairs across curbings and up stairs. Now I hear persons with disabilities complain of indignities implied by any different treatment, just because they move on wheels instead of legs. Civil rights laws have changed interracial relations. For evidence of how

---

[31]Concern for the poor is expressed 134 times in the Old and New Testaments.

consequential some changes can be, we need only consider the official change in psychologists' description of homosexuality, from a "pathology" to an "alternative lifestyle."

When we understand how social changes can affect our attitudes and relationships, we are better able to avoid negative outcomes. The Scriptures, illuminated by the Holy Spirit, help us see ourselves and others from God's perspective. Christian faith gives us insights, making us less subject to influence by social factors. The apostle Paul gives this advice: "Do not be conformed to this world—this age, fashioned after and adapted to its external, superficial customs. But be transformed (changed) by the [entire] renewal of your mind—by its new ideals and its new attitude—so that you may prove [for yourselves] what is the good and acceptable and perfect will of God" (Rom. 12:2, *The Amplified Bible*).

The Human Being of Scripture

We return to the question we began this chapter with: What is a real human being? Theologians explain the nature of the human race by reference to biblical language. For example, God created Adam from earth and Eve from Adam's body, separate from Himself and from the previously created animals. Also, human beings are a part of nature as God's highest creation, yet separate from nature as created in God's image. Terms used throughout the Old and New Testaments indicate that the words *Adam* and *man* include male and female, and they distinguish humans from God, angels, and animals. All people descended from Adam and Eve, and therefore we are all of one human race.

The question of human nature leads quickly to a further question: What components make up the person and how are these components related to one another? As you might expect, differences of opinion arise as various scholars discuss the components that make up a whole person. The Bible uses words translated *body*, *heart*, *mind*, *will*, *soul*, *spirit*, and several other body parts, such as *kidneys* and *bowels*. Noting that use of these terms is ambiguous, theologian Timothy Munyon questions whether it is possible to incorporate all of them into a single coherent model of the human person. He, along with most biblical scholars, identifies three positions:

Trichotomism. This interpretation views human beings as made up of three parts: body, soul, and spirit. The body refers to physical existence and unites the human to all other living creation. The soul is the personality principle, including sensations and emotions. The spirit is the higher power that distinguishes humans from all other life forms and enables the person to fellowship with God.

Dichotomism (or *dualism*). This interpretation views human beings as two parts: material and immaterial, distinguishing the physical body from the nonphysical mental and emotional qualities. Historically, this interpretation has been the most widely held view among evangelical theologians.

Monism. This interpretation views human beings as an indivisible unity.[32] The person is a unified being rather than so many components. Many modern scholars prefer this interpretation of the biblical record. They caution, however, that the person is a *conditional* unity, meaning that body, soul, and spirit are aspects of the whole, not a joining of separate parts.[33]

Christian scholars in the fields of psychology and sociology consistently remind us that the Bible is not a science book. It is an account of God and His relationship with His creation. It is a book of stories, teachings, and examples for living. Many of these scholars have translated and interpreted biblical passages to compose descriptions of human nature. While they have not achieved unanimity, they seem to be converging on the following conclusions.

> **"The body is just as much 'the person' as the soul is."**
> —*Vincent Rush*

To begin with, the Bible offers a general psychosocial (i.e., personal and relational) model of the human being. Human nature is a psychophysical (i.e., flesh animated by soul) unity. References to the body and to the inner person do not indicate separate parts; rather they seem to refer to certain functions of human nature. The body is the world-conscious aspect of our being. It was created by God and is not to be considered evil in itself. We do not have a body. We are a body. As Vincent Rush has pointed out, "*the body is just as much 'the person' as the soul is.*"[34]

Second, the word translated *soul* is used in various ways. It means a living creature, physically alive, a tangible, real person. The concept *soul* often refers to intellect, emotions, and will. Our soul defines our being, defines who we are. We do not *have* a soul. We *are* a soul.

Third, mind and emotions are not separate from the body. All are inextricably linked as the person.

Fourth, *spirit* refers to our relationship to the unseen spirit world. It is our God-consciousness. Paul often uses *spirit* and *flesh* not to refer to two parts of the person, but to two attitudes and styles of living.

Finally, earthly life for Christians will be followed by a resurrected body and renewal of life. We do not know the exact

---

[32]The view presented here as monism is sometimes also known by the name *hylomorphism.* See Vincent Rush, "What Is It To Be Human?," chap. 2 in *The Responsible Christian* (Chicago: Loyola University Press, 1984), 25–73.

[33]Timothy Munyon, "The Creation of the Universe and Humankind," in *Systematic Theology,* ed. Stanley M. Horton (Springfield, Mo.: Logion Press, 1994), 238–245.

[34]Rush, *The Responsible Christian,* 29.

details. The New Testament image is of a restored and perfected mind-body unit.[35]

THE IMAGE OF GOD

Most Christian scholars in philosophy and the social and behavioral sciences are compelled to address the concept *image of God*, because every theory involves the question of human nature. Exactly what do the biblical words mean? One generalized answer is that they refer to the way human nature reflects something of God's nature. They refer to elements of personality and selfhood, the existence of potential, possibility for development, freedom to choose, moral responsibility, creative abilities, the capacity for love and holiness.

C. Stephen Evans says, "The image of God consists of that complex of activities that are distinctively and uniquely human." Then he proposes a list to amplify his meaning. First on the list is the concept of *action*. God makes decisions, has plans and purposes, and acts on them. Next is the concept of an *agent*, a whole person, purposive, valuing, rational, morally responsible, social, passionate, and creative.[36]

It is characteristic of Christian sociologists to see in the *image of God* concept not only substance but also relationship. Because we are made in the image of the triune God, we are made to be interpersonal, relational. Besides having Godlike qualities and capacities, human beings reflect the image of God both when they respond to God's love and when they relate in godly ways in their world. Abilities and capacities reflect *the nature of God*. Relationships are *the dynamic expression of His nature*.[37]

SOCIAL THOUGHT IN THE OLD TESTAMENT

The plural form in biblical language (as in God's use of *us* and *we* in reference to Himself) implies an association, similar to the English concept *social*. *Elohim*, the name used in Scripture more often than any except *Yahweh*, is a plural form. *Yahweh* is God's covenant-keeping name. It is connected with the promise, "I will be with you." Hebrew society began as a tightly joined nomadic people pledged to distance themselves from the multigod religions of others and have no God but Yahweh. The original Covenant Code (the Ten Commandments and further exposition of God's instructions, recorded in Exodus 20 through 23) has two main themes. One is the relationship between God and people. The other is regulation of social organization and rela-

---

[35]See Menzies and Horton, *Bible Doctrines*, 84–85; Myers and Jeeves, *Psychology*, 24–30.

[36]C. Stephen Evans, *Preserving the Person* (Downers Grove, Ill.: InterVarsity Press, 1977), 144–145.

[37]Fraser and Campolo, *Sociology Through the Eyes of Faith*, 250–252.

tionships among people. Extended families were to provide for their members under the leadership of a father. The community was to care for its own disadvantaged persons and reach out in hospitality to include strangers. Those who had more material goods were expected to share with those who had less.

Eventually, as the Hebrews settled and developed a flourishing economy, extreme class divisions resulted. The wealthy lived in extravagance. They violated the Covenant Code, ignoring the plight of the poor. In the midst of this situation, the prophets Amos, Hosea, and Micah appeared and cried out against social injustice as well as spiritual decline. These eighth-century B.C. prophets reasserted the values of brotherhood and denounced social stratification. They emphasized the ethical aspect of serving God and established for future Christianity the truth that our religion must be practiced in human relationships. As later Christian sociologists have said it, God hates both idolatry and injustice.[38]

SOCIAL THOUGHT IN THE NEW TESTAMENT

Probably the most overlooked lesson on social concern is embodied in Luke's account of John the Baptist's ministry. Many people summarize this passage as preaching repentance and proclaiming the way of salvation. They forget how John answered people who asked what they should do if their tradition as children of Abraham was not sufficient. John answered bluntly, in words remote from religious ritual: "The person with two coats should share with someone who has none. The person with extra food should share." He told them to be fair and honest in all their dealings with people, as individuals and as representatives of society. His message did not stop with an admonition to repent. In every account of his ministry his point is to repent and "produce fruit in keeping with repentance." Luke's added details show this fruit includes personal caring and social justice.

> "The prophets Amos, Hosea, and Micah appeared and cried out against social injustice as well as spiritual decline."

Although Jesus' teachings emphasize the value of individuals as eternal souls, His life is a model for human relationships here and now. By His words and deeds He presents the person as a child of God, chosen to be in fellowship with Him. Each person is infinitely precious, without regard to natural barriers and differences, such as race, nationality, or social position. In Jesus we understand the true meaning of self-esteem, an appreciation of self in Christian context, without self-indulgent individualism.

Jesus turned away from social reform movements because His unique purpose was to demonstrate that the values of

---

[38]Ibid., 238.

God's kingdom are distinct from the values of human political and economic systems. Although His teachings do not advocate a struggle against social oppression, they do require those who have advantages to share with the needy. He does not hesitate to speak out against hypocrisy. He strongly upholds the sanctity of marriage. His way of life is family, brotherhood, and community.

Paul and the other apostles carried on with Jesus' teachings about the equality of individuals before God. They recognized the inevitable inequalities of the fallen world and taught that Christians should be willing to accept and adapt themselves to some of them. To this extent acceptance of existing social conditions was looked upon as submission to God and His will. Yet submission is never an excuse for Christians to be apathetic. We are never in any way to support perpetuating anything that harms people. We are to monitor our own attitudes and actions, and speak out against all forms of evil. The Apostolic teachings about love, equality, and justice laid foundations for later social action. Today, Christians who think and write about social issues are convinced that both Old and New Testament teachings are clear on this point: Persons are social beings, and we cannot be all God intends us to be as individual humans unless we grasp the fact that we are social—that is, relational—and accept our social responsibilities.

> "We are never in any way to support perpetuating anything that harms people."

What Have We Learned From the Answers?

Modern scholars and social thinkers complain that the disciplines of *psychology* and *sociology* are fragmented into schools of thought, conflicting theories, and diversified specializations. They say there is much reason to doubt that any single theory will explain both the biological aspects of mental processes and human introspection, emotions, and motivations. No unified, reliable body of answers to questions of human nature and behavior has emerged. The split between clinician-practitioners and social activists on the one hand and academician-scientists on the other grows wider.[39] While this may be a problem to secular theorists, who want neat packages to fit the natural science model, it may be a source of reinforcement to Christian scholars in the behavioral sciences. Like Heddendorf said of the hidden threads, I am thrilled when secular scientists admit their limitations. There is joy in knowing the unifying and overarching truths that form the basis for any adequate search for the whole truth.

---

[39]Morton Hunt, *The Story of Psychology* (New York: Doubleday, 1993), 641–643.

This insight brings us to our main conclusion: *Listening to the scholars is wise and profitable if we keep our Christian perspective.* If we remember that the basic error in all the social and behavioral sciences lies in their failure to deal with human purpose as God's creation, we can study them profitably and in the process learn much about ourselves and others. What makes us, or the sources of our behavior, are many and complex. We can summarize briefly that psychology and sociology generally explain human nature by naming three sources of behavior.

Biological. As human beings and as individuals we are born with physical characteristics and conditions that affect both how we respond to stimuli (i.e., learn) and how we develop as persons.

Psychological. People perceive their world in selective ways because of their experiences. They make decisions and act on the basis of the information they have or think they have. Each experience affects other perceptions, feelings, emotions, attitudes, and motivations.

Socialization and social determinism. People acquire the beliefs, customs, values, and attitudes of their social group and culture. They learn what they are expected to do and say, whom to respect and fear. Their lifestyle choices may be severely restricted by environmental factors. Their actions may reflect social influence and situations more than reflecting their own decisions.

The principles embodied in this secular explanation of behavior are basically true, so the theories are useful. But they are incomplete and hence misleading in that they imply totally human explanations. They omit two fundamental sources of behavior: the impact of sin and the guidance of the Holy Spirit.

A major misunderstanding between Christian and non-Christian psychologists involves the meaning of *sin*. Therapists and social workers are especially unhappy with the word because they think of it as a disparaging term directed at persons in reference to specific behavior. The scriptural truth is that sin is humanity's fallen nature. As a result of the Fall, sin is our first state and a primary source of human behavior. We all suffer the consequences of Adam's sin, our own sins, and the sins of others.

Holy Spirit guidance is the major ideal source of Christian behavior. The Holy Spirit draws us to awareness of God's love and makes us conscious of sin. He arouses our needs for purpose and meaning in life. The work of the Holy Spirit is to open the door through which we can enter, and have assurance and belonging, as persons in Christian community.

My First and Best Answer

I began this chapter by telling how I came to ask the question that I later found to be among the most challenging inquiries ever voiced by humans. When I was about seven years old I discovered the clue that would lead me to the answer. It happened like this:

Somewhere as we followed the migrant stream to another crop we pitched our tent beside a river. In those days you could drive off the highway and find a suitable campsite, where you could build a fire, cook a pot of beans, and use river water for washing dishes and clothes.

"This is a good spot," my father said, "We'll stay here over Sunday."

In the morning I saw children passing on the bridge. "Where are they going, all dressed up?" Real people. Incredible as it sounds to modern middle-class persons, I was more curious than afraid. I had been on their territory before, selling baskets. I followed them, all the way to a small church at the edge of the village, and finally into a Sunday school class.

It was there I heard the first direct answer to the question in my heart.

"You are children of God," the teacher said, facing us all with a small inclusive gesture. It was as though she reached out, like a fairy with a wand, and granted me identity. I was a child of God.

Most people feel like migrants sometimes, wandering and confused. Some feel guilty and self-blaming because of events, situations, perceived failures. Some think they are rejected by others. Some are unfulfilled, pressed into roles or obligations that seem meaningless, or trapped by unknown forces in conditions they can't explain. They are looking for meaning, purpose, a place to belong, asking, Why am I like this? Who am I really? What makes people like they are?

After 60 years of study, research, and teaching in the behavioral sciences, I know that the first answer I received was the pivotal one, the one all other truth about human nature depends on. If we keep it in mind, we can gain insights and wisdom from psychology and sociology and every other universe of knowledge. That, in part, is what we mean by a Christian worldview.

Review and Discussion Questions

1. Explain why scholars have difficulty defining *psychology.*

2. Why does methodology depend on some assumptions about human nature?

3. Describe the basic differences among experimental, clinical, and humanistic psychology.

4. Has the material on humanistic psychology enlightened you on the concept *humanism* as it is used in behavioral sciences? Explain. Do you believe we can be Christian humanists?

5. Write a comprehensive definition of *sociology.* What are the two major objectives of sociology? How can knowledge in both areas be applied to Christian life and service?

6. Explain why failing to consider human purpose is the major flaw in psychological and sociological theories.

7. Margaret Paloma believes both naturalistic and humanistic assumptions are partially compatible with the biblical image of person. Explain her reasoning.

8. Russell Heddendorf introduces the idea of "hidden threads" of Scriptural truth in academic theories. Look over the needs models of Maslow and Brill and point out some hidden threads.

9. The author suggests that being a "marginal person" helped her to look for answers and gain insights concerning human nature and relationships. How can we apply this concept to gain the most from both academic and Christian experiences?

10. Enumerate some ways our view of human nature affects our own self-concept and our social attitudes and relationships

Extended Project for Reflection

As you study for courses in any of the social and behavioral sciences (psychology, sociology, anthropology, social work, counseling, government, history) look for the "hidden threads" that either support Scriptural truth or oppose it. In church services and Sunday school classes look for ideas, concepts, assumptions, about human nature that are either compatible with human studies or cause you to question secular teaching. Keeping alert in these areas will help you get the most from both secular education and religion.

Selected Bibliography

Ashley, David, and David Michael Orenstein. *Sociological Theory: Classical Statements*. Boston: Allyn and Bacon. 1985.

Becker, Howard, and Harry Elmer Barnes. *Social Thought from Lore to Science*. New York: Dover Publications, 1961.

Brill, Naomi I. *Working With People: The Helping Process*. New York: Longman, 1985.

Burke, Thomas J., ed. *Man and Mind: A Christian Theory of Personality*. Hillsdale, Mich.: Hillsdale College Press, 1987.

Collins, Gary R. *The Biblical Basis of Christian Counseling for People Helpers*. Colorado Springs, Colo.: Navpress, 1993.

_____. *The Rebuilding of Psychology*. Wheaton, Ill.: Tyndale House Publishers, Inc., 1976.

Davis, Billie. *Renewing Hope: Helps for Helping Others*. Springfield, Mo.: Gospel Publishing House, 1995.

_____. *The Dynamic Classroom*. Springfield, Mo.: Gospel Publishing House, 1987.

Denny, M. Ray, and Robert H. Davis. *Understanding Behavior—Foundations and Applications*. Geneva, Ill.: Paladin House Publishers, 1981.

Downing, Lester N. *Counseling Theories and Techniques: Summarized and Critiqued.* Chicago: Nelson-Hall, 1975.

Evans, C. Stephen. *Preserving the Person.* Downers Grove, Ill.: InterVarsity Press, 1977.

Fraser, David A., and Tony Campolo. *Sociology through the Eyes of Faith.* San Francisco: Harper/SanFrancisco, 1992.

Glen, Joshua. "Sociology on the Skids." *Utne Reader* (November/December 1995).

Grunlan, Stephen A., and Marvin K. Mayers. *Cultural Anthropology: A Christian Perspective.* 2d. ed. Grand Rapids: Zondervan Publishing House, 1988.

Heddendorf, Russell. *Hidden Threads: Social Thought for Christians.* Dallas: Probe Books, 1990.

Henry, Carl F. H. *The Christian Mindset in a Secular Society.* Portland, Ore.: Multnomah Press, 1984.

Hunt, Morton. *The Story of Psychology.* New York: Doubleday, 1993.

Kendler, Howard H. *Historical Foundations of Modern Psychology.* Chicago: Dorsey Press, 1987.

Kinget, G. Marian. *On Being Human—A Systematic View.* New York: Harcourt Brace Jovanovich, 1975.

Leming, Michael R., Raymond G. DeVries, and Brendan F. J. Furnish, eds. *The Sociological Perspective: A Value Committed Introduction.* Grand Rapids: Zondervan Publishing House, 1989.

McKenna, David, *The Psychology of Jesus: The Dynamics of Christian Wholeness.* Waco, Tex.: Word Books, 1977.

Maslow, Abraham H. *Motivation and Personality.* New York: Harper and Row, 1970.

Munyon, Timothy. "The Creation of the Universe and Humankind." In *Systematic Theology,* edited by Stanley M. Horton. Springfield, Mo.: Logion Press, 1994.

Myers, David G., and Malcolm A. Jeeves. *Psychology Through the Eyes of Faith.* San Francisco: Harper and Row Publishers, 1987.

Paloma, Margaret. "Theoretical Models of Person in Contemporary Sociology: Toward Christian Sociological Theory." In *A Reader in Sociology: Christian Perspectives,* edited by Charles P. De Santo, Calvin Redekop, and William L. Smith-Hinds. Scottdale, Pa.: Herald Press, 1980.

Perkins, Richard. *Looking Both Ways: Exploring the Interface between Christianity and Sociology.* Grand Rapids: Baker Book House, 1987.

Pinker, Steven. *The Language Instinct.* New York: William Morrow, 1994.

Ritzer, George. *Sociological Theory*. 3d ed. New York: McGraw-Hill. 1992.

Rush, Vincent. *The Responsible Christian*. Chicago: Loyola University Press, 1984.

Sider, Ronald J. *One-sided Christianity? Uniting the Church to Heal a Lost and Broken World*. Grand Rapids: Zondervan Publishing House, 1993.

Vitz, Paul C. "A Christian Theory of Personality: Covenant Theory." In *Man and Mind: A Christian Theory of Personality*. ed. Thomas J. Burke. Hillsdale, Mich.: Hillsdale College Press, 1987.

Wirt, Sherwood Eliot. *The Social Conscience of the Evangelical*. New York: Harper and Row, 1968.

6
Work

Miroslav Volf

There is a famous character in Russian literature, Count Oblomov, who suffered a peculiar kind of illness: He was lazy. While most of us are occasionally affected by this illness, with him it had become chronic. He developed a general distaste for all activity. He lived off his large estate, but even that was too much work for him. He had to oversee management of his possessions, pay visits to people, get up and get dressed, chew his food and swallow it. In a word, he had to live. But his monumental laziness rebelled against all concessions. So he decided to draw back into complete apathy—he gave up overseeing his possessions, refused to see any visitors, left all mail unopened, and would not even open his windows to let in the light of day. Yet all this was in vain. There was still too much hustle and bustle in his inactivity, Oblomov felt. Even when he decided to do absolutely nothing, there still remained one thing he could not cease doing, one business he could never stop attending to, one burden he could not cease carrying, and that is the business and the burden of existence itself. As Alain Finkielkraut, from whom I borrowed this story, says in his book *Wisdom of Love,* "One can go on strike against everything, but not against one's existence. Oblomov removes all hindrances that stand in the way of his radical laziness, only to come up against this one immovable barrier. His laziness is but a useless sigh."[1] It takes work just to exist. No work, no life—this summarizes the lesson we learn from Oblomov's futile attempt to do absolutely nothing.

For many of us today, however, the question is not how lazy you can get without ceasing to exist but how much work you can do without breaking down. Some of us are addicted to work, but most of us feel we are forced to work; some of us need work in order to achieve, but most of us must work in order to survive. And so we work, day in and day out. In the book *The Overworked American*, Juliet B. Schor points out that people in industrialized societies are caught in the "insidious cycle of 'work-and-spend.'"[2] She writes, "Employers ask for long hours. The pay creates a high level of consumption. People buy houses and go into debt; luxuries become necessities; Smiths keep up with Joneses. Each year, 'progress,' in the form of annual productivity increases, is doled out by employers as extra income rather than time off. Work-and-spend has become a powerful dynamic keeping us from a more relaxed and leisured way of life."[3] Our "having" is in a race with our "wanting," but our "wanting," is swifter than our "having." And so we seem victims of Lewis Carroll's curse: "Here, you see, it takes all the run-

[1]Alain Finkielkraut, *Die Weisheit der Liebe,* translated from Russian by N. Volland (Reinbeck bei Hamburg: Rowohlt Verlag, 1989), 17.

[2]Juliet B. Schor, *The Overworked American: The Unexpected Decline of Leisure* (New York: Basic Books, 1992), 11.

[3]Ibid., 9f.

ning you can do, to keep in the same place." As John Kenneth Galbraith put it in his classic *The Affluent Society*, our struggle to satisfy wants is like the effort "of the squirrel to keep abreast of the wheel that is propelled by his own efforts."[4]

If Oblomov almost "lazied" himself to death, many people today are, in Schor's words, "literally working themselves to death—as jobs contribute to heart disease, hypertension, gastric problems, depression, exhaustion, and a variety of other ailments."[5] Too little work, and we cannot survive; too much work, and life is sucked out of us. Work is our blessing and work is our curse.

> **"Our 'having' is in a race with our 'wanting,' but our 'wanting' is swifter than our 'having.'"**

Caught between work as a blessing and work as a curse, how do we live? What help can the Bible give us as we struggle daily with our work? How does work relate to who God created us to be? What is the place of work in God's purposes with our lives? What kind of work is below our human dignity? What kind of impact does the cumulative work of humanity have upon our environment? These are important questions, but they usually go unasked. And yet most of us spend much of our time working. Before I try to answer them,[6] let me state briefly what I mean by *work*.

What Is Work?

"If no one asks of me, I know; if I wish to explain to him who asks, I know not." This was how Augustine expressed his difficulty with defining "time." The same seems true of "work." We think we know what work is, yet when we try to put into words what we think we know work is, we stammer.

I will begin explaining what work is by pointing out some things it is not. First, though often very strenuous, work is *not simply toil and drudgery*, as some people tend to think, partly wrongly interpreting Genesis 3. Many people in fact enjoy their

---

[4]John K. Galbraith, *The Affluent Society* (Boston: Houghton Mifflin, 1958), 154.

[5]Schor, *The Overworked American*, 11.

[6]I have intentionally left out some aspects of human work, such as the relationship between work and rest or leisure, because they are addressed in another chapter. In the following text I will not make extensive references to secondary literature. For a more extensive treatment of the themes that I here address, see especially Miroslav Volf, *Work in the Spirit: Toward a Theology of Work* (New York: Oxford UP, 1991). See also "Eschaton, Creation, and Social Ethics," *Calvin Theological Journal* 30 (1995), 130–143; "Work and the Gifts of the Spirit," in *Christianity and Economics in the Post-Cold War Era: The Oxford Declaration and Beyond*, ed. Herbert Schlossberg et al. (Grand Rapids: Eerdmans, 1994), 33–56; "On Human Work: An Evaluation of the Key Ideas of the Encyclical *Laborem Exercens*," *Scottish Journal of Theology* 36 (1984), 65–79.

work, and those who do are often the best workers. Would it not be strange to say that the best workers do not work? Second, work is *not simply gainful employment*. Though the majority of people in industrialized societies are gainfully employed, many work hard without pay. Take, for instance, housewives (rarely househusbands) who spend almost all of their waking hours keeping a household in order and raising children. Many of them rightly resent when people insinuate that they do not work; this is adding insult ("you do not work") to injury (they are not paid).

We need a broad definition of work, one that will include both work that is enjoyed and work that is suffered, work that is paid and work that is voluntary. A very simple definition of work would be "an activity that serves to satisfy human needs": You cook a meal in order to have something to eat; you type manuscripts in order to get a paycheck. In contrast, the purpose of play is play: You play tennis because you like playing tennis; you read a book because you like reading books. Of course, cooking can be your hobby; then you cook because you like cooking, and filling empty stomachs is then a useful side-benefit. Similarly, playing tennis (if you are a professional player) or reading books (if you are a student or professor) can be your work; then you play because you need money or recognition, and you read books because you need to pass an exam or prepare a lecture; the sheer fun of playing or reading is then a happy coincidence. Work, then, is an instrumental activity: It is done not for its own sake but to satisfy human needs.

Why Do We Work?

Remembering Oblomov's futile attempts to do nothing, a quick response to the question Why do we work? would be, Because we could not survive without working. Yet this answer, though correct on one level, would state not so much the reason we work as the purpose of our work. So I will return to work viewed as a means of "keeping body and soul together" in the next section when I address the purpose of work. For Christians, the question Why do we work? has a more profound answer.

First, *God created human beings to work.* Consider the two accounts of creation in the first chapters of Genesis. In Genesis 1:26 we read that God created human beings as male and female to "rule over" all the earth. Two verses later God blessed the first human pair and commanded them to "subdue" the earth and "rule over" all living beings (which, by the way, did not give them license to destroy the environment, something I will address later). "Dominion," which can be exercised only through work, is *the purpose for which God created human beings* (not the only purpose, but one purpose). That it is mentioned here explicitly is surely significant. Work, we can conclude, belongs essentially to the very nature of human beings as originally created by

God. This is why we find personal fulfillment in meaningful work, and, on the other hand, if we cannot work we find our lives empty and without meaning.

The same idea is underscored even more forcefully in the second account of creation (Gen. 2:4b–3:24). When we read this text we often concentrate on its important "spiritual" lessons and overlook the fact that work is one of its central themes. The account starts with the observation that there was no one to "work the ground" (Gen. 2:5) and concludes with the statement that God sent man out of the Garden of Eden "to work the ground from which he had been taken" (Gen. 3:23). Within this framework the narrative speaks, on the one hand, of Adam's "working" and "taking care" of the Garden (2:15) and, on the other hand, of the work "in the sweat of his brow" outside of the Garden (3:17–19). As Goran Agrell argued in *Work, Toil and Sustenance*, how the paradisaical work in Eden became the exhausting toil outside of it is a major theme of the narrative.[7]

For our purposes here it is important to note that, after creating man, God placed him in the Garden with an explicit purpose: "to work it and take care of it" (2:15). The Hebrew idea that humankind was supposed to *work* in paradise stands in marked contrast to Greek images of paradise. In *Works and*

> **"Work belongs essentially to the very nature of human beings created by God."**

Days the Greek poet Hesiod, for instance, insisted that in paradise human beings should live like gods, "free from work and toil," that the bountiful earth should of itself provide them with its fruits. Not so in the Bible. From the very beginning, human beings were created to work. Besides life without work not being possible, life without work for all those physically and mentally capable of working would not be meaningful. Indeed, such a life would not be properly human. Work belongs to the very nature of humanity. In that human beings "go out to their work" (Ps. 104:23), they fulfill the original plan of the Creator for their lives.

For Greeks, living like gods meant living without work. For Hebrews, living like God meant having meaningful work. The most striking feature of the Old Testament account of creation is not so much that human beings are meant to work, but that *God* works.[8] The first time the word *work* occurs in the Bible it does not refer to human work but to divine work: "By the sev-

---

[7]See Goran Agrell, *Work, Toil and Sustenance: An examination of the View of Work in the New Testament, taking into Consideration Views Found in Old Testament, Intertestamental and Early Rabbinic Writings* (Lund: Verbum/Hakan Ohlssons, 1976), 8.

[8]On the issue of divine work see Robert J. Banks, *God the Worker: Journeys into the Mind, Heart, and Imagination of God* (Claremont: Albatros, 1992).

enth day God had finished the work he had been doing: so on the seventh day he rested from all his work" (Gen. 2:2). The same word for work (Heb. m*ela'khto*) here used to describe God's activity is elsewhere used to describe ordinary human work, for instance, of Joseph, who "went into the house to attend to his duties [Heb. m*ela'khto*]" (Gen. 39:11). Because the God of the Bible is a worker, work has human dignity, not just economic value. Human beings, created in the image of God, work because their God works.

> "Because the God of the Bible is a worker, work has human dignity, not just economic value."

Second, we work because *God gifts and calls us to work*. We should expect that God who has created human beings to work will also impart to them gifts to do various tasks and call them to these tasks. And this is exactly what we find in the Old Testament. The Spirit of God inspired craftsmen and artists who designed, constructed, and adorned the tabernacle and the temple. "See, the Lord has chosen Bezalel . . . he has filled him with the Spirit of God, with skill, ability and knowledge in all kinds of crafts . . . And he has given . . . him . . . the ability to teach" (Exod. 35:30–34). "Then David gave his son Solomon . . . the plans of all that the Spirit had put in his mind for the courts of the temple of the Lord" (1 Chron. 28:11–12). Moreover, judges and kings in Israel are often said to do their task under the anointing of the Spirit of God (see Judg. 3:10; 1 Sam. 16:13; 23:2; Prov. 16:10).

When we come to the New Testament, the first thing to note is that all God's people are gifted and called to various tasks by the Spirit of God (see Acts 2:17; 1 Cor. 12:7), not just special people like temple artisans, kings, or prophets. Placed in the context of the new covenant, the above passages from the Old Testament provide biblical illustrations for a charismatic understanding of all the basic types of human work: All human work, however complicated or simple, is made possible by the operation of the Spirit of God in the working person. How could it be different? If the whole life of a Christian is by definition a life in the Spirit, then work cannot be an exception, whether that work is church work or secular work, "spiritual" work or mundane work. In other words, *work in the Spirit is one dimension of the Christian walk in the Spirit* (see Rom. 8:4; Gal. 5:16–25).

God desires all Christians to employ through their work various gifts God has given them. God calls people to enter the kingdom of God and to live a life in accordance with its demands. When they respond, God enables them to bear the fruit of the Spirit and endows them individually with multiple gifts of the Spirit. As those who are gifted by the Spirit and guided by the demands of love, Christians should do their work in the service of God and humanity.

If God created people to work and if God endows them with gifts to accomplish various tasks, two important consequences follow. First, work is not merely a means to an end. It is not simply a chore to be endured for the sake of meeting needs and satisfying desires. If you recall our definition of work, you will know that work will always remain an instrument, will always be a means. Yet this is not all work is, and this is not what the best work is. Because work is essential to our humanity, work *also has an intrinsic value.*

Second, all types of work have equal dignity. Religious work (such as preaching or teaching in a seminary) is not better than secular work (such as baking bread or building bridges); both are equally good if done in response to the gift and the call of the Spirit of God. The equality of all work was one of the basic insights of the great Protestant reformer Martin Luther. Along with the idea that a person is justified by faith alone, he discovered that everyday work should be done in response to a call of God. All Christians, not just monks, he insisted, have a "calling," and every type of work performed by Christians, not just religious service, can be a calling. He was right. For God is not only the God of redemption but also the God of creation; not simply the God of our soul but also the God of our bodies; not simply the God of the heavens but the God of the heavens and the earth.

The Purpose of Work

We work, I have argued, because we are created and gifted by God to work. The reason why we work lies in the very nature of who we are as human beings and what our purpose is on this earth. What about the *purpose* of work?

The first and foremost purpose of work is *to obtain necessities of life.* According to the apostle Paul, Christians should work "and earn the bread they eat" (2 Thess. 3:12); they should work in order not to "be dependent on anybody" (1 Thess. 4:12b). As Karl Barth put it, the first thing at issue in all fields of human work is the need of human beings "to earn their daily bread and a little more."

> "Every type of work performed by Christians, not just religious service, can be a calling."

The need to work to provide for necessities of life lies behind the duty to work. For Paul, this duty is of primary importance, so much so that it was part of the original instruction that Paul gave to the Thessalonians when he first evangelized them: "Even when we were with you, we gave you this rule: 'If a man will not work, he shall not eat'" (2 Thess. 3:10), a portion of the Bible that was quoted even in the Constitution of the old Soviet Union! Moreover, we have no reason to think that the Thessalonians were in this respect an exception. Other Pauline churches received similar instruction. For this was part of the teaching or "tradition" (2 Thess. 3:6) about the Christian manner of life.

The second, and closely related, purpose of work is *to provide for the needy.* In Ephesians, Christians are exhorted to "work, doing something useful" with their own hands, so as to have something "to share with those in need" (4:28). The exhortation echoes the belief and experience of the early Church that there should be "no needy persons among them" (Acts 4:34), an ideal inspired, no doubt, by the teaching of Jesus and the promises of the Old Testament (see Deut. 15:4). Similarly, in Paul's farewell address at Miletus, the primary purpose of work is to help the economically weak: "In everything I did, I showed you that by this kind of hard work we must help the weak, remembering the words the Lord Jesus himself said: 'It is more blessed to give than to receive'" (Acts 20:35). This verse is radical. It commands more than just helping the poor if we can; it commands laboring strenuously (which is the meaning of *kopiôntas*, the Greek word used) in order to have the necessary means to help. Moreover, supporting the needy through diligent work was not simply an act of generosity; rather, it was a demand of justice. For example, Paul calls the financial help of Gentile Christians for destitute Christians of Palestine explicitly "justice" or "righteousness" (Gk. *dikaiosunê*; 2 Cor. 9:9). This echoes the Old Testament view that almsgiving is not simply charity but justice. As we read in Psalms of the righteous, they have "scattered abroad" their "gifts to the poor," their "righteousness endures forever" (112:9).

The third purpose of work is *the development of culture.* On the surface, this purpose of work is not as obvious as the other two. Nevertheless, it is no less significant. The best way to get at it is to contrast what the Old Testament says about human work and what the Mesopotamian creation myths say about it. In the Atra-Hasis epic, the story of human creation starts with a description of an episode in the lives of the gods, the lower ones called Igigi and the higher ones called Anunnaki:

> When gods were like men,
> Bore the work and suffered the toil,
> The toil of the gods was great,
> The work was heavy, the distress was much.
> The Seven great Anunnaki
> Were making the Igigi suffer the work.[9]

The Igigi gods were, of course, unhappy with their lot; they were "complaining" and "backbiting." They even decided to rebel—they set fire to their tools and started besieging the temple of the great god Enlil. Through negotiations, however, a solution was found: the creation of human beings. Human beings should "bear the yoke" and "carry the toil of the gods." So the goddess Mami created human beings. After finishing the job she addressed the gods:

---

[9]*Atra-Hasis: The Babylonian Story of the Flood*, ed. W. G. Lambert and A. R. Millard (Oxford: Clarendon Press, 1969), 43.

I have removed your heavy work,
I have imposed your toil on man.
You raised a cry for mankind,
I have loosed the yoke, I have established freedom.[10]

Human beings were created to liberate gods from strenuous labor; human beings are a solution to the problem created by lower gods going on strike.[11] When humans work, they serve gods by doing the work gods were supposed to do. Human work is immediately related to service of the gods. Work is a cultic activity.

Contrast this with the Old Testament account of creation. Far from humans being created to liberate gods from strenuous work, in Genesis 2 it is God who works for human beings: God plants the garden for human provision (v. 8). In Genesis 1, moreover, the purpose of human creation concerns quite worldly things: It has to do with ruling over animals and subduing the earth. Human work is, if you please, "demythologized": It is divorced from its immediate connection with the cult and put into the service of *culture*.[12] Work is not a cultic, but a cultural, activity.

The fourth purpose of work is *cooperation with God*.[13] Genesis 2:5 suggests that there is a mutual dependence between God and human beings in the task of conserving creation. God's work and human work are related in the text when the reason is given why at the beginning "no shrub of the field had yet appeared on the earth and no plant of the field had yet sprung up: the LORD God had not sent rain on the earth" (v. 5). The reason was twofold: first, "the LORD God had not caused it to rain upon the earth," and second, there was no one "to work the ground" (v. 5). It takes the cooperation of God who sends rain and human beings who till the soil for plants to grow. Thus, far from being beasts of burden for the gods as in Mesopotamian myths, in the Bible human beings are coworkers with God. On the one hand, human beings are dependent on God, for "Unless the LORD builds the house, its builders labor in vain" (Ps. 127:1). On the other hand, God made human work a means by which to accomplish his work in the world. As Luther puts it, human

---

[10]*Atra-Hasis*, 59f.

[11]See Walter Zimmerli, "Mensch und Arbeit im Alten Testament," *Recht auf Arbeit—Sinn der Arbeit*, ed. Jürgen Moltmann (München: Christian Kaiser, 1979), 52.

[12]Jürgen Ebach, "Zum Thema: Arbeit und Ruhe im Alten Testament. Eine Utopische Erinnerung," *Zeitschrift für Evangelische Ethik* 24 (1980), 17.

[13]Against Stanley Hauerwas, "Work as Co-Creation: A Critique of a Remarkably Bad Idea," in *Co-Creation and Capitalism: John Paul II's Laborem Exercens*, ed. J. W. Houck and O. F. Williams (Lanham, Md.: University Press of America, 1983), 48.

work is "God's mask behind which he hides himself and rules everything magnificently in the world."

In *Issues Facing Christians Today*, John Stott tells a story that illustrates well the cooperation between God and human beings in mundane work.

"A cockney gardener was showing a parson the beauty of his garden, with its herbaceous borders in full summer bloom. Duly impressed, the parson broke out into spontaneous praise of God. The gardener was not very pleased, however, that God should get all the credit. 'You should 'ave seen 'ere garden,' he said, 'when God 'ad it all to 'isself.'"

"He was right," continues Stott. "His theology was entirely correct. Without a human cultivator, every garden quickly degenerates into a wilderness."[14]

There is yet another purpose of human work which we can touch here only briefly: It is *cooperation with God in the transformation of creation.* When we place cooperation with God in preservation of creation in the light of the promised new creation, then it becomes clear that human beings also cooperate with God in anticipation of God's eschatological transformation of the world. True, we are not ushering in the kingdom of God, building the "new heavens and a new earth;" only God can do that. Much like the original creation, the new creation is first of all a *gift* of God's grace, not a result of human effort.

Yet the God who gives is also the God who commands and inspires. Expectation of the kingdom is not contrary to participation with God who is already at work building the kingdom. If we work in the power of the Spirit who is "the first installment" of the eschatological glory (see 2 Cor. 1:22; Rom. 8:23), then our work in which we cooperate with God is active anticipation of the kingdom of God. Placed in the context of kingdom-participation, mundane work for worldly betterment, though it may be slight and imperfect, though needing divine purification, becomes a contribution to the eschatological kingdom, which will come ultimately through God's action. As Jürgen Moltmann puts it in the article "The Right to Work," in their daily work human beings are "co-workers in God's kingdom, which completes creation and renews heaven and earth."[15] God will purify, transfigure, and receive into his eternal kingdom all good and beautiful things that human hands have created.

> "Human work is 'God's mask behind which he rules everything magnificently in the world.'"
> —*Martin Luther*

---

[14]John Stott, *Issues Facing Christians Today* (Basingstoke, England: Marshalls, 1984), 160.

[15]Jürgen Moltmann, "The Right to Work," *On Human Dignity: Political Theology and Ethics*, tr. D. Meeks (Philadelphia: Fortress Press, 1984), 45.

Against the idea that work is cooperation with God in preservation and transformation of the world, one can object that it excessively glorifies work. It is therefore important to keep in mind that the notion of work as collaboration with God is *not a general theory of work*, applicable to any and every kind of work. Often human work is done in cooperation with evil powers, which scheme to ruin God's good creation. Just think of all the hard work that was done to uphold Hitler's Germany, Stalin's Russia, or Pinochet's Chile. Human work is not only a place where the glory of human beings as God's coworkers shines forth. It is also a place where the misery of human beings as impeders of God's purposes becomes visible. Like the test of fire, God's judgment will bring to light the work that has ultimate significance because it was done in cooperation with God. But it will also manifest the ultimate insignificance of work done in cooperation with those demonic powers that scheme to ruin God's good creation (see 1 Cor. 3:12–15).

> "Often human work is done in cooperation with evil powers, which scheme to ruin God's good creation."

Human Work and God's Curse

Except for the previous paragraph, so far I have emphasized only the positive side of work: Work is essential to our humanity and through work we not only keep together our neighbor's soul and body as well as our own, but we also cooperate with God in preservation and transformation of our world. As we all know, however, there is also a seamy side of work. Since the Bible does not gloss over it, it would be highly inappropriate if theologians did. Theology of work is not an ideology designed to glorify work but a tool to help us transform work so that it corresponds to the will of God for His creation.

Consider what the second account of creation (Genesis 2 through 3), a text, it will be remembered, in which work figures very prominently, has to say about the seamy side of work. In the same text in which we read that God created human beings and placed them in the Garden to till and keep it we also read about human toil outside the Garden. Between the fulfilling work and drudgery stands an inexorable mystery of human sin. The text does not attempt to explain that mystery; it only tells of sin's appearance, human responsibility for it, and sin's consequences on human beings. One of the consequences has to do with human work. God says to Adam: "Cursed is the ground because of you; through painful toil you will eat of it all the days of your life. It will produce thorns and thistles for you, and you will eat the plants of the field. By the sweat of your brow you will eat your food until you return to the ground, since from it you were taken; for dust you are and to dust you will return" (Gen. 3:17–19).

Notice two things about this text. First, what is cursed is the ground, not Adam or his work. It is still sometimes stated that the Old Testament sees work as a curse; some philosophers, such as Jürgen Habermas, like to speak of "the biblical curse of necessary work."[16] For one, such an interpretation flies in the face of Genesis 1:26–31 and Genesis 2:15, where work is clearly a fundamental dimension of human life. More importantly, however, in Genesis 3:17–19 itself there is no suggestion that work is a curse. Rather, as a consequence of *the curse against the ground* work has become toil.

> **"Toil, like oppression, is surely a consequence of sin. But sin should never be used to justify toil and oppression."**

Second, for work to be toil means that it is no longer easy and fulfilling; rather human beings must till the ground in the sweat of their brow. Moreover, after the Fall even the most strenuous work cannot prevent thorns and thistles from growing in the crop. Work often results in failure, and all the toil is sometimes in vain. One could object that this is a rather pessimistic view of work. And yet will one remove the sweat from work of most human beings by complaining about the pessimism of this passage? Will thorns be taken from the products of work if we take them from the biblical text? My sense is that the passage is *realistic*, rather than pessimistic.

We have to be careful, however, what we do with the realism of this passage. Often enough in the history of Christianity the passage has been misused by the powerful to justify exploiting the weak: After the Fall, it was claimed, you have to suffer the drudgery of work, put up with its toil, not seek to better your condition. Yet this is clearly a misuse of the passage. Almost without exception, the Old Testament censures forced labor, for instance. The first six chapters of Exodus, which tell the story of Israel's slavery in Egypt, testify clearly to that.

> "The Egyptians . . . worked them ruthlessly. They made their lives bitter with hard labor in brick and mortar and with all kinds of work in the fields" (1:12–13).

How did God react to Israel's oppression?

> "The LORD said, 'I have indeed seen the misery of my people in Egypt. I have heard them crying out because of their slave drivers, and I am concerned about their suffering. So I have come down to rescue them from the hand of the Egyptians" (3:7–8).

Or consider what happened when the great King Solomon levied forced labor on his subjects in order to build the house of the Lord, his own palaces, and fortifications of the city (see

---

[16]Jürgen Habermas, *Erkenntnis und Interesse* (Frankfurt A.M.: Suhrkamp, 1979), 80.

1 Kings 9:15). Solomon's treatment of workers caused his successor, Rehoboam, to lose great portions of the kingdom (1 Kings 12:1–24). The king was supposed to be a "servant to this people," not their slave driver (1 Kings 12:7). Similarly, the prophets vehemently attacked the kings of Israel for exploiting their subjects. A good example are Jeremiah's words to the Davidic king, Jehoiakim:

> Woe to him who builds his palace by unrighteousness,
> his upper rooms by injustice,
> making his countrymen work for nothing,
> not paying them for their labor.
> He says, "I will build myself a great palace with spacious
> upper rooms."
> So he makes large windows in it, panels it with cedar
> and decorates it in red.
> "Does it make you a king to have more and more cedar?
> Did not your father have food and drink?
> He did what was right and just,
> so all went well with him.
> He defended the cause of the poor and needy,
> and so all went well.
> Is that not what it means to know me?" declares the
> LORD.
> "But your eyes and your heart are set only on dishonest
> gain,
> on shedding innocent blood
> and on oppression and extortion" (Jer. 22:13–17).

Toil, like oppression, is surely a consequence of sin. But sin should never be used to justify toil and oppression; rather, because toil and oppression are consequences of sin, they ought to be fought against. Toil and oppression must cease. This is the message inscribed in God's deliverance of his people from Egyptian slavery; this is the message proclaimed boldly by the prophets.

Bad Work, Good Work

Let us look at some significant negative aspects of work and examine how the Bible instructs us to react to them. What we are after here is how to make the bad work that we often experience into the good work that God intends us to do.

First, *exploitation*. Many people around the globe work long hours for low pay, contracts are nonexistent, sexual harassment occurs, and health and safety regulations are flouted. It is quite appropriate to speak of "exploitation" and "oppression" in such situations. As indicated in the previous section, the God of the Bible is the God who is intent on liberating people from forced labor and slavery (compare Deut. 26:6–8). Moreover, God's liberation of the exploited and oppressed is a model of how God's people should treat the exploited and oppressed in their midst (see Lev. 25:39ff.).

As an indication that God wants exploitation and oppression removed from the face of the earth, consider prophetic visions about the new age of salvation. In the prophecy about the new heavens and new earth, Isaiah not only speaks of a special nearness of people to God and of a peace in nature, but also of a new kind of work people will do. "They will build houses and dwell in them, they will plant vineyards and eat their fruit. No longer will they build houses and others live in them, or plant and others eat . . . They will not toil in vain or bear children doomed to misfortune" (Isa. 65:21–23). The contrast is stark: If today people work and others enjoy the fruit of their labor, in the age of salvation that God is to bring about, those who work will also reap the benefits of their labor. The message is clear: no more exploitation, no more oppression.

Second, *drudgery.* For many people in many parts of the world, work is an "arduous good," as John Paul II says in the encyclical letter *Laborem Exercens.* It is good because it helps feed their mouths and give meaning to their lives; it is arduous, however, because they suffer greatly under its burden, often working under the most appalling conditions. This is against the will of God the creator and redeemer. Human beings are created by God as persons endowed with gifts which God calls them to exercise freely. Consider the way God wanted the tabernacle in the wilderness built. In contrast to the forced labor that Solomon imposed while building the temple (1 Kings 9:15) as well as to the cruel slavery in Egypt, Moses not only asked for contributions of valuable materials from only those "of a generous heart" (see Exod. 35:5), but insisted that the work itself should be an act of freewill offering too. For we read that Moses called "every skilled person to whom the LORD has given skill and ability to know how to carry out all the work" (Exod. 36:2).

> "Human beings are created by God as persons endowed with gifts which God calls them to exercise freely."

To put it more abstractly, as a fundamental dimension of human existence, work is a personal activity. People ought therefore to work freely, and should never be treated as mere means. We must resist any tendency to treat workers as labor input. Rather, people should enjoy the work they do. The Reformers were quite right in stressing not only that human beings were originally created to work, but also that they were intended to work "without inconvenience" and, "as it were, in play and with the greatest delight."[17]

Third, *self-centeredness.* It was never easy to work for the common good. People always preferred to be served than to serve

---

[17]Martin Luther, *Martin Luthers Werke. Kritische Gesamtausgabe* (Weimar: H. Böhlau, 1883–), XLII, 78.

(see Mark 10:45) and therefore needed to be encouraged to serve others, especially the needy, through their work (Eph. 4:28). In contemporary societies, however, powerful forces contribute to the general shift from concern for community to preoccupation with self. We consider ourselves as autonomous individuals interacting with other autonomous individuals. Moreover, the stress on individual autonomy is accompanied by an equal stress on the pursuit of self-interest. We like to think that it is good to be "inner-directed," and that if we take care of ourselves first, we will be able and willing to take care of others. So we work for ourselves, caught in the web of our own desires and social expectations. Our work has personal utility, but no moral meaning.

> **"Legitimate self-interest must be accompanied by the pursuit of the good of others."**

Contrast this with what we find in the New Testament. There too we are encouraged to work for our own sustenance (2 Thess. 3:12), yet we are also called to work for needy fellow-human beings. As Ephesians puts it, we should work honestly with our own hands, so as to "have something to share with those in need" (Eph. 4:28). Commenting on Ephesians 4:28, John Calvin wrote: "It is not enough when a man can say, 'Oh, I labor, I have my craft,' or 'I have such a trade.' That is not enough. But we must see whether it is good and profitable for the common good, and whether his neighbors may fare the better for it."[18] For Calvin as well as for most of the Christian tradition, in addition to personal utility, work also had a moral dimension.

God calls people to use their gifts for the benefit of the whole community. Human work should be a contribution to the common good. Individual self-interest can legitimately be pursued. In a world of scarce resources that must be adapted to human needs if humans are to survive, there is an important sense in which every self must be "self-ish." Yet the legitimate self-interest must be accompanied by the pursuit of the good of others. These two pursuits are complementary, not contradictory. As we can see from Ephesians 5:25–28, the New Testament sees no contradiction when a person "gives himself up" for someone and "loves himself" at the same time.

Fourth, *discrimination*. Despite the significant gains that have been made toward gender equality in many countries, discrimination in work (as well as outside it) continues for many women. Women are "either pushed or pulled into a narrow range of occupations"[19] that are often underpaid and offer little status, security, advancement, or fringe benefits.

---

[18]John Calvin, *Sermons on the Epistle to the Ephesians* (Edinburgh: Banner of Truth, 1973), 457.

[19]W. T. Bielby and J. N. Baron, "Men and Women at Work: Sex Segregation and Statistical Discrimination," *American Journal of Sociology* 91 (1986): 760.

Though men and women were created different, they are equal before God. Eve was created directly by God, just as Adam was. The fact she was to be a help does not mean inferiority or subordination in any sense. The same word "help" (Heb. `ezer) is most often used of God as a help to His people. Moreover, in the community of faith there is no longer male and female, just like there is no longer slave or master (Gal. 3:28). Women should, therefore, be recognized and treated as equal to men in social and economic life.

Work in a Fragile Environment

After six days of work, God created the world and pronounced it "very good" (Gen. 1:31). In Isaiah we read that God will in the end create new heavens and a new earth (Isa. 65:17). Why will this new creation be necessary if the original creation was created good, as we are explicitly told? Because today, on account of human sin, creation is "groaning as in pains of childbirth" (Rom. 8:22).

> "The fact Eve was to be a help does not mean inferiority or subordination in any sense."

Through greed and violence sinful human beings have spoiled God's good creation. We have abused the earth's resources. Our planet is facing a crisis of the ecological system, which is due mostly to the cumulative acts of generations, especially after the Industrial Revolution. If we—mainly those of us who live in economically developed nations—continue to use the world's resources at the current rate, we will not only cause disastrous instability within the global ecosystem but will also deplete resources essential to the well-being of future generations. The earth's ecology will no longer sustain an indefinite expansion of productive forces.[20] What we call the "environmental crisis" is not simply a crisis of the environment; it is a crisis of life on this planet. How did we create a crisis of life on the planet? The answer is: through work! So if we are to redress the problem, we must rethink how work relates to environment.

Critics have blamed the Christian faith for the progressive destruction of the environment after the beginning of industrialization. At the center of their criticism was God's mandate in Genesis 1 "to subdue the earth" and have "dominion over it." In its larger context the mandate is problematic on three counts, it is claimed. First, the mandate to subdue the earth presupposes uniqueness of human beings, their separateness from the rest of creation, which in turn encourages their destructive behavior. Second, the whole text of Genesis 1 is centered on human beings: They are the crown of creation. This, it is argued, devalues the

---

[20]Partly on these grounds, Christopher Lasch has argued that we have to rethink the idea of progress. See his *True and Only Heaven: Progress and Its Critics* (New York: Norton & Co., 1991).

rest of creation. Third, this demand to subdue gives license to the destruction of the environment. Let us look briefly at these objections.

First, *human uniqueness.* No doubt, human beings are unique in creation, and not simply in the trite sense that every species is unique. Humans have a special place in creation. This seems rather obvious if for no other reason than for the fact that they alone can reflect about their position in creation. The biblical texts underline human uniqueness by stating that human beings were created after special deliberation on the part of God. All other creatures God simply makes; when it comes to human beings, God says, "Let us make" humankind "in our image," and then proceeds to make man and woman (Gen. 1:26–27).

The uniqueness of human beings notwithstanding, it would be a mistake to concentrate only on what distinguishes them from the rest of creation. Of all the things that we are told about human beings, probably the most fundamental one is that they are "creatures," standing alongside the other creatures over against God. Created on the sixth day, they are part of the sequence of creative acts of God. Similarly in Psalm 104, where the psalmist worships God by looking at the marvel of creation, human beings and nature comprise an inseparable unity.[21] As Karl Barth expressed it, in the creation human beings are "first among equals."

Second, *anthropocentrism.* The "Oxford Declaration on Christian Faith and Economics" gives an excellent brief response to the charge levied against the Christian faith that it is anthropocentric, concerned only with human beings rather than with the rest of creation:

> Biblical life and worldview is not centered on humanity. It is God-centered. Nonhuman creation was not made exclusively for human beings. We are repeatedly told in the Scripture that all things, human beings and the environment in which they live, were "for God" (Romans 11:36; 1 Corinthians 8:6; Colossians 1:16). Correspondingly, nature is not merely the raw material for human activity. Though only human beings have been created in the image of God, non-human creation has a dignity of its own, so much so that after the flood God established a covenant not only with Noah and his descendants, but also "with every living creature that is with you" (Genesis 9:9). Similarly, the Christian hope for the future includes also creation. "The creation itself [i.e., the whole of non-human creation] will be set free from its bondage to decay and obtain the glorious liberty of the children of God" (Romans 8:21).[22]

---

[21]See O. H. Steck, *Welt und Umwelt* (Stuttgart: Kohlhammer, 1978), 68.

[22]"The Oxford Declaration on Christian Faith and Economics," in *Christianity and Economics in the Post-Cold War Era: The Oxford Declaration and Beyond*, ed. Herbert Schlossberg et al. (Grand Rapids: Eerdmans, 1994), 13f.

The term *modernity* refers to the new civilization developed in Europe and North American over the last several centuries and fully evident by the early twentieth century. The modern outlook is characterized by confidence in human reason to exercise technological control over nature and to advance human knowledge by means of the scientific method. For a more extensive treatment of modernity, see Lawrence Cahoone, ed., *From Modernism to Postmodernism: An Anthology* (Cambridge, Mass.: Blackwell Publishers, 1996)

It is indisputable that the Christian civilization after the onset of modernity devalued nature. It is, however, equally indisputable that devaluation of nature cannot be done with the Bible, but only against the Bible.

Third, the *meaning of dominion*. It is true that the verbs used in Genesis 1:26 and 28 are violent; to rule or have dominion (Heb. *radhah*) is used of treading the vine press (Joel 4:13) or of one country's subjugating another (Num. 24:19). The crucial question, however, is whether these verbs have violent connotations in Genesis 1. Do they give human beings unlimited rule over the earth?[23] Do human beings remain in "every case and at every phase" of mastering the earth "within the Creator's original ordering," as we read in the encyclical from John Paul II, *Laborem Exercens*?[24] Everything speaks against such an understanding of Genesis 1.

1. Even though "dominion" sometimes has connotations of violence, in Genesis 1 it refers to animals which were *not originally given to human beings as food* (cf. Gen. 1:29–30). It therefore does not include the killing of animals. Some commentators think it refers to their domestication.[25]

2. The Old Testament uses *radhah* to designate kingly rule (see 1 Kings 5:4; Ps. 110:2). In subduing the earth, human beings are exercising their royal responsibility. We should understand this rule in the context of Israel's ideal of a king. A king should be a "servant" of the people and care for their good (1 Kings 12:7). Moreover, as rulers over the earth, human beings are responsible to God who created them in His image. They must rule in accordance with God's will for God's creation (Gen. 1:31).

3. It is important to note that Genesis 1:26–28 relates the mandate to have dominion closely to God's blessing. Through their royal rule, human beings should mediate God's blessing to creation. And that blessing effects well-being rather than destruction.

4. Human beings are created in the image of God as community, not simply as isolated individuals (Gen. 1:26–28). Hence, they have to exercise dominion in responsibility to the whole human community, the global community in the chain of generations.

The second account of creation confirms this interpretation of dominion. Here we read that God placed human beings in the Garden of Eden not only to till (or work) it (*'avadh*) but also to

---

[23]See, for instance. B. Jacob, *Das erste Buch der Tora. Genesis* (Berlin: Shocken, 1934), 61.

[24]*Laborem Exercens. Encyclical Letter of the Supreme Pontiff John Paul II on Human Work* (London: Catholic Trust Society, 1981), no. 4.

[25]See Norbert Lohfink, "Macht euch die Erde Untertan?" *Orientierung* 38 (1974), 139; Claus Westermann, *Schöpfung* (Stuttgart: Kreuz Verlag, 1979), 78.

keep it (*shamar*) (Gen. 2:15). Consequently, human dominion consists in the twofold task of "working" and "taking care" of the creation. Working and taking care are two complementary aspects of human activity. All work must have not only a productive but also a protective aspect. Human beings rule over creation in accordance with the Creator's intentions only when their rule helps preserve the wholeness of God's creation. How else could their work be cooperation with God?

One final comment on the nature of dominion. At the beginning of modernity Francis Bacon recognized that "man fell from his state of innocence and from his dominion over creation" as a result of sin. But whereas he believed that innocence can be regained "by religion and faith," he maintained that for regaining dominion, the "arts and sciences" would suffice.[26] He granted that the exercise of technological power should be governed not only by sound reason but by religion. But it did not take long before God was forgotten and dominion was perverted into the exercise of brute technological power guided by instrumental reason alone.

Today we *need to rediscover the religious and moral dimensions of dominion over nature*. Reformers were aware that dominion based simply on arts and sciences is an inferior dominion. Only "upright" human beings can exercise true dominion over nature. Could this be the point of the statement in Mark that during Jesus' temptation in the wilderness He "was with the wild animals" but did not need to tame them (1:13)? Did not His communion with the wild beasts, the communion of Him who conquered the temptation to misuse power for self-aggrandizement, anticipate the future peace between human beings and nonhuman creation, a peace that will be the fruit of righteousness (see Isa. 11:6–8; 65:25)?

In Place of a Conclusion: The Warning of Albert Speer

In *Truthfulness and Tragedy* Stanley Hauerwas tells the story of Albert Speer, Hitler's architect and later minister of armaments. How could an intelligent young man like Speer go along with Hitler? Speer explains to his daughter:

> You must realize that at the age of thirty-two, in my capacity as an architect, I had the most splendid assignments of which I could dream. Hitler said to your mother one day that her husband could design buildings the like of which had not been seen for two thousand years. One would have had to be morally very stoical to reject the proposal. But *I was not at all like that*.[27]

The expression "instrumental reason" refers to one of the important uses of human reason. Specifically, it refers to the way human beings attempt to solve problems or reach goals by means of rational inquiry. In this sense, reason is the means, the *instrument*, for solving a problem or reaching a goal. By contrast, human beings also sometimes think about final things: e.g., the meaning of life or one's moral obligations. Reason, so employed, is *reflective* or *contemplative*, not instrumental. Thus, instrumental reason considers means to ends while reflective reason considers the ends themselves.

---

[26]Cited by W. Leiss, *The Domination of Nature* (New York: Georges Braziller, 1972), 49.

[27]Cited by Stanley Hauerwas, Richard Bondi, and David B. Burrell, *Truthfulness and Tragedy: Further Investigations in Christian Ethics* (Notre Dame: University of Notre Dame Press, 1977), 88ff.

Speer was "above all an architect" and out of "fear of discovering something which might have made me turn from my course" he chose not to know. "I had closed my eyes," he writes. With his eyes shut, he was oblivious to the crimes of the system he served, unable even to "see any moral ground outside the system where I should have taken my stand."[28]

Speer's temptations might have been greater because the Empire he worked for was more sinister, but they are basically no different from ours. In *The Gamesman: Winning and Losing the Career Game*, Michael Maccoby points out that careerism results in a loss of the self:

> Overly concerned with adapting himself to others, to marketing himself, the careerist constantly betrays himself, since he must ignore idealistic, compassionate, and courageous impulses that might jeopardize his career. As a result, he never develops an inner center, a strong, independent sense of self, and eventually he loses touch with his deepest strivings.[29]

The greatness and tragedy of Albert Speer, that consummate careerist, are one and the same: He was "above all an architect." Being "above all an architect" was his greatness because the singular devotion to his career made him an exceptionally good architect. Being "above all an architect" was his tragedy because the singular devotion to his career made him an exceptionally bad human being.

Work is dangerous. If you do not watch, it will split your professional excellence from your personal excellence, nurturing one and killing the other. It may lure you to strive to gain the whole world while blinding you to the fact that you are thereby losing your very soul (see Mark 8:36). The only way to be a good worker and a good person at the same time is to forget about gaining the "whole world" and strive instead for God's "kingdom and his righteousness" (Matt. 6:33).

Review and Discussion Questions

1. What does Volf mean when he says, "Work is our blessing and work is our curse"?

2. How does Volf define work? What does he think work is *not*?

3. Volf distinguishes between the *reason why* we work and the *purpose for* which we work. Explain this distinction. What is his answer to the question, Why do we work?

4. How does Volf explain the *purpose* of work? Actually he cites several purposes. What are they?

---

[28]Ibid., 90.

[29]Michael Maccoby, *The Gamesman: Winning and Losing the Career Game* (New York: Simon and Schuster, 1976), 204–205.

5. In the section entitled "Human Work and God's Curse," Volf describes the curse associated with the Fall. How does he relate the curse to human work?

6. The author identifies four negative aspects of work: exploitation, drudgery, self-centeredness, and discrimination. Summarize and illustrate one of these.

7. Critics have blamed the Christian faith for the progressive destruction of the environment after the beginning of industrialization. What evidence do the critics cite for their conclusion? Summarize Volf's response to the critics.

8. What is the point of telling the story of Albert Speer? Specifically, what does this man's story have to do with work?

Selected Bibliography

Hardy, Lee. *The Fabric of This World: Inquiries into Calling, Career Choice, and the Design of Human Work.* Grand Rapids: Eerdmans, 1990.

Laborem Exercens: Encyclical Letter of the Supreme Pontiff John Paul II on Human Work. London: Catholic Trust Society, 1981.

Jürgen Moltmann. "The Right to Work." In *On Human Dignity: Political Theology and Ethics,* D. Meeks, trans. Philadelphia: Fortress Press, 1984.

"The Oxford Declaration on Christian Faith and Economics." In *Christianity and Economics in the Post-Cold War Era: The Oxford Delaration and Beyond,* ed. H. Schlossberg et al. Grand Rapids: Eerdmans, 1994.

John Stott. "Work and Unemployment." In *Issues Facing Christians Today.* Basingstoke, England: Marshalls, 1984.

Miroslav Volf. *Work in the Spirit: Toward a Theology of Work.* New York: Oxford UP, 1991)

7

Entering Into "Divine Rest": Toward a Christian View of Leisure

Charles W. Nienkirchen

There was a boy who grew up in a small Canadian town. As part of a tightly-knit, working-class German subculture, his family taught him early to believe in work—its necessity, its moral value, and its rewards. Leisure and rest were rarely mentioned or modeled. The boy came to view all of life through the window of work. Everything, including his self-image, derived its worth from its relationship to work. "Working for God" became the premise that shaped his spiritual life. Believing that God was always asking him to do more by way of service, his lifestyle became one of highly extroverted, Christian activism. He evaluated spiritual success in terms of quantity of work and productivity—the only criteria he knew.

Years passed. "Workaholism" remained the reigning pattern of his life. During graduate studies, an interest in Christian history led him to explore Christian origins in the Middle East. A series of dialogues with monks who lived in the deserts of Egypt and Israel arrested him. He was intrigued by the motivations of a particular monk who had lived on the side of the Mount of Temptation outside of Jericho for over forty years. Amused by the monk's eccentricity and convinced of the irrelevance of his life, the young man engaged the monk in dialogue. He asked, "How does your life fulfill the Great Commission?" With equal directness, the monk retorted, "How do you follow Christ into the desert?—And furthermore, I am not flying around the world polluting the atmosphere!"

> **"I had no knowledge or experience of the 'desert Christ,' called into restful communion with his Father."**

I was that young man. The desert father had discerned my heart. I had no knowledge or experience of the "desert Christ," called into restful communion with his Father. The Spirit had taken me out of the comfortable familiarity of my western culture and religious tradition. The same Spirit was poised to begin a new chapter of His renewing work in my life. The encounter with the desert father launched me on a fifteen-year excursion into the world of "contemplative living" and "holy leisure." In the following pages I set forth some of the themes that seem central to understanding holy leisure and integrating it into daily life.

The Historical Rise of the Leisure Society

The Industrial Revolution of the eighteenth and nineteenth centuries drastically altered the economies of western Europe. In the two centuries since, much of the world has pursued industrialization. Societies have been built whose inhabitants have come to expect disposable wealth, disposable goods, and disposable time.[1] Relentless technological innovation has created an "age of leisure." Once the privilege of only the rich, leisure now extends to the laboring classes. This is evident in many aspects of life: shorter workweeks, more holidays, longer vacations, extended pre-work education, earlier retirement, longer life spans. The rapid growth of labor-saving, technological devices, including household appliances, and improved transportation and communication have made leisure more available to the average person. In addition, work is now generally separated both physically and psychologically from where people live. All these factors have combined to fill the lives of the working middle-class with a quantity of leisure and relaxation apparently unprecedented in world history.[2]

Numerous social observers, however, have called attention to a paradox of a late twentieth-century western world: People work hard at leisure. Writing at mid-century, Walter Kerr bemoaned the "decline of pleasure" in the industrial society. He acknowledged that the "dream of leisure" had undeniably been realized. Still, he lamented that the twentieth century had "in a contrary and perhaps rather cruel way . . . relieved us of labor without at the same time relieving us of the conviction that only labor is meaningful."[3] The British writer Jeremy Seabrook, writing in the late 1980s, saw western culture's descent into a "restless search for entertainment and escape" as corrupting leisure. In his view, leisure has been reduced to "a perpetuation of the never-completed task of work in mine, mill, or factory."[4] Far from being an experience of creative relaxation, leisure was seen

---

[1]The global impact of Europe's Industrial Revolution is substantiated in Fernand Braudel, *A History of Civilizations,* trans. Richard Mayne (London: Penguin, 1994), 373–398. On the development of Anglo-American leisure from industrialization to nineteenth-century "leisure for the masses," see Gary Cross, *A Social History of Leisure Since 1600* (State College, Pa.: Venture, 1990), 39–139. Hugh Cunningham, *Leisure in the Industrial Revolution ca.1780–ca.1880* (London: Croom Helm, 1980), 140–191, identifies the leisure patterns of modern industrial urban society that began to take shape in the mid-nineteenth century as (1) more regular work patterns, (2) clearer separation between work and leisure, and (3) shorter hours of work and a growing demand for leisure.

[2]The spread of leisure and "fun" in the twentieth-century English context is succinctly analyzed in John Armitage, *Man at Play: Nine Centuries of Pleasure Making* (London: Frederick Warne, 1977), 134–184. The emergence of leisure as a major item on the western social agenda of the late twentieth century is substantiated by A. J. Veal, *Leisure and the Future* (London: Allen and Unwin, 1987).

[3]See the intriguingly entitled chapter "Some Observations on the Oddness of Our Lives," in Walter Kerr's *The Decline of Pleasure* (New York: Simon and Schuster, 1962), 11–42, esp. 40.

[4]Jeremy Seabrook, *The Leisure Society* (Oxford/New York: Basil Blackwell, 1988), 5.

by Seabrook as bearing "an extraordinary resemblance to the feverish activity of capitalist labour."[5] More recently, Mary Bateson, an anthropologist, has captured her late twentieth-century fellow Americans working hard at play: "We are a restlessly busy society, with little capacity to loaf in the sun (though we work hard at getting tans) or laze in bed (where 'joy' is a serious obligation). We are as bullied by the obese Sunday paper as our . . . ancestors were by two-hour sermons."[6] All of this commentary reminds us of the incisive musings of the nineteenth-century English cynic Leslie Stephen. Stephen lampooned the pretentious use of leisure time supposedly created by the Industrial Revolution: "thousands of persons at the present moment

The Puritan Ethic

What goes by the name of "the Protestant ethic" today is nearly the opposite of what the original Protestants [Calvin, Luther, the Puritans] actually advocated and practiced. Only when the religious conscience and theological framework had been removed did the original Protestant ethic acquire the traits that are mistakenly attributed to it.

The common stereotype about the Protestant ethic is right in one regard: it *did* assert the value of industrious work . . . we might note . . . that the original Protestants did not advocate work because it was inherently meritorious but because it was God's appointed means of providing for human needs.

A main emphasis of the original Protestant ethic was to delineate the motivations and rewards of work. The rewards of work were overwhelmingly conceived as spiritual and moral . . . In addition to providing a balanced Christian view of the goals and rewards of work, the Protestant work ethic aimed at an ideal of moderation in work.

Most of the modern charges against the Puritans are either untrue or exaggerated. They tend to be based on the Puritans' bias against selected *manifestations* of leisure activities that were acceptable to the Puritans *in principle*. Within their religious and moral framework, the Puritans engaged in a healthy range of leisure activities.

Without the restraining influence of Protestant belief in the primacy of the spiritual, the tenets of the original Protestant ethic became perverted into a creed of personal success. This secularized perversion is what most people today mean when they speak glibly of "the Protestant ethic." The truth is that the people of the Reformation era would be horrified by what goes under the banner of "the Protestant ethic."

Material taken from Leland Ryken, *Work and Leisure in Christian Perspective* (Portland, Ore.: Multnomah, 1987) 92, 93, 97, 99, 104, 69.

---

[5]Seabrook, *Leisure Society*, 5.
[6]Mary C. Bateson, *Composing a Life* (New York: Plume, 1990), 125.

are . . . pretending to themselves that they are enjoying a holiday. They will come back almost tired to death of their pleasures and delighting to return to their business. . . . yet they will persuade themselves and others that they have passed an inconceivably agreeable vacation."[7] The widely-held claim that industrialization gave the gift of leisure to the working masses of western society during the eighteenth and nineteenth centuries is misleading. It may well be more true that industrialization imposed upon society a new concept of time that actually reduced leisure, not increased it.

Scholars have increasingly revised the commonly held view that the Industrial Revolution created leisure. Historian Richard Kraus, for instance, argues that the Industrial Revolution actually intensified the Puritan glorification of work and condemnation of leisure and play. He draws attention to the strong connections made by nineteenth-century religious leaders between work, discipline, and wholesome living. He concludes that "Americans became more consciously dedicated to the Protestant work ethic than Europeans ever had been."[8] Along similar lines, certain Protestants have exalted work and economic productivity. In their view, work has sanctifying and purifying value. C. Wright Mills, for instance, in his survey of the history of work, insisted that before the twentieth century a "gospel of work" dictated the image America had of itself as well as the image held by the rest of the world.[9]

Some overly optimistic futurists continue to forecast the decline of work. They contend that work will be "reworked" to incorporate more leisure into work schedules.[10] Other voices,

---

[7]A cynic [Leslie Stephen], "Vacations," in *Mass Leisure,* ed. Eric Larrabee and Rolf Meyersohn (Glencoe, Ill.: Free Press, 1958), 284.

[8]Richard Kraus, *Recreation and Leisure in Modern Society,* 4th ed. (New York: Harper Collins, 1990), 147; cf. Clive Jenkins and Barrie Sherman, *The Leisure Shock* (London: Eyre Methuen, 1981), 2, regarding the Industrial Revolution's glorification of work. In defense of the original Protestant work ethic and Puritan views of recreation, note Leland Ryken's *Work* (featured in the sidebar on the previous page), 87–115.

[9]C. Wright Mills, "The Meaning of Work Throughout History," in *The Future of Work,* ed. Fred Best (Englewood Cliffs, N.J.: Prentice-Hall, 1973), 9; cf. D. Rogers, *The Work Ethic in Industrial America 1850–1920* (London: University of Chicago, 1978), 14: "The central premise of the work ethic was that work was the core of moral life."

[10]On these themes, see Ken Dychtwald and Joe Flower, *Age Wave* (New York: Bantam, 1990), 115–145, 173–207; Russell Chandler, *Racing Toward 2001* (Grand Rapids/San Francisco: Zondervan/Harper 1992), 82–89. For predictions of leisure steadily eroding work towards the end of the twentieth century, see Marion Clawson, "How Much Leisure, Now and in the Future?" in *Leisure in America: Blessing or Curse?* ed. James C. Charlesworth (Philadelphia: American Academy of Political and Social Science, 1964), 12; John K. Galbraith, *The Affluent Society,* 2d ed. (Boston: Houghton Mifflin, 1969), 297–310, especially 302–303 and especially the forecasts of the Hudson Institute, regarding the future "leisure-oriented" society. Herman Kahn and Anthony J. Weiner, *The Year 2000* (New York: MacMillan, 1967), 186–197.

however, contend that work is actually increasing. There is some evidence, for example, that the number of working hours is increasing compared to forty years ago.[11] Alvin Toffler, in *The Third Wave*, discussed the rise of the "prosumer." A prosumer, it seems, is someone who without compensation spends much so-called leisure time in the voluntary production of goods and services.[12] In the view of some, leisure has so completely evaporated from society that the distinction between work and leisure may not even be meaningful anymore.[13] Some laboring groups actually claim to have no leisure time at all.[14] Even as certain trends (some of which have been brought on by economic recessions) indicate a revival of work, numerous western countries have witnessed the rise of the enigmatic "leisure industry." In the United States, the leisure industry is surpassed only by the automobile industry in gross retail sales.[15] Some Christian critics, while espousing that leisure has its legitimate place in society, have attributed the rapid growth of the leisure industry during the 1970s and 1980s to the corruption of the American work ethic.[16] In short, while no one would dispute the reversal

> **"In the United States, the leisure industry is surpassed only by the automobile industry in gross retail sales."**

[11]Juliet B. Schor, *The Overworked American: The Unexpected Decline of Leisure* (New York: Basic Books, 1991), 51, attributes this trend to the "work and spend" syndrome in which "money" takes precedence over "time off." Cf. Robert Wuthnow, *Christianity in the 21st Century* (New York/Oxford: Oxford University, 1993), 194–196, for a similar discussion of the "maladies of the middle class." For a similar observation in a Canadian setting, see William G. Watson, *National Pastimes, The Economics of Canadian Leisure* (Singapore: The Fraser Institute, 1988), 10–11.

[12]Alvin Toffler, *The Third Wave* (New York: William Morrow, 1980), 282–305.

[13]Ibid., 294.

[14]On the dilemma of women who work outside the home, see John Naisbitt and Patricia Aburdene, *Re-inventing the Corporation* (New York: Warner, 1985), 251.

[15]See Howard W. Kelley, "A New Century Dawns," *Leisure Management* 13 (October 1993): 46. On the industrialization of leisure in Britain, Europe, and Australia, see Bill Martin and Sandra Mason, "Research Note: Current Trends in Leisure: the Changing Face of Leisure Provision," *Leisure Studies* (January 1992): 81–86; "The Leisure Industry and the Single European Market," *Leisure Studies* 10 (January 1991): 1–6; J. R. Brehaut and K. C. Poole, "The Industrialization of Leisure," *Leisure Studies* 1 (January 1982): 95–107. According to John Naisbitt, *Global Paradox* (New York: Avon, 1994), 133, travel/tourism, the world's largest industry, is the United State's "number one source of foreign exchange earnings."

[16]Chuck Colson and Jack Eckerd, *Why America Doesn't Work* (Dallas: Word, 1991), 52–53.

in work and play that occurred in America from 1800–1950, at this point in the century the "age of leisure" may be more illusion than reality.[17] If so, the illusion is nowhere more painfully symbolized than in the loss of childhood as a social phenomenon.[18] Neil Postman has observed the "adultification" of American society since the 1950s as shown in the media, clothing styles, eating habits, games, sports and entertainment, language, sexual practices, and the criminalization of youth.[19]

Another complication is that in current literature the term "leisure" lacks a clear definition. No consensus has been reached regarding a working definition of the term.[20] At least three factors seem responsible. First, some people employ superficial concepts and spurious distinctions (are *leisure* and *recreation* the same or different?). Second, the "planned" version of leisure promoted by state and other social agencies often gets undue attention. Third, some definitions of the term are simply deficient.[21] What, for instance, is the relationship between leisure and certain kindred activities such as play, fun, enjoyment, and consumption? (For that matter, what are we to make of the debate that revolves around the projections of a coming "leisure society?"[22]) Its essential meaning is obscured further when used in phrases such as "leisure industry," "leisure time," "leisure travel," and "leisure management." All of these expressions associate leisure with some kind of activity. In its etymology, however, the term *leisure* (derived from the Latin *licere*) has to do with freedom, in a sense denoting an interior state of reflection and contempla-

> **"In its etymology, however, the term *leisure* (derived from the Latin *licere*) has to do with freedom."**

---

[17]On the continuation of the old work ethic and its conditioning of leisure, see Gene Quarrick, *Our Sweetest Hours* (Jefferson, N.C.: McFarland, 1989), 14,15.

[18]A provocative work on this theme is David Elkind, *The Hurried Child* (Reading, Mass./Don Mills, Ont.: Addison-Wesley, 1981).

[19]Neil Postman, *The Disappearance of Childhood* (New York: Laurel, 1982), 67–80.

[20]This observation is made in Peter Emerson, "Leisure Counseling: A Call to Order," *Career Planning and Adult Development Journal* 8 (Spring 1992): 5.

[21]Harry Van Moorst, "Leisure and Social Theory," *Leisure Studies* 1 (1982): 157.

[22]See the attempts to bring conceptual order out of definitional chaos by Sheila Mullett, "Leisure and Consumption: Incompatible Concepts?" *Leisure Studies* 7 (1988): 241–253; Walter Podilchak, "Distinctions of Fun, Enjoyment and Leisure," *Leisure Studies* 10 (1991): 133–148; cf. Otto Newman, "The Coming of a Leisure Society," *Leisure Studies* 2 (1983): 97–109.

tion combined with external quietness. For the philosopher Bertrand Russell, true leisure, defined contemplatively, is the only remedy for the fatigue, unhappiness, and nervous strain that makes modern, urban life a "pilgrimage in the desert."[23]

Much of recreational leisure is a quest for relaxation through activities that are not a part of one's normal, daily routines. By contrast, contemplation, or "holy leisure," is not a relaxation exercise. Physical relaxation is a by-product of contemplation. In the Christian tradition, contemplation has to do with developing a prayerful lifestyle that is continually aware of and open to the Divine presence. It is an attitude of receptivity to the transforming work of the Holy Spirit that embraces the whole of life, not just the time off from work. It is living confidently in a restful way, committing all of one's life to the care of God and submitting unreservedly to the Divine will. Body, mind, and spirit are peacefully integrated in a life of obedience.

> "Contemplation, or 'holy leisure,' is not a relaxation exercise. Physical relaxation is a by-product of contemplation."

At least two other distractions arise when we consider leisure. The first is the tendency to associate it with free time and entertainment. The second is to treat it as either preparation for work, reward for work, or rest from work. But, of course, if we define leisure in these ways, we simply perpetuate the urban wasteland that Russell so aptly described. This is so because leisure, so defined, is deprived of an integrative role in culture. It gets reduced to being a single part of life rather than a lifestyle. Moreover, if we confine leisure to a restricted period of time, we undermine its primary value in spiritual experience in favor of its social and economic benefits.[24] For example, most college students would sooner equate leisure with spring break, ski week, or fun-in-the-sun than with going to class, that is, a *leisurely* pursuit of truth and ultimate meaning.

Frank Buckley provides a more meaningful perspective on leisure. He describes it as "the experience of restful coming-together and easeful presence." His idea is helpful because it transcends social conditions of various cultures and time periods. It applies equally well whether we are thinking of leisure as

---

[23]See Bertrand Russell's discussion of the malaise of modern life in *The Conquest of Happiness* (New York: Bantam, 1968), 3–4, esp. 43. For Russell, leisure has to do with things "not of practical importance in one's own life" (160).

[24]See the treatment of leisure as a "form of activity" in James F. Murphy, *Concepts of Leisure: Philosophical Implications* (Englewood Cliffs, N.J.: Prentice-Hall, 1974), 109–116; cf. Richard Kraus, *Recreation and Leisure in Modern Society* (New York: Appleton-Century-Crofts, 1971), 256. Charles K. Brightbill and Tony A. Bobley, *Education for Leisure-Centered Living* 2d ed. (New York/Santa Barbara: John Wiley and Sons, 1977), 8, define leisure as "discretionary time that is best outlined in the quantitative model."

"time-off" in an industrial society or in the undifferentiated, cyclical time of preindustrial life. For Buckley, all of life—whether "free time" or "work time"—is meant to flow from an "authentic leisurely attitude."[25]

In 1899, the American sociologist and economist Thorstein Veblen published *The Theory of the Leisure Class*.[26] In it he heralded a century of leisure which spawned a leisure-based culture. A fascinating recent study by Glenn Uminowicz shows how American Protestants of various denominations at the turn of the twentieth century tried to incorporate the so-called leisure revolution into their overall vision of a Christian civilization. By establishing a network of "respectable resorts," they aimed at combining their quest for holiness with the opportunities

> "Sociologically, the Scriptures are unfamiliar with the 'age of leisure' that Veblen anticipated."

for relaxation, play, and amusement which a new century seemed to promise.[27] These resorts were the forerunners of the modern religious theme park. Unfortunately, they unwittingly denigrated the spiritual life by wedding it to the consumer ethic in the context of a "Christian Disneyland."

Sociologically, the Scriptures are unfamiliar with the "age of leisure" that Veblen anticipated. At the same time, a biblically-based view of spirituality is a necessity for the believer facing the rise of leisure in North American culture. Such a spirituality would define leisure and give it both focus and meaning within a Christian worldview.

If leisure raises spiritual issues, it also raises moral issues. One of them is the morality of the indulgent consumption of material goods encouraged by the leisure business.[28] In his masterful history of the "simple life" in America, David Shi highlights the tension in American society during the last three decades between two types of persons. One type takes a consumer approach to life. People of this type are committed to the excessive level of material consumption engendered by the American dream. A second type advocates a simpler, less

---

[25]Frank M. Buckley, "The Everyday Struggle For The Leisurely Attitude," *Humanitas* 8 (1972): 310–311.

[26]Thorstein Veblen, *The Theory of the Leisure Class* (Franklin Center, Pa.: Franklin Library, 1979).

[27]Glen Uminowicz, "Recreation in a Christian America: Ocean Grove and Asbury Park, New Jersey, 1869–1914," in *Hard at Play: Leisure in America, 1840–1940*, ed. Kathryn Grover (Amherst, Mass.: University of Massachusetts, 1992), 8–38.

[28]This trend harmonizes well with the preference of Americans for individual economic enterprise and private consumption over public welfare identified in Robert N. Bellah et al., *The Good Society* (New York: Alfred A. Knopf, 1991), 86–90; cf. John K. Galbraith, *The Culture of Contentment* (Boston: Houghton Mifflin, 1992).

acquisitive approach to life. People of this type search for a more leisurely, simple lifestyle grounded in spiritual integrity and displaying ecological awareness.[29] Significantly, both the consumptive and simple living ethics have found their outspoken advocates in evangelicals, Pentecostals, and charismatics.[30]

A full analysis of leisure would invariably touch on philosophical, theological, sociological, psychological, historical, and economic issues. Many of these issues are quite technical and lie beyond the scope of this chapter.[31] We focus our attention here primarily on biblical, theological, and historical themes.

The Ancient Biblical Concept of Rest

Seen through our eyes, the Hebrew and Greco-Roman worlds of the Old and New Testaments were work-societies.[32] Within the Hebrew tradition, however, the interplay of work and rest, rooted in the Genesis creation narrative (Gen. 2:3), was intrinsic to their society.[33] The fourth commandment, pertaining to the Sabbath and the related laws regarding the sabbath year and the year of Jubilee (Exodus. 20:8–11; 23:10–19; Lev. 25:1–17), enshrined rest for everyone governed by the legal code of Israel.[34] To be sure, this code was not always adhered to throughout Israelite history. Still, at the heart of the Mosaic law lay a

---

[29]See the discussion of "affluence and anxiety" in David E. Shi, *The Simple Life* (New York: Oxford University, 1985), 248–276.

[30]For example, see the collection of evangelical and charismatic advocates of simplicity in *Lifestyle in the Eighties,* ed. Ronald J. Sider (Philadelphia: Westminster, 1982), as well as the call for charismatics and evangelicals to reject materialism in Jeremy Rifkin with Ted Howard, *The Emerging Order* (New York: G.P. Putnam's Sons, 1979), 211–272.

[31]For a recent overview of the multidisciplinary literature on the work-leisure relationship alone, see J. Zuzanek and R. Mannell, "Work-leisure Relationships from a Sociological and Social Psychological Perspective," *Leisure Studies* 2 (1983): 327–344.

[32]Of course, the recreational notion of leisure was certainly articulated by Greek and Roman philosophers and enjoyed by the rich and powerful who exploited the masses under them. The Greco-Roman philosophical concept of leisure as an ideal life beyond labor for the minority, based on the work of the majority, is discussed in Sebastian De Grazia, *Of Time, Work, and Leisure* (Garden City, N.Y.: Doubleday, 1964), 9–30; Byron Dare, George Welton, William Coe, *Concepts of Leisure in Western Thought: A Critical and Historical Analysis* (Dubuque: Iowa, Kendall/Hunt, 1987), xiii–2, 27–44.

[33]See James M. Houston's reference to the "rest/restlessness" dialectic in human civilization as rooted in the rhythms of creation. *I Believe in the Creator* (Grand Rapids: Eerdmans, 1980), 217–219, esp. 219.

[34]See Gerhard Von Rad's foundational study (1933) of "rest" as a "benefit of redemption," "There Remains Still a Rest for the People of God," in *The Problem of the Hexateuch and other Essays*, trans. E. W. Trueman Dicken (New York: McGraw, 1966), 94–102, and more recently, Walter C. Kaiser, Jr., "The Promise Theme and the Theology of Rest," *Bibliotheca Sacra* 130 (April 1973): 135–150.

"leisurely" vision of life, making provision for regular personal, societal, and environmental renewal. In the Hebrew tradition, the moral and legal commitment to rest expressed two central themes. First, it reflected a view of a God who both understood and practiced leisure. Second, it compensated for four centuries of unremitting slave labor endured in Egypt (Deut. 5:15). The fact that Sabbath-breaking was treated as a capital offense (Exod. 31:14; Num. 15:32–36) shows what weight the Scriptures give to the original vision of the Sabbath. Tellingly the seventy-year length of the Israelite exile in Babylon was the exact equivalent of the years of failure to observe the sabbatical year (2 Chron. 36:20–21).

The Old Testament institution of the weekly Sabbath conveyed several meanings. First, it certainly recalled life in Eden. In this sense, it entailed cessation of physical labor, contemplation and remembrance of the Holy, restoration of energy for humans and animals alike, and recognition of ethical responsibility.[35] Second, it served as a sign of the covenant. In this sense, it looked ahead to the restful life in the reign of the Messiah.[36] Third, it seems to have mandated joyful play and celebration.[37] Evidence for this view appears in passages

[35]On the significance of the Sabbath, see Hans Walter Wolff, "The Day of Rest in the Old Testament," *Concordia Theological Monthly* 43 (September 1972): 498–506; Paul K. Jewett, *The Lord's Day: A Theological Guide to the Christian Day of Leisure* (Grand Rapids: Eerdmans, 1971), 13–28; Harold H. P. Dressler, "The Sabbath in the Old Testa-ment," in *From Sabbath to Lord's Day: A Biblical, Historical and Theological Investigation,* ed. D. A. Carson (Grand Rapids: Zondervan, 1982), 21–42. Willard M. Swartley, *Slavery, Sabbath, War and Women* (Scottdale, Pa.: Herald, 1983), 65–95 gives a useful survey of the sabbath debate in recent literature. Regarding the sabbath as a cure for some of the ills of modernity (purposelessness, competition, and unrest), see W. Gunther Plaut, "The Sabbath as Protest: Thoughts on Work and Leisure in the Automated Society," in *Tradition and Change in Jewish Experience,* ed. A. Leland Jamison (Syracuse, N.Y.: Syracuse University, 1978), 169–183, esp. 176–178. The psychological and physical benefits of sabbath observance are explored in Alan D. Goldberg, "The Sabbath: Implications for Mental Health," *Counseling and Values* 31 (April 1987): 147–156; *Influence of the Weekly Rest-Day on Human Welfare* (New York: The New York Sabbath Committee, 1927).

[36]Jürgen Moltmann, *The Church in the Power of the Spirit* (New York: Harper and Row, 1977), 269–270; cf. Jürgen Moltmann, *The Passion for Life: A Messianic Lifestyle* (Philadelphia: Fortress, 1978), 76.

[37]In her superb, holistic study of the sabbath, Marva J. Dawn sees it as an opportunity for "feasting on the eternal." See *Keeping the Sabbath Wholly* (Grand Rapids: Eerdmans, 1989), 151–202. Niels-Erik A. Andreasen, *The Christian Use of Time* (Nashville: Abingdon Press), 71, sees "the Sabbath" a daring "non-doing and a festive playfulness" which transcends the world of work. Robert K. Johnson, *The Christian at Play* (Grand Rapids: Eerdmans, 1983), 88–93, sees the "rest of the Sabbath" as analogous to play. The classic study by Johan Huizinga, *Homo Ludens: A Study of the Play Element in Culture* (Boston: Beacon, 1955), discusses religious festivity as a form of play.

of sabbatical legislation for feasts (Exod. 23:10–19) and in passages that discuss the Year of Jubilee (Lev. 25:8–55). Sabbath rest is rightly termed the rhythmic counterpoint of the other six days.[38]

As with all the commandments, the commandment to keep the Sabbath was meant to liberate, not to repress. This liberation derives its significance from the monumental event of redemption in the Exodus (Deut. 5:15) and underscores that all time is a gift of God. The whole of life was to be lived in a spirit of liberation against the backdrop of the Sabbath.[39] To ignore the Sabbath invited various forms of psychological, social, and economic oppression. In addition, to ignore the Sabbath meant denying the providential care of God for His creatures. Throughout the Old Testament, prophetic voices decried violations of the Sabbath. Such violations eroded the gift of leisure that benefited all Israelites (Isa. 58:13f.; Jer. 17:21ff.; Amos 8:5; 4:4ff.; 5:21ff.). The obsession with work, whether for maximizing economic profit or simply achieving personal security, was a trend to be resisted since it reduced life to a struggle for earthly existence. By contrast, the Sabbath pointed to an eternal order of things. Jürgen Moltmann has rightly concluded: "The sabbath is not

The Sabbatical and Jubilee Year Traditions

Among the many benefits of redemption offered to man by Holy Scripture, that of "rest" has been almost overlooked in biblical theology, despite the fact that theologically speaking, it expresses a highly characteristic notion. In various books of the Old Testament, compiled at different periods, the belief is expressed that God will give, or has given, "rest" to his people.

This notion of "rest" now comes to occupy an important place in the religious thought of Israel. It is thought of as a rest found by a weary nation through the grace of God in the land he has promised them.

The singular characteristic of Genesis 1 through 2:4a is that it ventures, starting from faith in the God of the covenant, to draw a conclusion with regard to God the creator of all things . . . This is most plainly seen in the statement which connects God's rest from the work of creation with the institution of a seventh day, a day of rest which is contrasted with the days of creation. The statement asserts that the world is no longer being created but that it has already been given rest by God . . . Above all, however, the sentence makes so bold as to declare that even the living, creative God is at rest!

The preceding comments are drawn from Gerhard Von Rad's seminal essay, "There Remains Still a Rest for the People of God" (see note 34).

---

[38]John C. Haughey, *Converting Nine to Five* (New York: Crossroad, 1989), 47.

[39]On the intention of the Mosaic Law that the spirit of the sabbath suffuse the whole of life rather than compartmentalize life by observing a "special Day" set apart from the others, see S. R. Hirsch, *Horeb: A Philosophy of Jewish Laws and Observances* (New York: Soncino, 1962).

there for the sake of the work; the work is there for the sake of the feast." God's rest is not merely cessation from "strenuous work." It is the pinnacle of creation.[40]

Moses' legislation of leisure expressed a theology of rest, which permeates the Old Testament. Rest in its spiritual, social, and military facets was viewed as the chief redemptive benefit to God's people living in the land of promise. A leisurely life was the fruit of trusting in the salvation of God. It was understood holistically—as deliverance from sin, as provision for one's daily material needs, and as protection from one's enemies.

We do not know for sure to what extent the ancient Hebrew concept of the Sabbath carried over into New Testament times.[41] Certainly Sabbath-keeping was part of Jesus' lifestyle. For instance, He attended the synagogue on the Sabbath (Mark. 1:21). But he also set aside Sabbath traditions and encouraged others to do the same (Matt. 12:1–14). The allegedly scandalous actions of Jesus on the Sabbath are in effect the revival of an ancient sabbatarian ideal. According to this ideal, the Sabbath functioned as a means of caring for the physical needs of the weak and needy who were especially vulnerable to economic oppression (Mark 2:27–28).

Legitimate scholarly discussion will continue over the precise degree to which Jesus' views of the Sabbath conform to Old Testament teachings about the Sabbath. What is not in dispute, however, is that Jesus emphasized sabbath themes of rest and renewal both in His lifestyle and in His teaching. In his daily rule of life, He modeled the integration of the active life (work) and the contemplative life (leisure). For him, the deserted places He regularly withdrew to were not only places of testing and temptation but also places of opportunity for rest and renewal. In these places He was reenergized to meet the feverish demands of ministry in the marketplace.[42] Robert K. Johnston, while acknowledging that no fully developed theology of leisure can be found in the New

> **"Moses' legislation of leisure expressed a theology of rest, which permeates the Old Testament."**

---

[40]Moltmann, *The Church in the Power of the Spirit*, 269.

[41]This issue is comprehensively studied by D. A. Carson, "Jesus and the Sabbath in the Four Gospels;" M. Max B. Turner, "The Sabbath, Sunday and the Law in Luke/Acts;" and D. R. de Lacey, "The Sabbath/Sunday Question and the Law in the Pauline Corpus," *From Sabbath to Lord's Day,*ed. D. A. Carson (Grand Rapids: Zondervan, 1982), 57–196.

[42]The significance of the desert as a place of spiritual renewal and restoration and not just a place of rebellion and judgement is developed in Kenneth Leech, *Experiencing God: Theology as Spirituality* (San Francisco: Harper and Row, 1985), 35–38, 127–161.

Testament, has intriguingly suggested that in the network of Jesus' friendships one can see evidence of a "convivial life-style."[43]

Admittedly, the image of the "leisurely Christ" does not fit easily with traditional western stereotypes of Christ. However, certain aspects of the western intellectual and religious tradition would understandably fail to pay adequate attention to the biblical depiction of a contemplative, leisurely Christ. This would be true, for example, of the Protestant work ethic, which extols work and tends to downplay contemplative and celebrative dimensions of life. Portraying Christ as a contemplative figure is much more in tune with the way cultures of the East view him.[44] Oriental societies have traditionally affirmed the value of what the Indian writer Vandana Mataji calls "ascetical leisure."[45] The image of Jesus "on vacation" is alien to Scripture; the picture of a Christ "in contemplation" is not.[46] A western-styled "shortened work week" was never part of the Incarnation; "resting in God" was. For the earthly Jesus, work done in the setting of contemplation was ordered by the same exhausting dawn to dusk routine familiar to many in undeveloped or developing nations today.

> **"Admittedly, the image of the 'leisurely Christ' does not fit easily with traditional western stereotypes of Christ."**

The substance of Jesus' teaching supports the practice of his life. Two major themes of his message are consistent with the deep-seated needs of the tiresome human condition. He offers *spiritual renewal* and he offers *rest*. Both of these gifts are experienced through conversion (John 3:1–15; Matt. 11:28–30).[47] More generally, the gospel is in itself a form of Sabbath. As such it

---

[43]Johnston, *Christian at Play*, 119–125, esp. 120. Elton Trueblood, the Quaker, documents the playfulness of Jesus in *The Humor of Christ* (New York: Harper and Row, 1964). C. S. Lewis sees the miracle at Cana as "sanctifying . . . a recreational use of culture" in *Christian Reflections* (Grand Rapids: Eerdmans, 1967), 15.

[44]Jaroslav Pelikan's *Jesus Through the Centuries* (New York/San Francisco: Harper and Row, 1987) surveys the historical tendency to diversely depict Christ according to cultural presuppositions; cf. Priscilla Pope-Levison and John R. Levison, *Jesus in Global Contexts* (Louisville, Ky.: Westminster/John Knox, 1992).

[45]Vandana Mataji, *Gurus, Ashrams and Christians* (Bombay: St. Paul, 1978), 59–63, 66, calls for a contemplative style of Christianity, and presumably a corresponding image of Christ more appropriate to the needs of Asian culture.

[46]On the "desert/contemplative Christ" see William McNamara, *Mystical Passion: Spirituality for a Bored Society* (New York/Ramsey, N.J.: Paulist, 1977), 94; John R. Sheets, "Graced-Life as Contemplative," *Contemplative and the Charismatic Renewal*, ed. Paul Hinnebusch (New York/Mahwah, N.J.: Paulist, 1986), 40–43.

[47]See Charles Cummings, *The Mystery of the Ordinary* (San Francisco: Harper and Row, 1982), 75–79, on the importance of "rest" in the teaching and lifestyle of Jesus.

makes provision for the basic spiritual needs of human beings described as "hunger" and "thirst" (Matt. 5:6; John 4:1–15). It delivers needy human beings from all forms of bondage and oppression. Indeed, the self-proclaimed mission of Jesus is articulated (on a Sabbath) in prophetic language that recalls the Year of Jubilee (Luke 4:18). The clear suggestion is that his life and work were the personal embodiment of what had originally been expressed in Jewish law.[48]

As first a Jewish renewal movement, the first generation of Christians utilized the Jewish Sabbath like their leader, a Jewish prophet and teacher, did. They continued to observe the Sabbath for purposes of worship and prayer as well as the proclamation of Jesus' teachings (Acts 13:13–48; 16:13ff.; 18:4). The significance of Old Testament Sabbath laws and institutions, however, gradually diminished to the status of "shadows." Christ himself emerged as the "substance" (Col. 2:16–17). This shift of emphasis affected the way Christians viewed rest. Over time, they quit thinking of rest within the framework of the Jewish calendar. Instead, rest became a main ingredient of life lived in the power of the spirit of the Messiah.

For a period of time in the first century, Old Testament Sabbath legislation favorably affected Jew and Christian alike. By stipulating days and seasons of rest it humanized ancient life, made the toil more bearable. As Christianity spread beyond Palestine, and when the Jewish political state was dissolved in the last third of the first century A.D., Old Testament Sabbath legislation became increasingly irrelevant to Christians. However, the abiding prophetic significance of the Sabbath itself was never lost for early Christians. They saw the ultimate destiny of God's people, regardless of their specific geographical location, as participation in the future "rest of God," a rest beyond mortal life (Heb. 4:9–10).[49] Fittingly, the New Testament canon concludes where the Old Testament canon begins—with an idyllic garden scene, a setting for human leisure made possible by a divine act of creation (Gen. 1; Rev. 22:1–5). In Genesis, the Garden of Eden, a place of intimate leisurely communion with the Creator, is supplanted by a world of sweaty work and urbanization due to the impact of evil. In the Book of Revelation, the new heavens

> **"For a period of time in the first century, Old Testament Sabbath legislation favorably affected Jew and Christian alike."**

---

[48]The intent and historicity of Jubilee legislation in Lev. 25 is analyzed in Robert North, *The Sociology of the Jubilee Year* (Rome: Pontifical Biblical Institute, 1954).

[49]F. F. Bruce makes this point in his commentary on Heb. 4:9–10, *Commentary on the Epistle to the Hebrews* (Grand Rapids: Eerdmans, 1964), 77–79.

and earth feature the return of the garden to the redeemed city. In the new city, sin-cursed work, reflecting the darkness of the human experience, is transformed back into holy leisure, enjoyed in a world of inextinguishable light.[50] In this life, leisurely rhythms of contemplative prayer and celebrative play, more so than industry and work, seem to foreshadow the essence of life in the eternal state. The call of the gospel, then, is not to observe one Sabbath per week, though this is not precluded. Rather it is a call to live a life of leisurely Sabbath-keeping. Only in answering this call can we redeem our tendencies to compulsive work and compulsive recreation. In effect, a proper understanding of rest (Sabbath) even transforms our view of work.

In the Scriptures, then, the notions of leisure and work are intimately interrelated. Christians in every period since the first century have attempted to grasp and explain the relationship between them.

The Christian Tradition of Holy Leisure and Holy Time

A Christian view of leisure in postmodern North American society can be profitably informed by a concept found in the writings of the Early Church Fathers. The concept is known as holy leisure *(otium sanctum).* According to the Fathers in both the eastern and western Christian traditions, an authentically Christian life was one in which action alternates with contemplation, doing with seeing, and service with worship. Work

Gregory of Nyssa

Gregory of Nyssa (ca. 330–95) was a Christian theologian at the time of transition from the Early to the Medieval Period of Church history. Influenced by his brother Basil and friend Gregory of Nazianzus, he entered monastic life. The youngest of the Cappadocian Fathers from Asia Minor (modern Turkey), he eventually became Bishop of Cappadocia in eastern Central Turkey. At the First Council of Constantinople (381), he argued against the Arians, championing the Nicene doctrine of the single substance *(ousia)* of the members of the Trinity. His writings include numerous anti-Arian tracts and apologies for rigorous Christian asceticism.

---

[50]My thinking in this regard has been stimulated by Jacques Ellul's thesis regarding the redemption of the city in *The Meaning of the City* (Grand Rapids: Eerdmans, 1970). On the importance of gardens in scripture and in urban civilization, see Matthew Fox, *The Reinvention of Work* (San Francisco: Harper, 1994), 160. Fox helpfully notes the derivation of the word *paradise* from the Persian term for *garden.*

without holy leisure was said to destroy one's spiritual attentiveness. As a result, work itself was dehumanized. In his allegorical discussion of the symbolic meaning of priestly garments, Gregory of Nyssa reflected the broad consensus of the Fathers in his statement that "the heart becomes the symbol of contemplation, and the arms, of works."[51] For him, earthly life was best lived as the day of preparation for the eternal Sabbath to come.[52]

The fifth-century Julianus Pomerius of Gaul delivered a discourse on the ideals of the contemplative and active lives, lauding holy leisure as the interior state in which one can "conduct the business of his soul."[53] The active life was perfected, completed, through the contemplative life. Leisure, Pomerius thought, transcends work rather than negating it.[54] Much of his thought on holy leisure was inspired by Augustine (A.D. 354–430).

Following his conversion, Augustine had been attracted to a monastic life. He even authored a rule for religious communal life (ca. A.D. 397). Unexpected circumstances, however, did not permit Augustine to realize his dream of a contemplative life. Still, he continued to affirm the value of holy leisure in his later writings. His *City of God* (A.D. 413–436), a defense of Christianity prompted by the fall of Rome, exhorted Christians to integrate the active and contemplative dimensions of their lives. Neither was to be pursued at the expense of the other. For Augustine, the love of truth stimulates the desire for "holy leisure." The "sweets of contemplation" were to be preserved and enjoyed in the midst of a call to a pressured life of social service. Otherwise the burdens of existence could prove unbearable.[55] Augustine believed human history would be completed and perfected when an unending "great Sabbath" was ushered in. With this culmination of history, eternal life would consist of "rest . . . love and praise." In other words, it would consist of uninterrupted "holy leisure."[56] In his *Confessions*, Augustine anticipated the "eternal Sabbath" as a time when God would *rest* in his creatures just as he now *works* in his creatures.[57] His vision of human destiny placed work in time and rest in eternity.

---

[51]Gregory of Nyssa, *The Life of Moses*, trans. Abraham J. Malherbe and Everett Ferguson (New York/Ramsey, N.J.: Paulist, 1978), 106.

[52]Ibid., 89.

[53]Julianus Pomerius, *The Contemplative Life*, trans. Mary J. Suelzer (New York/Ramsey, N.J.: Newman, 1947), 28.

[54]Ibid., 31–33.

[55]Augustine, *The City of God* (Grand Rapids: Eerdmans, 1973), 414.

[56]Ibid., 511.

[57]Augustine, *Confessions*, trans. R. S. Pine-Coffin (Harmondsworth, England: Penguin, 1961), 37, 38.

The fourth and fifth-century sayings of the Desert Fathers summarized the spiritual experiences of monks in the Egyptian desert in a form of folk wisdom. City dwellers, then and now, may be prone to conclude from the sayings that these secluded desert monks devoted themselves only to contemplation and spiritual exercises. But if we read the sayings carefully, we see clearly that the monks attempted to find a balance between manual work and "holy leisure." A story sharpens the point. In it a man named Abba John the Dwarf is corrected for trying to gain a life of leisure that eliminates work.

> It was said of Abba John the Dwarf, that one day he said to his elder brother, "I should like to be free of all care, like the angels, who do not work, but ceaselessly offer worship to God." So he took off his cloak and went away into the desert. After a week he came back to his brother. When he knocked on the door, he heard his brother say, before he opened it "Who are you?" He said, "I am John, your brother." But he replied, "John has become an angel, and henceforth he is no longer among men." Then the other begged him saying, "It is I." However, his brother did not let him in, but left him there in distress until morning. Then, opening the door, he said to him, "You are a man and you must once again work in order to eat." Then John made a prostration before him, saying, "Forgive me."[58]

In the eyes of most people, monks live a life radically set apart from normal societal routine. However, the story above shows that even in a life motivated to seek God without worldly distractions leisure cannot be distorted so as to preclude work. Rather, the call of the desert monk was to engage in "leisurely work."

The western monastic tradition similarly recognized the benefits of balancing work with leisure on a daily basis. In the eastern monastic tradition, work served contemplation. In the western tradition, by contrast, the synthesis of the two tipped in the direction of work. The Rule of Benedict (ca. A.D. 540), a charter document for monasticism in the West, prescribed a daily schedule of what it deemed an appropriate blend of manual work, spiritual reading, and contemplation (ch. 48). Benedictine monasticism did in fact acknowledge the value of leisure. However, the Benedictine motto *laborare est orare* (to work is to pray) amounted to a "glorification of work." This emphasis on work was played out to

---

[58]*The Desert Christian: The Sayings of the Desert Fathers*, trans. Benedicta Ward (New York: Macmillian, 1975), 86. Cf. the commentary on the story of Abba Silvanus's understanding of the Mary–Martha relationship (*Desert Christian*, 223) in Rembert Sorg, *Towards a Benedictine Theology of Manual Labor* (Lisle, Ill.: St. Procopus Abbey, 1951), 20; Robert Taft, *The Liturgy of the Hours in East and West* (Collegeville, Minn.: Liturgical Press, 1986), 68–69.

its full limits in later centuries of European civilization.[59]

From the time of Augustine onwards, Christian writers discussed the relationship between work and holy leisure in the context of the way they thought about Martha and Mary, the sisters of Lazarus and friends of Jesus.[60] They were often seen as personifications of the active and contemplative lives. Until the twelfth century, Martha symbolized the life taken up with the activities of pastoral care; Mary represented those who gave themselves to prayer and waiting on God in a cloistered setting.[61]

In the twentieth century, advocates of the ancient Christian notion of holy leisure have suggested that the nurture of the inner life, leisure, and spirituality have a close kinship. The Swiss scholar Josef Pieper in *Leisure, The Basis of Culture* (1952) described leisure in interior terms as "a mental and spiritual attitude." This attitude cannot simply be reduced to the product of "external factors" such as easing working conditions. More specifically, he called it a "condition of soul." This state, he thought, was impossible to experience apart from an inner state of calm and quietude almost to the point of falling asleep. As such, leisure is the antithesis of both work and idleness, whose corollary sins are the despair and disquietude that rob one of entering the internal state of leisure. Not only does leisure constitute the foundation of culture but it belongs to a "higher order than the *vita activa* [active life]." Quite simply, leisure, for Pieper, is an experiential companion of the contemplation and celebration that draw one into mystical union with the Creator and his creation.[62] Thus, in the English translation of Pieper's *Musse und Kult,*

> **"The nurture of the inner life, leisure, and spirituality have a close kinship."**

---

[59]On the Benedictine glorification of labor, contra the meditative work of the eastern monastic tradition, see Herbert B. Workman, *The Evolution of the Monastic Ideal* (Boston: Beacon, 1963), 165–158. Prayer, study, and work corresponding to the polarities of spirit, mind, and body is discussed in Brian C. Taylor, *Spiritually For Everyday Living* (Collegeville, Minn.: Liturgical Press, 1989), 30–46.

[60]Cuthbert Butler, *Western Mysticism,* 2d ed. (London: Constable, 1927), 159–160.

[61]This type of lifestyle, we should note, was not always positively viewed even in monastic circles. See the discussion of the relative value of Martha the "fruitful active" versus Mary the "sterile contemplative" among twelfth-century Cistercian writers in Christopher J. Holdsworth, "The Blessings of Work: The Cistercian View," *Sanctity and Secularity: The Church and the World,* ed. Derek Baker (Oxford: Basil Blackwell, 1973), 65.

[62]Josef Pieper, *Leisure, the Basis of Culture,* trans. Alexander Dru (New York: Random House, 1963), 38–45.

Psalm 46:10 says, "Have leisure and know that I am God."[63]

Holy leisure necessarily embraces work, rather than excluding it from life. For Thomas Merton, the American Trappist writer, leisure enlivens work, increases its fruitfulness. Leisure even converts work into a form of prayer.[64] In a similar vein, Evelyn Underhill speaks of the "leisure of Eternity." According to Underhill, if allowed to infuse the workplace, leisure (properly understood) serves several purposes. For instance, it seems to inhibit dishonesty. In addition, it militates against nervous anxiety, the subservience to the tyranny of time, and the tendency to avoid dull aspects of one's job—all expressions of work's dark side.[65] The absence of this holy leisure in the heart of western culture strips work of its spiritual significance and

The Christian Calendar

The Christian calendar is a direct inheritance from the Jewish religion in which the keeping of regular commemorations and observances had long been important . . . It is from [the Jewish] calendar that the Christian Church took the concept of great festivals like the Passover and Pentecost . . . Of course they gave new significance to the old feasts. The Passover became Easter and Pentecost . . . From very early times, the Church adopted also the Jewish custom of a seven-day week with regular occurring fasts on Wednesdays and Fridays . . . Only the Jewish Sabbath was changed by the Christians. They chose as their Holy Day the day of the Resurrection, the Lord's Day . . . [The Romans] divided the year into twelve months and therefore when the Church began to institute festivals which were of unique importance for itself and not originally Jewish they were observed on dates in the Roman calendar. These included the saints' days . . . and later Christmas Day.

From L. W. Cowie and John Selwyn Gummer, *The Christian Calendar* (Springfield, Mass.: G and C Merriam Co, 1974), 7.

---

[63]Pieper, *Leisure*, 19. The best analysis of the *vita activa* and the *vita contemplative* in western civilization and "the reversal of the hierarchical order" between the two is Hannah Arendt, *The Human Condition* (Chicago: University of Chicago, 1958), esp. 289–292. Arendt terms the displacement of the *vita contemplative* "perhaps the most momentous of the spiritual consequences" of modernity (289). Also useful is Robert Bellah, "To Kill and Survive or To Die and Become: The Active Life and Contemplative as Ways of Being Adult," in *Adulthood*, Erik Erikson (New York: Norton, 1978), 61–80, esp. 76–78, on the need to recover the contemplative life in America modeled by Thomas Jefferson and Abraham Lincoln—two great "contemplatives in action."

[64]Thomas Merton, *Spiritual Direction and Meditation* (Collegeville, Minn.: Liturgical Press, 1960), 76–77. For the early Christian roots of the "work as prayer" tradition see Origen's treatise "On Prayer," *Origen* trans. Rowan A. Greer (New York/Ramsey, N.J.: Paulist, 1979), 104.

[65]Evelyn Underhill, *The Spiritual Life*, reprint ed. (London/Oxford: Mowbray, 1984), 97–98.

psychologically alienates the laborer from his or her labor.[66] By contrast, regard for leisure imbues the worker and the materials of work with meaning beyond their utility.[67] Work, as a

Notable Events in the Traditional Christian Calendar

Advent (Coming): This time in the church calendar begins four Sundays before Christmas. During advent, Christians recall the Old Testament Messianic prophecies. Some Christians also observe advent as a period of prayer and fasting.

Christmas: This is the time Christians mark the birth of Jesus. Protestants and Roman Catholics celebrate Christmas on December 25. The Easter Orthodox Church celebrates Christmas on January 7.

Epiphany: Often celebrated as a festival, this time commemorates the coming of the Magi as the first manifestation of Christ to the Gentiles. In the Eastern Orthodox Church it commemorates the baptism of Christ. January 6 is the customary date for celebrating the epiphany.

Ash Wednesday: Ash Wednesday is the first day of the Lenten season.

Lent: Lent is the name given to the forty weekdays from Ash Wednesday to Easter. It is observed by the Roman Catholic, Eastern Orthodox, and some Protestant churches as a period of penitence and fasting.

Palm Sunday: This Sunday, one week before Easter, commemorates Jesus' triumphal entry into Jerusalem.

Good Friday: This day marks the death of Jesus, which Christians believe to be the sacrifice that makes possible the reconciliation of God and humankind.

Easter: Easter commemorates the resurrection of Jesus. It is generally regarded as the most important day in the Christian calendar. In the Roman Catholic and Protestant Churches, Easter is customarily celebrated on the first Sunday after the first full moon after the vernal equinox. The Eastern Orthodox Church celebrates Easter twenty-eight days later.

Ascension Day: This day, the Thursday forty days after Easter, is observed in commemoration of Christ's ascension into Heaven.

Pentecost: Pentecost is the time Christians celebrate the descent of the Holy Spirit on the apostles. It is customarily observed (and sometimes celebrated as a feast) on the seventh Sunday after Easter.

Trinity Sunday: Trinity Sunday occurs on the Sunday following Pentecost Sunday. It is celebrated in honor of the Trinity.

Feast of the Transfiguration: August 6 is a feast date set aside to celebrate the occasion when Jesus led Peter, James, and John up a mountain, His physical appearance changed, and He was bathed in light.

Reformation Day: In the Protestant tradition, October 31 recalls the beginning of the Reformation in 1517. The Reformation is characterized by two trends in the sixteenth Century: (1) the rejection or modification of some Roman Catholic doctrines and practices; (2) the establishment of the Protestant churches.

All Saints Day: November 1 is observed in Western liturgical churches as a Christian feast in honor of all the saints.

---

[66]On the lack of contemplation/leisure in the West see Douglas Steere's essay "Contemplation and Leisure," *Together in Solitude* (New York: Crossroad, 1982), 112–113.

[67]On discovering the essence of life through contemplation, Maisie Ward quotes a letter of G. K. Chesterton (1899) in which he refers to being excited and intoxicated by the "startling wetness of water," the "fieriness of fire," the "steeliness of steel," and the "unutterable muddiness of mud." *Gilbert Keith Chesterton* (New York: Sheed and Ward, 1943), 108–109.

type of the active life, locates human beings in time and space. Leisure permits the worker to touch the eternal even if he or she is unable to grasp it fully.

The ancient Christian traditions of holy leisure and holy time were mutually supportive. Early Christians patterned their observance of holy time after the ancient Hebrews, who structured their life around a yearly calendar of holy days. The calendar included six annual religious festivals and three pilgrimages to Jerusalem. Christians during the early and later Middle Ages developed their own version of a religious calendar, which sanctified time for them. The Christian calendar came to revolve around two focal points: the season of Advent, Christmas, Epiphany; and the season of Lent, Easter, Pentecost. These two seasons enabled the church to reflect on and celebrate the whole mystery of God acting in human history. Intrinsic to the yearly rhythms of Christian worship was the weekly cycle. The cycle began and ended with the Lord's Day and embodied the themes of creation, resurrection, and the peace of God in the coming re-creation. Even more fundamental to the sanctification of time was the observance of prayer hours that interspersed labor with rest on a daily basis.[68]

> "The ancient Christian traditions of holy leisure and holy time were mutually supportive."

Seen in their totality, the daily, weekly, and yearly rhythms of prayer, reflection, and celebration in the Christian calendar were regular invitations to enter into holy leisure and to be refreshed by it. Christians were encouraged to remember the divine drama of redemption and to anticipate its unfinished events. Doing so was intended to be a source of new energy in the midst of intense societal pressures and personal sufferings. It also protected Christians in a later age of religious freedom under the Roman emperor Constantine from compromising with the pagan beliefs and customs which were woven into the fabric of political and civil life. The calendar provided a regular rhythm of alternative Christ-centered festivities.[69]

Life in medieval Europe came to be ruled by the church's view of holy time. Eventually, however, this notion of time was overturned by the rise of mechanical time-measurement devices

[68]On the Christian calendar as the "sanctification of time" and the early Christian notion of "keeping time" see Dom Gregory Dix, *The Shape of the Liturgy,* 2d ed. (London: Dacre/Adam and Charles Black, 1945), 303–396; John Westerhoff III and William H. Willimon, *Liturgy and Learning Through the Life Cycle* (New York: Seabury, 1980), 55–72. The origin of the divine office is briefly but competently explained by G. J. Cuming, "The First Three Centuries," in *The Study of Liturgy,* ed. Cheslyn Jones, Geoffrey Wainwright, Edward Yarnold (New York: Oxford University, 1978), 353–357.

[69]For the full calendar of Greco-Roman festivals see Nigel Pennick, *The Pagan Book of Days* (Rochester, Vt.: Destiny, 1992).

which catered to the demand of the factory system for increased precision, promptness, and regularity.[70] Industrial schedules—not Christian feasts—became the new liturgies of western culture during the eighteenth and nineteenth centuries. During the Industrial Revolution, time itself was "industrialized." The forces of economic production were installed as the new deities to be worshiped on the altar of work. In this connection, John Farina has called attention to two important points. First, he noted that the "quality of time" is "culturally determined." This means it is tied to cultural values. Second, he observed that the tendency of most societies is to dichotomize time. Western culture does so in terms of "work" and "non-work."[71] With "industrial" (work) time, "free" (nonwork) time was also born, but it had no intrinsic value. It was simply the cessation of work. By contrast, when preindustrial life was governed by natural seasonal rhythms, time was inherently leisurely.[72] In preindustrial times, work was accompanied by a personal sense of joy and spiritual renewal (true leisure). This experience of time seems to be what industrialized laborers seek to find in separate leisure time as a compensation for the void they experience in work.[73] Presently in North America, one must look to fringe Christian traditions such as the Amish and Shakers and to the continent's native inhabitants to recover a perspective on time that views it cyclically and in sympathy with the rhythms of nature and ancient traditions. These groups attempt to live in preindustrial time within their own countercultural communities.[74]

---

[70]On the transition from natural to mechanical or industrial time and the corresponding effect on work and leisure, see Robert Banks, *The Tyranny of Time* (Downers Grove, Ill.: InterVarsity, 1983), 116–145.

[71]John Farina, "Perceptions of Time," in *Recreation and Leisure: Issues in An Era of Change,* ed. Thomas L. Goodale and Peter A. Witt (State College, Pa.: Venture, 1980), 23.

[72]I am indebted to James Murphy's distinctions between "cyclical," "mechanical," and "psychological" time in *Concepts of Leisure,* 5–9. Thomas Green, *Work, Leisure and the American Schools* (New York: Random House, 1968), 48–60, differentiates between "diurnal" and "clock" time.

[73]On the affinity of true leisure with true work, see Wayne Stormann, "Work: True Leisure's Home," *Leisure Studies* 8 (1989): 25–33.

[74]Charles S. Rice and John B. Shenk, *Meet the Amish* (New Brunswick, N.J.: Rutgers, 1947), 1, refer to Lancaster County, Pennsylvania, a showcase of Amish culture as "the Garden Spot of America." Regarding the Amish closeness to nature and the rhythms of their communal life as governed by "agricultural" and "holy" time, see John A. Hostetler, *Amish Society,* 3d ed. (Baltimore, Md.: John Hopkins, 1980), 89–92, 136–138, 220–222. On the Shaker commitment to simplicity of life, stillness, and a mainly agricultural economy, see Mark Holloway, *Heavens on Earth,* 2d ed. (New York: Dover, 1966), 71–74. More generally on Shaker theology and spirituality, see *The Shakers,* ed. Robley E. Whitson (New York/Ramsey/Toronto: Paulist Press, 1983), 4–32. For aboriginal concepts of "cyclical time" contra "linear time" see Peter Knudtson and David Suzuki, *Wisdom of the Elders* (Toronto: Stoddart, 1992), 142–154.

In summary, the concepts of holy leisure and holy time were two vital components of ancient and medieval Christianity's strategy for the spiritual formation of its adherents. Daily, weekly, and yearly cycles of holy time led Christians into the festive experience of holy leisure and allowed them to contemplate and participate more fully in the life of Christ. By this process, the mundane aspects of life were given a sense of the sacred and the transcendent. "Holy resting," a legacy of Judaism, was the key to spiritual empowerment. Invited by holy time into "holy leisure," the church collectively in its seasons of the Christian year, and Christians individually in their life cycles, repeated experiences of dying, rising, and being anointed by the Spirit for service to the church and society. Considering the sacredness of time, Noële Denis-Boulet underscores the reasons for the continued use of the Christian calendar: "[I]t is because our human time, subject to the rhythm of natural recurrence, tends toward eternity in its own way, that we need a liturgical year, that we cannot live our Christian life without the Christian calendar."[75] A Christian view of leisure requires as its foundation a Christian view of time. Without such a view, leisure loses its spiritual focus. The current widespread revival of interest in "spirituality" (much of which has non-Christian origins) among people who are also seeking a more leisurely lifestyle speaks to us powerfully. It demands that we find an appropriate place for leisure in any culturally-relevant discussion of spirituality.

Towards a Contemporary Spirituality of Leisure

The term *spirituality* is quickly associated by ordinary minds with extraordinary persons—saints and mystics who have accomplished extraordinary spiritual feats and lived on a plateau of perfection beyond the attainment of the vast majority of people. Defined within a biblical framework, however, "spirituality" refers to the work of the Holy Spirit in any believer's life, from which his or her inner attitudes and outer actions ultimately derive. Dallas Willard aptly proposes that "spirituality is simply the holistic quality of human life as it was meant to be, at the center of which is our relation to God."[76] Willard's view of spirituality places a spirituality of leisure squarely within the domain of everyday life where one is renewed by the Holy Spirit in the image of Jesus Christ. The

> "A Christian view of leisure requires as its foundation a Christian view of time."

---

[75]Noële M. Denis-Boulet, *The Christian Calendar* (New York: Hawthorn, 1960), 199.

[76]Dallas Willard, *The Spirit of the Disciplines* (San Francisco: Harper and Row, 1988), 77.

presence of the *imago Dei* (the image of God) in every human life makes life, even in its leisurely dimensions, intrinsically spiritual. In the same vein, spiritual theology (the study of spirituality) may be defined not as an intellectual act that lies beyond the reach of ordinary people but as "simply the act of reflecting on the mystery of God and his relationship with the created universe, especially the human experience of God."[77]

The concerns of leisure (even if defined functionally as "free time") and spirituality necessarily overlap. Both domains of life have as their goal to promote personal well-being and self-actualization. Further, they afford an opportunity for the expression of one's deliberate choices and inner desires. Lastly, each in its own way directs one's attention to the need for recreation and restoration so as to live a fruitful life, while resisting the pressure to define a "fruitful life" solely in terms of utility.[78] Leisure and spirituality can help people see that they must resist culture's pressure to define the "fruitful life" solely in terms of usefulness. (For something to be nonuseful does not necessarily make it *useless* in the sense of having no worth, meaning, or purpose.) But people also need to take the next step and act on the need for recreation and restoration so life might indeed be fruitful.

> **"The experience of leisure prompts one to consider the meaning of life and to reconnect with one's innermost yearnings."**

To live in a leisurely fashion is not the exclusive right of those seeking a spiritual life. Moreover, a spirituality devoid of any respect for leisure is not adequate to meet the spiritual needs of human beings. A religion without leisure is destined to degenerate into a mediocre, anxious existence. Any experience of life as an occasion for renewal or as an expression of human creativity will be smothered by a fatiguing sense of dullness and boredom.[79] Ironically, non-Christians at home with the contemplative side of life may actually live with more spiritual integrity than frantic, stressed Christians who do not know how to rest. The experience of leisure prompts one to consider the meaning of life and to reconnect with one's innermost yearnings. From these deepest instincts come the vital energy for living. The same instincts determine the purpose and direction of one's life.[80]

---

[77]Robin Maas and Gabriel O'Donnell, *Spiritual Traditions for the Contemporary Church* (Nashville: Abingdon Press, 1990), 12.

[78]My thinking was stimulated on this subject by Stanley Parker, *The Sociology of Leisure* (London: George Allen and Unwin, 1976), 103–113.

[79]On the importance of quiet restraint and relaxing play in living a spiritual life see Klaus Bockmuehl, *Living by the Gospel* (Colorado Springs, Colo.: Helmers and Howard, 1986), 49–50; Adrian Van Kaam, *Am I Living a Spiritual Life?* (Denville, N.J.: Dimension, 1978), 83–87.

[80]On leisure as an experience of personal, psychological/spiritual integration, see Elaine Smurawa, "Leisure: An Integrative Attitude," *Humanitas* 8 (1972): 323–346.

Leisure is, at the same time, a profoundly human and spiritual experience. A contemporary theology of leisure should respond both to the North American cultural situation and to its spiritual needs. An adequate theology of leisure should include at least the following three themes: the definition of leisure as an interior state, leisure as the integration of two kinds of time, and the revival of sabbatical living.

THE DEFINITION OF LEISURE AS AN INTERIOR STATE

As we have noted already, leisure is understood by many today as an active use of "free-time" in a recreational sense. Taken this way, leisure has little spiritual significance. However, if leisure is identified with an inner contemplative state (as many writers on the spiritual life have done), it becomes indispensable to the nurture of an authentically Christian spirituality. In the words of Dietrich Bonhoeffer, a truly leisurely existence is reflected in "the simplicity of the carefree life" envisioned by Christ in the Sermon on the Mount. Such a disposition contrasts sharply with an acquisitive striving after "daily bread," which cannot be "secured" by "anxiety or work."[81] Leisure as the inner, patient repose in the providence of God is a clear indicator of the quality of life in the kingdom of God that distinguishes believers from unbelievers. It separates those who rest in God from those who strive frenetically to provide security for themselves. The seventeenth-century English Puritan preacher John Flavel commended the "due consideration of Providence." He regarded such "consideration" as a means of nurturing an "inward tranquillity" of the mind stabilizing one "amidst the vicissitudes and revolutions of things in [an] unstable, vain world."[82]

> "Leisure as the inner, patient repose in the providence of God is a clear indicator of the quality of life in the kingdom of God."

Defining leisure in terms of the inner life makes it an all-encompassing Christian expression closely akin to prayer. Moreover, this way of viewing leisure resists a tendency common in secular studies of recreational leisure: dividing life artificially into compartments of "work" and "leisure."[83] In his book *Sabbath Time* (1992), Tilden Edwards constructs a series of images of sabbath time and work and ministry

---

[81]Dietrich Bonhoeffer, *The Cost of Discipleship*, rev. ed. (London: SCM, 1959), 154ff. One of the best recent treatments of Christian simplicity is Richard Foster, *Freedom of Simplicity* (San Francisco: Harper and Row, 1981).

[82]John Flavel, *The Mystery of Providence* (London: Banner of Truth Trust, 1963), 167.

[83]See Judith Brook, "Leisure Meanings and Comparisons with Work," *Leisure Studies* 12 (April 1993): 149–162.

time. They show work, play, and prayer not as dissociated from each other but as interrelated and connected—though they appear to be opposite rhythms of one life.[84] Karl Rahner, the German Jesuit theologian, has aptly commented that "every human activity which involves the whole man in any way and to any degree is both work and leisure."[85] Holy leisure according to an ancient Christian tradition is part of the *opus Dei* (work of God), not something separate from it. Holy leisure relates to fulfilling the apostle Paul's command "to pray

> **"'Activity which involves the whole man in any way is both work and leisure.'"**
> —*Karl Rahner*

without ceasing" (1 Thess. 5:17). The same theme appears in the classic seventeenth century call of Brother Lawrence, the Carmelite, who calls us "to practice the presence of God" in all things.[86] The recognition of leisure's affinity with the contemplative "prayer of rest" tradition in Christianity reinforces the vital contribution the discussion of leisure can make to today's world. In particular, such a recognition reinforces the contribution such a discussion can make to renewing the spiritual life of a high-tech culture dominated by activism, whether in its secular or religious variation.[87]

Leisure defined in terms of the inner life begins to form a Christian response to a society overcome by addictions and preoccupied with recovery programs. Addictions of varying kinds can be properly regarded as the inevitable result of the loss of leisure. Loss of leisure is actually a loss of

---

[84]Tilden Edwards, *Sabbath Time*, 41, 42. I have also been helped in my thinking about the relationship between work and leisure by the Japanese sociologist Kunio Odaka's five possible ways of defining the work–leisure relationship: (1) work-oriented-unilateral (life consists of work); (2) leisure-oriented-unilateral (life consists of work for a living and leisure for enjoyment which makes life worth living; (3) identity (no distinction between work and leisure); (4) split (work is work and leisure is leisure); (5) integrated (work makes leisure pleasurable and leisure gives new energy to work). "Work and Leisure: As Viewed by Japanese Industrial Workers," quoted in Stanley Parker, *The Future of Work and Leisure* (New York: Praeger, 1971), 70.

[85]Karl Rahner, *Theological Investigations*, trans. Kevin Smyth (Baltimore/London: Helicon/Daron Longman and Todd, 1966), 4: 379.

[86]Brother Lawrence, *The Practice of the Presence of God*, trans. E. M. Blaiklock (Nashville: Thomas Nelson, 1982).

[87]See Richard Foster, *Prayer, Finding the Heart's True Home* (San Francisco: Harper 1992), 93–103, for a helpful identification and explanation of the "prayer of rest" as understood by a variety of spiritual writers. For a recent more general spirituality of leisure, see Leonard Doohan, *Leisure A Spiritual Need* (Notre Dame: Ave Maria, 1990).

interior freedom. It is part of what James Houston has described as the "ghastly process of 'losing one's soul'."[88] The psychiatrist Scott Peck interprets certain addictions (to alcohol and other drugs) as "sacred diseases." They reflect a misdirected attempt on the part of the addict to gain the leisure of a lost Eden or future heaven.[89] Understandably, the recovery of leisure becomes the concern of physicians of the soul—psychotherapists, counselors, and spiritual directors alike.

Ironically, the "great malady" of the twentieth-century age of leisure has been diagnosed as "loss of soul." Thomas Moore, a well-known student of the Swiss psychotherapist Carl Jung, has made an astute observation: "[W]hen soul is neglected, it doesn't just go away; it appears symptomatically in obsessions, addictions, violence, and loss of meaning."[90] A society troubled by violence, materialism, and pornographic images of life has lost its capacity for leisure. When defined as an inner state, however, leisure functions as a powerful corrective. It mends lifestyles of unbridled sensuality, in which people surrender their personal freedom and with it the capacity to develop moral virtue. Christian conversion aims at the transformation of the heart with its affective energies and power of the will, resulting in a life of self-control. The leisurely life then is one in which the heart is set free to do what it was created to do—worship the Creator, enjoy the fruits of creation, and love one's neighbor.

> "Ironically, the 'great malady' of the twentieth-century age of leisure has been diagnosed as 'loss of soul.'"

---

[88]James Houston, *The Heart's Desire: A Guide to Personal Fulfillment* (Oxford: Lion, 1992), 53. Addiction as the opposite of freedom is more fully analyzed in Gerald May, *Addiction and Grace* (San Francisco: Harper and Row, 1988), 1–15. As a case in point, see Richard Foster's discussion of the interior freedom of simplicity as a force for breaking an addiction to money in *The Challenge of the Discipline Life* (San Francisco: Harper and Row, 1985), 71–87.

[89]Scott Peck, *Further Along the Road Less Traveled* (New York: Simon and Schuster, 1993), 136–137.

[90]Thomas Moore, *Care of the Soul* (New York: Harper Perennial, 1992), xi. His observation of modern "soullessness" was anticipated in his mentor Carl Jung; see his *Modern Man in Search of a Soul,* reprint ed. (Orlando, Fla.: Harcourt Brace Jovanich, 1933), 196–220. See also Martin Luther King, *Where Do We Go From Here? Chaos or Community?* (Boston: Beacon Press, 1967), 186, for a discernment of the relationship of materialism and spiritual problems such as racism and militarism. More recently, see Jim Wallis, *The Soul of Politics* (New York: New Press/Orbis, 1994), 126–144, for an exposé of the consumer credo "I shop, therefore I am" and a recognition of the connection between consumerism, violence, and sexual exploitation. Wallis argues that consumerism promotes the "commodification of life" and has even usurped the place of "citizenship" in America.

LEISURE AS THE INTEGRATION OF TWO KINDS OF TIME

The presence or lack of leisure in life has direct bearing on the perception of time, in its use and significance. Christian reflection on time, influenced by classical Greek thought, has traditionally distinguished between two kinds of time. The first we shall call *chronos*-time. It is measured time, time calculated by duration. The Scriptures have little to say about *chronos*-time. The second we shall call *kairos*-time. It is the "right time," time evaluated by content. *Kairos*-time is poetically expressed in the times and seasons of the third chapter of Ecclesiastes.[91] Though not totally blind to *kairos*-time, modern life in the West is very much ordered by *chronos*-time. The Scriptural thought of "redeeming the time" (Eph. 5:16) and the modern thought of saving time are quite different. Scripture sees time as a gift and opportunity to be used under the guidance of the Holy Spirit. We redeem the time in order to accomplish those things that accord with God's purposes. The modern view of time is as a commodity, which can be efficiently or inefficiently used, raced against, managed, saved, lost, or even converted into money.[92] *Kairos*-time promotes a relaxed awareness and discernment of the opportunities for living provided by time.[93] *Chronos*-time is prone to being compulsively bullied by a frenetic scheduling of life. Aiming at affluence, economic productivity, and living efficiently fosters the sense of being rushed, the hallmark of societies ruled by *chronos*-time.[94]

> **"The presence or lack of leisure in life has direct bearing on the perception of time, in its use and significance."**

While one lives in a culture dominated by *chronos*-time, leisure opens one up to the *kairos* potential of every *chronos* moment. It also demolishes the artificial barrier, undermining the unity of life, between "secular" and "sacred" time. Moments exist not to be crowded into Day-Timers and crammed into digital watches. Rather, they exist to be listened to for the wisdom they contain regarding the movements of the Spirit in the often

[91]See John McInnes, *New Pilgrims* (Palm Springs, Calif.: Ronald N. Haynes Pub. Inc., 1981), 18–35; Robert Banks, *Tyranny of Time*, 168–177, regarding the *kairos/chronos* distinction; and Jean M. Blomquist, "Holy Time, Holy Timing," *Weavings* 6 (Jan/Feb, 1991): 7–13.

[92]See Benjamin Franklin's commercialization of time with his famous dictum "time is money" in his essay "Advice to a Young Tradesman (1748)," *The Autobiography of Benjamin Franklin* (New York: Random House, Modern Library 1944), 232.

[93]Interesting in this regard is the observation in Staffan B. Linder, *The Harried Leisure Class* (New York: Columbia University, 1970), 17, that cultures with "superfluity of time" are found in the poorest countries where much of time has no productive significance.

[94]See the survey, "Rapid Growth in Rushin' Americans," *American Demographics* 15 (April 1993): 26; Nancy Gibbs, "How America Has Run Out of Time," *Time* (24 April, 1989), 48–55.

boring, frazzled, and stressed areas of our lives. Leisure allows us to hear in each of life's seasons—childhood, adolescence, early adulthood, midlife, and old age—the issues that face us and the opportunities given to us.[95] Moreover, the voice of the Spirit can be sharpened through the genuine experience of leisure in times of transition and dislocation, when the familiar structures and movements of life are uprooted and altered.

The place of leisure in a Christian spirituality is inextricably linked to the question of time. This being so, the challenge for contemporary North American Christians is to build into their lifestyle what James Whitehead has called "an asceticism of time."[96] Whitehead's phrase refers to how we allow for serendipitous breakthroughs of the Spirit. Leisure, though it looks (and often feels) like wasting time, actually fosters sensitivity to these divine encounters. In the setting of leisure, all time is God's time. *Chronos*-time and *kairos*-time meet in every moment. A truly Charismatic spirituality requires an ongoing leisurely sensitivity to the voice and stirring of the Spirit in which the will of God is communicated to the Christian. Without this sensitivity no claim to spirituality can remain faithful to its vision of nurturing life in the fullness of the Holy Spirit. The authenticity, effectiveness, and longevity of charismatically empowered ministry depends in no small

*C*hronos and Kairos Time

Chronos is duration, *kairos* is opportunity. We cooly measure *chronos* with clocks and calendars; we passionately lose ourselves in *kairos* by falling in love or leaping into faith . . . If we are dominated by a sense of *chronos*, the future is a source of anxiety, leeching energy from the present, or leaving us whiningly discontent with the present . . . But if we are dominated by a sense of *kairos*, the future is a source of expectation that pours energy into the present. An obsession with *chronos*—rigid schedules, carefully planned timetables—is a defense against God's *kairos*, the unexpected and uncontrolled mysteries of grace.

From Eugene Peterson, *Reversed Thunder* (San Francisco: Harper and Row, 1988), 192,193.

---

[95]Each part of the life cycle poses its own challenges to living leisurely. The constraints on leisure which accompany each season of life are the focus of part three of *Constraints on Leisure,* ed. Michael G. Wade (Springfield, Ill.: Charles C. Thomas, 1985), 289–353.

[96]James Whitehead, "An Asceticism of Time," *Review for Religious* 39 (January 1980):16–17.

way on the depth of holy leisure, which undergirds it and out of which it is born. In *The Spirit of Life*, the German Lutheran theologian Jürgen Moltmann recognizes the interrelationship between these two themes. He follows his treatment of the "charismatic" (including speaking with tongues) with a consideration of the value of meditation and contemplation in terms of the deepening of one's experience of the Spirit. Without the self-awareness which comes in holy leisure, religious activists of any kind invariably fall into a trap. They "pass on . . . the infection of their own egoism, the aggression generated by their own ideology," all of which are demons of the soul which inhabit an inner wasteland.[97] By contrast, living in the *kairos* moment is described by Sue Monk Kidd as "spilling over with life and God." Living in the *kairos* moment ushers one into deepening "stages in contemplative awareness of attunement."[98]

> **"Secularization in western culture has eroded the sensitivity of society as a whole to the value of *kairos*-time."**

There is a corollary to what we have been saying: Secularization in western culture has eroded the sensitivity of society as a whole (and that of many Christians) to the value of *kairos*-time. The same process by which the skyscrapers of financial institutions and sports stadiums have displaced Gothic cathedrals at the hub of urban life has led to the suppression of the ecclesiastical calendar as a socially acceptable means of keeping time. In modern life, where there is no method of instituting "holy time," secular *chronos*-time frequently runs roughshod over sacred *kairos*-time.

The recent trend toward resurrecting the church calendar, even in churches unaccustomed to liturgical worship, however, illustrates the need of many to liberate their daily lives from the bondage of *chronos*-time. In increasing numbers, people feel a need to open their schedules to holy *kairos* moments, stimulated by an observance of the seasons of the church year.[99] For the past couple of centuries the "holiday" has

---

[97]Jürgen Moltmann, *The Spirit of Life* (Minneapolis: Fortress, 1992), 199–205, esp. 201–202.

[98]See the superbly eloquent description of the three stages of "contemplative awareness" whereby a person is transformed from *listening* to music to *being* music in Sue Monk Kidd, *When the Heart Waits* (San Francisco: Harper, 1990), 194–196; cf. the evangelical Anglican author Joyce Huggett, *The Joy of Listening to God* (Downer's Grove, Ill.: InterVarsity, 1986), 41–74, for the stages of her journey into the experience of contemplation.

[99]For illustration of this trend, see *Stories for the Christian Year*, ed. Eugene H. Peterson (New York: Macmillian, 1992). Robert Webber discusses the "phenomenon of convergence" in liturgical and charismatic churches as it affects the revival of the church calendar, in *Signs of Wonder* (Nashville: Abbott Martyn, 1992), 99–115.

triumphed over the "holy day," but the latter is making its return to combat the effects of a totally secular outlook.[100]

LEISURE AND THE REVIVAL OF SABBATICAL LIVING

Admittedly, the sociological situation of the modern North American differs substantially from that of the ancient Hebrew to whom the divinely originated "rest" legislation was given. Vacations, weekends, and nine-to-five workdays were as alien to the world of the Old Testament as strict Sabbath observances

Augustine on Leisure and the Revival of Sabbatical Living

Suppose . . . that the tumult of a man's flesh were to cease and all that his thoughts can conceive, of earth, of water, and of air, should no longer speak to him; suppose that the heavens and even his own soul were silent, no longer thinking of itself but passing beyond; suppose that his dreams and the visions of his imagination spoke no more and that every tongue and every sign and all that is transient grew silent—for all these things have the same message to tell, if only we can hear it, and their message is this: We did not make ourselves but he who abides forever made us. Suppose, we said, that after giving us this message and bidding us listen to him who made them, they fell silent and he alone should speak to us not through them but in his own voice, so that we should hear him speaking, not by any tongue of the flesh or by an angel's voice, not in the sound of thunder or in some veiled parable, but in his own voice, the voice of the one whom we love in all these created things; suppose that we heard him himself, with none of these things between ourselves and him, just as in that brief moment . . . I had reached out in thought and touched the eternal Wisdom which abides over all things; suppose that this state were to continue and all other visions of things inferior were to be removed, so that this single vision entranced and absorbed the one who beheld it and enveloped him in inward joys in such a way that for him life was eternally the same as that instant of understanding for which we had longed so much—would not this be what we are to understand by the words "Come and share the joy of your Lord?"

From Augustine, *Confessions* Book 9:10.

---

[100]Bruce Lockerbie makes a case for the value of the liturgical year in spiritual formation in "Living and Growing in the Church Year," in *The Christian Educator's Handbook on Spiritual Formation,* ed. Kenneth Gangel and James C. Wilhoit (Wheaton, Ill.: Victor, 1994), 130–142; cf. the call to replace "entertainment" with authentic leisure and the revival of social feastivals in Fox, *Reinvention of Work,* 161. Fox (34–37) also suggests a relationship between addictive work and television watching in both American and Japanese culture.

are to the world of our high-tech western culture, when the land rarely lies fallow and sabbaticals (for the few who enjoy them) are often used to produce more, not less. What relevance do "rest rhythms" devised for a primitive Middle Eastern, preindustrial culture have for a postmodern western, technological, fast-paced, seven-days-a-week, consumer-oriented society? What relevance do they have in a day when "creation" is understood as *production*, "chronic fatigue syndrome" struggles to gain status as a legitimate disease, and "burnout" pervades the workplace?

In response to these modern trends, a growing number of Christian writers in recent decades have sought to revitalize the nearly forgotten institution of the Sabbath, recovering the ethic of Sabbath living. This response has largely come out of recognition that regular rhythms of rest and relaxation, whether or not they translate into a traditional observance of the Sabbath day, are still essential ingredients of a spiritual life.[101] The ancient notion of rest is presently undergoing a resurgence. At the same time, many people have developed a renewed interest in the classical spiritual disciplines that formed a routine part of daily life prior to the advent of the industrial society: prayer, meditation, solitude, silence, journal keeping, and autobiographical writing.[102]

The practice of these disciplines has frequently been tied together in a religious sense with the essence of the Sabbath. In a secular sense, they have been linked with the need of modern people to find relaxation and leisure in the midst of their stressful, harried lives, when even holidays and vacations show the symptoms of workaholism rather than a strategy for recreation.[103] Some have proposed that we rethink the nature and purpose of vacations. They believe we should view them as opportunities for genuine rest and renewal and thus as a means

---

[101]For evangelical Protestant writers recovering the sabbath see Karen B. Mains, *Making Sunday Special* (Waco, Tex.: Word, 1987); Eugene H. Peterson, *Working the Angles* (Grand Rapids: Eerdmans, 1987), 44–58; Gordon MacDonald, *Restoring Your Spiritual Passion* (Nashville: Oliver Nelson, 1986), 157–171, and (Protestant turned Catholic) Ernest Boyer, Jr., *A Way in the World* (San Francisco: Harper & Row, 1984), 101–105; cf. the Catholic Thomas Ryan, *Disciplines For Christian Living* (New York/Mahwah, N.J.: Paulist, 1993), 69–102.

[102]For example, see Richard Foster, *Celebration of Discipline,* revised ed. (San Francisco: Harper and Row, 1988); Henri J. M. Nouwen, *The Way of the Heart* (New York: Ballantine, 1981); Susan A. Muto, *Pathways of Spiritual Living* (Garden City, N.Y.: Double Day, Image Books, 1984).

[103]See Harvey Cox's recognition of meditation as an expression of the essence of "sabbath-keeping" in *Turning East* (New York: Simon and Schuster, 1977), 63–73. In his bestseller, *The Relaxation Response* (New York: Avon, 1975), Herbert Benson promoted a "secular" mode of meditation for relieving stress and then combined his religiously-neutral method with a "faith-factor" in *Beyond the Relaxation Response* (New York: Berkeley, 1984).

to curb the individual and societal "drivenness" engendered by a work ethic gone awry.[104]

In preparing for a sabbatical in 1989, I received a strong inner sense during times of silent prayer that the break from professional duties was to be a period of renewing rest for myself and my family. It was to be lived in the spirit of the Old Testament sabbatical year and not to be abused by overwork and an excessively scheduled life—as academics are prone to do. As I submitted to the leisurely study of Christian prayer—or, perhaps more correctly, allowed the numerous traditions of Christian prayer to speak to me—a course was birthed. I called it "Prayer Paths to God." It was not so much the product of my efforts as it was the fruit of the Spirit's work in me, to be given away as a gift to many students in various schools seeking direction in their inner lives.

> **"Work is not the enemy. The enemy is a lifestyle that revolves _solely_ around work."**

Christian theologians have long affirmed that for life to attain its full spiritual potential, it must be lived in a dialectical, rhythmic way.[105] Leisure and work deserve proportionate amounts of time and energy. In this way the soul can be nurtured in contemplation and the body engaged in work.[106] Work is not the enemy. The enemy is a lifestyle that revolves _solely_ around work.[107] Wholeness in life comes from recognizing and experiencing the interplay of work, rest, worship, and

---

[104]Tim Hansel, _When I Relax I feel Guilty_ (Elgin, Ill.: David C. Cook, 1979), 109–142, coins the phrase "active rest" for his strategy of refashioning vacations along more leisurely lines. Cf. Gordon MacDonald, _Ordering Your Private World_ (Nashville: Oliver Nelson, 1984), 33–38, for the characteristics of "driven" persons who live on the verge of the "sinkhole syndrome" (13–18). The earlier booklet by Charles E. Hummel, _Tyranny of the Urgent_ (Downers Grove, Ill.: InterVarsity, 1967), endeavors to lead evangelical "activists" into a more leisurely lifestyle.

[105]For example, see Questions 179–182, second part of the second part, on the active and contemplative life in Thomas Aquinas, _Summa Theologica_, vol. 2 (New York: Benziger Bros., 1947), 1929–1946. The classic work (originally published in 1920) by A. G. Sertillanges, _The Intellectual Life_, 5th ed. (Westminster, Md.: Christian Classics, 1980), 66–68, 87–93, extols the restorative and rejuvenating potential of solitude and rest to enhance the fertility of one's intellectual life.

[106]Karl Rahner, _Theological Investigations_, 4:378, lists "recreation, play, liturgy, creative thinking, poetry and art, and similar concepts" as leisure activities. Sport, however, he calls a "peculiar mixture of leisure and work" (379).

[107]Of course, some have also seen leisure as a serious peril to civilization. The president of Colgate University, George B. Cutten, in _The Threat of Leisure_ (Washington DC: McGrath, 1926), 87–99, listed physical and mental degeneracy, moral decline, boredom, love of pleasure, excessive wealth, perpetuation of moronic elements, sexual laxity, and decline of the fine arts as the deleterious effects of leisure.

play rhythms. It comes from recognizing their capacity to revitalize each other when given their due place. A return to sabbath rhythms has refreshing implications for individuals, families, and society alike, though integrating them with the hectic, consumptive patterns of life in the late twentieth century will test the resolve of even the most devoted.[108]

The burgeoning of the retreat movement across North America during the past two decades illustrates a notable point. A significant part of the population today is making a serious effort to incorporate rhythms of interior retirement into their lifestyles so as to counter addictions to the noise and activity generated by an overly extroverted society. Formal "retreating" was introduced into Christian history during the sixteenth century by the Society of Jesus, founded by Ignatius of Loyola. However, the importance of solitude in Judeo-Christian spirituality has been affirmed since ancient times. The list of persons throughout Christian history who have maximized the value of periodic experiences of solitude includes many notable persons: Paul, Anthony, Benedict, Francis, Ignatius, Jonathan Edwards, David Brainerd, Hudson Taylor, A. W. Tozer. In recent times, the retreat movement has spread around the world and been embraced by a broad range of Christian traditions.[109]

A retreat is a temporary, structured withdrawal from normal living. As such, it expresses the sabbath ideal. It is literally a "retreating" of life in the presence of God within a context of silence so as to get in touch with transcendent realities. The solitude and silence of the retreat center creates an environment in which a change of attitude toward one's daily world can occur. At the same time it allows personal creativity to blossom.[110]

---

[108]The challenge of developing a more passive, contemplative spirituality in an impatient action-oriented culture is well addressed in W. H. Vanstone, *The Stature of Waiting* (London: Darton, Longman and Todd, 1982), 52–68, 101–115. Similar sentiments are expressed in Henri J. Nouwen, "A Spirituality of Waiting: Being Alert to God's Presence in Our Lives," *Weavings* 2 (January/February, 1987): 7–17, esp. 7–8. Barbara Killinger, *Workaholics: The Respectable Addicts* (Toronto: Key Porter, 1991), 7,6, suggests that play, meditation, and spiritual exercises at the heart of life are an effective remedy for workaholism.

[109]On the origin and development of the retreat movement see N. W. Goodacre, "Retreats," *A Dictionary of Christian Spirituality,* ed. Gordon Wakefield (London: SCM, 1983), 335–336. The various nuances of "retreat" are considered in Anthony Starr, *Solitude* (London: Flamingo/ Fontana, 1989), 32–41. On the historic attempts of affluent western urban dwellers to find "retreat" see Witold Rybczynski, *Waiting for the Weekend* (New York: Penguin, 1991), 162–185.

[110]The purpose and pattern of retreating is thoroughly discussed in John L. Casteel, *Renewal in Retreats* (New York: Association Press, 1959). More recently, see the excellent personal retreat program by Brother Ramon, *Heaven on Earth* (London: Marshall Pickering, 1991), and the more religiously eclectic discussion of retreating by David A. Cooper, *Silence, Simplicity and Solitude* (New York: Bell Tower, 1992).

Retreat centers have been described as "sacred landscapes," where the process of getting in touch with one's own soul is married to the search for God, the consideration of the meaning of life, and a reflection on the common good.[111] The purposes of the ancient Jewish Sabbath—rest, relaxation, contemplation, and play—are also those of the retreat center. The tranquil atmosphere of retreat facilities, often enhanced by beautiful settings, heightens the spiritual awareness of those who make themselves available. Sensitive to the cry for "holy leisure," which is growing louder in society at large, some secluded retreat centers and monasteries now advertise "holiday retreats" as remedies for the speed, stress, and secularity of modern life. In short, they represent a meaningful alternative to the typical vacation.[112] The power of the sacred place to induce a sense of inner sacredness is also being recognized by increasing numbers of people for whom a sense of connectedness with the land has been eroded by urban sprawl.[113] Ironically, a recognition of the renewing power of nature in its unspoiled beauty is being recovered at a time when wilderness areas are being depleted by industrial tourism and the encroachment of urbanites.[114]

---

[111]Regarding the mission of retreat centers, see Tom Gedeon, "Holding Environments for the Blue Planet in Our Search for God, for Meaning, for the Common Good," *Newsletter* (Retreats International), Winter, 92/93, 3–5.

[112]See the travel article "Holiday Retreats," *Good Housekeeping,* July, 1989, 138–140, and the Sanctuaries series of vacationers' guides to monasteries, abbeys, and retreat centers by Harmony Books; Jack and Marcia Kelly, *Sanctuaries, The Northeast* (New York: Bell Tower, 1991); *Sanctuaries, The West Coast and Southwest* (New York: Bell Tower, 1993).

[113]On the impact of physical geography on various American spiritual movements and mentors, see Belden Lane, *Landscapes of the Sacred* (New York/Mahwah, N.J.: Paulist, 1988). Aboriginal understandings of "sacred space" are surveyed in Knudtson and Suzuki, *Wisdom of the Elders*, 121–141. On the renewed sense among urban Americans of the power of place to shape experience, see the sociologist Ray Oldenberg, *The Great Good Place* (New York: Paragon, 1989), 294–296.

[114]Irene M. Spry, "The Prospects for Leisure in a Conserver Society," in *Recreation and Leisure: Issues In an Era of Change,* ed. Thomas L. Goodale and Peter A. Witt (State College, Pa.: Venture, 1980), 152. Regarding the assault on national parks, see John G. Mitchell, "Our National Parks," *National Geographic* 186 (October 1994): 2–55. On the nineteenth-century "millenialist" origins of the American assault against the wilderness, see the eco-theologian Thomas Berry, *The Dream of the Earth* (San Francisco: Sierra Club Books, 1990), 114–116. Henry G. Bugbee, "Wilderness in America," *Journal of the American Academy of Religion* 42 (December 1974): 614–620, sees the American "wilderness tradition/ethos" with its associated spirituality as being in "dialectical contrariety" to the technological and mechanical culture which breeds consumerism. He calls for people and nature to live in "mutuality."

Conclusion—Divine Rest and the Renewal of Life

In his classic twentieth-century work on the Sabbath, the Jewish philosopher Abraham Heschel summons his readers to live "beyond civilization." His metaphors for the Sabbath as the archetypal symbol of divine rest and human leisure are eloquent—"palace in time," "great cathedral," "spirit in the form of time," cornerstone in an "architecture of time." For Heschel, modern civilization has a technological caste. This does not mean merely that we are surrounded by a growing number of technological devices. It means that in a very basic way we are concerned with the control and management of natural forces and resources. But Heschel believes we are called to something higher. We are called, he believes, to a kind of "spiritual living" that leads each of us "to face sacred moments." The spiritual life of any civilization starts to decay when daily human existence no longer regularly experiences "intuitions of eternity." By entering into the earthly experience of eternal rest—though brief and passing—humans do not renounce a technologically-based civilization. Instead, they "surpass" civilized life and affirm their independence of it. In doing so, they contribute to its spiritual renewal. Heschel concludes by asserting that the "answer to the problem of civilization" is not a flight "from the realm of space." Rather the answer is to discover a way of life that is "in love with eternity."[115]

In the closing decades of the twentieth century, a growing body of eminent persons in the West have resonated with Heschel's concern to preserve the sanctity of time and space in the midst of the dominance of technology. The French sociologist Jacques Ellul has offered a thoughtful analysis of the secularization of western civilization. In his view, any sense of the sacred that we might still have is now no longer derived from nature but from society and "technique." The "new demons" which have contributed to the loss of a sense of sacred mystery Ellul identified as materialism, scientific rationalism, and technical administration. The net effect of these secularizing forces is to strip western civilization of any sense of soul beyond that gained from society itself. Ellul harshly criticized Christian theologians. He believed they married Christianity to secularism. Against this he called for the resurrection of a Christian worldview that reinstates the biblical Creator-God at the center of the world.[116] In order to escape the technological system, Ellul claimed we need something beyond ourselves:

---

[115]Abraham J. Heschel, *The Earth is the Lord's and the Sabbath* (New York: Harper and Row, 1966), 8, 13–32.

[116]Jacques Ellul, *The New Demons* (New York: Seabury, 1975).

"We . . . need a transcendence. . . . Only something that belongs to neither our history nor our world can do this. . . . We are faced with technology as our fate or the existence of a transcendent. The existence of this transcendent permits us to evaluate the world in which we find ourselves."[117]

A finite, human life reaches its fullest potential and sense of meaning only by realizing its rootedness in the world of the infinite. Otherwise, humans merely become slaves of all they invent.

Without doubt our technological approach has brought a vast number of improvements and creature-comforts to life in the West as well as in other parts of the world. But as a frame of reference such an approach is capable only of building a civilization based on work. It cannot produce inner contentment. It cannot give rest to the soul. In fact, the technological society strips its participants of the capacity to experience "profound religious affection."[118] Unavoidably, leisure is robbed of its creative power. Its restorative qualities are blunted by the all-encompassing demands of technology, which prevent workers from discovering their true personalities.[119] The experience of holy leisure must be stimulated by other sources. The distinguished German economist E. F. Schumacher concluded that

Making Room for Sabbatical Living

Perhaps the hardest part of Sabbath for young people is its often slower, more reflective pace, away from the frenetic activities of many of their peers. Their sheer physiological conditioning to that speed may make it difficult to adapt for a long period of time. Because they are usually kept so hyped in our culture, with the way that can obliterate any spaces for God's Spirit to be recognized in their lives, it is that much more worth the effort. They can adapt for *some* period of time, even happily so, if what is done remains sensitive to their capacities.

From Tilden Edwards, *Sabbath Time* (Nashville: Upper Room, 1992), 103.

---

[117]Jacques Ellul, *Perspectives on Our Age* (Toronto: Canadian Broadcasting Corporation, 1981), 101.

[118]The factors contributing to desacralization in the industrial society are elucidated in S. S. Acquaviva, *The Decline of the Sacred in Industrial Society* (Oxford: Basil Blackwell, 1979), 133–141. Acquaviva suggests that industrialization even sterilizes the emotional life of society (146).

[119]Jacques Ellul, *The Technological Society*, trans. John Wilkinson (New York: Random House, Vintage Books, 1964), 401–402, on the destruction of leisure by the technological society.

three hundred years of being consumed by the accumulation of knowledge for exploitative ends, to the neglect of traditional wisdom, left Western civilization "rich in means and poor in ends."[120] Shortly before his death, Schumacher converted to Christianity. His personal journey led him to discover and embrace the "Jesus Prayer" in the Russian spiritual classic *The Way of a Pilgrim* (1884).[121] He called for the West to return to its contemplative Christian roots in order to avoid catastrophe. In his view, we need to renew our spiritual life, damaged by a materialistic outlook. The remedy he recommended is a return to holy contemplation.

> "At the personal level, Christians in the West (especially Protestants) must recover a theology of the contemplative life."

The development of a Christian view of leisure is indispensable to the cause of personal, societal, and environmental renewal. At the personal level, Christians in the West (especially Protestants) must recover a theology of the contemplative life. In so doing, they may be freed from being unwitting allies of some of the sins most common to our era. Fortunately, some Protestant theologians in the West have begun to address this deficiency.[122] The recovery of "holy leisure," "holy time," and "divine rest" as necessary and desirable rhythms in a Christian's life has several benefits. It stems unhealthy activism, it tempers uncontrolled materialism, and it fosters an atmosphere in which spiritual vitality can be continually renewed. In Stephen Covey's recent bestseller *The 7 Habits of Highly Effective People* (1989), he highlighted holy leisure as important to personal transformation. Covey's model of leisure calls for the renewal of the spiritual, mental, social, and physical dimensions of life. It differs importantly from today's dependence on personality, attitudes, skills, techniques, and public image. What is really at stake for Covey in the experience of leisure is the restoration of a "character ethic" to society.[123] A character ethic involves nurturing personal integrity as the means to success.

We have been defining leisure in classical contemplative language, drawn from the Christian tradition that focuses on the inner life. We have called attention to its benefits for personal

---

[120]Schumacher, *A Guide for the Perplexed* (London: Jonathan Cape, 1977), 68.

[121]Ibid., 73–91, esp. 88.

[122]For example, see the Anglican, John Macquarrie, *Paths in Spirituality,* 2d ed. (Harrisburg, Penn.: Morehouse, 1992), 140–152. Theologians of play are also helping in this regard. Cf. Jürgen Moltmann, *Theology of Play* (New York: Harper and Row, 1972), and the earlier Hugo Rahner, *Man at Play* (New York: Herder and Herder, 1967).

[123]Stephen R. Covey, *The 7 Habits of Highly Effective People* (New York: Simon and Schuster, 1989), 287–307, 18–21.

renewal. An added benefit is that defining leisure in this way places leisure in a context not controlled by the more secular work-related criteria for determining leisure—"free time," "length of work week," "number of working days per year." All of these points of reference are subject to the rise and decline of economic fortunes of industrialized nations. (Notably, social theorists who appeal to ever-changing data sources often contradict each other in their attempts to prove that work is actually declining or increasing.[124]) People in nations experiencing economic depressions and high rates of unemployment become responsive to preindustrial modes of time keeping. They seek a notion of time that does not artificially separate work and leisure in the way that dominates modern industry. As a result, they often come to appreciate time in a way not unlike the ancient biblical notion of *kairos*-time.

At stake also in the formulation and proclamation of a Christian view of leisure is the renewal of culture as a whole. In many respects the America portrayed in Neil Postman's *Amusing Ourselves to Death* (1985) is a society that has lost the meaning and art of true leisure.[125] It is out of touch with its own soul and thus vulnerable to the "spiritual devastations of tyranny." In recent decades, our collective character, ethic, and public conscience have been increasingly eroded by the public media and entertainment industry. These elements of our social existence can be restored only when thoughtful individuals enter into "divine rest" and experience the rebirth of their own moral imagination.[126] From the posture of a renewed "Christian mind" they can then lead the reformation of the larger social agenda.

Lastly, consider the staggering array of ecological crises created in North America and beyond. These crises have been brought about by the way industrial production has tried to keep pace with the demands of consumers. As a result, the earth cries for rest. Human civilization is now about to enter the twenty-first century. The threats to the natural environment—air, earth, and water—seem greater than ever. Moreover, they seem likely to increase unless there is a return to and respect for the restful rhythms of creation by which nature is able to replenish itself.[127]

---

[124]The difficulty of determining American workers' time-income tradeoff preferences due to the differing types of data used by analysts is noted in Fred Best, *Flexible Life Scheduling* (New York: Praeger, 1980), 107–108.

[125]Neil Postman, *Amusing Ourselves to Death* (New York: Penguin, 1985).

[126]On the descent of America into a "new dark age," see Charles Colson, *Against the Night* (Ann Arbor, Mich.: Servant, 1989).

[127]Regarding the projected strain which industrialization will place on the natural environment in the twenty-first century, see Paul Kennedy, *Preparing For the Twenty-First Century* (New York: Harper, 1993), 95–121.

Overconsumption of resources on many fronts threatens the planet with apocalyptic possibilities too frightful to envision. Environmental issues are ultimately all leisure-related. Will the earth be allowed to rest? Will human beings rest so the earth will be allowed to rest? Will Christians realize their eternal destiny as people of rest? The survival of entire societies, if not the whole human race, may well depend on our willingness to enter again into "divine rest."

While the curtain falls on the twentieth century, the monks continue to proclaim their message of restfulness to the modern world. Recently, the Spanish Benedictine monks of Santo Domingo de Silos, singing their centuries-old Gregorian chants of "holy leisure," found themselves at the top of the pop music charts—after hundreds of years of not trying! Their success, ironic as it is, illustrates well the timeless appeal of "ancient rest" in an age of restlessness.

Review and Discussion Questions

1. Do you regard work as part of your spiritual journey? Try to explain your answer using reasons and examples from your own experience or from what you have read or heard about.

2. Is leisure part of your spiritual journey? Here again try to explain your answer drawing on reasons and examples from your own experience. Also try to incorporate into your answer some reflection on the difference in the way Nienkirchen uses the term *leisure* and the way you used the term before reading his chapter.

3. What relevance does "sabbath" have in modern American culture? Try to draw on some of the points Nienkirchen makes about sabbath. In what ways do you think American culture may be missing something important—even crucial—to its well-being by ignoring sabbath rhythms?

4. How could sabbath rhythms be integrated into society as a whole? into your lifestyle?

5. Where does "leisure/recreation" fit in a Christian worldview? Are playing and praying compatible?

6. What is your philosophy of "time"? Is the *kairos/chronos*-time distinction meaningful to you? Could you integrate it with a Day-Timer?

7. How would you make use of a day of solitude?

8. Can you integrate the concept of "holy time" into your lifestyle? List a few specific examples and try to explain what might be gained by such an integration. Do you know of people who have actually tried some of the ideas you set forth?

9. Explain the difference between a "secular" and a "Christian" view of leisure.

Selected Bibliography

Robert Banks. *The Tyranny of Time*. Downers Grove, Ill.: 1983.

Marva J. Dawn. *Keeping The Sabbath Wholly*. Grand Rapids: Eerdmans, 1989.

Leonard Doohan. *Leisure, A Spiritual Need*. Notre Dame: Ave Maria Press, 1990.

Jean Fleming. *Between Walden and the Whirlwind*. Colorado Springs, Colo.: Nav Press, 1985.

Richard Foster. *The Freedom of Simplicity*. San Francisco: Harper & Row, 1981.

Tim Hansel. *When I Relax I Feel Guilty*. Elgin, Ill.: David C. Cook Publishing, 1979.

Harold D. Lehman. *In Praise of Leisure*. Scottdale, Pa.: Herald Press, 1974.

Josef Pieper. *Leisure, The Basis of Culture*. New York: New American Library, 1963.

Witold Rybczynski. *Waiting For The Weekend*. New York: Penguin Books, 1992.

Leland Ryken. *Work and Leisure in Christian Perspective*. Portland, Ore.: Multnomah Press, 1987.

8

The Ethics of Being: Character, Community, Praxis

Cheryl Bridges Johns and
Vardaman W. White

Jeff, a college freshman, considers himself a Christian. He attends a private Christian college where he is active in a campus choir and academic clubs. Jeff attends church and volunteers his time with the youth group. He has never used drugs and does not drink alcohol. Yet, Jeff and his girlfriend are sexually active. Having grown up around people who hold the Scriptures in high regard, Jeff is familiar with scriptural statements forbidding sex outside of marriage. However, in his moments of reflection, he tells himself that this behavior is not sinful because he and his girlfriend love each other and plan to be married. To him, sex before marriage is morally wrong if one is promiscuous or if there is no long-term commitment involved.

Even though he confesses Christianity, Jeff is a product of his culture. He is what may be called a "postmodern person." In recent years there have been cultural and social shifts of such magnitude that many people speculate that we are in an era radically different from previous generations. People used to believe that there existed a core of truth which defined for everyone a unified vision of right and wrong. That is no longer the case. Jeff has grown up in a world in which behavioral norms are regarded as human inventions. They are no longer believed to derive from a source beyond humankind (God). Truth, too, has become relative and individualized. Even reality itself is seen as a construction and not a given. Hence, persons today are encouraged to live by their *own* rules, define truth for themselves, and make their *own* world. As if sewing a patchwork quilt, we are being encouraged to blend together symbols which in times past were thought to be incompatible. Today, for example, it is said that one may take elements from many different religions and lifestyles and blend them together in order to create a unique and individualized expression of truth.

In such a world, how does one know how to define right and wrong? Of course, the Scriptures provide an important basis for answering such questions. Throughout the centuries and across many cultures, Christians have derived moral rules from the Scriptures. Jeff, too, has a basic familiarity with moral rules derived from the Scriptures. But Jeff needs something more than a list of rules—even if those rules come from the Bible—in order to navigate the maze of moral decisions he faces in daily life. The mere fact that he knows certain rules does not yet mean he is equipped to meet the challenges of a postmodern social context populated by competing worldviews. Jeff needs something that will center his life, unifying it, so that he will not only *have* Christian beliefs and actions but that he will *be* a Christian. Jeff needs to have the heart and the mind of a Christian, which will transform his view of reality.

An Ethics of Being

One way to begin to talk about morality is to focus on human action and the observance of rules. The central question in this approach is, What should I do? Answering this question inevitably leads one to consider such issues as duty or obligation,

Biblical Ethics

Although it is obvious that "biblical ethics" refers to the ethics as found in the Bible, it is not obvious as to whether or not there is one consistent ethic espoused in Scripture. The Bible was written over a great many years by different authors addressing diverse individuals and communities. However, if the Bible is revelation of God inspired by His Spirit, then it is reasonable to believe that there is some consistency in what it reveals concerning the nature of being human, the nature of human relationships with each other and with God, and the nature of human actions. Within this relative consistency, however, are diverse ethical emphases, different communities facing different problems, various points in history which dealt with new problems, and so forth. This acknowledgment does not relativize ethics but forces us to deal honestly and sensitively with the narratives and instructions we find in Scripture. We must remind ourselves that treating biblical ethics as a whole or treating them so briefly is simplistic.

The Old Testament is especially difficult to characterize. Walter Kaiser, Jr., however, identifies five elements of Old Testament ethics: It is personal, theistic, internal, future-oriented, and universal (*Toward Old Testament Ethics*). Based on God and His relationship with humankind, it stresses human dispositions, attitudes, intentions and motivations, offers both hope and judgment at some future time, and applies God's standard to all people. The Old Testament also stresses the following: God's character, especially as holy; the covenant between God and His people; just societal and personal relations; family and the community; and the Law of Moses.

The New Testament emphasizes responding to Jesus and to His message. Jesus' ethics are found in the response to the inbreaking kingdom of God. So Allen Verhey writes: "That is the first and fundamental thesis with respect to the ethic of Jesus: it is an ethic of response, response to the apocalyptic action of God, which is at hand and already making its power felt" (*The Great Reversal*, 15). The correct response to the Kingdom is repentance. The law is fulfilled by love, which is "a disposition that drives towards its own concretion in works of love" (24). Thus, one responds to God in repentance and love, and one then acts according to that love. Paul recognizes that in Christ something new has been created, that the Christian is oriented toward a new life and participates in Christ's work and being. Christians are free from bondage to sin, death, and law. One is free not to practice libertinism but to practice love, which is the fulfillment of the law (108).

the characteristics of a satisfactory code of ethical rules, the justification for making exceptions to rules, the methods for determining priorities among the rules, and the sanctions for reinforcing rules.

To be sure, it seems natural and even necessary to answer the question What should I do? In traditional moral theory, the answer to this question has taken two general forms: (1) I should do (or refrain from doing) action *A* because I am duty-bound to do so, or (2) I should do (or refrain from doing) action *A* because of the consequences it will bring about. The first is called a *deontological* approach; the second, a *consequentialist* approach. (See the sidebars on deontological ethics and consequentialist ethics for brief treatments of these approaches to ethical issues.)

It is worth noting, however, that the very nature of the question What should I do? focuses attention on *action* and the rules governing it, and we are left to wonder about the person who

Deontological Ethics

The word *deontology* derives from a Greek verb *dei* meaning "it is necessary." A deontological approach to ethics emphasizes what is necessary: duty or obligation. Rather than seeking ends or consequences, a moral agent should act out of duty or obligation. A deontological ethical theory thus claims that an action or rule is right for a reason other than the consequence of the action or rule (e.g., it is commanded by God, it is inherently right) (Frankena, *Ethics*, 15).

Immanuel Kant (1724–1804) took a deontological approach to ethics. He held that an action must be done from duty in order to have moral worth. For Kant, to act from duty means to act out of respect for the moral law. Without that respect, the action is not done from duty. Of course, Kant recognized that people do not always act from proper motivation. Sometimes they do things that are consistent with what duty requires but are motivated by something other than duty. Their motivation, for example, may

be selfishness. Actions of this sort are said to be done not *from duty* but merely in *accordance with* duty. According to Kant, such actions have no moral worth and deserve no moral praise. For example, if duty commands telling the truth and if a certain person tells the truth simply out of a selfish motive, then that act of truth-telling lacks moral worth.

At the heart of Kant's moral theory is something called the *categorical imperative*. An imperative is a command. Some commands have an if-then form and are called hypothetical imperatives; e.g., "If you want to have friends, then be a friend." The command here is "be a friend." But the command is binding only on the specific condition that you want to have friends. According to Kant, morality is based on a command that has no such conditions attached to it. The command of morality is binding without qualification. Simply put, the command of morality is *categorical* (i.e., unconditional).

carries out the actions—the *agent*. Surely no action is whole or complete apart from reference to a person doing the action.[1] This insight provides a point of departure for criticizing the focus on human action with its emphasis on rules. According to this criticism, the prior question does not so much concern what I should *do*, but rather what kind of person I should *be*. Answering this question requires that we consider not only what it means to be human but also what is worth seeking in life. (For instance, Jeff's behavior regarding sex before marriage reflects more than just not following the rules of Christian behavior. It reflects something of Jeff himself—his beliefs,

---

[1]As Stanley Hauerwas writes: "'Problems' or 'situations' are not abstract entities that exist apart from our character; they become such abstractions to the extent that we refuse to be other than we are." See *Vision and Virtue: Essays in Christian Ethical Reflection* (Fides Publishers, 1974; Notre Dame: University of Notre Dame Press, 1981), 49.

Kant held that there is only one *categorical imperative:* "Act only according to that maxim by which you can at the same time will that it should become a universal law." This version of the categorical imperative uses the term *maxim*. A maxim is a private rule of action or a private reason for acting. Kant believed that people have reasons for what they do. The categorical imperative states that in order for one's action to be moral, one's reason for acting (the maxim) must be one that everyone could act on. Kant's meaning can be made clearer by considering cases of theft. Suppose I see a pen on my secretary's desk. I need a pen for my own use, but my secretary is not present, so I consider stealing her pen. My maxim (my private rule of action) might be something like, "Whenever I need something, I am free to take it from any available source, even if I have to steal it." Now the test of the morality of my proposed action is whether or not the maxim that under-lies it can become a universal law (a law for everyone). A moment's reflection shows that my maxim cannot become a universal law. It is not possible for me to will that my maxim authorizing theft should be the basis for everyone's actions. Even though I propose to steal my secretary's pen, I do not want other people to steal from me. Nor do I want other people to even suspect that I am a thief. Quite simply, I want everyone else to refrain from theft, but I want an exception made for myself. My maxim cannot become a "universal law." It is therefore not a moral maxim. I should not act on it.

There are deontological elements in the Bible. God is the giver of the Law. God's people are expected to obey God's command regardless of the consequences. In addition, deontological principles may be abstracted from Scripture, e.g., the principle of loving one's neighbor, the principle of the sanctity of human life.

habits, feelings, character. It reflects something of his *being*.) Of course, when we set out to consider these issues, we do not altogether ignore rules or the concept of duty. But the emphasis does shift to a concern with character development, the role played by the virtues and vices, and the components in our spiritual, biological, and psychological nature that are affected by and influence moral growth. In short, the focus shifts from a primary concern over *action* (and its emphasis on rules and obligations) to a primary concern over *being* (with its basic thrust toward character transformation and formation).

In a postmodern world in which there is little given or assumed that would prescribe what one should do, it is imperative that Christian ethics begin with the transformation of being. Jeff must become someone distinctively Christian before he can express in action a clear Christian lifestyle. In other words, Jeff must develop the character of a Christian.

How, we might ask, does an emphasis on character help us in ethics? First, character helps us respond in the particular situation because in the particular situation we are still us! Circumstances change, but the constant upon the shifting sands is the person facing the circumstances. That person's character, his or her dispositions, values, virtues, and vices, move with that person across the landscape of his or her life. Quite simply, character provides for consistency in action. Arthur Holmes notes that "a developed character makes behavior far more predictable than does the sudden impulse or passing inclination. It makes a person reliable, a responsible agent."[2] In short, we *do* what we *are*, and consistency of being translates into consistency of action. A person whose nature it is to be courageous will generally be courageous no matter the circumstance. He or she can be relied upon to be courageous because such courage is part of the person.

Second, events do not simply happen to us, but are interpreted by us. Hauerwas writes that "character determines circumstance, even when the circumstance may be forced upon us, by our very ability to interpret our actions in a story that accounts for moral activity."[3] Events are not simply past events, but are connected to each other to form stories. Humans are storytellers: They gain their identity and understanding of the world through the stories that make up their history. In a sense, then, we are stories,[4] or, perhaps better, stories are embodied in our

---

[2]Arthur Holmes, *Ethics: Approaching Moral Decisions*, Contours of Christian Philosophy Series (Downers Grove, Ill.: InterVarsity Press, 1984), 117.

[3]Stanley Hauerwas, *The Peaceable Kingdom: A Primer in Christian Ethics* (Notre Dame: University of Notre Dame Press, 1983), 8.

[4]Stanley Hauerwas, *Truthfulness and Tragedy: Further Investigations into Christian Ethics* (Notre Dame: University of Notre Dame Press, 1977), 78.

character.[5] The important point is that all events become part of our life-stories, part of how we describe ourselves, part of how we interpret our lives. The situation, then, is not some abstract "thing" separate from ourselves, but is also a part of our life-story, is one event in a history of events, and we face it in character, that is, as a person drawing upon personal history to respond to the present.

We cannot separate what we do from what we are; therefore, in ethics we must concentrate primarily upon the agent, not the act. If the being of the actor is well formed, then the actions that flow from it will likely be proper as well. The essential question of ethical theory, then, is not What ought I *do*? but What ought I *be*? In the following pages we will discuss three aspects pertaining to our being: character, community, and praxis.

Consequentialist Ethics

A consequentialist approach to ethics evaluates the moral worth of an action by reference to the consequences it produces. An act is right or good if it yields a certain result or consequence, wrong if it does not. An example of a consequentialist ethic is utilitarianism, articulated classically by Jeremy Bentham (1748–1832) and John Stuart Mill (1806–1873).

Bentham identified the good as pleasure. Among the alternative actions one might take in a situation, the moral act will have the consequence of producing the greatest amount of pleasure. Bentham's utilitarianism was quantitative. To this end he devised the *hedonic calculus*, a set of quantifiable elements (e.g., duration, intensity, extent) applied to the expected consequences of an action or policy according to which pleasure and pain could be measured.

Mill rejected Bentham's quantitative utilitarianism in favor of a more qualitative version. He wrote in *Utilitarianism*: "The creed which accepts as the foundation of morals 'utility' or the 'greatest happiness principle' holds that actions are right in proportion as they tend to promote happiness; wrong as they tend to produce the reverse of happiness. By happiness is intended pleasure and the absence of pain; by unhappiness, pain and the privation of pleasure." Mill believed, though, that people who have enjoyed both base pleasures and higher pleasures give a preference to the higher pleasures. He ascribes this to an innate dignity in humans. So he writes: "It is better to be a human being dissatisfied than a pig satisfied; better to be Socrates dissatisfied than a fool satisfied." Hence, his utilitarianism tends to be more qualitative than Bentham's.

Not all consequentialist ethics are utilitarian. For example, consequentialist elements may be noted in both Testaments of the Bible in the many references to a future time of blessing and judgment. The Scriptures lead us to expect judgment—and hence consequences—for our actions and dispositions.

---

[5]Richard Bondi, "The Elements of Character," *The Journal of Religious Ethics* 12 (Fall 1984): 209.

Character

The first and the most basic element of the triad is character. This section will explore what character is, why Christian character requires transformation and formation, the biblical language of sanctification, and aspects of character.

DEFINITION

There is an interrelatedness to our being that defines our character. For instance, Jeff is not just a composite of actions; rather, he is composed of a mysterious unity of actions, affections, and reasons. Craig Dykstra notes that these aspects of ourselves are expressed in the unfolding drama of the story of our lives. As dramas that have a past and a future, our current actions reflect how we perceive the past and what we intend to make of the future. Having a well-formed character is living out a story that is intelligible, that truthfully corresponds to reality.[6]

The story of our character shines through our lives. It is composed of our convictions: "those tenacious beliefs which when held give definiteness to the character of a person or of a community, so that if they were surrendered, the person or community would be significantly changed."[7] In other words, we are our convictions.

Convictions are acquired through the dynamics of formation (gradual growth). Indeed, our convictions are constantly being shaped by a host of forces. For instance, Jeff's convictions have been shaped by his family, his experiences at school and church, and the larger society as reflected in the media. But Jeff also needs transformation in order to know and worship God rightly. He needs to have his desires transformed because his desires, bent by sin, provide him with little sense of what he should rightly want. It is the Christian claim that "faith in Christ along with God's grace have a transforming effect on human nature in general and on each Christian in particular."[8] Contemporary Christian ethics must rest on this premise—which is the very basis of Christianity.

The Basis of Christianity

An approach to Christian ethics based on character stems from the nature of Christianity itself. Ethics is not reducible to what Christians do since Christianity is not reducible to what

---

[6]Craig Dykstra, *Vision and Character: A Christian Educator's Alternative to Kohlberg* (New York: Paulist Press, 1981), 52.

[7]James W. McClendon, *Biography as Theology* (Nashville: Abingdon Press, 1974), 34.

[8]*The Westminster Dictionary of Christian Ethics*, ed. James F. Childress and John Macquarrie (Philadelphia: The Westminister Press, 1986), s.v. "character."

Virtue and Virtues

From antiquity to the present, many different lists of virtues have been put forward. In several of his dialogues, the philosopher Plato (fourth century B.C.) finds reason to mention and discuss several of the classical Greek virtues: wisdom, piety, courage, temperance, and justice. In Galatians 5:22–23, St. Paul (first century A.D.) lists several virtues he calls fruit of the Spirit: love, joy, peace, patience, kindness, goodness, faithfulness, gentleness, self-control. The thirteenth century theologian Thomas Aquinas discusses many virtues, including four primary virtues (temperance, justice, fortitude, prudence) and three theological virtues (faith, hope, love). The eighteenth century theologian, Jonathan Edwards stresses love and holiness, noting that the religious life is one of affections according to which the Christian lives a life of love and loving the holy things of God. In the early 1990s, William Bennett published an anthology of folk stories under the title *The Book of Virtues*. In it he orders the stories according to ten virtues: self-discipline, compassion, responsibility, friendship, work, courage, perseverance, honesty, loyalty, and faith.

What is virtue? For Aristotle, virtue (*aretê* = excellence) is a disposition of the soul (a state of character) developed by habits which help a person achieve happiness (*eudaemonia*). Virtue aims at the intermediate: it is a mean between the vices of defect and excess. For example, the virtue courage lies in a mean between rashness (excess) and timidity (deficiency). Virtue is not a matter of determining an arithmetical mean between two vices and doing it. Rather, virtue always requires sensitivity to a context: doing the right *act* at the right *time* in the right *way* with respect to the right *people*.

In his *Summa Theologica*, Thomas Aquinas defines virtue as "a good quality of the mind, by which we live rightly, of which no one can make bad use, which God works in us without us." For an act to be virtuous, both *reason* and *desire* must be disposed toward the act. In other words, if someone knows that the act she is doing is a good act but desires to do something else, then she has not acted virtuously. Similarly, if someone acts in a good way but does not understand the moral quality of the act, then he has not acted virtuously. Thus, for Thomas, intellectual virtue (the perfection of our ability to know) and moral virtue (the perfection of our desires) are necessary, if we are to achieve our proper end, *beatitude*, vision of God.

Alasdair MacIntyre identifies three stages of virtues, the later stages presupposing the earlier ones. At the first stage, virtues make possible the attainment of goods internal to practices (e.g., sciences, games). At the second stage, virtues undergird us in seeking the good. The virtues provide knowledge of the self and of the good. At the third stage, virtues sustain a vital tradition. A person begins in and lives within a tradition and the quest for the good takes place within one's tradition. MacIntyre's notion of virtue is communal and teleological: virtue is the inculcation of or ordering of traits which assist the individual and the community of which the individual is a member in the quest for the good life.

In the Aristotelian-Thomistic tradition, carried into the present through people such as MacIntyre and Stanley Hauerwas, virtues are the perfections of activities, excellences which enable people to live successfully. They are the dispositions and skills embodied within a moral agent which are carried into any situation and which enable that agent to negotiate successfully that situation. (For additional information, see *Westminster Dictionary of Christian Ethics*, s.v. "virtue.")

Christians do. This discussion of the basis of Christianity presupposes certain tenets that cannot be investigated in this study: that humanity was created by God, for God, and in God's image; that humanity is sinful, alienated from God and God's purposes for their lives, thus from their own true being; that Jesus Christ was God incarnate, died, and was resurrected to effect humanity's reconciliation to God; that this reconciliation involves transformation of the whole person by the Holy Spirit into that which participates in the divine nature. Stated thus, the question may be asked: What can participate in the divine nature? The answer: That which is holy.

God's essential nature is holy. God's holiness qualifies all other qualities of God so that, for instance, God's power is a holy power and God's love a holy love.[9] For a person to be reconciled to God, he or she must come into the presence of the holy God. Since an essential aspect of holiness is separation from the unholy,[10] how can the unholy stand before the holy? Only by holiness itself, by the grace or gift of holiness given by the holy Himself, can this be accomplished. This "is a gift that betokens inner transformation to recognize 'what is good and acceptable and perfect' (Rom. 12:1–2)."[11] We must not only recognize the good and the perfect, but we must also *become* "good and acceptable and perfect." We are commanded to *be* holy, to *be* perfect.

> "Sanctification is an actual transformation of character in which we are made holy and righteous."

Only by this *becoming* can we avoid having a patchwork identity which pieces together moral choices based on what feels good or seems right for the moment. As we become holy and perfect we journey deeper in God and toward God. This does not mean that we never commit sin or that we are without any faults. Rather, it means that our affections and our desires become the affections and desires of God. Our thoughts and actions thus become that which reflects our hearts' desires as they are God's desires. Our holy being expresses itself through holy living, holy doing.

We become holy through the process of sanctification. There are several aspects of sanctification which should be noted. First, it is an act of God's gracious will toward us. It is God's gift to us, not something we have accomplished through our own ability. Second, it is an actual transformation of character in

---

[9]Paul Tillich, *Systematic Theology,* vol. 1 (Chicago: The University of Chicago Press, 1951), 272.

[10]Donald G. Bloesch, *Essentials of Evangelical Theology*, vol. 1, *God, Authority, & Salvation* (San Francisco: Harper & Row, 1978, 1982), 33.

[11]*The Westminister Dictionary of Christian Ethics*, ed. James F. Childress and John Macquarrie (Philadelphia: The Westminster Press, 1986), s.v. "holiness."

which we are made holy or righteous. This process entails cleansing and separation. It means, according to one scholar, "to be engrafted into the righteousness of God."[12] R. Hollis Gause writes: "It is a purging act of God provided to cleanse the nature of the believer and to set him free from the law of sin and death (Romans 8:2)."[13] Third, it produces holy living. Again, doing follows being.

Sanctification is not a wiping clean the slate of our life; rather, it is a process of cleansing, purging, making holy who we are. We who are holy participate in the divine nature. It is us, with our history, our story, our ideas, our character, encountering (and making ours) the history, story, ideas, and character of Christ and Christianity. We do not lose what is ours but instead acquire what has been absent and undergo a transformation of what has been corrupt.

TRANSFORMATION AND FORMATION

It was during his second semester in college that Jeff attended a revival service at his local church. That night the evangelist preached a powerful sermon regarding our inability to hide our sinfulness from God. During the sermon, Jeff knew that the Holy Spirit was scanning his life, revealing and bringing to light hidden areas of sin. During the altar call, he literally ran to the altar. He later testified that he felt as if the Lord was waiting on him with open arms, arms which he felt reached to embrace his sinfulness. He testified to a powerful cleansing and healing. From that night on, Jeff was a different person. After counseling, he ended the unhealthy relationship with his girlfriend and he began to desire time alone with God. He knew he had a journey ahead consisting of a daily walk with God and growth in his relationship with God, but he would always look back to that revival service as a turning point in his Christian life.

Sanctification is a transforming experience. Christianity itself is transforming. Transformation refers to change from one thing or characteristic to another. Christianity is not reducible to "belief" or "morality," but is *relationship* between Creator and creature, and, as has been seen, an essential aspect of this relationship is transformation. It is important for Christian ethics to reflect the nature and power of transformation. Simply because transformation is not something we *do* does not mean that it is unimportant or that it can be ignored. By understanding what takes place in transformation, we can better understand what we are supposed to be. Although transformation is vital, it is not itself the goal. Rather it occurs at strategic points along our journey, ever moving us toward

---

[12]Bloesch, *Essentials of Evangelical Theology*, vol. 2, *Life, Ministry, and Hope* (San Francisco: Harper & Row, 1982), 41.

[13]R. Hollis Gause, *Living in the Spirit: The Way of Salvation* (Cleveland, Tenn.: Pathway Press, 1980), 49.

our goal—God himself. By appreciating the goal of transformation, we can better claim for ourselves the life of the transformed being.

After Jeff's transformational experience during the revival service, he needed the regular experiences of formation such as Bible study, prayer, and worship. He needed to understand and appropriate the meaning of what had happened to him. Between transformational moments, character is also served through *formation*. The tasks of understanding, appreciating, and appropriating are not themselves transformational experiences, but are, instead, formational activities. Formation refers to development or maturation; a thing or characteristic is not changed into another thing or characteristic, but becomes stronger or greater or better.

> "Not only must we ask ourselves, *What are we being,* but also, *What are we being-toward?*"

Christian character is developed in our social environment. However, Christians are not mere products of their environment. After his transformational experience, Jeff had to accept or reject the social influences around him. This accepting and rejecting, this choosing, is self-determination or self-agency. Through the choices we make for certain actions "we not only reaffirm what we have been but also determine what we will be in the future."[14] In this way we actively utilize the character already formed to intentionally shape the character that we will have in the future. Since each person has so much to do with the formation of his or her character, each person is morally responsible for what is formed. What is essentially changed, made holy, in sanctification is the *character*. The Christian must then be responsible to develop the *character* according to its movement toward perfection.

Transformational experiences spread before us a vision of reality that enables us to press forward in our journey. From such experiences we have transformed understanding of ourselves and the world we live in. No longer are we held captive to a frame of reference that works against our character. Through transformational experiences we are set free to see what God sees and to become and to do God's intentions in this world. Our minds and our hearts are renewed into the mind of Christ (Romans 12:2). We are no longer conformists or patchwork persons; we are enabled to become overcomers.

What we do arises from what we see, thus forming what we are, finally shaping our vision. The movement of events is circular: from *vision*, to *action*, to *being* and so on throughout our life, propelling the character toward growth. Vision,

---

[14]Hauerwas, *Vision and Virtue*, 49.

springing from who we are, provides direction for this growth because what spreads before the core of our being is our perception of the future. Not only must we ask ourselves, What are we *being*, but also, What are we *being-toward*?[15]

This section has explored what character is, the need for both the transformation and formation of character, and sanctification. Within this framework, the basis of Christianity has been identified as relationship in which unholy beings are changed by God into holy beings for communion with Him. We have called attention to the importance of self-determination and noted the circular relationship of being, vision, and action. As important as these are to formation, however, they are not the only means of character formation. Christian character requires an environment in which it can be formed properly. This context is the topic of the next section.

Community

THE NECESSITY OF COMMUNITY

Christian ethics must consider the social setting in which transformation and formation occur. The setting required is *koinonia*. In this section we shall suggest some reasons for the necessity of *koinonia*, its definition, and nature.

After his experience during the revival Jeff found himself longing for a group of people with whom he could share his struggles and worship on a regular basis. Although he had been active working in the youth group, Jeff had never developed a regular habit of church attendance. He performed work for the church but he had never become part of the church fellowship. After the revival, he joined a small covenant group that met regularly for prayer and encouragement. (A covenant group consists of people who commit themselves to pray, support, strengthen, and bless each other.) He became more faithful in worship attendance. Immediately he noticed a difference in his life. He felt connected, needed, and loved. His covenant group encouraged him in his daily walk and provided regular fellowship with believers. Whenever he had a need, he knew he could call upon others to pray with him.

The covenant group that Jeff joined is built on the basic insight that human beings are social creatures. This means that they need interaction with other human beings in a community setting. In community, people share their experiences with each other and come to feel as though they belong to one another.[16] The desire for community is given to us by

---

[15]James W. Fowler, "Future Christians and Church Education," in *Hope for the Church: Moltmann in Dialogue with Practical Theology*, ed. Theodore Runyon (Nashville: Abingdon, 1979), 95.

[16]James Poling and Donald E. Miller, *Foundations for a Practical Theology of Ministry* (Nashville: Abingdon Press, 1985), 126.

God. Further, community is necessary for the development of the Christian. It is nearly impossible to develop a Christian lifestyle without the fellowship of the church;[17] indeed, "formation occurs in the context of relationships."[18] Only in community does one learn who one is, develop character, and live according to it. But the community must be a faithful community if it is to form us faithfully.[19]

DEFINITION

The New Testament word used to identify the type of community needed is *koinonia*. Paul used it to indicate "the fellowship of relatedness of Christians with Christ and consequently with one another."[20] *Koinonia* has the basic meaning of "to share with someone in something."[21] Thus for us *koinonia* is the fellowship of believers in Christ, which should be found in the church.

FEATURES OF KOINONIA

Howard Snyder names three aspects of Christian community important for this study: commitment and covenant, shared life, and transcendence.[22] It may be useful to apply these aspects of *koinonia* to the elements James McClendon suggests Christians need: stability (for the body), integrity (for the mind), and liberty (for the spirit). Christians need to be in an environment that will nurture body, mind, and spirit.[23]

Commitment and Covenant

Commitment and covenant refer to the bond between a person and God and, because of this, the bond between a person and other members of the Christian community. Snyder says of commitment and covenant: "There is no genuine Christian

---

[17]Stanley Hauerwas and William H. Willimon, "Embarrassed by God's Presence," *Christian Century* 30 (January 1985): 99.

[18]James W. Fowler, "Practical Theology and the Shaping of Christian Lives," in *Practical Theology*, ed. Don S. Browning (San Francisco: Harper & Row, 1983), 162.

[19]Stanley Hauerwas, "The Gesture of a Truthful Story," *Theology Today* 42 (July 1985): 187.

[20]Paul Lehmann, *Ethics in a Christian Context* (New York: Harper & Row, 1963), 86.

[21]Friedrich Hauck, s.v. "[Koinos]," in *Theological Dictionary of the New Testament*, eds. Gerhard Kittel and Gerhard Friedrich, trans. Geoffrey W. Bromiley (Grand Rapids: Wm. B. Eerdmans Publishing Company, 1965, 1982), 3: 808.

[22]Howard A. Snyder, *Liberating the Church: the Ecology of Church & Kingdom* (Downers Grove, Ill.: InterVarsity Press, 1983), 127-128.

[23]James W. McClendon, Jr., *Ethics: Systematic Theology*, vol. 1 (Nashville: Abingdon Press, 1986), 236.

community without a covenant. . . . Christian community cannot exist without commitment to Jesus as Lord and to each other as sister and brother."[24] Although the concept of *koinonia* as mystical organism is important, this fact does not negate the necessity of simple, personal loyalty within the community and among its members. James Nelson rightly emphasizes both the organic and the covenantal aspects of *koinonia*, but he notes that there is a danger of a person's individuality being lost if the community is seen only as organic. There must be unity, but it must be the result of members' consciously committing themselves to one another, being loyal and faithful to one another.[25]

It is important that the beauty and uniqueness of each individual be expressed in the Christian community. Legalism—the rigid and uncritical adherence to rules— is often a means of substituting conformity for genuine *koinonia*. It does not celebrate but rather fears individuality. However, legalism often provides a false sense of community by providing security for persons and by providing definite boundaries in a world in which there appears to be no boundaries. In a legalistic environment, persons don't have to be responsible for their actions. They do not have to bother with struggling to relate to those who may be different.

> **"*Koinonia* has the basic meaning of 'to share with someone in something.'"**

Because legalism does not change the internal nature of persons, the external dos and don'ts have to be ever present. People are judged and valued according to their conformity to rules and not according to their convictions. Thus, their "being" is not transformed by the relationships found in the community. What appears to be genuine Christian community is in fact quite the opposite!

A true community must be *convictional*; that is, its members must be united because they have thoughtfully chosen their deepest beliefs and values, not merely because they conform uncritically to a commonly held external code of behavior. A convictional community is one "that holds particular convictions, stories, language, rituals, and forms of action in common."[26] These elements of commonality are wondrously and mysteriously held together by the Holy Spirit, who makes *koinonia* a living reality. As persons (who are beings) relate to one another, they also find themselves relating to the Ultimate Being, God.

---

[24]Snyder, 127.

[25]James B. Nelson, *Moral Nexus: Ethics of Christian Identity and Community* (Philadelphia: Westminister Press, 1971), 119.

[26]Dykstra, *Vision and Character*, 57.

As the contemporary church has reacted against earlier forms of legalism (and the false notions of community resulting from it), it has experienced difficulty creating genuine convictional communities. Instead, contemporary Christianity has too often opted for an individualism which, like the dominant society, makes the moral life a private affair of the individual. Consequently, persons may attend a church and never be challenged regarding their lifestyles. They may not even know what others within a congregation believe about critical moral issues. Even worse, they may not even care to know the stories and beliefs of others.

If Jeff is to grow as a Christian, he does not need a legalistic community, which would force him to follow a list of rules and regulations. On the other hand, he also does not need a community that does not care enough to confront, instruct, and model for him the alternatives to the dominant society. Jeff needs a community characterized by commitment, covenant, and loyalty. Jeff needs others who are willing to share the Christian life with him in the bonds of *koinonia.*

Shared Life

Snyder describes shared life as "spending time together"[27] and says that "such life finds its real meaning in the balance of shared worship, nurture and witness."[28] Perhaps in the phrase "shared life" is the encapsulated meaning of *koinonia.* "Shared" implies plurality; there must be more than one in order to share. "Life" is singular. Lives are not so much shared as life is shared. *Koinonia* is an organic unity composed of many persons. The persons witness to one object of worship, partake of one essence, look to one experience, tell the same story, look to the same future, profess the same hope. They share in the one life. However, the persons remain distinct, bringing their own stories to the one story, bringing their own characteristics to the one essence.

Both covenant and shared life provide integrity. For McClendon, integrity "means society not propped chiefly upon lies; it means opportunity for education that nurtures openness of mind, critical examination of current beliefs, coherent or integral ways of thought for each consistent with the item next to follow, full spiritual liberty."[29] For integrity to be fostered, persons must commit themselves to, and share their lives with, each other.

Such commitment and sharing also lead to loyalty. Loyalty is not blind obedience or naive trust but critical faithfulness born

---

[27]Snyder, 127.

[28]Ibid., 128.

[29]McClendon, 236.

out of the veracity proven in testing. Hauerwas writes: "No society can be just or good that is built on falsehood. The first task of Christian social ethics, therefore, is . . . to help Christian people form their community consistent with their conviction that the story of Christ is a truthful account of our existence."[30] People are loyal to each other and to God when they know that their community is based upon what is true and that their convictions are true.

Integrity and loyalty, then, are reciprocal. The Christian and the community have integrity and become loyal by being true to the story of Christ; God has integrity and demonstrates loyalty by providing a story that is true.

Transcendence

True *koinonia* is beyond the ability of human beings to produce it. We do not create *koinonia*; it is given to us. As such it is a gift. Not only this, but Christians share both with Christ and with other Christians. All of this is *koinonia*, especially as understood by New Testament writers, and they saw all of these aspects of *koinonia* as deriving from Christ and the Holy Spirit.[31] Hollis Gause explains: "In a spiritual and real sense, the presence of Christ provides a twofold pattern. First, as he indwells the Father, the believers are to indwell Christ. Second, as Christ indwells the believers, they are to indwell each other. This is the biblical pattern of unity which is the experience and practice of holiness."[32] For *koinonia* to exist, Christians must not only experience the presence of each other and commit themselves to each other, they must also experience the presence of God and commit themselves unreservedly to Him.

CHRISTIAN LIBERTY

Following Jeff's transformational experience, he remarked to a friend that he no longer felt bound by the standards of the prevailing popular culture. He felt a new freedom to say no to what is evil and yes to what is righteous. His participation in the body of Christ also gave him the courage to *be* what before he was unable to be. Jeff was free. He was free to be victorious over sin and temptation, not just someone who was barely getting by. He continued to have struggles, but these struggles did not have power over him as they once did. Shame and guilt were no longer his constant companions.

The spirit needs freedom (as do the body and mind), and reli-

---

[30]Hauerwas, *A Community of Character: Toward a Constructive Christian Social Ethics* (Notre Dame: University of Notre Dame Press, 1981), 10.

[31]Eric G. Jay, *The Church: Its Changing Image through Twenty Centuries* (London: SPCK; Atlanta: John Knox Press, 1977, 1978), 23–24.

[32]Gause, 56.

gious freedom is an important facet of social life. Freedom is not limited to social structures, however. Gerhard Lohfink warns: "It is impossible to liberate others unless freedom radiates within one's own group. It is not possible to preach social repentance to others unless one lives in a community which takes seriously the new society of the reign of God."[33] How can those in chains unlock the chains of others? How can those living in a community that is unjust, prejudiced, unforgiving, unloving, and uncaring model the virtues of God's kingdom? The Christian community must first evidence God's reign before Christians can call other communities to submit to that reign.

> "Freedom is the power to be a Christian, to do the will of God, to act according to one's holy nature."

Although this freedom within the community has a social element, it is essentially freedom based upon a relationship with God. Groome correctly notes that "it is by the freedom of our 'spirit' that we can transcend the mundane and passing to reach out for union with the ultimate Transcendent."[34] This freedom transforms and is the product of transformation; it is a freedom of being which reflects the nature of *koinonia*. This can be seen if Hauerwas's definition of freedom is accepted: "From our perspective of an ethic of virtue, therefore, freedom is more like having power than having a choice . . . For the virtuous person, being free does not imply a choice but the ability that what was or was not done was one's own."[35]

Freedom is the power to be Christian, to do the will of God, to act according to one's holy nature. Transcendence is especially important to the concept of freedom, for freedom emanates from what God has done in the forming of *koinonia*. It is a gift, coming from God. It begins in transformation and is perpetuated in formation. It is firstly from God and secondly recognized and fostered by the community.

God transforms and forms not only Christian character, but also Christian community. Ethics must attend to both, making sure that the goals of each are articulated and grasped. Neither can survive without the other: Community cannot exist without a constituency of individual persons; character will not develop without an appropriate social environment that will provide for the transmission, inculcation, and living of Christian faith. There must be a narrative, a story, a character, an identity, a sharing that is Christian, in order to nurture immature Christian being toward growth.

---

[33]Gerhard Lohfink, *Jesus and Community: The Social Dimensions of the Christian Faith*, trans. John Galvin (London: SPCK, 1985), 138.

[34]Groome, 96. Groome identifies three dimensions of freedom: the "spiritual"; the "personal," which is the interior, psychological aspect of freedom; and the "social/political" (96).

[35]Hauerwas, *Community and Character*, 115.

Faith is not something Christians merely *have* but something that is *lived*. The next section looks at what emanates from character and community: praxis.

Praxis

During the summer following his freshman year Jeff participated in a short-term missions trip to South America. What an experience! His days were filled with conducting Christian classes in neighborhoods where children lived in abject poverty. In the evenings he joined his Latin American brothers and sisters in worship. Unbelievable worship! His month of living and working and worshiping in a Two-Thirds world setting radically changed Jeff's concept of Christianity. He began to understand that serving Christ involves more than merely attending church. It is a way of life that demands purposeful, informed, and circumspect action in the world. As Jeff discovered during his stay in Latin America, such action reveals one's real values and beliefs.

In this section, we shall investigate the relationship between *doing* and *being* as it relates to *praxis*. We will explore how *doing* is not merely an option but instead a mandate for the development of a Christian ethic. We will also discuss the ways in which *praxis* forms Christian being and community.

DEFINITION

Praxis is not simply action or practice. Rather, it is "reflective action,"[36] that is, practice that is informed by theoretical reflection. In order to understand praxis one must first consciously move away from separating theory from practice. This does not mean that theory and practice should be reduced to each other or that they are identical. Rather, this approach seeks to hold them together so that practice is not viewed as simply the application of theory. In praxis, theory and practice are joined.[37] What we think about our social setting is to be reflected in our actions within that social setting. Conversely, our actions (for good or bad) reveal our thinking about the things we act upon. What is ultimately revealed by our actions is our being—who we are—our character. Consequently, Christian character is both revealed and shaped by our actions.

THE RELATIONSHIP OF PRAXIS TO CHARACTER AND COMMUNITY

Praxis arises out of character and community. Thinking and doing are not separate from who and what we are, from our character, from our story.

---

[36]Groome, xvii, note.

[37]Ibid., 152.

Although what we are is not reducible to what we do, what we do nevertheless reflects and is grounded in what we are. Also, although faith is not reducible to what we do, what we do reflects our faith and is grounded in it. Action, then, is a necessary ingredient of faith. Faith implies response. It is not only participation in the divine nature through the transformation of character. It is also *participation in the divine work which arises from that participation in the divine nature.*

If action (response) is one side of the *praxis* coin, the other side is critical thinking. Like action, critical thinking is integral to faith. Steve Land claims that "sound doctrine produces and maintains sound or healthy Christians" and that it "is primarily concerned with the cultivation of a community with the character and virtues of Christ."[38] Christian doctrine, as well as critical reflection upon the Christian narrative, the stories of the community and the individuals within the community, the mission of the community, the virtues fostered within the community—all are expressions of faith. Faith is expressed in what we *think* as well as in what we *do*. Indeed, in the expression of faith, thought and action influence each other. What we think not only helps shape what we are, but also issues from what we are. Our critical thinking is not done in a vacuum but, like any other aspect of our lives, is done against the background of our experiences.

Praxis arises also from community. Poling and Miller speak of praxis as "the reflection of a community upon that interaction in which it is already engaged."[39] In fact, Groome calls the community "a group of people who share together in a common effort to live Christian *praxis*."[40] *Praxis,* then, reflects not only individual character, but also the character of the community.

As we change, develop, and become what we will be, our development takes place in response to our actions.[41] In other words, what we do is not simply the outgrowth of a fully formed character; our deeds form us as well. Hauerwas refers to actions as "acts of self-determination; in them we not only reaffirm what we have been but also determine what we will be in the future."[42] By understanding who we are and who we need to be, we self-consciously choose what we do (reflective action). By what we do we self-consciously choose who and what we will be (active reflection).

---

[38]Steven J. Land, "Modest Appearance," in *A Life Style to His Glory* (Cleveland, Tenn.: Pathway Press, 1988), 115.

[39]Poling and Miller, 65.

[40]Groome, 122.

[41]Dermot A. Lane, *Foundations for a Social Theology: Praxis, Process and Salvation* (New York: Paulist Press, 1984), 3.

[42]Hauerwas, *Vision and Virtue*, 49.

THE RESULTS OF PRAXIS

Both the individual and the Christian community exist within a larger social context—the world. What do they have to say to the world? What responsibilities do they have to society? In this section, we develop the view that in *praxis* both the individual and the community meet the world.

Context and Responsibility

Whether Christians like it or not, they exist within the context of the world. The situation is simply that Christianity exists on earth, that Christians live their faith in the world, that the Christian community is one among many communities, and that it both influences and is influenced by the broader society. Aspects of the broader society, such as economics or politics, are part of the Christian's world. There is no Christian life apart from life in this world.

There is also unavoidable responsibility due to the nature of Christianity itself. Lehmann builds a case for God as "politician." He argues that "the God whom in the *koinonia* we come to know as real, as the only God there is, the only God worth talking about, is not divided but one; and the God who is one is the God of politics."[43] By this he means that God is active in human life in the world. His community is political because it is active in the world it inhabits. *Praxis* is the active reflection/ reflective action of Christianity living in, dialoguing with, and impacting the world.

During his stay in Latin America Jeff heard stories of fellow Christians who had "disappeared" because they had spoken against the violent treatment of the indigenous Indians. He began to see that a true Christian cannot help but relate to the political-social dimensions of this world, though he or she often pays a price for such involvement. Upon his return to the U.S. Jeff began to work as a construction volunteer in a local chapter of Habitat for Humanity. He also became more aware of the rise of pornography in his hometown and helped organize a campaign to close businesses that profited from it.

Knowing the Truth

How do we know whether or not our *praxis*, or reflection-action in the world, reflects the mind and will of God? How can we be sure that our actions do not reflect self-invested interests under the guise of religion? Human reflection-action, while important, is distorted and may become self-serving. Without an authority beyond the self that transcends and at times even negates reflection-action, we are left with the possibility, despite

---

[43]Lehmann, 82–83.

our best intentions, of sinful *praxis*. For instance, those persons who bomb abortion clinics claim to be doing righteous war against the evils of abortion. However, their violence only makes worse the alienation and anger found in our society. Such bombings have accomplished nothing righteous related to the problem of abortion.

Daniel Schipani has reformulated *praxis* to a way of knowing and engaging the world, a reformulation which embodies discipleship as "the dynamic, dialogical, and discerning following of Jesus."[44] He further notes that the truth that we practice must ultimately be revealed to us.[45] Therefore, our practicing the truth is a matter of loving obedience to the known will of God.

> "Like Adam and Eve who hid in the Garden, we do not want to face the truth about ourselves and our world."

But how do we know the truth? How do we discern the known will of God? Often a gap exists between ourselves and the truth. In fact, we often go to great efforts to hide from the truth. As Parker Palmer notes, we "hide from the transforming power of truth; we evade truth's quest for us."[46] We do so because this truth knows us. Like Adam and Eve who hid in the Garden, we do not want to face the truth about ourselves and our world. However, this truth is not inert, it is active. It seeks us out. It pursues us. Why? Because truth is most clearly found in God, who desires a personal relationship with us. Jesus' words, "I am the way and the truth and the life" (John 14: 6a), reveal not only that God is truth but that He has made a way for us to know the truth. Through Christ we can know God, and this knowledge of God reveals the truth about ourselves.

The Bible speaks of a way of knowing God that is more than simply having a knowledge about Him. The Hebrew word for "to know" is *yada'*, which conveys a knowledge that comes through experience. It implies that there is a specific relationship between the knower and what is to be known. This way of knowing has a strong affective component. Rather than simply a matter of the mind, it is also experiential. Notably *yada'* was used as a euphemism for lovemaking; another form of the word *yada'* was used for friend, or confidant.

To the biblical writers, if a person knew God, he or she was encountered by a God who lived in the midst of history and who initiated a covenant relationship that called for a response of the whole person. One could not know God and not be in a

---

[44]Daniel Schipani, *Religious Education Encounters Liberation Theology* (Birmingham, Ala.: Religious Education Press, 1988), 125.

[45]Schipani, 136.

[46]Parker Palmer, *To Know As We Are Known: A Spirituality of Education* (San Francisco: Harper & Row, 1983), 59.

relationship with Him. The measure of whether or not a person knew God would be how that person was living in response to Him. Therefore, to know God is to love and to obey him!

In contrast, certain Greek thinkers explained knowledge much differently: standing back from something in order to know it objectively. You might say that a person would be fearful of "getting her or his hands dirty" by what was to be known. Our word *theory* comes from the Greek *theoros,* or "spectator." It suggests a sort of knowledge about the world characterized by a theater audience. What is to be known is "out there," on stage, and we relate to it at a distance. Parker Palmer gives an insightful description of knowledge when viewed in this light:

> Our knowledge does not draw us into relationship with the known, into participation in the drama. Instead, it holds us at arm's length as detached analysts, commentators, evaluators of each other and the world. Like theater-goers we are free to watch, applaud, hiss and boo, but we do not understand ourselves as an integral part of the action.[47]

The object is something exterior to the knowing subject; it is to be viewed, identified, catalogued, its parts related to other parts, and judged.

John's first epistle provides a stark contrast to this "audience" way of knowing. He seems intentionally to play against this understanding of knowledge and attacks its implications for the Christian life, namely, that it is possible to know about Jesus without conforming to him. For John, knowledge of God is grounded in a loving relationship (1 John 4:3,16,20), and this knowledge is manifested through obedience to the known will of God.

> We know that we have come to know him if we obey his commands. The man who says, "I know him," but does not do what he commands is a liar, and the truth is not in him. But if anyone obeys his word, God's love is truly made complete in him. This is how we know we are in him: Whoever claims to live in him must walk as Jesus did (1 John 2:3–6).

Quite simply, knowing God involves something more than having a correct theory about Him; it also involves experiencing Him, obeying Him, and being challenged and changed by that experiential knowledge of Him.

Jeff's involvement in the life of the church and his involvement as a Christian in the larger world reflect a change in his view of his relationship with God. No longer could he be "part of the audience," observing the Christian drama from a distance. Jeff became part of the drama and became part of its

---

[47]Palmer, 23.

story. His knowledge of God became direct and personal and it nurtured him in a lifestyle of obedience.

It is more comfortable, however, to be in the audience, to watch while others worship, to observe others testify, to gaze from a distance while others enter the world with the Christian witness. It is much easier to give verbal assent to a Christian ethic than to embody and live a Christian ethic! We all must make the crucial decision as to whether we will be experientially acquainted with God or just settle for knowing about God.

Accepting the Challenge

Not only must individuals make the decision to have an active faith, but the church as a corporate body must make this same decision. When the agenda is set by the prevailing popular culture, the church fails to have the influence it should have. The church is the church, not popular culture. Therefore, its *praxis* should remain true to its character.

The church remains true to its character by preserving its *distinctiveness*. It does society no favor by adapting itself to the prevailing popular culture, for it fails in its task precisely at the point at which it fails to be itself. As Hauerwas rightfully contends, "The church does not have a social ethic, but is a social ethic . . . insofar as it is a community that can clearly be distinguished from the world. For the world is not a community and has no such story, since it is based on the assumption that human beings, not God, rule history."[48] For the church to adopt a social ethic formed by the prevailing popular culture is to deny the nature of the church. Rather, the church must express the social ethic that it already embodies; it must carry forward the story of Christ, a story that continually impacts the social relations of human beings.

The church must be itself for the sake of humankind. It is the role of the church to serve and transform society and its institutions. To accomplish this task the church must be the church and not assimilate itself to the prevailing popular culture. Only a Christianity that is not embarrassed to be itself can do this.

Being "for humankind" means being true to the message of the church. As John Westerhoff asserts: "It is . . . as a *witnessing community* that the church must be understood. The church has a story to tell, a vision to share, good news to proclaim. And that story, vision, and good news are communicated best through its life, its word-actions in the world."[49] The church, then, is the physical manifestation of the story of Christ; it points to God beyond itself. It is a testimony to God's action in history.

---

[48]Hauerwas, "Gesture of a Truthful Story," 182.

[49]John Westerhoff, *Will Our Children Have Faith?* (San Francisco: Harper & Row, 1976), 48.

Through the actions and words of the church, people ought to see the intentions, actions, and character of Christ himself.

Christianity can only show the world what it lacks and can only retain its distinctiveness by being a contrast-society, or a counterculture. What is a contrast-society, or counterculture? Snyder defines a subculture as one that agrees basically with the dominant culture regarding primary values, and differs in less important values, whereas a counterculture may agree with a dominant culture concerning less important values but diverges from the dominant culture at the point of its primary values.[50] The church functions as a subculture when, for instance, it adopts a value such as individualism to the point that it fails to

> **"It is the role of the church to serve and transform society and its institutions."**

reach out to people in distress, but varies from the world in how that individualism may be expressed. (For example, it may condemn the "right to privacy" individualism of abortion rights advocates but laud the individualism that says that the community has no responsibility to help women who become pregnant because of their sin.) The church functions as a counterculture, however, when secondary values are shared (such as wearing similar clothes or participating in common entertainment) but challenges the dominant culture in its core beliefs and its fundamental values (such as by reminding the society that it is subject to a power greater than itself or that might does not make right). Snyder considers the church in North America to be largely a subculture, not a counterculture.[51]

The contrast-society is one which stands against many of the commonly accepted goals and practices of today's popular culture. For instance, it rejects the false images (such as stereotypical and demeaning portrayals of women) projected by the popular entertainment media and stands against the self-delusion of those who advocate autonomy but not responsibility. Instead, the contrast-society stands for the truth revealed in Jesus Christ and lived in the Christian faith, stands for the reconciliation of all people to God, and stands for a standard of living in conformity to the holiness of God. It does *not* expect society to conform, but it models holy living through the lives of individual Christians. Holiness is inherently antithetical to the unregenerate elements of popular culture. Only as a sanctified community does the church function as a contrast-society to the world.[52]

This understanding of contrast-society as sanctified community complements Jackie Johns's statement that "the (ancient)

---

[50]Snyder, 120.

[51]Ibid.

[52]Lohfink, 130.

church understood the impetus of its existence as a contrast society to be its infusion with the Spirit of God."[53] The same point can be made for the Church in the postmodern era. Nothing stands in greater contrast to certain commonly accepted goals and practices of today's culture than holiness. The church must recognize the fundamental differences between itself and the institutions that have so captured the hearts and minds of people in the present era.

The holiness of the church issues in *praxis*. This *praxis* is specifically prophetic in nature. It is not just the task of individuals to be prophetic witnesses, but it is the commission of the church to exist as a prophetic, holy community. Only in this way can people everywhere see the light of the Kingdom shining in the darkness.

During his mission trip, Jeff experienced life in prophetic communities of people whose *koinonia* welcomed him in the bonds of Christian love and whose *praxis* challenged him to make visible the Christian faith. Jeff made a transition in his thinking about the relationship between the Christian and the world. He moved away from being part of a Christian subculture toward becoming part of a contrast-society. This move represented a major shift in his way of being in the world. For Jeff, there was now a marked difference between a Christian worldview and other worldviews prevalent in the culture. Whereas before he only saw Christianity as increasing the quality of his life, he now saw his faith as radically altering his life. His life was altered in such a way as to express a prophetic calling.

In order to express truly this calling, however, Jeff needs to be part of a prophetic community of believers who exist as a contrast society. Such communities are found wherever there are Christians who corporately seek to be the people of God no matter what the cost. Such communities exist all around the world. Some are paying a great price for their prophetic witness.

In North America, while there is no overt persecution of Christians, believers such as Jeff nevertheless stand in contrast to the rapidly secularizing society. Their Christian *praxis* will become more and more at odds with what Stephen Carter calls "the culture of disbelief."[54] In this culture God is viewed as a hobby. Carter notes that "The message of contemporary culture seems to be that it is perfectly all right to *believe* that stuff—we have freedom of conscience, . . . but you really ought to keep it to yourself, especially if your beliefs are the sort that cause you

---

[53]Jackie Johns, *The Pedagogy of the Holy Spirit According to Early Christian Tradition*, (Ed.D. dissertation, The Southern Baptist Theological Seminary, 1986), 169.

[54]Stephen L. Carter, *The Culture of Disbelief* (New York: BasicBooks, 1993).

to act in ways that are . . . a bit unorthodox."[55] Those who take their Christian faith more seriously than a mere hobby risk being labeled "fanatics" or "religious fundamentalists." Such labels indicate the level of fear present in our society toward prophetic Christianity. Carter observes that such fear is understandable because "religion is really an alien way of knowing the world—alien, at least, in a political and legal culture in which reason supposedly rules. . . ."[56] He considers religion to be subversive, especially in nations where it is the norm to discount the religious view as irrelevant.[57] The contemporary American church must accept the risk of being misunderstood, labeled, and even actively persecuted. Only then can its prophetic witness be clearly seen.

VIRTUES OF THE DISCIPLINES

Being a person of virtue is not easy or automatic. Many persons come to Christ with ingrained habits of sin. While transforming encounters free us from the bondage and tyranny of sin, the Holy Spirit desires to continue the transformational work of re-creation from within. For centuries the *praxis* of the Christian disciplines have been a means whereby believers have overcome sin and have the character of Christ deeply ingrained in their innermost being.

The disciplines themselves do not transform, but Richard Foster observes that they "allow us to place ourselves before God so that He can transform us."[58] Foster compares the spiritual disciplines to the farmer doing all that he can humanly do to provide the right conditions for the growing of grain: the Spirit sows through the disciplines, planting us in soil that God may change us from within. Thus, the disciplines do nothing in themselves; they are means God uses for our benefit.[59]

Foster divides the disciplines into three categories: the inward disciplines, consisting of meditation, prayer, fasting, and study; the outward disciplines, consisting of simplicity, solitude, submission, and service; and the corporate disciplines, consisting of confession, worship, guidance, and celebration. The *praxis* of the disciplines take us deeper into God, and as we journey we find that we have made our heart to be at home in His presence.

---

[55]Carter, 25.

[56]Ibid., 43.

[57]Ibid.

[58]Richard Foster, *Celebration of Discipline* (San Francisco: Harper & Row Publishers, 1978), 6.

[59]Ibid.

The Journey Ahead

Beginning his sophomore year, Jeff reflects back over his eventful freshman year and realizes that he was a very different person. A year ago, he had felt and responded to the voice of the Holy Spirit who led him into a deeper walk with Christ. Along the way he learned that *being* was foremost in importance. Now his moral choices and ethical decisions are no longer based on a patchwork of values and beliefs. Rather, they flow from a well-formed and unified self. Jeff's character now, more than before, reflects the *character* of God. Jeff began his freshman year loosely connected to the body of Christ. Now as a sophomore, he is actively part of a local church where he finds brothers and sisters to share in the *koinonia* of the Holy Spirit. Finally, Jeff's life now reflects the *praxis* of the Christian life. His actions as a Christian are more consistent with who he is as a believer in Christ.

Jeff is on an amazing journey. It is a journey toward God. It is a journey in God and with God. On the way, there is the possibility of further transformation and continual growth. While the journey takes him into an uncertain future, Jeff faces it with assurance that he, like the apostle Paul, can finish the race knowing that there is a crown of righteousness awaiting him (2 Tim. 4:7,8).

Review and Discussion Questions

1. What is a "postmodern person"? What problems does the contemporary world pose for Christians regarding morality?

2. Distinguish between deontological, consequentialist, and character ethics. Identify elements of each in your personal ethics and in specifically Christian ethics.

3. What is sanctification? What is the relationship between sanctification and transformation? How does sanctification affect one's character?

4. How does one's vision affect one's character? Does a stress on vision mean that character ethics is ultimately consequentialist?

5. Why are integrity and loyalty important for Christian community, and why are both important for the development of Christian character? Is the commitment and covenant found in *koinonia* different from what may be found in other communities?

6. Describe your Christian community. Is it true *koinonia*? Do you find commitment and covenant, shared life, and transcendence in your community? Do you find stability, integrity, and liberty in your community?

7. Does freedom imply the freedom to sin? Would not true freedom mean that no action is sinful if it is performed by a Christian?

8. What does it mean to think of God as "politician"? What does this imply for Christian involvement in social issues?

9. How does the church differ from the world? What can the church do for the world or tell the world? What should the agenda of the church be? Is it the same agenda as that of the world? If not, how do they differ? Is there only one agenda for the church? Is there only one agenda for the world?

10. Identify the spiritual disciplines. Do you see them operative in your life? How?

11. Jeff changed in many ways during his freshman-year journey. Describe his changes. Why did he change? What affected him?

Extended Projects for Reflection

1. Tell your story. Who are you? What is your dominant tradition? What do you value? Where are you going? Identify the experiences that are most important in your life, that have helped you become who you are.

2. The postmodern worldview often characterizes truth as relative. What is the relationship between the Christian and truth? How can Christians know the truth and know that their beliefs are true? Explain to the postmodern mind how your Christian claims are true.

Selected Bibliography

CLASSICAL READINGS IN MORAL THEORY

Thomas Aquinas. *Treatise on Happiness.* Trans. John A. Oesterle. Prentice Hall, 1964; Notre Dame: University of Notre Dame Press, 1983.

Thomas Aquinas. *Treatise on the Virtues.* Trans. John A. Oesterle. Englewood Cliffs, N.J.: Prentice Hall, 1966; Notre Dame: University of Notre Dame Press, 1984.

Aristotle. *Nicomachean Ethics.* Trans. David Ross. Indianapolis: Bobbs Merrill Company, 1962.

Augustine. *City of God.* Abridged. Ed. Vernon J. Bourke. New York: Doubleday, 1958.

Augustine. *Confessions.* Trans. John K. Ryan. New York: Doubleday, 1960.

Didache. In *Early Christian Fathers.* Ed. Cyril Richardson. New York: Macmillan Publishing Company, 1970.

Edwards, Jonathan. "Dissertation Concerning the Nature of True Virtue." In *The Works of Jonathan Edwards.* Vol. 1. Carlisle, Pa.: The Banner of Truth Trust, 1974.

Luther, Martin. *The Bondage of the Will.* Trans. James I. Packer and O. R. Johnston. Grand Rapids: Fleming H. Revell, 1957.

Kant, Immanuel. *Groundwork of the Metaphysics of Morals.* Trans. H. J. Paton. New York: Harper and Row, 1964.

Kierkegaard, Søren. *Works of Love*. Trans. Howard Hong and Edna Hong. New York: Harper Torchbooks, 1962.

Mill, John Stuart. *Utilitarianism*. Indianapolis: Hackett Publishing, 1979.

CONTEMPORARY READINGS IN MORAL THEORY

Childress, James F., and John Macquarrie, eds. *The Westminster Dictionary of Christian Ethics*. Philadelphia: Westminster Press, 1986.

Frankena, William K. *Ethics*. Englewood Cliffs, N.J.: Prentice-Hall, 1973.

Gause, R. Hollis. *Living in the Spirit: The Way of Salvation*. Cleveland, Tenn.: Pathway Press, 1980.

Groome, Thomas. *Christian Religious Education: Sharing Our Story and Vision*. San Francisco: Harper & Row, 1980, 1981.

Harrison, R. K., ed. *Encyclopedia of Biblical and Christian Ethics*. Nashville: Thomas Nelson Publishers, 1987.

Hauerwas, Stanley. *The Peaceable Kingdom: A Primer in Christian Ethics*. Notre Dame.: University of Notre Dame Press, 1983.

Holmes, Arthur. *Ethics: Approaching Moral Decisions*. Contours of Christian Philosophy Series. Downers Grove, Ill.: Inter-Varsity Press, 1984.

Kaiser, Walter C., Jr. *Toward Old Testament Ethics*. Grand Rapids: Zondervan, Academie Books, 1983.

MacIntyre, Alasdair. *After Virtue*. Notre Dame.: University of Notre Dame Press, 1981, 1984.

Niebuhr, H. Richard. *The Responsible Self: An Essay in Christian Moral Philosophy*. San Francisco: Harper and Row, 1963, 1978.

Niebuhr, Reinhold. *An Interpretation of Christian Ethics*. San Francisco: Harper and Row, 1935.

_____. *Moral Man and Immoral Society: A Study in Ethics and Politics*. New York: Charles Scribner's Sons, 1932, 1960.

Nygren, Anders. *Agape and Eros*. Trans. Philip S. Watson. Philadelphia: Westminster Press, 1953.

Outka, Gene. *Agape: An Ethical Analysis*. New Haven, Conn.: Yale University Press, 1972.

Schnackenburg, Rudolf. *The Moral Teaching of the New Testament*. Herder KG, 1965; New York: Seabury Press, 1979.

Verhey, Allen. *The Great Reversal: Ethics and the New Testament*. Grand Rapids: Eerdmans, 1984.

9

Music From the Heart of Faith

Johnathan David Horton

Let the word of Christ dwell in you richly in all wisdom; teaching and admonishing one another in psalms and hymns and spiritual songs, singing with grace in your hearts to the Lord.

—Paul the Apostle

To have a world without music would be like having a world without meaning. Music gives evidence to mankind's deepest feelings and aspirations.

—Norman Dello Joio

Prelude: The Power of Music

I was a brand new college freshman attending my first solo vocal recital. The auditorium seemed huge and there were people everywhere. Making my way up the stairs, I found my seat near the front of the balcony about midway across. The excitement seemed almost palpable, hanging over the crowd like a dense fog. Sitting alone in the middle of a crowd, I was caught up in the expectancy of the moment. This would be no ordinary concert.

George London, the guest soloist, had recently returned from Moscow where he had sung at the Bolshoi Opera Theater in that most famous of all Russian operas, *Boris Godunov*. London performed during the middle of the cold war when relations were strained between the USA and the USSR. This foreigner, this American, had sung the title role. Although the Russians had not initially wanted to like him, they were completely captured by the beauty of his voice and the strength of his character. His performance was hailed as a triumph! The story of his success had been carried by the American media, and he had become a national hero, an overnight celebrity. We could hardly wait to hear this famous *basso* sing.

A hush filled the auditorium as the lights were dimmed. Mr. London mounted the stage to the thunder of applause. And what singing!—song poured forth from his very soul. The expressiveness of his singing built a bond of communication between singer and audience that transcended verbal expression.

Toward the end of the program he sang the little English folk song *Lord Randall*. This song is a dialogue between a mother and her dying son. Though simple enough that it could have been sung by any voice student in the audience, he breathed a life into the song that stirred the depths of the soul. As the song unfolded, he sang with a thinner and thinner, and softer yet softer voice. The song ended in a mere whisper as we, the audience, felt the pain of Lord Randall's death. The silence that followed was the longest I have ever heard in a concert. The audience sat transfixed, staring at the stage through tears.

At long last an explosion of applause rolled across the auditorium in wave after wave after wave. Completely overwhelmed by the emotion of the moment, I sat in stunned stillness, unable to raise my hands to applaud. I thought, *I must write a letter to my mother and tell her, 'Tonight I discovered the power of music!'*

Music has the power to influence our lives in profound ways. As we consider that influence, we might ask ourselves the following questions: How important is music in the life of the individual? What is music's role in society? What is the source of music? What is its purpose? How do we assign meaning to an abstract assortment of sounds and silence? How can we get more out of music? What is the impact of music as part and parcel of the popular media? And, finally, are there guidelines that can help us make moral and artistic choices about music? This chapter is organized around these questions. We begin with the place of music in the life of the individual and in society.

The Preeminence of Music

It would seem unlikely, a priori, *that the whole human race should be endowed with the faculty to enjoy beauty unless it achieved some noble consummation.*

—H. E. Huntley

Music surrounds us. It saturates the fabric of our lives. Music is an almost constant companion in public and in private. If we go shopping for groceries at the super market, we hear music. If we go for a drive in the car, music is the sound coming from our dashboard. If we get together with a few friends in the dormitory for a study session, music is the study monitor. Music enhances and heightens our times of celebration. It lightens the load of our work. It comforts us when we feel alone. Music expresses our faith in God. And music gives expression to our thoughts and emotions, from the most trivial whim to the loftiest insight.

There are many styles of music. Indeed, it seems there are almost as many styles as there are people. Nowhere is the diversity of styles more apparent than in the great urban centers of America. If you surf the radio waves you will discover stations that specialize in particular styles of music: Top 40, mainstream rock, heavy metal, alternative rock, rap, soul, soft rock, reggae, jazz, blues, country, southern gospel, contemporary Christian music, inspirational, classical, New Age, and various national and ethnic music styles. It has often been said that music is a universal language, but we soon discover that it is also a language of diversity. (See Appendix 4, "Music and the Performing Space," on p. 474.)

Most of us are familiar with one or more styles of music. We have learned to love and appreciate the music that we understand; it makes sense to us. We understand its syntax—the structure of its meaning. People often say, "I don't know much about music, but I know what I like." What they really mean is, "I like what I know." Sometimes we hear unfamiliar music and respond, "Why, that's not even music!" What we probably mean is, "I don't understand this music, and it makes me uncomfortable." When we restrict ourselves to only the music we know and understand, we cut ourselves off from new worlds of potential pleasure and insight.

Not only is music an essential element of American culture, music is a vital part of every culture around the globe—past and present. Music is integral to every society, from the most primitive tribe to the most complex urban community. Through music, people express every human emotion, from ecstasy and happiness to grief and despair. Weddings, funerals, parties, civic ceremonies—wherever people gather, there will be music.

Though few would question the pervasive quality of the musical experiences that fill our lives, the question is inevitably raised, Is music a necessity for life? In a strictly biological sense, what do we need to sustain life? We need air—we can live about three minutes without air. We need water—we can live about three days without water. We need food—we can live about three weeks without food. But if we need music, how long can we live without it—a day, a week, a lifetime? It's a philosophical question that doesn't yield to a simple answer.

Consider the following question instead: What is the longest time in your waking hours that you do not experience music? I often pose this question to my students. Their answers are amazingly consistent! Some say they experience music almost continuously, others say that no more than fifteen minutes goes by without experiencing music, and a few report that two hours

Classical Music

The expression "classical" has several usages and has been applied to a broad range of music. In one of its more common usages, it refers to chamber music, opera, and symphonic music in the educated European tradition. In this sense, it picks out types of music which, in their technical sophistication and level of culture, differ from folk or popular music. Sometimes "classical music" refers more narrowly to European music of the late eighteenth and early nineteenth centuries. Sometimes its use is extended to include symphonic and other technically sophisticated and serious music of the late nineteenth and twentieth century.

or more goes by with no music. The most frequent answer students give is that no more than thirty minutes passes each day without music!

Stop and ask yourself the same question: What is the longest time in your waking hours that *you* do not experience music? As you consider this question, you should include all the music you hear in live performance, all the music you hear on radio or television, and all the music you hear on cassette or CD. In addition, you should include all the music you hear on film, all the music you hear on elevators, in stores, and at parties. Finally, include all the music you hear inside your head even when there is no physical sound! It seems that music is as prevalent as language.

The value of understanding language, both spoken and written, is apparent to almost everyone. We use spoken and written language in our everyday lives for interpersonal communication, commerce, and self-expression. Mastery of language skills is understood to be fundamental to successful living in today's world. But how apparent is the value of the mastery of musical knowledge and skills? Strangely, it is the very ubiquity of music that leads some to deny the need to acquire a systematic knowledge of music. If people already love and appreciate music, the argument goes, why study it? They fail to see that music education is "less an imparting of love for music than a stretching and reforming of a love that already exists."[1]

> "Strangely, it is the very ubiquity of music that leads some to deny the need to acquire a systematic knowledge of music."

Will knowing more about music enhance our enjoyment of it? We talk of music appreciation, but no one speaks of football appreciation, for example. It is generally understood that the more one knows about football, the more one is likely to enjoy watching a football game. While it is true that there is not a one to one correlation between knowledge of football and enjoyment of the game, there is a notable connection between the two: knowledge begets appreciation. No doubt the same principle applies to music, especially when the knowledge is directly connected to the music itself. Some knowledge of music is necessary for one to understand the many different worlds of music, to develop the skills necessary to make music, to deepen the intellectual and aesthetic understanding of the art of music. Arguably, some knowledge of music is necessary even to express one's innermost thoughts and feelings through music. If these claims are true, what must we know to enhance our appreciation of music?

To begin with, appreciation is likely to deepen proportionally to one's knowledge in the following three areas: (1) the great

---

[1]Harold M. Best. *Music Through the Eyes of Faith* (San Francisco: Harper, 1993), 69.

and enduring musical landmarks of one's own civilization— cultural heritage; (2) the fundamentals of music, including analysis, composition, and performance—the craft of music; and (3) the expressive, or affective, nature of music—the aesthetics of music. William J. Bennett, former secretary of the Department of Education, expressed the foundational nature of music knowledge this way: "No education is complete without awareness of music; music is an essential expression of the character of a society."[2]

OUR CULTURAL HERITAGE

A well-educated American citizen should be conversant with at least some of the monumental musical accomplishments of Western civilization. Music of the ancient past has been forever lost to us, but music from the medieval period to the present is a part of our musical heritage. The great composers of the past have given us insight into the human condition of their time and of our time as well. It is interesting to note that the subject matter of musical texts—the lyrics—remains amazingly constant from generation to generation.

Bach and Handel, Haydn and Mozart, Beethoven and Brahms, Debussy and Stravinsky, and others besides have shaped the music of the everyday world.[3] The study of the music of these masters of the past will yield a harvest of enrichment and enjoyment as well as a greater understanding of the music of the present. "The whole claim for the importance of the classics rests on the basis that there is no substitute for firsthand knowledge."[4] A solid knowledge of the classics should include familiarity with representative masterpieces of the major genre—such as symphony, overture, opera, ballet, oratorio, concerto—including an understanding of their form, style, and thematic development.

Study of the popular music of America—folk, Top 40, jazz, blues, rock, Broadway show, country, gospel, contemporary Christian music—should also be included in a well-rounded music education. Our popular musical heritage includes the folk music of many countries and cultures. In addition, America itself has proven a fertile ground for producing new musics through the cross-pollination of its many and varied musical cultures. American popular music, in its many forms, has made a notable mark throughout the world.

THE CRAFT OF MUSIC

In an ideal world, everyone would learn to read music, to sing, and to play an instrument. Indeed, the door to the world of musical performance swings open wide to the person who

---

[2]Alice Potosky, ed., *Testimony to Music* (Reston, Va.: MENC, 1986), 15.

[3]This is not to imply that all their music had lyrics.

[4]Alfred North Whitehead. *The Aims of Education* (New York: The Macmillan Company, 1929), 79.

can read music and who knows the rudiments of singing and/or playing an instrument. Musical performance is itself a kind of knowing. All of the listening and analysis in the world can never fully duplicate the understanding inherent in musical performance.

Knowledge of melody, harmonic structure, rhythm, and meter is essential to a full understanding of music. Knowledge of musical form, which is by nature rhythm on a grand scale, is necessary to understand many of the musical monuments of Western civilization. The more one learns of the inner workings of music, the more sense the music makes. Each aspect of musical structure may be used to express what is in the mind and heart of the composer and performer. In short, knowing the craft of music facilitates one's appreciation of music.

THE AESTHETICS OF MUSIC

We have been developing the view that one's love of music grows proportionately as one's understanding of music deepens. Engaging our cultural heritage and grasping some of the technical aspects of the craft of music mark important steps toward the sort of understanding that enhances appreciation. But while the aesthetics of music is related to both of these it is identical to neither. Musical aesthetics goes beyond the historical, cultural, and technical aspects of music and speaks to its essential nature.

Some theories of aesthetics call for a distancing of oneself from the musical experience in order to make aesthetic judgments.[5] Such a point of view creates a listener who is a critic rather that a participant. As a musician, however, I regard involvement in the musical moment as the essence of the aesthetic experience. In this connection, we must appreciate fully the fact that music is more than notes or sounds. It is more than melody, harmony, rhythm, and counterpoint. As one artist has observed, "Music is first an expression of the spirit—otherwise it is merely pretty noise."[6] Music springs from deep within the spirit of the performer and speaks to the depths of the spirit of the listener in ways that elude words. The listener who is fully attuned to the music is, in the words of H. E. Huntley, "re-enacting the creative act and, attracted by beauty, is experiencing himself the joy of creative activity. He is, in fact, in Kepler's phrase, 'thinking God's thoughts after Him.'"[7] What Huntley describes so poetically represents at its core a profound pro-

---

[5]Abraham A. Schwandron. *Aesthetics: Dimensions for Music Education* (Washington: MENC, 1967), 17.

[6]Interview with David Van Koevering, Mighty Horn Ministries, Cleveland, Tenn., May 1985.

[7]H. E. Huntley,*The Divine Proportion* (New York: Dover Publications, 1970), 22.

duction and exchange of meaning. The aesthetics of music has to do with making sense of this profound production and exchange of meaning. We shall describe it more fully later in this chapter when we respond to the question, What does music mean?

The Source of Music

Where were you when I laid the earth's foundation?
. . . while the morning stars sang together and all the
angels shouted for joy?

—Job 38:4–7

Most current music history texts do not attempt to trace the origins of music. They choose to begin with recorded history. *The Encyclopedia Britannica* states that every known ancient society "entered historical times with a flourishing musical culture."[8] Early writers speculated that what we now know as music began as a rudimentary form of communication, that it eased the burden of communal labor, and that it was a powerful element of religious ceremony. Indeed, most early writers spoke of music in terms of legend and myth. Those who do not accept biblical revelation can only see the origin of music shrouded in a mystical haze.

The source of music can be discovered through the revelation of Scripture. God said to Job: "Where were you when I laid the earth's foundation? . . . while the morning stars sang together and all the angels shouted for joy?" (Job 38:4–7). While this is clearly a poetic passage dealing with creation, the truth of God's revelation is nonetheless real—music existed before human beings were created! God, the creator of the cosmos, is the creator of music.

We are made in the image of God. This means that we are endowed with God's *attributes*. God is spirit, therefore, we are endowed with a spirit. God has personality, so we have a personality. God is creative; we too are creative. It is true that only God can create *ex nihilo*, that is, He alone can take nothing and create something out of it. But we humans can take something and create something entirely new—something that did not exist before. God is infinite in each of his characteristics; humans are finite. Nonetheless, being made in the image of God, we possess (albeit in limited measure) his characteristics.[9]

God is musical. The Bible gives us a clear record that God the Father, God the Son, and God the Holy Spirit sing. Upon the day of the Lord, God the Father will sing over His children with great joy (Zeph. 3:17). Concluding the last Passover celebration with His disciples, God the Son sang a hymn with them (Mark

---

[8]*Encyclopedia Britannica*, 15th ed., s.v. "Music, Western."

[9]Francis A. Schaeffer, *Art and the Bible* (Downers Grove, Ill.: Inter-Varsity Press, 1973), 34.

14:26, Matt. 26:30). And God the Holy Spirit sings in the heart of the believer (1 Cor. 14:15).

Because God is musical and we are created in His image, we too are musical.[10] The musical creativity of the human family seems almost boundless. One person can take the twelve tones of the chromatic scale[11] and create a sublimely stirring symphony. Another person can take those same twelve tones and create an earthy country song. Another can create an intricate jazz piece, and yet another, a romantic ballad. Using only such an apparently limited palette of twelve musical tones, composer after composer has found a limitless range of musical possibilities.

How does the musician, the composer, create music? Paul Hindemith, one of the twentieth century's most influential composers, describes musical inspiration in this way: "Something—you know not what—drops into your mind—you know not whence—and there it grows—you know not how—into some form—you know not why."[12] If the professional composer does not know the sources of musical inspiration, it is no wonder that the general public views composing as such a mystery.

Some would have it that musical creativity is limited to those with a high degree of musical training or to those who are especially gifted. Yet ordinary people commonly experience moments of musical inspiration when a fragment of a melody or a piece of a new song comes into their consciousness. Regardless of the quality of these little moments of musical inspiration, most people think of their bit of music and forget it. Without the discipline of musical training it is difficult to preserve these musical inspirations or to transform them into something memorable.

> **"Because God is musical and we are created in His image, we too are musical."**

Two differences between the average person and the genius in regard to musical creation are the tenacity of the genius to develop the idea and the vision to turn that idea into something of true significance.[13] The truly gifted composer is driven to pursue every musical idea that comes to mind. During every waking hour some part of the composer's brain is searching for potentially valuable bits of musical flotsam and jetsam on the

---

[10]Stanley M. Horton, ed., *Systematic Theology* (Springfield, Mo.: Logion Press, 1994), 250–253.

[11]In music of the western world each octave is divided into twelve equal half steps, which then repeat for each octave. The octave is a naturally occurring phenomenon in which notes sound "alike" when they vibrate in multiples of two, e.g., A = 440 is one octave higher than A = 220. There are, therefore, only twelve notes and their octave duplications to create music from.

[12]Paul Hindemith. *A Composer's World* (Cambridge, Mass.: Harvard University Press, 1952), 57.

[13]Ibid., 60.

sea of inspiration. When these musical ideas come, the composer seizes and treasures them. To the composer who is consumed by the passion for creating music, these musical ideas, in the words of Aaron Copeland, "seem to be begging for their own life, asking their creator, the composer, to find the ideal envelope for them, to evolve a shape and color and content that will most fully exploit their creative potential." Through these musical inspirations our deepest hopes and dreams may be "embodied in a pellucid fabric of sonorous materials."[14]

Most people who have a serious interest in music are capable of creating music. Just as one does not need to be a world class chef to enjoy the art of cooking and to benefit from it, so one does not have to be a musical genius to enjoy composing music and to receive its benefits. Every serious musician, amateur and professional alike, should be encouraged to grasp those moments of musical inspiration that spring into consciousness and develop each one to the fullest. Composing music is a relatively unexplored territory in the world of musical enjoyment for most musicians.

The Purpose of Music

Preposterous ass, that never read so far
To know the cause why music was ordained
Was it not to refresh the mind of man,
After his studies or his usual pain.

—Shakespeare

Thou art worthy, O Lord, to receive glory and honor
and power: for thou hast created all things, and for
thy pleasure they are and were created.

—Revelation 4:11, KJV

William Faulkner, recipient of the Nobel Prize for Literature in 1954, addressed the purpose of his writing in the foreword of his collected works *The Faulkner Reader*. He said that he had not written his novels merely to entertain, or to make money, or to become famous, or even to create great art. Rather he had written his stories to "uplift man's heart."[15] It was his desire to help his readers transcend their everyday world. As a secular writer, he was seeking to touch and, perhaps, to transform the spiritual lives of his readers. This view represents a high and beautiful human aspiration. Yet as worthy as such a goal may be, there is a higher and yet more noble purpose for music.

---

[14]Aaron Copeland, *Copeland on Music* (New York: W. W. Norton and Co., Inc., 1960), 63.

[15]William Faulkner, *The Faulkner Reader* (New York: The Modern Library, 1954), ix.

Music is a gift from God. God gave us music so that we might commune with Him. Music can and does serve many varied purposes, but the Bible makes it clear that its most important function is worship. The song of the elders is instructive: "Thou art worthy, O Lord, to receive glory and honor and power: for thou hast created all things, and for thy pleasure they are and were created" (Rev. 4:11, KJV). God is the source of all creation, and all of creation, including music, is designed for His pleasure.

Music was designed first and foremost for worship, and that is its highest and most noble purpose. This point does not mean, however, that all music should be church music. Neither does it mean that all music should be religious. It is perfectly appropriate for Christians to compose, arrange, perform, and listen to secular music. The Bible itself contains secular art.[16] King David's song of lament for Saul and Jonathan is one such example. It celebrates the lives of these two heroes of Israel (2 Sam. 1:19–27). The Bible also celebrates human love. The Song of Solomon, although it is commonly interpreted allegorically (representing Christ and the Church), is first of all a love poem. (See Appendix 5, "Worship Music and Style," on p. 478.)

In general, then, the music of romance, love, family, friendship, and all the subjects of life are appropriate for the Christian, and they all have merit. However, the overarching perspective for our music is this: God is the primary audience! Whether we sing a song of worship directly to God, listen to "our song" with our sweetheart, play a Mozart horn concerto in the practice room, or simply find ourselves "jammin' out" with some friends, we do it all with an awareness that there is a God who sees us. We do not have to go to Him in prayer, like the little child saying "Look, Mommy," to inform Him of what we have done. He sees it all, and He understands the intent of our hearts even more than our parents or our closest friends (see Psalm 139). We offer all of our music as an act of worship. If it cannot be a glory to the Lord, it has no place in the life of a Christian.

Clearly, God is interested in our worship. Jesus gives us wonderful insight into the heart of worship in his conversation with the woman at the well (John 4). Worship, Jesus tells her, is not a matter of location but a matter of proper orientation to God: "God is spirit, and his worshipers must worship in spirit and in truth" (John 4:24).

What do we mean when we say to worship God in spirit? Because God is spirit, and because we are made in his image, we too are spiritual beings. Our spiritual dimension makes us quite distinctive from other life on earth. Therefore, when we worship God in spirit, we worship Him in a way that is dis-

---

[16]Schaeffer, *Art*, 21.

tinctive to our humanity (among created beings) and yet in a way that truly highlights how we are like God. In true spiritual worship there can be no sham, no pretense. Worship in spirit must be honest and sincere, because God sees right to the core of our hearts (1 Sam. 16:7).

To worship in truth, we must worship according to the patterns and principles found in Scripture. Because few subjects generate greater differences of opinion than music and worship, we will begin with this presupposition: Every opinion must submit to the authority of Scripture. Our worship too—including worship that incorporates music—must be guided by the principles of Scripture. What, then, do the Scriptures say about worship, in particular, worship that involves music?

First, God is interested in our music. We know of His interest because the Bible is filled with music. There are literally hundreds of references to music and worship throughout the Bible, from Genesis 4:21, where we meet Jubal who is the "father of all who play the harp and flute," to Revelation 15:2–4, where we see those who overcame the beast singing "the song of Moses the servant of God and the song of the Lamb." Psalms is the great hymnbook of the Bible. Most scholars agree that the psalms were meant to be sung. Further, the Book of Psalms provides a wealth of information about music and worship—it is a virtual worship manual for God's people.

> **"God is interested in our music. We know of His interest because the Bible is filled with music."**

Second, singing praises to God is not a suggestion, it is a divine directive. Psalm 149 is particularly instructive: (1) "Sing a new song to the LORD;" God wants our worship to be fresh. He does not want our worship music to become rutted in tradition or mired in familiarity. (2) Sing his praise in "the assembly of the saints;" whenever God's people gather, it is His desire that we join our voices and our hearts in the unity of song. And (3) "sing for joy on [your bed];" God's people should sing songs of praise wherever they are, whether alone or in a company. Worship is not something that takes place only within the church building. Worship is a lifestyle! All of our lives should be an offering of worship to the Lord. All of our music, both sacred and secular, should be a praise, a glory, to the Lord! (See 1 Cor. 10:31.)

Third, the Bible implies that music plays a teaching role. Because when we sing we memorize without really trying to do so, we are instructed to use music to "teach and admonish one another with all wisdom, . . . as [we] sing psalms, hymns and spiritual songs with gratitude in [our] hearts to God" (Col. 3:16). The living theology of a congregation is revealed as much in the songs that are sung as in the sermons that are preached. The lyrics of the songs remain long after the sermon is forgotten.

Some would argue that the church today must rely solely upon the New Testament for guidance in matters of worship. This view does not harmonize with Scripture. Let us examine what the New Testament says about the Old Testament and particularly the Book of Psalms. First, Jesus makes repeated references to the Psalms, thus establishing their reliability. Second, each section of the New Testament—the Gospels, the Book of Acts, the Epistles, and the Book of Revelation—quotes from the Book of Psalms. Third, the apostle Paul is referring to the Old Testament, the then-contemporary canon of Scripture, when he writes, "All Scripture is God-breathed and is useful for teaching, rebuking, correcting and training in righteousness, so that the man of God may be thoroughly equipped for every good work" (2 Tim. 3:16–17).

In addition, the prophet Amos (Amos 9:15) and the apostle James (Acts 15:16) both tell us that in the last days God will rebuild the tabernacle of David. When the ark of the covenant, the very symbol of the presence of God, was returned to Israel, David did not return it to Shiloh where it had stood during the settling of the land, nor did he return the ark to the new location of the tabernacle at Gibeon, where burnt offerings and music were offered up by the priests. The ark of the covenant was brought to Jerusalem and placed in a new tent—the tabernacle of David. This new tabernacle featured a new order of worship. Although burnt offerings and fellowship offerings were presented before the Lord, the instructions for the worship leaders were simple and direct: Make petition, give thanks, and praise the Lord. The worship centered around two activities—prayer and musical worship.

> He appointed some of the Levites to minister before the ark of the Lord, to make petition, to give thanks, and to praise the Lord, the God of Israel: Asaph was the chief, Zechariah second, then Jeiel, Shemiramoth, Jehiel, Mattithiah, Eliab, Benaiah, Obed-Edom and Jeiel. They were to play the lyres and harps, Asaph was to sound the cymbals, and Benaiah and Jahaziel the priests were to blow the trumpets regularly before the ark of the covenant of God (1 Chron. 16:4–6).

Clearly, musical worship lay at the very heart of the activities surrounding the presence of God. Many believe that the tent, unlike the tabernacle before it, was an open structure allowing the Levites access to the ark of the covenant where the glory of God dwelt between the cherubim. Likewise, many believe that the tabernacle of David is being restored spiritually with respect to musical expression in worship in this generation.

God is concerned about the content of the songs we sing and the thoughtfulness with which we sing them. In Psalm 47 we are instructed to sing songs of praise to God, our King. Examine the insistent repetition of these verses: "Sing praises to God, sing praises: sing praises unto our King, sing praises. For God is the King of all the earth: sing ye praises with understanding"

(Ps. 47:6–7, KJV). Evidently, if we wish to please God with our song then we must understand who He is. If we truly understand that He is King of all the earth, we will not sing thoughtlessly.

In the sincere act of worship, the Holy Spirit permeates every aspect of music. As LaMar Boschman reminds us, "He not only calls us to worship but enables us to worship. The Holy Spirit gives us the music of worship, the lyrics of worship and the desire to worship."[17] It is the anointing of the Holy Spirit that causes the music to penetrate with life-changing force. Music alone does not change hearts for the better; only when enlivened by the Holy Spirit does it have such benefit.

What Does Music Mean?

Talking about music is like dancing about architecture.

—Thelonious Monk

When composer Robert Schumann was asked to explain a difficult etude, he sat down at the piano and played the etude again. Since no words could adequately explain the meaning, he used none. Did the questioner have a better understanding of the etude after hearing it the second time? We cannot know the answer, but the likelihood for additional insight was greater after a second hearing than after a verbal explanation. "When it speaks of music, language is lame."[18]

The heart of the difficulty is that meaning in music is essentially nonverbal. What music means cannot be reduced to words; musical meaning does not yield readily to propositional discourse. This point holds true even of songs with lyrics. The music may enhance the meaning of the words, or the music may be in conflict with the meaning of the words, but, in any case, the music does not merely mean what the words mean.

Composers of the Baroque Era believed in a concept called the doctrine of affections. They believed that certain specific rhythms and specific melodic patterns have a particular meaning which can be used to enhance the meaning of the text.[19] From Plato to the present many have believed that music has an inherent meaning. In other words, some theorists have believed that the melody and rhythm of the music communicate a specific meaning to the hearer at some level.[20] By contrast, others

An *etude* is a piece of music written to exploit or develop a particular technique. It is designed as a study piece but is often played in concert.

---

[17]LaMar Boschman, *A Heart of Worship* (Orlando, Fla.: Creation House, 1994), 38.

[18]George Steiner, *Real Presences* (Chicago: The University of Chicago Press, 1989), 19.

[19]Joseph Machlis and Kristine Forney, *The Enjoyment of Music,* 6th ed. (New York: W. W. Norton & Company, Inc., 1960), 260.

[20]Calvin Johansson, *Discipling Music Ministry: Twenty-first Century Directions* (Peabody, Mass.: Hendrickson Publishers, 1992), vi.

have held that music primarily expresses the inner self and is not a vessel for meaning.[21] In this chapter we shall chart a course different from both views.

Leonard Bernstein suggests that there are four levels of meaning in music: (1) narrative-literary meanings, (2) atmospheric-pictorial meanings, (3) affective-reactive meanings, and (4) purely musical meanings.[22] Upon further examination we see that each of the first three can be grouped under the category program music, that is, instrumental music that has been given verbal or visual associations. Meaning is suggested by a title or an explanatory "program" provided by the composer or the publisher. The nature of the supplied meaning may be a story, an idea, a location, a mood, or something else. The fourth category that Mr. Bernstein suggests is frequently called absolute music, or pure music. Pure music has no extra-musical meaning.

MEANING THROUGH ASSOCIATION

Music is frequently called the universal language, yet it is not possible to transmit a verbal thought through the music itself. The composer, through his music alone, cannot communicate a precise meaning (concept, idea, thought). A single musical idea or an entire composition may gain meaning by association, but such meaning is dependent upon the knowledge of the individual hearer.

Meanings gained through association are not universal. For example, two-beat southern gospel music may be the sound of camp meeting and spiritual renewal to one person, yet to another that same two-beat music may be the sound of the honky tonk, totally unsuitable for use in worship. For some people the sound of the pipe organ is the epitome of spiritual music; to others it is the very essence of dead and lifeless formalism. These meanings are not inherent in the music. Rather, they are the product of personal associations with the music or musical style.

> "Meaning is suggested by a title or an explanatory 'program' provided by the composer or the publisher."

Meaning through association is learned meaning. When people see a picture of the ocean on the TV screen and hear over and over a low-pitched, accented half-step movement of two notes, how do they know that a shark is about to attack? Those who have seen the movie *Jaws* know it because they have learned to associate this very distinctive musical motive with the great white shark in the movie; it sounds ominous only because it is associated with an ominous event.

---

[21]Ralph Vaughn Williams, *The Making of Music* (Ithaca, N.Y.: Cornell University Press, 1955), 55.

[22]Leonard Bernstein, *The Joy of Music* (New York: Simon and Schuster, 1954), 15.

Such associations are dynamic, not static. Our understanding of the meaning of certain musical motives or styles is constantly changing. Many people have associated the sound of the minor mode with sadness. Yet most people who hear the currently popular Christmas song *Mary Did You Know* think of it as warm and happy in its mood. The music of Elvis and the music of the Beatles was the sound of rebellion when these performers burst on the scene. Now they are the stuff of elevator music. They evoke the comfort of nostalgia. Not long ago I was listening to a conservative Christian radio station. I was surprised to hear an oldie, which ten years ago had a Top-40 sound! When it was newly released it wouldn't have been played on that radio station because of being too "worldly;" now it was on their playlist. Had the song become sanctified by age?

PURE MUSIC

What is "pure music"? According to Malcolm Budd, "It is the art of sounds that are not given a nonauditory interpretation."[23] Morse Code is an example of sounds that are given a nonauditory interpretation, since it is made up of sounds organized for the express purpose of communicating a verbal message. However, these sounds serve no artistic or aesthetic purpose. By contrast, the sounds of pure music have no nonauditory (i.e., linguistic, or verbal) meanings. They are purely musical meanings.

Meaning in music is not anti-intellectual, but it could be described as nonlinguistic or nonconceptual. Although composing, arranging, and performing require high order intellectual activity, the meaning of music is not primarily cognitive. No one can explain how mere sound waves falling on the human ear can cause the transmittal of nerve impulses to the brain "so that we emerge from engulfment in that orderly presentation of sound stimuli as if we had lived through a simulacrum of life, the instinctive life of the emotions."[24]

MEANING VERSUS A MEANING

David Pass has suggested that the meaning does not reside in the artifact (the piece of music). Instead, meaning emerges from the interaction of what the performer intends and the insight that the listener brings to the listening experience. He has suggested the following model: designer/producer—artifact—interpreter. In this model the designer is the one who creates the music and the producer is the one who performs the music. The designer/producer may or may not be one and the same person. The notes, rests, articulation, expression marks, and instructions

---

[23]Malcolm Budd, *Music and the Emotions: The Philosophical Theories* (New York: Routledge, 1985, 1992), ix.

[24]Copeland, *On Music*, 24.

comprise the artifact itself. The interpreter is the one who hears the music and ascertains its meaning. It must be stated, however, that it is not possible to intend anything without the presence of an artifact.[25] Let us consider for a moment the intent of the designer/producer and the artifact as a given. What the listener—the interpreter—will receive from the music is dependent upon the understandings, experiences, and personal taste that he or she brings to the listening experience.[26] Each person comes to the musical moment with a unique personal history. That history will, of necessity, have a powerful impact on one's perception of the

A New Model for Meaning in Music

Designer/Producer	Artifact	Interpreter
The composer/performer	The music itself	The hearer

meaning of the music. Just as no two histories are alike, no two interpretations of meaning will be alike.

Why does one piece of music yield such conflicting reactions in a variety of listeners? Susanne Langer gives this explanation, "[M]*usic at its highest, though clearly a symbolic form, is an unconsummated symbol . . . for the assignment of one rather than another possible meaning to each form is never explicitly made.*"[27]

Music is not just sounds, it is an expression of the spirit. While sound is the vehicle of that expression, music can never be explained by the physical alone. The spiritual expression of the performer communicates to the spirit of the listener in a way that transcends language. Although the skill of the composer and the skill of the performer will influence how effectively the spiritual message is communicated, it is not technique that speaks, it is spirit. Music that speaks to the spirit must originate in the spirit. This is true regardless of the intent of the performer.

Hearing As Performance

> A "hearing" is itself a performance, an active process of making meaning.
>
> —Jeanne Bamberger

The average young person in America spends many hours each week listening to recordings, attending concerts, and watching television programs and movies that feature music. After hearing all that music, do we really need help learning to listen to music? There is little doubt that a greater knowledge of music will enhance the quality of musical perception. As Jeanne

---

[25]Pass, *Music*, 42–43.

[26]Ibid.

[27]Susanne K. Langer, *Philosophy in a New Key: A Study in the Symbolism of Reason, Rite, and Art* (Cambridge, Mass.: Harvard University Press, 1942, 1951), 200.

Bamberger observes, "What we hear depends on what we are able to think of to hear—even though we are quite unaware that thinking is going on at all."[28] Her comment makes sense if you reflect on the last time you found yourself at a party where the "background" music was at rock concert level. Perhaps you were asked the name of a song that was playing but could only respond, "I'm sorry, I don't know; I wasn't listening." You heard the sounds, but you had not listened to the music. Active, attentive listening requires focusing mental attention on the music.

But by itself, paying attention is not enough. The listener needs both knowledge of, and significant exposure to, the music in order to comprehend what that music has to offer. If I were standing in my back yard on a clear night gazing into the sky, an astronomer might ask me, "Do you see the stars?" Perhaps he means, Do you see the constellations and the planets? I might very well answer, "Yes, I see the stars," but as a novice I would not see what the trained astronomer sees. To find the constellations and the planets, I need the knowledge of what to look for in the stars. Similarly, to hear the details of the structure of music, I need to know how the music is put together.

You probably already have many important listening skills, and you may have a greater knowledge of music than you think you do. Consider the example of the student who says she enjoys music. If someone asked her, she would admit that she can "clap simple rhythms, recognize tunes she has heard before, even sing or whistle at least some of them."[29] Nonetheless, she would probably be quick to add, "I really don't know much about music." In fact, clapping rhythms and recognizing and performing melodies are high order skills. If you already have these skills you have a solid foundation to build on.

Most people have learned to make sense of the music that they know and love. Although they may not understand the precise terminology of the musician, the music that they know makes sense to them. They understand the syntax—the structure of its meaning. Just as children learn the syntax of spoken language long before they begin formal language study, so too we learn the syntax of music aurally and intuitively even if we have not formally studied music.

However, we do not all hear music the same way. Some people consider melody the key to music: They hear music horizontally. Some hear music vertically: They think of chords and harmony. They concentrate on the sounds that occur at the same time. Still others are fascinated by the rhythm, or the form, or the tonal colors of the instruments in all their combinations and permutations.

---

[28]Jeanne Bamberger, *The Mind Behind the Musical Ear: How Children Develop Musical Intelligence* (Cambridge, Mass.: Harvard University Press, 1991), 5.

[29]Ibid., 7.

There are many different things to listen for in music. Suppose we were to compare listening to music with looking at a panoramic landscape. We can choose to view it in several ways: from left to right, from right to left, up close. We might even try to take in the entire panorama at once. What we see is affected to a great extent by where we choose to focus our attention. So it is with music.[30] We listen to music in at least three ways: the sensual/emotional level, the cognitive/intellectual level, and the spiritual level.

THE SENSUOUS/EMOTIONAL LEVEL

Sometimes we listen to music and simply allow it to wash over us like warm sunshine. We listen passively without any effort. At other times we allow the music to stir our emotions. We allow our deepest feelings to rise to the surface. Those emotions become a part of the listening experience. At this level repeated hearings give a sense of comfortableness, a sense of familiarity, to the listening experience. The listener is able to relax and enjoy the music with a reasonable knowledge of what is coming next.

THE COGNITIVE/INTELLECTUAL LEVEL

Sometimes we listen for the way the music is put together, i.e., the inner workings of the music. We listen for the melody, the harmony, the counterpoint. We consider the form, the structure, of the music. We take pleasure in music as art. We enjoy the creative gifts of the composer and the performer. Sometimes we enjoy the context of the music as much as the music itself. In opera and ballet (which has a story line) and in program music (music endowed with a literary or pictorial association), we sometimes listen for the plot or the extra-musical aspects to supply the key to the music. It is at this level, particularly, that greater knowledge is essential. The more one understands the inner workings of the music, the more one is able to hear the context of the spiritual message.

THE SPIRITUAL LEVEL

Music has a remarkable if not unique ability to speak directly to the spirit. We are always affected by the spiritual content of the music. Melody, harmony, form, and other technical features of music exist for the purpose of conveying spiritual content. This is true whether the music is sacred or secular. The spiritual content may well touch the emotions, but the spiritual and the emotional are not one and the same. Music speaks to the deepest part of the individual and utters the unutterable language of the spirit.

---

[30]Jay D. Zorn, *Listening to Music* (Englewood Cliffs, N.J.: Prentice Hall, 1991), 3.

Counterpoint is the combining of two or more independent melodic lines at the same time. Most music is made up of one dominant melody accompanied in the other voices by harmony.

Music and the Popular Media

For me, the music I choose to listen to or skate to is important because it reaches my spirit and affects my life.

—Janet Lynn Salomon

Music and the popular media influence our lives in numerous and complex ways. In general, the greater the exposure, the greater the impact. Constantly changing trends in hairstyles, clothing, and fast food all affect us at a superficial, ephemeral level. Changes in social attitudes concerning matters of morality, on the other hand, affect us at a profound, eternal level. What effect do changes in music have on us?

That there is an important effect seems clear. Precisely how and in what way it occurs is less clear. A television executive testified before a congressional hearing that it was absurd to believe that music could influence the behavior of young people. Just a few weeks later in a bulletin to potential advertisers, the executive guaranteed increased sales to any company that would advertise on its programs. The executive was able to offer a guarantee because he is convinced that the medium, with its use of music and video, has an effect on the audience. He was able to discount the effect of music during the congressional hearing because the precise mechanisms of the effect are not well known.

The difficulty comes in trying to establish a cause and effect relationship between hearing a certain song and then behaving in a particular way. Human behavior is simply not that predictable. Causal effects are often subtle and complex. Changes of attitude and behavior occur incrementally—little by little, one small step at a time. But if the impact and causal influences of music in the popular media are subtle and complex, making them virtually imperceptible, that does not mean they are therefore unreal or unimportant. The listener may be unaware of the influences at work in popular contemporary music and yet be influenced nonetheless. The media guru of the 1960s Marshall McLuhan recognized this fact in a much less sophisticated era of radio and television: "The effects of Technology do not occur at the level of opinions or concepts, but alter sense ratios or patterns of perception steadily and without resistance."[31]

One of the most powerful influences in the present generation is Music Television: MTV has essentially created a new, nonlinear art form. It is a marriage of rock music and fast-paced film. Whereas the typical television program has plot and continuity, MTV music video programming relies on mood and emotion. The idea is to make the listener feel a certain way, not

---

[31]Marshall McLuhan, *Understanding Media: The Extensions of Man* (New York: Signet Books, 1964), 33.

think a certain way. MTV is itself a context that attempts to abolish the idea of context. Images appear so rapidly that it is impossible for the viewer to edit or filter the experience.[32] It is not possible to think through the morality of the situation as it is presented. The viewer/listener can only follow the stream of consciousness as it flows. The morality of MTV infiltrates—infects—the morality of the viewer/listener as subtly and silently as a virus does the body.

Music, the media, and MTV are shaping the attitudes of young Americans. In a recent survey of young people from evangelical and Pentecostal churches, researchers discovered that the young people who were regular church attendees held attitudes toward morality that were not markedly different from their unchurched counterparts. The core values of both groups were apparently affected more by the music, the media, and MTV than by their parents or their churches.[33]

The struggle between good and evil is perennial. Music is but one of the arenas of that struggle. Still, it is an extremely important arena because it has the capacity to affect both the soul (including intellect and emotions) and the spirit. Music and the popular media may have a positive influence, or a negative influence. Its most enduring influence on today's generation of young people, however, may be that it merely serves as diversion. Kenneth Meyers seems to make this point when he observes that there is something new about popular culture today, including its music: "Modern popular culture is not just the latest in a series of diversions. It is rather a *culture of diversion*."[34] Bob Sorge paints a graphic and sobering picture of this culture of diversion for the Christian:

> You don't hear Him because you're hearing too many other things. Oprah Winfrey, Sally Jesse Raphael, Phil Donahue. You're licking your fingers on the delicacies of Babylon. An evening that could be spent hearing the words of Jesus is squandered before the tube. "As the World Burns." Pity the Christian who has rationalized watching soap operas. It's vultures' food.
>
> You get in your car in the morning, and on the way to work tune into your "Contemporary Adult Rock" music station. Jiving to the jingles of Babylon. Humming the melodies of the Great Harlot. And then you cry, "Oh Lord, I want to hear You." "No you don't." Did you know that in the Book of Revelation they mourn the death of the songs of Babylon.[35]

---

[32]Quentin J. Schultze et al., *Dancing in the Dark: Youth, Popular Culture and the Electronic Media* (Grand Rapids: Wm. B. Eerdmans Publishing Co., 1991), 203–207.

[33]Josh McDowell and Bob Hostetler, *Right from Wrong* (Dallas: Word Publishing, 1994), 8–9.

[34]Kenneth A. Myers, *All God's Children and Blue Suede Shoes: Christians and Popular Culture* (Westchester, Ill.: Crossway Books, 1989), 56.

[35]Bob Sorge, *In His Face* (Canandaigua, N.Y.: Oasis House, 1994), 56.

Sorge's words implicitly bear witness to the need to attentively attend the details of what everyday life has to offer. To float through life passively absorbing the messages, musical and otherwise, of the contemporary popular culture is to live a life diverted from what finally and ultimately matters in life.

Postlude: Making Choices

As we listen to unfamiliar musical styles, we do well to ask ourselves: What is this music all about? What does it mean? Until we understand the music, we are not qualified to evaluate its worth. Of course, we cannot avoid having an initial emotional response to the music we hear. Still, we should realize that our initial response to a new piece of music is as much about the music we have heard in the past as it is about the music we are hearing at the moment!

Can the nonmusician ever be qualified to make a judgment about the value of a musical work? In a practical sense each of us makes such judgments every day. We form an opinion based on knowledge or on ignorance, but we do make judgments. If our judgment is to have validity, however, we must listen to a sufficient number of pieces of a particular musical style, or genre, before forming a final judgment on a specific work. As Francis Schaeffer has pointed out, "The highest quality of a particular style can best be determined not by listening to the pronouncements of others, but by listening to a sufficient quantity of the whole in order to make your own judgments."[36] Direct acquaintance with representative pieces of a certain genre of music, then, is an indispensable requisite for forming a sound judgment about a particular piece of music in that genre. Quite simply this principle means that as an initial frame of reference, we should evaluate a specific piece of jazz, folk, rock, rhythm and blues, Gregorian chant, or baroque by comparing it to other pieces of the same genre that we have direct experience with.

The flip side of this principle is we should not choose music simply because of its popularity. The standard for "worthy" is primarily the piece's technical merit. If we choose to listen to a Mozart Symphony played by the New York Philharmonic, an Irish folk song by The Chieftains, a big band jazz riff by Stan Kenton, a country ballad by Ricky Skaggs, a blues rendition by B. B. King, or a gospel song by Alvin Slaughter, our initial question should be the same: Is this a worthy example of its genre?

A second frame of reference calls for us to focus on the worldview presented in the music. In particular, we are interested in the ideology and moral norms, explicit or implied, in the piece. With respect to this frame of reference, both serious and popular music should be evaluated in the same way we evaluate other works of art. A common but mistaken perception is that

---

[36]Schaeffer, *Art*, 41.

serious music and the fine arts have a higher level of morality than popular music and the popular arts. This is simply not true. Every composer, musician, and artist has a worldview. That worldview may harmonize with Scripture, or it may not. We do not endorse a piece of music or a work of art as ideologically sound or morally good simply because it satisfies a high standard of technical merit. "As Christians, we must see that just because an artist—even a great artist—portrays a worldview in writing or on canvas, it does not mean that we should automatically accept that worldview."[37]

The Westminster Shorter Catechism tells us that the chief aim of every human being is "to glorify God and to enjoy Him forever." The music you choose should glorify God and enhance your enjoyment of Him. First Corinthians 10:31 says, "[W]hatever you do, do it all for the glory of God." God has given music for us to enjoy—both sacred and secular. The world of music is open before you. You are invited on a journey, an incredible adventure, to experience glorious new worlds of music.

Francis Schaeffer

Francis Schaeffer suggested four basic standards for evaluating a work of art. Though Schaeffer speaks primarily of painting, the standards easily apply to music.

1. *Technical excellence.* The technical quality of the music should be considered quite apart from its message or its worldview. Is the music well crafted—melody, harmonic structure, rhythm, form, instrumentation/orchestration, counterpoint, unity/contrast, and so forth? There may be varying degrees of technical excellence in each of these aspects. All other things being equal, the more one knows about music, the more accurate one's assessment of the music's technical quality will be.

2. *Validity.* Is the musician honest to himself, to the genre of the music, and to his worldview? The issue here has to do with the musician's integrity. If the artist is creating a work of art only for money or for the sake of being accepted, his work lacks validity. Does the music flow from the real self—the authentic self?

3. *Intellectual content.* All artists have a worldview which will show through in the work. No matter how great or famous the artist or musician, the body of her work must be judged by the light of scriptural truth. In fact, the greater the artist, the greater the impact of a negative worldview.

4. *The integration of content and vehicle.* How well is the musical form and style suited to the content of the worldview? How well do the various aspects of the music fit together? A four voice fugue in the style of J. S. Bach performed on kazoos would sound ridiculous even if the composition were first rate and the performance impeccable. (Schaeffer, *Art & The Bible* [Downers Grove, Ill.: InterVarsity Press, 1973], 41–48.)

---

[37]Best, *Music*, 73.

Review and Discussion Questions

1. When someone says, "That music is so worshipful," what style of music do you immediately think about? What music would your mother think about? Your grandmother?

2. In regards to musical style in worship, how do we reconcile the seemingly contradictory principles of 1 Timothy 4:4–5 and 1 Corinthians 8:9–13?

3. Is the same style of music appropriate for every culture? Why or why not?

4. Does every culture need a variety of styles to express the full range of worship? Explain.

5. What does the author mean when he says: "[T]he music of romance, love, family, friendship, and all the subjects of life are appropriate for the Christian, and they all have merit. However, the overarching principle for our music is this: God is the primary audience!"?

6. What do you think Thelonius Monk might have meant when he said, "Talking about music is like dancing about architecture"? Do you agree?

7. What does the author mean when he speaks of hearing as performance? Illustrate.

8. Assess Francis Schaeffer's four criteria for evaluating a piece of art by using two pieces of music you are familiar with—one sacred, one secular.

Selected Bibliography

Bernstein, Leonard. *The Joy of Music.* New York: Simon and Schuster, Inc., 1954.

Best, Harold M. *Music Through the Eyes of Faith.* San Francisco: Harper, 1993.

Budd, Malcolm. *Music and the Emotions: The Philosophical Theories.* New York: Routledge, Inc., 1985, 1992.

Floyd, Samuel A., Jr. *The Power of Black Music.* New York: Oxford University Press, 1995.

Hoffer, Charles R. *The Understanding of Music,* 5th ed. Belmont, Calif.: Wadsworth Publishing Company, 1985.

Johansson, Calvin. *Discipling Music Ministry: Twenty-first Century Directions.* Peabody, Mass.: Hendrickson Publishers, 1992.

Langer, Susanne K. *Philosophy in a New Key: A Study in the Symbolism of Reason, Rite, and Art.* Cambridge, Mass.: Harvard University Press, 1942, 1951.

Lawhead, Steve. *Rock Reconsidered.* Downers Grove, Ill.: InterVarsity Press, 1981.

Myers, Kenneth A. *All God's Children and Blue Suede Shoes: Christians and Popular Culture.* Westchester, Ill.: Crossway Books, 1989.

Pass, David B. *Music in the Church: A Theology of Church Music.* Nashville: Broadman Press, 1989.

Schultze, Quentin J. et al., *Dancing in the Dark: Youth, Popular Culture and the Electronic Media.* Grand Rapids: Wm. B. Eerdmans Publishing Co., 1991.

Sorge, Bob. *In His Face.* Canandaigua, N.Y.: Oasis House, 1994.

Stolba, Marie K. *The Development of Western Music: A History.* Madison, Wis.: Brown and Benchmark Publishers, 1992.

Zorn, Jay D. *Listening to Music.* Englewood Cliffs, N.J.: Prentice Hall, 1991.

10

The Place of Literature in a Christian Worldview

Twila Brown Edwards

In the beginning was the Word . . . and the Word was God.

—John 1:1

Jesus was not a theologian. He was God who told stories.

—Madeleine L'Engle[1]

Recently my husband and I browsed in a large, new Barnes & Noble bookstore. So many books and millions of words! Books about religion, archaeology, computers, travel, and gardening. Imaginative storybooks, drama, and poetry. Children's books, some of heavy cardboard, some of cloth so they can be washed, many others with exquisite illustrations. We have come a long way since the first large book, the Gutenberg Bible, was printed in movable type in 1456. Although we have a highly technological society, books are amazingly important to us. Friendships are born and nurtured by sharing books. Books cause us to laugh, to cry, sometimes even to make dramatic changes in our lives. Our family traveled frequently when our son was young, so we spent many hours together on the road reading books, mostly imaginative literature. We laughed hilariously over the escapades of Huck Finn and Tom Sawyer. We sat in wonder and silence at the end of Madeleine L'Engle's description of the birth of a unicorn.[2] We softly wept together when we realized that Laura Ingalls' sister, Mary, would see no more. We often felt ourselves drawing closer as a family because of shared reading experiences. Browsing now in this huge bookstore, we thought about the place of reading books in the life of the Christian. With so many books available, how do Christians make wise choices? Or do many Christians choose not to read imaginative literature at all? Is it easier to watch television than to read? In this chapter I develop a Christian approach toward imaginative literature. I believe that reading great literature is an essential part of the development of a wholesome Christian worldview.

My belief in the importance of literature is founded upon the cornerstone of literature itself—the Word. The powerful signifi-

---

[1]Madeleine L'Engle, *Walking on Water: Reflections on Faith and Art* (Wheaton, Ill.: Harold Shaw, 1980), 54.

[2]Madeleine L'Engle, *A Swiftly Tilting Planet* (New York: Dell, 1978), 156–57. In this fantasy story, Charles Wallace and Gaudior, a unicorn, are bleeding and worn out from an encounter with evil forces known as Echthroi. The wise unicorn realizes they must be restored before further engagements to overcome the evil, so he allows Charles to ride on his back to the home of the unicorns where the snow and ice have miraculous healing properties. While in this land where humans have never before visited, Charles has the inspiring experience of seeing a baby unicorn hatched from its shell. The unicorns' only food is starlight and moonlight.

cance of literature to a Christian worldview has to do with the connection I see between the literary word and the Divine Word. Michael Edwards has also suggested the crucial connection between God and literary language: "God not only has a language but . . . *he is language*, or at least . . . one way of describing him, or an aspect of him, is to call him 'the Word.'"[3] Edwards believes,

> It is not only the second Person of the Trinity but the third who has this linguistic reference, for God is also the Spirit, or the Breath, and although pneuma [spirit, breath] has an absorbing variety of meaning, as has logos [word, expression], it does suggest the breath that is the basis of speech. One even notices in the creation story that opens the Bible that the account of the Spirit or Breath of God "moving on the face of the waters" is followed immediately by his speaking: "And God said, 'Let there be light,'" as if his breath were moving partly for the purpose of voicing those words.[4]

God, then, created the world by the Word. Furthermore, when the world—including language—fell, He redeemed the world through the Word, Jesus Christ. Literature is important because literary artists are "subcreators." They use words to create an imaginary world we enter as readers in order to see ourselves and each other more clearly—as divinely created, as sinfully fallen, and as redeemed by the Word—so that when we return to our own world, we may live richer lives.[5]

This chapter will explore the way literature connects with four important doctrines of the Christian faith: Creation, Fall, Redemption, and Pentecost. I will attempt to answer the following questions: (1) Why is the creativity of the literary artist important to the Christian? (2) Why are literary representations of the Fall important to the Christian? (3) Why are literary depictions of Redemption important to the Christian? (4) Why is literature that employs the images of Pentecost important to the Christian?

Creation

IMPORTANCE OF THE LITERARY ARTIST'S CREATIVITY

God begins His story by describing the creative power of words over chaos: "Now the earth was formless and empty, darkness was over the surface of the deep, and the Spirit of God was hovering over the waters. And God *said*, 'Let there be light,' and there was light" (Gen. 1:2–3, my emphasis). In God's account of creation, the setting, the earth, was

---

[3]Michael Edwards, *Towards a Christian Poetics* (Grand Rapids: Eerdmans, 1984), 217. This work has been influential in shaping my views in this chapter.

[4]Ibid., 217.

[5]J. R. R. Tolkien, "On Fairy-Stories," in *The Tolkien Reader* (New York: Ballantine, 1966), 40.

without distinguishing characteristics, without inhabitants, and dark. The first mention of the Spirit portrays the breath of God speaking powerful Words, birthing a world of order out of chaos.

The world of our lives is also often chaotic. The importance of the literary artists' creativity is directly related to our chaotic darkness. Into that darkness literary artists—not unlike God in whose divine image they are created—come with their world of story, shaped and created by structure and form that speaks to the chaos within us. By entering the literary artists' created world even though it may be a fallen Eden, we often are able to recover and reshape some of our own lost Eden. For example, the artist participates in the creativity of God himself when he shapes a world where a beast, like us, may be loved by a princess whose kiss transforms some of our ugliness into beauty. The story heals some of our chaotic inner being. The beauty of the structure and form created by the God-given talent of the artist returns to us some of the beauty of our own lost Eden.

Not only, however, did God control chaos and make our world, but He also created humankind in His divine image. As Michael Edwards points out, God, as Creator, formed us "characters" by His language and breath. By His Word he made us in His image; and by His breathing into our nostrils, He gave us the breath of life. "Our very existence depends on an act of language." Furthermore, the apostle Peter explains that believers are "'born again . . . through the living and enduring word of God' and adds that "this is the *word* that was preached to you" (1 Pet. 1:23–25, my emphasis).[6] God, therefore, gave us birth and rebirth in his image through His Word and Breath. If the literary artist is true in his observations of human nature, he creatively gives birth to imaginary characters who will help us, as we read, to find the image of God in ourselves.

> **"By entering the literary artists' created world we often are able to recover and reshape some of our own lost Eden."**

Not only in the creation of worlds, therefore, but also in the creation of characters, the earthly artist is a subcreator who imitates God. By their God-given talents, literary artists create characters that remind us we are created in God's image, even if we view ourselves as abominably fallen. Reading fairy tales, for example, can help a despondent mother realize that she doesn't always appear to her children as a wicked stepmother or even a witch, but she sometimes actually appears as the good and beautiful fairy godmother.

Fairy tales can also help children make sense of the chaos in their world. Walter Wangerin, Jr., for instance, tells how the

---

[6]Michael Edwards, *Towards a Christian Poetics*, 218.

fairy tales helped him process his confusion about the good and bad moods of his mother when he was a small child.[7] When his mother lovingly kissed him goodnight, she smelled of roses, and he felt contented and secure by her loving embrace. He arose in the morning expecting to encounter the same loving responses from her. Instead, however, he was confronted by a woman who scolded him because he had risen late, heckled him to dress quickly for school, and threatened (and carried out the threat) to make him walk to school if he were not dressed on time. He felt rejected, guilty, and confused. He became withdrawn, not knowing how to process his "two mothers." One day the teacher read to the class the story of "Snow White" with its "two mothers, an original and a stepmother." This fairy tale stimulated the imagination of young Walter, releasing him from the fear that there was something in him that caused the awful change in his "morning mother" from his "night mother." He subconsciously was able to process the fact that the same human being, even a mother, is sometimes extremely loving and at other times tense and unthoughtful. He could now avoid turning the unkindness of another inward upon himself in a destructive way. The fairy tale had communicated to the child something important about humankind. I contend that, in doctrinal terms, the Truth (God's Truth) that the child learned through this fairy tale was that his "morning mother" was the woman who was allowing the Fall to get the better of her, while his "night mother" was the woman who was allowing her created image to shine through her fallen nature.

> **"'The story that shapes a child's universe also shapes the child—and by the child, the man thereafter.'"**
> —*Walter Wangerin, Jr.*

Most mothers reading Wangerin can identify strongly, perhaps redemptively, with that twofold response to their children. The story helps remind the mother that she is not only miserably fallen but also created in God's image, and it helps the child establish order in his chaotic world. "The story that shapes a child's universe also shapes the child—and by the child, the man thereafter. The memory of a burning fairy tale can govern behavior."[8]

Thus far I have attempted to base my argument for the importance of literature upon the theology of Creation by establishing parallels between the divine creation of a good order in the world and in humanity and the literary creation of a good order in the worlds and lives of characters and readers. My third Scriptural foundation for our argument reveals an exciting

---

[7]Walter Wangerin, Jr., "Hans Christian Andersen: Shaping the Child's Universe," in *Reality and the Vision*, ed. Philip Yancy (Dallas: Word, 1990), 2–5.

[8]Ibid., 5.

intersection of these divine-literary parallels. For in the Genesis Creation story, God himself, who has just created the universe by *naming* it, grants the power of naming, of language, of words (the foundation of literature), to humans. After He had created the animals, "The Lord God . . . brought them to the man . . . and whatever the man called [or named] each living creature, that was its name" (Gen. 2.19). Just as God had creatively spoken "'Let there be light' and it was so," so Adam creatively spoke "Let this be called 'Lion'" and it was so." At the naming, therefore, the world, which was derived from God's language and was God's (spoken) text, now became Adam's text also."[9] Michael Edwards affirms that although it is God's language that creates the animals, Adam's "naming" helps identify the nature of these creatures. "After God's all-powerful divine language had created the world, Adam's powerful human language, by naming it, could mingle with it and modify it."[10]

Literary artists can participate in this powerful naming quality of human language. This naming portion of the biblical

Gilbert Keith "G. K." Chesterton

G. K. Chesterton (1874–1936), an important Christian writer, believed that fairy tales prepared him to believe Christianity. "My first and last philosophy, that which I believe in with unbroken certainty, I learnt in the nursery . . . The things I believed most then, the things I believe most now, are the things called fairy tales" (49). Chesterton learned ethics and philosophy from "being fed on fairy tales. If I were describing them in detail I could note many noble and healthy principles that arise from them . . . There is the lesson of 'Cinderella,' which is the same as that of the Magnificat— *exaltavit humiles* [exaltation of humility]. There is the great lesson of 'Beauty and the Beast;' that a thing must be loved *before* it is loveable. There is the terrible alle-

gory of the 'Sleeping Beauty,' which tells how the human creature was blessed with all birthday gifts, yet cursed with death; and how death also may perhaps be softened to a sleep. But I am not concerned with any of the separate statutes of elfland, but with the whole spirit of its law, which I learnt before I could speak, and shall retain when I cannot write. I am concerned with a certain way of looking at life, which was created in me by the fairy tales" (50). For more on his view about fairy tales, see Appendix 6, "G. K. Chesterton on the Power of Fairy Tales," p. 483.

Taken from Gilbert K. Chesterton "The Ethics of Elfland," in *Orthodoxy*. Doubleday, Image Bks., New York, N.Y., 1973.

---

[9]Edwards, *Towards a Christian Poetics*, 9.
[10]Ibid., 8–9.

Creation passage helps us to integrate our theology with our literary theory and to give a forceful reply to the question opening this first section: Why is the creativity of the literary artist important to the Christian? First, the literary artist's creativity often helps to overcome our chaos and to restore us in some sense to an Edenic order. Second, the creativity of the literary artist helps us to realize the divinely created image in each of us. And third, creative literature may be viewed as a continuation of the divine commission to use language to name, or identify, the true nature of ourselves and the universe around us.

I conclude this discussion of Creation with two examples from literary artists who have fulfilled that original commission by focusing creatively on the naming power of the literary word. In retelling the creation story for children, Jean Richards humorously and imaginatively portrays Adam's effort at naming the butterfly:

> God thought
> He would make
> something different.
> He took a pinch of clay
> and made a tiny body
> with a tiny head and six miniature legs.
>
> Then He added two wings.
> God thought that the wings looked too plain,
> so he painted them with bright colors.
>
> He placed it in the air,
> and the creature began to flap its wings.
> "How exquisite!" said Man.
> "I think I shall name it
> Butterdog."
>
> But God frowned.
> Man thought and thought.
> Maybe Butterdog was not the right name.
> "I have it!" he cried.
> "Butterfly!"
>
> The minute Man
> said the word,
> Butterfly took off gracefully
> into the sky.[11]

Even a child can understand that calling something (or someone) a quality that it is not is a dishonest use of language. There is a peculiar power in naming that precisely identifies true nature. By accurately naming qualities in a character, the literary artist sometimes helps our hidden abilities and talents to take flight. Literature, therefore, can help us to understand ourselves and our world, thereby identifying and developing those good qualities that God has made inherent in us and in all His creation. Psychologists tell us, for example, that intelligent children who are frequently

---

[11]Jean Richards, *God's Gift* (New York: Delacourte, 1993).

named "dumb" or "ignorant" may develop their minds far below their potential. Just as God would wince at the name "butterdog" for a creature made to fly, so He would frown on us when we name others in a way that narrows their possibilities of discovering the divine image in themselves. Properly naming each other and ourselves, an activity in which the literary artist can greatly assist us, helps us realize our potential as creatures made in God's image.

Madeleine L'Engle, who says that "all great works of art are icons of Naming,"[12] is also interested in helping her readers realize their divine potential through creative naming. In her novel *A Wind in the Door*, L'Engle creates characters who suggest that we can either pigeonhole each other by our hateful acts or name each other by our loving acts. Meg, a young woman who has repeatedly had negative experiences with her school principal, is faced with a choice: dwelling on Mr. Jenkins' bad qualities or remembering the nicest thing she has ever known about him. Although she prefers to hate Mr. Jenkins, she finally brings herself to remember his kindest act. Calvin, Meg's good friend, is an extremely poor young man who had told her about a kind act Mr. Jenkins had once done for him. Calvin had been forced to wear to school some shoes his mom had bought for him at a thrift shop. Meg remembers Calvin's story:

> They cost her [Calvin's mother] a dollar, which was more than she could spare, and they were women's Oxfords, the kind of black laced shoes old women wear, and at least three sizes too small for me. . . . When I saw them, I cried, and then my mother cried. . . . I got a saw and hacked off the heels, and cut the toes out so I could jam my feet in, and went to school. . . . After a few days Mr. Jenkins called me into his office and said he'd noticed I'd outgrown my shoes, and he just happened to have an extra pair he thought would fit me. He'd gone to a lot of trouble to make them look used, as though he hadn't gone out and bought them for me.[13]

While Meg prefers to tell one of the many negative stories she knows about Mr. Jenkins, she repeats instead the story of his kind gift of shoes. Meg's choice to name instead of pigeonhole Mr. Jenkins calls forth the best in the principal's nature, helping him and the community he lives in to grow in goodness rather than remain entrapped in their hatred. The reader of such a story is also named since the storyteller helps us to see our naming power of good over evil. Naming by the literary artist, therefore, helps develop character in the reader. Like the powerful naming language of Adam, the naming of the literary artist helps to restore some of the image of God in us that was broken at the Fall.

---

[12]L'Engle, *Walking on Water*, 46.

[13]Madeleine L'Engle, *A Wind in the Door* (New York: Dell, 1973), 114.

God, therefore, created the world by His Word and Breath and shared language with Adam, giving him the power of language to name. We read great creative literature because the literary artist creates a secondary world that we enter to help us see ourselves and each other more clearly. Creative stories help bring order and form to lives filled with chaos and darkness. These artists also create characters that help us to see and to name God's image both in ourselves and in our fellow human

John Milton

John Milton (1608–1674) lived during turbulent times: the beheading of Charles I as King of England, the beginning and ending of the Commonwealth under Cromwell, and the reinstallation of the monarchy under Charles II. His father liberally educated John, expecting him to become a clergyman. The brilliant young man, however, gradually felt a call to become a poet. He later wrote "an inward prompting now grew daily upon me, that by labour and intent study . . . joined with the strong propensity of nature, I might perhaps leave something so written to aftertimes as they should not willingly let it die" ("Church Government" 668). Certainly that inward prompting was a true voice because Milton's *Paradise Lost* is considered one of the greatest poems in the English language.

Milton composed poetry in Latin when he was ten-years-old and was an accomplished English poet at twenty-four. He later became fluent in four more languages—Greek, French, Italian, and Hebrew. He believed that if a person wanted to be a good poet, he "ought himself to be a true poem" ("Apology for a Pamphlet" 694). Being a good poet to Milton first meant being a good person. He believed the poet had a power similar to that of a clergyman to instill in people the desire for virtue. Milton, therefore, used his

mighty pen to try to bring religious, social, political, and personal freedom to humankind. Because he wrote in favor of the Commonwealth and against the return of the monarchy, Milton narrowly escaped being condemned to death when Charles II returned to the throne. Although the new monarchy publicly burned Milton's books and he himself was imprisoned  for a time, Milton miraculously survived to write one of our two great English epics: *Paradise Lost*.

Although I have not quoted from *Paradise Lost* in this chapter, this epic poem deals extensively with the themes of Creation and the Fall. I highly recommend Milton's poetic insights on these two doctrines, which are important to the discussion of the place of literature in a Christian worldview.

Milton's idea of learning in a Christian worldview:

"The end then of learning is to repair the ruins of our first parents by regaining to know God aright, and out of that knowledge to love him, to imitate him, to be like him" ("Of Education" 631).

Milton quotations taken from the Merritt Y. Hughes edition of *John Milton: Complete Poems and Major Prose.* Odyssey Press, 1957.

beings. What John Milton says about education applies to literature: Stories help to "repair the ruins caused by our first parents."[14]

The Fall

IMPORTANCE OF LITERARY REPRESENTATIONS OF THE FALL

Part One: The Importance of Reading Literature About the Fall

Although God's powerful language brought a glorious world into existence and His breath poured life into Adam, and although human language was used to name God's creatures, language (and by extension, literature) also participates in the Fall. "Between the languages of God and of man there intrudes the language of the serpent."[15] At first, as Michael Edwards reminds us, the serpent tries only to arouse suspicion of God's words: "Did God really say, 'You must *not* eat from any tree in the garden?'" Eve answers, "God did say, 'You must *not* eat fruit from the tree that is in the middle of the garden, . . . *or* you *will* die.'" Becoming bolder, Satan flatly contradicts God's words: "You *will not* surely die" (vv. 1–4, emphasis added). Edwards further comments on this event:

> It is another momentous deploying of language, which reverses the greatness of Adam's naming into the wretchedness of contradiction and ambiguity. In contradicting the words of God, the serpent produces a language at odds with the world, opposed, that is, to its Creator and to its fact, since Adam and Eve will die, and also at odds with language itself. . . . The serpent's phrase is the beginning of semantic obscurity, and since it was effective it has left us a world in which meaning is no longer evident, and a language equally uncertain, as we interpret it and as we use it.[16]

After Adam and Eve participated in the lie of the serpent, "the eyes of both of them were opened, and they realized they were naked." When God walks in the garden and asks where they are, Adam replies, "I was afraid because I was naked; so I hid" (Gen. 3:7–10). The naked transparency of Adam and Eve's relationship with each other and with God is gone. Because Adam participated in the serpent's lie, he tries to hide himself with fig leaves and in fallen, deceptive language. Adam's language, powerful though it was in its creativity in naming the animals, is now characterized by falsity and self-deception. He has distorted God's image in himself.

In the Genesis account Adam and Eve must leave the garden and continue their marriage in much less than ideal circumstances. Their transparent relationship, as well as their language,

---

[14]John Milton, "Of Education," in *John Milton: Complete Poems and Major Prose*, ed. Merritt Y. Hughes (New York: Odyssey, 1957), 664.

[15]Edwards, *Towards a Christian Poetics*, 10.

[16]Ibid.

William Shakespeare

William Shakespeare (1564–1616) is the greatest playwright of all time. He also ranks as one of the greatest poets of all time, probably along with Dante and Milton.

Shakespeare's thirty-seven plays form a corpus greater than that of all other playwrights for several reasons. (1) He wrote renowned plays in every dramatic form: tragedy, comedy, history, romance, and tragicomedy. (2) While many other playwrights have written exceptional works of art, no one else has composed so many plays with such enduring dramatic power. (3) His works reveal a penetrating knowledge of human nature in astonishing variety.

Shakespeare has created memorable female characters. Beatrice (*Much Ado About Nothing*), logical and witty, delights us with her joking jabs at her lover while at the same time falling in love with him. Viola (*Twelfth Night*), ingeniously imaginative, protects her purity and fools even her master with her male disguise, all the while deftly, but also playfully, advancing the plot.

Complex characters like Hamlet (*Hamlet*) and Prospero (*The Tempest*) help us probe the mystery of human personality. Shakespeare frightens us with intimate studies of villains like Richard III (*Richard III*) who mercilessly kills his nephews to gain the power of the throne. But he also elicits our boisterous laughter with a character like Dogberry (*Much Ado*) who mispronounces words and bumbles his efforts to enact justice. And among his characters are some of the most famous lovers in Western literature: Romeo and Juliet,

Antony and Cleopatra, the first pair young and innocent, the second mature and lustful.

Shakespeare's characters are always set in plots that demand moral honesty. Neither Richard II (*Richard II*) nor Richard III (*Richard III*) gets away with abuse of royal power. Lady Macbeth's complicity in the murder of King Duncan (*Macbeth*) contributes to her psychosis and suicide. Malvolio's vaunting pride is punished by his isolation from society (*Twelfth Night*). Shake-  speare's genius in creating characters has entertained us and given us models to imitate; but he has also helped us to be repulsed by evil.

Perhaps the most obvious measure of Shakespeare's penetration of Western culture is our quoting him—often unconsciously—to define ourselves and our situations. These quotations will remind us of the enduring quality of his characters' sayings:

"It was Greek to me."
"To be, or not to be: that is the question."
"What's in a name? that which we call a rose
By any other name would smell as sweet."

Shakespeare has left us an enduring legacy by his creation of a world peopled with memorable characters: both fallen and redeemed.

has been forever marred. "An abuse of language . . . brings about the Fall, and it is a fallen language that the now mortal pair take with them into exile."[17]

Edwards suggests that the literary artist also experiences the consequences of this linguistic fall. T. S. Eliot, one of the most significant poets of the twentieth century, expresses the painful efforts of the writer to give shape and power to story through language only to discover this result of the curse: words "slip, slide, perish."[18] Whereas before the Fall language was a vehicle of creative energy, humans now have to struggle to convey meaning. In spite of this linguistic curse, however, literary artists (perhaps better than any of us) have retained the creative gift of naming. In the Creation section of this chapter we saw the imaginative writer's ability to name the goodness of humanity as created in God's image. Here we are interested in the literary artist's ability to truthfully name the fallenness of humankind.

The Christian's highest calling is to know the truth. Ultimately, of course, that means knowing Christ, who characterized Himself thus: "I am the Truth" (John 14:6). Knowing Christ, however, also means knowing the persons He died to save. Although reading about grossly fallen individuals can be uncomfortable to Christians, understanding the Fall is, nevertheless, also a part of the truth of human nature. Truth is not always beautiful. If we are faithful to our call to know the truth, we cannot avoid the horrifying ugliness of the Fall. We read such literature, therefore, to help us understand the truth of sin's power. We are called to know God's truth—all of it, even the part that is ugly and fallen.

I will argue in this section, therefore, that Christians should read literature about the ugliness of the Fall for two basic reasons: (1) for the benefits to oneself and (2) for the benefits to one's neighbor. First, by naming fallen humanity truthfully in great art, writers may assist us in seeing sin in its naked ugliness and thereby help us to be repulsed by (rather than temptingly attracted to) fallen behavior.[19] Second, by naming fallen humanity truthfully, great artists may give us insights into specific fallen behaviors that may aid us in better understanding and bearing witness[20] to our fallen neighbors.

---

[17]Ibid.

[18]T. S. Eliot, "Four Quartets" in *T. S. Eliot: Collected Poems 1909–1962* (New York: Harcourt, 1963), 180.

[19]Even the Bible records the fallen behavior of humankind (e.g., David and Bathsheba, Cain and Abel, the wicked kings of Israel).

[20]We are not using the term *witnessing* narrowly to mean "evangelizing" only, but rather to include the admonition of the Great Commission of Jesus to "make disciples" and "to teach" His commands (Matthew 8:19–20).

First, I will discuss the self-benefits of reading great literature that warns us against the effects of the Fall. William Shakespeare, the greatest dramatist in the English language, provides a compelling example of naming the disastrous consequences of the Fall in his tragedy *Othello*. Shakespeare makes it clear in this play that the tragic ending of the marriage between Othello and Desdemona is based upon a lie of the serpent. Othello, a general in the Venetian army and a Moor, has won the love of the beautiful Desdemona and married her against the wishes of her powerful Christian father. Othello has promoted Cassio instead of Iago to the office of lieutenant. Jealous and angry that he did not receive the promotion, Iago contrives and acts on a vengeful scheme: He plants doubts in Othello's mind concerning the faithfulness of his wife. Throughout the early part of the drama, Shakespeare demonstrates the fallenness of language by having many of the characters call (or name) Iago "honest Iago." All the while, however, Iago's dishonest language ensnares both the husband and the wife, ultimately destroying the marriage. Shakespeare's use of irony allows the reader to participate in the ambiguity of language, caused by the lie of the serpent. The disparity between what Iago says and what he means powerfully portrays for the reader the deceitful use of language. The reader feels he has been forced out of the Garden of Eden, where the word was equated with reality, and has entered the fallen world where language "slips and slides" and causes death. Although lies do not always cause physical death, they do often cause psychological, social, and spiritual death.

> **"We are called to know God's truth—all of it, even the part that is ugly and fallen."**

Iago suggests to Othello that Desdemona is having an affair with Cassio. By having Desdemona's handkerchief (which had been given to her by her loving husband) planted in Cassio's room, Iago leads Othello to believe the lie about her infidelity. The scenes between Iago and Othello are frightening. This villain carefully suggests to Othello that his wife is unfaithful and then quickly retracts his statements just enough to make Othello think he is honestly trying to protect Othello from becoming jealous. Iago's calculated mixture of truth and lies spins a web of doubt that causes a mad jealousy in the unsuspecting husband, who ends his marriage by killing his wife and then himself because he believes Iago's lie. Like the serpent, Iago has contradicted the words of truth and destroyed a husband and wife. Shakespeare's portrayal of Iago's deceit leads the reader to be repulsed by a character who uses language to divide meaning from reality. Reading literature like Shakespeare's, which reveals the cruelty of this fallen character, helps Christians to identify the ugliness of the Fall and to shun evil deceptions. We are told by Paul to "resist the devil, and he will flee from you" (James 4:7). It is much easier to resist the temptation to use the lies of the serpent when we heed the voice of literary artists who reveal the vileness of fallen human nature.

Not only does the artistic naming of evil help Christians to be repulsed by evil as it occurs in others' character (for example, in Iago's), but it also helps Christians to identify the same fallen traits in themselves. Unfortunately, Christians are sometimes deluded into thinking that they are immune to evil. Artistic characterizations show the power and deceit of sin. Othello was a good man. He had been faithful on the job; he had commanded the Venetian army well; he was honest with the men under him; he was a law-abiding citizen; he was an excellent friend to Iago; he loved Desdemona dearly. Nevertheless, he allowed himself to be seized by sin and deceived into murdering his own dearly-loved wife. Thoughtful Christians, who allow themselves to be confronted by the artist's works, will pause in reading such a story and not only think *There but for the grace of God go I* but also realize *I, too, am capable of destructive evil.* An antidote to being beguiled by evil is to study—sensitively and reflectively—its deadly nature in fictional characters. Fallen Christians are no less sinful than fallen non-Christians. Great literature can help us know ourselves and perhaps better resist our fallen tendencies.

The second major reason why I think Christians should read literature about the Fall has to do with the benefits to our non-believing neighbors. Although reading literature does have intrinsic value for Christian readers themselves, Christians may also become better witnesses to God's truth and grace if such reading helps them to understand the fallen behavior of nonbelievers. Certainly Christians should not themselves participate in sin to understand the sinner better. But by reading about a fallen character, the Christian can gain insights that when shared may help the sinner consider seriously the merits of faith in Christ. I once taught a young woman who had been reared in a Christian home where she had been sheltered from the most hideous of fallen humanity. When she married a man who was called to an inner-city ministry, she was completely unprepared for the depths of fallenness she found on the streets. Reading novels that characterized the kinds of personalities she was to encounter might have helped to prepare this woman for ministry in the city.

> "An antidote to being beguiled by evil is to study—sensitively and reflectively—its deadly nature in fictional characters."

Part Two: The Importance of Reading Responsibly

Fully believing that reading literature results in these two benefits (to ourselves and to nonbelievers), I have asked students to read works of literature about fallen humans. Some students have objected, "Why should Christian students be forced to read great literature if it portrays the Fall through the language of corrupt characters?"

I have responded that to be great, literature must be true to the human condition. From a Christian perspective that includes at least two things: (1) human beings have enormous potential for good because they are made in the image of God and have been given "common grace"; but (2) humans also have potential for evil because of the Fall. Characters in great literature, therefore, will be complex. Even an evil person will manifest good qualities; and the best of persons may exhibit a tragic flaw. Literary artists must be true to both the image of God *and* the Fall in the characters they create.

> "Characters in great literature, therefore will be complex. Even an evil person will manifest good qualities."

Many of my students would prefer to read only about "good" characters. However, if we are to understand the truth about the human condition, is it not necessary for us to read also about the truly fallen—the wife abuser, the serial killer, the fraud who cons senior citizens out of their meager savings? In creating characters of this kind, the writer must be true to the personalities of those characters. A drug addict who has lived for many years on the streets will not talk like a Sunday school teacher who has devoted his life to making Bible stories come alive. The writer would engage in a certain dishonesty if he portrayed such a character otherwise. Would the writer not also be participating in the lie of the serpent?

Although my students are often helped by this response, many of them are still troubled by reading literature containing such frank depictions of fallen behavior. Their resistance might be summarized in the following question: "Might not the potential benefits of reading such 'sinful' literature be outweighed by the probable harm caused to the readers' faith?" Most simply put, the answer is "Yes." I believe the solution to this dilemma, however, lies in responsible reading. In the second part of this section I will attempt to address this valid concern by answering these related questions: What should responsible Christians read? How should responsible Christians read? When is it more responsible not to read?

What Responsible Christians Should Read

First, let us think about our responsibility for what we read. The Christian worldview demands that we be good stewards of our time; therefore, we should read only great art. Poorly-written fiction is not worth our time. Dorothy Sayers, a novelist who eloquently defended the Christian faith, distinguished between great art and "mere entertainment." A definition of great art, however, is not easy. Imaginative writers and critics through the centuries have struggled to explain great art. I do not intend to survey all these ideas in this chapter, but a few comparisons between great art and mere entertainment will help us to distinguish what kind of literature is worth the Christian's time and effort.

Great art helps us recognize the eternal in the temporal. When we read *Othello*, we feel Shakespeare is writing about something far larger than the story of this one man and his wife. He is reaching through the story to a larger reality, a reality that includes all love relationships, all jealousies, all betrayals. We sense Shakespeare is reaching into the eternal where someday all betrayals and jealousies will be removed and the great mar-

Dorothy Sayers

In his biography of Dorothy L. Sayers (1893–1957), David Coomes refers to this remarkable woman as "an apologist for the Christian faith in closely argued books like *The Mind of the Maker*, epic-proportioned plays like *The Zeal of Thy House*," and as "the imaginative translator of Dante's *The Divine Comedy*. . . . She was kind, generous, enthusiastic, robust, opinionated, self-deprecating, contradictory. . . . Christianity, it is fair to say, dominated most of Sayers' life" (7). She wrote several detective novels, of which Lord Peter Whimsey is the hero. She wrote a BBC radio series on the life of Christ named *The Man Born to Be King*. The series was extremely popular and effective since it puts the Lord's life in a realistic human setting.

In *Creed or Chaos*, a collection of essays, Sayers comments on the language of plays about Jesus, "We do him singularly little honour by watering down His personality till it could not offend a fly. Surely it is not the business of the Church to adapt

Christ to men, but adapt men to Christ" (24). In *The Mind of the Maker*, a theological essay, she accuses her fellow Englishmen of having made no progress since the Middle Ages in their ability to describe the Christian faith. As Sayers observes, "Words are understood in a wholly mistaken sense, statements of fact and opinion are misread and distorted in repetition, arguments founded in misapprehension are accepted without examination" (xi). The consequence of this sloppiness is that the ordinary mind is swamped with an illogical and unlikely mishmash of mythology parading as Christian truth. Sayers proposed in a pamphlet entitled "The Lost Tools of Learning" an educational remedy for this linguistic tragedy: "[V]erse and prose can be learned by heart, and the pupil's memory should be stored with stories of every kind—classical, myth, English legend, and so forth" (18). She counsels Christians to engage children and youth in rigorous education, which necessarily includes the responsible reading of significant literature.

riage relationship between Christ and His bride will last for eternity.

Dorothy Sayers presents us with a difficult but important concept about great art: that it transforms the abstract into the concrete. She further believes that Christianity contains a divine model for this concept.[21] For example, it is difficult for us to know God because He is spirit; in a sense, He is abstract. God decided we need to see Him concretely, to touch Him, to hear Him talk. So He sent Jesus into the world in a material body. Reflecting on this fact, the writer to the Hebrews called Jesus the "express image"[22] of the Father (Heb. 1:3, KJV). In modern language we might say Jesus was the photocopy of the Father. By looking at Jesus, we now know God is kind, loving, and forgiving; He also is appalled by sin. God, therefore, revealed His nature to us by His express image ("exact representation," NIV), Jesus. Similarly, in great art if a poet wants to explain to us an abstract human experience, like "love," he also uses concrete images. Robert Burns, for example, wanting to explain his love for a woman, writes, "My love is like a red, red rose." By saying his love is like a rose, this great artist has given his love a material body. The rose image is helpful because it immediately explains the softness, the fragrance, the beauty (yes, the thorniness!) of love in a way that the abstract word "love" cannot. As a subcreator, therefore, the true literary artist reveals Truth to us through images. The artist's activity, of course, is not God's creation-out-of-nothing because "the human artist is in the universe and bound by its conditions. He can create only within that framework and out of that material which the universe supplies."[23] Nevertheless, just as God incarnated the truth about Himself through His express image, or exact representation, Jesus, so in great literature the artist incarnates in words his experience, giving it a material body.

> **"In great literature the artist incarnates in words his experience, giving it a material body."**

As a further way of defining what great art is, Sayers explains how this incarnation of the artist's experience can help us as we read great literature: "In the image of *his* experience, we can *recognize* the image of some experience of our own—something that had happened to us, but which we had never understood, never formulated, or expressed to ourselves, and therefore never known as a real experience."[24] For example, which one of us,

---

[21]Dorothy L. Sayers, "Toward a Christian Aesthetic," in *Christian Letters to a Post-Christian World: A Selection of Essays* (Grand Rapids: William B. Eerdmans Publishing Co., 1969), 77.

[22]In the original language this expression often referred to the impress or etching on a coin.

[23]Ibid., 77–78.

[24]Ibid., 80.

experiencing the artistry in *Beauty and the Beast,* has not had that moment of recognition that we too have some beastliness within us that needs to be transformed by someone's loving kiss? Sayers says this recognition of experience that occurs when we read true art "is as though a light were turned on inside us":

> Now that the artist has . . . imaged it forth . . . for me, I can possess and take hold of it and make it my own, and turn it into a source of knowledge and strength. . . . This recognition of the truth that we get in the artist's work comes to us as a revelation of new truth. . . . [This work of literature] puts a new knowledge of ourselves within our grasp. It is new, startling, and perhaps shattering.[25]

These startling, shattering revelations are important to Christians who desire to understand themselves and God's world. And this important recognition of reality occurs only when we read *true* art. Samuel Coleridge, a nineteenth-century poet, calls the incarnational revelation that occurs in great art the "translucence of the eternal through and in the temporal."[26] The great writer has made an eternal idea understandable through a temporal image. A Christian worldview demands that we not go through life just allowing events to happen to us. Rather we must "think about such things" (Phil. 4:8), deeply experiencing and understanding God, ourselves, other human beings—God's entire created world. In Coleridge's terms, through great art we are seeing the eternal in and through the temporal image—certainly a necessary activity for the Christian.

Although great art is what the Christian should read, Sayers points out that the typical reader often does not read this "creative and Christian kind of art." Typically, most readers (perhaps even most Christian readers) do not want "to be upset by sudden revelations about [themselves]. . . . [They] want entertainment."[27] I agree with Sayers that mere entertainment is what Christians *should not* read.

What is wrong with a diet of mere entertainment? Pseudo-art gives us "the enjoyment of the emotions which usually accompany experience without having had the experience."[28] Mere entertainment stories are like soap operas, providing us with some of the blood-and-gore emotions of the murders at the end of *Othello* without our having experienced the agonizing destruction of jealousy that Shakespeare's play demands of us. The pseudo-art thrillers prevalent in our culture fail to develop significant character within us because the focus is wholly on

---

[25]Ibid.

[26]Samuel Taylor Coleridge, "The Statesman's Manual," in *The Norton Anthology of English Literature,* 6th ed., vol. 2, ed. M. H. Abrams et al. (New York: Norton, 1993), 399.

[27]Sayers, *Christian Letters,* 81.

[28]Ibid.

the action rather than on the building of character. For example, if *Beauty and the Beast* had been produced as pseudo-art, Beauty would have the glorious experience of the kiss that transforms the Beast into the Prince without having gone through the grueling—but character-developing—experience of having loved and responded again and again to the beast in his ugliness.

Sayers eloquently explains why "mere entertainment" should be avoided by the Christian:

> It does not reveal us to ourselves: it merely projects on to a mental screen a picture of ourselves as we already fancy ourselves to be—only bigger and brighter. The manufacturer of this kind of entertainment is not by any means interpreting and revealing his own experience to himself and us—he is either indulging in his own day-dreams, or—still more falsely and venially—he is saying "What is it the audience think they would like to have experienced? Let us show them that, so that they can wallow in emotion by pretending to have experienced it." This kind of pseudo art is "wish-fulfillment" or "escape" literature in the worst sense—it is an escape . . . from reality and experience into a world of merely external events. . . . For occasional relaxation this is all right; but it can be carried to the point where, not merely art, but the whole universe of phenomena becomes a screen on which we see the magnified projection of our unreal selves, as the object of equally unreal emotions. This brings about the complete corruption of the consciousness, which can no longer recognize reality in experience. When things come to this pass, we have a civilization which "lives for amusement"—a civilization without guts, without experience, and out of touch with reality.[29]

Life is too short to read even the great literature. We do well to avoid mere entertainment, which may cause us to lose touch with the repugnant nature of evil and thus contribute to the deterioration of the moral conscience, which is the foundation of our civilization. Therefore, Christians should avoid mere entertainment and read great art.

How Responsible Christians Should Read

If Christians should read great art—which includes fallen characters—then *how* should Christians read about these immoral people? The Christian reader bears a responsibility to focus on the eternal truth (as it is presented in and through the fallen, temporal characters), rather than to focus on the fallen actions of the characters themselves. We may read, for example, with the intent of understanding the horror of using another person as a physical object, of the unfairness of taking from another human being what does not belong to him unless he is willing to make a lifelong commitment. Or we may read and wallow in the descriptions of the immoral actions themselves. A writer of mere entertainment emphasizes the sinful actions of the fallen, often with little concern about character growth or

---

[29]Ibid., p. 81–82.

the consequences of sin. A great artist, on the other hand, focuses on the character of the fallen. Christian readers, if they do not pay attention to the alternatives, may wrongly focus on the act rather than the character, even when reading great art. To focus only on the act is to take sin too lightly and to condone rather than grieve over the tragedy of what that sin is doing to the soul of the character. But our Christian worldview demands that we read responsibly, looking for the "eternal truth" in the character of the fallen individual. Christians, therefore, must responsibly choose *what* they read (limiting themselves to great art) and *how* they read (focusing on the eternal truths behind the sinful acts, not on the acts themselves).

When It Is More Responsible Not to Read

One final question needs to be addressed concerning the reading of literature which describes fallen characters: Should some Christians completely avoid reading certain great works of literature if these works contain depictions of fallen human beings? The biblical answer appears to be, "Yes." *When*, then, is it more responsible for a Christian not to read such works of literature? Paul says that Christians should not subject themselves to activities that condemn them: "Blessed are those who have no reason to condemn themselves because of what they approve. But those who have doubts are condemned if they eat [meat offered to idols], because they do not act from faith; for whatever does not proceed from faith is sin" (Rom. 14:22–23, NRSV). We must know ourselves and avoid even some pieces of great literature that may be destructive to us. This is not because there is anything intrinsically evil about good art. Quite to the contrary. I have spent this entire chapter detailing the benefits that can come from great art. But (as with the meat offered to idols in Paul's writing) persons should not read a piece of literature if doing so would cause *them* to stumble. Even those who, in Paul's words, are not condemned but feel called to understand the fallen world must be careful what and how they read. Flannery O'Connor, a twentieth-century Christian writer, gives a caution in a slightly different context that may be helpful to us here. In counseling how to build up faith she suggests that "for every book you read that is anti-Christian, make it your business to read one that presents the other side of the picture."[30] I, of course, am not speaking of books that are "anti-Christian" but rather of characters that are evil. But O'Connor's wariness is an important word of caution to all of us to know ourselves and to

> "We must know ourselves and avoid even some pieces of great literature that may be destructive to us."

---

[30]Flannery O'Connor, "Letters," in *Flannery O'Connor: Collected Works* (New York: Library of America, 1988), 1165.

be vigilant about what, how, and when we read. Why? So that we may responsibly read great literature about the Fall in order to reap powerful benefits for ourselves and our nonbelieving neighbors.

Redemption

IMPORTANCE OF LITERARY DEPICTIONS OF REDEMPTION

I have suggested that the major contribution of the doctrine of Creation to our theory of literature is to remind fallen readers that they are created in God's image. Conversely, I have argued that the doctrine of the Fall as it is represented in literature reminds those of us who act as though we have perfected God's image in us that we are indeed fallen. Another way of describing the function of the Fall in literature is to say that it is a vehicle of the Spirit to help convict us of our fallen sinfulness and remind us that we are in need of redemption. An additional reason why Christians should read great literature, therefore, is that art strongly portrays both our need for, and the powerful possibilities of, redemptive transformation. In Michael Edwards's words, "If the biblical reading of life is in any way true, literature will be drawn strongly towards it. Eden, Fall, Transformation, in whatever guise, will emerge in literature as everywhere else."[31]

This archetypal "Transformation," or what we more commonly refer to as the doctrine of Redemption or Salvation, is probably the most familiar to us as Christian readers. Let us not forget, however, that the central redemptive figure in this salvation story was an "abstract," divine Spirit who has been made concrete in the Word. Furthermore, this Jesus realized what it has taken human psychology almost two thousand years to discover: that words, used as concrete images in stories, are a powerful means of helping men and women change behavior. Paul Watzlawick has summarized the work of the noted psychologist Milton H. Erickson and other psychologists who attempt to determine ways to help patients transform their lives into better ones. They discovered the power of redemptive elements in the concrete images of stories. Erickson's work showed that lasting change in the behavior of his patients occurred most frequently when he appealed not to logic, but to metaphor, symbol, and image.[32] Could the energy of concrete images be one reason why Jesus came as the express image of God the Father? By imitating the Image, we become more like the Father. It is one thing to understand our fallenness; it is

> "'If the biblical reading of life is in any way true, literature will be drawn strongly towards it.'"
> —*Michael Edwards*

---

[31]Edwards, *Towards a Christian Poetics*, 12.

[32]Paul Watzlawick, *The Language of Change: Elements of Therapeutic Communication* (New York: Basic Books, 1978), 56–69.

another to know how to cooperate with the Holy Spirit to transform our behavior. This is a major reason why Jesus told stories. He knew, for instance, the power of the image of a father running with open arms toward a prodigal son. This image conveys the unconditional, redemptive love of God much more forcefully than a propositional statement like "God loves us even when we go astray." Many of us have been transformed deep in the recesses of our being by the image of the father putting a new robe on a son previously clothed in foul-smelling rags. And who among us can read of that great feast of the fatted calf and want to return to the pigpen and eat cornhusks? And as we read the images of that feast provided by the earthly father, a deep longing arises in us for an even greater Feast, the marriage supper of the Lamb, when our redemption will be complete. In the New Jerusalem we shall eat heavenly food and drink nectar from the trees of life growing along the river that flows from the throne of our heavenly Bridegroom. The redemptive ways that Jesus uses words in this parable reach through the temporal to the eternal, transforming us through their images that help us experience the embrace of God's grace. This is what Madeleine L'Engle meant in the passage we have chosen as an epigraph for our chapter: "Jesus was not a theologian. He was God who told stories."

> **"In order to become the 'God who told stories,' the true and divine Word became flesh."**

For the purposes of this chapter, therefore, I might summarize the doctrine of Redemption in the following way. In order to become the "God who told stories," the true and divine Word became flesh; He used our language and was tempted, as we are, to speak the lie of the Serpent. Jesus, the divine Word, however, lived a perfect life using language only for good, always attempting to restore His followers to their original God-given image through His words. Ultimately, the Word redeemed us through His grueling self-sacrifice on the cross and His glorious resurrection. He made it possible for us "to put on the new self, created to be like God in true righteousness and holiness" (Eph. 4:24).

Throughout this chapter I have drawn parallels between the actions of the Godhead and the literary artist. I am not suggesting, of course, that the literary artist has the same power of redemption (or salvation) as Christ, *the* Word. However, I am convinced that as a creature—created in the divine image of the Word and empowered by the Word as a namer—the literary artist may become a powerful instrument of divine redemption. The great literary artist embodies Truth in his words and may help to bring about a gloriously redemptive transformation of the reader through a composing process that, in many cases, involves long, grueling hours of self-sacrificial attention to his literary words.

One of the reasons that literary depictions of redemption are so important to Christians is that when literary artists do give such self-sacrificial attention to redemptive themes, they help to give us hope that our fallenness can be redeemed. Many literary artists, for example, have given their attention to the story of St. George and the Dragon: authors of fairy tales, children's stories, and epics (like Edmund Spenser's), as well as illustrators and visual artists the world over. The redemptive elements are

> **"We seem born knowing dragons exist. Even children sense and fear the evil in the world symbolized by the dragon."**

strong in this story. Surely this repetition of the St. George story helps to satisfy our deep need to hear over and over again that the "dragon" in us can be slain, and we can be redeemed. It seems we are born knowing the dragon exists. Even small children sense and fear the evil in the world symbolized by the dragon. Psychologists have suggested that literature which portrays the defeat of evil by someone good is necessary for the mental health of children. Children know the dragon exists, but if they do not read the fairy tales, they might not easily learn that there is a St. George who can kill the dragon.[33]

Here again the great literary artists show us the eternal through the temporal. St. George is often a symbol of Christ, the Deliverer who will come riding on a white horse. Out of His mouth will come a sharp sword, to forever defeat the Dragon, Satan, who will be cast into the lake of burning sulfur.[34] The story of St. George and the Dragon clearly reflects the Christian doctrine of redemption. Indeed, St. George and the Dragon—and many other stories—speak to our need to read literature which assures us that the evil in us and in the world can be defeated. Repetition of the hope of redemption needs to sink deeply into the fabric of our lives. Why is it important for Christians to read great redemptive literature? Reading such literature, whether the redemption story is overt or not (and often it is not), has compelling value because this literature reiterates that the Fall is not the final word for human beings. These stories proclaim the good news that we have glorious possibilities for transformation.

The story told in the novel and in the film *Schindler's List* also illustrates well these redemptive elements. The story is full of cruelties that people perpetrate on one another. But within this tragedy of torture, sexual abuse, and mass executions comes the gradual transformation of one man's heart that results in the preservation of 1,200 Jews.[35] Schindler himself was no saint. He

[33]See Bruno Bettelheim, *The Uses of Enchantment: The Meaning and Importance of Fairy Tales* (New York: Knopf, 1977), 122–123.

[34]See Revelation 19:11,15 and 20:10.

[35]Thomas Keneally, *Schindler's List* (New York: Simon & Schuster, 1982), 394.

was a greedy, womanizing, self-serving opportunist. Yet he also had God-given possibilities for goodness that gradually caused him to regard life as precious and dignified. In a Christian worldview, actions that recognize the dignity of life come from God and are made possible by his "common grace," no matter how flawed the person. Not uncommonly, redemption comes in strange ways and under the pall of wickedness: Jesus hanging on a cross beneath a cloud obliterating the sun is a central image of our Christian worldview. Human beings, both Christians and unbelievers, need to read great literature for its constant repetition of these redemptive elements, which can shine through the Fall in us, at least partially redeeming the image of God in us.

We have just looked at some pieces of literature that contain some clear redemptive elements. But why should the Christian read great works of literature that do not seem to have any overt redemptive qualities? For example, why should the Christian read a tragedy that seems to end in destruction rather than redemption? Or why should the believer read a comedy that doesn't seem to take anything seriously, especially such a serious subject as the doctrine of Redemption? I will address these questions and close this section by returning to Shakespeare. Shakespeare's tragedy *Romeo and Juliet* and his comedy *A Midsummer Night's Dream*, will help us to explain how the Christian can find redemption even in the most unlikely places and, once again, why great literature is so vitally important to the Christian.

Although it may not be obvious at first, the push toward redemption is strong even in stories of tragedy. Family feuds, such as the one Shakespeare portrays in *Romeo and Juliet*, are quite common. Shakespeare eloquently portrays the hatred caused by the Fall. But his play also features a strong drive toward redemption:

> Hatred is a condition of our corrupted wills, of our fall from grace, and it attempts to destroy what is gracious in human beings. In this cosmic strife, love must pay the sacrifice, as Romeo and Juliet do with their lives, but because their deaths are finally perceived as the cost of so much hatred, the two families come to terms with their collective guilt and resolve henceforth to be worthy of the sacrifice.[36]

Not unlike the "tragedy" of the Gospel drama, the potential for redemption in this Shakespearean play arises out of sacrificial death.

For many years the Capulets, the family of Juliet, have been the bitterest enemies of the Montagues, the family of Romeo. Ironically, a Capulet and a Montague fall in love without realizing their family connections. When Juliet Capulet learns Romeo is a Montague, the fall and the powerful love of redemption unite in her cry:

---

[36]David Bevington, "Introduction to Romeo and Juliet," in *The Complete Works of Shakespeare*, 3d ed., ed. David Bevington (New York: Harper, 1980), 993.

> My only love sprung from my only hate!
> Too early seen unknown, and known too late!
> Prodigious birth of love it is to me,
> That I must love a loathed enemy.[37]

In spite of their families' mutual hatred, two innocent young people experience love that will ultimately redeem both families. When, unknown to their families, Romeo and Juliet beg Friar Laurence to marry them, he consents, expressing hope that this marriage may ultimately be redemptive:

> I'll thy assistant be;
> For this alliance may so happy prove,
> To turn your household's rancor to pure love.[38]

But the holy union does not immediately heal the wounds of hatred.

Before redemptive healing can take place, a catastrophe occurs. Juliet's earlier fear, "My grave is like to be my wedding bed,"[39] does indeed come true. In a street brawl between the Montagues and Capulets, Romeo kills one of Juliet's relatives and is banished from his homeland. Friar Laurence devises a plan to bring the young lovers together again by giving Juliet a potion that will make her appear dead, but in reality she will be in a deep sleep. A message is sent to Romeo to come and find the sleeping Juliet in the family tomb, but Romeo never receives the explanation. He later steals into the tomb, thinks Juliet is indeed dead, and kills himself. When Juliet awakens and sees her beloved Romeo dead at her side, she also ends her life. Family hatred has brought tragic results for these two young lovers. But just as redemptive hope arises out of death in the Christian story, so, too, love and reconciliation arise out of death at the end of Shakespeare's story. Both families stand over the dead bodies of the young lovers as the Prince berates them:

> Capulet! Montague!
> See what a scourge is laid upon your hate,
> That heaven finds means to kill your joys with love.[40]

The two families shake hands in redeemed friendship over the sacrificed bodies of their children. Reconciliation has been costly but effective. A symbol of the redemptive union of these two families had occurred during the one night Romeo and Juliet had together before he fled from his home city. There should have been many more nights of love for this idealistic young couple, but their lives have been sacrificed. Out of their deaths, however, come redemptive love and reconciliation. A Christian

---

[37]William Shakespeare, "Romeo and Juliet," in *The Complete Works of Shakespeare*, ed. Hardin Craig (Chicago: Scott, Foresman, 1961), 1.5.140–43.

[38]Ibid., 2.3.90–93.

[39]Ibid., 1.5.137.

[40]Ibid., 5.3.291.93.

reader finds great artists communicating such redemptive truths through the most tragic of stories.

Stories of comedy also often proclaim deep redemptive truths, frequently through the character of the Fool or the Clown. The Clown causes us to laugh at the character flaws he displays, and thereby we see the foolishness of our own fallen condition. But he also helps us to realize our redemptive possibilities:

> The Fool or Clown sets up a total dynamic, from our degradation to our possibility of redemption. It is surely in part the fact that he descends, comically, into our fears about ourselves and the world and, comically, lifts us, that draws us to him so powerfully. In [Charlie] Chaplin's dress, the baggy trousers, overtight jacket and oversize boots are countered by bowler, bow tie, walking stick and mustache. The tramp is also a dandy. A circus clown almost fails to climb the steps up to it, then walks across a rope with a show of panic clumsiness that belies a thrilling virtuosity. Suddenly terrified, Harlequin turns a backward somersault, without spilling a drop from the wineglass.[41]

The clown simultaneously reveals our crippled condition and holds out hope for our potential to be restored to our original virtuoso image and abilities.

Through the clownish character of Bottom, in *Midsummer Night's Dream*, Shakespeare projects for us on stage the foolish, bumbling nature of our fallen condition but also the desire to be loved back into our original condition. Oberon, King of the fairies, desires to punish his wife, Titania. Oberon asks the conniving Puck (a fairy who loves to play tricks on others) to put on Titania's eyes a love potion that will cause her to fall in love with the first creature she sees when she awakens. Meanwhile, Puck finds Bottom, a comical weaver, and fastens on him a donkey's head. Shakespeare intends for us to see the humor of our fallen condition in Bottom.[42] His scapegoat role is evident from Bottom's words when his friend Snout first sees him and is astounded at Bottom's transformation into a donkey:

> Snout: O Bottom, thou art changed! what do I see on Thee?
>
> Bottom: What do you see? you see an ass-head *of your own*, do you?[43]

Bottom, unaware of his changed condition, frightens all his friends off the stage. Readers of this play recognize in Bottom's donkey-like buffoonery their own bumbling, fallen nature. I do not mean that sin is funny or lighthearted. But Bottom's silliness can make us realize how far we have strayed from God's noble image in us. By laughing at Bottom, we can image forth our fears about our own fallenness and raise our hopes of transformation.

---

[41]Edwards, *Towards a Christian Poetics*, 54.

[42]Ibid., 53.

[43]William Shakespeare, "Midsummer Night's Dream," in *The Complete Works of Shakespeare*, ed. Hardin Craig (Chicago: Scott, Foresman, 1961), 3.1.117–18, italics mine.

When Titania awakens, sees Bottom, and immediately expresses love for him, her words bring hope of transformation from his donkey condition. "I will purge thy mortal grossness," she tells Bottom, "so / That thou shalt like an airy spirit go."[44] The reader also longs to escape his "mortal grossness," caused by the serpent's lie, and fly to that heavenly garden of restored beauty and innocence. Later, when the donkey's head has been removed, Bottom awakens from what he believes was a dream:

> I have had a most rare vision. I have had a dream, past the wit of man to say what dream it was: man is but an ass, if he go about to expound this dream. Methought I was—there is no man can tell what. Methought I was —and methought I had,—but man is but a patched fool, if he will offer to say what methought I had. The eye of man hath not heard, the ear of man hath not seen, man's hand is not able to taste, his tongue to conceive, nor his heart to report, what my dream was.[45]

We laugh at Bottom's disfigurement, his clouded sensibilities, and the confusion in his language. But we are also relieved to see his animal head transformed into a human one again. If Bottom has recovered the image of a human being, perhaps there is hope that his confused language and sensibilities will also be redeemed. Shakespeare has given us a hilarious story that images forth the Fall but also gives hope for transfiguration. The story brings us hope that our fallenness, too, can be redeemed, that our ugliness can be transformed into beauty, that our fallen language will experience a "new tongue," that our donkey-like nature can once again be transformed into God's image.

Christians, then, should read great comedies because humor and laughter have the potential to describe (and perhaps even effect) miraculous, redemptive transformations. Michael Edwards believes that comedy leads to or "opens to miracle. . . . Laughter is one of the means by which we seem to . . . [move beyond this world]. Laughter is the perception of possibility."[46] Edwards suggests that the Abraham and Sarah story is an example of laughter that "opens to miracle." That a hundred-year-old man and a ninety-year-old woman could give birth to a child certainly approaches the realm of comedy. When God tells Abraham that the barren Sarah will be the "mother of nations," Abraham falls on his face and laughs at the ridiculousness of the suggestion. God turns Abraham's laughter into redemptive possibility by looking ahead to the naming of their son: "You will call him Isaac [which means laughter]!" (Genesis 17:19). God here uses the language of "naming" and transforms the ridiculous into the real. Later, when Sarah hears the LORD prophesy to Abraham, "About this time next year, . . . Sarah

---

[44]Ibid., 3.1.153–64.

[45]Ibid., 4.1.208–117.

[46]Edwards, *Towards a Christian Poetics*, 69.

your wife will have a son" (Gen. 18:10), Sarah also laughs at the ridiculousness of birth from her decaying body. But Sarah's scornful laugh is transformed into the miracle of her joyous laughter on the day of Isaac's birth. On that day Sarah said, "God has brought me laughter." And Sarah realizes that her joyous laughter will be multiplied and extended into the future as she predicts the laughter of all of us as we perceive the miracle of her aged body giving birth. Sarah declares, "Everyone who hears about this will laugh with me" (Gen. 21:6). Sarah was right. The reader laughs because such stories of comedy open us to the miracle of rebirth, renewal, redemption. This comedy in particular brings even greater joyous laughter when the reader realizes that the laughing Sarah was not only the mother of Isaac ("Laughter" himself), but also thereby the "mother" of Christ (Redemption himself).

Why, therefore, should a Christian worldview demand reading great redemptive literature—even literature like tragedy and comedy in which redemption is not overt? A tragedy is frequently diagrammed as a falling line. The fortunes of the protagonist begin high but fall towards a final death because of a flaw in the main character. Othello is at the top of the Venetian army and has married his beloved, but because of his jealousy, at the end of the play he and his wife lie dead on stage. A comedy, on the other hand, is commonly diagrammed as an ascending line. The fortunes of the protagonist begin low, but rise dramatically, often ending with a wedding. Sometimes the rise is helped by the intervention of another character. Cinderella is in rags, cannot go to the celebration, but the fairy godmother intervenes and transforms her into a lovely belle who at the end of the story marries the Prince. The Christian story is both a tragedy and a comedy. Human beings began as high as possible—breathed into existence by the Breath and Word of God into an idyllic Garden, as we saw in our study of the doctrine of Creation. But as we noted in our discussion of the Fall, the diagram of the human story falls sharply because of the lie of the serpent. The whole human race was headed for death, but there is a dramatic V-shaped turn[47] as our story is transformed into a comedy by the catastrophic death of Jesus Christ. J. R. R. Tolkien, the famous Christian fantasy writer, defines this event as a eucatastrophe ("good catastrophe"), the death and resurrection of the Word made flesh.[48] On the cross, Jesus dramatically changed the tragic human story into a comedy that will end—as comedies traditionally do—in a joyous wedding between Christ and His followers. The same

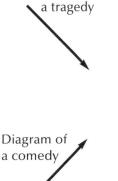

Diagram of a tragedy

Diagram of a comedy

Diagram of the Christian Story

---

[47]Northrop Frye, *The Great Code: The Bible and Literature* (New York: Harcourt, 1982), 169.

[48]Tolkien, "On Fairy-Stories," 68.

voice that spoke at Creation and came as the Word will speak again. John says, "I heard a loud voice from the throne saying… 'I am making everything new!'" (Revelation 21:5). The biblical story begins in a garden with a tree of life and ends in a city with many trees of life. In the middle is a tragic fall that is mirrored in our stories of tragedy. But in these same stories are strong redemptive (or comedic) elements. Both tragic and comic stories, therefore, reflect the larger reality of Eden, the Fall, and Redemption. Redemptive elements in great literature direct us toward that final Redemption, which will end in a joyous wedding when our salvation and the divine comedy will be complete. In the meantime, the renewing of the redemptive process continues in us through the renewing and empowering language of Pentecost, the final doctrine I wish to discuss in this chapter.

Pentecost

IMPORTANCE OF LITERATURE THAT EMPLOYS IMAGES OF PENTECOST

As I conclude this chapter, I would like to glance at one final doctrine of the Church: Pentecost. This is a vital doctrine for our purposes in this chapter because this biblical story focuses heavily upon language and is, therefore, crucial to completing our discussion of a Christian approach to reading literature. Michael Edwards asserts, "On this occasion [at Pentecost] . . . language is foregrounded as never before. For if the Spirit comes at Pentecost as a beginning and a pledge of the future transformation of the world, his sign is the miraculous transformation, very pointedly, of the apostles' speech."[49] Pentecost, a scene that contrasts sharply with the scene at Babel, depicts a "renewing of language, and beyond." Writers participate in this renewing of language and beyond "in acts of renaming."[50]

In the Book of Acts the apostles (and by extension the entire Church) are given the Pentecostal commission to go into all the world and renew it by teaching the Word. Along with this commission, Jesus promised to send the Holy Spirit to empower us to complete our goal: "You will receive power when the Holy Spirit comes on you: and you will be my witnesses in Jerusalem, and in all Judea and Samaria, and to the ends of the earth" (Acts 1:8). Not long after this, on the Day of Pentecost, God fulfilled His promise by descending in the person of the Holy Spirit upon the apostles like tongues of fire: "Suddenly a sound like the blowing of a violent wind came from heaven and filled the whole house where they were sitting. They saw what seemed to be tongues of fire that separated and came to rest on each of

---

[49]Edwards, *Towards a Christian Poetics*, 12.

[50]Ibid., 65.

them. All of them were filled with the Holy Spirit and began to speak in other tongues as the Spirit enabled them" (Acts 2:2–4). On that day the Holy Spirit empowered the Church to rename—or translate into other tongues—the truth of the gospel of Christ. On the day of Pentecost the name of Jesus Christ was literally "renamed" in the languages of the "Parthians, Medes and Elamites; residents of Mesopotamia, Judea and Cappadocia, Pontus and Asia, Phrygia and Pamphylia, Egypt and the parts of Libya near Cyrene; . . . Rome; Cretans and Arabs" (Acts 2:9–11).

This divine gift of renaming is directly parallel to the divine gift of naming given to Adam. At creation God identified humankind by naming them in his image. But capitulation to the lie of the serpent led Adam and Eve to try to hide their fallenness. The identity given them by God became confused. Redemption began the restoration of the image of God in humankind; Pentecost provides the energy for carrying the redemptive message. I believe that literary artists are among those who have been commissioned and spiritually empowered to renew and rename their readers through the fiery use of literary language that explicitly or implicitly teaches the gospel of Creation, the Fall, and Redemption. I also believe that the concrete images through which the Scripture communicates the story of Pentecost deserve special attention: "the blowing of a violent wind" and "tongues of fire." First, I will briefly discuss the significance of this Pentecostal imagery. Finally, we will examine the question of why Christians should read such great literature by considering one of the many texts in which literary artists use these images of Pentecost to create powerful stories that help to rename and renew us.

Both the Hebrew and Greek word for "wind" can also be translated "breath" or "spirit." Linguistically, therefore, this passage at Pentecost is allied to God's breathing into Adam the breath of life on the birthday of humankind. On the birthday of the Church here in Acts, God breathed a renewed language into His apostles and the rest of the 120 who must now proclaim the saving grace of Christ since He has ascended to the Father.

On the heads of those disciples waiting in the upper room rested a "tongue of fire." Fire imagery in Scripture frequently connotes the presence of God. Of the numerous images, two examples follow. Moses' call to be the deliverer of Israel out of Egyptian bondage comes from a burning bush. This story evokes awe in the reader as the voice from the fiery bush uses intensified language to express the nature of God who is calling and empowering Moses: "I AM THAT I AM." The words from the fire, which does not consume, convince Moses to lead a deliverance that has become the archetype of all deliverances from oppression in our world today. Before the burning bush experience, Moses had "named" himself "slow of speech and tongue" (Exodus 4:10), but God says "I will help you speak and will teach you what to say" (Exod. 4:12). After Moses' fiery experience he led slaves out of bondage to be renamed God's chosen people.

A second example of the image of fire as representing God's presence is portrayed in the fiery furnace experience of Shadrach, Meshach, and Abednego (Dan. 3). Northrop Frye believes the fire image, as an indication of the presence of God, is so prevalent in the Bible that it almost seems like God wants the believer to live in fire.[51] Certainly this story would support Frye's intuition. The fiery furnace, intended for the destruction of the three Hebrew children (and indeed it does consume those who throw them in), is easily endured by these faithful men. They walk in fire accompanied by a figure Nebuchadnezzar described as "like a son of the gods." These three Hebrews live in fire but, like the burning bush encountered by Moses, they are not consumed. Similarly, in the story of Pentecost, God's fiery presence touches language as His Spirit now comes to dwell in human bodies. And the wind, fire, and Word of God unite to indicate God's newest invasion into the story of humankind.

Definition of "Archetype"

According to Northrop Frye, an *archetype* is "a typical or recurring image . . . a symbol, which connects one poem with another and thereby helps to unify and integrate our literary experience" (*Anatomy of Criticism: Four Essays*. Princeton: Princeton University Press, 1957, p. 99). Leland Ryken defines an *archetype* as "an image, character type, or plot motif that recurs throughout literature (as well as throughout life). Archetypes are the building blocks of literature and the ingredients of our own lives" (*Words of Life: A Literary Introduction to the New Testament*. Grand Rapids: Baker Book House, 1987, p. 22). The journey archetype is an example. Characters going on a journey to find another country are portrayed in a wide variety of literature: Odysseus' journeying from Troy back home to Ithaca; Abraham's leaving his homeland in search of the promised land; the children of Israel's wandering around in the desert in search of a new country; Huckleberry Finn's traveling down the Mississippi, a journey into a mature understanding of his friendship with Jim, the African American whom his elders had mistreated; the Joad family's traveling from Oklahoma to California, searching for a better land to improve their economic conditions; Jesus' journey from heaven to earth and back to heaven again at his Ascension. Perhaps the journey archetype is prevalent in literature because it parallels our own journey from birth through life to death.

---

[51]Frye, *Great Code*, 162.

As we have seen throughout this chapter, the literary artist often uses, participates in, or becomes the instrument of the key forces of each of the major biblical doctrines we have studied. Such is the case for Pentecost as well. C. S. Lewis, one of the greatest Christian writers of the twentieth century, for example, effectively uses these images of Pentecost to renew and rename his readers in *The Magician's Nephew*, one of the *Narnia Chronicles*. In this story, the lion Aslan (a symbol of Christ) sings the world of Narnia into existence in a voice "so beautiful" that those who listen "could hardly bear it."[52] Lewis convincingly portrays Aslan's creative power through the language of music. Polly, one of the children in the story, begins to see "the connection between the music [of Aslan] and the things that are happening. When a line of dark fir trees spring up on a ridge about a hundred yards away she feels that they are connected with a series of deep, prolonged notes the Lion had sung a second before. And when he bursts into a rapid series of lighter notes she is not surprised to see primroses suddenly appearing in every direction."[53] Later the Lion's song changes again: "It was more like what we should call a tune, but it was also far wilder. It made you want to run and jump and climb. It made you want

Clive Staples "C.S." Lewis

C. S. Lewis (1898–1963) was an English author, noted for his exposition of Christian tenets. For many years of his life, he was an atheist. His journey toward Christianity began when he read George MacDonald's *Phantastes*, a fantasy novel which Lewis says "baptized his imagination." Through this personal experience Lewis came to understand the redemptive power of imaginative literature. Having struggled through to belief in God, Lewis became influential in explaining Christianity to intellectuals.

His *Mere Christianity* is consid-ered one of the most notable popular apologies for the Christian faith written in the twentieth century. Many of the theological ideas contained in *Mere Christianity*, Lewis also expressed fictionally in the seven novels that comprise *The Chronicles of Narnia*. Other important works include *The Allegory of Love* (1936), on medieval romantic love, and the ironic *Screwtape Letters* (1942). He also wrote outer-planet fantasies with moral overtones, e.g., *Out of the Silent Planet* (1938), and criticism.

For additional information on Lewis, see Appendix 7, "C. S. Lewis," on p 485.

---

[52]C. S. Lewis, *The Magician's Nephew* (New York: Collier, 1986), 99.

[53]Ibid., 107.

to shout."[54] Aslan's voice gradually transforms the dark, empty Nothingness into a fertile world where happy animals bray and neigh, bark and bleat with joyous life, joining their voices with Aslan's in happy song.

Lewis then unites the power of Aslan's voice at creation to the power of the renewing of language at Pentecost, combining the breath, fire, and wind images reminiscent of the outpouring of the Holy Spirit on the birthday of the church. At Pentecost the apostles' speech has a miraculous touch that seems to give them a power beyond themselves to proclaim the gospel. In a similar way, Aslan breathes on some of the animals of Narnia, giving them human speech:

> The Lion opened his mouth, but no sound came from it; he was *breathing* out a long, warm *breath*; it seemed to sway all the beasts as the *wind* sways a line of trees. . . . Then there came a swift flash like *fire (but it burnt nobody)* either from the sky or from the Lion itself . . . and the deepest, wildest voice they had ever heard was saying: "Narnia, Narnia, Narnia, awake. Love. Think. *Speak*. . . . Be *talking* beasts."[55]

The animal language of the Narnians is touched by the creative breath of Aslan, set afire by the wind of God's presence, which empowered but did not consume. The Narnian animals are given human language, a gift far beyond their animal nature. The reader also participates in Creation and Pentecost, helping to renew and remake his character. By responding to Aslan's fiery words, the reader, too, is encouraged to come more fully awake, to love, to think, to speak, to be.

After this linguistic commissioning of the animals, Aslan's creative Word literally remakes another character in the novel, Cabby (formerly a cab driver in London) into the new King of Narnia. After also calling Cabby's wife into the newly-created Narnia, Aslan speaks the fiery words that rename these two characters: "'My children,' said Aslan, fixing his eye on both of them, 'you are to be the first King and Queen of Narnia.'" Aslan's fiery tongue transforms this character from a cab driver to a king! Even Cabby's horse, Strawberry, receives a new name and becomes a new creature. After asking the shy Strawberry if he would like to be a winged horse, Aslan speaks with his tongue of fire: "'Be winged. Be the father of all flying horses,' roared Aslan in a voice that shook the ground. 'Your name is Fledge.'" The transformation in Strawberry as he is renamed is startling: "The horse shied. . . . And then . . . there burst out from the shoulders of Fledge wings that spread and grew, larger than eagles', larger than swans', larger than angels' wings in church windows. . . . He gave a great sweep with them and leaped into

---

[54]Ibid., 113.

[55] Ibid., 116. Italics mine.

the air."[56] Readers of this great piece of literature are led to believe that they too could be renamed, could lose some of the beastliness of the Fall and soar closer to that original image of God at Creation. The language of Aslan has been touched with renaming fire, causing Cabby and his wife to ascend the throne, and giving Strawberry the gift of language and wings to fly, helping him to transcend his beastliness.

Once again in light of a biblical doctrine, this time that of Pentecost, I ask the question Why should Christians read literature? Because God often seems to touch the language of the literary artist with His creative breath and tongue of fire. Often the artist is inspired (the etymology of "inspired" includes *breathing life into*) to write words beyond what is usually humanly possible. Often the storyteller is given a "fiery tongue" beyond his usual human language to shape characters that speak new life to the inner recesses of our beings. Literature can make us come more fully alive.

Conclusion

When the French poet St.-John Perse gave his acceptance of the Nobel Prize for literature, he spoke of the power of the poet: "The poet . . . hold[s] up before the spirit a mirror more sensitive to his spiritual possibilities . . . [and] evoke[s] . . . a vision of the human condition more worthy of man as he was created."[57] St.-John Perse was right. God has always placed a premium on the power of the Word. With His words, He spoke the worlds into existence. His Word had power to produce oak trees and hippopotamuses, and the sun and moon and stars. His prophets had the Word of the Lord burning in their bones as they proclaimed His punishment and His mercy. He sent His son, incarnate as the Word, to dwell among us. At Pentecost He showed us that He wanted to share that powerful Word with us when He came as a flaming tongue of fire and rested on the disciples. Someday He is coming again, and His name shall be called the Word of God (Rev. 19:13). Out of His mouth will come a sharp, two-edged sword, the symbol of His Word; and the sin of the Fall and the confusion of Babel shall be destroyed forever. In the meantime, He inspires ("in-breathes") literary artists to keep reminding us of the doctrines of Creation, the Fall, Redemption, and Pentecost. Why then should Christians read great literature? We read great literature about Creation to allow the Spirit to restore some of the image of God in us. We read artistic stories about the Fall to recognize and understand the nature of evil in an attempt to avoid temptation in our own lives and to bear witness to our fallen neighbors. We read great literature

---

[56]Ibid., 144–45.

[57]St.-John Perse, *Two Addresses* (New York: Bollingen Foundation, 1966), 14.

about Redemption to immerse ourselves in the good news that we have glorious possibilities for transformation. And we read stories with Pentecostal imagery to experience the renaming and renewing power of fiery language.

Christians, I conclude, have the happy privilege, indeed the responsibility, to read and encourage others to read great literature that participates in God's creativity, that tells the truth about the Fall, that helps us understand the good news of redemption, and that empowers us with Pentecost's fiery language of spiritual renewal and renaming. I chose to begin this chapter with the inspiring first verse of the Gospel of John: "In the beginning was the Word, and the Word was with God, and the Word was God." I close the chapter with a reference to John 1:14. For I imagine that had John cowritten it, he might have concluded in this manner: And the Word has become embodied in great literature and dwells among us; and we behold His glory, the glory as of the only begotten of the Father full of grace and truth about Creation, the Fall, Redemption, and Pentecost.[58]

Review and Discussion Questions

IMPORTANCE OF THE LITERARY ARTIST'S CREATIVITY

1. At creation God brought order out of chaos. Discuss how a well-known form like the fairy tale can help bring order into the life of a child. If you have had helpful experiences in your own life by reading fairy tales or other forms of literature, describe those experiences using concepts developed in the chapter.

2. How does the author use the word *naming*? Discuss the difference between "pigeonholing" and "naming" another person.

3. How does the "naming" by a literary artist help to restore some of the image of God in us? Describe any positive experiences you may have had of being "named" by reading an imaginative piece of literature.

IMPORTANCE OF LITERARY REPRESENTATIONS OF THE FALL

1. Why must the literary artist tell the truth about the Fall?

2. How can literature help us to understand better the nonbeliever?

3. What kind of literature should Christians read? Why? Discuss examples.

---

[58]This chapter is not about the nature of the Bible as literature. I believe it is the greatest literature ever written just as I believe it is the inspired Word of God. The Bible, of course, is written in literary forms like poetry, proverbs, apocalypse, etc. Since the 1970s there have been numerous books and essays analyzing the Bible as literature by literary and biblical scholars holding a broad range of theological positions. Readers wishing to explore this topic further are directed to begin with a work such as Leyland Ryken's *Literature of the Bible* (Grand Rapids: Zondervan Publishing House, 1974).

4. Dorothy Sayers describes some writings as "mere entertainment." Explain and illustrate what she means.

5. *How* should responsible Christians read? In other words, what criteria should they apply when they evaluate imaginative literature? Discuss a specific example of your reading a novel or short story in a responsible manner.

IMPORTANCE OF LITERARY DEPICTIONS OF REDEMPTION

1. Discuss how the use of literary images helps remind us of Redemption. For example, explain the function of the image of the father's welcoming back the prodigal son in Jesus' parable.

2. Explain how Shakespeare's tragedy *Romeo and Juliet* reminds us that Redemption often comes through sacrifice. Discuss any other examples of literary works which remind us that Redemption comes through sacrifice.

IMPORTANCE OF LITERATURE THAT EMPLOYS IMAGES OF PENTECOST

1. Explain how language was affected at Pentecost.

2. What are the predominant images accompanying the coming of the Holy Spirit on the Day of Pentecost (Acts 2:1–4)? Explain how C. S. Lewis uses these images in the creation of Narnia in *The Magician's Nephew.*

Extended Projects for Reflection

1. Read Flannery O'Connor's short story "Revelation." This story can be found in *Flannery O'Connor: The Complete Stories,* published by Farrar, Straus and Giroux, New York, 1971. Then answer the following questions:

   A. What does Mrs. Turpin think of herself in the first part of the story?

   B. What happens to Mrs. Turpin's understanding of herself after Mary Grace strikes her with the book in the doctor's office?

   C. What is the significance of Mary Grace's "naming" Mrs. Turpin a "wart hog"?

   D. When Mrs. Turpin has the vision of souls "rumbling toward heaven," why do you think she is "bringing up the end of the procession"?

   E. What is the significance of Mrs. Turpin's having her vision while standing on the side of the pigpen?

   F. Does Mrs. Turpin's vision of her own sinfulness give you hope for her redemption?

   G. Did the story help you to see some attitude of your own that needs Christ's forgiveness and healing? Name the attitude and discuss ways to be healed with a friend who will keep your confidence.

2. Discuss other literary works that use images associated with Pentecost: wind, fire, language.

A. For example, read *That Hideous Strength*, by C. S. Lewis. Notice the scene where Ransom and Merlin are conversing in an upper room and suddenly the window blows open, and a wind rushes into the room. Ransom finds himself "sitting within the very heart of language, in the white-hot furnace of essential speech. All fact was broken, splashed into cataracts, caught, . . . slain, and reborn as [true] meaning" (321–322). Could this magnificent description indicate what our language might be like if all the serpent's lies were removed from our tongues?

B. Read also *The Final Beast* by Frederick Buechner. Notice the many images of the Holy Spirit used in this book as the main character, a minister, prepares a sermon to preach on the Day of Pentecost.

Selected Bibliography

PRIMARY WORKS

Dante's *The Divine Comedy* (Ciardi's translation)
Spenser's *The Faerie Queen*
Shakespeare's *Macbeth*
Milton's *Paradise Lost*
Swift's *Gulliver's Travels*
Dickens' *David Copperfield*
Ibsen's *Hedda Gabler*
Shaw's *Saint Joan*
Flannery O'Connor's *Complete Short Stories*

SECONDARY WORKS

Chesterton, Gilbert K. "The Ethics of Elfland." *Orthodoxy*. Garden City, N.J.: Doubleday, 1959.

Edwards, Michael. *Towards a Christian Poetics*. Grand Rapids: William B. Eerdmans Publishing Co., 1984.

Gaebelein, Frank, E. *The Christian, The Arts, and Truth*. Portland, Ore.: Multnomah, 1973.

Holmes, Arthur, ed. *The Making of a Christian Mind: A Christian World View & the Academic Enterprise*. Downers Grove, Ill.: InterVarsity Press, 1985.

Ryken, Leland. *The Liberated Imagination: Thinking Christianly About the Arts*. Wheaton, Ill.: Shaw, 1989.

Sayers, Dorothy. *The Mind of the Maker*. San Francisco: Harper & Row, 1941.

Yancey, Philip, Ed. *Reality and the Vision: 18 Contemporary Writers Tell Who They Read and Why*. Dallas: Word, 1990.

11

Christians and the Entertainment Media Culture

Terrence R. Lindvall
and
J. Matthew Melton

s that a rug you're wearing?" she asked him, pointing to his head.

"Yeah, and what do you call that, a shower cap?" he fired back.

So it went. Two icons of pop culture, Madonna and David Letterman, were slugging it out on late-night television. Letterman, on one side, was in a unique position. The man who made a niche for himself by being outrageous found he had more than he could handle in the queen of shock-and-roll. On her side, Madonna was making the network world squirm with her tasteless comments through commercial breaks and then well past her time to leave.

When it was all mercifully over and Madonna was gone, Letterman framed the entire episode as he cracked, "Our next guest is Mother Teresa." The mountain of tension dissolved into laughter, not at Mother Teresa but at the massive incongruity of the thought of someone widely regarded as a saint appearing on the same television program as Madonna. Perhaps without intending to, Letterman pointed up a major concern for contemporary believers. Just how massive is the gap between Christianity and contemporary popular culture, and what kinds of challenges does this gap present?

What should be the relationship between Christians and popular culture? What biblical analogies and principles provide us with perspectives on how to relate to the wild sea of media entertainment we find ourselves floating in? This chapter deliberately limits itself to the popular culture of entertainment media. Film and television provide the literature and drama of contemporary society and by their pervasiveness and pumped-up volume almost drown out the voices of other popular culture productions. This generation is dominated by the visual entertainment media, which deserves special attention. Through stories of how Daniel, the people of Israel, the apostle Paul, and the historical church dealt with their surrounding cultures, I will try to derive an understanding of our contemporary predicament. In doing so, I wish to accomplish two things: (1) to articulate a position of critical discernment for those whose response to popular culture is either dread of "contamination" or, at the other extreme, complacent consumption and (2) to recommend a redemptive approach that seeks to transform culture.

Before we immerse ourselves in this discussion, it is worthwhile to affirm the central place of our Christian faith. I echo C. S. Lewis when he asserts that "the Christian knows from the outset that the salvation of a single soul is more important than the production or preservation of all the epics and tragedies of the world."[1] Christianity confesses the centrality of faith in Jesus Christ. Our lives are to be lived in happy submission to this per-

---

[1] C. S. Lewis, *The Weight of Glory* (Grand Rapids: Eerdmans, 1949), 14–15.

son, including an understanding of our rights and responsibilities as Christians. Probing a tension between the right to produce or review art and the responsibility to evaluate it, especially with regard to motion pictures, Mortimer Adler contrasted two ways suggested by Christianity. "It is not in the spirit of Savonarola that the arts must be scourged and expunged, but in the spirit of St. Thomas who, at the end of his life and in religious ecstasy, could say of his own *Summa Theologica*—incontestably magnificent as a production of human art—'It seems to me rubbish.'"[2] St. Thomas recognized that the glorious objects of culture are transitory and will pass away. In contrast, the holiest object presented to us, other than God himself, is our human neighbor; for he or she has been created in the image of God and for eternity. Our enjoyment and contemplation of culture must faithfully keep this set of priorities.

Defining Culture

"Culture," derived from the Latin *cultura*, refers to those social customs and products invented by humans and reflecting their beliefs and values. As currently interpreted, culture is characterized by the arts, habits, and behaviors of a social group. Thus the Victorian girls of the 1890s were as constrained by their culture as were the material girls of the 1980s. Both followed the fads and fashions that made up the popular culture, whether the "low" culture of the masses or the "high" culture of the elite.

In the nineteenth century, Matthew Arnold, English poet and critic, described culture as the normative act of "acquainting ourselves with the best that has been known and said in the world."[3] People then tended to view culture as "cultivating" the best and brightest, the highest ideals of taste and refinement, the good things one hoped to be associated with: good books, good company, good clothes, good music, good theater, and the like. Goodness included both moral and aesthetic dimensions: One could be instructed about good things and simultaneously find delight.

Below the ideal of high culture is the culture that the mass of people actually want. Contemporary popular culture rarely concerns itself with what is "good." It has become more associated with what is held in common in a given society or what will sell. Culture that is consumed on a large scale becomes "popular, or pop, culture." Michael Jackson's album *Thriller*, James Cameron's *Titanic*, and Stephen Spielberg's *Jurassic Park*

---

[2]Mortimer J. Adler, *Art and Prudence* (New York: Arno Press, 1979), 92.

[3]Matthew Arnold, *Literature and Dogma: An Essay Towards A Better Understanding of the Bible* (London: Macmillan, 1924), Preface.

qualify—not necessarily because they are intrinsically good, but because they are enormously popular. These media arts appeal to the masses and do not require a high degree of intellectual sophistication or cultural refinement.[4]

The popular culture we address here is visual entertainment: film, television, video, and the new forms of techno-culture, such as interactive video games. In many ways, these image-based media exert a sometimes overt, sometimes subtle, but always powerful influence over the development of our culture. In this connection, Neil Postman sees the question of whether visual media shape or reflect culture as antiquated. In his view,

Popular Culture and the Church

George Lucas, director of the movie *Star Wars* and consequently a modern myth-maker, declares that film and television have supplanted the church as the great communicator of values and beliefs. (See Dale Pollack, *Skywalking: The Life and Films of George Lucas* [New York: Harmony Books, 1973], 139–144.) Introducing the 1994 PBS series *American Cinema*, John Belton paralleled going to the movies with a religious, ecstatic experience. Even the great 6,200-seat Roxy Theater in New York was advertised as "the cathedral of the motion picture." (*American Cinema/American Culture* [New York: McGraw-Hill, 1994], 3–4.) "The fact is incontrovertible," wrote William Kuhns. "People today live 'by the media' whereas they once lived 'by the book'" (*The Electronic Gospel: Religion and Media* [New York: Herder and Herder, 1969]). The possibility that the media replaces the pivotal role historically played by the church in shaping the values of a community is disconcerting, but understandable. The movies have become a virtual church for many.

Even within our own homes, one may find family devotions being supplanted by electronic household gods. Television can function as a private shrine to the god of images—a Greek or Olympian hearth god of ESPN, a personal Buddha of Public Broadcasting, or a Dionysian god of X-rated cable. Each one offers its own view of the good life. And often we lie prostrate before our god, even becoming couch potatoes.

The transformation from an oral, word-centered culture to an electronic, image-centered culture presents a special challenge to Christian scholars and students, especially in light of the now recognized power of images. The values promoted in the popular culture of television and film are seldom those of the Christian faith. Egotism, hedonism, covetousness, revenge, lust, pride, and a legion of other vices compete only too successfully with the Spirit's fruit of love, joy, peace, patience, kindness, goodness, faithfulness, gentleness, and self-control (Gal. 5:22–23). The task of Christians is to discover whether any of these scriptural values exist in particular

---

[4]Two pivotal works by John Fiske attest to the dominance of the entertainment media in shaping popular culture: *Television Culture* (New York: Routledge, 1987) and *Reading the Popular* (New York: Routledge, 1989). One of the most lucid and cogent Christian perspectives is Kenneth A. Myers's *All God's Children and Blue Suede Shoes: Christians and Popular Culture* (Wheaton, Ill.: Crossway, 1989).

television and film have become our culture.[5]

If Postman's assessment is slightly exaggerated, his assessment of the influence of visual media on contemporary culture undoubtedly raises basic questions for people of faith. For example, do we truly grasp the extent to which our lives and worldview are influenced by visual media—particularly by image-based entertainment media? Also, what responses should a Postman-like view of culture elicit from us? Thoughtful Christians have attempted to shape their responses within their understanding of the Scriptures. It is to some of these central scriptural issues that we now briefly turn.

expressions of popular culture, to expose the false, and to celebrate the good and true. In this connection, Paul's recommendation to the Christians at Philippi holds true: "Finally, brothers, whatever is true, whatever is noble, whatever is right, whatever is pure, whatever is lovely, whatever is admirable—if anything is excellent or praiseworthy—think about such things" (Phil. 4:8). Our contributions to popular culture as either viewers (consumers) or artists (producers) should follow Paul's exhortation to embrace integrity, virtue, and beauty in our thoughts and actions in spite of the popular culture's all-too-common emphasis on opposite values.

We have said that contemporary popular culture rarely concerns itself with what is good. Therefore, Christians must be extremely selective in the activities of popular culture they choose to participate in. Although a choice between what is popular and what is scripturally appropriate may not be easy, it may be necessary in order to maintain a healthy relationship with the Lord.

Works to consult: In her provocative study *The Electronic Golden Calf: Images, Religion, and the Making of Meaning* (Cambridge, Mass.: Cowley, 1990), Gregor T. Goethals penetrates the popular visual arts, exposing how they mediate values and shape character. William D. Romanowski expertly analyzes the religious role of entertainment in American life in his lively *Pop Culture Wars* (Downers Grove, Ill.: Inter-Varsity Press, 1996). Three articles that explore the idea, promise, and threat of Christians and contemporary films are, respectively, Mark Coppenger's "Christian Perspective on Film" in Leland Ryken's *Christian Imagination* (Grand Rapids: Baker, 1981), 285–302; Terry Lindvall's "Spectacular Transcendance: Cinematic Representation of African American Christianity," *The Howard Journal of Communications* 7, no. 5 (1996): 205–220; and Roy M. Anker's "Yikes! Nightmares From Hollywood," *Christianity Today*, 16 June 1989, 18–23.

---

[5]Neil Postman, *Amusing Ourselves to Death* (New York: Penguin, 1985).

Creation and the Fall

An understanding of the Christian's relationship to culture can be grounded in two biblical doctrines: Creation and the Fall. Each emphasizes a particular truth regarding the human condition that seems to contradict or oppose the other. However, both are true and should exist in a healthy, fruitful tension. Otherwise, if we align ourselves with either doctrine, our responses to culture will differ considerably, and if we interpret either doctrine in isolation from the other or propose either doctrine as the exclusive means for dealing with popular culture, its meaning can be skewed and abused. I have chosen to label these two responses: creationist and conversionist.[6]

On one side we place the doctrine of God as Creator. The Scriptures declare, as does nature itself, that God created everything, and that He created it all good and pleasing. The Apostles' Creed confesses belief in God the Father, Maker of heaven and earth. In studying the doctrine of Creation, we discover from Genesis the good foundation for all of life. The Psalmist declares the glory of God in Creation (Psalm 19), and Paul points out that all men and women can clearly understand the divine nature by contemplating the created order (Rom. 1:19–20). Traces, clues, hints, whispers, and rumors of God's power and grace are scattered about this world, and human beings, according to Paul, have the vision to see the beauty of God's goodness. Every bush, if we could just see it as a burning bush, is a message from God to us as it was to Moses.

The creationist approach celebrates goodness in everything. It tends to be optimistic, romantic, at times even naive, in approaching life. Looking out of prison bars, it looks at the stars. It is a response full of gladness and gratitude, hope and delight, knowing that God himself made this world and that everything in it is good. The creationist receives the world with rejoicing, for he or she has eyes of faith to see God working for the good of those who love Him and are called according to His purposes (Rom. 8:28). However, the creationist may neglect the problem of sin, evil, and the Fall, preferring, like Forrest Gump, to see goodness in all things.

Beside this affirming doctrine of God's most excellent handiwork is the clear, biblical doctrine of the Fall. That which was created good has become "depraved" (John Calvin's term) or "eclipsed" (Augustine's term).[7] The Scriptures declare that be-

---

[6]I am indebted to H. Richard Niebuhr, *Christ and Culture* (New York: Harper Torchbooks, 1951), for my understanding of the relations of these two doctrines to culture.

[7]John Calvin, *A Compendium of the Institutes of the Christian Religion*, ed. Hugh T. Kerr (Philadelphia: Westminster Press, 1964), 48–49, and St. Augustine, *Confessions*, trans. R. S. Pine-Coffin (Baltimore: Penguin Classics, 1961), 133.

cause Adam and Eve ate fruit from the tree of knowledge of good and evil, their descendants and all creation itself were cursed and placed under the judgment of God. This being so, all creation must wait and groan for its redemption (Rom. 3:10; 8:22). In studying the doctrine of the Fall, we discover the tendency of all things to rot, or go bad, the human imagination as much as egg salad. Thus we are rightly suspicious of the corruption and perversion of human sin. Informed by the doctrine of the Fall, the conversionist sees the need for all things to be changed and made right.

Related to both Creation and Fall is the nature of human beings, creatures who are made in the image of God but who repudiate their Maker. The fact of the Fall calls for redemption; people need to be converted, transformed, made new. The conversionist notes Paul's observation in Romans where he points out that even though the sublime grandeur of God is evident, His human creation refused to give Him honor or thanks. They "exchanged the glory of the immortal God for images made to look like mortal man and birds and animals and reptiles" (Rom. 1:23). Humankind worshiped its own false images rather than God himself. And so all of us became slaves to perversion and depravity, desperately needing to be redeemed and rescued from our sin. The conversionist believes that even believers live in a corrupt and fallen world, with traps and snares set before our feet. We are in a dangerous world and must be wary, for Satan is on the prowl, seeking to devour us.

Creation and the Fall—these two doctrines define our predicament. We were created good, but we fell. We still bear the image of God, but it has been marred. Making us like himself, the God who speaks (or, as Francis Schaeffer wrote, *He Is There and He Is Not Silent*) gave us an important feature of His nature: He made us communicators. He also made us, in Tolkien's word, sub-creators.[8] And as subcreators, our handi-work of communication is culture. The first culture of the human (as recounted by Scripture) was agriculture, the call to cultivate a garden, to put it in order. Then,

> "Creation and the Fall—these two doctrines define our predicament. We were created good, but we fell."

in the garden, Adam, not God, named the animals, creating a culture of human language. And Adam and Eve were given "dominion," the responsibility to maintain order in their garden culture. God blessed Adam and Eve with a cultural mandate to rule over Creation, which He saw as very good (Gen. 1:31).

Though the Fall subverted the wholly good results of the cultural mandate, it did not change the mandate itself. The very first chapter of Genesis enjoins us to attend to the whole of cre-

---

[8]J. R. R. Tolkien, "On Fairy Stories," in *Essays Presented To Charles Williams*, ed. C. S. Lewis (Grand Rapids: Eerdmans, 1966), 57.

ation and to rule as regents in the name of God and for His glory.[9] Regardless of the Fall, we humans have been given this special calling to be subcreators of culture, to be namers and identifiers of our fellow creatures. And we are still vested with the challenge to maintain the earthly order. But the Fall has made both cultural tasks infinitely more difficult. There is a confusion of tongues, so to speak, in the current practice of "naming," and the rampant selfishness that resulted from the Fall has made the development of a redeemed culture an ongoing challenge.

> **"Though the Fall subverted the wholly good results of the cultural mandate, it did not change the mandate itself."**

Disagreements between creationist and conversionist views about popular culture stem from attitudes about the effects of the Fall. Ingrid Shafer characterizes the two groups as those who primarily "see the world fractured by original sin versus those who see the world connected by original blessing."[10] The creationist position embraces a Garden of Eden perspective in which goodness and beauty are seen to be at the center of, or the basis of, all popular art and culture. The conversionist, on the other hand, sees a corrupt world in dire straits. Anything done or made by human effort is no better than dung (Philip. 3:8). Our best response, conversionists would say, is to be separate from the world, to reject it and its products.

Christians need to recognize the validity of both perspectives. At times we need to flee the pleasure offered us, as Joseph did (and Pinocchio on Pleasure Island did not). At other times we should freely partake of what is presented to us, enjoying the moonlight of popular culture, but recognizing that it is only sunlight secondhand. In today's world of cinema, the pleasure of watching the amazing ways of a man with a maiden (as Prov. 30:18–19 puts it) tastes like juicy grapes in such romantic comedies as Frank Capra's 1934 *It Happened One Night* or the 1987 Steve Martin comedy *Roxanne*.

The justification for Christians participating in popular culture derives from the principles of freedom and discernment. Each of us is invited not only to enjoy God but to enjoy His creation and His creatures. We can work *and* play to the glory of God, being free and wary. In later sections we shall consider

---

[9]The subject of the cultural mandate has been addressed in the truly wise and insightful words of Gene Edward Veith, Jr., in two works: *The Gift of Art* (Downers Grove, Ill.: Inter-Varsity, 1983) and *State of the Arts* (Wheaton, Ill.: Crossway, 1991). See also Kenneth A. Myers, *All God's Children and Blue Suede Shoes: Christians and Popular Culture* (Westchester, Ill.: Crossway, 1989), and Leland Ryken, *Culture in Christian Perspective* (Portland, Ore.: Multnomah Press, 1986).

[10]Ingrid Shafer, "Introduction: The Catholic Imagination in Popular Film and Television," *Journal of Popular Film and Television* 19 (Summer 1991): 50–51.

two models for engaging popular culture. Our goal is to find a balanced model that integrates the two doctrines of Creation and the Fall and that will shape our souls and our appetites. At the same time, I am reminded of the mistake of the worldly-wise man of Bunyan's *Pilgrim's Progress* who savored the doctrines of the world and let them shape his soul as much as his stomach. We therefore turn our attention first to the task of discerning cultural values and the related problem of popular culture's power to seduce.

Discerning Cultural Values

The entertainment media culture can be defined as a value-packed commodity. Christians entering the temples of popular entertainment must become aware of what ideology and values are being sold to them, what message Hollywood is trying to sell. To become discriminating about these products one must first become discerning. Yet some people ask a preliminary question: whether we should even come into contact with popular culture. For the Christian all things, including interacting with the entertainment media, are lawful, but not all are necessarily profitable or edifying (1 Cor. 10:23; 16:12). Thus while God grants permission to the spiritually mature to explore and enjoy our world, wisdom dictates that we exercise prudence and discrimination. Can we attend all films to the glory of God? Certainly not. Many films would be a definite hindrance to our spiritual development. Will exercising our freedom offend some people? Probably so. Thus we must seek the good of our neighbor in making conscious choices about the entertainment we view. And we must ask ourselves, Is this worth my time and/or money from a scriptural perspective? Yet we cannot simply turn off the television set and consider ourselves safe from its impact. Millions of others don't turn it off and, like it or not, they become channels of its values. Moreover, some Christians may be called

> **"We must ask ourselves, Is this worth my time and/or money from a scriptural perspective?"**

to work in the entertainment culture, either as artists or critics—to produce entertainment media or to critique it in all its beauty and ugliness. These are divinely sanctioned vocations, calls from God to interact with an industry whose ideologies and values often conflict with those of orthodox Christianity. It is thus crucial to be prepared, through sound teaching and with the full armor of God, to live and do battle in such a business that challenges Christian principles.

Culture often turns its signposts toward the ideals of truth, wisdom, and beauty. In the medieval era, talented dramatists presented morality plays that entertained while they instructed, and today William Bennett's *Book of Virtues* offers a fascinating compilation of old and new tales that enrich the human soul. In contemporary culture, however, vandals have marred the signs, even twisted them to point the wrong way. Some of the new signs are made of neon, flashing but not illuminating: They do not help us understand which way we should go. They point to physical attractiveness, material success, and individual accomplishment rather than eternal good. In soap operas like *Dynasty* and *Beverly Hills 90210*, viewers are intrigued by the plastic perils of the rich and beautiful. An astounding aspect of such shows is that we make gods and goddesses of their actors, many of whom portray greed, adultery, pride, and various vices, in a contemporary cult of celebrity.

> **"Every popular cultural medium from feature films to music videos communicates a belief or value."**

Every popular cultural medium from feature films to music videos communicates a belief or value. All express an ideology or, as Richard Weaver points out, preach a sermon of sorts.[11] Some media messages may be overt—clearly showing the values they recommend. Obviously, classic Christian films like John Schmidt's *SuperChristian* are straightforward in their presentation, as is a multileveled cinematic masterpiece like Steven Spielberg's *Schindler's List*. They are uncompromisingly explicit vehicles of communication. *SuperChristian* preaches that the inner person is much more important to God than the flashy external image; it says that image *isn't* everything. *Schindler's List* portrays the horror of the Jewish Holocaust, pounding into our consciousness that we must never forget the inhumanity mankind is capable of, the cruelty, the suffering. We must remember. One walks away from such films not only entertained but challenged to think about the message.

Other media, just as intentional, communicate indirectly. Producers, writers, and directors often communicate their values in parables, stimulating audience reflection through subtlety, irony, and ambiguity. Some directors intend audiences to wrestle with their material and discover for themselves the values planted in their stories.

Finally, cultural messages can be unintentional but no less significant. Regardless of whether one is producing *Nightmare on Elm Street Part VI*, *Jerry Springer*, *Married With Children*, or a Diet Dr. Pepper commercial, specific ideological viewpoints with aesthetic and moral values are being expressed. Audiences can read moral attitudes in any image, even if the message is ultimately nonsensical. As the Duchess said to Alice: "Tut, tut, child. Everything's got a moral if only you can find it."[12]

---

[11]Richard Weaver, *Language Is Sermonic* (Baton Rouge, La.: Louisiana State Press, 1970), 201–225.

[12]Lewis Carroll, *Alice's Adventures in Wonderland* (New York: New American Library, 1960), 84.

A seemingly mindless program like *Beavis and Butthead* recommends a certain way of looking at reality. Although it is intended as a satire on its own MTV audience, viewers, especially children, can still read other moral messages into it, as did the young boy who set another child on fire after watching a particular episode. The entertainment media culture recommends a certain way of looking at the world and offers specific behaviors as models.[13] Christians who view the entertainment media culture must learn how to read those images and reject the ones that are incompatible with Christian standards and Scripture.

Seduction of Culture

Culture, like nature, abhors a vacuum. It rushes in to fill the void of human longing. In the process people can be seduced by the appearances of popular culture, which are counterfeits of the voice of God. The spiritual vacuum of the heart (which Augustine viewed as restless until it rests in God) may be quickly, but frothily filled with the fake religion of popular culture, involving the worship of money, sex, power, objects, and fame. In this section I shall script a bleak scenario so that we do not blithely dismiss the dangers of our subject. But remember, while this discussion deals with the darker side of our subject, even the darkness should not deter children of the light. Christians are meant to be the light of the world, which includes the darkness of an often godless entertainment culture.

Simulacra, or virtually real images, can easily seduce us. We have begun a slow, mindless move into cyberspace, an artificial, seemingly infinite world where humans travel on information highways and interface digitally rather than face-to-face. This new "reality" is almost neognostic (denying the reality of evil), exalting a new kind of spirituality, an electronic version, over the ordinary world. Its citizens prefer an artificial image to a person of flesh and blood, because the image is easier to manipulate, usually for one's own pleasure.

> **"In ancient Israel, the primary bearers of ideological and narrative messages were the prophets and priests."**

In ancient Israel, the primary bearers of ideological and narrative messages were the prophets and priests. One temptation of the Hebrew people was to surrender this vital function to pagan influences. Hebrew prophets repeatedly warned

---

[13]The fact that even frothy television sitcoms provide social and political meanings is brought out in Darrell Y. Hamamoto's *Nervous Laughter: Television Situation Comedy and Liberal Democratic Ideology* (New York: Praeger, 1989). The book provides important critical analyses of how different decades of television comedies have preached competing versions of the American dream.

them that heathen idols were mere sticks and stones; even so, these sticks and stones were often found seductive. Similarly, film images have the capacity to seduce. They create a way of looking at the world and shape the unwitting spectator into their kind of viewer. Like ancient idols of wood and stone, our celluloid and digitized images trigger emotions and physiological responses that properly belong to real life and true worship.

> "Today, video and electronic media have become the primary bearers of ideology and morality."

Today, video and electronic media have become the primary bearers of ideology and morality. The entertainment media seek to squeeze out the church and be the dominant authority in communicating values. But even more significant is that these new authorities have a hold on our attention that is more powerful, pervasive, and compelling than that of the church. The statues and stained-glass windows in the Notre Dame and Chartres cathedrals seem mute and silent compared to the explosive images created by the film industry.[14]

Popular culture is particularly potent in its visual impact in other ways as well. By presenting the female form as an image to be consumed by spectators, for example, it reduces every woman to an erotic commodity and reconstructs the man into a voyeur, or peeping Tom, who commits adultery with the image.[15] Asherah (see sidebar) is reborn on screen. We dwell in a culture of unbelief, sex, violence, and death. We dwell in a world of advertising, artifice, and personality cults. What is frightfully disturbing is that most viewers know more about celebrities than about their next-door neighbors, or possibly even their own families.

The entertainment culture continually offers us narratives celebrating the Pelagian heresy, the false doctrine that human beings are essentially good people. This ancient, yet modern, heresy permeates the American popular culture of the twentieth century. Classical Hollywood cinema is grounded in the American dream, in which an individual can, by wit,

---

[14]Consider, for example, such films as *Die Hard* and *Waterworld*.

[15]Scott MacDonald points out that a key aspect of Hollywood film is the promotion of adultery. Citing feminist articles, he demonstrates that "the gaze in the movie theater is, for all practical purposes, gendered male: the pay off for the viewer, as often as not, is the eroticized female body, and the very fact of looking at conventional films becomes a form of repressed adultery. Just as so many men *in* films have sex with more than one woman, the male . . . spectator comes to 'know' the women in films in addition to whatever women they know in real life" ("From Zygote to Global Via Sue Friedrich's Films," *Journal of Film and Video* 44 [Spring/Summer 1992]: 31). This observation by secular critic MacDonald does sound a lot like Jesus' words in Matthew 5:27–28.

muscle, luck, inherent goodness, or mere grit, determine his or her (usually his) own salvation and destiny. Western rationalism, individualism, a dogmatic belief in the goodness of heroes, and self-determinism govern the narrative pattern of most Hollywood films. Heroes (usually male) shoot the villains, win the girls, destroy the evil universe, and triumph by their own skill and pluck. They are masters of their lives and fictional universe. Whatever Rambo or Rocky wills, he can do. But such ideology runs counter to the Christian doctrine of being lost in sin and in desperate need of God's grace and each other in the community of the church. Yet

Asherim

Asherim (plural for Asherah) were living trees or tree-like poles set up as sexual objects or high places for the devotion of ancient people. They symbolized fertility and the female principle in nature religions. Near most Phoenician altars, there existed an Asherah site promoting a worship of sexuality, offering soothing aromas to all their idols. Yet the worship was more akin to gross immorality than to reverence or praise. Incense was burned and sacrifices made at these high places on the mountain. Even in the city, Ezekiel cried out, "At the head of every street you built your lofty shrines and degraded your beauty, offering your body with increasing promiscuity to anyone who passed by. You engaged in prostitution with the Egyptians, your lustful neighbors, and provoked me to anger with your increasing promiscuity" (Ezek. 16:25–26).

The Book of Deuteronomy forbade such practice. "Do not set up any wooden Asherah pole beside the altar you build to the Lord your God, and do not erect a sacred stone, for these the Lord your God hates" (Deut. 16:21–22). Forsaking the Lord, the people of God would bow down to these gods of carnality. Even King Solomon slipped from his wisdom and went after foreign women (700 wives and 300 concubines). He found his heart turned away after their gods, such as Ashtoreth, the fertility goddess of the Sidonians.

Yet, pagan worship was not characterized only by the unrestrained sexuality around these giant phallic symbols. It was also marked by an obsession with violence. Human sacrifice was required by the national Moabite god, Chemosh (also set up by Solomon), and the Ammonite fire god, Molech, including children. And it was not unusual for adherents to whip themselves into a frenzy, like the pagan prophets in the super Baal contest with Elijah (Kings 17).

The idols, symbols, and graven images surrounding such worship portrayed and abetted sexual immorality and violence. It is only a  stone's throw from such graven images of wood, silver, and gold to our own photographic and electronic images that portray and encourage contemporary forms of erotic lust and aggression.

many films and television programs preach otherwise.[16]

Seduction by the media can occur in theological, ethical, or even aesthetic realms. Film and television may tempt us with views of the world that are nihilistic or utopian. They may tease us with stories that say that our actions have no moral consequences, that we may escape the wages of pride, revenge, lust, theft, and other sins. Or they may try to mesmerize us with images that are excessively romantic or disgusting.

Yet this seductive power is not bad in itself but in the purposes it is used for. Films can also seduce, charm, or persuade us into goodness, courage, charity, hope, faithfulness, holiness, and delight. Films as diverse as *Forrest Gump*, *The Lion King*, *The Elephant Man*, *Prince of Egypt*, *Amistad*, and *Schindler's List* have stimulated wholesome reflection and discussion.[17]

Recognizing popular culture's power to persuade, affect, influence—and, yes, seduce—what models are available and useful to us as we engage popular culture? Based on our earlier discussion of the biblical doctrines of Creation and the Fall, I now set forth two scriptural models that give clear warning of the dangers of popular culture and careful guidelines for participating in it.

Daniel's Model of Discernment

The history of God's people interacting with popular culture has teetered between creationist and conversionist, the extreme versions of which are the hopelessly naive and the rigidly legalistic. There is a problem with taking only one perspective.

---

[16]In their groundbreaking study *The Classical Hollywood Cinema* (New York: Columbia University Press, 1985), David Bordwell, Janet Staiger, and Kristin Thompson exegeted the narratives of classical Hollywood films to reveal goal-oriented protagonists as a "reflection of an ideology of American individualism and enterprise" (p. 16). People create or "cause" their own destinies. In contrast to such personal causality, classical Soviet films assumed stories were caused by the social and political factors of the collective. Other genres, such as film noir, operate in a fatalistic universe, in which treachery, existential despair, and inescapable determinism control the script. What is most remarkable and encouraging is a trend in which a few films, including *Forrest Gump, The Mission, Chariots of Fire, Babbette's Feast*, and even *The Time Bandits*, do acknowledge the possibility of divine causality, that Someone outside the natural narrative may be involved in the outcome.

[17]The positive critical reviews of these films and others can be attained by subscribing to Ted Baehr's *Movieguide* (c/o The Christian Film & Television Commission, P.O. Box 190010, Atlanta, GA 31119) and various other cultural and art magazines that provide a biblical base, such as *Books & Culture* (P.O. Box 37011, Boone, IA 50037-2011), *The Alpha-Omega Film Report* (P.O. Box 25605, Colorado Springs, CO 80936), and *Inklings* (P.O. Box 12181, Denver, CO 80212-0181). I especially recommend the valuable insights of critic Michael Medved on PBS's "Sneak Previews." You should know what kind of film you are going to see before surrendering yourself to its seductive and hypnotic influences. Wisely choose which images may sleep in your imagination.

Neither model is satisfactory by itself. The creationist may be too naive and not notice the effects of the Fall upon all human beings. All of us have fallen away from goodness and none of us is immune to temptation. But the optimism of the creationist is a necessary check and balance to the pessimism of the conversionist. Knowing sin in the world and in ourselves, we tend to react legalistically and then to become judgmental. We seek to separate ourselves from cultures that are different from our own.[18]

Babylon was the center of an ancient Near Eastern empire that established a level of artistic and architectural splendor and beauty unequaled in the pagan world. The Babylonian gardens stood as one of the seven (cultural) wonders of the ancient world. The city's buildings were remarkable for their architecture and its walls stood impregnable and proud. King Nebuchadnezzar boasted, "Is not this the great Babylon I have built as the royal residence, by my mighty power and for the glory of my majesty?" (Dan. 4:30) Into this powerful and prestigious center of culture came certain bright sons of Israel to be civil servants of the royal administration. One of them, Daniel, excelled the others. He represents one model for exploring the delicate and controversial issue of how the people of God can relate to popular culture.

> **"All of us have fallen away from goodness and none of us is immune to temptation."**

The culture of Babylon, like ours, was overwhelmingly image-oriented. The dominant aesthetic of Babylonian culture could be seen in Nebuchadnezzar's construction of a spectacular golden image of himself. Graven images of gold, silver, bronze, iron, wood, stone, and brightly colored paints could be found in every nook and cranny, guiding and governing the life of the great empire. Also like ours, their culture found solace in mysticism, with soothsayers, magicians, astrologers, conjurers, and all manner of diviners.[19] Yet, such "wisdom" could not prevent Nebuchadnezzar from going crazy and grazing like a cow (Dan. 5:28–33).

The culture of Babylon stressed beauty, excellence, innovation, vanity, and excess. It could easily have seduced a godly young man dropped into its luxurious lap. Yet Daniel created a consistent counterculture that transcended Babylonian opulence. In a country of overwhelming and attractive paganism,

---

[18]The etymological root of the word Pharisee is *parash,* meaning to "cleave, divide, separate." The Pharisee is one who separates himself or herself from the contamination of others and their culture. Their "separateness" is often revealed in a self-righteous posture.

[19]This suggests that New Age pop culture with all the celebrity psychic hotlines may be only the Old Age cultic religions dressed up in modern fashion.

this young Israelite stedfastly refused royal food and favors. However, his refusal was anything but a purist's asceticism. It was a clear statement about things that really mattered—his faith and Hebrew heritage.[20]

Two key principles may be extracted from Daniel's example. First, he was well-established in his faith. He knew the law of God intimately. After years in captivity, Daniel and his companions remained solidly faithful to the Word of God, not only when their obedience meant running counter to the dominant culture, but also when it meant they might die for it.

The second principle, even more remarkable, was that Daniel saw and understood the Babylonian culture more clearly than did the most enlightened of his Babylonian contemporaries. He was a man who possessed "a spirit of the holy gods," as Belshazzar's queen described him. He was said to be full of "illumination, insight, and wisdom." God had given him and his friends knowledge and intelligence in every branch of literature and wisdom; Daniel even understood all kinds of visions and dreams (Dan. 1:17). Daniel was the last word, the best media critic around. He could even describe and interpret dreams he had not seen, previews of coming imperial attractions. As such, Daniel stood as a commendable prototype for God's people seeking to interact with popular culture, a balance between the creationist and conversionist approaches.

Like the creationist, Daniel was open to learning from all life and from studying the cultural practices, philosophies, and dreams of other people, even pagans. Yet like the conversionist, Daniel critically evaluated the truth and goodness of their lifestyles. Even with the availability of the king's choice foods and wine, Daniel chose not to defile himself, but through self-control restricted his diet to vegetables and water. His knowledge of the fool, the sluggard, and the drunk of the *Book of Proverbs* from his own culture made him aware of the dangers of temptation in a foreign culture. He was in Babylon, but not of Babylon.

> **"Daniel was the last word, the best media critic around."**

Daniel tested his views of the Babylonian world in the light of his holy faith. He accepted the Babylonian culture for what it was and sought to understand it better than its own citizens understood it. But when it demanded his worship of the king or of anything his Hebrew faith found unacceptable, he rejected it. He was granted by God the gift of discerning the Babylonian culture and of knowing what was good and what was not. Surely Daniel's life of prayer, Scripture study, and circumspect judgment serves contemporary Christians as a commendable example of how to interact with popular culture.

---

[20]At the very least his vegetarian experiment proved healthier than the more sumptuous Babylonian diet.

Paul's Transformational Model

A persistent problem confronting God's people has been the utter hegemonic power of the surrounding pagan cultures. (Hegemony can be understood as the informal but pervasive influence of culture over the values and attitudes of a group of people. Thus, as Michael Medved demonstrates in his book *Hollywood vs. America,* the media elite of Hollywood have hegemonic power over what is accepted as normal in our society.) Time and again, Israel compromised its faith and accommodated itself to the gods of the Philistines, Edomites, and others. These cultures were hostile to the Hebrew faith and culture. Rather than prohibiting the construction and worship of graven images, they encouraged it.[21]

> "A persistent problem confronting God's peple has been the utter hegemonic power of the surrounding pagan cultures."

The focus of cultural antagonism was the worship of Baal or Ashtoreth, cults fraught with the visual imagery of debasing rituals, including mutilation and murder. The popular cultic worship of the female Ashtoreth as religious prostitute and bloodthirsty war-goddess combined the familiar emphases of sex and violence that characterize much of contemporary popular culture. The role of the worshiper was his or her willingness to be seduced into unrestrained immorality through suggestive symbols. The writer of Proverbs continually warned young men against entering the seductive shrine of the prostitute, likening it to an ox going to slaughter (Prov. 7:21–22).[22]

Literal idols and orgiastic rituals appear to be one thing—but much the same thing occurs symbolically when a culture itself becomes an idol, a deity, requiring its own form of ritualistic sacrifice. Referring to Israel's problem, the apostle Paul warned: "Do not be idolaters, as some of them were; as it is written: 'The people sat down to eat and drink and got up to indulge in pagan revelry.' We should not commit sexual immorality, as some of them did—and in one day twenty-three thousand of

---

[21]Gene Edward Veith, Jr., offers insightful studies of the biblical foundations of art in his *State of the Arts* (Wheaton, Ill.: Crossway Books, 1991). It must be pointed out that all artistic images were not forbidden to the Hebrews. They made room for visible religious items with the Tabernacle and priesthood, but they were primarily a people of the Word. The Tabernacle in all its symbolic splendor was overshadowed by a culture of poems, parables, psalms, and prophecies.

[22]This image was brought out graphically in a 1987 melodrama produced by Adrian Lyne in which a brazen adulteress character seduced a married male character. She lived directly above a slaughterhouse, which foreshadowed the brutal slaughter of a pet rabbit and the climactic attempt to butcher his wife. The movie was a vivid and disturbing warning to anyone tempted to cheat on his or her spouse. It truly spelled out that the consequence of sin is death—as the terrible warning of the seventh chapter of Proverbs points out.

them died" (1 Cor. 10:7–8). Paul insightfully called attention to the tendency of a pagan culture first to seduce its participants and then to swallow them in its excess and spit out their bones.

> "The redemptive approach to popular culture flowers in the work of the apostle Paul."

Anyone who has ever been part of the frenzy of a rock concert knows how easily the pulsating beat can reduce a listener to what the prophet described as a mule in heat (Jer. 2:24; Ezek. 23:20). Proverb 6:26 uses another metaphor: "For the prostitute reduces you to a loaf of bread."[23] These considerations all point to what E. Michael Jones has called "Hollywood's Guilty Secret," the tendency of the media to propagate a Dionysian frenzy of sex, violence, and horror.[24] The gods of pagan popular culture lead to destruction. As God warned the ancient Israelites, "The worship of their gods will certainly be a snare to you" (Exod. 23:35).

In Paul's visit to Lystra (Acts 14), we see how the Hellenistic culture of his time had been deified. Culture itself became a god with its own cult following. After the miraculous healing of a lame man, the multitudes were certain Paul and Barnabas were really the Greek gods Hermes and Zeus. The temple priest of Zeus hastened to sacrifice oxen and garlands to these men who performed divine miracles. The crowds interpreted what was marvelous to them and tried to cram it into their cultural-religious worldview. Paul and Barnabas corrected the mistake, but only with great difficulty, thus showing us another approach to popular culture. This approach is called *redemptive* or *transformational*. It is rooted in the cultural mandate of Genesis and flowers in the work of the apostle Paul.

The redemptive approach recognizes the truth of both doctrines of Creation and the Fall. Yet it also recognizes that as Christ has redeemed us from being children of the dark to being children of the light, so we can be light in our culture: "Therefore do not be partners with them. For you were once darkness, but now you are light in the Lord. Live as children of light (for the fruit of the light consists in all goodness, righteousness and

---

[23]The adversarial relation of the Christian faith to the film and television industries has been spelled out in pamphlets by conservatives like A. W. Tozer's *Menace of the Religious Movie* (Wisconsin Rapids, Wis.: Rapids Christian Press, Inc.) and Gordon Lindsay's *Should Christians Attend the Movies?* (Dallas: The Voice of Healing Publishing Company, 1964). What is fascinating is that postmodernists are echoing the concerns of these Christians of a previous generation. Of particular interest are the works of Jean Baudrillard, whose titles indicate his view of the entertainment media: *Seduction* (New York: St. Martin's Press, 1979) and *The Evil Demon of Images* (University of Sydney, Australia: The Power Institute, 1988).

[24]E. Michael Jones, "Hollywood's Guilty Secret: How the Fetus Became a Monster; How Sex Became a Horror," *Culture Wars* 1, no. 1 (June 1995): 25–37.

truth) and find out what pleases the Lord. Have nothing to do with the fruitless deeds of darkness, but rather expose them. For it is shameful even to mention what the disobedient do in secret. But everything exposed by the light becomes visible, for it is light that makes everything visible" (Eph. 5:7–13).

Christians are called children of light, even as we seek to usher light into a world of dark shadows and to bring out the results of the light. Paul was adept at finding openings for the gospel in the popular culture of his day. His communicative strategy of "becoming all things to all people" was put into practice at the Areopagus, where a Greek obsession, the worship of an unknown god, became a striking opportunity. Quoting Greek poets and referring to Greek games, races, and boxing matches, Paul took the Athenian culture as a starting point for introducing the light of the gospel. Rather than separating himself from their culture or consuming it uncritically, Paul explored it and found ways to adapt it to his own purposes. In this way he redeemed and transformed the popular culture of his day.

Sometimes confrontation was necessary. Paul realized that the profit motive underlay many of the cultural values in pagan society. Mammon (money: shekels, talents, drachma, dollar) was the real god behind most pagan gods. When Paul challenged Demetrius, the silversmith who made the figurines of Artemis, Demetrius rallied his associates with words any modern-day capitalist would embrace: "He called them together, along with the workmen in related trades, and said: 'Men, you know we receive a good income from this business'" (Acts 19:25). Paul subverted the culture of the money-merchants, attacking the source of profit by exposing the base values advertised in Ephesus. Prophetic critics today may also cause such riots among the commercial sponsors of our popular culture, especially when they convince audiences of the seductive power of the images employed by the mass media.[25] For Americans indeed spend an inordinate amount of money on entertainment.

> "Christians are called children of light, even as we seek to usher light into a world of dark shadows."

Confrontation was not the only way to deal with the popular culture, as Paul demonstrated in other situations. The Book of Acts portrays apostolic interaction with the world as open, free, and transforming, though aware of the danger of false teachers coming in like savage wolves (Acts 20:29–31). Jesus' model of incarnational communication—of

---

[25]Editorials attacked movie critic Michael Medved after his exposé of the movie industry's moral bankruptcy, *Hollywood vs. America: Popular Culture and the War on Traditional Values* (New York: Harper Collins, 1992). And the threat of not having lunch in the business anymore might well have struck K. L. Billingsley for his "Christian Critique of the World of Film," in *The Seductive Image* (Westchester, Ill.: Crossway Books, 1989).

coming into the world but remaining unstained by it—enables men and women of God to experience a breadth and diversity of cultural life without losing what is essential to our Christian life and testimony.

People of God do not easily accept cultural differences. It took a dramatic vision for Peter to be open to another culture. God commanded Peter to receive the unclean Gentiles into God's gracious Kingdom without changing their diet or most cultural practices (Acts 10:9–16; 11:1–18). The Council at Jerusalem agreed to overlook certain external matters of culture, such as circumcision, and asked only that Gentiles "abstain from food sacrificed to idols, from blood, from the meat of strangled animals and from sexual immorality" (Acts 15:29). Paul was concerned that no unnecessary cultural yoke was to be hung on believers' necks.[26]

As people of faith, we are permitted both to enjoy popular culture and to use its raw materials to produce ennobling and beautiful works of art. In other words, we are permitted to interact with the treasures of popular culture and marvel at what is good and lovely in them. We can take a simple entertaining film like *Home Alone* and find ourselves refreshed in watching a lost boy found and comforted in the confines of a church at Christmastime. We may also utilize the media to produce wholesome products in and through them, much as Ken Wales produced the television version of Catherine Marshall's inspiring book *Christy*.

Yet with a freedom to enjoy the gold and silver of pagan society, visual culture itself became a sort of stumbling block for the church. Early Christians found themselves walking a fine line between the dangers of idolatry and the advantages of imagery. In 725 Emperor Leo III of Constantinople sought to purge the church of what he saw as superstitious pagan influences. He banned the use of icons and religious pictures in worship.[27] Leo commanded his subjects to swear a hatred of images (imperial

---

[26]Paul's sentiments would be echoed centuries later by Augustine in his discussion of "Egyptian gold" in *On Christian Doctrine*: "Just as the Egyptians had not only idols which the people of Israel detested and avoided, so also they had vases and ornaments of gold and silver and clothing which the Israelites took with them secretly when they fled, as if to put them to better use. They did not do this on their own authority but at God's commandment, while the Egyptians unwittingly supplied them with things which they themselves did not use well. In the same way, all the teaching of the pagans contain . . . also liberal disciplines more suited to the uses of truth . . . These are, as it were, their gold and silver." When Christians separate themselves in spirit from their miserable society, they should take the enemy's treasure with them. When good or neutral things, whether ancient rhetoric or modern film, are "perversely and injuriously abused in the worship of demons" (as Augustine put it), the Christian should seize them and convert them to wholesome uses.

[27]This is where the term *iconoclast*, "one who breaks images and smashes icons," comes from.

portraits were permitted, however). His proclamation was opposed vigorously, however, by many artists and monks, and Pope Gregory of Rome rose up and excommunicated the iconoclasts. The use of images for and by the church was affirmed and celebrated.

The rejection of cultural images and icons was rooted in the dualism of the Manicheans (who sought to be more spiritual than God by condemning the visible world as evil) and in the worldviews of both the Jew and Moslem, who held the veneration of images to be idolatrous. Pope Gregory resisted these

Myth-Making and the Story of Stories

Often films are constructed from the stories of human experience, stories that are thought to be universal and what we may call mythic (See chap. 1, pp. 41–44). For example, the theme in Chris Columbus's hilarious slapstick *Home Alone* offers a variation on a age-old myth of being lost and then found. Myth must not be taken as meaning "lie" or "falsehood." Myth is not the opposite of truth. In art myth must be understood in its original sense, derived from the Greek *mythos*, as "story" or "tale." For C. S. Lewis, myth reaches deep into the heart of humanity and touches some transcendent reality that the forms of discursive thought cannot fully convey. The myth, or universal story, of a god who descends to earth and takes on human form can be found in many cultures, according to Lewis. In Christianity, however, one finds this story matched with historical fact. The myth actually happened in the real historical person of Jesus Christ. Such ancient myths as a corn god dying and coming back to life dimly parallel the true event of our own crucified and resurrected Lord. The fact that this curious story is repeated in various societies is evidence of its ultimate truthfulness, for one expects to see shadows and reflections of a genuine light. Indeed, some popular myths can whet the human appetite for the Christian faith, whether it be the messianic undertones in the movie *ET* or the hope of love, trans-

formation, and rebirth in *Beauty and the Beast*.

For a more extensive treatment of myth, see the following works:

C. S. Lewis, "Myth Become Fact" and "Christian Apologetics" in *God in the Dock: Essays on Theology and Ethics*, ed. Walter Hooper (Grand Rapids: Eerdmans, 1970), 89–103.

Peter L. Berger, *A Rumor of Angels: Modern Society and the Rediscovery of the Supernatural* (Garden City, N.Y.: Archer Books, 1970).

Frank McConnell, *Storytelling & Mythmaking* (New York: Oxford UP, 1979).

George Gerbner, "Television: Modern Myth-maker," *Media & Values*, 40–41, (Summer/Fall, 1987), 8–9.

William F. Fore, *Mythmakers: Gospel, Culture and the Media* (New York: Friendship Press, 1990).

Geoffrey Hill, *Illuminating Shadows: The Mythic Power of Film* (Boston: Shambhala, 1992).

Bernard Brandon Scott, *Hollywood Dreams and Biblical Stories* (Minneapolis: Fortress Press, 1994).

Bruce Babington and Peter William Evans, *Biblical Epics: Sacred Narrative in the Hollywood Cinema* (Manchester: Manchester UP, 1993).

Joel W. Martin and Conrad E. Ostwalt Jr's, eds., *Screening the Sacred: Religion, Myth and Ideology in Popular American Film* (Oxford: Westview Press, 1995).

negative opinions by championing a positive use of such cultural signs and symbols. The Council of Nicaea resolved the issue in 787, decreeing: "pictures, the cross, and the Gospels should be given due salutation and honorable reverence, not indeed that true worship, which pertains alone to the divine nature . . . For the honor which is paid to the image passes on to that which the image represents, and he who shows reverence to the image shows reverence to the subject represented in it."[28]

The image was justified in that it honored the historical realities of God working in human events. Rather than forbidding images, the church used icons in worship and teaching as a vital means of communication. Later, in the fourteenth century, Nicholas of Lyra articulated in his *Praeceptorium* three reasons for the institution of images. First, most people could not read words, but they could read images. Second, people remembered what they saw but forgot what they heard. And third, since human emotions were sluggish, images would move people into devotion. As the church recognized the value of attracting its congregation through visual means, it produced cycles of morality and miracle plays. However, the use of icons did result in some people putting more faith in the images rather than God. Contemporary Bible-believing Christians do not venerate icons but put their faith in Christ and have a personal relationship with Him.

The key for transforming the popular culture is to recognize, with the Apostle Paul, that one can adapt the vehicles of communication for one's audience. What that means for the church in the twentieth and twenty-first centuries is that we must speak truth through visual images as well as through the spoken and written word.

Creating Media Culture

The arguments for and against Christian involvement in popular culture have not changed much over the centuries. Tensions between creationists and conversionists surfaced early in church history and are still with us today. An early twentieth-century example bears this out. Christian response to the advent of film was divided between a reaction against and a creative involvement with the new medium. The church recognized both dangers and opportunities in the new technology (a perspective that wisely recommends itself as CD-ROM, interactive media, and innovative forms of digital technology invade our worlds).[29]

On one hand, the church condemned the technique and content of the "moving picture." Films were viewed as "the Devil's Camera," projecting the world, the flesh, and the devil into dark and dirty dens of iniquity. The church traditions that empha-

---

[28]John Bright, *A History of Israel* (Philadelphia: Westminster Press, 1959), 149.

[29]Creative work is being done with the new technology by the American Bible Society in New York City.

sized human sinfulness and the need for repentance attempted to keep their congregations from all worldly amusements, including movies.

On the other hand, as early as 1898 Colonel Henry Hadley, an evangelist, saw moving pictures as a new and dynamic means of declaring the good news through visual parables. Hadley used films extensively in his evangelistic crusades in Atlantic City and the East Coast, drawing thousands of people to see his illustrated sermons. He believed that "these moving pictures are going to be the best teachers and the best preachers in the history of the world."[30]

The value of popular culture for creativity as well as evangelism was not lost on keen observers. Writing in his 1922 book *Photoplay Writing*, William Lord Wright declared, "Nearly every plot element can be found in the Bible. Romance, adventure, sex problems—all can be found within the covers of the Book of Books, if you but know how to look for them. Shakespeare knew this and a number of his plots are but variations of the old, old parables and stories which the Bible presents."[31]

By 1920 over 2,000 churches used motion pictures, combining entertainment, education, and evangelism.[32] Conservative Christians like Billy Sunday saw fresh potential in the popular new medium. His hope regarding its possibility for good was matched by his evangelistic boldness in mixing with the Hollywood community. In 1915 director Allen Dwan was directing a film entitled *Jordan Is a Hard Road*. Since one of his actors was to play an evangelist, Dwan recalled:

> [I] got a fellow named Billy Sunday who was a well-known evangelist, like today's Billy Graham, and used him as my technical advisor. We put up a huge tent over in Hollywood across from the studio and filled it full of extras—not professional ones—just people off the streets. Now, in the story, Campeau is supposed to harangue them about religion and make them come to God, but I got Billy Sunday up there and he let them have one of his best hot lectures, and I had about three cameras filming only the audience. And pretty soon these people began to feel it, and the first thing you know, they were crawling up the aisles on their knees, coming up to Billy Sunday to be saved, hollering "Hallelujah" and going into hysteria. A terrific scene. No bunch of million-dollar actors could have done it. You could see the frenzy in their faces. And after we cut, he actually went on with a religious revival right there. Then I was able to put Campeau up there and let him go through the gestures of talk, cutting back all the time to these people I'd already shot. The effect was astonishing.[33]

---

[30]Terry Ramsage, *A Million and One Nights* (New York: Simon and Schuster, 1926), 375.

[31]William Lord Wright, *Photoplay Writing* (New York: Falk, 1922).

[32]G. William Jones, *Sunday Night at the Movies* (Richmond, Va.: John Knox Press, 1967), 25.

[33]Peter Bogdonovitch, *Allen Dwan: The Last Pioneer* (New York: Praeger, 1971).

Here Billy Sunday models a healthy and encouraging enthusiasm, showing how a Bible-believing preacher would see his role of taking the good news everywhere, even to a film set.

In the earliest days of film industry, however, the Church was divided regarding the value of the new technology. Some questioned its worth. Other churches readily incorporated it for attracting and ministering to those outside their walls. In 1910 a minister named Reverend Jump envisioned the possibilities of what God might be able to do with film in the church. In his pamphlet *The Religious Possibilities of the Motion Picture,* Jump argued that when Jesus set forth the essential meaning of Christianity in a universal language that should speak to men of every age and all races, he chose a dramatic story. He told the

Interactive Christians

Dr. William J. Brown

When one of the first revolutionary communication technologies, the telegraph, made its debut, the prophetic message that Samuel Morse launched for public meditation was, "What hath God wrought?" We should be asking the same question today with the explosion of new interactive communication technologies.

After decades of research on the antisocial effects of media, nations around the world have discovered the powerful positive impact of prosocial entertainment during the 1980s and 1990s. Television soap operas have been used to promote literacy in Mexico, women's status in India, and agricultural innovation in Kenya. Popular music videos have encouraged teenage sexual abstinence in Latin America and the Philippines. Blockbuster films have improved health practices in Bangladesh and India.

The use of entertainment for education is rapidly diffusing in western countries too. Unfortunately, the pornographer is again creating a suspicion of the new media frontiers

like the Internet. Instead of allowing the potential corrupting uses of communication technology to make us retreat from the giants in the Canaan of Cyberspace, God's people should be aggressively seeking to know how He intends to use CD-ROMs, interactive virtual reality, and the World Wide Web for His purposes. Shouldn't we Christians assume that God has allowed us to use new digital imaging processes for more than simply visualizing interactions of ex-presidents with Forrest Gump or Elvis with Pizza Lovers?

Since God is the most creative being in the universe, Christians should be at the forefront of creatively exploring new communication technologies as means of propagating ideas, crafting messages, and communicating truth. The American Bible Society is using videotapes and CD-ROM to help believers visualize Scripture. The Christian Broadcasting Network is using animation to bring Bible stories to millions of television viewers in over forty nations. Ark Multimedia Publishing is teaching cre-

parable of the Good Samaritan, and then gave an example of ideal preaching, which many preachers of the present day seem to have completely overlooked:

> Note some of the details of that sermon-story. It was not taken from the Torah, but from contemporary experience. It was an exciting robber story. It frankly introduced morally negative elements and left them negative almost to the end of the story. Was it not dangerous to the church establishment of that day to have its priest and Levite held up to ridicule as hypocrites and *poseurs*? And as for the robbers, not only did the story realistically describe their violent crime, but it left them victorious in their wickedness. They scurried off with their booty, unrepentant of their sins, chuckling at a man foolish enough to venture out alone on the notorious Jerusalem-Jericho road. Despite not being scriptural to

ationism, Project Light is teaching Bible-based language phonics, and Jubilee Tech International is teaching Bible in other languages, all on interactive CD-ROM. Beyond CD-ROM technology, we have an even more powerful means of communication: an international, decentralized, integrated, digital network capable of transmitting text, graphics, sound, and visual images across the globe at the speed of light.

Dr. Harry Sova of Blue Ridge Interactive, Inc., advises creative Christian artists to invade the digital world:

"You can now produce your own multimedia movies, interactive games, reference materials, etc., with a minimum of equipment, expense, staff, and probably do all of this in a room over your garage or in your garage. Only a handful of people are now needed to take a project from writing stage to distribution. Production is no longer defined by the size of your studios, equipment, or how many power lunches were consumed in order to finance your last mega project. Use your God-given talents and produce a music video, a family-oriented game, an epic motion picture, or a full-color magazine. Publish them on CD-ROM, videotape, digital audio, or the World Wide Web."

Some Christian students will be called to be the new creative artists to impact our world for Christ through the new media. Just as C. S. Lewis and J. R. R. Tolkien were literary Christian thinkers who influenced many generations through their written work, God wants to gather an army of innovative Christians who will fuse imagination with the visual image to tell stories that redeem both our culture and individuals within it. New media technologies should be viewed as an exciting opportunity for Christians to use the power of entertainment-education to promote biblical values and beliefs and open electronic windows in our popular culture and let in the Light.

—*Dr. William J. Brown, Dean, College of Communication and the Arts, Regent University.*

the people who heard it, despite its level of excitement and its realistic and morally negative features, who dares assert that the story of the Good Samaritan has wrought harm in the world? Rather, it has earned for itself recognition as being the central parable of all Jesus' teachings.[34]

This parable needed only a new title like "The Adventures of a Highwayman" or "Raiders of the Lost Samaritan" to make it a splendid movie. Jump believed that the church could easily adopt the form of visual media and communicate in a way commensurate with Jesus' own style. The church could pour new wine into new wineskins.

Christians are called to seize opportunities to translate their faith into the vernacular of the day, to communicate with the secular age through their visual media and challenge them on their own ground. In the lead article of the Fall 1993 issue of *Journal of Popular Film and Television*, Bill Brown investigated what has been called "prosocial entertainment." Brown noted the internationally popular work of CBN's animated Super-Book series in its influence upon audience members' beliefs. In exploring the expanding influence of the entertainment media to address societal problems and promote ethical behaviors, he showcased filmmaking at Regent University:

> In 1991, a popular award-winning film called *Turtle Races* was produced to tell the story of a young long-distance runner who works with handicapped children through the Special Olympics program. The film, intended to promote a better understanding and treatment of the physically impaired, was entirely produced by film students at Regent University in Virginia. A year later, film students at Regent produced *Crowning Glory*, another award-winning film about the struggles of a family helping their daughter fight the physical and emotional battles of cancer.[35]

What was important about these two movies was a firm conviction that the media are not only persuasive for evil but for good as well. If we believe the media can change our attitudes about saving rain forests or wearing seatbelts or buying toothpaste, can they not also persuade us regarding integrity, chastity, faithfulness to God and to our families, and other positive virtues?

Scripture affirms both the liberty and the call of the people of God to go into the world. Missionary Elisabeth Elliot wrote of Naaman who, after his healing, inquired of Elijah whether it

---

[34]Reverend Herbert A. Jump, *The Religious Possibilities of the Motion Picture* (New Britain, Conn.: South Congregational Church, 1911).

[35]William J. Brown and Arvind Singhal, "Ethical Considerations of Promoting Prosocial Messages Through the Popular Media," *Journal of Popular Film and Television 21*, no. 3 (Fall 1993): 92–99. In "Using Pop Culture to Fight Teen Violence," *The Chronicle of Higher Education* (21 July 1995), A5, Amy Magaro Rubin argues that positive proactive messages, as designed by Jay Winsten, director of Harvard's Center for Health Communication, have a powerful impact on youth.

was now possible or appropriate for him to go into the temple of pagan gods and help his master in his heathen worship. Elijah's words were simply, "Go in peace." The Christian likewise is called to go into the world, but not be of it. Some saints, exercising appropriate care and wisdom and with appropriate grounding in Scripture, may be called to go into Hollywood and work.[36] In doing so, they can be cultural tentmakers, the Bezalels of the media, not only putting out overtly religious propaganda, but weaving subtle, good stories for the cultural marketplace. This creative work has been done and is being done by Christians: David Puttnam (*Chariots of Fire*, *The Mission*), Matt Williams (*Home Improvement*), Don Hahn (*Beauty and the Beast*, *The Lion King*), Martha Williamson (*Touched By An Angel*), Chris Auer (*Big Brother Jake*), Peter Engel (*Saved By The Bell*), and others who have leavened the Hollywood culture with media of virtue and wholesome delight.[37] The challenge now is for future generations of Christian artists to pick up the torch and take the light of God (the Father of natural as well as spiritual lights) into the darkness of the twenty-first century.

> "Scripture affirms both the liberty and the call of the people of God to go into the world."

When British journalist G. K. Chesterton visited America in 1927, he noted that Americans fell short of being true peasants like those in Oberammergau, Austria, who produced the Passion Play for their community. The defect in Americans is that "they do not produce their own spiritual food in the same sense as their own material food. They do not, like some peasantries, create other kinds of culture besides the kind called agriculture. Their culture all comes from the great cities; and that is where all the evil comes from. You would hardly find in Oklahoma, what was found in Oberammergau. What goes to Oklahoma is not the peasant play but the cinema. And the objection to the cinema is not so much that it goes to Oklahoma as that it does not come from Oklahoma."[38] Christians from

---

[36]Jesus prayed that God would not take His disciples out of the world but that they would be kept from the evil one (John 17:15). In this connection, I must acknowledge the vanguard work of Francis A. Schaeffer and his daring son Franky Schaeffer for providing spirited apologetics for Christians to be involved in the arts. See especially Francis A. Schaeffer, *Art and the Bible* (Downers Grove, Ill.: InterVarsity, 1979), and Franky Schaeffer, *Sham Pearls for Real Swine* (Brentwood, Tenn.: Wolgemuth and Hyatt, 1990). However, I am more indebted to C.S. Lewis and his essays, especially "Christianity and Literature" and "Christianity and Culture" in *Christian Reflections* (Grand Rapids: Eerdmans, 1967).

[37]Michael Medved, "Elites in Hollywood Rediscovering Traditional Religion," *Washington Times,* National Weekly Edition (May 1–7, 1995), 23.

[38]G. K. Chesterton, "What I Saw In America," in *G. K. Chesterton: Collected Works*, 21 (San Francisco: Ignatius Press, 1990), 106.

Oklahoma, Missouri, and around the world must begin to produce wholesome, nutritious, and nourishing entertainment culture. We are called to sow our faith in the media and bring forth hearty and delicious fruit.

Critiquing Media Culture

We have been talking about utilizing the technical tools of the entertainment industry to *produce* worthwhile and morally

---

The Joy of Discernment

Dr. Ted Baehr

"I saw this movie the other night, and it was awful!" I hear these sentiments constantly from Christians who have distasteful experiences with the mass media of entertainment but seem clueless about how to find the good and exercise the critical awareness and discernment skills to get the most enjoyment out of a movie.

To give credit to the disenchanted, there is no doubt that there are many rotten movies out there, but the good news is that there were more good films coming out of Hollywood in 1994 and 1995 than had been released since the late 1960s. Whereas there were only a handful of family and wholesome mature audience movies released in 1990, in 1994 forty percent of the films released were aimed at families, and there were many films like *While You Were Sleeping, Clear And Present Danger, Shadowlands*, and *The Madness Of King George* which were aimed at mature audiences but contained no perverse sex, little or moderate violence and few foul words. The key is knowing about the movie you are about to see and then understanding the grammar of the movie to get the most out of it.

Christians must think about each movie in several ways: what are its artistic values; for example, how does it amuse the audience? What kind of language does it use? and, how does it depict violence and sexual behavior? Further, what are its moral values; for example, how do the characters relate to each other? how accurate is it in presenting historical events? what is its worldview? and, what is its overall message? Is this movie appropriate for children? Teenagers? Adults? How does this movie compare with similar movies in its attitude toward society, politics, authority figures, and the causes and solutions of individual and social problems? For the Christian, of course, the message of every movie must ultimately be compared with the message of the Bible.

The key to this analysis and to developing critical media awareness skills is asking the right questions to gain discernment of the movie. The good news is that movies and other entertainment can be enjoyable and even fun if you have trustworthy guidance in choosing the good and if you have developed the media awareness skills to get the most out of the movie without being manipulated by it.

—Dr. Ted Baehr, publisher, Movie-guide, *Atlanta, Georgia.*

ennobling alternatives. But another question remains: What practical steps can we take to avoid being contaminated when *consuming* popular culture? Several responses come to mind.

First, our minds must be set on the things above (Col. 3:1–2). Our priorities in life must be to serve God and our neighbors. Many of us become so preoccupied with a televised music video or an NBA basketball game that we meet any interruption with growls, grunts, stony silences, or other "don't bother me" responses. If we become so obsessed with our own entertainment that God or one of His servants cannot call us out from it, we have sold our lives to a love of the world. The media, even produced by Christians or celebrating a Christian message, must always be put aside for truly important human interactions. We should not swallow popular entertainment junk food merely because we have nothing else to do. We may watch to enjoy ourselves, but not just because it is there—lest we become too easily what Jerry Kozinski called "videots."[39]

Second, having put love of Christ and our neighbors at the center of our lives, we must critically assess our own worldview and our own character. Daniel's intimate experience with the living God and his studied understanding of his faith and religious tradition equipped him to meet any foreign culture. Do we know what our moral, spiritual, and aesthetic norms are? If not, we are obligated to discover them. In addition, we should become aware of and confess those weaknesses and temptations we are prone to. How are we affected by scenes featuring profanity, nudity, violence, or sex? How do images of the horrific and the occult affect us? Do we have an inordinate fascination with grief or suffering, even romantic suffering? Do films tempt us to covet certain lifestyles? Let us examine our own motives for watching. Against which standards do we measure what we will watch? Scriptural or popular culture? God has set those twinges of conscience and guilt in our hearts for a reason. Through its media the world offers the temptations of the lust of the flesh, the lust of the eyes, and the pride of life. And they are not called temptations for nothing. There *is* something perversely fascinating and inviting about portrayals of sex, violence, heroism, and success in the media. It is foolish for Christians to expose themselves to what may haunt or hurt them. Likewise, let us recognize what ennobles and encourages us. Are there certain narratives that help us recognize human dignity, encourage us, breathe compassion into us, or enable us to see aspects of life that we need to see (but would rather not)?

Third, we cannot merely watch passively, chomping "the chewing gum for the eyes;" rather, we should learn to critically apply aesthetic, ethical, and theological categories to distinguish good from bad entertainment. A film may be technically

---

[39]Jerry Kozinski, *Being There* (New York: Harcourt, Brace, Jovanovich, 1970).

brilliant or a model of superb acting, but at the same time morally destructive. On the other hand, a program may be theologically sound but aesthetically dull and inferior. One could possibly enjoy a film for its entertainment and yet find it reprehensible for its worldview. We must realize that the film or program we are about to see is implicitly arguing for some particular way of viewing life. It promotes a certain way of looking at revenge, forgiveness, religion, parents, the opposite sex, perhaps even the value of a college education. (On this last point, it is pertinent to ask how *The Absent-Minded Professor*, acceptable to most Christians, differs from *Animal House*.) Quentin Schultze argues that each television and film story *"functions* as the Bible for millions of people."[40] In what ways do these products of the entertainment media form the bases for people to conduct their lives? The mind must be kept alert. Many films seek to subvert the workings of the mind by appealing exclusively to the senses, the gut, the imagination. Some films arouse, disturb, or excite even to the point of prompting unthoughtful viewers to act out what they see, just like the viewer of Beavis and Butthead. One is what one eats. Walt Whitman wrote that there was a child who went forth and everything he saw became a part of him. What is becoming a part of us? We must remain ever vigilant, even in the leisure of our casual entertainment.[41]

> **"We should learn to critically apply aesthetic, ethical, and theological categories to distinguish good from bad entertainment."**

We don't need to view much of entertainment media to find out if it is bad. Our standards based on Scripture (not the standards of popular culture), plus the witness of the Holy Spirit within us, should screen many products of popular culture from our consideration, to say nothing of our attendance.

Polishing our critical skills for viewing requires us to acquire a basic grammar and understanding of production. We can learn to recognize the rhetorical and emotional effects that the choice of actors and actresses, music, lighting, film angles, and a host of other editing techniques have on our responses to different films or television programs. We can probe as well the explicit and implicit values of the film. What, for instance, is its view of human nature and the human dilemma? What moral or intellectual positions does it take? Is its view of life relativistic, existentially meaningless, deterministic, romanticized? How

---

[40]Quentin Schultze, *Television: Manna From Hollywood?* (Grand Rapids: Zondervan, 1986).

[41]Bob Briner has crafted a very sensible set of action steps for dealing with media criticism in his *Roaring Lambs: A Gentle Plan to Radically Change Your World* (Grand Rapids: Zondervan, 1993). He also showcases Regent University alumnus Frank Schroeder as an independent director of quality family films (*Pistol Pete*) who helps to introduce wholesome entertainment into the media marketplace.

does it portray religion, God, church, or Christianity? Does it contribute to our perceptions of life as more violent or ridiculous or sublime? Finally, our perspectives on the media should be continually tested within or against a community of family, friends, church, professors, and other Christians. Such candid and open interaction of discussion and debate is certain to leave a greater impact on us than the program itself.

Conclusion

Ultimately our call as Christians in a multicultural world must not only be to critically discern and enjoy the cultures of other people and learn from them, but to bring forth our own cultural fruit. We are under a cultural mandate as Christians to be salt and light in this world, not only to be followers of Christ but to be redemptive agents in our society. In the early days of silent film, Presbyterian biblical scholar J. Gresham Machen preached that Christianity must remain connected to and pervade all areas of human activity. "Any branch of human endeavor . . . must be brought into some relation to the gospel. It must be studied either to be demonstrated as false or in order to be made useful in advancing the Kingdom of God."[42] We should ask ourselves, Do our choices lead us toward God or away from God?

The whole of human life must be brought into subjection to the wisdom and light of God. We must not naively consume film, television, or video games; rather we must seek not only to understand what persuasive messages these media convey but also how to use them to communicate biblical truths.

These two challenges exist for Christians: (1) to be circumspect about what we both consume and produce in the popular entertainment culture and (2) to serve Living Bread to a world sated with moral junk food. The church may interrupt the world's cultural agenda by producing Christian artists who entertain an audience willing to hear and ponder a parable. Servants of God like Daniel were able not only to interpret the dreams of pagans but to receive their own dramatic dreams as well and communicate them in compelling ways to fascinated audiences.

In conclusion let us consider the collapse of the Tower of Babel, confusing tongues and culture, and another biblical event: Pentecost, which brought together many tongues and cultures in the proclamation of the gospel. Cultures can find their proper place in the kingdom of God. Though we do not escape from culture, we are not to be conformed to it. Redeemed and transformed, we obey the cultural mandate to enjoy what is good and beautiful and to exercise our own gifts and talents in contributing to everything that glorifies God. When

---

[42]J. Gresham Machen, "Christianity and Culture" in *The Banner of Truth* (June 1969).

we place culture under the Lordship of Christ we find a freedom to enjoy and cultivate it. We find that as we work and worship to the glory of God, we may also engage our culture—both as consumers and producers of culture—to the glory of God. With this understanding in mind, Mother Teresa following Madonna on *Letterman* might not have been so odd after all. In fact, the humble but tough little saint of God might well have entered the entertainer's life as an answer to prayer.[43]

Review and Discussion Questions

1. How does Lindvall define "culture," "high culture," "popular culture," and "visual entertainment popular culture"? What are the relationships among these notions of culture?

2. Explain what is meant when William Kuhns says, "The fact is incontrovertible. People live 'by the media' whereas they once lived 'by the book.'" Do you agree with Kuhns?

3. Lindvall says that all popular entertainment media communicate beliefs and values. What does this mean? How does it occur? Give examples from television, videos, or films.

4. "The image has the capacity to seduce." What does Lindvall mean by this comment? Is the term *seduce* too strong a word for what he means? Explain your response and provide examples from the entertainment media to make your point.

5. Explain Lindvall's notions of the creationist and conversionist approaches to contemporary entertainment media. Are these two approaches compatible with each other or do they represent completely separate approaches?

6. What does Lindvall mean when he speaks of Daniel's "model of discernment"? What are the strengths and weaknesses of trying to apply Daniel's experience in ancient Babylon to our situation in today's world? Are the situations sufficiently similar to make a valuable comparison?

7. What is the "transformational model" that the author describes? How does it exemplify the doctrines of Creation and the Fall? Describe how it might work when applied to a process such as television or film production?

8. In your opinion, has the Christian community mastered or even competently used the production technology associated with television and film? Is it appropriate for the Christian community to do so? If so, under what circumstances and for what purposes?

9. In one way or another, most of us are *consumers* of products

---

[43]Gary Liddle, Associate Professor of Biblical Studies at Evangel University and Michael Palmer, Professor of Philosophy at Evangel University provided extensive, valuable editorial assistance. Dayton Kingsriter, a member of the editorial board of Logion Press, provided thorough commentary on all aspects of the manuscript, for which I thank him.

created and distributed by the entertainment media. Sumarize Lindvall's recommendations for avoiding being contaminated by what we consume. How would you evaluate his recommendations? Can you think of additional recommendations?

10. Lindvall says, "Contemporary popular culture rarely concerns itself with what is 'good,'" and "[t]he values promoted in the popular culture of television and film are seldom those of the Christian faith." What are the implications for Christians contemplating participation in such a culture?

Extended Projects for Reflection

1. If you have viewed a film or television program recently, develop a critique of it using either Lindvall's recommendations or some guidelines of your own. If you use your own guidelines, explain why they are useful and adequate for such a task.

2. Think of a film or television program that exemplifies values that ennoble us, accentuates human dignity, or in some way articulates a message of hope, compassion, justice, or love. Explain how the film or TV program articulates its message.

3. Suppose you are a film producer. Describe a film that you will produce that meets the following criteria:
   a. It is intended to attract a contemporary college-age audience
   b. It presents a Christian theme and assumes a Christian worldview
   c. It deals realistically with evil
   d. It is an artistic film (not a documentary)
How will your film attempt to satisfy these criteria?

Selected Bibliography

Adler, Mortimer J. *Art and Prudence.* New York: Arno Press, 1979, 1992.

Billingsley, K. L. *The Seductive Image: A Christian Critique of the World of Film.* Westchester, Ill.: Crossway Books, 1989.

Briner, Bob. *Roaring Lambs.* Grand Rapids.: Zondervan Publishing House, 1993.

Drew, Donald J. *Images of Man: A Critique of the Contemporary Cinema.* Downer's Grove, Ill: InterVarsity Press, 1974.

Ellul, Jacques. *The New Demons.* New York: Seabury Press, 1975.

Hattemer, Barbara, and Robert Showers. *Don't Touch That Dial.* Lafayette: Huntington House Publishers, 1993.

Holloway, Ronald. *Beyond the Image: Approaches to the Religious Dimensions in the Cinema.* Geneva: WCC, 1977.

Jewett, Robert. *Saint Paul at the Movies.* Louisville: Westminister/ John Knox Press, 1993.

Lane, Chris, and Melodie Lane. *Parenting by Remote Control: How to Make the Media Work For Rather Than Against Your Family*. Ann Arbor, Mich.: Vine Books, 1991.

May, Larry. *Screening Out the Past*. Chicago: University of Chicago Press, 1980.

Medved, Michael. *Hollywood vs. America*. New York: Harper Collins, 1992.

Muggeridge, Malcolm. *Christ and the Media*. London: Hodder & Stoughton, 1977.

Myers, Kenneth A. *All God's Children and Blue Suede Shoes: Christians and Popular Culture*. Westchester, Ill.: Crossway Books, 1989.

Niebuhr, H. Richard. *Christ and Culture*. New York: Harper Torchbooks, 1951.

O'Brien, Tom. *The Screening of America*. New York: Continuum, 1990.

Schaeffer, Franky. *Sham Pearls for Real Swine*. Brentwood, Tenn.: Wolgemuth & Hyatt, 1990.

Schultze, Quentin J., ed. *Dancing in the Dark: Youth, Popular Culture and the Electronic Media*. Grand Rapids: William B. Eerdmans, 1991.

Scott, Bernard Brandon. *Hollywood Dreams and Biblical Stories*. Minneapolis: Fortress Press, 1994.

Swartz, Tony. *Media: The Second God*. New York: Random House, 1981.

Veith, Gene Edward, Jr. *The Gift of Art*. Downers Grove, Ill.: InterVarsity Press, 1983.

12

Politics for Christians (and Other Sinners)

Dennis McNutt

I n the good old days when I had enough hair to make a trip to a barber shop worthwhile, I learned one of the rules of that unique institution. Discuss fishing, football, the weather, or the economy at will, but venture into the topic of either religion or politics only if you were sure everyone would agree with you. You could too easily start a heated discussion that would disturb the quiet atmosphere. We are all "experts" in these topics having to do with some of the greatest issues of human life—right and wrong, the meaning of life and death, justice and politics. We also tend to have strong opinions about them. Religion and politics aren't topics for casual banter. When we discuss either of them, they arouse our deepest passions and convictions; when we combine them, we stir up an explosive brew.

Well, combining politics and theology is exactly what I intend to do in this chapter. It might be true that only the ignorant or arrogant would try that in public. After all, even the greatest minds can become expert in only one or the other of these great topics, let alone master them both. Nevertheless I will venture into both topics. To be human is to be involved in politics. And to be Christian is to bring all our life under the claims of the gospel, and that includes politics. Every time we vote or express an opinion about a political matter, such as gun control, prayer in public schools, or whether abortion should be legal, we are operating in both fields. So we inevitably combine politics and theology.

Thinking About Politics for Christians

Unfortunately for Christian scholars, the Bible is not a textbook on political theology for the modern world. It gives us few explicit passages on the proper role of governments. Romans 13:1–6 does tell us that governments are ordained by God and Christians should submit to governmental authority. That seems clear enough, but then early in Acts we find that Peter and the apostles were arrested and jailed for preaching the gospel and performing signs and wonders. Then an angel of the Lord arranged a jailbreak for them and ordered them to go back into the public arena and continue breaking the law by preaching the gospel. When hauled back before the authorities, they declared, "We must obey God rather than men!" (Acts 5:12–29). Here the Bible seems to teach that in some circumstances we must defy government's authority. Jesus' cryptic pronouncement that we should "Give to Caesar what is Caesar's, and to God what is God's" (Matt. 22:21 and Mark 12:13–17) doesn't help much either, other than to tell us that government has the authority to tax for legitimate purposes, whatever they may be. The Bible does not clearly define the limits of this authority.

When we read the best scholars on what the Bible teaches about Christians and the political arena we find nearly as many opinions as writers. So some of us head off to college or seminary to study in the "original Greek," hoping we will finally discover the answer. Unfortunately, we forget that the biblical scholars have also studied the original languages of the biblical manuscripts, and they still have many disagreements. Reading the best political scientists, even Christian ones, will not give us a single answer; they also disagree about political philosophy, and they aren't trained biblical scholars.

Faced with this lack of consensus, it would be understandable if we just threw up our hands and declared the whole enterprise overwhelming. But don't despair! The Bible doesn't call us to be perfect in our understanding, only faithful to the understandings we have (Rom. 14:4–5). Biblical scholars and Christian political scientists do agree in many areas of this subject, and the areas of agreement provide enough to keep any Christian busy trying to live a faithful life, whether as a citizen, scholar, political activist, or public official. Bold in the assurance that we can agree on many areas of political theology, we should remember the complexity of our challenge and the many great Christian thinkers who have disagreed with one another over the centuries.

ACKNOWLEDGING OUR LIMITATIONS

As we acknowledge our differences with other Christians, we will do well to be tolerant of them, because we just might be wrong. We have much to learn from other members of the community of faith. As difficult as it might be, we must be fervent in trying to understand what the Bible commands while staying humble before the limitations of our understanding. We must continually remind ourselves that we may have blind spots in our thinking that make some claims of the gospel hard to recognize.

Even with our opinions harnessed by humility, we face a difficult task. The incompleteness of the Bible's teaching on governments and politics is complicated by the ambiguity of much that we must try to understand. Ideas such as justice, righteousness, equality, liberty, peace, democracy, human rights, the image of God, and redemption are grand generalities. We need terms like these for our conversation. But generalities carry ambiguity and vagueness, and that almost always leads to confusion.

THINKING IN SPECIFICS

Christians often easily agree with each other as long as the discussion stays at the level of generality. We all believe in the general principles of liberty and justice. When we get down to concrete cases, however, we often discover how much our agreement at the general level hides a host of disagreements over how the principles are to be applied. For example, we agree that we should love our neighbor, but what does that mean when we are faced with how to respond to the illegal immigrants who were injured or lost their possessions in the 1994 Los Angeles earthquake? Should we give them free medical care for their injuries? Should we subsidize rebuilding their homes and pay for temporary housing as we do for legal residents? Or should we just depend on private charities and the churches to provide their needs? Should we simply round them up as "criminals" who are here illegally and export them across the border? Should we treat them differently if they and their children have been attending our church and are brothers and sisters in Christ? Should our response be any different if the earthquake damage had occurred just across the United States border in Tijuana, Mexico?

The idea of equality presents similar difficulties in understanding and agreement. Equality seems like a great idea until we ask whether women should be drafted into the military, or whether they should be allowed to fight as front line soldiers or fly jet fighters in combat. Should the rights of homosexuals be identical to those of heterosexuals? What about the effort to make sure African-Americans have full equality with other Americans? Is equality of opportunity enough? Will we allow blacks to become police officers only if they pass the same examinations as other applicants? Or should we sponsor affirmative action programs that give blacks preferential treatment in hiring to make the percentage of black officers equal to the percentage of black citizens in the surrounding population? Should women firefighters be required to pass the same physical tests as men? How heavy a load must both male and female applicants be able to carry up a two-story ladder—25, 55, 90 pounds? If we set the standard higher than what might be encountered in the actual job conditions, will the requirement unfairly discriminate against women?

HEARING THE WHOLE GOSPEL

Even when we Christians agree on the specifics, we also have a problem hearing all of the gospel. The Bible commands us both to love God and to love our neighbors (Lev. 19:20 and Mark 12:30–31). We are commanded to do both equally. How well we hear each of these two commands is influenced by whether we are theologically conservative or liberal. Theological conservatives—evangelicals, Fundamentalists, Pentecostals, and charismatics—seem to take the first command more to heart than the second. Their libraries are crammed with books on how to draw closer to God and become more spiritual. They wish to become more Christlike and more sanctified. They diligently study doctrine and theology. They read books on finding God's will for their lives and for developing their spiritual gifts. But while they take seriously their duty to love God, some tend to pay less attention to the biblical teachings on concern for the poor, the stranger, the widowed, and the oppressed. The Bible teaches that they also, as much as the family next door, are our neighbors. Theological liberals are inclined to hear the Bible's call for social justice, but they tend not to be as concerned with personal piety. To the extent liberals and conservatives each emphasize one side of the Bible's teaching, they suffer from an artificial division in their spirituality. A full Christian life must recognize that both our relationship to God and our relationship to others, personally and politically, are essential parts of the Christian life.

This view of the Christian life will give our spirituality two dimensions. In a narrow sense spirituality means strengthening our personal relationship with God. The Bible contains an abundance of admonitions to seek God's face, so much so that when one man said that before he could go with Jesus he must first bury his father, Jesus responded, "Follow me, and let the dead bury their own dead" (Matt. 8:21–22). In its broader sense, spirituality includes working out our relationships with other humans.[1] We might call these two dimensions of spirituality the "pietistic" and the "applied." "Pietistic" spirituality may lead us to withdraw from the world of daily activities and seek God's face in a quiet place. Monks, prayer warriors, and those who spend hours a day studying their Bible live this kind of spirituality. "Applied" spirituality involves acting in all our relationships with other humans in ways that show we love them "as ourselves." I know how to love myself. When my breathing is restricted, I fight for air. When thirsty, I immediately search for water. When I need money, I strive to get some. When threatened, I try to eliminate the threat or escape from it. When my freedom is threatened, I fight to preserve it. When sick, I search for a good hospital, doctor, and medications. Here is the challenge: If the Scripture passage about loving my neighbor as myself means what it says, I must do the same for my neighbor.

> **"In its broader sense, spirituality includes working out our relationships with other humans."**

We Christians think we know who God is, but who actually is our neighbor? Only the family living next door? The person across town? The members of our local congregation? The larger denomination? The whole body of Christ? All humans? Even the starving people in Somalia and Haiti? The implication is that if our neighborhood extends around the world, our concern must also extend around the world.

Conservative Christians sometimes criticize liberals for not paying enough attention to personal piety. However, they may be too eager to pluck the mote from the eyes of their liberal

---

[1]Glenn Tinder, *The Political Meaning of Christianity* (San Francisco: HarperCollins Publishers. 1989), 197–198.

neighbors. While theological liberals may have erred by neglecting personal piety, they do have it partially right: The gospel *is* good news to the poor and oppressed. Liberals properly understand that Christian citizens have a responsibility for just laws and a just social system. They led the way in America in the fight against segregation of the public schools and for equality of all citizens, whatever their color. They worked for reforms that required government and businesses to treat persons, as Martin Luther King, Jr., said we should, according to the content of their character rather than the color of their skin. For a reminder of God's concern for the disadvantaged, you may wish to read Psalm 146. Its eloquent poetry declares that God is on the side of the oppressed, the hungry, prisoners, the blind, and those who are "bowed down." God watches over the foreigners, sustains the fatherless and the widows. So the gospel calls us to both a personal and public spirituality.

Steven Monsma illustrates this public dimension of spirituality with a revised story of the Good Samaritan. In his version, the traveler has been beaten and robbed, but a band of robbers have bribed the local centurion to look the other way. Monsma argues that helping the victim is clearly a Christian duty. But, he also argues, personally helping the victim would only be treating the symptom. The robbers will go on beating and robbing while the centurion looks the other way. The individual robbery is evil, but the corruption of the centurion is a greater evil because it allows the robberies to continue under the protection of those who are supposed to protect society. In this case, we should eliminate the cause—the system of corrupt "centurions" who protect the evildoers.[2]

Psalm 146

¹Praise the LORD. Praise the LORD, O my soul.

²I will praise the LORD all my life; I will sing praise to my God as long as I live.

³Do not put your trust in princes, in mortal men, who cannot save.

⁴When their spirit departs, they return to the ground; on that very day their plans come to nothing.

⁵Blessed is he whose help is the God of Jacob, whose hope is in the LORD his God,

⁶the Maker of heaven and earth, the sea, and everything in them—the LORD, who remains faithful forever.

⁷He upholds the cause of the oppressed and gives food to the hungry. The LORD sets prisoners free,

⁸The LORD gives sight to the blind, the LORD lifts up those who are bowed down, the LORD loves the righteous.

⁹The LORD watches over the alien and sustains the fatherless and the widow, but he frustrates the ways of the wicked.

¹⁰The LORD reigns forever, your God, O Zion, for all generations. Praise the LORD.

---

[2]*Pursuing Justice in a Sinful World* (Grand Rapids: Wm. B. Eerdmans Publishing Co., 1984), 9–11.

As Christians concerned with the public sphere, we must not settle for only individual acts of decency and charity towards our neighbors. Under proper circumstances, Christians should, for example, support raising taxes to pay for a new water treatment plant. Our taxes can contribute to improved health for our neighbors. But even in supporting a new water treatment plant, we must be certain that we are not simply treating a symptom rather than the cause of the pollution. The source of the problem may be factories that discharge toxic wastes upstream, in the river from which the town must pump its water. Or the problem may be caused by manufacturing plants that dump toxic chemicals into open pits. These poisons leach into the underground water supply and become diffused throughout a community. In dealing with a polluted water supply, building a new water treatment plant may be only part of the solution. The polluters may be imposing costs of building a new treatment plant on the larger community rather than safely disposing of their wastes. Dumping poisons into the river or open pits eliminates expenditure on waste treatment, increasing company profits; the owners save money but the local citizens may have to pay higher taxes and may well suffer health problems. Economists describe polluting practices such as this as "externalizing" the costs of production. That is, businesses shift some of their costs of operation to members of the surrounding communities. In some cases, externalizing the costs this way may result in children being born with severe physical deformities.

When we learn that companies are externalizing their costs this way, Christians cannot say, "We are not our brother's keepers." In the final great reckoning the Lord will hardly be satisfied with our explanation that we didn't work to eliminate social evils such as these because we were so busy being spiritual. We will not please God by saying that during our days on Earth we lived a dichotomized faith by emphasizing either personal piety or social justice. He will require us to give account of both our personal relationship with God and how we loved our neighbors as ourselves.

Loving Through Politics

When we love our neighbor enough to defend the victims of a polluted water supply, we may find that the best way to deal with the problem is through political action. Most of us will find it awkward to think of politics as a way to love our neighbors. We more easily think of love being expressed through private actions. Yet if we are compassionate toward the innocent persons harmed by corrupt police or laws that allow pollution, we will need to resort to political action to change governmental policies. Through politics we may be able to bring about police reforms and change the law to punish polluters. Additionally, if the town's water supply is contaminated, we can support a tax increase to pay for a new water treatment plant.

Here is another example of how we can love through politics. Prosecutors exercise a great degree of discretion in how they implement their authority to file criminal charges. For instance, they have the power to decide whether to ask for the death penalty or a lesser sentence in a particular homicide case. The history of American justice shows that African-Americans who committed premeditated murder have been more likely to face a death sentence than Caucasian offenders who committed the same crime. Such injustices should be a stench in a Christian's nostrils as they are in God's. If we love our brothers and sisters as ourselves, we should work to bring about legal reform. Our democratic system of government makes this possible. If a person named John Smith were charged with a crime in California, the case would be called, *People of California versus John Smith.* The title of this case shows that the citizens of California are making the criminal charges against John Smith. The district attorney prosecutes the accused in the name of the citizens. That is, the prosecutor acts on my behalf, since I am a citizen of California. I have joined with other citizens to bring our combined powers to bear on a single person. To the extent that I am able to influence what police and prosecutors do in my name, I am morally accountable for their actions and for their injustices.

> "Most of us will find it awkward to think of politics as a way to love our neighbors."

If we Christians are to love our neighbors, we have a duty to monitor the police and courts that bring their awesome powers to bear on our neighbors. The public authorities deserve our support when they protect the innocent and punish wrongdoers. When they go wrong—such as when they give blacks the death sentence far more often than whites for the same crimes—we must demand reforms. Working for justice in the legal system is an act of high spirituality every bit as much as fasting, praying, paying tithes, or going to the mission field, for this is one way we can love our neighbor.

SEARCHING FOR UNIVERSAL PRINCIPLES

In developing a Christian approach to politics we must avoid defining politics too narrowly. Politics takes many forms; it shows up in all types of human organizations, from the smallest to the largest. Our thinking about political power must consider all the forms of organizations, both formal and informal, large and small. For example, we must account for how politics operates in families, partnerships, corporations, clubs, churches, denominations, labor unions, city governments, athletic teams, chambers of commerce, nonprofit organizations, Christian colleges and universities, student governments, political parties, and the international political system. Christians live their lives at all these levels of social organization. And these organizations all involve political processes, as I will explain later in the discussion.

Further, our principles must apply to a wide variety of cultures. We must be particularly wary of developing a political theology out of the narrowness of the American political experience. For example, white, middle-class Americans may have a generous view of governments because their government serves them well. Quite understandably they will believe that the police are to be respected and the laws obeyed. But many Christians in other parts of the world live under governments that are undemocratic, corrupt, and even tyrannical. If we forget this, we may too easily interpret Romans 13:1–6, which says, "He who rebels against the authority is rebelling against what God has instituted," as a nearly unlimited grant of divine authority to governments. American middle-class Christians may too easily assume that resistance against government is both spiritual and political rebellion. Our political theology must make sense in constitutional democracies, tribal political systems, radical Islamic tyrannies, a fascist state like Hitler's Germany, and corrupt military dictatorships. We should not be surprised that Christians in Bangladesh, Uganda, Brazil, or Russia might read and interpret the Scripture a bit differently than we do. The problem is that Christians tend to apply biblical principles in culturally biased ways.

A few years ago I attended a church service in the black section of Pretoria, South Africa, when blacks and mixed-race persons were forced to live in segregation from the whites. My black brothers and sisters simply read the Scripture differently than I was inclined to do as a middle-class, white American. They knew that God was on the side of the poor and the oppressed. In this church, one wasn't likely to hear much preaching about how living a life of faith would make them healthy and wealthy; their songs were prayers for deliverance and their sermons were about living under political oppression. Thumbing through their Bibles, they paused at the verses that spoke to their particular spiritual needs. Comfortable Americans do the same; both sets of believers naturally savor different portions of the Scripture. So we will need to struggle to overcome the limitations of our experience, race, gender, and nationality if we are to allow the gospel its full authority in speaking to our hearts. Our biblical principles must make sense both in Pretoria, South Africa, and Peoria, Illinois.

If we are to think constructively as Christians about politics, we must avoid the common errors of thinking about a biblical view of politics. We don't easily understand what the Bible intends in political matters, since it is not a how-to book on politics. We may have a difficult time keeping a proper balance between the biblical requirements of personal and public spirituality. Nonetheless, we have seen that God has established governments for more than providing security from external foes and internal disorder. Governments are the sole organizations that exercise society-wide authoritative power. As such, they can help to balance the scales of justice between the powerful and the powerless. With this in mind, we can undertake further thinking about a Christian understanding of how humans interact politically.

Human Nature and Politics

At the core of all political philosophies are assumptions about human nature and human rights. Different assumptions about human nature account for much of the disagreement between American political liberals and political conservatives. Liberals tend to emphasize the decency of human beings and their potential for improvement, while conservatives tend to focus on the human tendency toward selfishness and evil. In constructing a Christian foundation for political thinking, we must build on a proper understanding of human beings. In doing this we must answer two central questions. The first is, What is it to be human? The second is, How does God expect humans to relate to each other? The first question can be answered in a more or less objective way. It has to do with the facts of how humans are constructed biologically and emotionally. Believers and nonbelievers can find much to agree on here. The second is a theological question. It starts and ends with Christian faith. Consequently, nonbelievers will not necessarily agree with us here.

An Anthropological Perspective

Any political theory will fail if it ignores the reality of human nature. This was Karl Marx's problem: He presumed that human nature was a product of the surrounding economic and social environment. (See sidebar on Marx in chapter 1, p. 32, and Appendix 3, "Karl Marx," p. 470.) In his view, criminal behavior was caused by the exploitative circumstances of a decadent capitalist system. Therefore, criminal behavior could be cured by overthrowing the exploitative capitalistic system and the corrupt government that served it. Marx's new socialist society would reform human nature. All citizens would be molded into naturally decent and just "comrades." A noble vision it was, but the experiment in the Soviet Union proved Marx was terribly wrong about human nature. The "old man" that the Apostle Paul warned us about was not eradicated by seventy years of totalitarian brainwashing. Marx built his house on the sand of faulty assumptions. We must do better.

We can think of human nature as the building material of a political system. Architects must know the characteristics of construction materials, such as steel, lumber, and concrete blocks. If they don't, their buildings will fall down or will leak when it rains. By analogy, as we think about designing a political system, we must pay attention to the nature of the human building materials. So what are these materials we build political systems from?

First, our biology makes us *self-centered*. Each of us lives in a single body. This naturally gives us a primary concern for our own comfort, health, and security. I feel the pain of the hypodermic needle being jabbed into my arm more than any sympathy I might feel if it was going into yours. Humans are built like that. Seeking pleasure and avoiding pain for ourselves is natural. This is the reason we make heroes out of the occasional brave souls who endanger their own lives to save others—risking one's life is so contrary to human instincts.

We are *social beings*. Except for the occasional hermit, we like to live together for mutual affection, a sense of security, and enjoyment. Some things we can do best by ourselves, while others require working together with others. This fact explains (in part) why we form corporations and establish governments. A corporation can pull together large sums of capital and a variety of human talents to produce products far more complex than individuals could produce by themselves. Governments can help a group of humans do things not easily done by either individuals or corporations. We enjoy belonging to groups—such as computer clubs, professional associations, and softball teams—to pursue interests we share with others.

Associations of humans serve many useful purposes, but they bring their own dangers. When we join with others to create organizations, our individual selfishness can become group selfishness. Humans not only look out for themselves as individuals but naturally look out for the well-being of the groups they belong to. In its constructive form this produces loyalty to our families, colleges, employers, ethnic groups— even our local churches. (Have you ever noticed how intense the competition can become between softball teams from two local churches?) On the national level our inclination to feel loyalty to others like us becomes love for our country. In proper proportion, patriotism can help build up a nation, but in excess it becomes a dark and evil force of hatred toward other nations. Being concerned with our own well-being cannot be entirely evil. God gave us that instinct to help us survive. The problem lies in finding the balance between "looking out for number one" and having a proper concern for our neighbors, near and far.

> **"As we think about designing a political system, we must pay attention to the nature of the human building materials."**

Humans are *reasoning beings*. We don't live simply by instinct, but we collect information, learn from others and from experience. This allows us to think about various courses of action and their consequences. The reasoning process shapes what we do and don't do. The quality of our thinking depends upon both how much we know and how well we process that information intellectually.

Humans are *moral beings.* The sense in which we are all *moral beings* does not mean, of course, that we are always good or that we behave in morally correct ways. It means only that we are members of the moral community, and that we make judgments about behavior according to some standard of right or wrong. This is equally true of Mongolian nomads, upscale dwellers of New York City, Indians living in the remoteness of the Amazon forest, and members of inner city gangs in South Central Los Angeles. Humans derive their moral codes from many different sources, such as tradition, reason, or simply what everyone else is doing. In some instances they also derive it from religious teaching. Whatever the code's source, humans continually think about and debate the rightness or wrongness of actions. In fact one of the first activities of a new organization is to create a code of behavior for its members.

A few years ago I learned that some Christians were setting up a type of commune in a nearby house. I walked over to meet the leaders and ask about their ministry. One young man told me that it was a communal home. I asked if they had any rules about how to manage all the details of administering the group. He assured me that they didn't need any; they would all seek the Lord together and would bless each other by sharing the housekeeping chores. I told him I was surprised at the lack of formal rules but wished them well in their efforts. As I left, I asked if he would mind if I checked in occasionally to see how the experiment was going. About a month later, I knocked at the front door and was welcomed inside. A bulletin posted on the living room wall immediately caught my eye. It turned out to be a list of assorted rules. It set forth which rooms were off limits to each gender. A set of chores was outlined for each member. I admit a little smugness came over me because I had predicted that rules would be needed. Nevertheless, I felt a twinge of sadness as I sensed the disappointment of the leaders in finding rules necessary.

Rule-making illustrates our capacity to reason together about right and wrong and to restrict our self-centered impulses so we can mutually enjoy the benefits of social life. Our capacity for both self-centeredness and concern for others must be properly considered when we design organizations. This is why Christians should favor democracy over other forms of government. In the words of Rienhold Niebuhr, "Man's capacity for justice makes democracy possible; but man's inclination to injustice makes democracy necessary."[3]

---

[3]*The Children of Light and the Children of Darkness* (London: Nisbet, 1945), vi.

Christians emphasize human fallenness and depravity. But they often fail to understand adequately that through God's gift of common grace sinners can also act decently and rationally for the common good.[4] Many non-Christians tend toward the opposite error. They recognize the human potential for decency and the possibilities for humans to reason together to solve social problems. At the same time, they often fail to understand adequately the potential in humans for self-serving behavior.

This brief sketch of the central traits of human nature—self-centeredness, sociability, reasoning, and capacity for moral evaluation—should give us a preliminary sense of the political problem. When self-centered persons form social institutions, individual desires inevitably come into conflict with the desires of other persons or with the interest of the community as a whole. Even when we try to act unselfishly, each of us may have different information and different skills to use in our thinking. Differences in our information and intellectual abilities also lead to disagreements. For example, which is the best way to build a road across a river? A bridge or a tunnel? A bridge may be more susceptible to ice in the winter; but a tunnel would be more expensive. Choices such as these involve honest and honorable disagreements.

Things get more sticky if we have conflicts over deeply held moral values. We may have the same facts and interpret them the same way, but profoundly disagree about whether something is right or wrong. The debate over abortion illustrates this type of conflict. The debate is not primarily over the facts; instead, this is a dispute over "oughts" and "ought nots." Here the conflict is over whether women *ought* to have "choice" or whether the government *ought* to protect the "rights of the unborn" by telling women they *ought not* have an abortion.

Many conflicts arise from our sinfulness, but not all. Even saints can disagree about the best way to do something or about which of several competing goals they should pursue. For example, a disagreement over whether to hire a contractor or use volunteer labor to build an addition to the church has nothing to do with sinfulness. Nor does a debate over whether to emphasize home missions or foreign missions. Both foreign and home missions are proper concerns, but doing more of one may mean doing less of the other. Devout Christians can honestly disagree over the proper balance between the two.

If we overemphasize the sinfulness of humans, we may see sin as the primary source of politics. Many political processes reflect nothing more than honest disagreements over the best way to do something. If I have properly summarized the human condition,

---

[4]For a good discussion of how evangelicals have overreacted to secularism's overly optimistic view of human nature, see Steven Monsma, *The Unraveling of America* (Downers Grove, Ill.: InterVarsity Press, 1974), 36–38.

we should not be surprised to find politics in nearly all of human life; we should expect to see imperfect humans struggling in imperfect ways to come to agreements so we can live and work together. In summary, we could say that in addition to the fact that human beings are self-centered, social, reasoning and moral beings, they are also *political beings.* Inevitably!

My students are often surprised when I shout out, "Thank God for politics!" I ask them if they believe I really mean it, or if they think I am just trying to start a discussion. I do mean it, for without politics, we could not be fully human. At least I'm in good company; I believe it was Aristotle who said that politics was the greatest invention of mankind. Of course the dark side of human nature does contaminate politics. We must admit this, and keep it in mind when thinking about political life.

A THEOLOGICAL PERSPECTIVE

A Christian political philosophy must have God's view of humans at its core. God doesn't believe humans are just intelligent animals. First, God created humans in His image (Gen. 1:27 and 9:6), and the Bible declares specific rights for humans. (See Appendix 10, "Rights," p. 497.) Second, we are objects of God's love. His love is so profound that He sent His Son to die for us. These theological truths offer two approaches to understanding how humans should treat each other.

The first approach starts from the doctrine that God created humans in His image. Scholars generally agree that this means that, like God, humans have a capacity for reason, we are capable of making moral judgments, and we are free to choose right and wrong. Since these traits are gifts from God, they are rights that humans must respect in each other. In addition to rights that flow from being made in the image of God, the Bible also establishes specific rights. The Bible lists many of them, such as the right to a fair trial, to asylum, not to be tortured, and a right to good working conditions.[5]

---

[5]John Warwick Montgomery, *Human Rights and Human Dignity* (Grand Rapids: Zondervan, 1986), 167–169. Although the Bible does not speak about individual rights in precisely the same manner as do modern scholars, it does clearly announce laws an individual could rely on as if they were spelled out as legal rights. The following examples illustrate this point: the right to a fair trial before impartial judges (I Tim. 5:21, Deut. 16:18–19; Deut. 17:6); the right to fair compensation for one's labor and to be paid each day before the sun sets (Luke 10:7; Deut. 24:14–15); the right for an accidental slayer to have asylum from a blood avenger (Num. 35:11, 15; Deut. 4:42); the right of a divorced woman to receive a bill of divorce from her husband (Deut. 24:1–3); the right to a good reputation (Deut. 13 through 19); the right to be free from sexual assault (Deut. 22:25–27); widows' rights (Deut. 25:5–6); the right to be protected against unjust weights in commercial transactions (Deut. 25:13–15).

A second approach starts by recognizing humans as objects of God's love. God loves us, and He commands us to love one another. That gives humans divine worth and dignity. It also creates a duty for each of us to respect the dignity and rights of others. According to Carl F. H. Henry, "The Bible has a doctrine of divinely imposed duties; what moderns call human rights are the contingent flipside of those duties."[6] (See sidebar on Henry in chapter 3, p. 140.) In Henry's view, instead of listing rights that individuals can assert against others, the Bible announces duties to be performed. The summary of the law, according to Jesus, is that we are to love God with all our heart and soul and our neighbor as ourself (Matt. 22:37–40). Commanded to love our neighbors, we must respect their needs as our own.

> **"God loves us, and He commands us to love one another. That gives humans divine worth and dignity."**

Therefore, persons wishing to protest their mistreatment by others would not claim a right but would point out the immorality of others failing their duty to them. In Henry's view, these biblical duties imply corresponding rights.[7]

Whether we take the first approach or the second one, we end up with much the same responsibilities toward others. God created persons whom He commands us to love and whose dignity and freedom we must respect. We must see all persons in this light. This does not depend on whether they are like or unlike us, or whether they are saints or sinners. Scripture does not give us a simple checklist of all specific human rights or explain how they should be protected in all circumstances. Nevertheless, human rights can be deduced from the idea of divinely created humans as objects of God's love and grace, who as autonomous, rational beings exercise moral choice. To deny such persons the freedom necessary for them to exercise their divinely given attributes would destroy precious rights granted directly by the Almighty.[8] To gain a sense of the divine importance of this gift of free will, remember that God gave humans the freedom even to reject Him! According to John Warwick Montgomery, "Jesus never forces Himself on man, and the true Christian believer can hardly justify doing what his Master will

---

[6]Carl F. Henry, "The Judeo-Christian Heritage and Human Rights," in *Religious Beliefs and the Moral Foundation of Western Democracy*, ed. Carl H. Esbeck (Columbia, Mo.: University of Missouri, 1986), 27–40.

[7]Ibid., 30.

[8]Montgomery takes this approach; see pp. 206–217. See also Lewis Smedes, *Mere Morality* (Grand Rapids: Wm. B. Eerdmans Publishing Co., 1983), 34–37, 219, 223 and 235. For an example from a Roman Catholic moral theologian, see Bernard Häring, *The Law of Christ* (Paramus, N.J.: The Newman Press, 1966), 1: 99–103, 120–121, and 3: 148–149. Also see his *Free and Faithful in Christ: Moral Theology for Clergy and Laity* (New York: Crossroad Publishing Co., 1981), 3: 360.

not do."[9] Accordingly, we must give at least as much respect for human freedom as God does.

Another important element of God's view of persons is that He doesn't play favorites (Acts 10:34). He did choose the nation of Israel to be His servant when the rest of the world turned their backs on Him. But when the Israelites became smug about it, God rebuked them by asking, "Are not you Israelites the same to me as the Cushites?" (Amos 9:7) He loves us all

Free Will

The term *free will* is both widely used and potentially misleading. When we say of someone, "He acted of his own free will," we normally mean that the person in question was not coerced, physically forced, to perform a certain action. For example, if Hamlet *acted of his own free will* when he attempted to kill the king by thrusting his dagger through the curtain, we mean merely that no one forced him to make a thrusting motion with his dagger. We should note, however, that "free will" cannot sensibly mean that the will is subject to no causes or influences of any kind. To say literally that the will is *free* of all causes or influences is tantamount to saying that the agent (the person acting) has no basis for any of his or her preferences, inclinations, desires, or intentions. For instance, we would have to say that the will is unfree even when rational thought guides its actions. But such a conclusion hardly makes sense. For this reason (and others besides), many scholars have elected to abandon the expression "free will" in favor of another term: *autonomy*.

"Autonomy" comes from two Greek words: *auto* (=self) and *nomos* (=law). Quite literally, the *autonomous* person is self-legislating. When Immanuel Kant, the eighteenth-century philosopher, used the term "autonomous," he meant that the person so described was not governed by external forces but by internal rational principles.

In other words, to act autonomously implies that the person acts according to good reasons and does not succumb to forces and influences (threats, inducements, and the like) exerted by another person or thing. More generally, autonomous persons act on the basis of decisions made voluntarily; that is, they act on the basis of decisions resulting from specific knowledge of the situation and control of their own bodily movements. In the best of circumstances the agent acts from deliberate choice—he or she considers his alternatives with care and circumspection. Autonomous persons are considered moral decision makers and are generally regarded as accountable for their actions.

To clarify these distinctions, consider two cases. In one case, a woman is pushed to the ground and raped. Clearly, her movements are controlled by another person. She is not behaving autonomously. In another case, a legislator is offered a substantial bribe to cast her vote in a certain way on an issue before the legislature. Moreover, she is told that if she refuses to comply, all political and financial support she might have expected in the close upcoming election will be thrown to her opponent. The stakes are high; the pressure to comply is great. If the legislator acts (votes) on the basis of her own reasons and not on the basis of external influences, she can be said to have acted autonomously.

---

[9]*Human Rights and Human Dignity* (Grand Rapids: Zondervan, 1986), 171.

deeply—and equally. The rights He gives to me and the right living He demands of me, He gives to you and demands of you identically. He doesn't favor Americans or Russians, men or women, blacks or whites, the healthy or the dying, straights or gays, young or old, rich or poor. He offers the same salvation, the same deliverance from sin, and the same help of the Holy Spirit to all. The radical equality of the Bible, if we take it seriously, will give our Christian political theology a revolutionary flavor.[10] Just think about the subversive power of this idea if we took it seriously in all our political organizations, large and small, even church organizations!

In developing a biblical approach to individual rights, we must apply general principles to concrete situations of political life. We were created as free individuals but are made to live in community, where our rights conflict with the rights of others.[11] When this happens we are forced to choose among them, and choosing among conflicting claims is what politics is all about. The challenge of political theory is to take the raw material of humans—self-centeredness, sociability, rationality, capacity for moral judgments—and design a political system that will take it all into consideration, producing the best society and highest protection for human rights. The problem is that our building materials are full of flaws. All institutions created by sinful individuals must inevitably be touched by sin. For example, if as individuals we are tainted by racism, the policies of our organizations and our government's laws will likely be racist. Understanding the sinfulness of humans should help us be realistic about not expecting perfection from our political institutions. But the decency and rationality of humans, those gifts of common grace that God has bestowed on all persons, do allow us to expect something good from each other.

The Nature and Problem of Power

Social life involves both harmony and cooperation on the one hand and conflict and the clashing of interests on the other. The way we work for harmony and resolve conflicts involves politics. At the center of politics is power. Before we examine the nature of politics, let us first consider some characteristics of power and how its exercise raises serious questions for Christians.

Christians hesitate to admit they use power, but all human relationships involve issues of power. Christians may be more comfortable talking about virtue and justice, but even if we

---

[10]Glenn Tinder, *The Political Meaning of Christianity* (San Francisco: HarperCollins Publishers, 1989), 165–180.

[11]Of course, any full understanding of human conflict must take into account the historical alienation of humankind from their Creator (Gen. 3).

avoid discussing power, we cannot escape using it. Nor should we, because power can be used for evil or good. Power is the ability to cause or influence another to behave as you wish. This definition is too simple but it will suffice for now. We need defensive power to protect ourselves from those who would do us harm. We might even use intervening power to protect someone from harm or injustice. We need economic power to care for our families and to prepare for our old age. Nations need military power to protect themselves against aggressors. We all swim in a sea of power. Therefore, not to call power by its real name and not to acknowledge its importance in human relationships is to be blind to the reality of power used against us and how we use it on others.

Fortunately most manifestations of power in social life take other forms than force. It operates more through influence than coercion. For example, economic power may be seen in the capacity to hire or fire someone, or to buy merchandise or services. Power may operate through the formal authority of an office in an organization. If decisions require a person's approval—such as a business manager's okaying the purchase of a new computer for the company—that person has official power. If a person is respected for wisdom and stature in a community, that person has social power. These forms of power are different from force in that they do not directly overpower the will of another by physical control. But they raise many of the same moral questions as does the use of force. For example, for an employer to fire a woman for refusing his sexual advances has the same financial effect as using a gun to take her purse.

We know well that power can be exploitative and aggressive. Let us also acknowledge its virtue. Power can serve decent purposes and help us to live with dignity. For instance, if we have economic power, we can rent an apartment, buy a coat for the winter, buy food, buy a car, pay for our children's teeth to be treated by a dentist, or pay tuition at a university. To the extent that the poor are unable to do these things, they suffer from powerlessness. If their poverty is severe enough, they will not only experience diminished power, they may also experience loss of personal dignity. So we must have compassion on the poor persons who lack power, because they cannot protect themselves or take care of their legitimate needs.

> "We know well that power can be exploitative and aggressive. Let us also acknowledge its virtue."

While power has many faces, the one we recognize most readily is *force*. A robber threatens force when he sticks a revolver to your ribs and demands your money. Even the most decent governments must use force. Police officers carry pistols and handcuffs. Judges are reinforced by marshals. Prisons are symbols of legal force in the form of guns, guards, locks, and steel bars.

The fundamental question is how to justify the use of force, the forceful overwhelming of a person's free will. If humans have a right to freedom, then using force to restrict the exercise of that right can be justified only by some higher principle. Governments have the right to use force to provide for the higher principle of providing for public safety and the general welfare. While most people accept the government's use of force to carry out the laws, we know that governments often use their power for evil. Such was the case in the Soviet Union during Stalin's era and in Germany under Hitler. Parents use force to control their children. We justify this by explaining that the parents know better than the child what is good for the child. After all, two-year-olds must be pulled back from the street, even if they kick and scream.

There is one notable fact about overt force, whether used by a police officer or a robber: At the very least we are unmistakably aware of it when it is used against us. The same cannot be said of indirect uses of force, such as hiding information or discriminating against women and minorities in hiring. In these cases the use of force is subtle and devious. The victim cannot easily know or prove that power was used unethically. For example, if you don't buy my products, is it because they do not suit your needs or because I am a Korean? Many scholars have argued that a "glass ceiling" blocks women from being promoted to the highest offices in American corporations. Does its existence prove that women face discrimination in promotions? Are there fewer women in the executive dining rooms because they lack the same training as men or because they take time off for bearing children? Or is it simply because they are women? Discrimination against women in the promotion process is difficult to prove. That makes it easy to get away with.

Control of information is another type of noncoercive power that often operates covertly. As we go about our daily activities we make numerous decisions about revealing and concealing information. Secrecy gives us power, and if we keep information from others who might want to know what we know, we gain power over their lives or increase our power to defend our own. If the information is about our private plans or personal health, we may wish to keep it private, hidden from prying eyes. If the information has to do with the church budget, and if we can keep it secret from others, we gain power and they lose it. If information is power, then secret information is well-nigh absolute power. While we reject the use of brute force in normal human relationships, other forms of power, such as secrecy, can also violate free will. But unless we first train ourselves to see these other forms of power in operation, we will not be able to challenge them or judge their morality.

The moral issue arises from how power affects human free will. Raw force attempts to overwhelm one's will directly. On the other hand, power based on respect has to be earned. Those who follow someone out of respect do so freely. For this reason, raw force is morally more problematical than the power that comes from respect. Power that operates through lying, propaganda, or secrecy may be justified in some extreme circumstances, but this has its own moral dangers; power in these forms is selected because it allows holders to control others by manipulating the information available to them. The liar gives another person false information under the guise that it is true, hoping to contaminate his or her reasoning processes and thereby controlling his or her behavior. The propagandist mixes a witch's brew of truths, conscious omissions, half-truths, and falsehoods hoping to shape the behavior of the audience in a manner that might not be possible with full and unadulterated truth. The manipulator of secrets withholds information from other persons, thereby denying them information their rational thinking processes depend on. The holder of the secret is thereby able to control the behavior of those kept uninformed. But such practices have much in common with raw force. If you wish to overwhelm the free will of another, as the wry saying goes, "Put a gun in his ear, and he will follow you anywhere." Manipulating the information available to other persons is just another technique for overcoming their free will and raises many of the same ethical questions as coercive actions. Individuals' wills can be directly overwhelmed or manipulated by deceiving or defrauding them, or by keeping them ignorant.

The use of power raises questions beyond the morality of controlling others. Power influences the holder as well as the subject. It gives the wielder a sense of importance. People with power are granted deference by others, their birthdays are celebrated by their subordinates, their offices are larger, and they have reserved parking places near the entrance to the office. The seduction of power is so alluring that few of us are immune to it. The old saying "His head grew too large for his hat" recognizes that our egos can become puffed up with a false sense of our own importance. Don't we all know people who have been overcome by their own importance after receiving a promotion?

The power of riches can delude us into an unbiblical self-reliance (Prov. 30:9). Even spiritual power can deceive us into an exalted view of ourselves. Paul gave a good chewing out to some members of the church at Corinth who had become arrogant because they thought they had power (1 Cor. 4:18–20), so the problem is not a new one for Christians. We need power to operate as leaders, but the very power we strive to own may come to own us.[12]

---

[12]For discussions of how power can come to possess Christians, see Anthony Campolo, *The Power Delusion* (Wheaton, Ill.: Victor Books, 1986); Jacques Ellul, *Money and Power* (Downers Grove, Ill.: Inter-Varsity Press, 1984); and Cheryl Forbes, *The Religion of Power* (Grand Rapids: Zondervan Publishing House, 1983).

Whatever form it takes, the question of the moral uses of power is central to political philosophy. We need power to create efficient organizations and governments. The challenge is to keep power virtuous.

THE NATURE OF POLITICS

The essence of politics is the struggle for power and influence. All social groups and institutions need ways to make decisions for their members. Politics helps us do that. The Greek word from which we get politics is *polis*, meaning "city." Politics in the classical sense involves the art of making a city function well. It also helps to operate our organizations and governments. When our political system is healthy, we maintain order, provide security, and gain the ability to do things as a community that we couldn't do well individually. We pass laws, have them enforced by the police, levy taxes for roads, sewer systems, public schools, and to support cancer research. Within our private organizations a healthy political system helps us to adopt budgets, evaluate personnel, establish and enforce policies and rules, and select leaders. At its best, politics improves the life of a group or community. Politics takes a variety of forms, such as elections, debates, bribery, campaign contributions, riots, or phone calls to senators. As you can see, I have listed both noble and ignoble ways to influence the decisions of a political system. Some of them are formal, such as elections, while others are informal, such as calling legislators and pressuring them to vote our way.

> **"I use the term *politics* to cover all the processes that allow decisions to be made for any group or institution."**

Notice that I am using "politics" in a broad sense. In many textbooks, the term *politics* refers to the processes used to make official decisions for an entire society. But I use the term to cover all the processes that allow decisions to be made for any group or institution. In this sense, we can properly speak of church politics, office politics, the politics of a Christian college or university, and even the politics of a family. Broadening the term beyond governmental politics allows us to notice the operations of power within any group. The broader meaning helps us to look for the struggle for power within an organization and ask questions about what this does to the rights of each member.

The use of power raises ethical questions in all our relationships and organizations. Therefore, I find it useful to analyze how power operates from the smallest units of social life, such as the family, to the worldwide scale of international politics. The New Testament discusses political struggles between both the largest and smallest units of social organization. It tells us of the disagreements between Peter and Paul, between the factions of the Corinthian church as well as the struggle of the Jewish revolutionaries against imperial Rome.

The problem of politics is that in the struggle for power we have winners and losers. The winners gain power and use it to control the losers. If a new law says you cannot throw gum on the sidewalk, and you support the law, you will obey it without having to be threatened with coercive force. Since you willingly comply, no great moral issue is at hand. But when the holders of power use it in ways that intrude on the God-given freedom of their subjects, the ethics of power becomes a crucial question.

> **"Organizations of the church have different purposes than governments but many of the same features."**

Many persons insist, "You can't legislate morality!" While it may be true that legislation cannot change hearts, it clearly can coerce persons into behaving in desired ways. Or laws can send them to prison if necessary. So politics raises the same questions as does any use of power: What higher values can justify the violation of someone's freedom rights? When rights come into conflict, how shall we decide which is the more important one? The sanctity of life clearly justifies taking away the liberty of a murderer. That's an easy call. But what's the proper punishment for a man who plays his stereo loudly after midnight and keeps his neighbors awake? Or what right does a state government have to force an elderly woman out of her home to make way for a new freeway? In each of these cases, power is exercised through a political process to enforce a moral calculation.

Is the right to life more precious than a murderer's right to freedom? Is the value of quiet at night in a residential neighborhood higher than the right of someone to enjoy loud music in the middle of the night? Is the need of the community to have an efficient road system a higher value than the right of an elderly woman to enjoy her private property? Each of these questions involves judgments about the relative value of conflicting rights. Such questions are commonly answered through political processes. The great issues of American public life in the 1990s illustrate making moral choices such as these through political procedures. Loggers in Oregon argue that their right to a job is higher than the rights of those who wish to preserve old-growth forests. The right of the poor to health care conflicts with the freedom of doctors and hospitals to charge whatever fees the market will bear.

The politics of ratification of the North American Free Trade Agreement (NAFTA) involved a struggle over the rights of American workers and business owners. Some unions wished to be protected from having to compete with low-wage workers in Mexico. Many companies wanted the right to seek the lowest manufacturing costs for their products. NAFTA also involved a clash between American workers and Mexican workers. In some low-wage industries, such as assembling electronic products, American workers feared they would lose their jobs to

Mexicans. In addition, the NAFTA issue involved a clash between what was good for the American economy as a whole and some industries in particular. In theory, by removing trade barriers between the United States and Mexico, NAFTA would improve the standard of living in both countries. However, even if both economies improve as NAFTA takes effect, some workers will lose their jobs while others will find new jobs opening up for them. In this complex case, we see that political processes were used to decide matters of great importance to workers and companies and to the American economy as a whole.

The issues in the NAFTA debate involved a moral calculus of great importance and complexity. And there were winners and losers. But that is the essence of politics. In the struggle for power, the winners impose their policies and opinions on the losers. We have come to expect this of the politics of governments, but we must be equally aware that power and politics operate in similar fashion in the institutions of the church.

Church *As* Politics

The politics of NAFTA as well as other issues of American national life are far more difficult to comprehend than the politics of a simpler institution, such as a church. Though organizations of the church have different purposes than governments, we can observe many features of the larger political system. Churches don't normally exercise coercive force,[13] but they do impose punishments, such as expelling members and removing ministerial credentials. They make decisions such as who will be the pastor and who will be accepted as members. In churches we can observe factions, rules, decision-making (such as adopting a budget), and policy formulation (such as deciding which programs will be added or discontinued). Running a church necessarily involves some type of politics; whether authoritarian, democratic, representative, or some mixture.

A church is a political organization from the day it is formed. Brought together by our need for fellowship and worship, we instinctively set up a structure of power and adopt procedures for making decisions for the congregation. In some cases this will be done under the authority of a denomination; in others it will produce an independent self-governing congregation.

---

[13]Unfortunately there are exceptions. During the Spanish Inquisition (15th century, A.D.), the Roman Catholic Church tortured and executed those whom it considered heretics. In the Salem Witch Trials in colonial New England (1690), church officials had women believed to be witches burned at the stake. Today, occasionally, members of the congregation or civil authorities may physically remove a person who disturbs a church meeting and refuses to be quiet or leave the sanctuary.

Unfortunately for many of us, the term *church politics* carries negative connotations. We use the term when we don't like the way decisions in our church are made. If we understood the necessity, indeed the inevitability, of politics inside the church, perhaps we would not shy away from observing politics in our churches. We then could discuss it freely and celebrate good church politics as much as we now bemoan bad church politics.

When my former pastor left my church for a denominational office, the church went on functioning and hardly missed a beat. He left our self-governing church well organized, with a sound constitution, a well-trained staff, and respected lay leaders. Our church political machinery was in good working order, so we went about the business of selecting a new pastor. Changing pastors can be deeply unsettling to a congregation if there isn't an atmosphere of mutual trust and some accepted procedures for selecting the new pastor. In this case the pastoral search committee carried out its work in a way that earned the respect of the congregation and helped us select a new pastor in an almost routine fashion. That was church politics at its best. Those who originally set up the procedures and all those who made them work so well blessed the church by making a political decision in a way that inspired trust.

Our local congregations look much like microgovernments. They have constitutions, bylaws, and parliamentary procedures to shape the governing process. And although they don't have armies, they do hire lawyers to protect their rights against outsiders. If we properly follow Matthew 18:15–18, the church also will have judicial functions for resolving disputes. For instance, if a brother sins against us, we are to go first to him privately and discuss the matter. If that doesn't resolve the matter, we are to discuss the dispute with him before witnesses. If the conflict remains unresolved, we are to tell it to the whole church. And if he refuses to listen even to the church, since the church has no prisons, he must be expelled and treated as an unbeliever.

Matthew 18:15-18

¹⁵"If your brother sins against you, go and show him his fault, just between the two of you. If he listens to you, you have won your brother over.

¹⁶"But if he will not listen, take one or two others along, so that 'every matter may be established by the testimony of two or three witnesses.'

¹⁷"If he refuses to listen to them, tell it to the church; and if he refuses to listen even to the church, treat him as you would a pagan or a tax collector.

¹⁸"I tell you the truth, whatever you bind on earth will be bound in heaven, and whatever you loose on earth will be loosed in heaven."

Paul admonished the Christians at Corinth for failing to accept the judicial authority of the church over disputes between believers. They apparently had been taking their disputes outside the church to be judged by "the ungodly." He shamed them, reminding them that if the church eventually was to judge angels, it should learn to judge the far less important conflicts of earthly life (1 Cor. 6:1–6). Paul's message here was that the church was to live as a model before the world. In that case we should pay more attention to how the political systems of our church organization operate. John Stott sums it up:

> [W]e have to take more seriously Christ's intention that the Christian community should set an example to other communities. . . . I am thinking particularly of the life of the local church, which is meant to be a sign of God's rule. The Church should be the one community in the world in which human dignity and equality are invariably recognized, and people's responsibility for one another is accepted; in which the rights of others are sought and never violated, while our own are often renounced; in which there is no partiality, favoritism or discrimination; in which the poor and the weak are defended, and human beings are free to be human as God made them and meant them to be.[14]

So we must not shy away from thinking about church politics. Organizations of the church are inevitably political. Additionally, if we are to be worthy of judging angels, we must first learn how to manage the mundane issues of earthly life. When we have learned to tend well the politics of our Christian organizations—local churches, denominations, evangelistic associations, and Christian colleges and universities—perhaps then we can aspire to serving our nation by participating in politics beyond the walls of the church.

Government, God's Servant

To most of us the word *politics* usually refers to the activities having to do with government. It brings to mind elections, campaigns, vetoes, filibusters, and deals done behind doors in smoky rooms. I earlier defined politics as a struggle for power to shape the decisions of an organization. That definition fits here because governments in a sense are indeed large organizations. But they are more than just large organizations. Governments have some traits and purposes that set them apart from private organizations, such the local Rotary Club, K-Mart Store, First Methodist Church, Teamsters Union, or the American Medical Association. The major difference is that government is the only institution that exercises power and authority over an entire society. This unique quality allows governments to meet three needs: (1) to provide national security against outsiders;

---

[14]John R. W. Stott, *Decisive Issues Facing Christians Today*, 2d ed. (Tarrytown, N.Y.: Fleming H. Revell, 1990), 161.

(2) to provide for internal order and peaceful resolution of conflicts between its citizens; and (3) to provide a mechanism for cooperative undertakings for its citizens.

Some political philosophers, such as Thomas Hobbes, have argued that the paramount purpose of government is to provide security for its citizens against attacks from foreign enemies. If citizens tried to defend themselves individually against a well organized attacker, they would live a dreadfully insecure—or short—life. So to protect their citizens, governments raise military forces through taxation and conscription. Citizens accept the burdens of paying taxes and military service because they value life and liberty so highly.

Even when there are no threats from invaders, internal conflicts must be resolved. The selfishness of humans often leads to conflicts that may lead to violence. If my neighbor starts building a fence twelve inches on my side of the property line, I will immediately try to set him straight. If he doesn't quickly see things my way and no government is available to help us settle the argument, I may lose land rightly mine and an injustice would result. Or, I could grab a baseball bat—people hear you better when you have one in hand! My neighbor may retreat, only to return to the discussion—gun in hand. You get the idea. We need government to help us resolve disputes between citizens. If my neighbor and I cannot resolve our dispute peacefully, we need to be able to turn to our government. An effective government would provide clear and fair laws governing real estate, courts to decide disputes, and police officers to enforce the decisions of the courts.

In addition to deciding disputes between neighbors, governments protect us against swindlers and murderers. An orderly society needs a system of criminal laws and proper enforcement. Without government we all would live in a state of anarchy and no one would be safe. Even a giant who is an evil

Thomas Hobbes

Thomas Hobbes (1588–1679) was an English philosopher and one of the greatest political theorists of the seventeenth century. At the early age of fourteen he entered Oxford University, graduating in 1608 with a bachelor's degree. In *Leviathan* (1651), his greatest work, he sets forth his social contract theory of justice. From the time it was published it was recognized as a powerful political treatise. Today it is regarded as one of the most important contributions to moral philosophy and political theory. For more information on Hobbes and his social contract theory of justice, see Appendix 8, "Thomas Hobbes and the Contract Theory of Justice," on p. 487.

genius would not live securely under anarchy. Just like the rest of us, he has to eat and sleep. Eating makes him vulnerable to poisoning, while sleeping makes him vulnerable to attack by someone weaker and even dumber than he.

As the supreme civil authority in society, governments have a monopoly on the right to use force (with a limited exception for self-defense). If a suspect will not submit peaceably to arresting officers, they are authorized to use physical force to bring him under control. In television documentaries on police work, we see suspects thrown to the ground, struck with batons, and handcuffed. While seeing this may turn the stomach of many citizens, it illustrates the power police are authorized to use in bringing suspected criminals under control and to prevent citizens from harming one another.

If my neighbor and I cannot resolve our dispute over the location of a fence, neither of us has a legal or biblical right to use a baseball bat or gun to resolve the dispute. Romans 13:1–6 states clearly that God intends for humans to submit to governments. God declares that the political authorities are his servants, who wield the sword against wrongdoers and who are authorized to collect taxes for the support of the government.

These two functions of government—providing external and internal security—are easily appreciated for their social value. The third function of government is equally valuable. Governments allow us to do things together we can't do as well otherwise. Some needs are society-wide, and government is uniquely able to meet them. For example, consider the problem of regulating the safety of air travel and the use of radio fre-

John Locke

John Locke (1632–1704) was an English philosopher and the architect of a philosophical point of view that came to be known as British empiricism. His family's religious tradition was Puritan. Locke himself remained a Christian and defender of Christian ideals his whole life.

Locke's two most important works, *Essay Concerning Human Understanding* and *Two Treatises of Government*, both appeared in print in 1690. They quickly established him as a leading philosopher and political theorist. His account of checks and balances in government provided a model for the framers of the United States Constitution, and colonial Americans paid attention to his arguments that revolution in some circumstances is not only a right but an obligation. His arguments for broad religious freedom have formed part of a long political discussion in Europe and America.

For additional discussion of his political theories, see Appendix 9, "John Locke and the Theory of Natural Rights," on p. 490.

quencies. The safety of airliners depends on invisible highways drawn in the sky by the Federal Aviation Agency. Radio and television broadcasts would interfere with each other if the Federal Communications Commission didn't regulate their broadcast frequencies. Preventing the spread of epidemics and agricultural pests and providing highways, sewer systems, and mosquito abatement are other functions that governments can fulfill better than institutions with a narrower scope of authority.

THE AUTHORITY OF GOVERNMENT

In carrying out its great responsibilities, a government will necessarily exercise great power. The problem is that a government's use of power may go beyond its God-given authority. If God appointed government as his "servant, an agent of wrath to bring punishment on the wrongdoer" (Rom. 13:4), we must be inclined to submit to it. But history gives us many examples of governments that have exceeded their divine grant of authority. In our earlier discussion we saw that governments have a claim on the legal use of force. At first thought, this is not a problem for Christians, because the passage in Romans 13 declares that rulers have the right to use the sword to carry out their proper duties. The problem comes in knowing where to draw the line between proper and improper use of governmental power. At some point, governments cross the line and move out from under the mantle of God-given authority. Beyond this line, governmental officials are tyrants, usurpers of the divine mandate.

This century alone gives us horrendous examples. In the

Romans 13:1–6

¹Everyone must submit himself to the governing authorities, for there is no authority except that which God has established. The authorities that exist have been established by God.

²Consequently, he who rebels against the authority is rebelling against what God has instituted, and those who do so will bring judgment on themselves.

³For rulers hold no terror for those who do right, but for those who do wrong. Do you want to be free from fear of the one in authority? Then do what is right and he will commend you.

⁴For he is God's servant to do you good. But if you do wrong, be afraid, for he does not bear the sword for nothing. He is God's servant, an agent of wrath to bring punishment on the wrongdoer.

⁵Therefore, it is necessary to submit to the authorities, not only because of possible punishment but also because of conscience.

⁶This is also why you pay taxes, for the authorities are God's servants, who give their full time to governing.

Thomas Aquinas on Law and Justice

Aquinas's *Treatise on Law* is taken from a longer work entitled the *Summa Theologica*. Like the rest of the *Summa*, the *Treatise on Law* is divided into short chapters called questions. Each question is a separate inquiry that is further subdivided into articles. In each article, Aquinas states his own view on the various questions he poses and tries to answer the major objections to it.

The *Treatise on Law* begins with a discussion in Question 90 of the *Summa Theologica* of the qualities that all laws must have. Aquinas argues first that all laws must be determined by reason. That is, laws cannot be senselessly arbitrary. Laws are made in order to achieve some end, and only by using our reason can we determine how we can achieve those ends. Thus, reason must enter into the making of all laws. Second, Aquinas argues that all laws must be designed to achieve the good of the whole society. We make laws in order to secure our happiness, but we can do so only if society as a whole is functioning well. It stands to reason, then, that if we are to achieve happiness, we must design our laws so that they will benefit the whole society. Third, Aquinas claims that only the people as a whole—or someone who is concerned with the good of the whole society—has the right to make laws. Laws must be designed to achieve the good of the whole society, so they must be made by someone who has this good in mind. But only the people as a whole or a representative acting on their behalf will keep the good of all society in mind. Fourth, Aquinas concludes that laws must be promulgated . . . must be made known to those who are to obey them. Otherwise, they will have no influence on our actions. So, Aquinas concludes, a rule can be counted as a true law only if (1) it is reasonable, (2) it is aimed at the good of the whole society, (3) it is made by the people as a whole or someone concerned with their good, and (4) it is enacted openly and not in secret.

We can clarify what Aquinas means by a true law if we look briefly at what was going on in Germany during World War II. When Hitler came to power, he declared that any decree or order he issued automatically became the law of Germany; subsequently he issued orders that began the war and secretly ordered the systematic killing of Jews. These orders often contradicted the German constitution, they were inconsistent with each other, and they violated basic judicial rights established by other laws. Thus, to the extent that Hitler's decrees were inconsistent, they were irrational: they did not have their source in reason but were simply the expression of his arbitrary will. Consequently, it is clear, first, that these decrees were not reasonable. Second, Hitler's decrees obviously were not aimed at the good of the whole society: they were designed to satisfy his own personal desires and those of his fellow Nazis. Third, these decrees were not made by a person concerned with the good of the whole society: They were made by a man dedicated only to the interests of a small group. And fourth, these decrees were not openly promulgated: They were so inhumane that many of them had to be enacted and carried out in secret. Hitler's decrees, then, did not have any of the characteristics of what Aquinas means by a true law. Thus, when the German leaders were brought before their judges after the armistice and tried as war criminals, they could not hold that in following Hitler's orders they were merely obeying the law. Aquinas would say they so clearly contradict our basic notions of what law is that they could not be counted as such.

This passage appeared first in Manuel Velasquez and Cynthia Rostankowski (ed.), *Ethics Theory and Practice* (Englewood Cliffs, N.J.: Prentice-Hall, Inc., 1985) 34–36. Reprinted by permission of Prentice-Hall.

1930s, Joseph Stalin authorized the slaughter of millions of his political opponents and pursued a policy of mass starvation in the Ukraine by manipulated food supplies. In the 1940s, Adolf Hitler not only authorized the killing of millions of civilians in aggressive wars against Germany's neighbors, but he tried to exterminate all Jews, gypsies, mentally retarded, and others in Germany. In the 1970s, the Pol Pot regime in Cambodia killed nearly half of the entire population of the country. His regime was so bestial that in order to save bullets he ordered his soldiers to kill political opponents with clubs, hammers, and rocks. These regimes earned the hatred—yes, that is the right word, for we are to hate evil—of civilized persons around the world. Such rulers have no divine blessing.

To put the question simply, how imperfect must a government be before Christians can refuse its authority? The simple answer is, quite a bit. God seems to give the benefit of doubt to governments. He knows that imperfect humans will create imperfect governments. Even so, in pursuing the well-being of their citizens, they carry out God's purpose on earth. But by what standard does God judge governments? God judges governments by how well they measure up to a fundamental value—justice. (See Appendix 11, "Justice," on p. 497.)

> **"In carrying out its great responsibilities, a government will necessarily exercise great power."**

To many American conservatives, the central domestic purpose of government is to provide order. When demonstrators became unruly during the civil rights struggle of the 1960s, conservatives shouted for law and order. The liberals responded with a call for law and justice. Both had it partly right and partly wrong. The conservatives sensed the value of an orderly society, but they were inadequately concerned with the racial injustices staring them in the face. Liberals sensed the need for justice, but sometimes forgot that justice requires an orderly society. If we combine the best of the two slogans, we get "law and order and justice." This combination captures somewhat the meaning of the Old Testament word *shalom*.[15] When *shalom* prevails, people live in harmonious relationships in a peaceful and just social order.

Justice, or fairness, means that persons are treated with dignity and granted maximum freedom consistent with the rights of others. They are allowed freedom of conscience, freedom to move their place of residence, freedom to earn a living, and freedom to change occupations. Justice means that persons are judged according to their merits, not their gender, physical abil-

---

[15]*Shalom* includes the ideas of peace, wholeness, well-being, prosperity, unaffectedness, intactness.

ities, or skin color. The basic needs of those who cannot provide for themselves, such as orphans, the disabled, and the elderly, are met. Under justice persons are held responsible to provide for themselves and their families; they cannot live as parasites on other productive citizens. When justice prevails, although not all persons will have equal powers, each will have enough power and independence to pursue lives of freedom and dignity. Questions of justice arise in any circumstance in which persons have disproportionate powers. There are too many possibilities to list here, but they include relationships such as those between landlords and renters, adults and children, rich and poor, police and citizens, and racial majorities and minorities. Carl F. H. Henry offered an example from the world of work. He condemned the assembly line that "degrades men into machines, and robs them of their destiny as sons of God."[16] A working environment that turns humans into robots or exposes them to danger must be condemned as unjust.

A just and orderly society is both the goal for governments and the biblical justification for their existence. Christians therefore should accept the obligation of continually pressing governments toward justice. In democracies that means we have both a constitutional right and a biblical duty to participate in the public arena. Since the nature of democracy is that one must gain the consent of the governed, we must learn to appeal to our opponents' reason, self-interest, and sense of justice.

We must learn not only the ins-and-outs of politics but will need to develop political good manners. We Christians are prone to moral arrogance because we believe we have absolute truth. Therefore we have a tendency to believe that anyone who disagrees with us only propagates error, or even worse, heresy. Richard J. Mouw argues that in the public arena of political debate Christians should practice "convicted civility." We must speak biblical truth to a fallen world but do so in a style that respects the legitimate arguments and rights of others to disagree with us.[17] Civility calls for us to respect the rights of others, even the right to live sinfully, as long as that does not violate the rights of others. He argues, however, that at some point we must move beyond civility, though "[w]e are never justified in engaging in a no-holds-barred crusade against our opponents."[18]

Because Christians ultimately answer to a higher authority, we live in tension with the authority of governments. We must

---

[16] Carl F. H. Henry, *Aspects of Christian Social Ethics* (Grand Rapids: Wm. B. Eerdmans Publishing Co., 1964), 57–58.

[17] Richard J. Mouw, *Uncommon Decency: Christian Civility in an Uncivil World* (Downers Grove, Ill.: InterVarsity Press, 1992).

[18] Ibid., 132.

constantly judge them by the biblical reason for their existence, so our loyalty can never be absolute. Glenn Tinder argues that obedience is our normal duty, but unconditional obedience would be idolatry.[19] So we must honor Corrie ten Boom's heroic refusal to obey the Nazi authorities when she hid Jews marked for extermination. She knew when a government must be defied.

The Politics of Nations

Politics at its greatest complexity takes place in the international arena. Here we also encounter power of the most awesome sort, power that raises the gravest issues for the moral life. All the elements of power already discussed can be observed in international politics, but at this level power operates across international boundaries and has the potential to lead to a nuclear war that destroys human civilization.

Richard Mouw on Civility

Rich Mouw is a Christian philosopher, ethicist and current president of Fuller Theological Seminary. In *Uncommon Decency: Christian Civility In an Uncivil World* (InterVarsity Press, 1992), he attempts to develop a theological basis for political pluralism and civility in public discourse with people whose political positions we find objectionable.

What is civility? Mouw's description of it makes it appear to be a kind of public virtue, a good habit, a disposition to behave toward others with a measure of reserve and consideration. He explains it this way:

> Civility is public politeness. It means that we display tact, moderation, refinement and good manners toward people who are different from us. It isn't enough, though, to make an outward show of politeness. Being civil has an "inner" side as well [p. 12]

For Mouw, civility lies at the heart of good citizenship, the art of working for the good of all in a way that recognizes, tolerates, and even values diversity of political opinion. We are not naturally good citizens. Citizenship is an acquired disposition, something we learn through practice.

> To be good citizens, we must learn to move beyond relationships that are based exclusively on familiarity and intimacy. We must learn how to behave among strangers, to treat people with courtesy not because we know them, but simply because we see them as human beings like ourselves [p. 14].

But won't civility dampen our convictions, weaken our resolve, making it seem that we stand for nothing? Mouw thinks not.

> I admit that trying to make believers gentler and more "tolerant" will strike some Christians as wrong-headed. What about the devout, passionate people who picket abortion clinics and organize boycotts against offensive television programs? They might worry that becoming civil will mean a weakening of their faith. I am convinced that this is not necessarily so.

---

[19]*The Political Meaning of Christianity* (San Francisco: HarperCollins Publishers, 1989), 205–211.

These characteristics of international politics create a problem for our understanding. The sheer complexity of international affairs pushes us to simplify the issues to make understanding possible. Simplification presents dangers for us when we try to think in a Christian way about international politics. Too often we look at the international politics as a matter of relations between governments. Focusing on governments as the actors on the international stage makes it easy to forget that governments are not abstract objects—they are associations of humans. Even more, they are organizations of persons whom God has created and whom He has made in His image.

Fully understanding that we are dealing with persons, and not simply governments, will cause us to approach international politics differently than those who do not start with a Christian worldview. A focus on human beings may help us to

---

Developing a convicted civility can help us become more mature Christians. Cultivating civility can make strong Christian convictions even stronger [p. 18].

Cultivating civility does not mean, according to Mouw, that we must abandon our principles or our point of view. Quite the contrary, the Christian cultivates civility precisely on the basis of principles and a thoughtful point of view.

No attempt to be civil will be biblically adequate if it downplays the reality of evil. Civility cannot mean relativism. All beliefs and values are not on a moral par. When we show kindness and reverence toward people with whom we disagree about important issues, it cannot be because we don't care about ultimate questions of truth and goodness [p. 143].

Cultivating civility also does not mean that we must abandon attempts to influence society through the legislative process. However, there are limits to our ability to effect changes of heart and mind through legislation.

I am wary of efforts to establish laws whose primary purpose is to force non-Christians to conform to Christian sexual norms. While it makes sense to construct legislative "fences" around certain practices of sexual exploitation, laws designed to make non-Christians conform grudgingly to Christian rules are not satisfactory. The Scriptures call human beings to offer God their free obedience. When they choose not to do so, we must respect their choices even if we find them regrettable [p. 90].

The American system of government is a representative democracy. This means, in part, that it is *not* a theocracy. Hence, "we have no automatic right to keep people from sinning" (p. 91). At the same time, we do have a responsibility to approach people like Christ himself would have done: "Treating other people with the gentleness and reverence of Jesus requires that we be deeply sensitive to the pain and brokenness of a creation that has not yet been fully delivered from its cursedness" (p. 155).

see world politics more like God sees it. If our analysis focuses only on governments, we may forget that we are not just Americans defending our interests against those of other nations, such as Iraq or Japan. We may not see that our governments exercise power that ultimately touches the lives of other people, whom God loves and has commanded us to love. That is, they also are neighbors we are to love as ourselves. Sending missionaries abroad illustrates our concern for their spiritual well-being, but we cannot stop there. As we love their souls, we must also show concern for their bodies, as we do our own. If they hunger, we must work to help them eat; if they live under oppression, we should help them escape it. Here again, of course, we will probably agree with these goals as long as our discussion stays safely at the level of generality. But how shall we solve Third World hunger? How shall we promote human rights in the People's Republic of China? Here's where the complexity begins and disagreements start.

For an illustration of the complexities of international relations, let us examine this last problem in a bit more detail. For decades American policy makers have been debating how best to deal with the People's Republic of China. In recent years, China has gradually allowed more economic freedom, including more commercial relationships with Western nations. In 1989, when tanks crushed the democratic protests in Tienanmen Square, American leaders were outraged. Some voices immediately called for severe sanctions against China. Many politicians suggested raising tariffs against Chinese imports to the United States. Others questioned whether this would cause the Chinese government to moderate its policies or rather would push it to crack down even harder on reformers. Some leaders, including then-President George Bush, argued that the best way to promote freedom in China was through expanding contacts with the West, not by reducing them. He believed this eventually would generate internal pressures that would lead to reforms. In the meantime, however, political dissidents would languish in prisons, and freedom would continue to be crushed. To complicate matters more, in 1994 President Bill Clinton was counting on China as an ally to pressure North Korea to cease developing nuclear weapons. China was important in this case not only because it was a powerful neighbor of North Korea but because it held veto power in the Security Council of the United Nations. Pushing China too hard on civil rights might result in losing an important ally against North Korea.

> **"We must understand how the structure of international power shapes international politics."**

We must not only recognize the complexity of world affairs, but we must understand how the structure of international power shapes international politics. Through a long historical process the peoples of various nations have sorted themselves into political units that exercise ultimate power—sovereignty—over all persons living inside their borders. International politics involves relations between governments that claim and vigorously defend their sovereignty. They resist granting power over their nation's affairs to any international organization, such as the United Nations. Consequently, there is nothing like a world government that is able to force peaceful resolution of disputes between two states. No international police force is available to arrest a sovereign state, drag it before an international court, and if it is convicted, haul it off to an international prison.

So if one state wishes to build a fence on its neighbor's land—that is, take some of its territory—neither country can force the other into court. Illustrations of the ineffectiveness of international organizations in resolving conflicts between sovereign states are readily found in the daily news. In 1995, Canada and Spain engaged in a dispute over fishing rights to a portion of the Atlantic Ocean near Newfoundland. The matter eventually resulted in Canada patrolling the area with warships to

> **"International politics involves relations between governments that claim and vigorously defend their sovereignty."**

enforce its claims. Spain backed down in the face of Canada's threat of force. The wars between the Croats, Bosnians, and Serbs in the territory of the disintegrated state of Yugoslavia continued in spite of the best efforts of the international community to prevent them. The United Nations found itself unable to form a unified alliance of member states willing to use lethal force to put a stop to the conflict. The problem is that sovereign states are unwilling to give any international organization sufficient power to decide relating to their individual national interest, except where the issue is considered minor. Moreover, international organizations (such as the World Court or the United Nations) lack sufficient enforcement power to coerce any but the weakest nations. The upshot is that when conflicts arise, nations are strongly tempted to follow an age-old pattern: One country grabs a baseball bat, the other grabs a gun, and the conflict easily escalates into war.

At first glance, having every country defend its own interests looks like anarchy. Great powers push around weaker powers or invade them. States do whatever they wish within their borders. Each state determines for itself what its interests are, decides on its own how to use its power, and judges itself by its own moral code. To call the international system anarchy, however, may overstate the matter. Even without a world government to enforce international law and establish order, most nations get along reasonably well with each other. Governments have mutual interests, so they negotiate treaties setting forth the privileges and obligations of the parties. Some treaties set forth rules governing international commerce and the rights of international travelers. Even without a higher authority to enforce treaties, most nations live up to their treaty obligations. They do so because each party to the treaty benefits; if circumstances had been otherwise the treaties wouldn't have been created in the first place. Nations also wish to honor their treaties because having a reputation for living up to its obligations helps a nation in negotiating future treaties.

> **"Most nations live up to their treaty obligations. They do so because each party to the treaty benefits."**

Christians should have no problem supporting an international treaty that benefits all parties, even if that treaty is based on the self-interest of the nations who signed the treaty. The happy coincidence of overlapping interests between nations allows them to work together, each for its own good. In agreeing to treaties, they are acting in much the same manner as neighbors who take care of each others' houses while they are away on vacation. The problem arises when sovereign nations have unequal military or economic power. Because of the anarchical quality of international politics, when the interests of nations conflict, each nation will use power in a self-serving way. One school of international politics, the so-called realist school, says this is the best we can expect from international politics. Nations inevitably feel their own pain and pleasure better than their neighbor's. (Remember the hypodermic needle?) And they judge their own actions by different moral codes. A Christian must find this repulsive because it sounds like "might makes right."

Power in international relations ultimately determines who will live, who will die, who will control land and natural resources, and who won't. A world map shows the existing order of sovereign states, each with its own boundaries. God didn't draw these lines; humans did. They are all products of power relationships, and power keeps them in their place. They also determine our loyalties.

An international border running between San Diego and Tijuana separates the United States from Mexico. I was fortunate to be born north of that line, so I am a United States citizen. I naturally share an affinity with other Americans, even those living in Boston, more than three thousand miles to the east. I don't easily feel as much concern for Tijuana's inhabitants, though they live only about one hundred miles to the south. That my loyalty to other Americans comes naturally may reflect more of my sinful nature than I wish to admit. Yet Mexicans were created by the same Heavenly Father. And some Mexicans are devout Christians, so we are brothers and sisters in the faith. My American patriotism, however, gets in the way of accepting this. I am more inclined to think of them as Mexicans than as brothers and sisters.

Focusing our thinking about international politics on persons rather than states will allow us to notice the individuals who make up the states. This will help us see them as human beings, as brothers and sisters, and as objects of God's love. We might even dream about the possibility of abolishing national borders so all the world's citizens could work for the common good. Given human nature, the eradication of national borders is impractical, so the existing order will likely continue until the Lord's return.

The problem of international politics is how to make governments act civilly toward other governments. They seem less able to do this than individuals. Governments combine the self-interest of millions of citizens into a group interest. Through governments we come to see ourselves as part of a larger community. In healthy amounts, identifying with other members of our nation manifests itself as patriotism—a feeling of belongingness and pride of country. Unfortunately, in excess patriotism can turn rancid, becoming an idolatrous worship of nation and hatred for other nations. Reinhold Niebuhr explained how this happens. He argued that individuals and groups operate out of different dynamics. Because individuals can feel sympathy for others, we can put aside our own interests to help our neighbors. Our capacity for reason allows us to develop a sense of justice. However, these traits of generosity and fairness become dulled when individuals combine into groups. Groups typically exhibit more selfishness than do members of the group acting as individuals; groups have less capacity to concern themselves with the needs of others; they are more inclined toward irrational acts and are more capable of evil than the individuals that make up the group.[20] As individuals we learn to apologize and even ask for forgiveness, but the larger the group, the more difficult this becomes. For entire nations, it is nearly impossible.

As American Christians, we are not immune to the excesses of patriotism. From childhood we are conditioned to see the world through patriotic eyes. We naturally wish the United States to be secure and prosperous. We learn

> **"As American Christians, we are not immune to the excesses of patriotism."**

about international affairs through the lenses of the American media and governmental officials. These sources seldom interpret the world through biblical principles, such as the divine kinship of all humans or loving our international neighbors as ourselves. Ideas such as these aren't readily accepted in the American marketplace of ideas. But as Christians, we at least can learn to ask if our government's policies serve a legitimate national interest. We can learn to consider whether American policies intrude on the right of other governments

[20]Reinhold Neibuhr, *Moral Man and Immoral Society* (New York: Charles Scribner's Sons, 1932 and 1960), xviii, xiv.

to provide for their citizens—our neighbors—and to help them live with freedom and dignity. Created by God, who loves all humans equally, the citizens of other nations have human rights that derive from the same divine source as ours. Simply learning to examine world affairs from this perspective can be one small step of faithfulness to our duty to love others as ourselves.

Conclusion

In this chapter I have touched on only a few aspects of the question of a Christian political philosophy. Much has been ignored or treated inadequately. But if we have learned a few ideas to help us face the challenge of living as Christians in a universally political world, we will have spent our time well.

All human relationships involve operations of power and influence. Power allows one person to control, manipulate, or influence the behavior of another. We need power, which appears in many forms, to operate human associations, from families to churches to national governments. Unfortunately, the power necessary for human life can be used for evil as well as good. The dual nature of power raises basic questions for Christians because God made us in his image and loves each of us deeply. When power demeans the value or violates the dignity of God's creations, we must protest, or be counted as accomplices.

We all live in networks of power relationships. So we have no choice but to involve ourselves in the moral questions of politics. Reinhold Niebuhr summarizes this well, "Politics will, until the end of history, be an area where conscience and power meet, where the ethical and coercive factors of human life will interpenetrate and work out their tentative and uneasy compromises."[21] If I am correct in saying that we all live in power relationships and if Niebuhr is correct in saying that conscience and power meet in politics, we have our task clearly before us: We must accept the burden of civilizing power with an informed Christian conscience.

Until the end of history, welcome to politics! Amen!

Review and Discussion Questions

1. What is it about the nature of humans that makes politics both inevitable and essential in human life?

2. If we believe that humans are objects of God's love and carriers of his image, how should that influence the way power should be exercised in an organization you currently belong to? You may wish to evaluate some specific practices you observe in your church, club, college, or university to see if they con-

---

[21]Ibid., 4.

form to a biblical view of humans and the use of power.

3. McNutt argues that politics occurs in all organizations, large and small. Pick a small organization you are familiar with and analyze it as a political entity. You may wish to discuss your family, student government, an athletic team, or a club in terms of how power operates within it, how decisions are made, and who wins and who loses.

4. Power takes many forms. To test your understanding of this statement, discuss the differences and similarities between coercive power and noncoercive power. How are they alike and unlike? How does the use of secrecy or deception raise many of the same ethical questions as the use of raw force?

5. If we can "love through politics," is it possible that a career in politics could be considered a Christian calling? If you answer affirmatively, explain some of the possible pitfalls of such a career.

6. Discuss the following statement: "If we are to have a sound political philosophy, we must have a proper view of both the sinfulness of humans and common grace."

7. Consider the following hypothetical situation: You take a group of Christians to an otherwise uninhabited tropical island that has an abundance of food, water, and shelter. There you and they establish a colony. Would your colony practice politics? Why or why not?

8. When we discuss international politics, we commonly focus on states (nations), both our own country and foreign countries. How does this focus on states/countries result in a degree of blindness to the reality of power in international politics?

9. The Bible commands us to love God and to love our neighbors as ourselves. Do you do both equally? If your answer is no, why not? Should you?

Selected Bibliography

CLASSICAL READINGS IN POLITICAL THEORY

Plato's *Republic*
Aristotle's *Politics*
Augustine's *City of God*
John Locke's *Two Treatises of Government*
Karl Marx's *The Economic & Philosophic Manuscripts of 1844*
Thomas Hobbes's *Leviathan*
The Federalist Papers
The Declaration of Independence
Jean Jacques Rousseau's *The Social Contract*

CONTEMPORARY READINGS

Campolo, Anthony. *The Power Delusion*. Wheaton, Ill.: Victor Books, 1978.

Cerillo, August, Jr., and Murray Dempster. *Salt and Light: Evangelical Political Thought in Modern America*. Grand Rapids: Baker Book House, 1989.

Cromartie, Michael, ed. *Evangelicals and Foreign Policy*. Washington, D.C.: Ethics and Public Policy Center, 1989.

Ellul, Jacques. *Money and Power*. Downers Grove, Ill.: Inter-Varsity Press, 1984.

Henry, Carl F.H. *Aspects of Christian Social Ethics*. Grand Rapids: William B. Eerdmans Publishing Co., 1954.

Montgomery, John Warwick. *Human Rights and Human Dignity*. Grand Rapids: Zondervan Publishing House, 1986.

Mott, Stephen Charles. *A Christian Perspective on Political Thought*. New York: Oxford University Press, 1993.

Mouw, Richard J. *Uncommon Decency: Christian Civility in an Uncivil World*. Downers Grove, Ill.: InterVarsity Press, 1992.

Tinder, Glenn. *The Political Meaning of Christianity: The Prophetic Stance*. San Francisco: HarperSanFrancisco, 1991.

Appendixes

Appendix 1
Reflections on the Meanings of Truth

Michael D. Palmer

"What is truth?" asked Pontius Pilate. Unfortunately, he seemed to be asking it rhetorically, not bothering to wait for a reply. So we are left to seek one for ourselves—What is the answer to this seemingly simple question? And why should you, as a Christian, be concerned about the answer?

To give a thoughtful response to these questions requires us to separate the different senses of the word; "truth" is used in different ways. We know, of course, that Jesus declared himself to be the truth: "I am the way and the *truth* and the life" (John 14:6). Moreover, when He prayed on behalf of His followers, He not only identified truth with himself but also with the Scriptures: "Sanctify them by the truth; your word is *truth*" (John 17:17). But the word *truth* has other uses as well. When we say "He is a true friend," we mean that the person in question really is a friend, not someone who merely pretends to be one. "She was true to her word" means that she kept her word. We also say *statements* are true: "What you just said is true"; "Truer words were never spoken"; "Do you swear that the testimony you are about to give is the truth, the whole truth, and nothing but the truth?" "Melville's characterization of Ishmael is true to human nature" means roughly that the character Ishmael in the novel *Moby Dick* is depicted as behaving in the way people of that kind generally behave under the circumstances described.

For our purposes the various uses and meanings of "truth" fall into four main categories:

1. Truth as it refers to a Christian worldview
2. Truth as it refers to the inner life or character of an individual human being
3. Truth as it refers to propositions (statements or judgments)
4. Truth as it refers to literary texts and works of art

When we have clarified these notable uses of "truth" for ourselves, we will be in a better position to explain why the topic of truth is important and why it should concern us.

Outline of a Christian Worldview

Jesus' pronouncement "I am the way and the *truth*, and the life" (John 14:6) is not simply one saying among others. For the Christian it represents a fundamental proclamation. Quite simply, it means that Jesus stands as the figure around whom one's life is centered. His purposes give meaning and coherence to the life devoted to His service. To commit oneself to the truth at this level involves committing oneself to an overall view of reality that touches every aspect of life. This commitment involves more than intellectual assent to a theory; it involves embarking unreservedly upon a way of life. Throughout this book the authors have called this kind of comprehensive view of reality (and the way of life based on it) a *worldview*.

As a worldview, Christianity has implications for who we human beings are, what we ought to do, how we can do it, and what we can hope to achieve. Psalm 8 identifies the place of humankind in a Christian worldview: "What is man that you are mindful of him. . . . You made him a little lower than the heavenly beings and crowned him with glory and honor." This passage presents humankind as created by a God who has distinct purposes for it. Moreover, if everyone is thus created, then God's purposes define what each of us ought to be and do. Of course, there are other features associated with one's assenting to and acting on Jesus' claim to be the truth—what I am here calling a Christian worldview. Since I discussed the six main elements of a Christian worldview at length in chapter 1, I shall limit myself here to a brief review of them with an eye toward discerning how they help us understand Jesus' claim to be the truth.

A Christian worldview, like other worldviews, expresses an *ideology*. An ideology, as noted in chapter 1, articulates the core beliefs of those who hold a certain worldview. It does so usually in philosophical propositions, statements of a creed, or other authoritative formulas. Christianity's core beliefs are found in its central doctrines, which provide (1) a general view about the nature of the universe—God is the creator of us and everything else; (2) a description of the essential nature of the individual human being—we are made in God's image;[1] (3) a diagnosis of what is wrong with humankind—through our choices we have become estranged from God; and (4) a prescription for the problem—we can be reconciled to God through Jesus.[2]

For many people, the truths of Christianity were made known to them first not through the profound (and often complex) intri-

---

[1]For a fuller treatment of this view of human nature, see chap. 5 by Billie Davis, "A Perspective on Human Nature."

[2]My use of the terms *general account of the universe, account of human nature, diagnosis,* and *prescription* follows Leslie Stevenson, "Rival Theories," chap. 1 in *Seven Theories of Human Nature,* second edition (Oxford: Oxford University Press, 1987). These features of an ideology correspond roughly to four traditional doctrines of the Church: creation, fall, redemption, and consummation. The doctrine of creation corresponds to the feature of a Christian worldview that says all things in the universe are created by God. The same doctrine reappears in the discussion of human nature: God created humankind in His own image. The doctrine of the fall appears in the feature of a Christian worldview that offers a diagnosis of the human condition. The doctrine of redemption corresponds to the prescriptive feature of a Christian worldview. Finally, the doctrine of consummation may be seen in the notions that the universe has a certain direction (natural and historical events are not merely random) and that its direction is toward a certain final culmination, or end (Gk. *telos*).

cacies of doctrinal statements but through the *narratives* found in the Bible. The narrative element of the Christian worldview, like that of other worldviews, expresses its core beliefs by example, image, story, symbol, parable, metaphor, archetype, and other literary and artistic devices.

To accept a Christian worldview means embracing and abiding by certain *norms*. Indeed, as was pointed out in chapter 8, it also means becoming a person whose character has been shaped in certain important ways. In the New Testament, Paul describes the ultimate norm for character formation as that of "conforming to the image of Christ"—by which he seems to mean assimilating and living out all the character traits exemplied in Jesus.

From the time of the founding of the Church in the first century, Christians have observed certain ceremonial acts. Of course, carrying out ceremonial acts—*rituals*, as they are called—is not unique to Christianity. (Most major worldviews encourage some form of ceremonial expression in order to integrate their patterns of belief into the fabric of the inner life and character of their adherents.) What *is* unique to Christianity, however, is the specific rituals it observes. In particular, the rituals of water baptism and Communion link the believer to certain profound beliefs central to the Christian faith: birth to a new life (baptism) and the resurrection of Jesus (Communion). The ritual of Communion reminds us of the remarkable—and startling—claim that in the life, death, and resurrection of the singular person Jesus, God has intervened in history to forgive humankind and to restore its ruptured relationship with Him. This claim lies at the heart of Jesus' worldview proclamation that He is the way, the *truth*, and the life.

Worldviews address more than the mind; they also speak to the affective side of human nature. This means that they evoke or encourage certain *experiences*. A Christian worldview specifically nurtures an encounter with God. The range of such experiences (as found in the Bible and in the records of the Church) is quite broad—from the animated to the subdued, from the fearful to the joyous. What the participants in these experiences commonly bear witness to, however, is the degree to which their experiences fortify their beliefs. This is not to say their experiences make their core beliefs true (make them truer than before, so to speak). They do, however, invest them with power and conviction.

The Church is the primary *social institution* of Christianity. Within its framework, doctrines and norms are worked out and clarified; narratives are told, retold, and protected; rituals are enacted; experiences with God encouraged and nurtured. Both historically and today, to be part of the Church means committing oneself to a community of people who acknowledge the centrality of the person Jesus and His claim to be the truth.

In sum, to accept Jesus' claim to be the truth involves much more than accepting a simple proposition or even a set of statements about the human condition. It involves thinking in terms of a comprehensive view of reality and entering fully into a way of life based on that view of reality. In short, to accept Jesus' claim means embracing and acting on a worldview that incorporates ideological, narrative, and normative elements as well as rituals, experiences, and social commitments.

Truth in the Inner Life

As was noted earlier, the English language exhibits a second use of the term *true,* as when we speak of someone being a *true* friend or being *true* to her word. In these instances the word refers to certain character traits of the persons in question. The true friend is *faithful*; the one who is true to her word has *integrity*.

The writer of Genesis understood this kind of truth. When Joseph, in Pharaoh's service, recognized his brothers, who had come to Egypt seeking grain, he tested them. He wanted to see if they had changed from the way they were when they conspired to sell him into slavery and then lied about it to their father, Jacob. Joseph accused them of being spies. In reply they explained their family background and insisted, "We are honest men." Pressing them further, Joseph demanded that the youngest brother be brought to him, so that "your words may be tested, whether there is *truth* in you" (Gen. 42:16, NASB). Clearly, Joseph was interested in something more than mere correctness. He wanted to test their words to see whether there was *truth* in his brothers. Spoken words represented an avenue for determining what was crucially important: the character of those who spoke them.

Truth in the inner life is neither a static nor a simple phenomenon; a virtuous character emerges slowly, over time, and on the basis of small choices made every day. Eventually it grows into a complex reality called the mature self. But often its origin can be traced to an occasion requiring the individual to reflect honestly on his own condition. In this respect, honesty about oneself is the initial and most basic phase of becoming a mature person exhibiting inward truth. All subsequent shaping of the inner life toward maturity and strength of character begins with a candid appraisal of one's own person.

The tax-collector mentioned by Luke recognized this point. That is why he went away from the temple "justified" and the Pharisee did not. Whereas the Pharisee proclaimed his own righteousness and boasted that he was not like other people (a swindler, unjust, an adulterer, or a tax-gatherer), the publican acknowledged his desperate condition. In simple, eloquent language, Luke tells us, "[T]he tax collector stood at a distance. He would not even look up to heaven, but beat his breast and said, 'God, have mercy on me, a sinner.'" (Luke 18:13).

The case of the tax collector points up a peculiar, almost paradoxical, relationship between truth as it refers to a person's inner life and truth as it refers to Jesus. No one who does not exhibit at least a measure of truth in the inner self can acknowledge in any fundamental way that Jesus is the truth. This means that acknowledging Jesus' true identity involves exercising a basic honesty with ourselves. In other words, unless we acknowledge our own status as a sinner, we cannot acknowledge the truth about Christ's redemption. Without our having the sort of candor or inward truth exhibited by the tax collector, Jesus can never become the truth for any of us. He will always remain only a distant figure who mouths unintelligible words. So for Jesus to become the truth, each person must welcome and cultivate truth in the most private recesses of life. But this cannot be done merely as a resolve of the will. It requires grace. Strangely, grace is at once easier and more difficult than we ordinarily view it.[3] It is easier, because, although we wish to pay or do something for it, it is free. It is harder, because it is regularly extended to us in ways we are least prepared to receive it. We wish to receive grace through familiar and comfortable channels. But Jesus extends grace in ways that force us to come to terms with the truth—both in ourselves and in Him—and sometimes His methods seem strange, even offensive. He extends grace to a Jew through the helping hands of a Samaritan, to a Canaanite woman through words about giving the children's food to a dog, to Peter by means of a dream about eating things traditionally called "unclean," to Paul through a blinding light.

Jesus, the truth, imparts grace through words and deeds. Through that grace we are empowered with sufficient honesty, with sufficient interior truth, to acknowledge the truth of the worldview based on His life. This pattern emerges clearly in the story of the woman at the well, of whom John speaks in the fourth chapter of his Gospel. When Jesus confronts her with the facts of her life, He is, in essence, speaking words of grace by presenting her with the opportunity to come to terms with herself. In a series of exchanges, the woman faces up to the dark reality of her past life and the depravity of her present condition. By doing so, she is able to listen to Jesus with increasing attentiveness until finally she is able to understand from Jesus' own lips that He is the Messiah, the anointed one.

We misunderstand the stories of the tax collector and the woman at the well if we take them as implying that truth dawns luminously in the inner life once and for all. The dawn of inward truth, like the practice of true worship, intensifies and matures as we give ourselves fully to it. In the moral sphere the pursuit of inward truth gradually leads to the reshaping of our

---

[3]Robert Funk, *Language, Hermeneutic, and Word of God* (New York: Harper and Row, 1965).

desires and affections toward the moral virtue and to the refining of our ability to make good choices, which is called intellectual virtue. In the spiritual realm the pursuit of inward truth gradually leads to a deepening and a purifying of our faith.

Propositional Truth

In everyday life as well as in technical fields of inquiry, such as physics, chemistry, mathematics, and logic, truth is commonly considered to be a property of our thoughts or the propositions (sometimes called statements or judgments) that express our thoughts. To understand this way of thinking about truth, I must make a distinction between *truth* and *fact*.

A fact is a state-of-affairs, that is, an object, a condition, a circumstance, or an event. Obviously, reality is composed of countless states-of-affairs. The drought that much of the Midwestern United States suffered during the summer of 1988 is a state-of-affairs, and as such is a fact. A satellite currently orbits the earth dragging a steel tether several miles long. (It broke loose from the space shuttle in 1996.) The satellite, with its tether, is a state-of-affairs and is therefore a fact. If your car has a crumpled right fender, that too is a state-of-affairs. The tree that grows in your front yard at home, the chemical in the laboratory beaker, the book on your desk, your teacher's bald head—these are all states-of-affairs, and as such they are all facts.

States-of-affairs, and hence facts, exist even if no one ever reports or describes them, and they exist independently of our language and thought. Furthermore, they are neither true nor false; they simply exist. But, of course, we can and do describe them, specifically in statements.

I said that truth is a property of the statements we make (or the thoughts expressed by them). When does a statement (or a thought) have this property? A statement is true when it describes a fact (a state-of-affairs that exists); or in the case of a statement about the past, when it describes a state-of-affairs that did occur; or in the case of the future, one that will occur. So if "There is a briefcase on the desk" describes an actual state-of-affairs, then the statement is true. In contrast, a false statement describes a state-of-affairs that does not (or did not or will not) exist.[4]

We may gain a richer appreciation of this definition of truth if we place it in the context of two related concepts: *belief* and *knowledge*.

---

[4]My definition of truth corresponds closely to the definition given by John Hospers in "Knowledge," chap. 1 in *An Introduction to Philosophical Analysis* (Englewood Cliffs, N.J.: Prentice Hall, 1988). The discussion of knowledge and warrantability that follows also owes much to Manuel Velasquez and Vincent Barry in "Truth,"chap. 6 in *Philosophy*, 3d ed. (Belmont, Calif.: Wadsworth Publishing Co., 1988), "Chapter Six: 265ff.

A *belief* (or opinion) is an attitude or state of mind in which one accepts, assents, or expresses conviction about the truth or actuality of something. We often express our beliefs in statements. For example:

"There's intelligent life in outer space."
"The moon is made of green cheese."
"Dante once lived."
"Bill Clinton was president before John F. Kennedy."
"Water is H_2O."

Clearly, while all of these statements express beliefs, only some of them are true. An important feature of beliefs is that, unlike facts, they are true or false. This does not mean that we always *know* whether our beliefs are true or false. (No one yet knows for sure whether there is intelligent life in outer space.) Nevertheless, regardless of our ability to demonstrate their truth value, all beliefs are either true or false.

Before defining *knowledge* I must pause briefly to clarify and reinforce a crucial distinction between facts and beliefs. Facts are simply states-of-affairs that exist. The liquid standing in the beaker is a *fact*; it is a state-of-affairs that exists. This fact is neither true nor false; it simply exists. Now a chemistry student may come along and express her *belief* about the nature of that liquid. "That liquid is water," she says, pointing to the contents of the beaker. Unlike the fact (the liquid standing in the beaker) which is neither true nor false, but simply exists, the chemistry student's belief (expressed in the statement "That liquid is water") must be true or false. If, upon closer examination, the liquid turns out to be water, her belief will be true. If it turns out to be some other substance, her belief will be false. With this distinction in mind between facts and beliefs, I turn to the topic of knowledge.

Knowledge is related to belief but differs importantly from it. It is related to belief to the extent that *knowing* something entails *believing* it. If you claim to know that your computer is in your room, you believe it. You don't just have a hunch. You have a positive belief. Your friends would think you very strange indeed if you said, "I know my computer is in my room, but I don't believe it." Of course, we sometimes *seem* to dissociate belief from knowledge, as in "I know the president has been assassinated, but I don't believe it." But this is a rhetorical expression. We actually do believe it; otherwise we would not be shocked. Intellectually we believe it, but emotionally we are incredulous. Employing the formal language that logicians prefer to use, we can express the relationship between knowledge and belief as follows: If p represents any proposition, then to assert that you know p involves believing that p is so. More succinctly, "I know p" implies "I believe p."

Of course, merely believing something is not the only requirement for saying we know it. We can and do believe all sorts of things: that there is life in outer space, that we are in excellent health, that the Green Bay Packers will once again make it to the Super Bowl, as they did in their glory days. But believing such things does not mean we know them to be the case. In short, knowledge implies belief, but belief does not imply knowledge.

Knowledge also requires evidence or justification. When you say, "I know that my computer is in my room," you mean not only that you believe what you said but that you have evidence for it. In general, then, "I know p" implies "I have evidence or justification for p." Suppose someone claims to know that southern California will be rocked by an earthquake next week. You would likely ask, "How do you know that?" If the person responded, "Because I believe it," you would not take the claim seriously. Belief merely expresses assent or indicates an attitude of conviction about something; it does not provide a justification. Only evidence can do that. A synonym for "evidence" or "justification" is *warrantability*. The person who claims to know that southern California will be rocked by an earthquake next week is implying that he has evidence or justification for what he believes. In other words, he is implying that his belief is *warranted*.

Is it correct, then, to speak of knowledge as warranted belief? No. Suppose southern California is not rocked by an earthquake next week. Clearly the person didn't know, but this does not mean that his belief was not warranted. It only suggests that knowledge implies more than warranted belief. It also implies *truth*. For you to know that your computer is in your room, it must actually be there. You may believe it, and your belief may be warranted. But to know it, you need something else in addition: the truth. So you may say that you know p only if p is actually true.

I am now in a position to define knowledge. *Knowledge is warranted, true belief.* To understand knowledge, then, we must not only understand truth, we must understand warrantability as well.

When is a belief warranted? When do I have justification for a belief? The answer depends on the kind of statement in question. Consider the following statements.

1. This rose is red.
2. Jefferson City is the capital of Missouri.
3. A bachelor is an unmarried male.
4. No circle is square.
5. The sum of the interior angles in a triangle is equal to two right angles.
6. The sum of the squares of the sides of a right triangle is equal to the square of the hypotenuse.
7. X is not non-X.
8. X is either Y or non-Y.

Each of these statements is warranted in suitable circumstances. We would be on solid ground if we believed them. Why?

Statements 1 and 2 are warranted by looking to the facts. If the rose in question is, as a matter of fact, red, then statement 1 is warranted. If Jefferson City is actually the capital of Missouri, then statement 2 is warranted. This kind of warrantability—which looks to the facts in order to provide evidence or justification—is called *empirical warrantability*. The scientific disciplines and courts of law have developed elaborate techniques for providing empirical warrants for some of their important claims. However, in less technical ways ordinary citizens also often seek empirical justification for claims that others put forward. For example, the store clerk who asks for a receipt when you return an item is asking for empirical evidence that you actually paid for what you are now returning.

But what about statements 3 and 4? Their warrantability cannot be established in the same way. Their warrantability lies in the meaning of their terms. Proposition 3 is true because the meaning of "unmarried" is included in the meaning of "bachelor." Similarly, in 4, the meaning of "circle" excludes the meaning of "square," and the statement asserts this exclusion. Statements 3 and 4 exemplify *semantic warrantability*: Their warrantability can be determined by analyzing the meaning of the terms used and the relations of these terms to each other.

The warrantability of statements 5 and 6 lies in their being theorems that we can deduce from the postulates and definitions of Euclidean geometry. The warrantability of these and other similar statements is furnished by the systems they belong to. In other words, they derive their warranty from the logical interdependence of all propositions in a deductive system. Propositions related in this way are said to have *systemic warrantability*.

Statements 7 and 8 are always warranted because to deny them brings a halt to all rational thought. If they are not warranted, thought itself cannot be reasonable, cannot be intelligent. Put another way, their denial is self-contradictory. Proposition 7 accords with the principle of identity: *A* is *A* (a statement that expresses the relationship anything has to itself). Everything we say presupposes that *A* is *A*. If you speak of a specific person, Jones, or a distant star, you presuppose that Jones is Jones and that the star is a star. If Jones were not Jones and the star not a star, of what could you even be speaking? Statement 8 accords with the principle of excluded middle: everything is either *A* or non-*A*. Thus, something is either Jones or not Jones; either a star or not a star. Logically, there can be no middle ground. Statements 7 and 8 are said to have *logical warrantability*; that is, they appeal to laws of logic that we consider necessarily true.[5]

---

[5]For additional information about the principles of identity and excluded middle, see Irving M. Copi and Carl Cohen, *Introduction to Logic,* 10th ed. (Upper Saddle River, N.J.: Prentice-Hall, 1998), 389–391.

The main points developed so far in this discussion of truth as it relates to propositions may be summarized as follows:

1. A fact is a state-of-affairs, that is, an object, a condition, a circumstance, or an event that exists.
2. Truth is not something that stands alone; it is a property of our statements (or the thoughts we express in statements).
3. A true statement describes a state-of-affairs; a statement that accurately and adequately describes a state-of-affairs has the property truth.
4. A belief is an attitude or state of mind in which one accepts, assents, or expresses conviction about the truth or actuality of something.
5. Knowledge is warranted true belief.
6. Warrantability is another name for justification or evidence.
7. Warrantability depends on whether the statement in question is empirical, semantic, or logical.

The discussion about truth as it refers to propositions is bound to raise questions about two other topics that concern the Christian: *wisdom* and *faith*.

Just as knowledge is not identical to belief, so too wisdom is not identical to knowledge. Solomon was not called the wisest man because he knew more than anyone else. He was wise because he had the ability (God-given) to make sound judgments about practical and moral matters. Indeed, the example of his life helps us define wisdom. Wisdom is a kind of insight or capacity to apply one's knowledge toward good ends in a prudent and circumspect way. In this connection the words of the writer of Proverbs resound like the peal of a bell: "Wisdom is the principal thing; therefore get wisdom: and with all thy getting get understanding" (Prov. 4:7, KJV). Important as the acquisition of ordinary or technical knowledge may be, becoming wise has higher priority in the life of one who aspires to live well.

Like wisdom, faith is not identical to knowledge. It is neither a technique for acquiring knowledge nor a source of knowledge. This means that it neither precludes nor represents a substitute for the reasoned pursuit of truth in the arts and sciences. Nor does entering into the life of faith exempt Christians from the ordinary requirements to make sense in their truth claims. Quite simply, faith is a way human beings make themselves available, unreservedly, to the revealed truth, which is God himself. Arthur Holmes puts the matter succinctly: "Faith is rather an openness and wholehearted response to God's self-revelation."[6] In this respect faith provides the context where inquiry into all kinds of truth takes place. To paraphrase the timeless

---

[6]Arthur F. Holmes, *The Idea of a Christian College*, rev. ed. (Grand Rapids: William B. Eerdmans Publishing Co., 1975 [rev. 1987]), 18.

words of St. Augustine: We do not seek understanding in order to have faith; we venture into faith in order to understand.

Truth in Literature and Art

When we begin to consider the question of truth in literature and the fine arts, we immediately encounter two seemingly incongruous facts. To begin with, works of literature and fine art do not necessarily depict reality accurately—at least they do not do so in a way that would satisfy a scientist's or a logician's requirements for precision and warrantability. Without question, works of literature and fine art exert enormous power in shaping the worldview of virtually every person and every culture. They accomplish this by means of a wide range of media and their elements: images, symbols, myths, legends, dramatic presentations, sculptures, paintings. All of these devices have an invented, or "made up," quality about them: Even those that are intended to represent or depict actual objects or events beyond themselves remain reconstructions of those actual objects or events. They are not identical to the realities themselves. Bach's *B-Minor Mass*, which so powerfully evokes the crucifixion and resurrection, presents the listener with sounds that never occur in nature. Besides artistic devices not being identical to actual events, persons, or things, at their best they may well distort and misrepresent them. Looking at the sculpted statues representing biblical prophets, kings, and queens that form the Royal Portal of the medieval Gothic cathedral in Chartres, France, is not the same as looking at actual persons.[7] Though lifelike, and in that sense "realistic," the figures are elongated to function as columns. Michelangelo's sculpture *Moses* is oversized and depicts Moses as having horns. As with literature and fine art generally, neither Bach's music nor the sculpted figures at the Chartres cathedral nor Michelangelo's sculpture of Moses represents reality with scientific or logical precision. In this sense they fail the test of propositional truth. At the same time (and here we see the other side of the paradox), even though works of literature and fine art are imaginary reconstructions of actual things and events and even though they distort and misrepresent actual things, persons, and events in certain ways, thoughtful persons recognize that in their highest and most subtle forms they convey truths that speak to some of the profoundest questions raised by human beings. With reference to Bach's *B-Minor Mass*, Frank Gaebelein says, "Bach puts into music the profound truths of Christ's passion and victory over death."[8] So the seeming incongruence is that even as

---

[7]Malcolm Miller, *Chartres Cathedral* (London: Pitkin Pictorials Ltd., 1985), 25, 26.

[8]Frank E. Gaebelein, *The Christian, the Arts, and Truth*, ed. D. Bruce Lockerbie (Portland, Ore.: Multnomah Press, 1985), 93.

great works of literature and fine art distort and misrepresent actual things and events, they nonetheless succeed in conveying truth. With a touch of hyperbole, Pablo Picasso articulated this incongruence this way: "Art is a lie that makes us realize truth."[9] How is this possible? How can literary and artistic devices, imaginary constructions that "distort" reality, convey truth and increase our awareness of it?

This question has no simple answer. To begin with, there are many genres of literature (e.g., novel, short story, poem) and several types of fine art (e.g., painting, music, drama). Artistic devices, therefore, will differ somewhat in kind and use from one genre or type to another. Furthermore, literature and art exhibit various types and levels of truth. There is a range of ways in which a literary text or work of art can be true or false. In what follows I shall limit the discussion to a few examples from literature, leaving it to the reader to make application of principles to other artistic endeavors. We shall discuss truth under two headings: valuational truth and implicit truth.

VALUATIONAL TRUTH

Literary works attempt to tell us the truth about those things that are of basic and vital importance in human experience, if not for all time then at least for certain epochs. They disclose human preoccupations, hopes, and fears—in short, they disclose human values. If we wish to learn what the people of a certain culture esteem or detest, hope for or fear, we can consult their stories and literature.

This phenomenon highlights one of the reasons for reading widely, both cross-culturally and historically. The complexity and practical urgencies that make up the everyday flow of events obscure the essential patterns and themes of life. Literary works attempt to focus our attention on the crucial features: pain and joy, love and hate, moral obligation, humankind's relationship to God. They seldom provide new information, or if they do provide new information, this is not their main function. Instead, they bring into the center of our field of vision ideas, principles, and themes, the truth of which may already be known to us but which has been crowded to the periphery of vision by the many routine activities of day to day existence.

A good deal of the so-called distortion in literature mentioned earlier derives from the author's need to strip away irrelevant and trivial details and to accentuate others in order to disclose the essential content of human experience. By means of this selectivity an author can arrive at the level of valuational truth. In this respect, a competent author can never remain at the level of mere "correctness" in her portrayal of human nature and reality. She must use highlighting, selectivity, omission, or

---

[9]Pablo Picasso, *The Arts*, May 1923, vol. 3, 315–326.

juxtaposition—each a kind of "distortion"—if she is to lay bare the truths that are worthy of our attention. Dante's *Divine Comedy* contains many curious images: dark woods, wild beasts, strangely frozen caverns, and a dead poet who leads Dante on a tour of hell. At the very bottom of hell itself is a grotesque monster frozen in ice to its waist, futilely flapping its expansive wings. In one respect these images misrepresent and distort reality, since they correspond only distantly to actual objects or else to nothing at all. Nevertheless, the images succeed in evoking other realities, such as sin, ambition, hell, human reason, and primally sinful Satan. Moreover, they vividly focus our attention on the important decisions that inevitably confront all of us. As one scholar has observed: "The imaginative details in a work of art are a lens or window through which we look at life."[10] The purpose of the lens is to magnify a small but noteworthy feature of human nature.

An author may be an astute observer of the human condition regardless of her worldview, philosophical commitments, or religious persuasion. We may judge her philosophical perspective to be misguided or wrong, but if she succeeds in accurately capturing the crucial contours of human experience or external reality, we must concede her writing conveys valuational truth. Joseph Conrad was probably not a Christian. Yet his *Heart of Darkness*, set in the heart of Africa (once called the Dark Continent), represents an insightful study of the real heart of darkness, the heart of men driven by acquisitive desires.

How do we know whether an author in describing human values has conveyed truth? Clearly, we are not concerned principally with the nonhuman factual information that literary works customarily contain. The merit of a literary work does not often depend on the truth of an astronomical system, such as the Ptolemaic astronomy employed by John Milton. Nor does it depend on the truth of geography, as in Lilliput and the other geographical falsehoods in Jonathan Swift's *Gulliver's Travels*. Nor does it even depend on the author's veracity in delineating historical facts. A historical drama can rearrange historical events or facts, as in the case of Shakespeare's *Henry IV*, and still be judged a great work of literature. But whether it is astronomically, geographically, or historically inaccurate, the great work of literature must nonetheless convey other more important truths. How can we tell whether a work accomplishes this task?

In judging the merit of a literary work, authorities, past and present, have held that the literary work must satisfy a criterion of authenticity or fidelity to human nature. This criterion was first stated explicitly by the Greek philosopher Aristotle, who observed that an author has a responsibility to say "the sort of

---

[10]Leland Ryken, "The Creative Arts," in *The Making of a Christian Mind*, ed. Arthur Holmes (Downers Grove, Ill.: InterVarsity Press, 1985), 105–131. See especially p. 127.

thing that a certain type of man will do or say either probably or necessarily [in the given circumstances]."[11] We may paraphrase Aristotle by stating the test of authenticity or "truth to human nature" in the following way: Would a person such as has been described in the novel or drama, act, think, feel, or be motivated in the way that the author describes given the circumstances described?[12]

Applying this test of "truth to human nature" is often difficult. The reader may lack sufficient knowledge of human nature to apply it, or the author may provide too few clues. But if the reader becomes convinced that the character in question would not behave in the way that the author describes, the reader will evaluate the characterization negatively. At the very least he will condemn the characterization with respect to the action in question as implausible. Of course, a negative evaluation of the authenticity of a characterization will in turn affect the reader's view of the work as a source of truth.

IMPLICIT TRUTH

Literary and dramatic works contain many explicitly stated propositions. The earlier discussion of propositional truth makes it clear that every proposition is either true or false. Since literary works contain many propositions, they also may contain truth in this obvious sense, if some of their propositions are true. For example, James Michener's historical novel *The Source* contains many true propositions about Palestine.

However, the most interesting and significant propositions in literature are implied, rather than explicitly stated. For instance, the overall worldview of a literary work is usually implicit and must be inferred from a careful reading of the text. Dante's *Divine Comedy* and Lucretius's *On the Nature of Things* are both poems. They do not announce their respective worldviews openly and directly. Nevertheless, what they say in poetic form implies propositions about a worldview. Only a careful reading of each reveals that Dante's is a Christian worldview and Lucretius's is a naturalistic (mechanistic) worldview.

Truth emerges implicitly in several other ways in literary works. Two of these are quite common and deserve special attention: metaphor and archetype. A metaphor is a figure of speech in which a word or phrase literally denoting one kind of object or idea is used in place of another to imply or suggest a likeness or analogy between them. We may think of metaphors as marking the convergence of two levels of meaning, a direct

---

[11]Aristotle, *The Poetics*, in *Aristotle XXIII,* The Loeb Classical Library (Cambridge, Mass.: Harvard University Press, 1923), Chapter 9, 1451b4.

[12]John Hospers, "Problems of Aesthetics," in *The Encyclopedia of Philosophy*, vol. 1, ed. Paul Edwards (New York: Macmillan Publishing Co., and The Free Press, 1967), 35–56. See especially p. 49.

or literal level and an indirect or implied level. If we were to say "the arm of God wrought miracles," the literal meaning of "arm" would be *bodily limb*. But the expression also implies a spiritual meaning. "The arm of God" means *God's power*. The literal meaning of the expression makes the statement in which it appears both false and meaningless: God does not have a bodily limb. But the implied meaning makes the statement both true and significant. God does have power, and His power is a notable point of attention for the believer.

An archetype is a recurring pattern of presentation and experience. (See the treatment of archetype on page 369.) Herman Melville opens his novel Moby Dick with these words:

> Call me Ishmael. Some years ago—never mind how long precisely—having little or no money in my purse, and nothing particular to interest me on shore, I thought I would sail about a little and see the watery part of the world.[13]

That Melville chose the name Ishmael is no accident. He expects the reader to recall the Genesis account of Ishmael, Abraham's son by Hagar. After Isaac's birth and upon the insistence of Sarah, Abraham sends Hagar and Ishmael away from the camp. The reader is told that she and the boy "departed, and wandered in the wilderness" (Gen. 21:14, KJV). Ishmael in the Genesis narrative has become an archetype of a wanderer, and the wilderness has become an archetype for an alien place in which no person can dwell and make a true home for himself. So Melville's Ishmael is an instance of Ishmael in the Genesis account; the sea on which Melville's Ishmael ventures forth is an instance of the wilderness Hagar and Ishmael are sent to wander in. The reader who sees the use of archetypes will be aware immediately of the implied truth that Melville wishes to convey: the Ishmael of *Moby Dick* is a displaced figure, who ventures forth to wander in a desolate, amorphous reality.

Thus, one measure of the greatness of a work of literature is its capacity to evoke connections with significant events or important texts through its use of metaphor and archetype.

Summary and Concluding Remarks

Our discussion has traversed four important meanings of "truth": as it refers to a Christian worldview, as it refers to the inward life, as it refers to propositions, and as it refers to the arts (specifically, literature). One question not yet touched on is the one I asked at the outset: Why should you concern yourself with the various meanings of truth? There are several good reasons, some of them philosophical, some practical. We shall consider only two practical ones.

First, issues having to do with the nature of truth relate to our

---

[13]Herman Melville, *Moby Dick,* ed. Harrison Hayford and Hershel Parker (New York: W. W. Norton & Company, 1967), 12.

beliefs. When we realize that our social interactions and self-image are affected by our beliefs and working assumptions, issues of truth quickly become more than philosophical abstractions. In science, morality, art, and politics, we hold beliefs that influence how we interact and respond to the world and how we live our lives. If we have no guidelines or principles for determining in what way these beliefs are true, or indeed whether they are true at all, we may feel unsure of ourselves. But if we know how to determine the truth value of our beliefs, then if they are not sound, we can abandon them. If our beliefs are sound, then we will be more likely to feel secure and confident in acting on them.

The second reason has to do with the biblical injunction about "handling accurately the word of truth" (2 Tim. 2:15, NASB). The person who knows little or nothing about the various kinds of truth is likely to engage in weak, if not outright inaccurate, exegesis of the Scriptures. All four of the principal types of truth discussed appear in the Bible. The Bible enunciates a Christian worldview, from which theologians derive, among other things, the doctrines of creation, fall, redemption, and consummation. Its message calls human beings into question and calls them to inward truth. It also contains many propositional truths. However, we must exercise great care at this point to note the literary nature of the Bible. Paul tells us that Scripture is useful for establishing sound doctrine. But the Bible is *not* what some Christians seem to assume: a theological treatise. Most of the texts of the Bible consist of narrative stories, poems, visions, and letters. The best-known words of Jesus are not theological propositions but parables, whose main characters probably do not correspond to any actual historical persons. Moreover, Jesus himself is virtually inaccessible in Scripture apart from the metaphors used to present Him: lamb of God, bread of life, servant, bridegroom, light of the world, the true light, the door, the true vine, king. And does not Paul recognize an archetypical relationship between Adam and Christ (Rom. 5:14)? We have here in the use of metaphor and archetype (and many other literary devices as well) nonpropositional ways the Scriptures disclose truth. They fall mainly under the fourth type of truth, literary truth. The reader of the Scriptures who fails to take account of the various ways the Biblical texts may present truth stands perilously close to defaulting on the injunction to handle correctly the word of truth. So the student of the Bible clearly has a stake in paying close attention to the meanings of truth.

Appendix 2
Jean-Paul Sartre

Michael D. Palmer

Jean-Paul Sartre (1905–1980) was a French philosopher, playwright, and novelist. He was born in Paris, where he was reared and educated until 1929. After 1929 he taught philosophy in several schools, both in Paris and elsewhere. From 1933 to 1935 he worked as a research student at universities in Berlin and Freiburg. From 1936 on he published philosophical studies and novels, the most notable being *Nausea* (1938) and *The Wall* (1939). In 1939, at the outbreak of World War II, he was called up by the French army. In 1940 he was captured by the Germans, but eventually he was released and returned to Paris where he resumed teaching philosophy until 1944. During the war years he completed his most important philosophical work, *Being and Nothingness* (1943). Partly because of his involvement with the French resistance and partly because of his philosophical brilliance, Sartre emerged after the war as the dominant figure in the French existentialist movement. During the early postwar years he wrote a number of novels and plays, which brought him worldwide fame.

The dominate themes of Sartre's early and mature (though not his later) philosophical writings are freedom of the individual human being and action. In *Being and Nothingness,* Sartre distinguishes between the being of things ("Being-in-itself") and the being of consciousness ("Being-for-itself"). Only consciousness, not things, has the ability to engage in the act of "secreting nothingness," by which Sartre means negating one's present circumstances and imagining alternatives.

This capacity to negate (to reject or deny boundaries and limitations) lies at the heart of Sartre's notion of human consciousness and reflects his way of describing human freedom. Freedom, Sartre asserts, is absolute—at least in the sense of being able to imagine or intend anything whatever. (I am always free to plan, to imagine, or to intend to revolt against my present circumstances in favor of something else; I may not always actually succeed in bringing about what I plan, imagine, or intend.)

The actual limitations to human freedom come from the specific features of the circumstances consciousness finds itself in, its so-called *facticity*. Facticity includes such things as personal facts (e.g., gender, race, physical limitations), social facts (e.g., family background, religious or political affiliation), and physical circumstances (e.g., geography, weather). At the point where one's *freedom* and one's *facticity* confront each other the central question of human existence emerges: "Who am I?" According to Sartre, any attempt to break the dynamic tension between one's freedom and one's facticity represents an act of "bad faith." In other words, to release the tension and settle the question "Who am I?" only on the basis of specific facts that make up one's life or only on the basis of one's freedom to imagine alternatives is to act in bad faith. The alternative to living in "bad faith" is to live "authentically"—to recognize both one's freedom and one's facticity.

Besides the temptation to succumb to bad faith, the chief threat to one's self-identify is other people. Sartre believes human relations to be conflicted. This is true, he thinks, not only in obvious cases such as hate relations, but also subtly in love and friendship relations. Sartre's most dramatic depiction of this interpretation of human relationships appears in his play *No Exit*, in which three people encounter each other in hell. After an extended period of interaction, one of the three characters concludes: "Hell is—other people."

Appendix 3
Karl Marx

Michael D. Palmer

Karl Marx (1818–1883) was a German social philosopher and revolutionary who lived and wrote at the height of the Industrial Revolution. He and Friedrich Engels (1820–1895) are generally regarded as the founders of modern socialism and communism. Marx was the son of a lawyer. His education included the study of law and philosophy. In 1844 he met Engels in Paris, where the two began a lifelong collaboration. With Engels he wrote the *Communist Manifesto* (1848) and other works that broke with the tradition of theorists, like John Locke, who appealed to natural rights to justify social reform. Marx invoked instead what he believed to be laws of history that lead inevitably to the triumph of the working class. Marx was exiled from Continental Europe after the revolutions of 1848. He settled in London, where he earned some money as a correspondent for the *New York Tribune.* However, he remained dependent on Engels's financial help while working on his monumental work *Capital* (3 vol., 1867–94), in which he presented a trenchant criticism of capitalism and developed his own economic theory.

Marx saw firsthand the exploitative effects that industrialization had upon the laboring peasant classes in England and Continental Europe. In *Capital*—using government reports, newspaper articles, and other forms of documentation—he wrote extensively about the suffering that workers were experiencing in various industries: exploitative working hours, pulmonary diseases and premature deaths caused by unsanitary factory conditions, child labor, excessively overcrowded working conditions for seamstresses in the sweatshops.

As bad as the conditions were for the working class, Marx believed them to be mere symptoms of a more fundamental problem, relating to the nature of capitalism itself. By his analysis, capitalism offers only two sources of income: sale of one's own labor and ownership of what he identified as "means of production" (factories, machinery, land, raw materials, and technology). Of course, workers, being poor, do not own the means of production. Because they cannot produce anything without access to the means of production, they must sell their labor for wages to those who do own the means of production. But Marx believed that the owners, instead of paying the workers the full value of their labor, pay them only enough to survive. What is left over—the difference between the full value of the workers' labor and what they are actually paid—the owners keep as profit. The workers feel compelled to comply with this arrangement because the owners have full control of the means of production and thus full control of the available jobs. Marx believed that as a result of this arrangement the owners will become increasingly wealthy even as the workers become increasingly impoverished.

In Marx's view, the capitalist system militates against the best interests of the workers, preventing them from developing their full productive capacity and preventing them from satisfying those needs that define them as human beings. Specifically, Marx held that capitalism generates four forms of "alienation," or ways in which human beings are separated from what is essentially theirs. First, the capitalist system alienates the worker from what he has made with his own hands. This happens, Marx thought, when the product of production (say, expensive clothing) is sold to others (members of the upper class) who use it for purposes antagonistic to the worker's interests (a social event such as a ball, which reinforces class differences). With respect to this first kind of alienation Marx says:

> [T]he worker is related to the *product of his labor* as to an alien object. . . . The *alienation* of the worker in his product means not only that his labor becomes an object, an *external* existence, but that it exists *outside him*, independently, as something alien to him, and that it becomes a power on its own confronting him. It means that the life which he has conferred on the object confronts him as something hostile and alien. . . .

> It is true that labor produces for the rich wonderful things—but for the worker it produces privation. It produces palaces—but for the worker, hovels. It produces beauty—but for the worker, deformity. It replaces labor by machines, but it throws a section of the workers back to a barbarous type of labor, and it turns the other workers into machines. It produces intelligence—but for the worker stupidity, cretinism. (108, 110)

Capitalism also alienates the worker from the most essential features of his own labor. He is compelled to sell his labor in order to feed his family and stay alive. But his labor holds no intrinsic reward for him and is essentially unfulfilling. It demeans rather than reinforces his human dignity.

What, then, constitutes the alienation of labor?

> First, the fact that labor is *external* to the worker, i.e., it does not belong to his essential being; that in his work, therefore, he does not affirm himself but denies himself, does not feel content but unhappy, does not develop freely his physical and mental energy but mortifies his body and ruins his mind. . . . Its alien character emerges clearly in the fact that as soon as no physical or other compulsion exists, labor is shunned like the plague. . . . [the worker's labor] is not his own, but someone else's, that it does not belong to him, that in it he belongs, not to himself, but to another. (110, 111)

The third way capitalism alienates workers is by instilling in them illusions about their real human needs. Capitalism leads workers to "renounce" what is truly in their best interest in favor of a false image of what is important. It makes money—*capital*—seem to be the ultimate object of desire. In Marx's words:

> Self-renunciation, the renunciation of life and of all human needs, is [capitalism's] principal thesis. The less you eat, drink and buy books; the less you go to the theater, the dance hall, the public house; the less you think, love, theorize, sing, paint, fence, etc., the more you *save*—the *greater* becomes your treasure which neither moths nor dust will devour—your *capital*. The less you *are*, the less you express your own life, the greater is your *alienated* life, the more you *have*, the greater is the store of your estranged being. (p. 150)

Finally, capitalism alienates people from each other. It sets one worker against another in a competitive grab for available employment opportunities, and it separates society into unequal and hostile social classes, which Marx names the *bourgeoisie* (middle-class property owners) and the *proletariat* (lower-class laborers).

> If the product of labor is alien to me, if it confronts me as an alien power, to whom then, does it belong? . . .
>   To a being *other* than myself.
>   Who is this being?
>   The gods? . . .
>   The *alien* being, to whom labor and the product of labor belongs, in whose service labor is done and for whose benefit the product of labor is provided, can only be *man* himself.

> If the product of labor does not belong to the worker, if it confronts him as an alien power, then this can only be because it belongs to some *other man than the worker*. If the worker's activity is a torment to him, to another it must be *delight* and his life's joy. Not the gods, not nature, but only man himself can be this alien power over man. (p. 115)

So, according to Marx, an unregulated capitalist economy inevitably yields disparities of wealth and power. To be sure, it produces freedom and wealth for those who own factories, land, raw materials, and technology. At the same time, however, it subjugates the laboring class of workers and alienates them from what they produce, from their own labor, from their own human needs, and from other human beings.

Marx sets forth his solution in his most famous programmatic work, the *Communist Manifesto*, in which he calls for a revolution. Government, in his view, cannot resolve the inequities and injustices of society, because it is designed to maintain the status quo. It protects the interests of those who are already vested in the current economic system. What is needed, argued Marx, is a revolution in which the working class takes control of the means of production, the so-called *economic substructure* of society. Only then can the more obvious arrangements in society—the so-called *social superstructure*: class structure, government, popular ideologies—be addressed adequately once and for all.

Marx's analysis of unrestrained capitalism proved to be more accurate and trenchant than his proposed solution. Virtually all capitalist economies around the world today have established some forms of regulation to mitigate the kind of abuses Marx identified. On the other hand, the social experiments in communism during the twentieth century have largely failed. Eastern Europe and the former Soviet Union give testimony to this failure.

The selections from Marx quoted here are found in Karl Marx, *The Economic & Philosophic Manuscripts of 1844*, edited with an introduction by Dirk J. Struik and translated by Martin Milligan (New York: International Publishers, 1964, 1973).

ADDITIONAL READINGS ON MARX

Heilbroner, Robert. *Marxism: For and Against*. New York: W. W. Norton & Co., Inc., 1980.

Mandel, Ernest. *An Introduction to Marxist Economic Theory*. New York: Pathfinder Press, 1970.

McLellan, David. *Karl Marx: His Life and Thought*. New York: Harper and Row Publishers, 1973.

Appendix 4
Music and the Performing Space

Johnathan David Horton

During a visit to the tropical island of Barbados, some friends and I came across an Anglican church that had been built in the 1600s. It was a small but delightful building with tall white walls, stained glass windows, and an impressive steeple. The inside of the church, with its high ceiling and beautiful wooden beams, was just as impressive as the exterior. As we approached the sanctuary, the sweet sound of music floated out to greet us.

The choir was in the middle of a rehearsal. Being careful not to disturb the singing, we stood in the back of the sanctuary relaxing in the cooling shade and the flowing melody. The hymn was familiar, but the tempo was much slower than I would have expected. Yet as we stood there listening to the choir, I was struck by how the music pulsed with life. The sound reverberated throughout the room, and every nook and cranny echoed with the sound of the choir and organ. The music was both beautiful and exciting!

After a few moments my thoughts turned to the rural American congregation that I had visited a few Sundays before. They had sung that same hymn but at a much faster tempo. The contrast was striking! Immediately the question came to mind, How would that rural American congregation have responded to the hymn sung at this tempo and in this style?

First of all, that rural church was quite different in construction—it had a low ceiling, padded pews, drapes on the windows, and a carpeted floor. Acoustically the two sanctuaries were quite different. A second question began to loom large, How would this Anglican congregation respond to the hymn in the tempo and style of the rural American congregation? After a few moments, a far more serious question rose in my mind, Does the acoustical environment affect the music that is performed in that environment?

First of all, how is music affected by the environment? The basic materials of music are sound and silence. Sound is created by (1) a vibrating medium, (2) an energy source, and (3) a means of transmission. Every musical instrument must include these three components. For example, the sound of the human voice is produced when the vocal cords, the vibrating medium, are set into vibration by the breath, the energy source, which is in turn activated by the musculature of the respiratory system. The vibrations of the vocal cords create sound waves that are carried through the air, the transmission medium, to the ear, which then transforms those sound waves into impulses to the brain, creating what we know as sound.

Acoustics is the science of sound, including the production, the transmission, and the effects of sound as well as the phenomenon of hearing. The study of acoustics provides us with much useful information, especially regarding music. Once a sound has been produced, it is affected by the environment it is produced in.

By way of example, let us examine the sound of a violin. The bow is drawn across the string, creating vibrations that are physically transmitted to the body of the violin. The body of the violin is set into vibration, which creates sound waves in the surrounding air. If the sound of the violin reached our ears in a single straight line, the science of acoustics would be ever so simple. However, the sound waves radiate from the body of the violin in a nearly 360-degree pattern.

Not only do we hear the sound of the violin directly, we also hear the sound of the violin reflected from many different surfaces and coming from many different directions. The number of the reflections, the strength of the reflections, the length of time between the initial sound and the first and ensuing reflections, and the length of time for a sound to die away—all of these factors, and more, directly impinge upon our perception of the sound. If this seems complicated, remember that we are talking about a single sound from a single instrument. Now imagine the complexity of a series of sounds from a host of different instruments. The possibilities boggle the mind.

Let us return to the rural church for a moment. The sound did not reverberate throughout the church. The lack of reverberation was a product of the sound absorbing characteristics of the carpet, the padded pews, the draperies, the low ceiling, the acoustical tile, and even the people. This "dry" acoustical environment required a public address system to amplify the sound of the music. In fact, the PA system had an electronic processor for adding artificial reverberation.

In this little church the slow tempo for this hymn as sung by the Anglican choir would not sound stately, it would just sound dead. The musicians could not depend upon reverberation to fill up the space with music; they had to create life in the music in some other way. They added drums, electric bass, guitar, piano with "runs" and "fills," and hand claps. The accompaniment and the tempo worked together to fill up the musical space with sound.

Let's turn the idea around. How would the tempo and style presented by the rural congregation fit here in this very reverberant setting? I thought about the rapid tempo, the many improvised notes of the pianist—it suddenly seemed funny. The music would not have sounded alive and exciting as it had that Sunday morning a few weeks earlier. Instead, it would sound muddled and confused as the reverberated sound would cause note to pile upon note to pile upon note until it would be as impossible to separate them as to untie the Gordian knot. If the music finished at noon, the reverberation would not have stopped before sunset!

Lest the point be missed, both presentations of the hymn had been appropriate to their circumstances. Both were responsive to the specific acoustical environment of their presentation. Yet neither presentation would have worked very effectively in an inhospitable acoustical environment.

Music is neither written nor performed in a vacuum. Many things influence the musical creation—the culture of the composer, the culture of the listeners, the age and musical background of the target audience, to name a few. The idea of musical space is seldom consciously considered, but it is a significant factor in the creation of the music. One of the keys to the differences in musical styles from culture to culture is the overwhelming variety of architectural spaces used for musical performances.

The composer or arranger creates music to fit the performance environment. The composer who is connected to the culture understands the kind of space where the music will be performed. If the arranger is writing music for a marching band, it is essential to understand the acoustical nature of the football stadium. If the composer is going to write an *a cappella* selection for a church choir, he or she must know something about the acoustical nature of a typical church sanctuary where the music will be performed.

Some composers have consciously exploited the characteristics of the acoustical space where their music was to be performed. Giovanni Gabrieli (1557–1612) is one such composer. The Cathedral of Saint Mark in Venice, Italy, where he served as organist-choirmaster, had several unusual architectural features. There were two organs, one on each side of the church, as well as several lofts throughout the church where vocalists and instrumentalists could perform.[1] Gabrieli wrote a significant amount of music for two, three, and more choirs. He would freely mix voices and instruments just as he would freely mix massive chordal structures with points of polyphonic imitation, that is, each voice following and imitating its predecessor. The impact of sounds coming from different directions added a dimension of drama to the performance that was exciting and new.[2]

Music must fit the instrument, or instruments, performing the music. Consider the music of the banjo. Irrespective of the acoustics of the room, the banjo itself simply will not sustain a note for more than a brief moment. To make the music of the

---

[1]Marie K. Stolba, *The Development of Western Music: A History* (Madison, Wis.: Brown and Benchmark Publishers, 1992), 236–237.

[2]Hoffer, Charles R. *The Understanding of Music*, 5th ed. (Belmont, Calif.: Wadsworth Publishing Company, 1965), 149.

banjo interesting, it is necessary to strike a new note before the first note dies away. That is why the banjo typically produces a nearly constant stream of notes.

The music makers of our generation have attempted to change the ground rules of musical acoustics. With the advent of high-tech public address systems, having sophisticated electronic-effects units, musicians can create the impression of any acoustical environment that is desired. The acoustician begins by designing a room that has little or no reverberation, or echo, in order to remove the limitations of a natural reverberation field. By altering the sound waves electronically, the engineer can create the effect of any acoustical environment, from a tiny room to a colossal stadium. Such electronic manipulation opens the door, at least in theory, to a much wider world of musical possibilities.

Appendix 5
Worship Music and Style

Johnathan David Horton

There is no such thing as a godly or an ungodly style.
—Francis A. Schaeffer

Every tune belongs to the Lord except the spittoon.
—Otis McCoy

I have always loved music. Many of my earliest childhood memories revolve around music. I remember a young lady with flowing black hair who began attending the church my father pastored in Charlotte, North Carolina. Everybody called her "Boots." Even though I was only five years old, it was love at first sight. She was the first trained soprano that I had ever heard. What a voice! When she sang "Down From His Glory," I fell in love with the music, too. What a glorious melody! It seemed the perfect vehicle to express what I felt in my heart.

I also remember how I felt the first time I heard Elvis sing that same melody with the words "It's Now or Never." I was a teenager and I listened to my share of rock and roll, but I thought, *The nerve of this guy, desecrating such a beautiful gospel song!* Imagine my chagrin when a few years later I discovered that the song that I loved so well did not begin its life as a sacred song. It is based on the tune of the popular Italian folk song "O sole mio."

The melody is a classic. It has been a favorite around the world for a long, long time. The appeal of its beauty is undeniable. But what does this melody really express: Is it the high, exalted love of "O sole mio"; is it the earthy, sensual love of "It's Now or Never"; is it the spiritual devotion of "Down From His Glory"; or is it something else altogether?

Musical style as a context for worship. Some believe that the ability of church music to communicate the gospel is not limited to the text of the music. They believe that "Church music proclaims the gospel through the actual music itself." Therefore, they contend, styles associated with secular music are wholly inappropriate for use in worship. To take the argument further: "The adoption and adaptation of secular music does not fulfill church music's overall purpose because it is incapable of doing so."[1]

Yet we know from a variety of sources that the history of church music is replete with examples of borrowing from secular music.[2] By way of example consider "the secular elements in

---

[1]Calvin, Johansson, *Discipling Music Ministry: Twenty-first Century Directions* (Peabody, Mass.: Hendrickson Publishers, 1992), vi.

[2]Erik Routley, *Twentieth Century Church Music* (Carol Stream, Ill.: Agape, 1964), 154.

the medieval carols, or the use of folk-song by Martin Luther as the basis for his Reformation hymns, or the use of music obviously derived from the *Beggar's Opera* by the Wesleys."[3] If the music itself carries the meaning, how do we account for the borrowing in *both* directions?[4]

The debate over what musical style is appropriate for worship has raged from the days of Martin Luther and the Council of Trent[5] to the present. Few subjects produce more dogmatic opinions based on such meager bits of evidence. Everyone seems to know what music is *spiritual*. Not amazingly, *spiritual music* is almost always "the music that I like."

The Bible, however, does not address the issue of musical style in a direct way. In the Old Testament era and in the New Testament era, we know of no certain distinctions between the musical styles of sacred and secular music. So far as we may know, neither the ancient Jew nor the early Christian created a new musical style. Since the Bible seems to be somewhat indifferent to musical style, why do church musicians, leaders, and theologians get so exercised over the issue of musical style in worship?

Which is not to say that individual worshipers are indifferent to musical style! Each of us has our individual preferences for musical styles in worship. Such views are frequently rather strongly held! Individual congregations have preferences, too. Worship styles and musical styles often more aptly define a congregation than does denominational affiliation.

Contemporary Christian Music. David Wilkerson, Jimmy Swaggert, Bob Larson, and others have condemned the use of rock music in the church. They believe that the form itself has been so tainted that it is not fit for the Master's use. But others believe that all forms are good if they have been sanctified through the word of God and prayer (see 1 Tim. 4:1–7). "Just because a form has been abused and associated with sub-Christian and anti-Christian influences does not mean that the form is invalid."[6]

Francis Schaeffer makes the point even clearer—we must not confuse message and style. "There is no such thing as a godly or an ungodly style. The more one tries to make such a distinction, the more confusing it becomes."[7] No musical style should be completely excluded from worship on the basis of its associ-

---

[3]Johansson, *Discipling*, 20.

[4]David B. Pass, *Music in the Church: A Theology of Church Music* (Nashville: Broadman Press, 1989), 44.

[5]The Council of Trent was an ecclesiastical council convened by the Roman Catholic church from 1543–63 as a response to the Protestant Reformation led by Martin Luther. Among other things, it laid down new rules for the use of music in worship.

[6]Pass, *Music*, 44.

[7]Francis Schaeffer, *Art & the Bible* (Downers Grove, Ill.: InterVarsity Press, 1973), 51.

ations, because we do not all have the same associations with *any* style of music.

The integrity of worship music. Some insist that our musical offering must be of the very highest quality possible or it is unworthy to be offered to the Lord. At first glance such a view seems sound, but deeper examination reveals a significant flaw. In the Old Testament the worshiper is commanded to make a burnt sacrifice of an unblemished male animal from his flock (Lev. 1:1–17). For those who were unable to afford the full offering, provision was made for a substitute. It is noteworthy that when Mary and Joseph brought the baby Jesus for his consecration ceremony, they offered the substitute, a pair of doves or two young pigeons (Luke 2:24). God was looking for the best that the worshiper had, not the best in all of Israel. As to music, the contemporary worshiper is still required to give the best that he or she has, but it should be music that comes from his or her heart and not music borrowed from some external authority.

Costliness is another qualification for our offering of musical worship. When the angel of the LORD stopped the destruction of Israel at the threshing floor of Araunah, King David went to build an altar to the Lord and sacrifice there. Araunah offered the land, the oxen, and everything else that was needed as a gift. But King David would not accept it. He said, "No, I insist on paying you for it. I will not sacrifice to the LORD my God burnt offerings that cost me nothing" (2 Sam. 24:24). True sacrifice is still costly. It costs our time; it costs our effort. Frequently it will cost much more than we can describe here.

Archibald T. Davidson, one of the most influential writers on Protestant church music in the early part of this century, took the view that church music should be quite unlike the music of our everyday lives. "The power and integrity of church music ought to be judged by the degree of its remoteness from the world."[8] He saw Gregorian chant as an ideal vehicle for worship. He viewed music of the everyday world as inhospitable to worship.

This point of view is diametrically opposed to current evangelical thought that seeks not a dualism but an integrity—a oneness—of life. Contemporary worshipers are seeking connections between their everyday lives and the realm of the eternal. They want to join the psalmist in singing, "I will extol the LORD at all times; his praise will always be on my lips" (Ps. 34:1). They are seeking for music and worship that integrates their lives—worship that is an honest reflection of who they are and who they can be through Christ!

The fathomless complexity of God's personality suggests that more than one approach to music style and worship may be appropriate. Let us consider only two aspects of His identity.

---

[8]Archibald T. Davidson, *Protestant Church Music in America* (Boston: E. C. Schirmer Music Co., 1933), 12.

First, He is *Jehovah shamah*, the God who is near. Second, He is *El Shaddai*, God Almighty. As *Jehovah shamah* He is the God who is *immanent*. He invites us into His throne room to bring our petitions and find grace in our time of our need (Heb. 4:24). As *El Shaddai* He is *omnipotent* (Gen. 17:1). He is the King of the universe—the righteous Judge, who deserves and demands our worship.

Our music should reflect both of these characteristics of God. Perhaps no one style of music can meet this demand. His *immanence* suggests songs in the familiar style of our everyday lives. Simple, direct choruses like "I Love You, Lord" or "I Sing Praises to Your Name" express devotion in a personal and direct way that is both unself-conscious and completely appropriate for the intimate worship before the throne of God. Whereas the exalted language of hymns such as "Praise to the Lord, the Almighty" and "All Hail the Power" give us a sense of His *omnipotence*. If we are to worship God with understanding, we need music that will help convey His full personality.

In other cultures or with people of different backgrounds, the musical examples might be quite different from those listed above. God wants every generation, every culture, every race, and every tongue to sing songs that spring from the heart. If our music is to have integrity it must be an honest reflection of who we are. This is true of the individual and it is true of the specific local congregation. An effective leader can, and will, teach new music and transmit the love of that music to the people until it becomes their own.

God did not use a cookie cutter to create the world. Because He is infinitely creative, God created a world of overwhelming variety. Is He, then, interested in only one style of music? Consider what an overwhelming variety of music is raised to the throne of God everyday, as His people sing His praises around the world! What makes people think that their favorite style is God's one and only choice for true worship?

Sing a new song unto the Lord. Every new revival movement, every new move of the Holy Spirit, is accompanied by a new hymnody.[9] Something about the fresh anointing of the Spirit seems to produce a new song. Every new revival in each new generation produces a new musical style as well. It is ironic that the people who were instrumental in the birth of the new hymnody of the previous revival are the very ones who are the most resistant to the new song of the new revival. But as certainly as a new move of God gives rise to a new hymnody, just as certainly new songs demand the new wineskin of a new

---

[9]For an extensive discussion of the history of worship music, see Donald P. Hustad, *Jubilate II: Church Music in Worship and Renewal* (Carol Stream, Ill.: Hope Publishing Company, 1981,1993), and Robert E. Webber, *Worship Old and New: A Biblical and Practical Introduction*, rev. ed. (Grand Rapids: Zondervan Publishing House, 1994).

musical style! As long as the church is here on earth, this cycle is likely to continue.

Anne Ortlund draws a very clear picture of the problem when she describes the day of Pentecost as it would have been if many of us had been there to hear the rushing mighty wind and to see the tongues of fire. "'Great! This is wonderful!' they cry. 'Quick! Shut the windows! Let's capture this glorious wind forever!'" Many years later, there they still sit, remembering the day that God showed up and determined to keep everything just like it was then.[10]

God is the forever contemporary. While He is the God of Abraham, of Isaac, and of Jacob, He is also the God of the present. He describes Himself as "I Am who I Am" (Exod. 3:14). The Spirit of God moves where He will, and so does His song. Like the children of Israel in the desert when the cloud of God's presence moved, we have a choice: We can move with God or be left behind!

---

[10]Anne Ortlund, *Up With Worship* (Glendale, Calif.: Regal Books, 1975), 7.

Appendix 6
G. K. Chesterton on the
Power of Fairy Tales

Twila Brown Edwards

G. K. Chesteron, an important early twentieth-century Christian writer, believed that fairy tales prepared him to believe Christianity. "My first and last philosophy, that which I believe in with unbroken certainty, I learnt in the nursery. . . .The things I believed most then, the things I believe most now, are the things called fairy tales" (49).

Chesterton further stated that fairy tales taught him a sense of wonder. Small children naturally have a deep sense of wonder: "A child of three is excited by being told that Tommy opened a door" (54). Fairy tales continue to nurture that wonder: "A child of seven is excited by being told that Tommy opened a door and saw a dragon" (54). However, adults soon lose that sense of wonder. But Chesterton believed fairy tales can help restore to adults this important quality, not only about dragons, but also concerning qualities of nature: He stated: "[Fairy tales] say that apples were golden only to refresh the forgotten moment when we found that they were green" (54). If, through story, adults enter fairyland and see an enchanted tree, when they return to our world, all trees will retain some of that enchantment. Adults, therefore, who read fairy tales will be much more apt to be good rulers over nature, taking care of the earth as intended in the creation mandate.

Chesterton also believed that fairy tales give us something he called the "Doctrine of Conditional Joy." In his case, the fairy tale prepared him to believe Christianity. "In elfin ethics all virtue is in an 'if.' The note of the fairy utterance always is, 'You may live in a palace of gold and sapphire, *if* you do not say the word 'cow'. . . . The vision always hangs upon a veto. All the dizzy and colossal things conceded depend upon one small thing withheld. All the wild and whirling things that are let loose, depend upon one thing that is forbidden" (55). Chesterton insisted that the condition need not be something the person thoroughly understands. "The true citizen of fairyland is obeying something that he does not understand at all. In the fairy tale an incomprehensible happiness rests upon an incomprehensible condition. A box is opened, and all evils fly out. A word is forgotten, and cities perish. A lamp is lit, and love flies away. A flower is plucked, and human lives are forfeited. An apple is eaten, and the hope of God is gone" (56).

Chesterton did not think these conditions were unjust. "Cinderella received a coach out of Wonderland and a coachman out of nowhere, but she received a command. . . . If Cinderella says 'How is it that I must leave the ball at twelve?' her godmother might answer, 'How is it that you are going there till twelve?'" (56–57). Rather than complaining about having to come home at twelve, Cinderella is filled with wonder that she gets to go to the ball at all. In Chesterton's view, fairy tales help humans to understand and accept that we live in a world of conditionality. If we obey the commands, we experience joy; if we disobey them, we suffer the consequences.

Fairy tales also helped Chesterton to believe there is a personal God. Because fairy tales contained so many acts of wonder, he began to believe there was Someone behind those acts. The fairy stories helped him to believe that "this world of ours has some purpose; and if there is a purpose, there is a person. I had always felt life first as a story: and if there is a story there is a story teller" (61). Chesterton reminisced: "I left the fairy tales lying on the floor of the nursery, and I have not found any books so sensible since" (58). Both he and C. S. Lewis began reading fairy tales again as adults and recommend that we never leave fairy tales in the nursery but continue reading them all our lives to our eternal benefit.

Quotations taken from Gilbert K. Chesterton, "The Ethics of Elfland," in *Orthodoxy* (Garden City, N.Y., 1959), 46–65.

Appendix 7
C. S. Lewis

Twila Brown Edwards

Clive Staples Lewis (1898–1963) was an atheist for many years of his life. His journey back toward Christianity began when he read George MacDonald's *Phantastes*, a fantasy novel which Lewis said "baptized [my] imagination." Through this personal experience Lewis came to understand the redemptive power of imaginative literature. Having struggled through to belief in God, Lewis became influential in explaining Christianity to intellectuals. By reading widely and studiously nurturing his talents, including his writing skills, Lewis developed the unusual ability to incorporate complex theological ideas into his non-fiction, as well as into his novels. His *Mere Christianity* is considered to be one of the greatest apologies for the Christian faith written in the twentieth century. Many of the theological ideas contained in *Mere Christianity,* Lewis also creatively embodied fictionally in the seven novels that compose *The Chronicles of Narnia.* These seven novels, which have been widely translated, have become favorites among children and adults alike from countries all over the world. Through these and other novels of his, Lewis himself has "baptized" the imagination of thousands of his readers.

Lewis was greatly attracted to myth, especially the heroic and romantic forms of myth. He also loved poetry. One of his friends tells of going on walking trips with Lewis when he would suddenly break forth quoting long passages of poetry that he had recently discovered and memorized. The romantic side of Lewis's personality was balanced by an unusual ability in logic. One of God's ironies is that Lewis' logical ability was greatly enhanced by one of his atheist teachers, W. T. Kirkpatrick, a man whom Lewis thought came the closest to being "a purely logical entity" as any man he had met. Any reader of Lewis will recognize his excellent use of logic in incisively setting forth relevant issues in the Christian faith.

When his mother became ill with cancer, the ten-year-old Lewis prayed earnestly she would be healed. His mother's death contributed to his journey into atheism. Later, as a man of fifty-eight and by that time a Christian, Lewis's faith was again severely tested when his wife, Joy Davidman Lewis, became ill with cancer. His book *A Grief Observed* is an honest confession of his struggle to believe in a benevolent God after the second important woman in his life succumbed to cancer. His novel *Till We Have Faces* also perceptively discusses our struggles with unbelief and belief.

C. S. Lewis died on November 22, 1963. His belief in the power of stories for the Christian here and in the hereafter can be seen by his writing at the end of *The Last Battle*. The children in the story have all died and gone to Aslan's land—Lewis's imaginative representation of heaven: "And for us this is the end of all the stories, and we can most truly say that they lived happily ever after. But for them it was only the beginning of the real story. All their life in this world and all their adventures in Narnia had only been the cover and the title page: now at last they were beginning Chapter One of the Great Story, which no one on earth has read: which goes on for ever: in which every chapter is better than the one before." (184)

LEWIS ON IMAGINATIVE LITERATURE

"What is the good of . . . occupying our hearts with stories of what never happened and entering vicariously into feelings which we should try to avoid having in our own person? . . . [W]e seek an enlargement of our being. We want to be more than ourselves. . . . We want to see with other eyes, to imagine with other imaginations, to feel with other hearts, as well as with our own. . . . We demand windows. Literature as Logos is a series of windows, even of doors. One of the things we feel after reading a great work is 'I have got out'. Or from another point of view, 'I have got in': pierced the shell of some other monad and discovered what it is like inside. . . . The . . . impulse is to go out of the self, to correct its provincialism and heal its loneliness. In love, in virtue, in the pursuit of knowledge, and *in the reception of the arts*, we are doing this. Obviously this process can be described either as an enlargement or as a temporary annihilation of the self. But that is an old paradox; 'he that loseth his life shall save it'. . . . Those of us who have been true readers all our life seldom fully realize the enormous extension of our being which we owe to authors. We realize it best when we talk with an unliterary friend. He may be full of goodness and good sense but he inhabits a tiny world. In it, we should be suffocated. The man who is contented to be only himself, and therefore less a self, is in prison. My own eyes are not enough for me; I will see through those of others. . . . Literary experience heals the wound, without undermining the privilege, of individuality. . . . In reading great literature I become a thousand men and yet remain myself. Like the night sky in the Greek poem, I see with a myriad eyes, but it is still I who see. Here, as in worship, in love, in moral action, and in knowing, I transcend myself; and am never more myself than when I do."

—C. S. Lewis, *An Experiment in Criticism*, pp. 137–141, italics mine

Appendix 8
Thomas Hobbes and the
Contract Theory of Justice

Michael D. Palmer

Thomas Hobbes was an English philosopher and one of the greatest political theorists of the seventeenth century. He was born in 1588 in England. At the age of fourteen he entered Oxford University, graduating in 1608 with a bachelor's degree. He died in 1679.

Hobbes's greatest work is entitled *Leviathan* (1651). In it he set forth his social contract theory of morality. Speaking of Hobbes's style, one scholar, H. W. Schneider, observed, it "reflects the light in the merry eyes of a wit and the dead earnest of a philosopher." From the time it was published it was recognized as a powerful political treatise. In subsequent generations it has come to take its place among the permanent important contributions to moral philosophy and political theory.

The name *Leviathan* refers to something large and formidable, such as a giant mythical sea animal. Hobbes used the name to refer to the political state. Specifically, he means a totalitarian state having absolute political power and control. The sovereign body politic, or commonwealth, according to Hobbes, is an "artificial animal"—a Leviathan or "mortal god"—constructed by the agreements ("compacts") human beings make with one another in the interests of security, justice, and peace.

Hobbes contended that human beings, driven by their desires for "gain," "safety," and "reputation," would experience continual conflict among themselves if there were no political force capable of enforcing civil agreements and moral rules. Without a powerful political regime, our situation would be a virtual "state of nature," by which he means "a War as is of every man against every man." In one of his most celebrated lines, Hobbes claimed that in this condition our lives would be "solitary, poor, nasty, brutish, and short." Fear of violent death is the principal motive that causes people to create a state by contracting to surrender their natural rights and to submit to the absolute authority of a "sovereign." By "sovereign" Hobbes had in mind a strong law-keeping force or government. Thus according to Hobbes, a government is formed when people in the state of nature agree "to confer all their power and strength upon one man, or upon one assembly of men" who "shall act . . . in those things which concern the common peace and safety."

Although the power of the sovereign, in Hobbes's theory, derives originally from the people—challenging the doctrine of the divine right of kings—Hobbes asserted that the sovereign's power is absolute and not subject to review by either subjects or ecclesiastical powers. Hobbes's concept of the Social Contract led to investigations by other political theorists, notably John Locke, Benedict Spinoza, and Jean Jacques Rousseau, who formulated their own quite distinctive theories of the social contract.

In the passage that follows, Hobbes presents his account of how a commonwealth comes into existence.

OF THE CAUSES, GENERATION, AND DEFINITION OF A COMMONWEALTH

The final cause, end, or design of men, who naturally love liberty and dominion over others, in the introduction of that restraint upon themselves in which we see them live in commonwealths is the foresight of their own preservation, and of a more contented life thereby—that is to say, of getting themselves out from that miserable condition of war which is necessarily consequent . . . to the natural passions of men when there is no visible power to keep them in awe and tie them by fear of punishment to the performance of their covenants and observation of those laws of nature set down [earlier] . . .

The only way to erect such a common power as may be able to defend them from the invasion of foreigners and the injuries of one another, and thereby to secure them in such sort as that by their own industry and by the fruits of the earth they may nourish themselves and live contentedly, is to confer all their power and strength upon one man, or upon one assembly of men that may reduce all their wills, by plurality of voices, unto one will; which is as much as to say, to appoint one man or assembly of men to bear their person, and everyone to own and acknowledge himself to be author of whatsoever he that so bears their person shall act or cause to be acted in those things which concern the common peace and safety, and therein to submit their wills every one to his will, and their judgments to his judgment. This is more than consent or concord; it is a real unity of them all in one and the same person, made by covenant of every man with every man, in such manner as if every man should say to every man, *I authorize and give up my right of governing myself to this man, or to this assembly of men, on this condition, that you give up your right to him and authorize all his actions in like manner.* This done, the multitude so united in one person is called a *commonwealth,* in Latin *civitas.* This is the generation of that great *leviathan* (or rather, to speak more reverently, of that *mortal god*) to which we owe, under the *immortal God,* our peace and defense. For by this authority, given him by every particular man in the commonwealth, he has the use of so much power and strength conferred on him that, by terror thereof, he is enabled to form the wills of them all to peace at home and mutual aid against their enemies abroad. And in him consists the essence of the commonwealth, which, to define it, is *one person, of whose acts a great multitude, by mutual covenants one with another, have made themselves every one the author, to the end he may use the strength and means of them all as he shall think expedient for their peace and common defense.* And he that carries this person is called *sovereign* and said to have *sovereign power;* and everyone besides, his subject.

—Thomas Hobbes, *Leviathan, Parts One and Two,* with an introduction by Herbert W. Schneider (Indianapolis: Bobbs-Merrill Co., 1958), 139, 142, 143.

Appendix 9
John Locke and the
Theory of Natural Rights

Michael D. Palmer

John Locke (1632–1704) was an English philosopher and the architect of a philosophical point of view that came to be known as British empiricism. He was born in the western region of England. His family was middle class, his father being a small property owner and an attorney. The family's religious tradition was Puritan; Locke himself remained a Christian and defender of Christian ideals his whole life. Early in life, Locke's father was his primary educational influence. Later, in 1652, after spending six years at Westminster School, he entered Christ Church, Oxford, where he began an association with that university that lasted some thirty years.

Locke's two most important works, *Essay Concerning Human Understanding* and *Two Treatises of Government*, both appeared in print in 1690. They quickly established his reputation as a leading philosopher and political theorist. In the *Essay* he took to task certain rationalists, like the French philosopher René Descartes (1596–1650), who advanced the view that the mind contains ideas even before birth (commonly called "innate ideas"). Locke advanced arguments instead that the mind, at our birth, completely lacks content. It is a virtual "blank slate" or "piece of white paper." Everything we come to know is inscribed upon it in the form of experience. In the *Essay*, Locke also distinguished between two kinds of qualities found in the things we encounter: *primary qualities* (e.g., extension, solidity, number) and *secondary qualities* (e.g., color, smell, sound). Primary qualities affect the sense organs mechanically, providing ideas that faithfully reflect reality. They are what science is concerned to discover. Secondary qualities, according to Locke, are produced by the interaction between objects in the world and our sense organs. Later empiricists such as David Hume (1711–1778) and George Berkeley (1685–1753) based their philosophical theories of knowledge largely on Locke's theory.

In political theory Locke was equally influential. For instance, his account of checks and balances in government provided a model for the framers of the United States Constitution; his formulation of the doctrine that revolution in some circumstances is not only a right but an obligation did not go unnoticed by colonial Americans; and his arguments for broad religious freedom have formed part of a long political discussion in Europe and America since he wrote them. In addition, many of the liberal social, economic, and ethical theories of the eighteenth century were rooted in Locke's social-contract theory. Indeed, one authority, Thomas Peardon, says of Locke that he is "probably the most representative thinker in the whole Anglo-American political tradition." He defends this assessment not on the grounds that Locke was particularly original in his political theory but on the grounds that he gave such clear and reasonable expression to beliefs that were the product of centuries of political experience.

Locke took his point of departure by rejecting Thomas Hobbes's views on several points, in particular his view of human nature. Says Peardon, "Locke viewed man as a pretty decent fellow, far removed from the quarrelsome, competitive, selfish creatures found in Hobbes." Contrary to Hobbes's assessment, Locke maintained that the state of nature (the condition of human beings prior to or apart from organized civil society and the constraints of government) was relatively happy and characterized by reason and tolerance. In the state of nature, all human beings were equal and free to pursue "life, health, liberty, and possessions."

Locke is generally credited with developing the idea that human beings enjoy two "natural rights": the natural right to *liberty* and the natural right to *private property*. In the state of nature each person would be the political equal of every other person. Moreover, in the state of nature each person would experience no constraints except the "law of nature," those principles established by God and available to human beings through their God-given reason. In the state of nature everyone would be free to do as he pleases except as his actions conflict with certain basic, God-given moral principles. In Locke's words:

> To understand political power right and derive it from its original, we must consider what state all men are naturally in, and that is a *state of perfect freedom* to order their actions and dispose of their possessions and persons as they think fit, within the bounds of the law of nature, without asking leave, or depending upon the will of any other man.

> A *state* also *of equality*, wherein all the power and jurisdiction is reciprocal, no one having more than another . . . without subordination or subjection [to another]. . . .

> But . . . the *state of nature* has a law of nature to govern it, which obliges everyone: and reason, which is that law, teaches all mankind, who will but consult it, that being all equal and independent, no one ought to harm another in his life, health, liberty, or possessions. (4,5)

In Locke's view, the law of nature "teaches" each person that he has a right to liberty. Therefore, "no one can be put out of this [natural] estate and subjected to the political power of another without his own consent." In addition, the law of nature teaches us that each person has rights of ownership over his own body, his own labor, and the products of his labor. He believed these rights to be natural, by which he meant that they are neither created by government nor achieved by any grant by government.

> Every man has a property in his own person: This nobody has a right to but himself. The labor of his body, and the work of his hands, we may say, are properly his. Whatsoever then he removes out of the state that nature has provided and left it in, he has mixed his labor with, and joined to it something is his own, and thereby makes it his property . . . [For] this labor being the unquestionable property of the laborer, no man but he can have a right to what that [labor] is once joined to. At least where there is enough, and as good, left in common for others. (17)

Despite the fact that everyone enjoys absolute freedom in the state of nature, such a condition is also fraught with peril due to the constant threat of danger posed by others.

Recognizing their insecure position, individuals organize themselves into a political body and create a government whose primary purpose is to provide the measure of protection of their natural rights that they lacked in the state of nature. Since government is created in the first instance to protect natural rights to liberty and property, "the power of the society or legislature constituted by them can never be supposed to extend farther" than what is necessary to protect these rights. In short, government has no authority to interfere with any citizen's natural rights to liberty and property except when necessary to protect one citizen's liberty or property from abuse by others.

—The selections quoted here have been taken from John Locke, *The Second Treatise of Government*, edited by Thomas P. Peardon (Indianapolis: Bobbs-Merrill Co., 1952). For an excellent resource on Locke, see Richard I. Aaron, *John Locke*, 3d ed. (Oxford University Press, 1971), 309–311.

Appendix 10
Rights

Michael D. Palmer

The concept of a "right" appears in many of the arguments and claims invoked in moral and political discussions. Land owners, for example, claim the right to use their property as they wish. Environmentalists argue for the right to clean air and drinkable water. Women assert the right to have "equal pay for equal work." Free press advocates proclaim the public's "right to know." In the political realm, certain legal documents employ the idea of a right. The first ten amendments to the Constitution of the United States, commonly referred to as the "Bill of Rights," stipulate certain duties of the federal government not to interfere in the activities of its citizens. The Declaration of Independence proclaims that "all men . . . are endowed by their Creator with certain unalienable rights . . . among these are life, liberty, and the pursuit of happiness."

The concept of rights appears even on the international scene. On December 20, 1948, the United Nations adopted a "Universal Declaration of Human Rights" containing some thirty articles. The first article reads: "All human beings are born free and equal in dignity and rights. They are endowed with reason and conscience and should act towards one another in a spirit of brotherhood." Among the rights identified in the remainder of the document are rights to life, liberty, and security of person; rights of freedom from enslavement and torture; the right to equal protection under the law; the right to be presumed innocent in legal proceedings until proved guilty; the right to freedom of movement; the right to own property; and the rights of free expression and religious belief and worship. Evidently the concept of a right and the correlative concept of duty stand at the center of much of our public discourse.

What does it mean to have a right? In general, when we speak of having a right we are not referring to a privilege but rather to an *entitlement* to something. We have this entitlement, this right, under two general circumstances: (1) being entitled to act in a certain way and(2) being entitled to have others act toward us in certain ways. Some entitlements come from a legal system: We are permitted or empowered to do something or we can expect others to behave in certain ways toward us due to specific legal provisions. In such cases the entitlement is called a *legal right,* or a *civil right.* The American constitution, for example, guarantees all citizens the right to "freedom of assembly." By contrast, the constitution of the People's Republic of China provides no similar legal right for its citizens. A cursory inquiry would confirm that the constitutions of different countries around the world differ widely in the kinds of protections and guarantees they provide their citizens. And of course the protections and guarantees provided for in the constitution of one country do not routinely apply to persons living in other countries under other constitutions. In short, legal, or civil, rights are limited to the particular jurisdiction within which the legal system is in force.

Not all entitlements derive from specific legal arrangements. Some come from a system of moral standards unrelated to any particular legal system. The rights to "freedom of conscience" and "freedom of expression," for example, are not guaranteed by the constitution of many of the world's countries. Nevertheless, many believe that these are rights that all human beings possess. Rights like these are called *moral rights*, or *human rights*. They are based on moral principles that either empower persons to do something or identify certain things others must do for them. Whereas legal rights are restricted to particular legal jurisdictions (like the boundaries of a city or nation), moral rights apply to everyone, everywhere, equally, at all times. Moreover, persons have moral rights simply by reason of being human. This means that social standing, ethnic heritage, race, gender, and other contingencies of life do not affect what moral rights a person has. For example, if humans beings have a moral right not to be enslaved, then this is a right that every person has regardless of nationality, social standing, ethnic heritage, race, or gender. In short, moral rights, unlike legal rights, are universal.

Rights—whether moral (human) rights or legal (civil) rights—are powerful devices. Their purpose is twofold: to enable the individual to pursue certain interests or activities, and to protect those pursuits. When we use the word "right" we generally have one or another of three things in mind. Sometimes we merely mean *absence of prohibitions* against doing something. I use the word in this sense whenever I claim to have a right to do whatever the law or morality does not positively forbid me to do. Clearly the enabling and protective functions are minimal in such cases. Other times we use the term *right* to identify certain *prerogatives that go with one's task responsibilities*. We use the word "right" in this way when we speak of a person being authorized or empowered to do something that secures the interests of others. An attorney, for example, acquires legal prerogatives to act in the interest of his client. The third use of the term "right" is to identify either the ways we *impose prohibitions or requirements on others* or the ways we *empower individuals to pursue their own interests*. When we use the word in this way we are normally attempting to identify activities or interests that the individual is empowered to pursue, or must be left free to pursue, or must be protected or helped to pursue. For example, since the Constitution of the United States guarantees the right to freedom of expression, the courts or law enforcement officials (or both) are expected to intervene whenever a citizen experiences an infringement of that right by others in the society.

Rights have the following three important features that define their enabling and protective functions.

First, rights are intimately linked with *duties*. How intimately the two are linked can be seen in the fact that we often define one person's rights in terms of the duties we impose on others. For example, my right to express political convictions can be, and often is, defined in terms of the moral and legal duties others have not to interfere in my verbal expression of those convictions. (The right in this case is called a *negative right* and the corresponding duty is called a *duty of non-interference*.) Also, the right to drinkable water can be defined in terms of the duty that government (or some other agent of society) has to ensure a clean water supply for its citizens. (The right in this case is called a *positive right* and the corresponding duty is called a *duty of positive performance*.) Duties, then, are generally the flip side of rights: like the two sides of a coin, wherever you find one, you will find the other.

Second, rights provide individuals with *freedom and equality* in the pursuit of their interests. This means three things: (1) To begin with, rights identify activities or interests that people must be left free (or helped) to pursue as they themselves choose. For example, my right to express my political convictions implies that I must be left free to express them if and as I choose. (2) But also, to enjoy freedom and equality in the pursuit of one's interests means that the pursuit of those interests or activities must not be subordinated to the interests of others except for the most compelling reasons. Thus, my decision to express my political convictions does not depend on gaining anyone's permission to do so. (3) Finally, having a right implies that I cannot generally be forced to stop expressing myself on the grounds that society will gain more benefits if I am kept quiet. Thus, the expression of my political convictions (when protected by a right) may not be impeded or stopped, even if others do not wish to hear me or even if they think they will gain something by silencing me. In general, then, recognizing a person's right implies an area in which that person is not subject to the wishes or interests of others. In short, a right defines an area within which each person stands as free as, and equal to, every other person.

Third, rights provide rational grounds for justifying one's actions and for invoking the protection or assistance of others. For example, if I want someone to cease interfering with me, I could draw on two lines of reasoning. First, because I have a right to engage in this activity (say, express my political convictions) my action is justified. But also, because I have a right to engage in this activity, no one is justified in interfering with me. On the other hand, if I need the protection or assistance of others (perhaps I am weak and cannot defend myself against my opponents), I could use a similar line of reasoning. The fact that I have a right to free expression justifies others in protecting or assisting me. But also, the fact that I have a right actually imposes a duty on others (it is not always clear whom) to protect or assist me.

FURTHER READING ON RIGHTS

Donnelly, Jack. *Universal Human Rights in Theory & Practice.* Ithaca, N.Y.: Cornell University Press, 1989.

Dworkin, Ronald. "Taking Rights Seriously." In *Taking Rights Seriously,* ed. Ronald Dworkin, 184–205. Cambridge, Mass.: Harvard University Press, 1978

Feinberg, Joel. *Social Philosophy.* Englewood Cliffs, N.J.: Prentice-Hall, 1973.

Martin, R., and J. W. Nickel. "Recent Work on the Concept of Rights." *American Philosophical Quarterly* 17, no. 3 (1980): 165–80.

McCloskey, H. J. "Rights." *The Philosophical Quarterly* 15 (1965): 115–121.

Wasserstrom, Richard. "Rights, Human Rights, and Racial Discrimination." *The Journal of Philosophy* 61 (29 October 1964): 628–41.

Appendix 11
Justice

Michael D. Palmer

Disputes in public discourse are often interlaced with references to "justice" or to "fairness." This occurs, for instance, when a person alleges that another party, say another citizen or the government, has made an "unjust" decision that affects him adversely. (Perhaps the government has reassessed property values and the dissatisfied person feels that his tax bill is too high compared to what his neighbors are paying.) Or it might occur when one person charges another with not sharing or participating in a "fair" way. (Perhaps in a group of workers one believes that she is carrying too much of the work burden compared to the others.) Sometimes we invoke the word *justice* with reference to a process: Someone complains of having been treated "unjustly" or "unfairly" as a process unfolded or in the application of a rule. (The defendant in a trial might complain that she has not received a "fair" trial and therefore that "justice" has not been served.) Commonly, these kinds of disputes require that we make comparative evaluations, since without comparisons we have no way of determining how the complaining person should have been treated. Indeed, justice and fairness are, at their core, *comparative concepts*. They require us to make comparisons in several general areas of human interaction: when we are trying to decide how to distribute benefits and burdens among the members of a group, when we are trying to administer rules or laws, when we are trying to decide the terms under which people should cooperate or compete with each other, when we are trying to determine how to compensate persons for injuries they have suffered, and when we are trying to determine appropriate punishment for wrongdoers. As for the terms themselves, "justice" and "fairness" are virtual synonyms: We often use them interchangeably. Whenever we do not use them interchangeably, we tend to prefer "justice" as the term more appropriate to weighty matters or formal situations.

Questions about justice usually fall into four main categories: *distributive justice, compensatory justice, procedural justice,* and *retributive justice.*

Distributive justice focuses on the fair distribution of benefits and burdens among the members of a group. The group might be a family, a community, or an entire society. Regardless of the size of the group, issues of distributive justice emerge when different members make conflicting claims on the group's resources and not all the claims are or can be met. The most prominent instances are ones where key benefits of the group are in short supply—such as food, housing, medical care, income, or jobs—compared to the number of people who want these benefits. A similar situation arises when burdens—such as laborious or dangerous tasks, substandard housing, or health risks—are distributed unequally among members of the group. If everyone could satisfy his or her desire for goods, or if everyone shouldered an appropriate level of the group's necessary burdens, conflicts among members of the group would not arise and distributive justice would be unnecessary. But, of course, conflicts of this very sort do arise, and a principle of distributive justice is indeed needed to resolve conflicting claims. What is that principle? Quite simply the principle of distributive justice requires that equals be treated equally and that unequals be treated unequally. More specifically, it requires that persons who are similar in all respects relevant to the issue under consideration should be given similar benefits and burdens. This principle applies even if the persons in question are unequal or different in certain irrelevant respects. For instance, suppose two students, Jill and John, submit term papers. If the papers are of equal quality, both students should receive the same grade, because in the academic context quality of writing—not bodily strength or good looks—should be the determining factor in assigning grades to term papers. On the other hand, the principle of distributive justice also requires that persons who are dissimilar in some respect relevant to the issue at hand should be treated differently—at least they should be treated differently in proportion to their dissimilarities. In the case of Jill and John, their term papers should be graded differently in proportion to the difference in quality of the papers. As a final comment on the principle of distributive justice, we should note that much of the debate over the principle has focused on defining what makes one person equal to (or different from) another. The main lines of the debate have centered on factors such as ability, need, and effort.

Compensatory justice concerns the just way of paying back, or compensating, people for what they lose when they are wronged or injured by others. Quite simply, a just compensation is one that in some sense is proportional to the loss suffered by the person being compensated. It attempts to provide restitution to the injured party. For instance, if your car collides with my parked car as you are backing out of a parking space, then you should pay for the repair of my car. The payment should be proportional to the cost of repairing the damage. If the repair bill is one thousand dollars (you were backing out very quickly), then it would be unfair to expect you to pay twelve hundred dollars and unfair to expect me to settle for eight hundred. Certain difficulties relating to the application of the principle of compensatory justice are well known. Some types of loss or damage are difficult or impossible to measure—as with the damage to one's good name when one is slandered. Sometimes full restoration is not possible—as with the loss of sight, hearing, a limb, or life itself.

Procedural justice concerns the just, or fair, application of the method of settling disputes or grievances. Procedural justice is the principle of *due process*. That is to say, procedural justice emphasizes the importance of a *process* and the *application of the rules* of the process. The most notable cases of procedural justice are found in our legal system. In the American legal system, for example, the Supreme Court has rule that persons charged with a crime should, at the time they are charged, be informed of their rights under the law. When an arresting officer informs a suspect of his legal rights, the officer is complying with a decision based on the principle of procedural justice. Many aspects of a criminal trial also rely on the principle of procedural justice. When a judge excludes a statement from testimony on the grounds that it is "hearsay," he is implicitly appealing to the principle of procedural justice. Of course, no one can guarantee that every application of rules will be without bias; the principle of procedural justice cannot be expected to meet such a lofty criterion. In general, procedural justice requires only that the *process* of applying rules and adjudicating cases be as fair as conditions permit and that they be consistent from one case to the next or from one person to the next. In this sense, procedural justice, like other forms of justice, is essentially comparative in nature.

Retributive justice refers to the just, or fair, imposition of punishments and penalties upon those who do wrong. A "just" punishment or penalty is one that in some sense is deserved by the person who does wrong. What, then, are the conditions under which a wrongdoer *deserves* to be punished or penalized? To begin with, the person must be causally connected with whatever went wrong. If mother's favorite crystal bowl has been broken, then I am *causally connected* to the broken bowl if I pushed it from the table. But two other factors will determine whether I deserve blame for the broken bowl: control and knowledge. Generally, if I have full control of my actions and if I know what I am doing, I should be held fully responsible for my actions. If I lacked control of my actions (say, someone bumped into me just as I was reaching for the bowl), then generally speaking I should not be blamed. Or if I am ignorant of relevant specific facts about the situation (say, I did not know that the floor near the table was wet and slippery), then generally I should not be blamed for breaking the bowl. Of course, negligence and pretended ignorance can be factors that actually increase my level of responsibility. As with other forms of justice, comparisons become important. Thus, once the facts of a case have been determined and the level of responsibility has been determined, the type and magnitude of punishment or penalty should be administered in a way that is consistent with other similar cases.

All four categories of justice are found in the Scriptures. In the Old Testament, the tithes were used in part to satisfy the needs of the Levites and the poor—a form of distributive justice. In the

New Testament, the Book of Acts (chap. 6) reports that as the church was growing in Jerusalem a complaint arose among the Hellenistic Jews against the native Jews: The Hellenistic Jews said their widows were being overlooked in the daily serving of food. Eventually a settlement was reached to ensure that everyone would be treated fairly in the serving of food—again, a form of distributive justice. A good bit of the Old Testament law explained the way in which land transactions should be handled. Under Levitical law land could not be sold permanently; it seems to have been considered an irrevocable family heritage. After a period of time, the first owner could buy it back. But so as to be fair to the current owner of the land who might be in jeopardy of losing some of his investment, the sale price was to be proportional to the number of years the current owner held title to the land (Lev. 25:13–17). Clearly, the principle of compensatory justice underlies the reasoning on this issue. Both Old and New Testament outline strategies for ensuring procedural justice. Perhaps the most prominent example appears in Matthew 18: 15–18 where procedures are established for expressing oneself to someone who is has sinned. Finally, the principle of retributive justice (deserved punishment) shows up in famous cases such as the destruction of Sodom (Gen. 18) and the death of Ananias and Sapphira (Acts 5).

For additional readings on the topic of justice, see the following works:

Feinberg, Joel. *Social Philosophy*. Englewood Cliffs, N.J.: Prentice-Hall, 1973.

Rawls, John. *A Theory of Justice*. Cambridge, Mass.: Harvard University Press, Belknap Press, 1971.

Rescher, Nicholas. *Distributive Justice*. New York: Bobbs-Merill, 1966.

Ryan, John A. *Distributive Justice*, 3d ed. New York: Macmillan, 1941.

Sterba, James P. *Justice, Alternative Political Perspectives*, 2d. ed. Belmont, Calif.: Wadsworth Publishing, 1992.

Indexes

Name Index

Subject Index